La Salle
Cadillac's Companion Car

Turner Publishing Company
Paducah, Kentucky

LaSalle
Cadillac's Companion Car

FIRST EDITION 2000

LIBRARY OF CONGRESS CATALOG CARD NUMBER: 00-102939
I.S.B.N. 1-56311-519-0

Copyright © 2000 by The Cadillac-LaSalle Club Museum and Research Center, Inc.
P. O. Box 1916, Lenoir, North Carolina 28645

No part of this book may be reproduced or transmitted in any form or by any means, electronic or mechanical, including photocopy, recording or any information storage or retrieval system now known or to be invented, without permission in writing from The Cadillac-LaSalle Club Museum and Research Center, Inc., except by a reviewer who wishes to quote brief passages in a review written for inclusion in a magazine, newspaper or broadcast.

The Cadillac-LaSalle Club Museum and Research Center, Inc., is a 501(c)(3) not-for-profit, charitable and educational organization and possesses all rights pertaining to this book.

TURNER PUBLISHING COMPANY
412 Broadway
Paducah, Kentucky 42002-3101

PRINTED IN THE
UNITED STATES OF AMERICA

La Salle
Cadillac's Companion Car

This book is dedicated to the separation of fact from fiction; the encouragement of collecting and preserving historical information; and the promotion of a genuine appreciation for the LaSalle automobile.

TABLE OF CONTENTS

INTRODUCTION *1*

LaSALLE *5*
    From A Designer's Point of View

HOW IT ALL BEGAN *7*
    Harley J. Earl
    Harley J. Earl, LaSalle and Styling
    Cadillac Welcomes LaSalle
    What's In A Name?
    March 4, 1927 . . . The Big Event

NINETEEN TWENTY-SEVEN *23*
    Series 303
    Proving Ground Tests
    Condensed Specifications (same as 1928)

NINETEEN TWENTY-EIGHT *39*
    Series 303
    Production Data
    Condensed Specifications

NINETEEN TWENTY-NINE *61*
    Series 328
    Production Data
    Condensed Specifications

NINETEEN THIRTY *87*
    Series 340
    Production Data
    Condensed Specifications

NINETEEN THIRTY-ONE *111*
    Series 345
    Production Data
    Condensed Specifications

NINETEEN THIRTY-TWO *133*
    Series 345-B
    Production Data

NINETEEN THIRTY-THREE *153*
    Series 345-C
    Production Data
    The Mystery Cars

NINETEEN THIRTY-FOUR *175*
    Series 350
    Decision to Drop LaSalle for 1934 Reversed
    Why the LaSalle Straight-8 Engine?
    Indianapolis 500 Pacemaker
    Production Data
    Condensed Specifications

NINETEEN THIRTY-FIVE *213*
    Series 50
    Production Data
    Condensed Specifications

NINETEEN THIRTY-SIX *235*
    Series 50
    Production Data

NINETEEN THIRTY-SEVEN ... 247
Series 50
Indianapolis 500 Pacemaker
Production Data
Specifications

NINETEEN THIRTY-EIGHT ... 271
Series 50
LaSalle 60 Special
Production Data
Specifications

NINETEEN THIRTY-NINE ... 297
Series 50
Bohman & Schwartz Convertible
Production Data
Condensed Specifications

NINETEEN FORTY ... 313
Series 50
Lifetime Warranty
Series 52 Special
Answers to Often Asked Questions
Explanation of the Codes
Production Data
Condensed Specifications

NINETEEN FORTY-ONE ... 351

NINETEEN FIFTY-FIVE ... 363
LaSalle II

NINETEEN SIXTY-THREE ... 369
XP-715
Riviera

NINETEEN SEVENTY-FIVE and ONE-HALF ... 373
Seville

EXPORTS ... 377
LaSalle in Australia
LaSalle in Europe
LaSalle Worldwide

FACTORY LITERATURE ... 387

CADILLAC - LaSALLE'S PARENT COMPANY ... 397
Penalty of Leadership
Cadillac-LaSalle Production Comparison

OVERVIEWS ... 399
Specifications
Price Ranges
Power Plants
Nomenclature
Identification Guide
Front Ensembles

EPILOGUE ... 416

ACKNOWLEDGEMENTS ... 417

INDEX ... 418

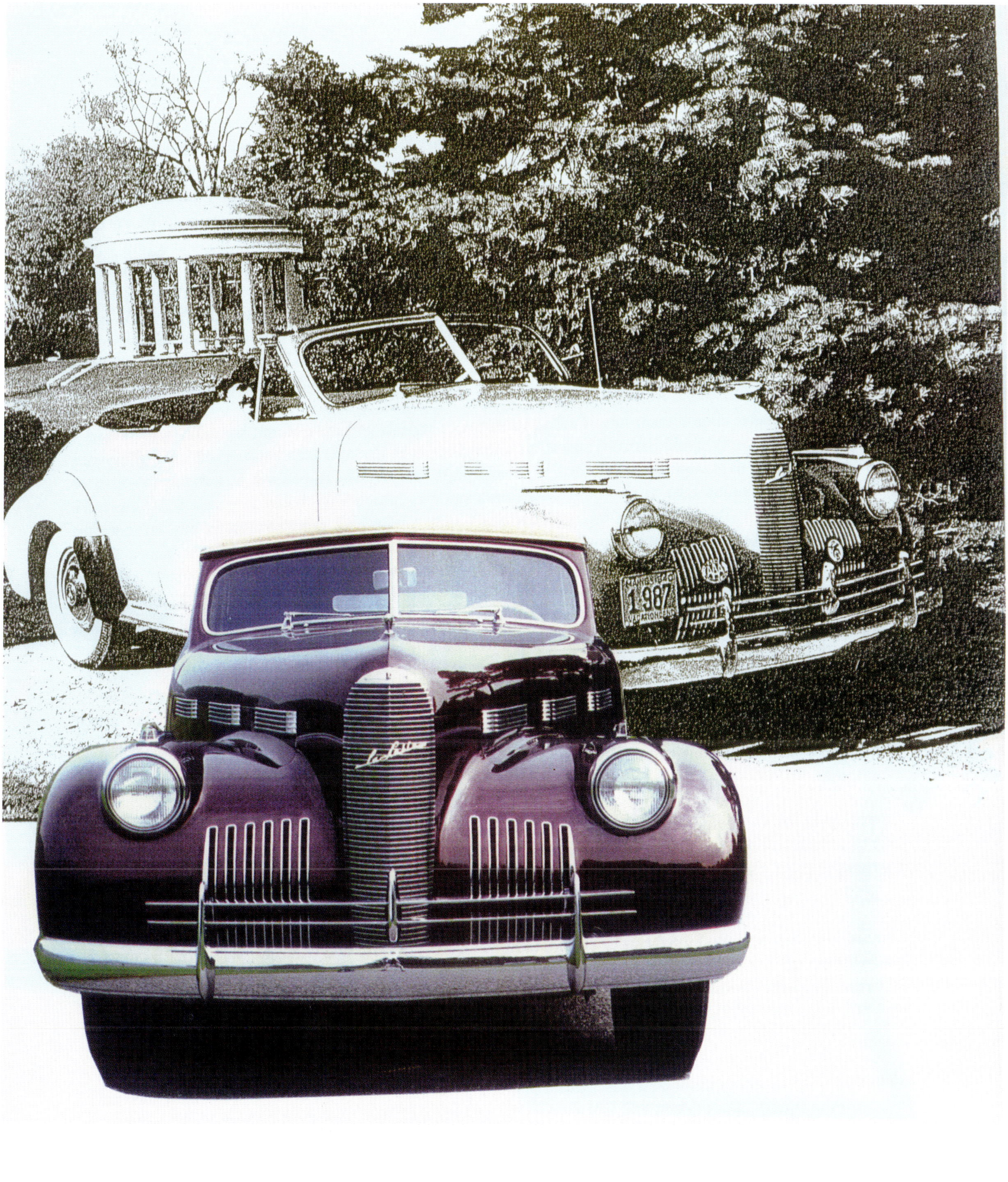

INTRODUCTION

HARLEY J. EARL

Any discussion, review or analysis of the LaSalle automobile would be incomplete and void of life without Harley Earl, stylist extraordinaire.

Harley J. Earl was born in Los Angeles in 1893 and spent a normal, happy childhood with three brothers and one sister in a rambling three-story house on five acres of orange groves at the corner of Hollywood and Bronson, four streets west of Hollywood and Vine. Harley Earl was bright, good looking, outgoing and had a natural affinity for attracting people around him. He was a good athlete and was very competitive. He was also very self assured, thoughtful and charming.

Harley was thought to have shared a lot of character traits with an uncle who had been a well-regarded and highly successful Mayor of Los Angeles. So, upon graduation from Hollywood High School in 1912, his father, J. W. Earl, had high hopes of having Harley become a lawyer and enter politics.

Harley Earl enrolled at the University of Southern California (USC) at his Dad's insistence. As it turned out, he spent a lot more time playing football and running track than studying. He quit USC after only one year and went to work for his father at the Earl Automobile Works, where he expressed his passion for automobile design.

In 1916, his father urged Harley to study law again and sent him to Stanford University. In class, once again he did more sketching and cartooning than studying. Harley preferred sports, where he demonstarted his competitiveness in track. However, one afternoon, he was cleated in the leg and developed an infection. It was sufficiently serious that he was sent home. College to no avail, he went back to his father's business.

Earl Carriage Works was a custom coach building shop catering to luminaries who wanted something different in which to be seen by their public. In 1910, the name was changed to the Earl Automobile Works as a reflection of the times and the growing automobile market. While working for his father, Harley Earl was able to develop his clay modeling ability—this, at a time when clay modeling was a fairly unusual styling demonstration medium. Most designers preferred to make side view renderings and sketches. Instead, Harley Earl sculpted scale models for prospective customers. He would ask them to come in person to approve his proposal or help make any changes. The three dimensional scale model approach helped his clients actually see what their cars would look like . . . what a powerful selling tool!

Harley Earl was able to conjure up lavish, bizarre and very individualistic coach works for Fatty Arbuckle, Tom Mix, Mary Pickford, Douglas Fairbanks, Pauline Fredericks and many others.

Don Lee was the highly successful Cadillac distributor for California. He had eyed the Earl Automobile Works for some time. He wanted to take advantage of this lucrative and growing business with the rich and famous who thrived on custom coach work. Don Lee had approached J. W. Earl several times to sell, but to no avail. Finally, when Don Lee was successful in buying the Earl Automobile Works from J. W. Earl in 1919, Harley Earl came with the deal. By that time, his father had given Harley the responsibility for the operation of the business. However, Don Lee had recognized Harley Earl's real talents as a designer and gave him the freedom to do more design work and less managing. Under that arrangement, Harley Earl was able to experiment and improve his abilities even more.

Harley Earl's custom body designs received a lot of attention. Some were shown back east at the Commodore and Plaza Hotels in New York and Chicago. His designs were imaginative and flamboyant, a far cry from those stodgy models emanating from the factory.

Don Lee (R) recognized Harley Earl's (L) design talents. Lee provided Earl with national exposure of his designs, which ultimately led to an invitation by General Motors to propose designs for the yet-to-be-named LaSalle.

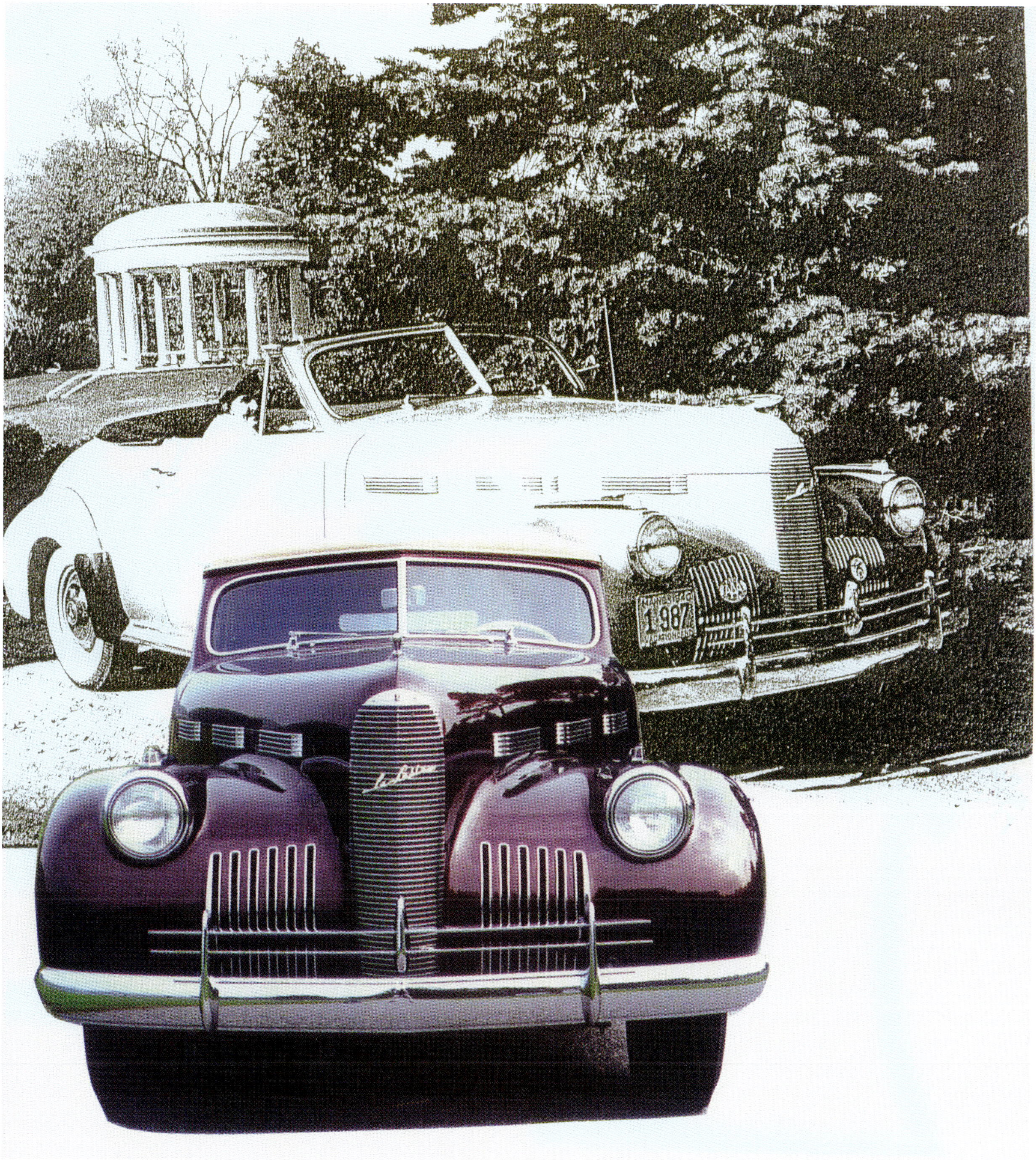

INTRODUCTION

INTRODUCTION

It all started when I bought a 1940 LaSalle Series 52 Coupe. Unfortunately, it was lost in a fire while being transported, and I tried to replace the Coupe with another Coupe. I soon found out how rare LaSalles had become because I could not find a suitable replacement, but I did stumble upon two other 1940 LaSalles— a Series 50 Convertible Sedan and a Series 52 Convertible Coupe. I decided to restore the Convertible Coupe first and soon realized that I needed a lot of help. Numerous people across the country came to my rescue and, in the process, I collected a list of current owners of 1940 Series 52 Convertible Coupes as a source for parts, mechanical tips and authenticity expertise. This evolved into a list of those cars with their original identification tags denoting body number, trim and paint. To confirm authenticity, I got in touch with the Cadillac Historical Collection, managed by Greg Wallace, and I also talked with Cadillac-LaSalle Club Technical Editor Matt Larson. All of that interaction made me realize that there was much information and misinformation about LaSalle, not just for 1940 but for all of the production years.

I had always admired the outstanding design qualities of LaSalle and these events whetted my appetite, especially after discussions with General Motors Director of Design (retired) David Holls. He added a large measure of passion to the beauty, design and significance of LaSalle's contribution to automotive history. That did it! I was motivated. If I could, in some small way, repay those who helped me by generating information and an appreciation for LaSalle, then I was willing. But how and what? Perhaps a magazine article would be in order. It could be a representative picture collection of surviving LaSalles. Such an article would be timely to celebrate the 70th Anniversary of LaSalle's introduction to the automotive world in 1927 by Cadillac. As I began collecting pictures and related information, it became obvious that a number of factory photographs had never been published and a lot of production data had never been researched. What to do now? "Publish a book and make the book bigger and more inclusive," friends urged, as did the Board of Directors of The Cadillac-LaSalle Club.

Thus, the contents evolved into a collection of owner photographs, factory photographs, advertisements, color reproductions, line drawings and other interesting tidbits. An effort has been made to feature different pictures, unusual information and new data, without ignoring the well-known material nor losing the flavor of the era in which they were new.

The information in some chapters and for some years is more extensive than others. Some comparisons, descriptions or analyses are more elaborate than others simply because of the availability, or not, of such information to the author. Conversely, some years had such a volume of information that it was impractical to use it all and some tough decisions had to be made.

A lot of pictures were obtained and gratefully received from owners of surviving LaSalles. Selecting suitable pictures to print was difficult at best. Certain body styles might have been listed as available but owner photos or factory illustrations could not be found, while others were in greater quantity than we could absorb in the book. The picture quality in the book reflects the quality of the materials as available and color has been used wherever possible.

This book does not pretend to be a restoration compendium; instead, it is a plethora of interesting information, history and design that, hopefully, will help anyone appreciate this fine automobile. Cadillac Motor Car Division distributed numerous factory publications including technical bulletins, preliminary shop manuals, owner's manuals, sales brochures, sales data books, accessory brochures and special need issues. Some of these have been referenced in the hope of stimulating their use. Fortunately, originals, or copies of originals, are still available to a limited degree on the open market. Advertisements in leading magazines are worth reading because they represent the flavor of the era and they, too, deserve preservation.

It should be noted that the reader will find inconsistencies in spelling and phraseology. For example, the name LaSalle had a variety of spellings: LaSalle, La Salle, LA SALLE and La SALLE. Other examples are the use of a different spelling for the new department of "Art and Colour" where the spelling of "color" is British rather than American, or the different spellings of the Australian body building company: Holden, Holden's, Holdens, etc. We tried to maintain its spelling and its use reflective of their era.

The line drawings by Bob Eng are a special feature. His attention to detail has pointed out relevant design differences between model years in a uniform, easy-to-compare, manner. The sprinkling of these fine drawings throughout the book has given us extra clarity and appreciation of the basic LaSalle design elements.

In my opinion, the feature of greatest historical significance is the Production section for each of the model years. This is a presentation of the factory data researched by Matt Larson. He spent untold hours during a three-year time frame meticulously looking at the original production records. He came up with facts, figures and information heretofore unknown or estimated. Over two hundred thousand individual records were reviewed. While seemingly trivial to some, it is the most comprehensive work to date and provides the basis for facts about LaSalle directly from the factory records. As you will find out, there were many fascinating surprises.

As best as can be determined, there are about 850 LaSalles still in existence worldwide. That represents less than a three percent survival rate of total production. Owners loved them and drove them and drove them, which explains their low survival rate. It is our desire through the publishing of this book to encourage their maintenance and preservation. We hope that the contents of this book will stimulate an interest in, provide a better understanding of and generate a passion for LaSalle as Cadillac's companion car.

Ron VanGelderen

At any gathering of LaSalle enthusiasts over the years, the subject has invariably turned to examination of body serial numbers and speculation about how many cars of a particular body style were built in various years. That information simply has never been available for the Fleetwood- or Fisher-bodied cars built from 1927 through 1937. Cadillac Motor Car Company must have kept that kind of records, but they are nowhere to be found. We resolved to determine the answers by looking for the highest body number for each style in the factory build sheet records. That approach was quickly found to be too simplistic. It did not account for passenger car and commercial chassis, skipped numbers, duplicate numbers, missing record sheets and multiple body styles that shared the same sequence of numbers. An in-depth examination ensued, the results of which are found with each chapter by year.

Even with access to the considerable material in the Cadillac Historical Collection, it has proven difficult to resolve owner questions like "What color and type of material is my car's interior supposed to be?" or "Was my car a special order color?" We have included that information as a help to the owners but primarily to demonstrate the unusual variety that was available to the LaSalle buyer. It was a time during which the customer was king and the company would build almost anything that the customer wanted.

We recognize that this book is not the final word on the subject of LaSalle automobiles. Many of our readers will have detailed knowledge about a particular model or a piece of information that makes the overall picture more complete. What you know may answer a question that other enthusiasts have searched for in vain. We are gathering material for a perpetual collection to benefit all hobbyists. Surely there are more surviving coachbuilt LaSalles than we have pictured in this book. There were hundreds of chassis shipped to Europe and other parts of the world. Please consider sharing your photographs, advertisements, literature, etc. We invite you to share that information with us so we can share it with others.

Matt Larson

THE LaSALLE
from a designer's point of view

David Holls, GM Director of Design (retired)

It was January 6, 1926. Harley Earl was leaving California for Detroit. He had just accepted the challenge, at the invitation from General Motors, to come up with a new design for Cadillac's new companion car in time for the next model year. A new design? And in so little time? But how? Harley Earl had been the key designer for the Don Lee Custom Body Works since 1919. Many Hollywood stars were proud owners of his flamboyant designs. So, in a record four months, he deftly combined some of the striking new shapes and forms he had developed at Don Lee with some very European, Hispano Suiza-like, overtones. The results were stunning, and the LaSalle introduced in March of 1927 was a roaring success, especially the open models, which were second to none in their beauty and flair.

LaSalle gave "Misterl," as he was often called, his credentials with GM and his entrée to do the entire line of cars for the largest corporation in the world. He would revolutionize the American automobile industry with a new key to the success of the American automobile—STYLE. In doing so, he created a new profession, the Automobile Designer. As Harley Earl gained prominence, he surrounded himself with the best. He very carefully hired young people who would meet his requirements, from all over America and, eventually, Europe. Virtually all the new Styling Departments formed by the other major manufacturers were headed by designers who had worked for Harley Earl. By the way, that was a one-way door. If you left GM Styling, you never returned. Mr. Earl ran a very tight organization and promoted from within that circle. The 1927 LaSalle had started all this, and it proved to be the perfect stepping stone for GM's entrance into the Classic era.

The Depression set new ground rules, old standards had to be changed. There were indulgences that could no longer be afforded. By 1933 GM had dropped all the other divisions' companion cars—Oldsmobile's Viking, Buick's Marquette and Oakland lost to Pontiac. Everyone knew LaSalle was next and the 1934 LaSalle proposal was merely a re-tagged Cadillac and far too expensive to sell in its designated price slot for that era.

Everyone was looking for a new standard—a new theme that was right for the times.

According to Mr. Earl, one of the most exciting days of his life occurred after his return from a business trip to Europe. It was not unusual for him to drop by the studios, regardless of the hour. This time, it was about 10 o'clock in the evening and he was alone, save for a few cleaning people. All of a sudden he stumbled upon a breathtaking design proposal for LaSalle casually left out by Jules Agramonte. It would become the all new 1934 LaSalle. Actually, it became much more; it would become GM's new trendsetter for the streamlined era. It was perfect—slender and light, with the most beautiful fender forms anyone had ever seen. It was like a modern racing plane. This car had no vestige with the old traditional "carriage trade" vehicles. This car was born to run on the new modern highways and appealed to the young and the old. Just like the original 1927 LaSalle, it was the right new car design for the times, but this time it was an original design and . . . totally American.

Work proceeded immediately on a full size model that Mr. Earl wanted shown to the Board of Directors at the new model preview show in the General Motors auditorium in August 1933. Mr. Earl reserved a spot toward the end of the program, after other GM cars had shown, for a special moment. Using the best of his Cecil B. De Mille Hollywood background, elaborate curtains raised, unveiling this all new vehicle. "This, gentlemen, is the LaSalle we will not be building!!!" The rest is history, of course. The LaSalle was saved, and a new design statement for the world was created. It was Harley Earl's finest hour. Introductions for the new 1934 LaSalle were planned, not just for the United States but for Europe as well. Wherever shown, LaSalle received lavish praise. It received international acclaim, and won many Concours d'Elegance awards in the major reviews on the continent. Imitation became the sincerest form of flattery. This was born out by the number of flagrant copies of LaSalle's design in Europe as well as the U.S.A. LaSalle made a statement; General Motors' Styling Section had arrived and had now become internationally known. From this point forward, there was no looking back. GM had established itself as the leading trendsetting Design Center in the world.

The fundamental design of the 1934 LaSalle remained intact for three years. Then, another new era emerged for LaSalle from 1937 to 1940. This time, sharing Cadillac's new high-performance engine. Quietly, these cars became the most desirable cars made in this country and somehow appealed to every discerning buyer, young or old. Not only were these cars fast and maneuverable, but they just looked sensational! They always had a new look each succeeding year, but somehow never gave up their continuous classic elegance of the other great design eras. They just kept looking better.

A raft of GM designers drove LaSalle, regardless of what they were designing in their studios. It was just THE car to own and drive. Bill Mitchell, who was largely responsible for the later designs always drove a LaSalle Convertible. His last was a 1940 Series 52 torpedo-bodied LaSalle painted white, especially for him.

LaSalles were just too good! Once again, they were outselling Cadillac but cost just as much to make. Although models had been proposed for 1941, no production cars would be produced. 1940 was LaSalle's last year. The financial decisions that dictated that choice were probably correct, but the automotive world will never forget those beautiful automobiles that graced this country with an air of elegance that may never be duplicated.

HOW IT ALL BEGAN . . .

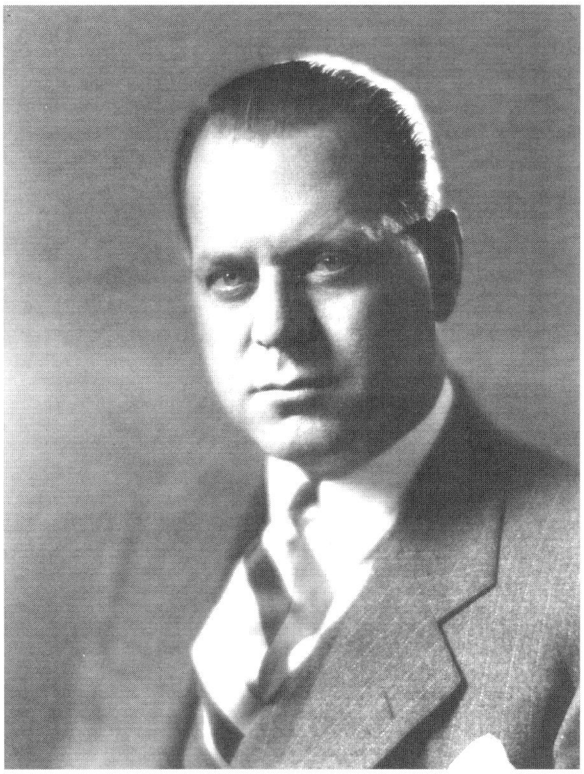

HARLEY J. EARL and LaSALLE

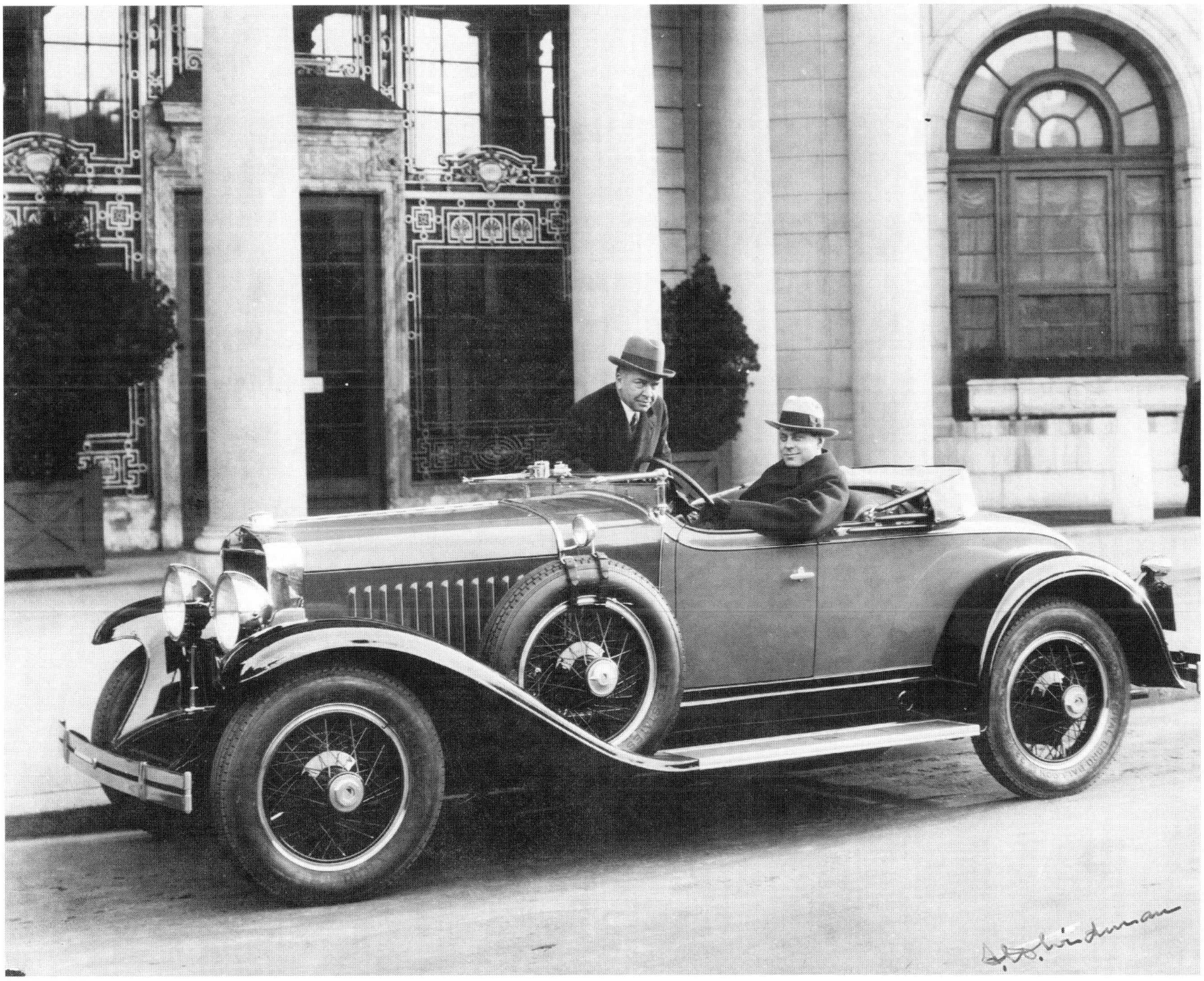

HARLEY J. EARL

Any discussion, review or analysis of the LaSalle automobile would be incomplete and void of life without Harley Earl, stylist extraordinaire.

Harley J. Earl was born in Los Angeles in 1893 and spent a normal, happy childhood with three brothers and one sister in a rambling three-story house on five acres of orange groves at the corner of Hollywood and Bronson, four streets west of Hollywood and Vine. Harley Earl was bright, good looking, outgoing and had a natural affinity for attracting people around him. He was a good athlete and was very competitive. He was also very self assured, thoughtful and charming.

Harley was thought to have shared a lot of character traits with an uncle who had been a well-regarded and highly successful Mayor of Los Angeles. So, upon graduation from Hollywood High School in 1912, his father, J. W. Earl, had high hopes of having Harley become a lawyer and enter politics.

Harley Earl enrolled at the University of Southern California (USC) at his Dad's insistence. As it turned out, he spent a lot more time playing football and running track than studying. He quit USC after only one year and went to work for his father at the Earl Automobile Works, where he expressed his passion for automobile design.

In 1916, his father urged Harley to study law again and sent him to Stanford University. In class, once again he did more sketching and cartooning than studying. Harley preferred sports, where he demonstarted his competitiveness in track. However, one afternoon, he was cleated in the leg and developed an infection. It was sufficiently serious that he was sent home. College to no avail, he went back to his father's business.

Earl Carriage Works was a custom coach building shop catering to luminaries who wanted something different in which to be seen by their public. In 1910, the name was changed to the Earl Automobile Works as a reflection of the times and the growing automobile market. While working for his father, Harley Earl was able to develop his clay modeling ability—this, at a time when clay modeling was a fairly unusual styling demonstration medium. Most designers preferred to make side view renderings and sketches. Instead, Harley Earl sculpted scale models for prospective customers. He would ask them to come in person to approve his proposal or help make any changes. The three dimensional scale model approach helped his clients actually see what their cars would look like . . . what a powerful selling tool!

Harley Earl was able to conjure up lavish, bizarre and very individualistic coach works for Fatty Arbuckle, Tom Mix, Mary Pickford, Douglas Fairbanks, Pauline Fredericks and many others.

Don Lee was the highly successful Cadillac distributor for California. He had eyed the Earl Automobile Works for some time. He wanted to take advantage of this lucrative and growing business with the rich and famous who thrived on custom coach work. Don Lee had approached J. W. Earl several times to sell, but to no avail. Finally, when Don Lee was successful in buying the Earl Automobile Works from J. W. Earl in 1919, Harley Earl came with the deal. By that time, his father had given Harley the responsibility for the operation of the business. However, Don Lee had recognized Harley Earl's real talents as a designer and gave him the freedom to do more design work and less managing. Under that arrangement, Harley Earl was able to experiment and improve his abilities even more.

Harley Earl's custom body designs received a lot of attention. Some were shown back east at the Commodore and Plaza Hotels in New York and Chicago. His designs were imaginative and flamboyant, a far cry from those stodgy models emanating from the factory.

Don Lee (R) recognized Harley Earl's (L) design talents. Lee provided Earl with national exposure of his designs, which ultimately led to an invitation by General Motors to propose designs for the yet-to-be-named LaSalle.

basis for a whole new approach to production automobile styling. It was the politically correct approach that avoided a conflict with the engineering department which, in the past, had been given the assignment of designing automobiles.

Harley Earl accepted the offered position as head of the Art and Colour department, even though he characterized the name as "sissy." From 1927 onward, the presence of a stylist as a separate and distinct function from engineering became increasingly apparent at General Motors. Harley Earl recognized the future of the concept and successfully used styling as a marketing strategy that would appeal to the automobile buying public worldwide. He knew that good looks would sell automobiles.

Harley Earl deserves full credit for the design of the first LaSalle and he deserves top billing for LaSalle's beautiful lines throughout the fourteen years of LaSalle's existence. Harley Earl was the primary source of styling inspiration, not only for LaSalle, but also for Cadillac and, ultimately, he influenced every General Motors' division until his mandatory retirement at age 65 in 1958.

Harley Earl had the daring to be different and the willingness to explore new concepts. He recognized a winning design when he saw it, he had the practical perspective to know what would be acceptable to the public and he had the unique sense on how to sell it to management. LaSalle was Harley Earl's first love. LaSalle was, and continued to be, his personal research and development exercise whenever a new style, a new idea, a new concept was to be explored. When others in the corporation were driving Cadillacs or the brand of the division for which they worked, Harley Earl often drove a LaSalle, when he could have had his pick of all divisions.

Without a doubt, it was the intuitive, yet pragmatic, styling genius of Harley J. Earl that catapulted LaSalle on its trendsetting journey.

Harley Earl was by far the most prominent figure in the industry, a giant among giants, a super ego among egomaniacs, legendary because he knew how to get things done.

Automobile historians now agree that Harley Earl initiated the concept of styling departments for production automobiles and that styling became a primary marketing strategy. His perspective generated a significant and permanent trend for the automobile industry. Harley Earl defined the role of the styling profession for the production automobile industry.

Without a doubt, Harley J. Earl, LaSalle and Production Styling will be inextricably linked in automotive history.

Harley J. Earl circa 1930.

THE SATURDAY EVENING POST — March 5, 1927

CADILLAC
welcomes
LaSalle

The LaSalle

A New CAR for CADILLAC HOMES

It has been apparent for a number of years that a very real need existed in this country for a companion-car of Cadillac calibre to fill a slightly varying field of usefulness.

There has been a very good reason why the need has not been met until this moment.

Another car of Cadillac calibre which could round out Cadillac service in Cadillac homes—supplying the same certainty of distinguished service and carrying the same social status—must of necessity be conceived and executed by the same minds and built by the same hands in the same inspirational environment which can alone produce Cadillac.

Only within the past twenty-four months has it been possible for Cadillac to look beyond its own particular field and arrange to satisfy this other great market—the thousands who have always looked forward to owning a car comparable to the Cadillac in engineering and manufacturing supremacy.

The congenial task of creating this other-brother to Cadillac has gone on carefully for nearly four years. It has proceeded with those inch-at-a-time precisions and precautions which exist only in the Cadillac engineering department and shops—supplemented by the facilities and resources of the General Motors laboratories and proving grounds.

The luminous result is a rarely beautiful car of most brilliant performance—the LaSalle—companion-car in every sense of the word to the Cadillac as *Sieur René Robert Chevalier* LaSalle himself was companion in distinguished achievement to that other great early-American, *Sieur Antoine de la Mothe* Cadillac.

Here is a second car which is as great as Cadillac—dedicated to slightly different uses and purposes but "bone of its bone and flesh of its flesh" in everything it is, and everything it is designed to do.

You will find that nothing even remotely resembling the LaSalle exists today because it has had incorporated into the very fibre of its manufacture the warp and woof, the lineage, the traditions, the high-breeding—if such a word is permissible—of Cadillac practice and Cadillac idealism.

The LaSalle is manufactured completely by Cadillac Motor Car Company within its own plant. Descriptive details will appear in the ensuing issue of the Post.

The first showing of the LaSalle will be at the Cadillac Spring Salon, March 5th to 12th, in cities throughout America

CADILLAC MOTOR CAR COMPANY
Detroit, Michigan - Oshawa, Canada
Division of General Motors Corporation

WHAT'S IN A NAME?

LaSalle was named after a noted French nobleman and explorer—René Robert Cavelier, Sieur de La Salle—who had claimed Louisiana for King Louis XIV in 1682. Naming LaSalle after a French explorer was fitting indeed because the builder of the car, Cadillac, was also named after a French explorer—Sieur Antoine de la Mothe Cadillac—who founded Detroit.

A noble name for a noble birth from a noble family characterized the aura and excitement of the times. France and the United States still had an active love affair. Anything French was immediately linked to new design, high fashion, color and excitement. For that matter, anything of an imported nature was fashionable. So, it was reasoned that the French foreign design characteristics of the new automobile should capitalize on this fashionability to attract those in the market niche as potential purchasers of the new LaSalle. LaSalle had all of the attributes advertising agencies would be able to promote with an uncommon flair to meet the vogue of the times.

The LaSalle was introduced to the public on March 5, 1927. It was an immediate success and exceeded expectations, winning numerous design awards and treated as an almost totally separate brand. Cadillac made sure, however, that the LaSalle would be promoted as "built by Cadillac" in the Cadillac factory. Kinship was considered essential. It was to fill a need without detracting from the prestige or clientele already faithful to Cadillac. Cadillac and LaSalle would be linked by name and by reputation. Hence, the very first advertisement in *The Saturday Evening Post* headlined, "Cadillac Welcomes La Salle . . . the new car for Cadillac homes."

LaSalle
a companion car to Cadillac

CARRYING FORWARD the policy of a quality car for every purse and purpose, General Motors saw the need for Cadillac's developing a high grade automobile which would be as socially acceptable as Cadillac itself, but with a slightly varying field of usefulness.

For this congenial task the Cadillac organization was invited to draw freely upon the entire resources of General Motors, including the Research Laboratories, the Department of Purchases, the Fisher Body Corporation and the Proving Ground.

The result is revealed in Cadillac showrooms this month—LaSalle, a fine motor car built wholly within Cadillac's plants, but, in the widest sense of the term, a "product of General Motors."

Those who travel much in Europe have realized that there was an opportunity to introduce a Continental style in the appearance of an American car. LaSalle has realized upon that opportunity. It is radically unlike any other automobile; yet the poise and the breeding of Cadillac are there!

Never was a car so rigidly tested in advance of its presentation to the public as LaSalle has been tested at the General Motors Proving Ground. It is a new car to you; it is a tried and proved car to us—as distinguished in performance as it is different in appearance. We present LaSalle with very great pride and invite you to view its six models.

GENERAL MOTORS

CHEVROLET · PONTIAC · OLDSMOBILE · OAKLAND
BUICK · LaSALLE · CADILLAC
GMC TRUCKS · YELLOW CABS, BUSES, TRUCKS
FRIGIDAIRE—The Electric Refrigerator

MARCH 4, 1927 . . . THE BIG EVENT . . . THE LaSALLE CHRISTENING CEREMONY

Clearing House, the cooperative bulletin of the Cadillac organization, provides a good overview of the events leading up to the christening and shortly thereafter. It is important to remember that LaSalle was intended as a companion car to Cadillac. Cadillac was still the parent company.

The factory's primary interest was to sell new Cadillacs. They were apprehensive about the possibility of LaSalle's good looks resulting in sales taken away from Cadillac rather than adding to Cadillac's sales volume. Getting salesmen in the right frame of mind, H. M. Stephens, National Sales Manager for Cadillac, in the February 24, 1927, issue of *Clearing House,* clearly stated, "There is a greater necessity for closer concentration on Cadillac sales than in previous years. LaSalle must not be sold to the exclusion of Cadillac. For you must remember that the Cadillac car is the backbone of our institution." "If we fail to give our biggest support to the car that has made us . . . then the prosperity of Cadillac, your own prosperity, and ours, accordingly, will suffer."

The foregoing quotes were in the same bulletin which introduced LaSalle to the Cadillac organization with great fanfare and enthusiasm.

So, it was crystal clear that LaSalle was viewed as a means of enhancing the sale of Cadillac automobiles and the Cadillac organization.

The emphasis was on companion car to Cadillac and that the demand was "for a slightly smaller car of Cadillac caliber for slightly different purposes." However, it was not to be regarded as a "little" Cadillac . . . "It is an entirely new car for a new purpose to fill a new field of usefulness."

Once introduced, incidentally, on the birthday anniversary of Sieur Antoine de la Mothe Cadillac, even Cadillac executives reveled in the success of the public's enthusiasm for this new companion car. "The reception of the LaSalle has been the most gratifying thing in my long experience with Cadillac," said Lynn McNaughton, Vice President. "The reception accorded the LaSalle exceeded the most optimistic expectations." The headline of the March 10, 1927, *Clearing House* bulletin stated, "Overwhelming enthusiasm greets introduction of LaSalle. Reception and actual sales far exceed expectations."

Note the change in the masthead of *Clearing House.* February 24, 1927, shows a Cadillac crest only. After the introduction, *Clearing House* actually showed the winged LaSalle crest with greater prominence. It was a hint of a change in attitude within the Cadillac organization. A change from LaSalle being "incidental" to a pride in its success, driven by public demand. Nevertheless, Cadillac took credit for this success, "For this flattering reception was due not because the LaSalle was a new car but because it was a car created by Cadillac."

To have a more thorough understanding of this entire event and the attitudes accompanying the introduction of the new LaSalle, we have enclosed copies of articles in those bulletins. Only by reading these articles in their entirety, written in the literary style of the times, can one appreciate the significance of this event. Also worth perusing are the numerous magazines in which LaSalle was promoted and all the sales literature published for the introduction, which, today, are highly prized possessions in the hands of collectors.

Festive was the occasion at the Copley-Plaza Hotel in Boston. Anna Danforth, daughter of the Boston, Massachusetts, dealership owner, christened the LaSalle with eloquent words and by breaking a bottle of champagne across the radiator, ship-launching style. Thereafter, Cadillac President L. P. Fisher presented her with the very same Convertible Coupe she had just christened.

Above all, the words of the christening spoken by Anna Danforth are prose of great eloquence befitting LaSalle: "And now, lovely creation of many minds and hearts and hands go forth into the highways and byways of the world, into the broad light of day, and beneath the starry skies, and may the record of your achievements bring new splendor to the glorious name we have given thee . . .

. . . I christen thee, LaSalle."

CLEARING HOUSE

Co-Operative Bulletin of — The Cadillac Organization

Thursday, February 24, 1927 — Volume XII, Number 30

Introducing LaSalle—Companion Car to Cadillac

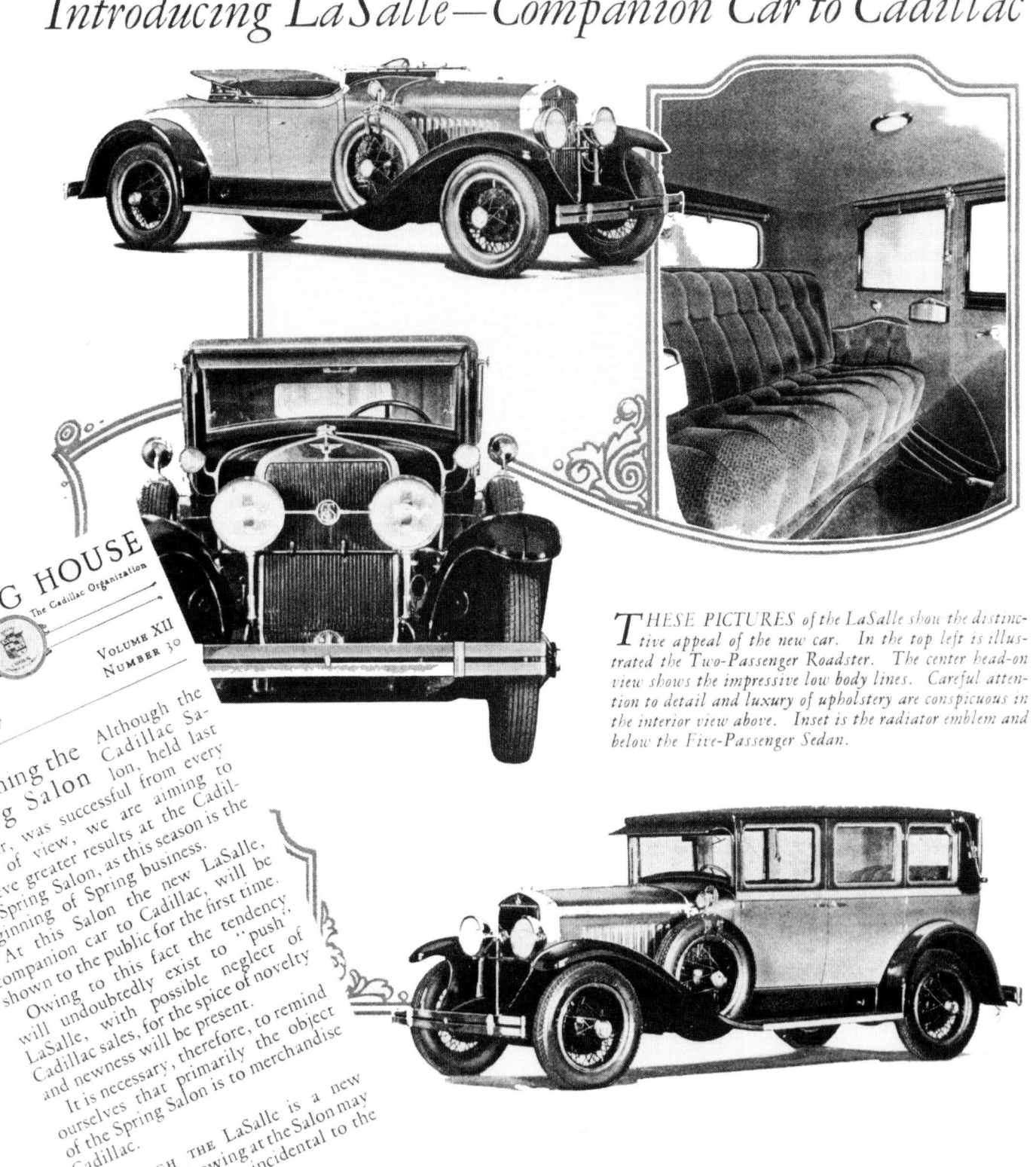

THESE PICTURES of the LaSalle show the distinctive appeal of the new car. In the top left is illustrated the Two-Passenger Roadster. The center head-on view shows the impressive low body lines. Careful attention to detail and luxury of upholstery are conspicuous in the interior view above. Inset is the radiator emblem and below the Five-Passenger Sedan.

Concerning the Spring Salon

Although the Cadillac Salon, held last October, was successful from every point of view, we are aiming to achieve greater results at the Cadillac Spring Salon, as this season is the beginning of Spring business.

At this Salon the new LaSalle, companion car to Cadillac, will be shown to the public for the first time.

Owing to this fact the tendency will undoubtedly exist to "push" LaSalle, with possible neglect of Cadillac sales, for the spice of novelty and newness will be present.

It is necessary, therefore, to remind ourselves that primarily the object of the Spring Salon is to merchandise Cadillac.

Although the LaSalle is a new car, its showing at the Salon may be regarded as only incidental to the Cadillac show.

CLEARING HOUSE

Co-Operative Bulletin of The Cadillac Organization

Thursday, March 10, 1927 — Volume XII, Number 32

Overwhelming Enthusiasm Greets Introduction of LaSalle Reception and Actual Sales Far Exceed Expectations

THE LaSalle, beautiful new companion car to Cadillac, was launched last week at the Cadillac Spring Salon on a tidal wave of enthusiasm that swept up a new record for attendance in every point where the car was shown.

In addition to the record breaking attendance all over the country, actual orders placed from the first moment when the Salon began were far in excess of all preliminary estimates, and while the complete figures as to total orders received to date are not available at this time, the amount was so large as to be astonishing.

And as this is written—on the fourth day of the Salon — reports from all sections of the country bear enthusiastic evidence of the fact that motordom has placed a most emphatic stamp of endorsement on the latest product of the Cadillac Motor Car Company.

The reception accorded the LaSalle has exceeded the most optimistic expectations. With the introduction of any new product in the automobile industry there are two important factors—how large a turnout the new car will receive and what sort of comment is made about it.

In the case of the LaSalle introduction, both these two factors were so favorable that a few hours after the Salon opened in the various points it became evident that the LaSalle was to prove all that was hoped for it.

In the first place, wherever the car was exhibited all attendance records for the introduction of a new car in the fine car field were broken. This, in itself, proved most significant. It indicated most clearly that the public was keenly interested in the advent of this car.

Of much more vital importance, however, was the enthusiastic outpouring of complimentary comment.

> THE reception of the LaSalle has been the most gratifying thing in my long experience with Cadillac. Although all of us who had anything to do with the design, production and introduction of this car were certain that we had really achieved the objective we were striving for, nevertheless, there still remained the public's reaction to be discovered. That America put such an instant, emphatic and unqualifiedly enthusiastic stamp of approval on this beautiful new companion car to Cadillac has proved in most thoroughly convincing manner just how right we were.
>
> Aside from the natural gratification that followed through a realization that in this car we have accomplished what we sought, one of the most gratifying features in connection with it has been that this tremendous wave of enthusiasm is an unmistakable tribute to the Cadillac Motor Car Company, for, after all, it was Cadillac's prestige, Cadillac's reputation as a designer and manufacturer of fine motor cars, that brought out such an overwhelming reaction of interest in the new car. Long before a line appeared in print about the LaSalle, interest was keen all over the country. Nothing was known of the car, what it was to be. But that it was being produced by Cadillac proved sufficient to stimulate the interest of motorists generally.
>
> I wish at this time to thank Cadillac distributors and dealers for the very splendid way in which they prepared for the introduction of this new car. The fact that the distributing organization all over the country worked in such close harmony with the factory and bent every effort to make the introduction a success was one of the biggest contributing factors to the event.
>
> LYNN McNAUGHTON,
> Vice President.

As was expected, the LaSalle captured visitors on sight. Its beauty of line, its perfect harmony and its brilliancy brought out the most flattering tributes of praise from all who saw it.

The LaSalle, in other words, has taken America by storm and has fully convinced motordom that it is, as we have stated, a car worthy to be a companion car to Cadillac.

The reception given the LaSalle by Cadillac distributors, dealers and salesmen was even more gratifying. That this body of men who are so well informed in things automotive and who through long experience with the Cadillac are accustomed to the best, should have hailed this new car with such unqualified enthusiasm is perhaps the best tribute that could have been paid the new product.

Therefore, this gratifying reception of Cadillac's companion car is a distinct tribute to the Cadillac Motor Car Company. It is a tribute to Cadillac's twenty-five years of prestige, to Cadillac's enviable record of success in fine car building. Furthermore, it is a notable triumph for Cadillac engineering and design. For this flattering reception was due not because the LaSalle was a new car but because it was a car created by Cadillac.

The record breaking attendance that followed the introduction of the LaSalle is all the more remarkable when it is remembered that not a line of advertising or

(Continued on page 128)

The La Salle, a New Automobile Introduced as a Companion Car To Cadillac, Will Be Shown to the Public at the Spring Salon

The LaSalle will be presented to the public at the Cadillac Spring Salon to be held simultaneously throughout the country from March 5th to 12th.

This new car has been produced by the Cadillac Motor Car Company in order to fill the demand which has existed in this country for some years for a slightly smaller car of Cadillac calibre for slightly different purposes.

It is a beautiful new car of brilliant performance, designed by Cadillac engineers and built by the Cadillac Motor Car Company entirely within its own plants as a companion car to Cadillac. It is not a "little" Cadillac —it is an entirely new car for a new purpose to fill a new field of usefulness.

Inherent in this car are the principles that have contributed so much to Cadillac's prestige, and the LaSalle may be characterized as the Cadillac principle applied in a new way.

It is powered with a ninety-degree V-type Eight, the same type of engine that has scored such a phenomenal success in the Cadillac car for thirteen years. This principle of engine design has been adapted to the particular needs of the LaSalle.

The La Salle line includes six models of distinctive beauty and charm: The Five-Passenger Sedan; the Four-Passenger Phaeton; Four-Passenger Victoria; Two-Passenger Convertible Coupe; Two-Passenger Roadster and the Two-Passenger Coupe. The last three models have dickey seats. The fact that the car is powered with the same type of engine as is the Cadillac is sufficient proof of the mechanical efficiency of the car.

The body work is of the same beautiful finish and luxurious appointments that have characterized the Cadillac; but a new note of originality in body line giving low, graceful and perfectly proportioned harmony, has been achieved, setting a new standard in American coachcraft.

Extensive advertising and publicity arrangements have been made to announce the LaSalle.

Prior to the actual showing of the car at the Cadillac Spring Salon, the first newspaper advertisement will appear on Thursday, March 3rd, throughout the country concurrently with a double page announcement in the *Saturday Evening Post* of the same week.

The newspaper advertisement will be on the Spring Salon and will also state that the LaSalle will be shown publicly for the first time on March 5th.

The *Saturday Evening Post* advertisement will introduce the LaSalle, briefly setting forth what the car is and why it has been produced.

In the *Literary Digest* of March 5th will appear a mention of the La Salle in a color advertisement.

The General Motors Corporation, on Sunday, March 6th, will also run a newspaper advertisement in all important towns and cities of the country, the keynote of which will be that although LaSalle is a new car to the public, it is, strictly speaking, four years old to the manufacturers, as it has been perfected over that period in the factory, laboratory and Proving Ground, and has the General Motors Corporation resources behind the product.

In addition to this advertising, the Cadillac Motor Car Company has engaged Radio Station WEAF, New York, for a concert between the hours of 8:00 and 9:00 p. m., Eastern time, Thursday, March 3rd, when the new LaSalle will be announced.

In order to fix in the mind of the public the thought that the two cars are essentially the product of the Cadillac Motor Car Company, in future advertising they will always be tied-up with the name of the company.

(Continued on page 120)

THE introduction of the LaSalle is an event which I know you all have long anticipated.

This new automobile is a car of quality worthy in every way of the Cadillac family, and we all are proud of it.

It is a car, radically different in many ways, which has been built in response to a specific demand on the part of a section of the motoring public for a companion car to Cadillac, of true Cadillac calibre.

With this potential market, with an automobile that we have built for, and which so obviously fits this demand, I have no doubt about your ability to merchandise LaSalle.

I even predict that sales will far exceed our production schedule for the first twelve months.

What I now wish to stress is that your efforts in merchandising Cadillac be not lessened in any way, for this is of the greatest importance.

You would not be human if you did not feel urged to exert your utmost in putting over LaSalle in a big way, with its appeal and its novelty of "something new."

But, although LaSalle is a new car, rather is there a greater necessity for closer concentration on Cadillac sales than in previous years.

LaSalle must not be sold to the exclusion of Cadillac.

For you must remember that the Cadillac car is the backbone of our institution.

If we fail to give our biggest support to the car that has made us, if we fail to visualize the whole situation in its true light and do not get the right conception of the position of LaSalle in the Cadillac picture—then the prosperity of Cadillac, your own prosperity and ours, accordingly, will suffer.

I hope all distributors and dealers will grasp the importance of this message.

H. M. STEPHENS

CLEARING HOUSE

Co-Operative Bulletin of The Cadillac Organization

Thursday, March 17, 1927   Volume XII, Number 33

Boston Welcomes The LaSalle At Christening Ceremony

The festive and enthusiastic scene that marked the christening of the LaSalle at the Copley-Plaza Hotel, Boston, on March 4, is shown above. Miss Danforth, who performed the ceremony, is seen to the right of the car which was afterwards presented to her by President L. P. Fisher

"AND NOW, lovely creation of many minds and hearts and hands go forth into the highways and byways of the world, into the broad light of day, and beneath the starry skies, and may the record of your achievements bring new splendor to the glorious name we have given thee. I christen thee, LaSalle."

With these words, followed by the crash of breaking glass, as a bottle of mock champagne was broken on the radiator, the LaSalle, companion car to Cadillac, was christened at the Copley-Plaza Hotel, Boston, on March 4, before an attendance of more than three hundred Cadillac distributors, dealers and salesmen, executives of the Cadillac Motor Car Company and representatives of the General Motors Corporation.

As Miss Anna Danforth, daughter of Albion L. Danforth, president of the Cadillac Automobile Company of Boston, performed the ceremony which symbolized the introduction of the new car to the automobile public, cheer upon cheer rang out and myriad colored lights flashed on the centre group showing the sleek, resplendent LaSalle roadster impressive in its suggestion of grace and hidden power.

Previous to the actual ceremony, the guests had gathered in other rooms in the hotel and now, marching behind a band of white-coated musicians, they entered the room in which was staged the new car draped and covered in silken cloth.

Around and around the room the men marched, finally pausing to witness the unveiling, which was accomplished by a group of girls in a manner not unlike the Maypole Dance.

It was an enthusiastic and impressive ceremony, fitting to the importance of the occasion, and unforgetable by reason of its impressiveness in the minds of all those present witnessing the christening.

(Continued on page 132)

CLEARING HOUSE

Co-Operative Bulletin of The Cadillac Organization

Thursday, June 9, 1927

Volume XII, No.

Tremendous Mileages Rolled Up By Standard LaSalle Cars

ONE OF THE facts responsible for the outstanding success of the LaSalle reflected by the instant acceptance, rapid and constantly increasing sales... the wonderful performance... the hands of private... Cadillac Motor C... lutely sure... ally...

...this page which confirms the fact that the La...

"Thoroughbreds Both" might be the title of this picture in which are seen "Miss LaSalle", a novice horse owned by Albion L. Danforth, president of the Cadillac Motor Car Company of Boston and the actual LaSalle, thoroughbred offspring of Cadillac, which was christened at the Copley Plaza Hotel, Boston by Miss Anna Danforth, daughter of Mr. Danforth. This horse has captured a blue ribbon at the Brooklyn Riding and Driving Club, Brooklyn, New York, and also a second and third prize at the Paul Revere Horse Show, Concord, Mass. Mounted on the "Miss LaSalle" is Albion Danforth; in the car, Miss Anna Danforth and her sister

"The Last Word in Automobile Design" Is The Enthusiastic Verdict of LaSalle Owner

HERE's another short account of LaSalle owner enthusiasm forwarded to us by the Uppercu Cadillac Corporation, Brooklyn, N. Y.

This owner, like all who are fortunate possessors of LaSalle, is so thoroughly "sold" on his car that words are not needed to elaborate on his genuine joy he derives from his car.

"It would be unusual," he said, "if I did not express my deep appreciation to each and every one in the Cadillac Automobile Company for delivering to me what I consider the last word in automobile design and construction."

A charming picture in which grace, style, beauty are all combined. Yes, the description applies both to the LaSalle and to the three maidens, the Misses Gloria, Bertha and Francesca Bragiotti, who run a dancing academy well known in social circles of Boston

NINETEEN TWENTY-SEVEN
Series 303

In surpassing smartness and in brilliancy of performance, the La Salle is as new as this morning's sun— but in its assurance of fine and unfeeling service, it is as old as Cadillac's own 25 years of reputation and responsibility.

The ardent admiration aroused everywhere by its charm of appearance is as nothing in comparison with the delight invariably inspired by the brilliant performance of the La Salle. It was only to be expected that America, with its quick and wholehearted appreciation of superiority in any field, should have accorded a warm welcome to La Salle.

How La Salle revives the desire to drive. Let a man or woman with even a shred of youthful enthusiasm spend an hour with a La Salle, and the whole concept of modern motoring is changed. For with the La Salle, driving again becomes an act of entrancing delight, and mere riding takes on an entirely new enjoyment.

—*from the 1927 sales brochure*

Près des Pyrénées

"AS REFRESHING AS A PARIS FROCK".. Says a smart weekly, of the La Salle

The La Salle was born to the Cadillac purple—with 250,000 Cadillacs as ancestors—with the latest 90-degree, V-type, eight-cylinder engine under its hood—with never a doubt as to its consequent performance. And its price makes a lesser car an extravagance.

FOR A SMALL DOWN PAYMENT—with the appraisal value of your used car acceptable as cash—you may possess a La Salle on the liberal term payment plan of the General Motors Acceptance Corporation—the famous G.M.A.C. plan.

From $2495 to $2685, f. o. b. Detroit

La Salle
CADILLAC MOTOR CAR COMPANY
DETROIT, MICHIGAN   OSHAWA, CANADA
Division of General Motors Corporation

NINETEEN TWENTY-SEVEN
Series 303

On Cadillac Motor Car Company's Silver Anniversary, a completely new automobile was introduced: the LaSalle, a companion car to Cadillac. Nobility and exploration were chosen as themes for the introduction. Noble would be its heritage, and exploration of new vistas, its destiny.

The first LaSalle was given an American-European look featuring a delicately peaked radiator shape, a LaSalle badge on the tiebar between the two headlights, graceful front fenders flowing into the running boards, and new dish-like headlights. Parking lights were mounted on the cowl and landau bars were prevalent on closed and transformable models. Three types of wheels were available . . . wire spokes, wooden spokes and solid discs. Aside from its lithe body style, Harley Earl introduced a wide palette of colors and dramatic two-tone exterior paint treatments.

Eleven body types were available on two Fisher-bodied chassis—125-inch wheelbase and 134-inch wheelbase. Another four were made by Fleetwood. The Series 303 was designated after the car's engine displacement of 303 cubic inches, in the European tradition.

Created to fill a void and to add, not take away, volume from Cadillac, LaSalle's marketing strategy was well thought out. Cadillac and LaSalle would be linked by name and by reputation. Yet LaSalle was promoted as a completely new car . . . one could argue a totally separate brand offering. Even though Cadillac built the LaSalle, there were very few interchangeable chassis or body components.

From a niche perspective, the introductory prices were ideally positioned from $2495 to $2685, right between the highest priced Buick and the lowest priced Cadillac. "Prices in value would be impossible if LaSalle were not the running mate to Cadillac—enjoying all the economies of their great joint volume of production."

The positioning of LaSalle from the very outset was significant. "This new car has been produced by the Cadillac Motor Car Company in order to fill the demand which has existed in this country for some years for a slightly smaller car of Cadillac caliber for slightly different purposes." "It is not a 'little' Cadillac—it is an entirely new car for a new purpose to fill a new field of usefulness." "LaSalle must not be sold to the exclusion of Cadillac." It was to tap a new market and increase sales for the Division as a whole.

All 1927-28 LaSalle advertising illustrations were created by Edward A. Wilson, who, as a commercial artist, had garnered a fine reputation with Pierce Arrow, Franklin, Victrola, etc. Wilson used the French foreign connection to the fullest. The settings were delightfully European and were truly works of art. A Victoria Coupe is pictured near a large windmill and labeled "le Moulin," and an open Roadster is entitled "The Hare and the Tortoise." The prose of the time was part of the subtitles "How LaSalle revived the desire to drive"; "quick, smooth, smart; why LaSalle demand grows—*and grows*." "When the new companion car to Cadillac made its debut last spring, its fresh grace and beauty won instant acceptance."

PERFORMANCE, as is understood among owners of fine cars, is not an excess of ability to be demonstrated on occasions. Rather, it is a superiority of routine behavior to be continuously enjoyed. It inheres in qualities which may be hard to define but which are instantly identified—positive qualities, which do not proclaim their presence, but whose lack is immediately and unmistakably felt.

It is in this, the true fine car sense, that the LaSalle interprets performance. It has an abundance of power for the most exceptional demands—surging acceleration, boundless speed—the maximum degree of riding comfort on a compact wheelbase —balance, perfected control, roadability—that refinement of behavior which is everywhere so highly prized, but which is to be gained only when sound principles are faithfully observed and correctly applied. The four-passenger Victoria applies them in a sumptuous model whose every appointment bespeaks luxury.

OF prime significance about the LaSalle is the fact that it is built by Cadillac. In its design and construction the intimate mastery of fine car requirements and possibilities, gleaned in a quarter century of successful building, finds expression.

Cadillac engineers designed the LaSalle, and perfected it in their own workshops, in the vast General Motors Engineering Laboratories, upon the General Motors Proving Ground. Characteristic Cadillac manufacturing practice prevails at every step. Seasoned Cadillac craftsmen form its parts and assemble and align them.

The result is a car fully meriting rank as companion car to Cadillac, yet distinctive and worthy of highest regard on its own account.

Under its hood is an engine precisely the same in principle as the one that, for nearly fourteen years, has made Cadillac the envied leader among fine cars—a compact, simple, 90-degree, V-type, eight-cylinder power plant, precisely adapted to the LaSalle weight and dimensions. Throughout its chassis the same guiding influence is seen again and again—the influence of those ideals, those influences, and that technical mastery which have made Cadillac great.

In the Convertible Coupe— two-passenger with folding seat in the rear deck—this mechanical excellence powers a car which fully accords with its brilliant abilities.

STRIKINGLY beautiful as it is, the LaSalle wins even more enthusiastic plaudits for its consummate riding ease. Even those who are most meticulous in this regard acclaim it. Those accustomed to the comforts inherent in extreme length are astounded that a 125-inch wheelbase can afford such complete relaxation.

This achievement is due to the rare mastery with which Cadillac engineering principles have been modified and applied in keeping with the LaSalle's size, weight, and designated field of usefulness.

In the Roadster, this roadability is emphatically in evidence. Here the essentially fine qualities of LaSalle performance are presented in a model which from the tall radiator to the gleaming rails upon the rear deck aptly symbolizes the vigor and vitality of modern youth.

". . . LaSalle was never an experiment . . ." On every ad, it listed Cadillac Motor Car Company and, in the ads, it said that "only Cadillac could have endowed LaSalle with its transcending beauty of line and appointment, its nimble fleetness, its sophisticated poise."

A great deal of literature was produced. One of the LaSalle showroom brochures was also illustrated by Wilson. All of the models are pictured in quaint scenes with a Convertible Coupe at a railroad crossing, and others in European villages. One ad entitled "In Springtime" shows country lanes lined with tall trees and rainbows on the horizon, and cupid pointing his bow and arrow towards the departing LaSalle. This beautiful 24-page booklet was in full color.

Wilson's work was fascinatingly beautiful. These works of art detailed with great splendor the European countryside, the architecture and the graceful lines of the LaSalle automobiles. A fitting tribute to LaSalle's first year.

Adequate power was essential in a lighter, smaller Cadillac. The engine was an 8-cylinder L-head V-type with a total displacement of 303 cubic inches, and a brake horsepower of 75 bhp. Connecting rods were ten inches long between centers and the location of the bearings were unlike Cadillac. Rods were placed side by side for each pair of cylinders with interchangeable bronze-backed babbitt lined bushings. There were two Morse silent-chains forward coming from the sprockets on the crankshaft. One was directly over the crankshaft, while the other drove the engine water pump.

LaSalle's Delco ignition system did not have any spark adjuster. Electrical failure would have to be aborted and was, by installing a supplementary vacuum pump driven from an eccentric on the camshaft, much like today's mechanical fuel pump. The Delco ignition system featured a distributor with two sets of contact points. The spark adjuster is mounted on the dash. Engine temperature was controlled by external shutters.

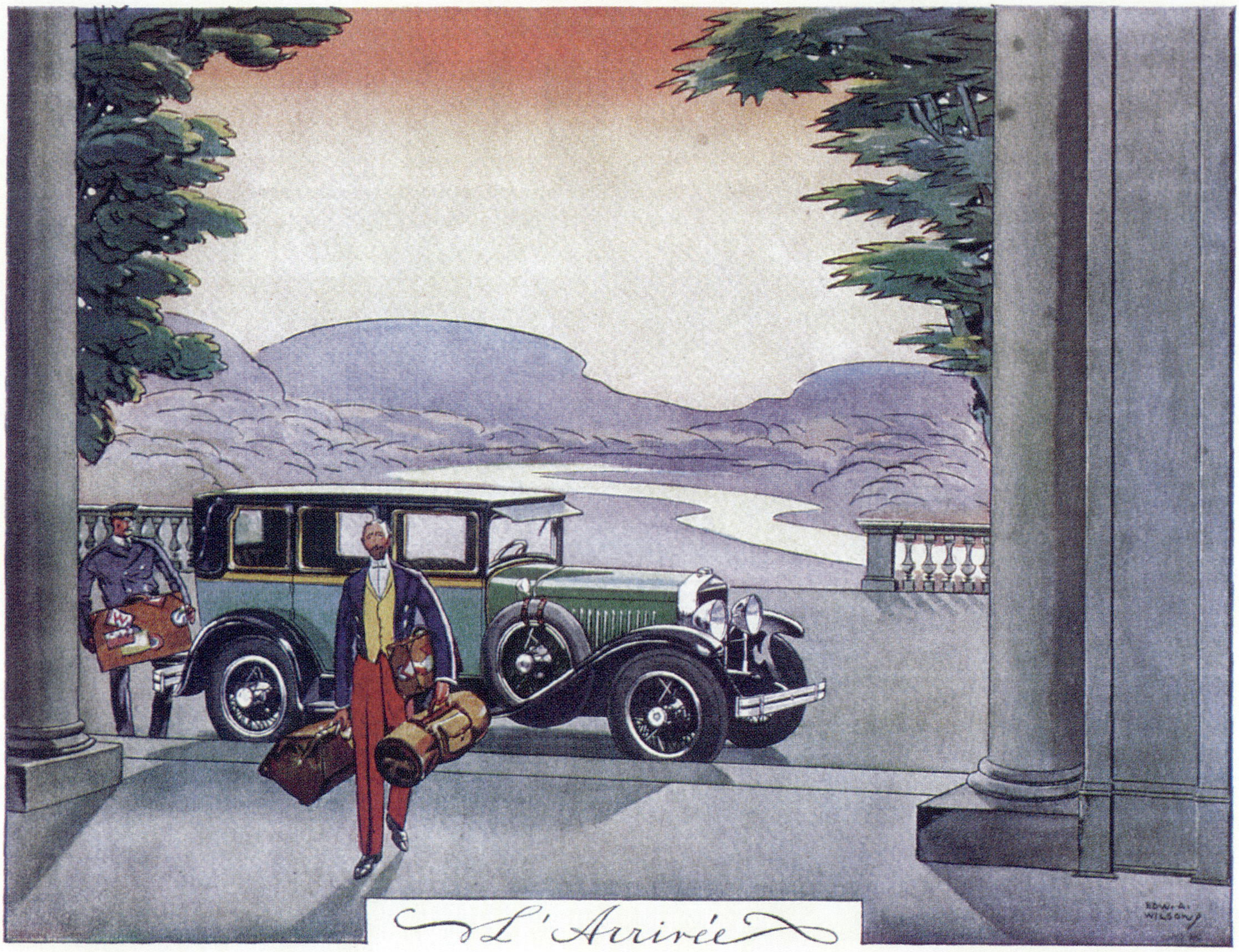
EDW. A. WILSON

L'Arrivée

WHY LaSALLE DEMAND GROWS—*AND GROWS*

When the new companion car to Cadillac made its début last spring, its fresh grace and beauty won instant acceptance. It was bought on sight by smart motorists the country over.

But only *performance* can account for the mounting La Salle sales in every community. The magical ease of handling, the rare smoothness of gear-shift, the new and delightful experience behind the steering wheel—these are La Salle attributes which have won thousands to its ownership, through the unsuppressed enthusiasm of pioneer purchasers.

Of course, the La Salle was never an experiment. It has a long line of ancestry in Cadillac, and shares with that car the distinction of being powered by the 90-degree V-type, eight-cylinder engine which knows no peer.

You may possess a La Salle on the liberal term-payment plan of the General Motors Acceptance Corporation—the famous G. M. A. C. plan

CADILLAC MOTOR CAR COMPANY

DETROIT, MICH. DIVISION OF GENERAL MOTORS CORPORATION OSHAWA, CAN.

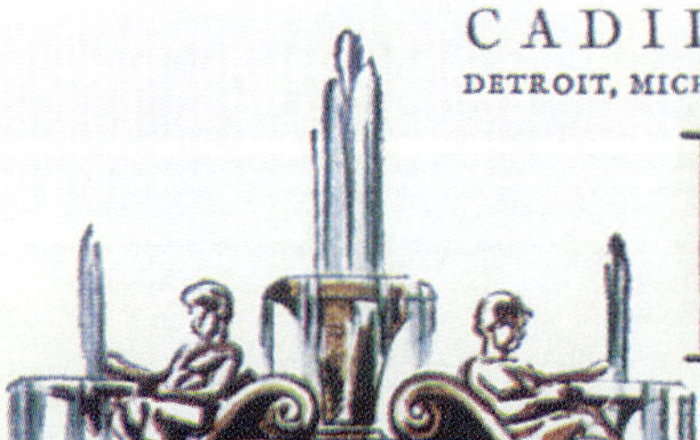

LA SALLE

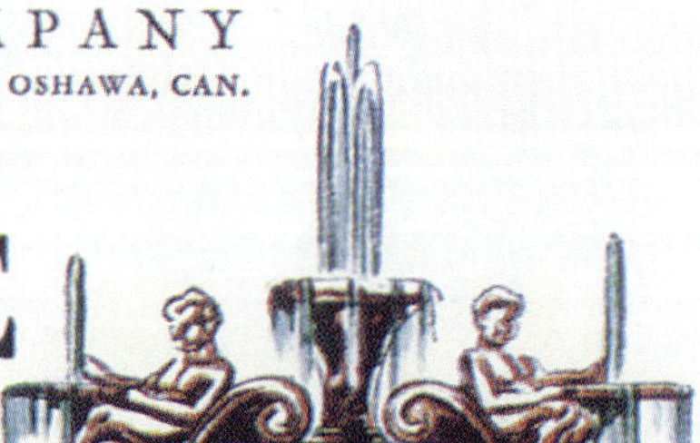

FROM $2495 *to* $2685 F.O.B. DETROIT

MANUFACTURED · COMPLETELY · BY · THE · CADILLAC · MOTOR · CAR · COMPANY · WITHIN · ITS · OWN · PLANTS

Lubrication was conventional with a provision for lubricating the valve stem with a system of small oil passages extending from the cylinder walls. Braking was accomplished by two independent systems in case of failure. Results . . . consumer confidence was high because it was linked to Cadillac's parenthood and reputation.

Further evidence of the mechanical reliability was demonstrated with a test run by twelve cars picked at random from the production line and driven over 300,000 miles during a four-month period of time. Not a single failure of a major component was reported.

Headline reports were enthusiastic: "Overwhelming enthusiasm greets introduction of LaSalle. Reception and actual sales far exceed expectations." "The LaSalle has taken America by storm and has fully convinced motordom that it is as we have stated, a car worthy to be a companion car to Cadillac."

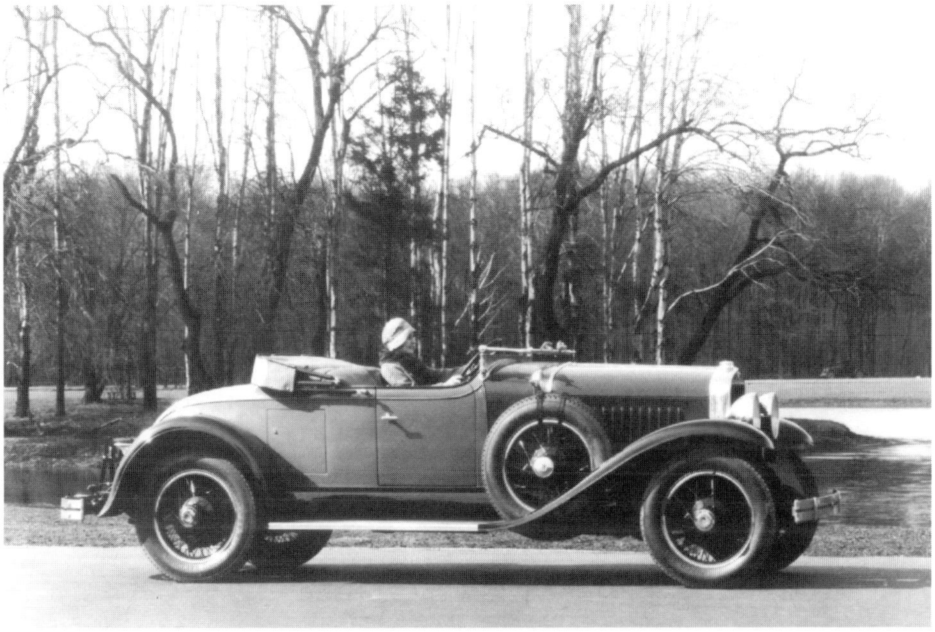

The Series 303 LaSalle Roadster in a two-tone color scheme with golf club door and rumble seat. "Light and lithe" were the most apt descriptions to give to this delightful car designed by Stylist Harley J. Earl. Its appeal to women was immediate and the factory promoted that purposefully in an attempt to draw a new clientele which would not take away from Cadillac sales.

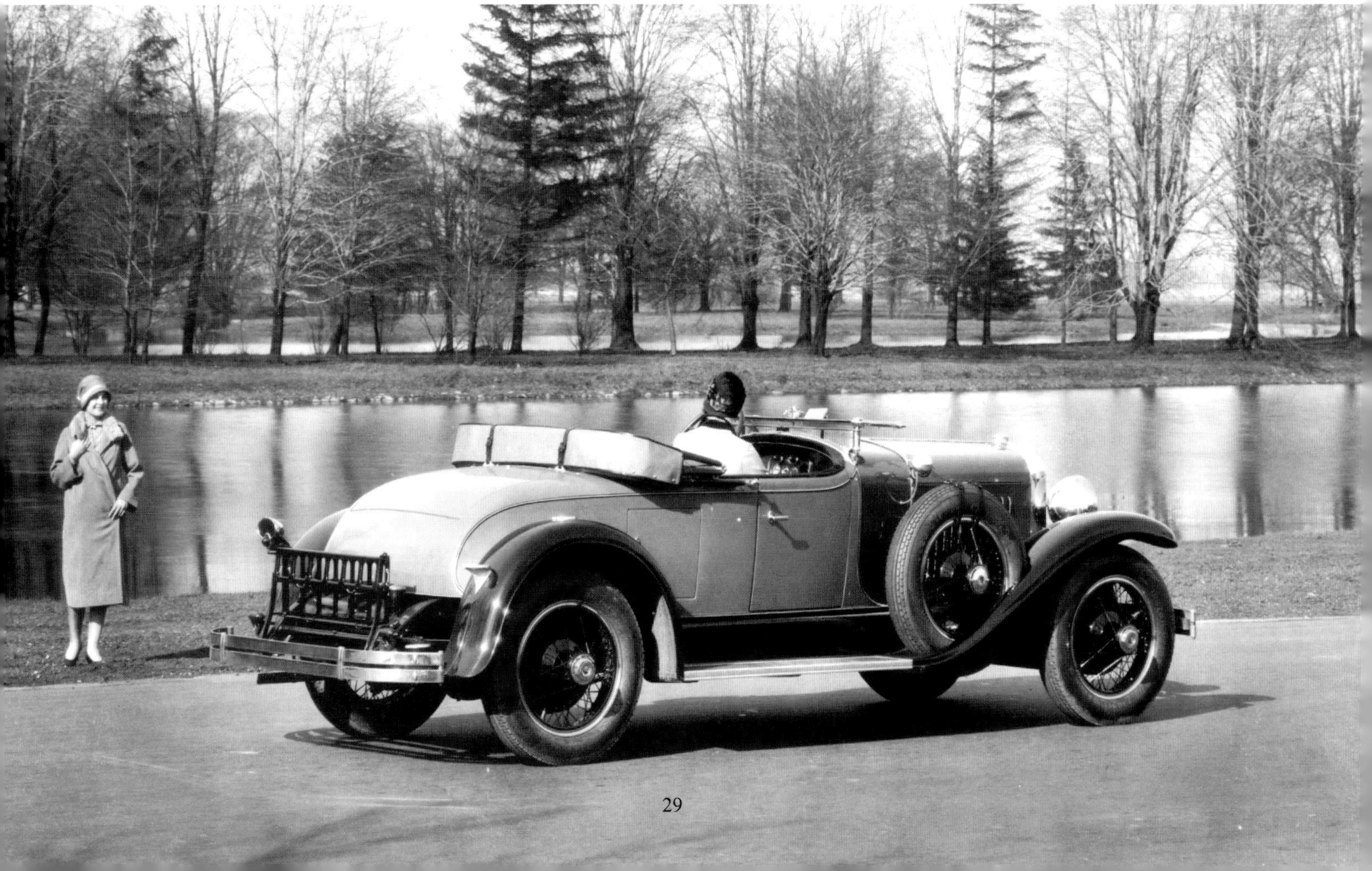

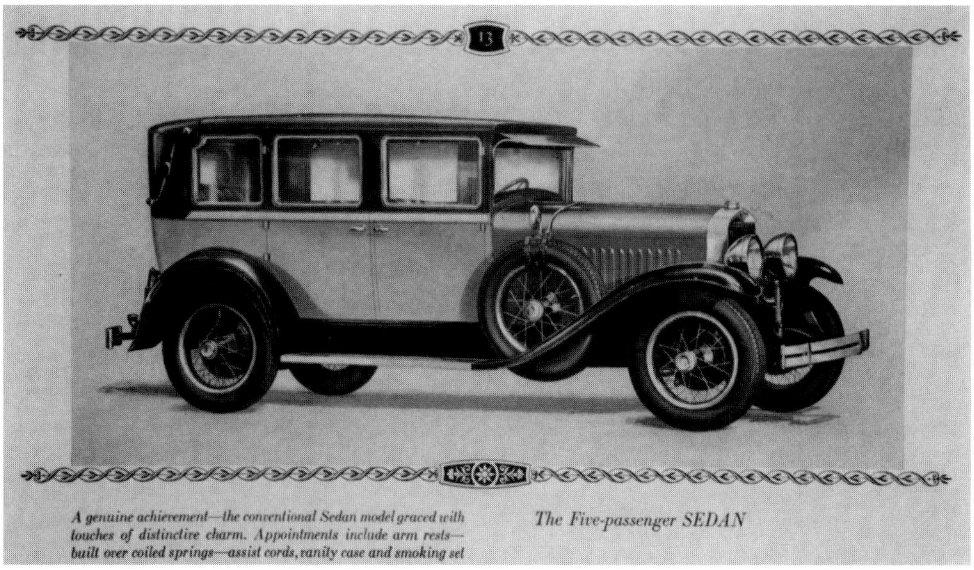
13
A genuine achievement—the conventional Sedan model graced with touches of distinctive charm. Appointments include arm rests—built over coiled springs—assist cords, vanity case and smoking set
The Five-passenger SEDAN

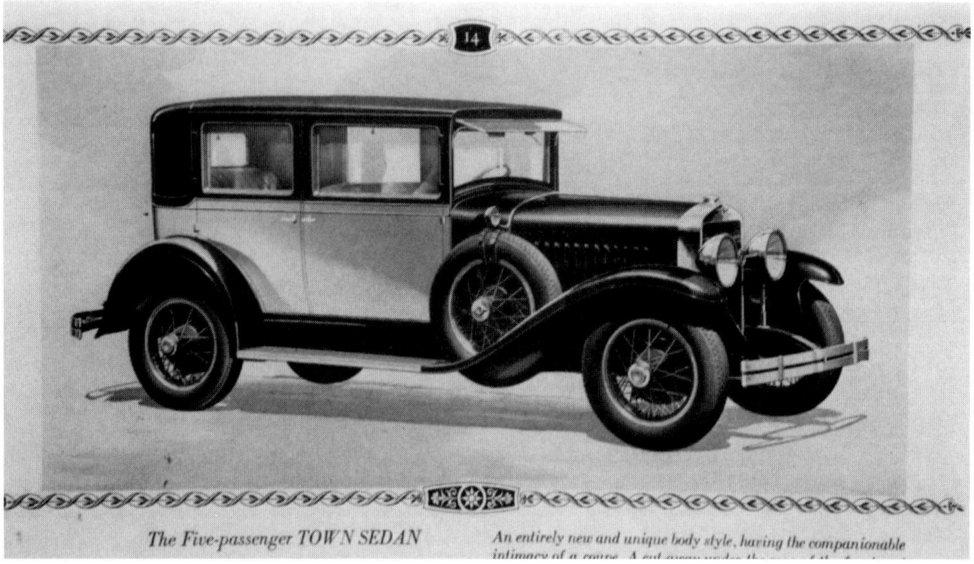
14
The Five-passenger TOWN SEDAN
An entirely new and unique body style, having the companionable

Three models are shown from the black and white sales brochure with realistic, almost photographic, proportions.

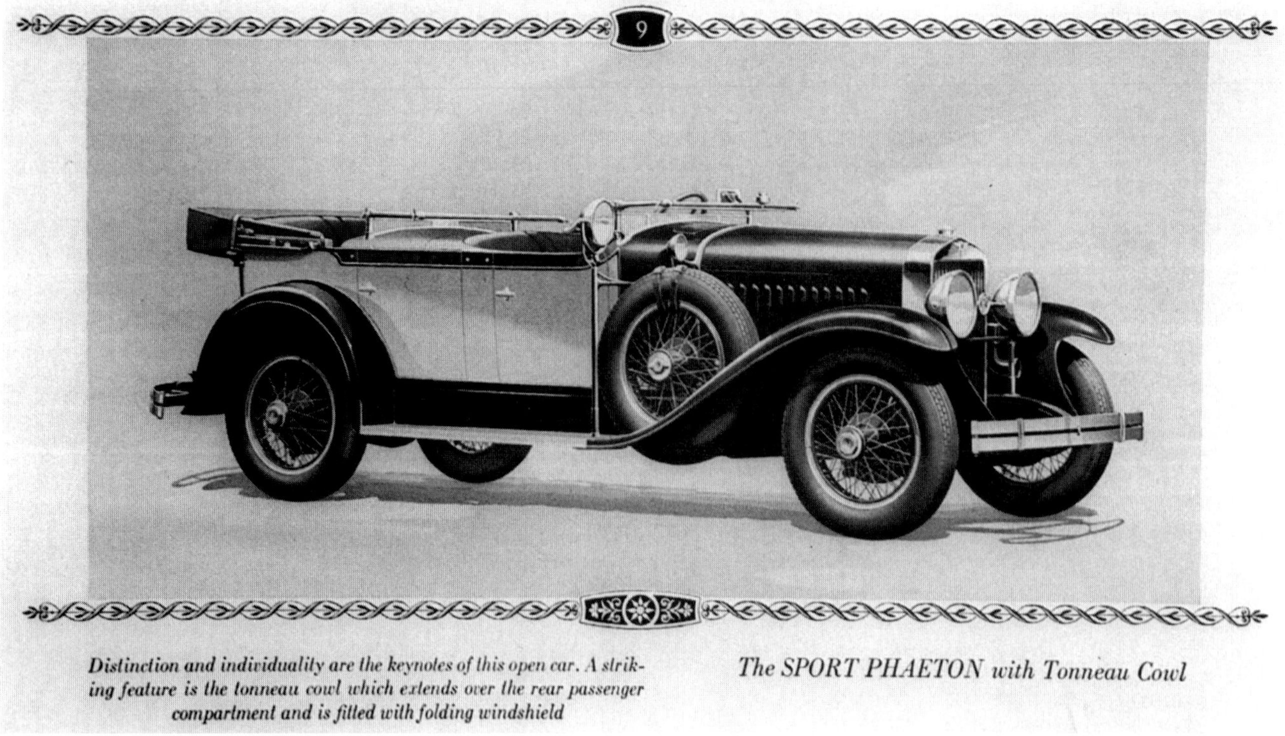
9
Distinction and individuality are the keynotes of this open car. A striking feature is the tonneau cowl which extends over the rear passenger compartment and is fitted with folding windshield
The SPORT PHAETON with Tonneau Cowl

Matchless grace and balance. Windows and windshield framed in nickeled moulding; nickel trimmed rear deck with rumble seat for two. When the top is in position the rear curtain may be folded upward out of the way

The Two-passenger CONVERTIBLE COUPE

The Four-passenger VICTORIA

Strikingly graceful model of widest utility. Curtains at quarter windows, dome light, combination vanity and smoking case, and assist cord on the right side are details in its complete appointment

Representative samples of the sales brochure shows all LaSalle models in a very realistic, non-artistic, black and white presentation.

A singularly vigorous open type. Nickel framed windshield, nickeled bars on the rear deck, nickel mounted top—sparkling, graceful, eager to go

The Two-passenger ROADSTER

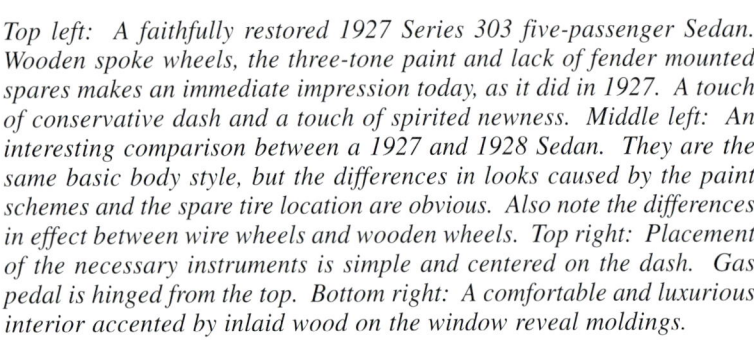

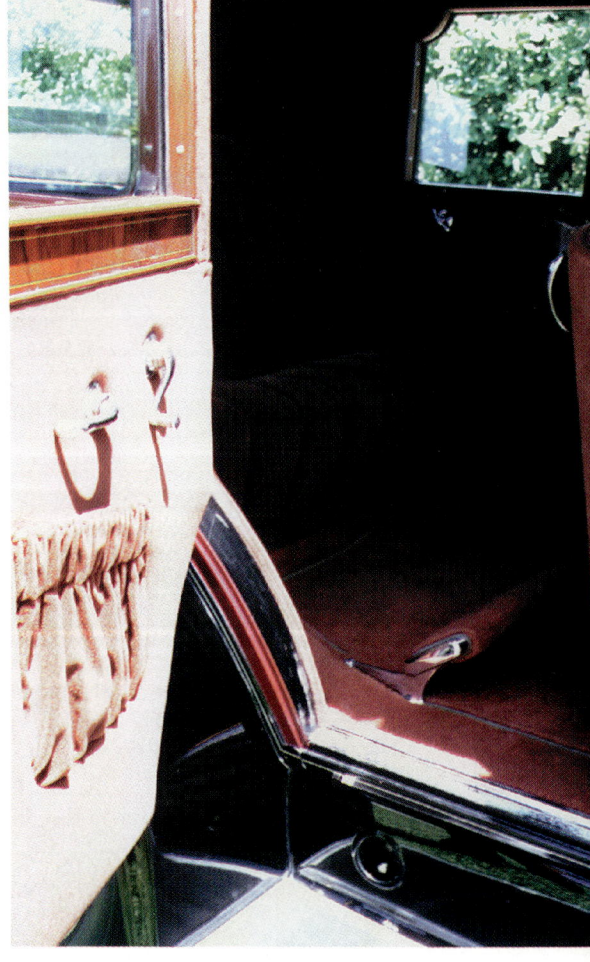

Top left: A faithfully restored 1927 Series 303 five-passenger Sedan. Wooden spoke wheels, the three-tone paint and lack of fender mounted spares makes an immediate impression today, as it did in 1927. A touch of conservative dash and a touch of spirited newness. Middle left: An interesting comparison between a 1927 and 1928 Sedan. They are the same basic body style, but the differences in looks caused by the paint schemes and the spare tire location are obvious. Also note the differences in effect between wire wheels and wooden wheels. Top right: Placement of the necessary instruments is simple and centered on the dash. Gas pedal is hinged from the top. Bottom right: A comfortable and luxurious interior accented by inlaid wood on the window reveal moldings.

Opposite page, clockwise. Top left: Distinctive ornamentation on the first LaSalle ... LaSalle, the nobleman, on the radiator cap; the coat of arms on the radiator; and the LaS on the tiebar between the headlights. Top right: The handsome front ensemble reminiscent of the Hispano-Suiza. The 1927 year model is easily identified by the cowl parking lights and twelve large hood ventilators. Middle right: Rear view shows the padded rear section and split rear bumper to accommodate the spare tire. Bottom right: A very handsome taillight assembly where LaSalle is briefly lit when the brake is engaged. Bottom left: Absence of the fender mounted spare exposes the cowl mounted parking lights.

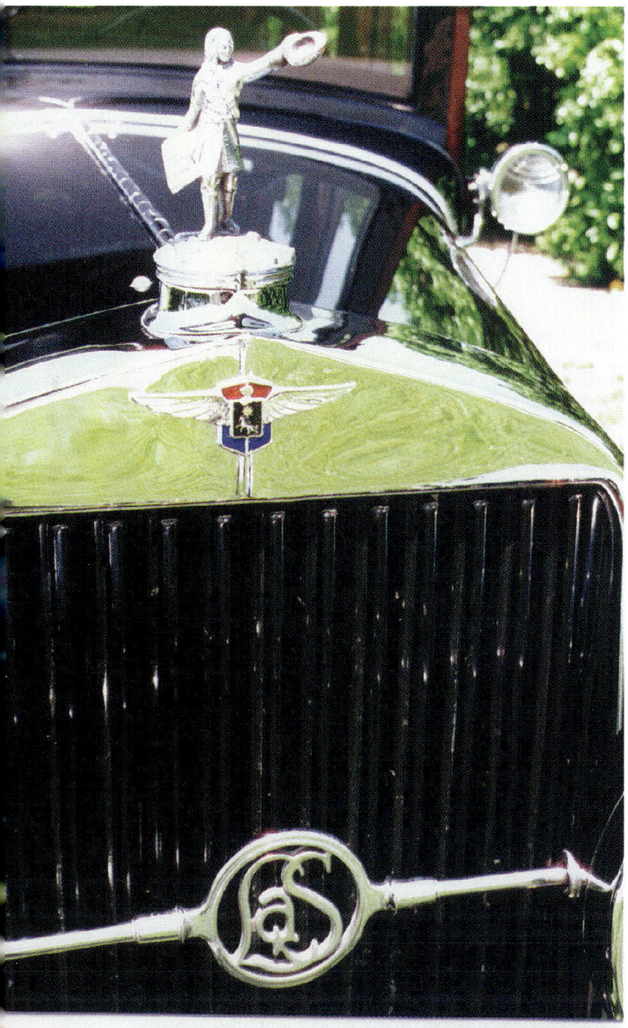

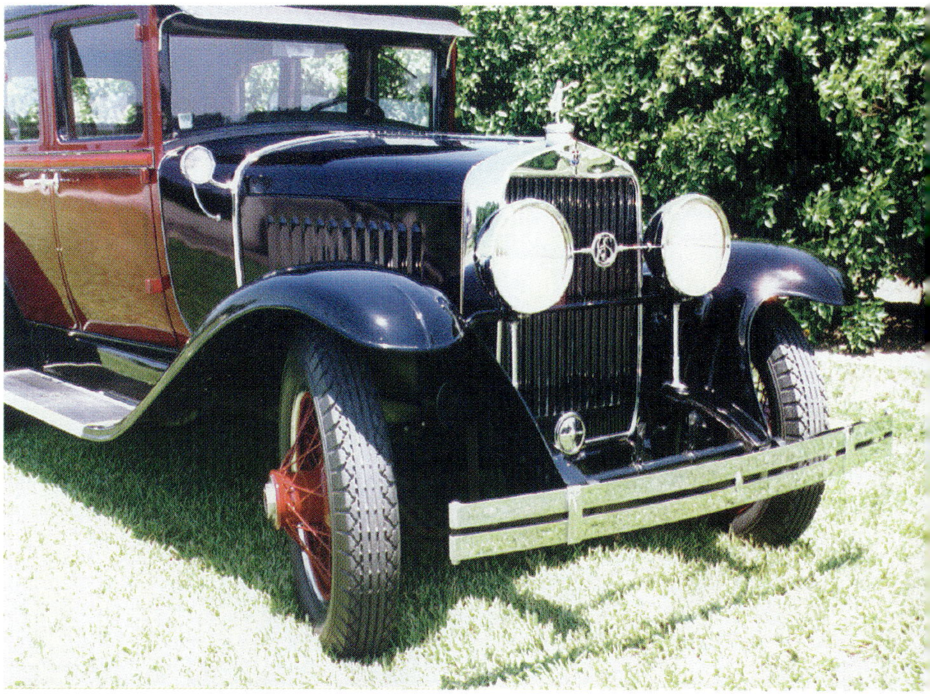

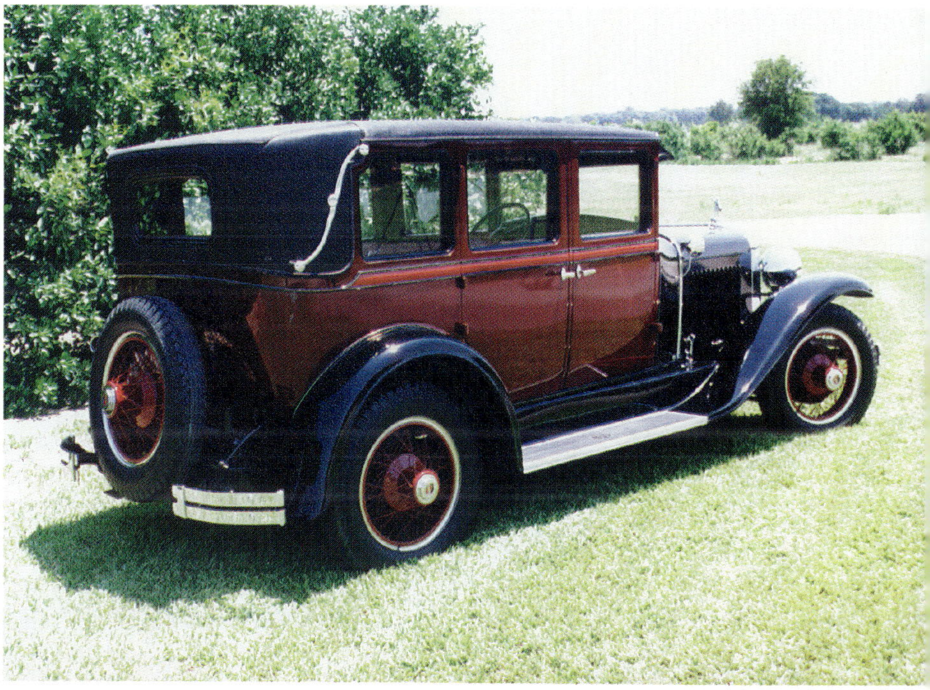

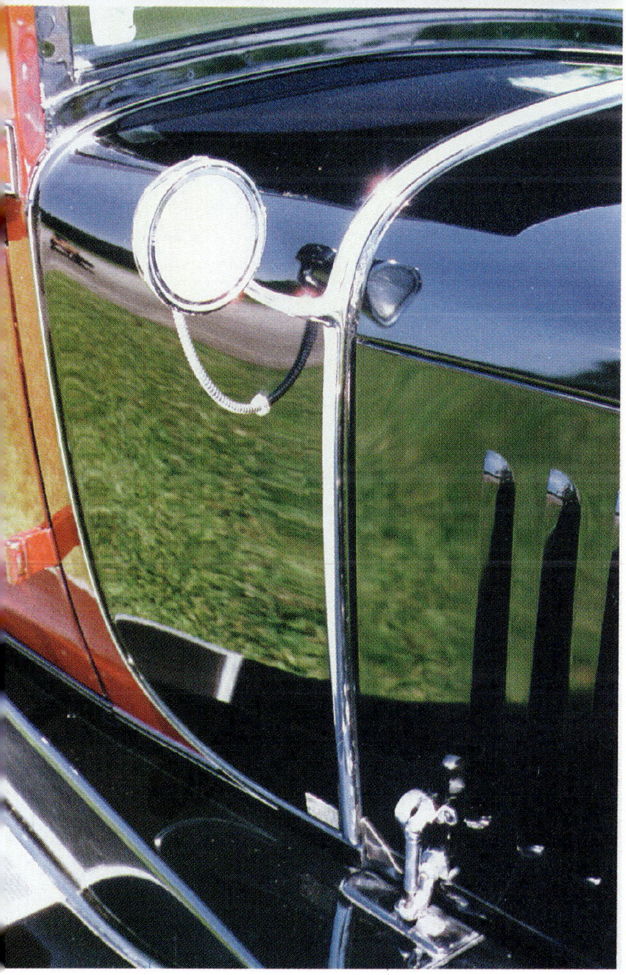

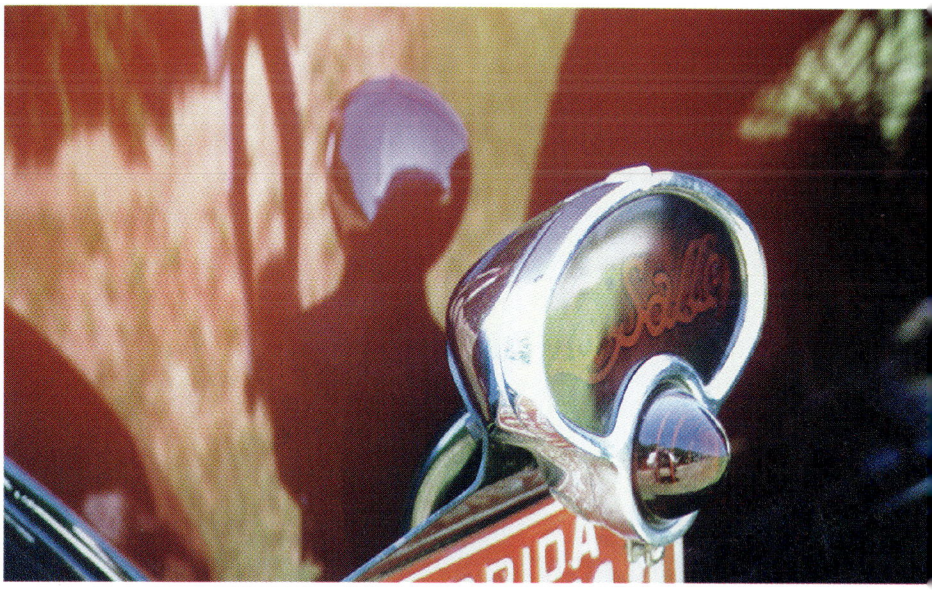

Two four-passenger Phaetons. Both have interesting paint schemes. Both have fender mounted spare tires. Both have been meticulously restored and maintained. Top: The dual cowl Sport Phaeton has a running board spotlight. Bottom: The Phaeton with side curtains mounted is located in Australia. A chrome radiator rock shield has been installed.

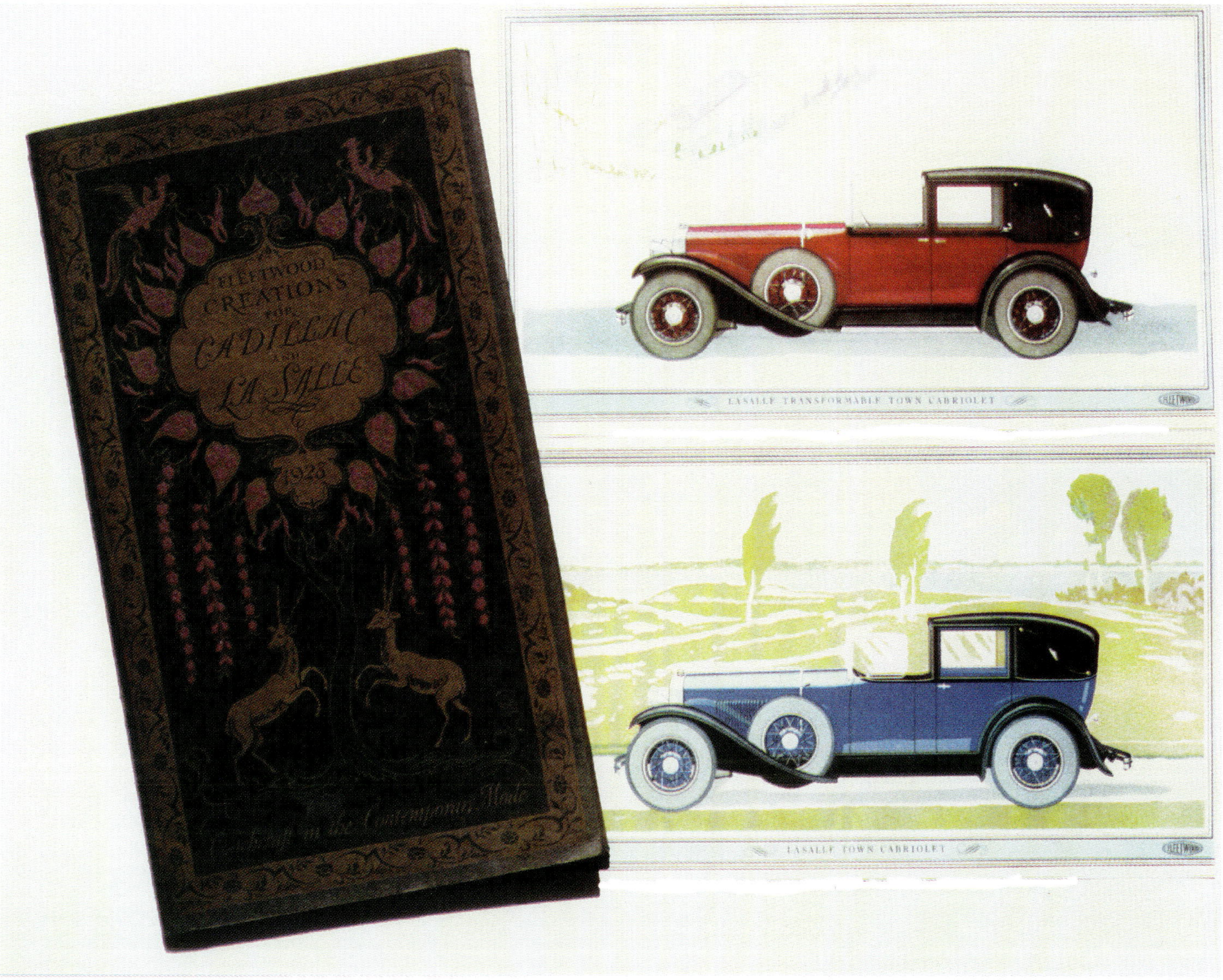
FLEETWOOD
CREATIONS
FOR
CADILLAC
AND
LA SALLE
1928
LASALLE TRANSFORMABLE TOWN CABRIOLET
LASALLE TOWN CABRIOLET

Top: A special Fleetwood "Creations for Cadillac and LaSalle" *book had portfolio inserts on individual models proposed by Fleetwood, primarily catering to the rich and famous. Most of the body styles were quite formal. Shown are a Transformable Town Cabriolet and a Town Cabriolet. Bottom: The 1928 sales brochure was elegant and artistic. LaSalle often beckoned the emerging women's market. To quote the brochure, "Women delight in its ease and beauty. The LaSalle obeys the feminine hand instantly, with only the slightest effort. This is one of the many reasons why it is so strongly favored by women."*

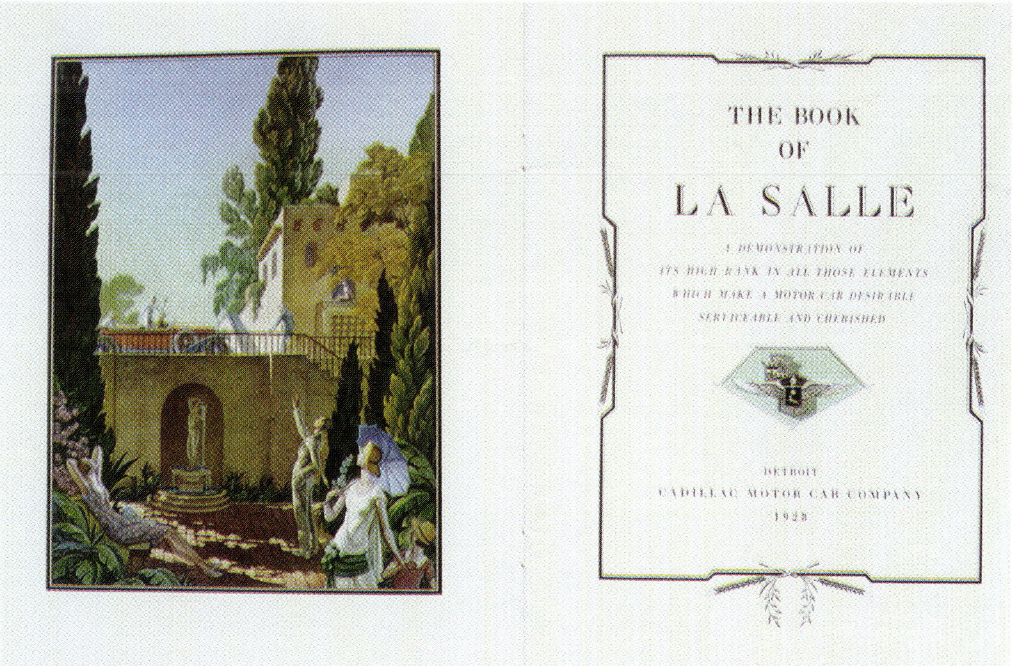
THE BOOK
OF
LA SALLE
A DEMONSTRATION OF
ITS HIGH RANK IN ALL THOSE ELEMENTS
WHICH MAKE A MOTOR CAR DESIRABLE
SERVICEABLE AND CHERISHED
DETROIT
CADILLAC MOTOR CAR COMPANY
1928

Hier – et aujourd'hui

LA SALLE—the spirited and modernistic interpretation of a critical public's ideas and ideals of the motor-car of today and tomorrow. There is nothing in motor-car manufacture today—excepting Cadillac itself—that can compare with *La Salle's* singular richness of performance, its fresh and fascinating lines, its ultra-modern sophistication. There is nothing in engineering which is newer or more progressive than *La Salle's* 90-degree, V-type, 8-cylinder, Cadillac-built engine. A single ride in *La Salle*—a single turn at its wheel—and you will be convinced of *La Salle's* surpassing excellence with a finality so compelling as to leave no room for doubt or debate.

Substantial reduction on the entire La Salle line—$2350 to $2875, f. o. b. Detroit. Five new models, including new five-passenger family sedan. If you prefer to buy out of income, the General Motors plan is very liberal. Appraisal value of your car acceptable as cash.

CADILLAC MOTOR CAR COMPANY
DETROIT, MICHIGAN   OSHAWA, CANADA

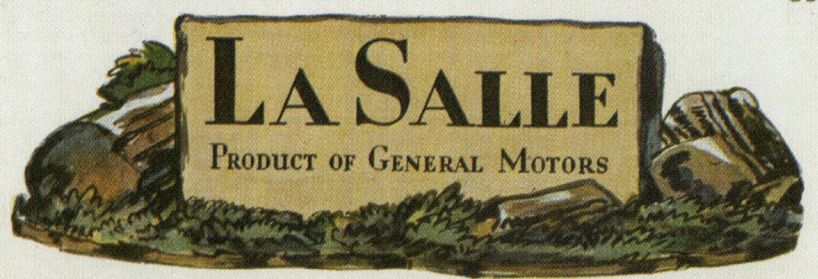

LA SALLE
PRODUCT OF GENERAL MOTORS

LASALLE SEVEN-PASSENGER STANDARD SEDAN

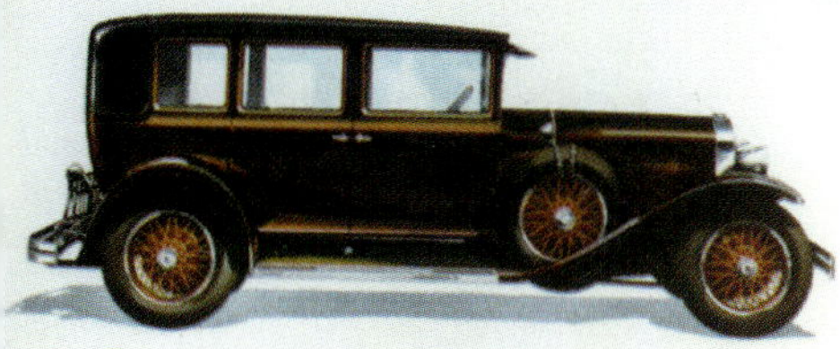

That buoyant grace so characteristic of La Salle is strikingly accentuated by its imposing length

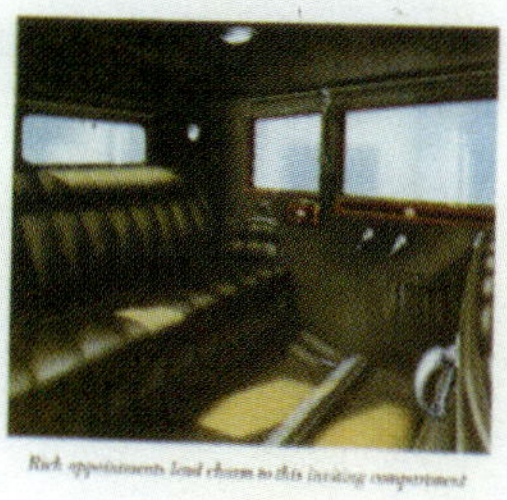

Rich appointments lend charm to this inviting compartment

LASALLE TWO-PASSENGER ROADSTER

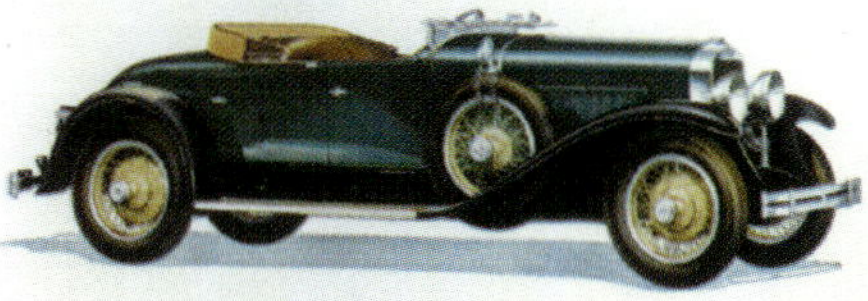

The sprightly grace of La Salle design harmonizes very happily with the character of the Roadster

LASALLE FOUR-PASSENGER PHAETON

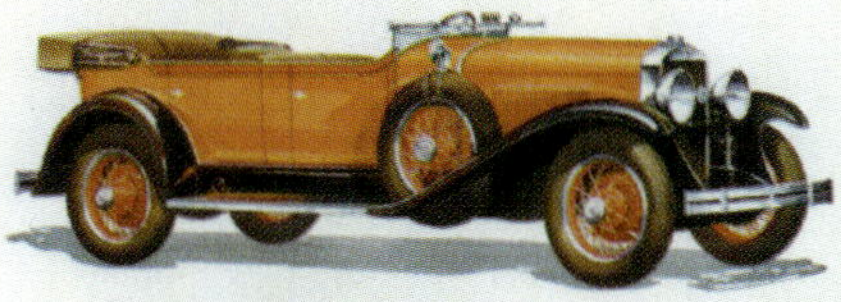

Long, graceful, low running, fleet, the Phaeton is typically La Salle, predominantly smart

LASALLE FIVE-PASSENGER CABRIOLET SEDAN

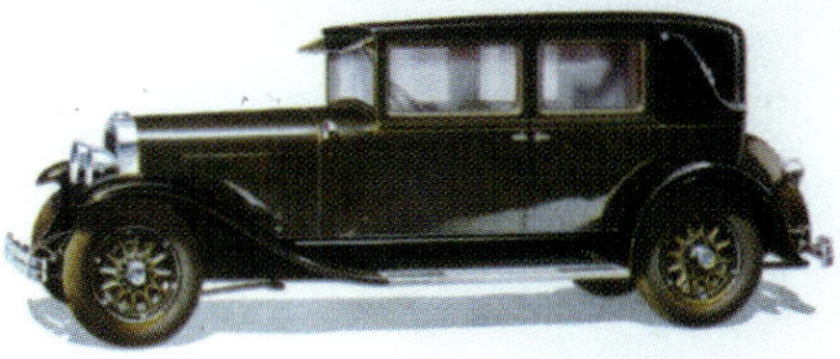

A long, graceful model, distinguished by leather rear quarter panels and appointed with true elegance

FLEETWOOD TRANSFORMABLE · STYLE 3051

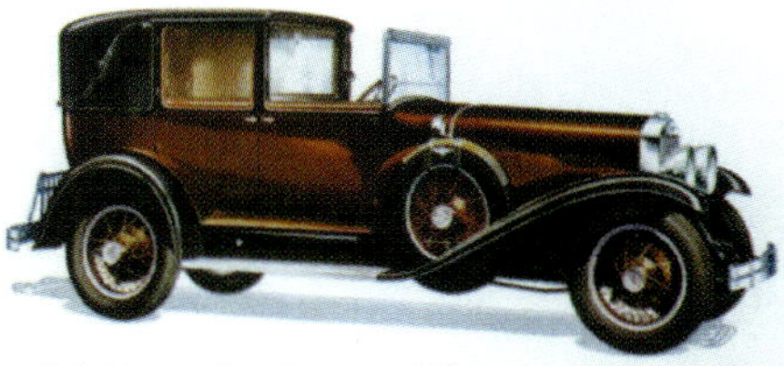

Patrician in its exclusive styling and rich appointments, it has the distinctive Fleetwood transformable feature

LASALLE TWO-PASSENGER STANDARD COUPE

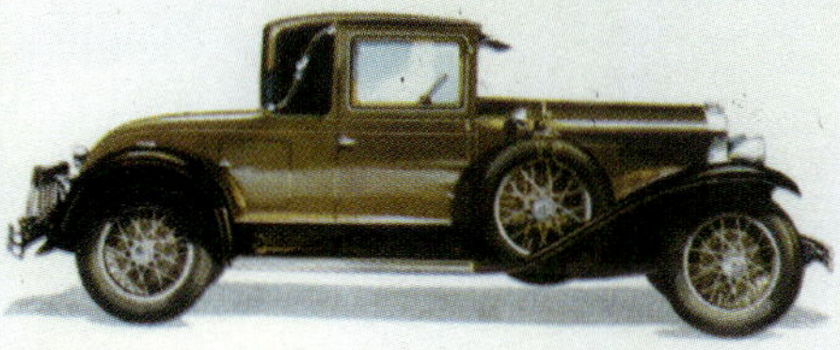

A personal car of signal charm and brilliant ability. It is fitted with upholstered rumble seat

LASALLE FIVE-PASSENGER TOWN SEDAN

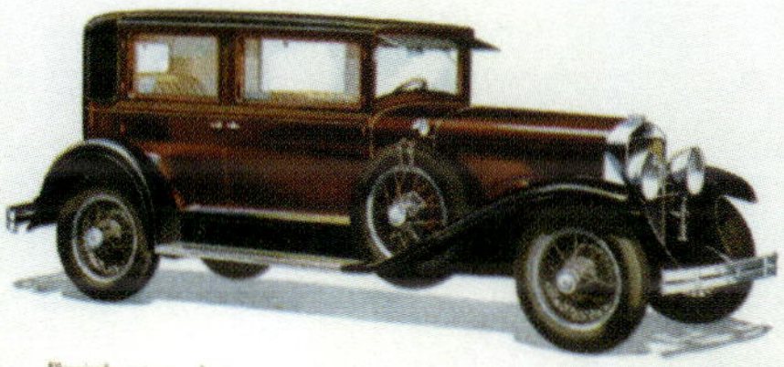

Pleasingly compact and intimate, yet with all the convenience which inheres in a four-door Sedan model

LASALLE FOUR-PASSENGER SPORT PHAETON

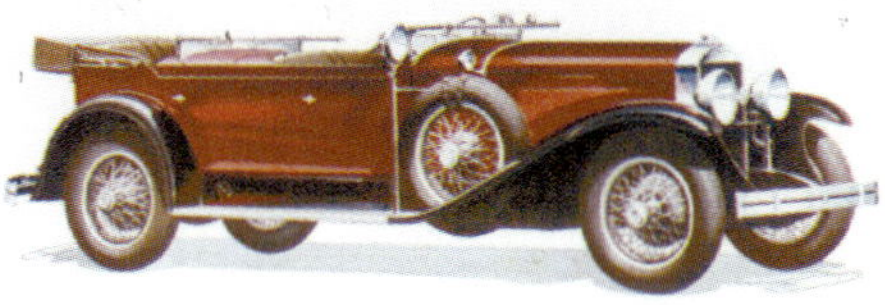

LASALLE TWO-PASSENGER CONVERTIBLE COUPE

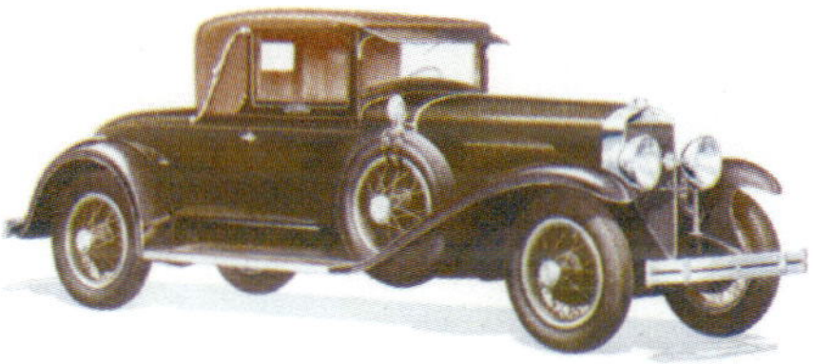

LASALLE FIVE-PASSENGER IMPERIAL

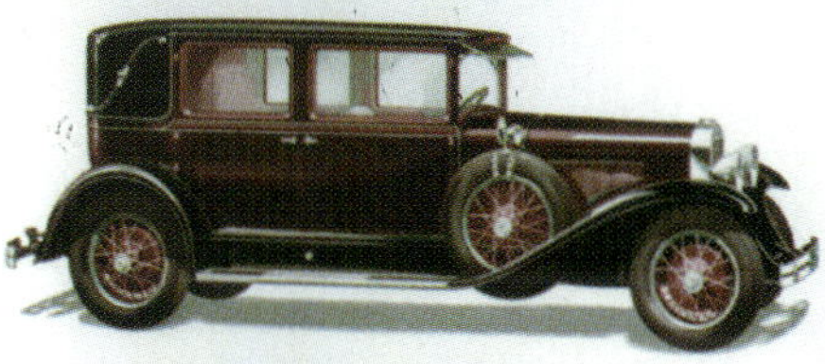

Equally adapted by an adjustable glass partition to owner-driven and formal, chauffeur-driven uses

LASALLE SEVEN-PASSENGER IMPERIAL

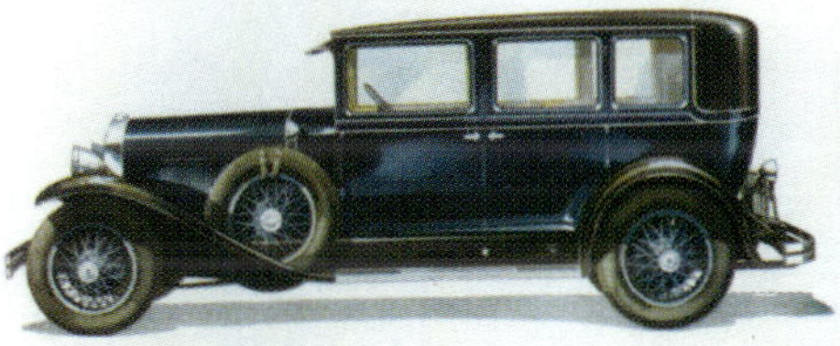

A counterpart of the Standard Seven-passenger Sedan with the addition of an adjustable glass partition

LASALLE FIVE-PASSENGER COUPE

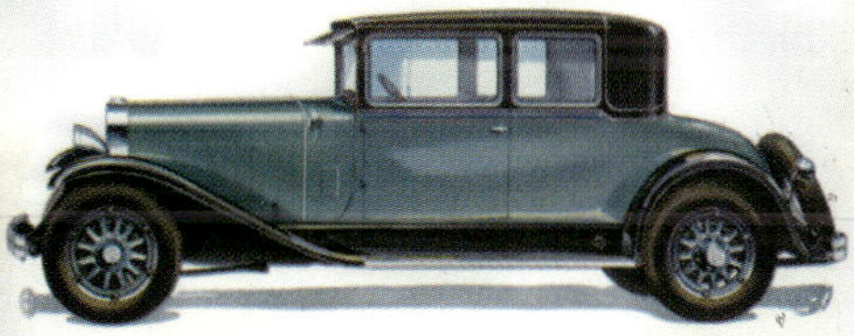

Mounted on the 134-inch chassis for generous space and sweeping grace of exterior appearance

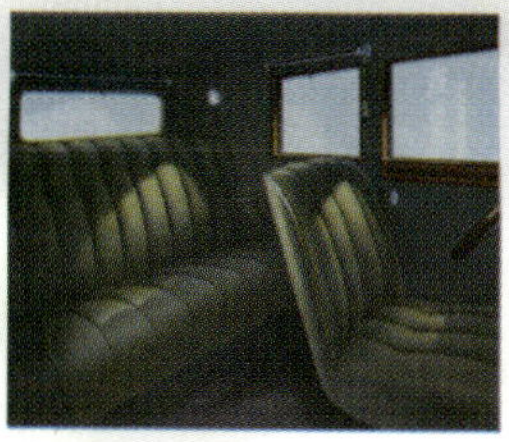

Compact and intimate, the interior is inviting and charming

LASALLE SEVEN-PASSENGER FAMILY SEDAN

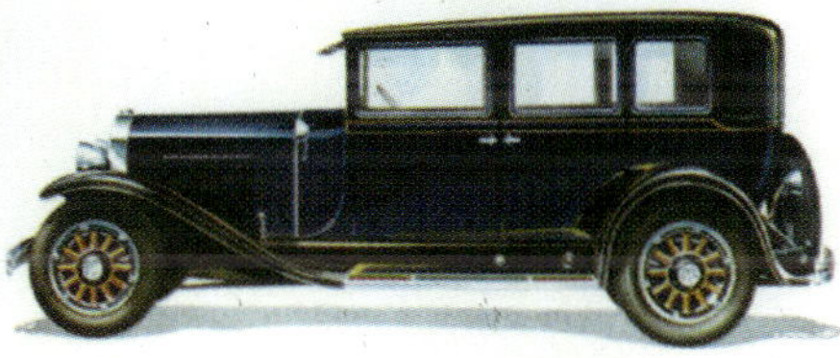

In outward grace, in inward charm, this model fitly exemplifies La Salle's refreshing features

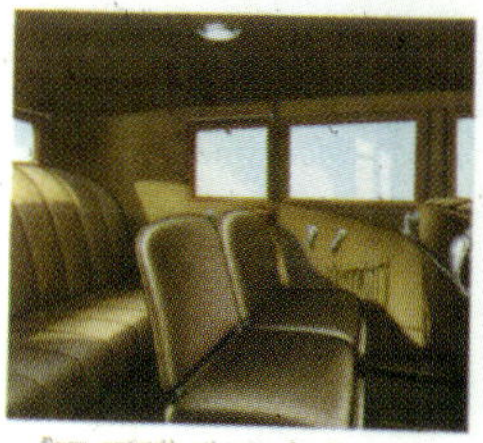

Roomy, comfortable, with inviting, homelike atmosphere

LASALLE SEVEN-PASSENGER STANDARD SEDAN

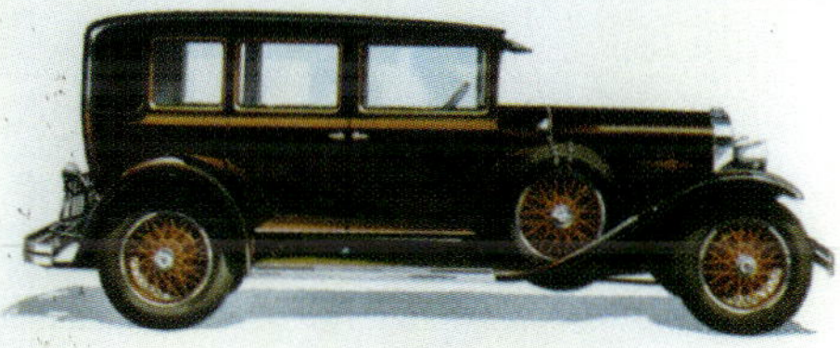

That buoyant grace so characteristic of La Salle is strikingly accentuated by its imposing length

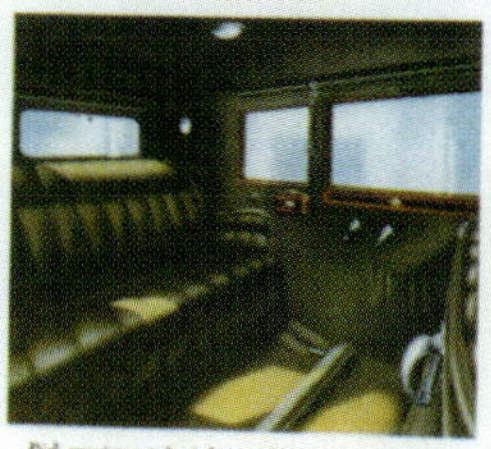

Rich appointments lend charm to this inviting compartment

LASALLE FIVE-PASSENGER COUPE

Mounted on the 134-inch chassis for generous space and sweeping grace of exterior appearance

Compact and intimate, the interior is inviting and charming

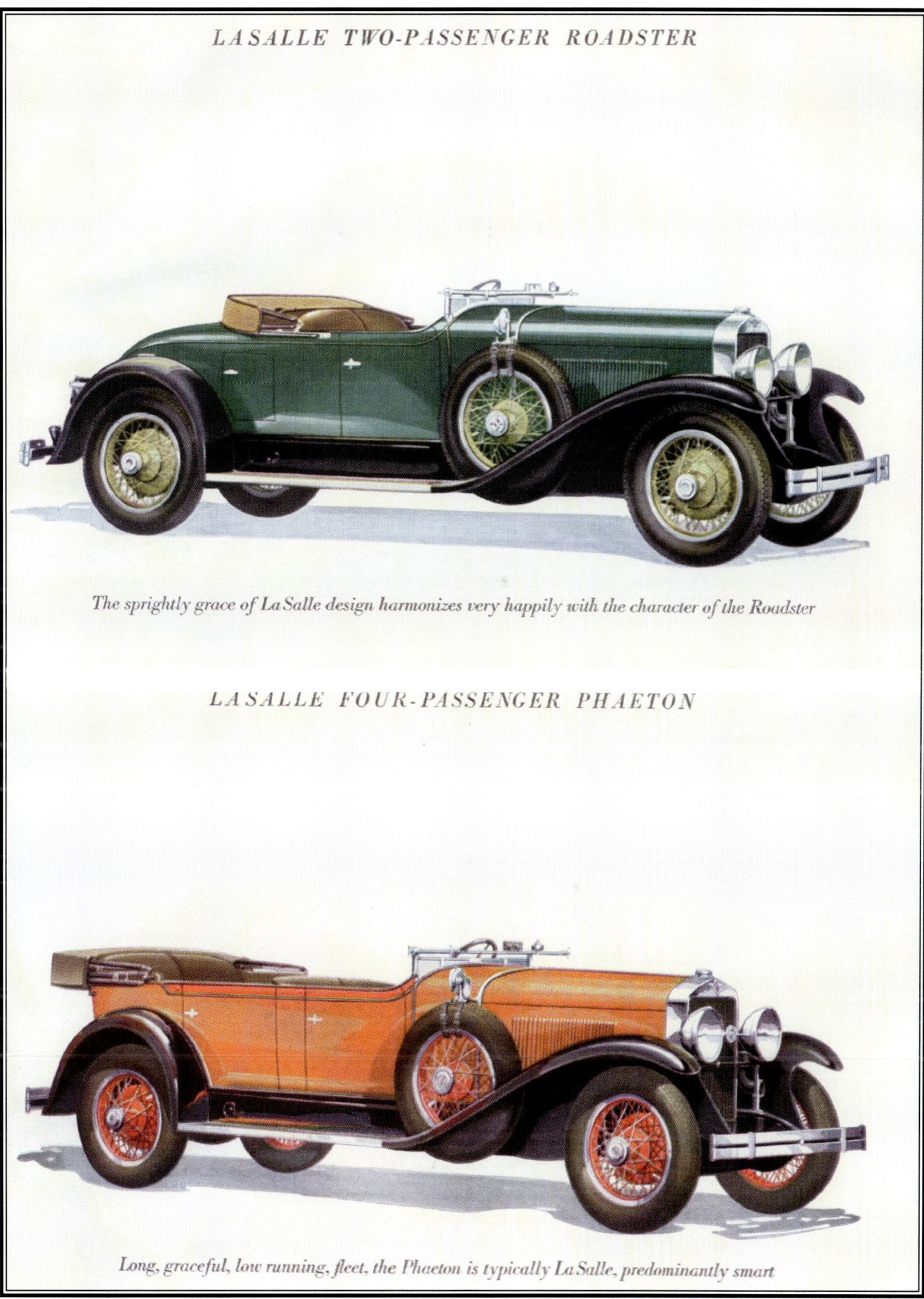

Vivid, intense, authentic in its application of curite hues

A MINERAL so modern as curite finds a most fitting counterpart in this La Salle Roadster, an essentially new, vigorous, timely motor car. The Ledge Orange and Ravine Yellow of body panels, fenders, and mouldings parallel the striking color series so intense in the stone; and the upholstery in genuine pigskin carries the same tones—a striking effect which is further emphasized by the instrument panel in bright Orange Duco. The striping is Watercourse Red.

La Salle Roadster
BODY BY FISHER

Handsome in showy armor—resplendent in radiant blue and gold

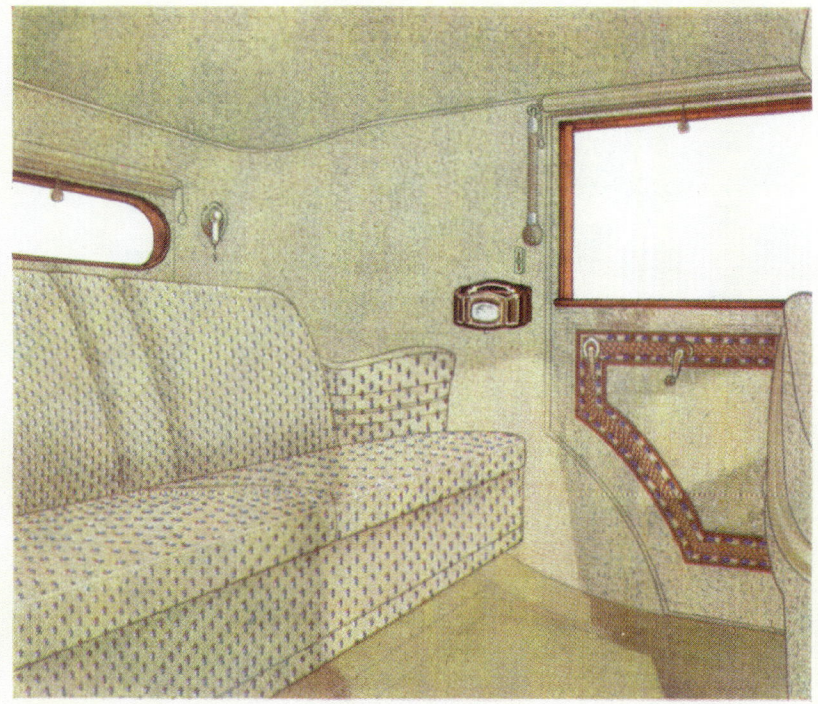

FINISHED all over in Nassau Sand with window reveals and stripings in Tidewater Blue, this La Salle Town Cabriolet adapts the lambent colorings of the Angel Fish to the uses of a fine car. The top, in tan leather, carries out the general color scheme, the hardware by Ternstedt is satin nickel inlaid with delicate blue, and the tan broadlace is enriched by touches of blue. Broad windshield wings flank the chauffeur's seat, and the rear compartment is fitted with two folding courtesy seats.

La Salle Town Cabriolet
BODY BY FLEETWOOD

A lustrous, handsome creation, rich as if carved from coral

This LaSalle Transformable Town Cabriolet glows with a living color—the Rose of precious Coral. Thrown into sharp contrast against ebony fenders, wheels, and upper panels, the soft hue of the gem is delightfully emphasized. Mouldings are Black with a vivid Coral stripe. The Coral strand is repeated throughout the pattern lace of the interior; and the satin gold hardware by Ternstedt is inlaid with Rose Coral. The driver's compartment may be changed at will from open to enclosed. Two folding occasional seats in the rear compartment face to the rear.

LaSalle Transformable Town Cabriolet
BODY BY FLEETWOOD

1927 - 1928 LaSalle Production

<u>Total Production</u>: 26,804 automobiles and chassis (three serial numbers not used.)

<u>Serial Numbers</u>: 1927 - 200001 thru 216850.
                               1928 - 216851 thru 226807.
The Vehicle (engine) serial number is stamped "On the name plate on the front face of the left side of the dash and on the crankcase just below the water inlet on the right-hand side."

<u>Chassis Numbers</u>: Start with prefix "2 -" and increase from the first unit, which has chassis number "2-27." The numbers are not sequential. Location of chassis unit number is "on the upper surface of the right-hand side bar just in front of the oil filter."

<u>Body Plates</u>: Fisher job/style number (e.g., 1168) or Fleetwood job number (e.g., 3751) and body serial number are on the body plate attached "to the front face of the left side of the dash" (in the engine compartment.)

Body Type and Style Numbers:	1927	List Price (various dates)	1928	List Price (Jan. 4, 1928)	W.B.	Production
<u>Series 303 (LaSalle) Fisher Bodies</u>						
4-Pass. Phaeton	1168	$2495.00	1168	$2485.00	125"	1575
4-Pass. Sport Phaeton (dual cowl)	1168-B	$2995.00	1168-B	$2975.00	125"	270
2-Pass. Roadster	1169	$2525.00	1169	$2485.00	125"	1184
5-Pass. Sedan (metal back)			8110	$2495.00	125"	763
5-Pass. Family Sedan (metal back)			8110-A	$2350.00	125"	2720
5-Pass. Sedan (leather back)	7380	$2685.00			125"	5001
5-Pass. Sedan (leather back)	8120		8120	$2495.00	125"	1823
4-Pass. Victoria (Coupe, leather back)	7390	$2635.00			125"	1250
4-Pass. Victoria (Coupe, leather back)	8130		8130	$2550.00	125"	405
2-Pass. Convertible Coupe	7400	$2635.00	7400	$2550.00	125"	3001
2-Pass. Coupe (leather or fabric back)	7410	$2585.00			125"	1100
2-Pass. Coupe (leather back)	8140		8140	$2450.00	125"	527
2-Pass. Business Coupe (leather back)			8140-A	$2350.00	125"	446
5-Pass. Town Sedan (metal back)	7420	$2650.00	7420	$2495.00	125"	1600
5-Pass. Coupe (metal back)			8050	$2625.00	134"	1001
7-Pass. Sedan (metal back)	8060	$2795.00	8060	$2775.00	134"	1666
7-Pass. Family Sedan (metal back)			8060-A	$2575.00	134"	1064
7-Pass. Imperial Sedan (div., metal back)	8070	$2895.00	8070	$2875.00	134"	485
5-Pass. Cabriolet Sedan (leather back, blind qtrs.)			8080	$2675.00	134"	500
5-Pass. Imperial Sedan (division, leather back, blind qtrs.)	8090	$2795.00	8090	$2775.00	134"	210
Touring (non-production body)				Not listed	134"	1
Chassis				Not listed	125"	55
Chassis				Not listed	134"	34
Unidentified units						65
<u>Series 303 (LaSalle) Fleetwood Bodies</u>						
5-Pass. Transformable Town Cabriolet (front door crank-up windows)	3051	$4700.00	3051	$4700.00	125"	9
2-Pass. Coupe	3110	$3600.00	3110	$4275.00	125"	12
5-Pass. Sedan	3120	$3800.00			125"	13
5-Pass. Town Cabriolet (front compartment wing windows)	3130	$5000.00	3130	$4500.00	125"	22
5-Pass. Transformable Town Cabriolet (front door crank-up windows)			3751	$4800.00	134"	2
					Total	26,804

<u>Canadian (Oshawa, Ontario) built units. (Identified units are included in the production totals above)</u>:

5-Pass. Sedan (leather back)	7380				125"	41
2-Pass. Convertible Coupe	7400		7400		125"	16
7-Pass. Sedan (metal back)	8060		8060		134"	18
5-Pass. Sedan (metal back)	8110		8110		125"	24
5-Pass. Sedan (leather back)			8120		125"	4
Unidentified						57
					Subtotal	160

Cars were assembled at Oshawa on complete chassis shipped from Detroit. Shipments of as few as three and as many as twenty-five chassis in a group are listed in the serial ledgers. Some cars were subsequently recorded in the Detroit records by body style, body number and other details. It is likely that many of the unidentified units were style 8110 5-passenger Sedans or style 8060 7-passenger Sedans, and account for most of the unidentified 65 cars in the overall production total.

Standard Color Combinations

Upper Panels	Paint #	Lower Panels	Paint #
Ardsley Green	2443038	Canoe Brook Green	2441638
Black		Black	
Black		Derby Red, Medium	2443336
Black		Vineyard Lake	2443089
Ching Blue	2441282	Norse Blue	2441467
La Force Gray	2441765	La Force Gray	2441765
Senator Green	2441306	Desert Sand	2441313

Fender set in black enamel is <u>standard with all body colors</u>, special color fenders at additional list charge of $85.00
Chassis is finished in black, but special color may be had at additional list charge of $15.00

Trim Options
LaSalle Fisher Bodies

<u>Open/Convertible bodies - job/style: 1168, 1168-B, 1169, 7400</u>   <u>Top:</u>   16 T 1527 Drab-duck (khaki)
18 T 1327 Green Leather   6 T 1527 Black (optional)
19 T 1327 Blue Leather   <u>Rumble Seat:</u>   35 T 1227 Black Imitation Leather
20 T 1327 Tan Leather (finish not indicated)
21 T 1327 Gray Leather
22 T 1327 Black Leather
23 T 1327 Red Leather
26 T 1327 Tan Leather (finish not indicated)

<u>Closed bodies - job/style: 7380, 7390, 7410, 7420, 8050, 8060, 8070, 8080, 8090, 8110, 8120, 8130, 8140</u>
68 T 127 Cloth (color and type not listed)   84 T 127 Brown & Tan Mohair
70 T 127 Green-Gray Mohair   85 T 127 Tan Mohair
71 T 127 Plush (Mohair, color not listed)   32 T 128 Blue Mohair
80 T 127 Blue-Gray Mohair   36 T 128 Bedford Cord Cloth (color not listed)
81 T 127 Taupe Mohair

<u>1928 Family Sedan and Business Coupe closed bodies - job/style: 8060-A, 8110-A, 8140-A</u>
112 T 128 Broadcloth (color and type not listed)

Note: The above trim numbers are from Trim Charts #1 and #2 of the Fifth Edition, *Cadillac Master Body Parts List*, March 1936, which does not contain material type and color descriptions. Descriptions are included where positive correlations from other records can be established. Factory documents describe available 1927-1928 Fisher body trims in general terms as Mohair, Wool Velour, Broadcloth or Worsted; two-tone Bedford Cords for owner driven cars; hair-line broadcloths, figured cloths, doeskin broadcloths in light drab shades for Cabriolets; Mohair Worsted Velvet and Cotton Velvet.

LaSalle Fleetwood Bodies

"Trim options include four broadcloth materials of special weave offered exclusively on Cadillac/LaSalle Fleetwood bodies:
    2423-24 Mouse-gray broadcloth   2427-28 Fawn-gray broadcloth
    2425-26 Tan broadcloth   2429-30 Gunmetal-gray broadcloth
In addition, two new mohair materials have been especially developed, one in fawn and the other in green." Source: *Distributors Convention*, August 30 - September 1, 1927

Standard and Optional Equipment

Standard Equipment: Five wood wheels (except Sport Phaeton), size 32 X 600/32 X 620; rear spare tire carrier.

Optional Equipment:
Wood wheels - natural (instead of painted)	$ 10.00
Five disc wheels, 32 X 600/32 X 620	No charge
Five wire wheels, 32 X 620	$ 95.00
Six disc wheels, fenderwells and 2 spare tires	$150.00
Six wire wheels, fenderwells and 2 spare tires (standard equipment on Sport Phaeton only)	$250.00
Fenderwells for wood wheels, 2 spare tires	$140.00
Folding Trunk Rack (standard equipment on Sport Phaeton only)	$ 35.00
Running Board Searchlight (standard equipment on Sport Phaeton only)	$125.00
Special Trunk	$ 75.00

"Cadillac Motor Car Co. announces it is offering high compression heads and a low gear ratio for LaSalle roadsters and phaetons. The new high compression heads will have a ratio of 5.1 to 1. The new gear ratios are 4.0 to 1. Extra cost for this equipment is $125.00. When such equipment is used, the factory recommends the purchase of wire wheels, due to the higher speeds and acceleration. These wheels are offered at $95.00 additional, bringing the total cost of this high speed equipment to $220.00." *Automobile Trade Journal*, September 1927.

<u>Research Methodology</u>: Microfilm copies of the ledger records of the as-built configuration of each serial number were individually viewed. All record sheets were accounted for. Three serial numbers were not used in production. All Fleetwood body styles were recorded by serial and body number to determine the quantity of each body style built. All chassis were recorded by serial number. Because of shared body number sequences and unusual body numbers, Fisher body styles 1168-B, 8060, 8060-A, 8110, 8110-A, 8120, 8130, 8140 and 8140-A were individually recorded to determine actual production totals. No attempt was made to construct cross reference lists of the other Fisher body numbers with corresponding engine numbers to account for the 65 unidentified vehicles. The Canadian assembled cars that are not identified by body style undoubtedly result in somewhat understated production totals by body style.

Notes on research findings:

1. <u>1927-1928 model distinctions</u>. There is a long running discussion among enthusiasts and automotive historians as to which cars are 1927 LaSalles and which are 1928's. Automotive historians have published differing views. All known factory records have been carefully studied in an attempt to resolve the discussion. We are all accustomed to thinking of cars as specific **model years**, irrespective of when they were built or shipped to the dealers. Cadillac Motor Car Company does not appear to have distinguished between 1927 and 1928 LaSalles by model year. Therein lies the problem. A cursory review of Cadillac serial numbers from 1902 through 1927 will demonstrate that model year designation was not the norm; automobile production was recorded by **calendar year**. Introduction of the LaSalle on March 5, 1927, with subsequent introduction of the new Cadillac series 341 on September 1, 1927, resulted in the model year confusion that was not clarified until the introduction of the 1929 models of both marques.

Production was continuous from the first 1927 LaSalle built through the last 1928, with no break in the engine serial numbers and many body style changes. In all subsequent years of LaSalle production, there is a distinct break between model years, with a change in the prefix of the engine serial number group (e.g., 4----- in 1929; 6----- in 1930; 220---- in 1935; 221---- in 1936.)

Undated factory distribution summaries, labeled *10 Day Pre-War*, list 1927 production of 10,767 LaSalles and 1928 production of 16,038 LaSalles, for a total of 26,805, which is within one car of matching the actual record count. Using the 10,767 number for the end of the 1927 LaSalle, (some historians have) would put the start of 1928 production in late July 1927, less than five months after the March 5, 1927, introduction. There is no apparent basis for selecting serial #210767 as a break between 1927 and 1928 cars. Serial numbers for all of the early body styles continue well beyond the 10,767 point; none of the additional or new-for-1928 body styles were ready for shipment and dealers had not seen or been able to order the new styles.

The Distributors Convention was held in Detroit from August 30-September 1, 1927. The new Cadillac series 341 models were on display, along with thirty-two LaSalle display models. The convention handouts indicate in part: "The number assigned to each specification corresponds with the number on the tag of each car and may be used for convenience in ordering duplicates on any job shown." "Three welcome additions to the LaSalle line are announced. The 5-passenger Imperial Sedan (style 8090), 7-passenger Sedan (style 8060) and 7-passenger Imperial Sedan (style 8070) are all mounted on the 134" wheelbase." Although no delivery dates are indicated, the implication is that LaSalle Distributors could immediately order the new body styles. The convention handouts show side views of body styles with features common to 1928 but do not say that the new LaSalle styles offered are 1928 models. Initial shipment of six added or changed body styles (8120, 8130, 8140, 8060, 8070 and 8090) commenced in late August/early September 1927. Early serial number cars in those styles can be considered to be 1927 models that continue into the new calendar year as 1928 LaSalles. A 1927 model year from March through December 1927 (out of 19 months of shipments) seems reasonable.

Record analysis reveals a series of running changes to various components (not unlike current manufacturing), with an overlap in the building of new body styles that are distinctly 1928 models and the phaseout of distinctly 1927 body styles. The running changes are reflected in the multiple editions of the LaSalle Operators Manual for the Series 303, which indicate applicability by engine serial number. Sales of the LaSalle were far greater than expected and all existing stocks of bodies and components were apparently utilized in a seamless transition to the 1928 LaSalle. "Due, the company says, to unexpected sales volume which the LaSalle has enjoyed since its introduction last March - 15,000 having been sold in nine months instead of a year as anticipated - it has been possible to materially lower the prices of the other LaSalle models." Source: *Automobile Topics*, January 7, 1928. Factory list prices for 1928 were reduced from the 1927 introductory level.

Although there is no perfect fit in terms of the introduction of additional body styles, discontinuation of early body styles, mechanical component changes, etc., accepting a break point recorded by Cadillac Motor Car Company is the only reasonable differentiation between 1927 and 1928 LaSalles. The records do not show the date that vehicles were built, only the date they were shipped. Cars were shipped as late as December 31, 1927, with serial #216954 being the highest number shipped in 1927. Shipments resumed on January 3, 1928. *Cadillac-LaSalle Facts*, a vest pocket booklet produced by Cadillac Motor Car Company in early 1928, lists both the Cadillac 341 and LaSalle 303 cars shipped through the end of the year as 1927 cars and lists 1927 LaSalle engine numbers as serial #200001 to #216955 (which was shipped on 2/14/28). The *Cadillac Master Parts List* shows engine serial #216851 as the first 1928 LaSalle. Serial #216851 is the **third** serial number shipped on January 3, 1928, which makes that change point appear to be totally arbitrary. Eighty-five cars with serial numbers higher than #216851 were shipped in December 1927 and thus obviously built sometime in 1927.

Initial shipments of six new body styles (8110, 8110-A, 8140-A, 8050, 8060-A and 8080) began between December 22, 1927, and January 17, 1928. Switching from a **calendar year** to a **model year** designation, beginning with the resumption of production in calendar 1928 and the sale of six new body styles, aligns the LaSalle with Cadillac designations for all future models. It is a logical choice. Lacking further documentation, the Cadillac-LaSalle Club, Inc., has chosen to accept the January 3, 1928, change point as the beginning of the 1928 LaSalle model year. Any date accepted necessarily results in some number of cars being improperly categorized when considered only on the basis of serial number, shipping date or body style.

2. <u>Body Styles</u>. The array of Fisher body styles is confusing at the very least, due to mid and late calendar year body style changes and additions, the appearance that Cadillac selected an arbitrary serial number to designate 1928 cars and the addition of distinctly 1928 body styles. A simplified breakdown follows:

1927 early Fisher body styles	Style #	W.B.	
4-Pass. Phaeton	1168	125"	Retained through 1928
4-Pass. Sport Phaeton (dual cowl)	1168-B	125"	Introduced in July 1927, retained through 1928
2-Pass. Roadster	1169	125"	Retained through 1928
5-Pass. Sedan (leather back)	7380	125"	Replaced by style 8120, Sept. 1927
4-Pass. Victoria (Coupe, leather back)	7390	125"	Replaced by style 8130, Sept. 1927
2-Pass. Convertible Coupe	7400	125"	Retained through 1928
2-Pass. Coupe (leather or fabric back)	7410	125"	Replaced by style 8140, Sept. 1927
5-Pass. Town Sedan (metal back)	7420	125"	Introduced in July 1927, retained through 1928

1927 late Fisher body styles, carried through 1928	Style #	W.B.	
5-Pass. Sedan (leather back)	8120	125"	Slight changes from style 7380, see note below
4-Pass. Victoria (Coupe, leather back)	8130	125"	Slight changes from style 7390, see note below
2-Pass. Coupe (leather back)	8140	125"	Slight changes from style 7410, see note below
7-Pass. Sedan (metal back)	8060	134"	Announced at Distributors Convention, Aug. 1927
7-Pass. Imperial Sedan (metal back)	8070	134"	Announced at Distributors Convention, Aug. 1927
5-Pass. Imperial Sedan (leather back, blind qtrs.)	8090	134"	Announced at Distributors Convention, Aug. 1927
1928 new Fisher body styles			
5-Pass. Sedan (metal back)	8110	125"	First car shipped December 31, 1927
5-Pass. Family Sedan (metal back)	8110-A	125"	Announced January 1928
2-Pass. Business Coupe (leather back)	8140-A	125"	Announced January 1928
5-Pass. Coupe (metal back)	8050	134"	Announced January 1928
7-Pass. Family Sedan (metal back)	8060-A	134"	Announced January 1928
5-Pass. Cabriolet Sedan (leather back, blind qtrs.)	8080	134"	Announced January 1928

Note: "Slight changes have been made in the 2-passenger Coupe, 4-passenger Victoria and 5-passenger Sedan. The radius of the curve at the rear of the roof has been slightly lessened, giving a lower appearance to the body; dark glass sun visors have been substituted; and cowl ventilators opening to the rear have been located on each side. These changes in design are made to correspond with the design of the three new models. Wide auxiliary seats are supplied in the 7-passenger Sedan and 7-passenger Imperial." Source: *Distributors Convention*, August 30 - September 1, 1927.

"Five new LaSalle models have been perfected and put on the 1928 market by Cadillac Motor Car Co." Source: *Automobile Topics*, January 7, 1928. (No mention of the style 8110 5-Pass. Sedan as a new model.)

Visually, the most recognizable distinction between early 1927 and late 1927/1928 models is the change from an engine hood with 12 louvers on each side for 1927, to a hood with 28 louvers on each side and the addition of cowl ventilators opening to the rear on closed body styles. There are surviving cars with serial numbers in the 1927 block that have the later hood, Electrolock ignition, carburetor heat control, new type chassis and brakes, etc. On the mechanical level, the 1928 units principally have the twin disc clutch instead of the eleven disc clutch, Lovejoy hydraulic shock absorbers instead of Watson stabilators and 16-inch front brake drums instead of 14-inch.

3. <u>Vehicle Records</u>. The 1927 and 1928 LaSalles are recorded as hand-written, single-line, two-page entries in large leather bound ledgers. The data elements listed are: Engine Number / Date Shipped / Shipped to Distributor at / Delivered to / City and State / Date Delivered / Type (style #) / Number (body #) / Upholstery / Top / Center & Lower Panels (color name) / Stripe / Moulding / Lock No. / Wheels - Type & Size, Color, Stripe, Hubs / Radiator & Lamps (nickel plated) / Gear Ratio / Frame Number / Engine Unit Number / Front Axle Number / Rear Axle Number / Transmission Number / Carburetor Number / Steering Number / Generator Number / Extra Equipment / Car Cover / Decking Charge.

In practice, the last three blocks of the ledger were used for notes including hood and cowl color, fenderwells and trunk rack, high compression cylinder heads if so equipped, etc.

Very few of the records were filled in to indicate the Delivered to / City and State / Date Delivered information. After serial #212000, those three data elements were eliminated in a new ledger. Less than one hundred vehicles are annotated with the name of the original purchaser; most of whom were factory or other General Motors employees. Harley Earl received a style 8090 5-Passenger Imperial Sedan. Nine vehicles were charged to the factory accounts of the Fisher brothers.

Some highly unusual record changes were entered in the vehicle ledgers, changing the body style notations as a result of modifications made by dealers. Two particularly odd entries are changes from a 7-Pass. Sedan (8060) and 7-Pass. Family Sedan (8060-A) to five-passenger styles 8110 and 8110-A with the notation "Auxiliary seats removed by Don Lee" (the Los Angeles based distributor). The seven-passenger body is physically longer than the five-passenger body and thus the style number change is inappropriate. Three 5-Pass. Imperial Sedans, style 8090, were annotated "Body style changed by dealer from Imp 5 Sedan to Cabrio." and the body style changed to 8080. Removal of the Imperial Partition would make that physical change and be an appropriate style number distinction. It is unlikely that any of the body tags were changed.

4. <u>Color</u>. No listing of standard color combinations for the complete 1927 and 1928 LaSalle model years could be located. To determine the probable standard colors and entire range of color combinations, body color listings (upper panel/lower panel) were recorded. Black is standard for all years. Six combinations are rubber stamped in the ledgers and are obviously standard. All other entries are hand written. Thirteen other combinations were found on more than 500 cars each, one on 463 cars, and one on 372 cars. All of those colors are probable standard colors and so listed below. New apparently standard colors were introduced throughout the production run. A total of 482 color combinations were found to have been applied to the 1927-1928 cars. Many of the combinations were special orders found on a single car. Other colors were found on as many as 174 cars, which is less than one percent of total production and thought to not represent a standard color.

Cadillac Motor Car Company maintained a policy of discouraging the use of what they considered to be non-durable paint colors, to the point of declining orders to paint cars in such finishes. Fifty-three cars (eleven body styles) were shipped to dealers with the body in primer "Rubbed out of rough stuff" for local finishing as arranged by the dealer or purchaser.

(probable) Standard Color Combinations

Upper Panels	Paint #	Lower Panels	Paint #
Algerian Blue	1254	Algerian Blue	1254
Black		Bolling Green	1331
Black		Calumet Blue	20235

Upper Panels	Paint #	Lower Panels	Paint #
Black		Phantom Gray	2443356
Black		Powder Blue	3116
Black		Wissahickon Green	20366
Bruce Green	2441723	Cape Smoke	2441482
Czarina Beige	2443009	Cossack Brown	2441322
Czarina Beige	2443009	Czarina Beige	2443009
Dustproof Gray	2441274	Dustproof Gray	2441274
English Gray	2441774	English Gray	2441774
Gettysburg Blue	2441205	Gettysburg Blue	2441205
Larchmont Blue	2441273	Pelham Blue	2441297 (Phaetons & Roadsters)
Lush Green	2441478	Canoe Brook Green	2441638 (Phaetons & Roadsters)
Royal Purple Lake	20528	Royal Purple Lake	20528

5. <u>Special Features</u>: Customer requests for non-standard upholstery material, deviations from the standard trimming methods (e.g., Cadillac style pleated and tufted), application of non-standard colors, etc., were handled by the assignment of a Fisher Order number with detailed written instructions to the body plant. None of those individual order records are known to exist for 1927-1928 LaSalles. Only a small fraction of the F.O. numbers are indicated in the ledgers, although there were many such orders as evidenced by the large volume of non-standard paint cars, which required a sixty-day delivery time. None of the individual orders for the Fleetwood bodied cars are known to exist.

Numerous cars were annotated "Natural cane work in belt panel." Four cars were fitted with a single fenderwell; three on the left side, one on the right side. A Phaeton charged to F. J. Fisher had all of the nickel parts (body and chassis) chromium plated, a precursor of the 1929 models. A style 7380 5-Pass. Sedan charged to the factory was equipped with nickel plated disc wheels and "Special walnut panels." It was probably a show car. An unorthodox combination was an 8060-A 7-Pass. Family Sedan (austere interior trim), painted Black with "Chromium plating on fenders."

Few truly custom Fisher Orders were done. A "Partition 5-Pass. Sedan 1153 LX," using a style 7380 body shell, was charged to the factory account of A. J. Fisher. The car featured: Weise cloth, Special Maroon top and body, special steering column, walnut door panels, fenderwells and trunk cover. A "Special 5-Pass. Sedan 1157LX," also using a style 7380 body shell, was built for an unknown buyer. No indication of the body modifications was listed, but the car was trimmed in "special cloth" and the body painted Willeys Pale Auto Yellow. Two special body cars were done with modified style 1168 Phaeton bodies and listed as "Double Cowl Phaeton." These likely were prototypes for the Sport Phaeton that went into production some 4600 cars later. One was charged to the factory account of John J. Raskob (GM Executive Committee). Cadillac cars were available in a 7-Pass. Touring body style that was not offered on LaSalle. A single "134" Chassis Touring, Non-Production LX1290" car, presumably a 7-passenger, was built and charged to the factory. A "134" Chassis 5 Coupe, Sample Body 1295 LX" is shown charged to the factory. An "8120 Special 5 Sedan" is listed with "Special body built for Eng. Dept." An "8080 Special 5 Cabrio. Sedan" was charged to the factory account of L. P. Fisher, but no details are listed.

6. <u>Factory installed accessories</u>: Very few cars had factory installed accessories other than the wire wheels, sidemounts and folding trunk rack option. Installed items were:

Heavy duty rear springs	Lovejoy Shock Absorbers (pre 1928)
High Compression cylinder heads	Special Camshaft
High Speed Equipment	Spotlight
Houdaille Shock Absorbers	Standard Trunk
Kelch Heater	Trunk Cover to match top (Drab Duck)

7. <u>Chassis</u>: Complete drivable chassis, in both the 125" and 134" wheelbases, were produced and sold to both domestic and foreign coachbuilders. Typically the units included the bumpers, radiator, hood and cowl, lights, dashboard, running boards, fenders (with or without fenderwells and trunk rack), etc. The finished vehicle would thus have a distinctly recognizable LaSalle origin. Chassis distribution was:

Alexandria, Egypt	3	London, England	11 (Right hand drive)
Antwerp, Belgium	8	Newark, New Jersey	1
Berlin, Germany	15	New York City, New York	1
Boston, Massachusetts	1	Oshawa, Canada	1
Buenos Aires, Argentina	3 (Right hand drive)	Paris, France	20
Buffalo, New York	2	Stockholm, Sweden	1
Chicago, Illinois	1	Utica, New York	2
Copenhagen, Denmark	3	Washington, D.C.	4
Factory, Detroit	12		

The first eleven LaSalle serial numbers are chassis indicated as "Factory - Experimental." At least one of those was eventually fitted with an unspecified body with center and lower panels in Cadillac Blue, Lt. Two "Cut Open Chassis" for show displays were done, one sent to Newark and one charged to the factory. The records give only a brief hint of the custom coachwork done on the LaSalle chassis. Serial #216545, a 134" wheelbase chassis, was shipped to Paris on 12/9/27. It was returned to the factory for credit and shipped to New York City on 6/11/28 with the record annotated "Hibbard & Darrin 5 Sedan." Serial #216741, a 134" wheelbase chassis, was shipped to Utica, New York, on 12/21/27. It was returned to the factory for credit on 6/11/28 with the record annotated "Willoughby body on chassis - 4 Sport Sedan." It is reasonable to guess that Willoughby, based in Utica, also built a body for the other chassis shipped to Utica.

8. <u>Export Cars</u>: Export sales rapidly became an important element of LaSalle production - the first export being a 5-passenger Sedan, serial #202641, to Copenhagen on April 6, 1927. Car and chassis exports totalled 1975 units; 1334 in 1927 and 641 in 1928. All LaSalle body styles were available in either left or right hand drive, a feature that was essential to international sales. Sales to Canada (in addition to the cars assembled in Oshawa) were not treated as exports, whereas, sales to Mexico were through the General Motors Export Division. Vehicles destined for the U.S. Territory of Hawaii were treated as exports. Right hand drive was a common feature for export cars destined for island nations plus Argentina, India and South Africa. Export totals by body style were:

Body Style	Style #	Qty.	Body Style	Style #	Qty.
4-Pass. Phaeton	1168	460	5-Pass. Cabriolet Sedan	8080	6
4-Pass. Sport Phaeton	1168-B	13	5-Pass. Imperial Sedan	8090	34
2-Pass. Roadster	1169	121	5-Pass. Sedan	8110	19
5-Pass. Sedan	7380	206	5-Pass. Family Sedan	8110-A	10
4-Pass. Victoria	7390	39	5-Pass. Sedan	8120	242
2-Pass. Convertible	7400	253	4-Pass. Victoria	8130	11
2-Pass. Coupe	4110	7	2-Pass. Coupe	8140	8
5-Pass. Town Sedan	7420	67	2-Pass. Business Coupe	8140-A	2
5-Pass. Coupe	8050	5	Chassis, 125" wheelbase		34
7-Pass. Sedan	8060	111	Chassis, 134" wheelbase		31
7-Pass Family Sedan	8060-A	8	5-Pass. Town Cabriolet, Fleetwood	3130	1
7-Pass. Imperial Sedan	8070	287			

Where did the exports go? Destinations are listed below (destination not indicated in the records for 10 units):

City	Qty.	City	Qty.	City	Qty.
Berlin, Germany	252	Osaka, Japan	41	Kingston, Jamaica	5
Antwerp, Belgium	205	Barranquilla, Columbia	39	Nairobi, Kenya	4
Paris, France	128	Havana, Cuba	39	Guatemala	3
Buenos Aires, Argentina	122	Melbourne, Australia	38	Lima, Peru	3
Alexandria, Egypt	118	Caracas, Venezuela	25	Perth, Australia	3
Madrid, Spain	109	Adelaide, Australia	22	Delhi, India	2
Copenhagen, Denmark	96	Brisbane, Australia	15	Leon, Mexico	2
London, England	91	Santo Domingo, Dom. Rep.	12	Madras, India	2
Stockholm, Sweden	69	Wellington, New Zealand	12	Rangoon, Burma	2
Honolulu, Territory of Hawaii	67	Montevideo, Uruguay	11	Recife, Brazil	2
Port Elizabeth, South Africa	67	Bombay, India	8	San Jose, Costa Rica	2
São Paulo, Brazil	58	Panama City, Panama	7	Torreon, Mexico	2
Sydney, Australia	55	Calcutta, India	6	Valparaiso, Chile	2
San Juan, Puerto Rico	51	Cali, Columbia	6	Barcelona, Spain	1
Mexico City, Mexico	49	Oruro, Bolivia	6	Port Au Prince, Haiti	1
Batavia, Java	48	San Salvador, El Salvador	6	Santiago, Chile	1
Manila, Philippine Islands	44	Colombo, Ceylon	5	Tampico, Mexico	1

9. Indianapolis: "Before a crowd estimated at 135,000, the LaSalle Roadster driven by "Big Boy" Rader paced the Indianapolis Memorial Day race and made a very splendid showing. The Roadster which Rader drove had a beautiful black finish and with its nickel work made a most impressive sight as it tore around the curve and flashed into the straight-away with the pack of 33 racing cars roaring at its heels." Source: *Clearing House*, June 2, 1927. Selection of the new LaSalle as the pace car provided a significant stamp of approval and publicity boost. LaSalle was destined to pace the Indianapolis race three times, an impressive record for a car that was built for only fourteen years. The identity of the 1927 pace car is not clear from factory records. Roadster serial #204256, body #340, is listed in the ledger as "For Indpls Speedway, Steve Hannagan" and was shipped on 4/23/27. That car, however, had Black upper panels and Derby Red Medium lower panels. There are no other indications of cars for the Speedway. Is the race account incorrect? Was serial #204256 repainted for the race, or was there a second Roadster that was the actual pace car?

10. <u>Serial numbers</u>. None of the body styles were assembled in body number sequence. For body styles that shared the same body number sequence, blocks of serial numbers were apparently assigned to a particular style and, when all were used, another block was assigned.

Fisher body styles.

First car built in each body series		Last car built	Highest body number	
1168	serial 200018, body 273	serial 226806, body 1489	1999	
1168-B	serial 208955, body 28	serial 226778, body 267	371	
1169	serial 200019, body 5	serial 226695, body 1173	1184	
7380	serial 200016, body 1074	serial 216160, body 2455	5001	
7390	serial 200028, body 77	serial 223991, body 1244	1250	
7400	serial 200015, body 239	serial 226741, body 2993	3001	
7410	serial 299924, body 11	serial 216772, body 1063	1100	
7420	serial 209192, body 30	serial 226807, body 1224	1600	
8050	serial 216947, body 3	serial 226732, body 992	1839	
8060	serial 212036, body 1264LX	serial 226805, body 2542	2826	Note 1
8060-A	serial 216911, body 1115	serial 226794, body 2463	3469	Note 1
8070	serial 212046, body 1266	serial 226529, body 480	1468	
8080	serial 217095, body 2	serial 226804, body 500	500	
8090	serial 212061, body 70	serial 226637, body 119	210	
8110	serial 208251, body 310	serial 226791, body 3067	3169	Note 2
8110-A	serial 217045, body 18	serial 226802, body 3513	7429	Note 2
8120	serial 205614, body 1452	serial 224558, body 1578	2110	
8130	serial 207102, body 154	serial 226749, body 275	1215	
8140	serial 211834, body 254	serial 226625, body 934	962	Note 3
8140-A	serial 216812, body 146	serial 226793, body 967	975	Note 3
Chassis 125"	serial 200001	serial 226636		
Chassis 134"	serial 214892	serial 222897		

Note 1: Body styles 8060 and 8060-A share the same body number sequence.
Note 2: Body styles 8110 and 8110-A share the same body number sequence.
Note 3: Body styles 8140 and 8140-A share the same body number sequence.

<u>Fleetwood body styles</u>. All of the Fleetwood bodies had body numbers assigned by the body works in Pennsylvania. The chassis were shipped to Fleetwood and returned to Cadillac Motor Car Company in Detroit with the body installed.

First car built		Last car built
3051	serial 204384, body 10322	serial 217223, body 10608
3110	serial 200012, body 10050	serial 217098, body 10061
3120	serial 200022, body 10189	serial 207761, body 10199
3130	serial 200013, body 10177	serial 217312, body 10611
3751	serial 219256, body 10941	serial 226002, body 10943

CONDENSED SPECIFICATIONS

POWER PLANT

Engine—Compensated eight-cylinder, V-type; 90-degree angle between cylinder blocks. Engine and transmission in unit; 3-point suspension. Piston displacement 303 cubic inches. Bore $3\frac{1}{8}$"; stroke $4\frac{15}{16}$". Horsepower S.A.E. rating 31.25; actually more than 75.

Cylinders—Cast in blocks of 4, with detachable heads.

Pistons—Nickel-iron, close grained and long wearing; 3 rings; lower ring special oil regulating type.

Connecting Rods—Drop-forged alloy steel, I-beam section; side by side, two on each pin. Bearings $2\frac{3}{8}$"x$1\frac{3}{8}$". Babbitt in rods.

Valves—Inlet $1\frac{1}{2}$", tungsten steel; exhaust $1\frac{1}{2}$", silico-chrome steel. Single spring. Automatically lubricated.

Crankcase—Special copper alloy aluminum; non-resonant.

Crankshaft—Diameter $2\frac{3}{8}$", length to outer ends of front and rear bearings $23\frac{25}{32}$". Supported on 3 main bearings, bronze-backed—Chadwick interchangeable. Crank throws 90 degrees apart, provided with compensators.

Camshaft—Single hollow shaft, with 16 cams; shaft supported on 4 bearings. Driven from crankshaft by silent chain.

Clutch—New dry-plate type with two discs, $9\frac{1}{2}$" in diameter. Positive release.

Transmission—Selective type with 3 speeds forward and 1 reverse. Alloy steel, oil-hardened gears and shafts. Faces of gear teeth accurately ground and ends of teeth chamfered to obtain easy and quiet gear shifting.

GASOLINE SYSTEM

Supply—20-gallon fuel tank located at rear of chassis. Feed is by vacuum to smaller tank on dash.

Vacuum Pump—Special design, located at rear of crankcase and driven by eccentric on the camshaft, provides vacuum necessary to lift gasoline to vacuum tank under all conditions.

Fuel Strainer—Straining device located between tank and the carburetor, cleans engine fuel before it enters the mixing chamber of the carburetor.

Carburetor—LaSalle design and manufacture; maximum efficiency and economy. Air valve, single jet type. Automatic Thermostatic mixture control. Intake header exhaust-heated. Valve in left exhaust manifold operated from instrument board, when closed deflects back exhaust gases from left cylinders through intake header jacket thus giving maximum heat for carburetor almost immediately. Manifold high turbulence type.

COOLING SYSTEM

Radiator—Copper with cellular core; nickeled casing.

Water Cooling—Capacity $5\frac{1}{4}$ gallons. Centrifugal pump mounted on right side of engine and driven by silent chain from crankshaft. Cylinder blocks interconnected. One drain plug for entire system; necessary to disconnect only 3 hose couplings to remove radiator.

Temperature Control—Thermostatically controlled by vertical balanced radiator shutter blades.

Fan—6 blades; driven at engine speed by a V-belt from camshaft. Hub carries gear oil pump and oil reservoir for its own lubrication.

LUBRICATING SYSTEM

Engine lubrication—Pressure circulation system employing gear pump carried in oil pan and driven by extension of the distributor shaft. Supply in 8-quart capacity steel reservoir with screen for cleaning oil. Oil manifold runs length of crankcase, with leads connecting main bearings, the rear camshaft bearing, the pressure gauge and filter. Hollow camshaft carries oil from rear to other camshaft bearings. Passages in crankshaft conduct oil from main bearings to connecting rod bearings. Pressure is regulated by adjustable piston valve, overflow from which lubricates chain mechanism. Valves automatically lubricated by ports in cylinder walls. Oil level gauge on top of crankcase at rear of cylinder blocks.

Crankcase Ventilation—An effective and unique system which prevents contamination of crankcase oil with water and unburned fuel.

Oil Filter—An effective filtering device for removing impurities in solid form.

ELECTRICAL SYSTEM

Ignition—Delco-Remy high tension system; ignition timer with two sets of contact points, induction coil and condenser. Jump-gap type distributor.

Generator—Two-pole Delco-Remy, mounted on right side of crankcase. Driven by same silent chain as water pump. Current regulated by automatic, thermostatic switch.

Starting Motor—Four-pole Delco-Remy, mounted horizontally at the right side of transmission case. Has exceptionally high stalling torque.

Battery—LaSalle-Exide, 100 ampere hour, 6-volt, 3 cells. Carried on right-hand side of frame under front seat.

Horn—Delco-Remy high frequency type, mounted on left side of radiator.

Lighting Equipment—Two headlamps, two side lamps; new design, bullet type; tail lamp, controlled from single lever at center of steering wheel. Stop signal lamp in unit with tail lamp, controlled by foot brake. Instrument board lighting controlled by light switch at center of steering wheel. Dome light in Two-passenger Coupe, Four-passenger Victoria and Five-passenger Sedan.

OPERATING CONTROLS

Gear Shift—Center.

Service Brakes—Two independent braking systems. Mechanically operated, internal expanding on front wheels and external contracting on rear wheels. Division of pedal pull automatically proportioned between front and rear systems. Both front brakes operate when straight ahead, outer brake released on turn.

Hand Brake—Internal expanding on rear wheels and will not require adjustment during life of brake lining.

Steering Gear—LaSalle design, worm and sector, completely adjustable; reduction $17\frac{1}{2}$ to 1. Steering wheel 18" in diameter, rubber composition with steel reinforcement; metal cast hub and spokes.

Engine Controls—Accelerator at right of brake pedal. Hand throttle lever built into central portion of steering wheel.

Automatic Spark Control—With manual lever located on instrument board directly in front of steering column.

Instrument Board—Special die cast panel; ignition switch with coincidental lock; ignition advance control; fuel gauge; ammeter; speedometer; oil pressure gauge; carburetor enriching button; intake header heat control; clock; motor heat meter and cigar lighter. Instrument lamps with separate switch.

MISCELLANEOUS

Axles—Rear axle, LaSalle design, three-quarter floating type with helical bevel gear and pinion. Shafts and pinion are alloy steel forgings. Front axle, reversed Elliott type; drop-forged special alloy steel with inclined king bolts. Drop-forged steering spindles with ball thrust bearing at lower end.

Drive—Solid steel propeller shaft $1\frac{5}{16}$" in diameter, turns in torque tube which completely seals assembly. Rear end rigidly connected to rear axle by splined sleeve; front end, to transmission shaft through universal joint. Torque tube is bolted to differential carrier at rear, and front end pivoted in ball-and-socket joint at rear of the transmission. Transmits drive of rear wheels to chassis and absorbs torque reactions due to acceleration and brakes.

Fenders—One-piece metal; oval contour.

Fender Wells—Optional, at extra charge.

Frame—Side bar channel section with wide top flange, carbon steel, maximum depth of side members $6\frac{1}{2}$"; 4 channel cross members and 2 tubular cross members.

Springs—Semi-elliptic suspension. Rear shackle tension type provided with ball-and-socket joint. Delco-Remy-Lovejoy shock absorbers are standard equipment. Front springs 39" x 2"; rear 58" x 2".

Tires—32" x 6.00" cord balloon.

Tire Carrier—Rim type mounted at rear of chassis.

Tools—Complete set of tools in compartment under front seat.

Wheelbase—125" and 134".

Wheels—Artillery type, 20" diameter, 12 hickory spokes with steel felloe; demountable split type rim. Wire wheels, and disc wheels having rim integral, optional at extra charge.

The Cadillac Motor Car Company reserves the right to make changes in specifications at any time without incurring any obligation to install same on cars previously sold

Harley Earl and a 1928 LaSalle Roadster in California.

NINETEEN TWENTY-NINE
Series 328

In all the history of the automobile industry there is no more brilliant record of an almost instantaneous and lasting success than the remarkable record of the La Salle. Striding boldly into a somewhat jaded acceptance of automobile design and style, this spirited and youthful conception of a newer and smarter motorcar at once swept aside all adherence to tradition and, overnight, established a vogue to which the whole industry now pays tribute. This vogue was so dynamic and so accurately mirrored motordom's subconscious desire that its influence has been profound and is everywhere evident.

—from the 1929 sales brochure

La Salle leadership takes on new impetus.

Now La Salle interprets the new vogue which it created in a beautiful and brilliant new line of cars. Retaining all the elements of style and modishness that made La Salle creator of today's vogue; refined and improved in accordance with the Cadillac Motor Car Company's well-known policy of continuous advancement, the new cars are larger and more luxurious than ever before, are capable of even more satisfying performance, and introduce to motordom a number of significant developments in automotive engineering that add greatly to the ease of operation and riding qualities and that contribute markedly to greater safety.

The La Salle name thus becomes more significant than ever in the fine car field. Its characteristic bent for vigorous styling has now a more untrammeled expression than ever. Its resources in power are augmented. Its amenability to control is refined and developed to new degrees of driving ease. Its safety factors are multiplied and strengthened.

La Salle thus intensifies its appeal to all discriminating motorists. Women drivers—the younger generation— the busy man of crowded affairs, all find in it qualities and abilities of utmost value. More emphatically than ever, La Salle reinterprets the prevailing requirements of fine motoring.

—from the 1929 sales brochure

NINETEEN TWENTY-NINE
Series 328

The Series 328 LaSalle was once again named, in the European manner, after the displacement of the engine, which was increased to 328 cubic inches.

Visual changes were extremely modest. Parking lamps on the LaSalle were relocated from the cowl to the top edge of the front fenders. Riding on the demand for longer wheelbase models, LaSalle responded with all models on a 134-inch wheelbase, except for the Roadster, two Phaetons and two Fleetwood styles. LaSalle also offered four fully custom Fleetwood bodies. Production had reached a record of almost 23,000. For the first time, LaSalle exceeded Cadillac production during a model year (by 5,000).

All LaSalles were fitted, for the first time, with chrome plated exterior brightwork and metallic paint became available. The variety of available combinations was almost without limit. Wheels were available in wooden artillery, spoke and disc configurations.

On October 20, 1928, in *The Saturday Evening Post*, a full page ad without illustrations promoted "revolutionary new features that meant infinitely greater safety, comfort and handling ease . . ." Ten new features were explained: "1. Syncro-Mesh transmission; 2. Duplex brake system; 3. nimbler steering gear; 4. Security-Plate Glass; 5. front seat adjustment; 6. 90 degree, V-type, Eight Cylinder engine improvements; 7. Pneumatic Control for maximum quietness; 8. Chromium plated; 9. unequalled body design; and 10. longer, wider and more luxuriously roomy closed bodies . . . eleven new Fisher body styles and two custom built Fleetwoods." The illustrated color ads maintained the French foreign flavor . . . stating "the smart, distinctive LaSalle design that created today's vogue in motorcars finds in the LaSalle a still richer and more fascinating expression excelled only by Cadillac itself and unequalled by any other car in the world." A black and white advertisement headlined "A distinguished symbol of social prestige." "You only have to pause where the smartest people congregate, you have only to check the social register, and you will inevitably discover a preponderance of Cadillacs and LaSalles." It seems evident that a great connection in the public eye was desired by Cadillac with LaSalle. Common safety factors, mechanical features and common prestige connections were the very essence of beauty, chic, smartness and luxury. The artistic touch was aimed at the quality of life and lifestyles enjoyed by those with considerable means. LaSalle and Cadillac shared a sales brochure as well . . . quite a change of marketing strategy from the words of H. M. Stephens, who, at LaSalle's introduction, urged keeping the two marques separate and apart. One could argue that Cadillac was hurting and that LaSalle was gaining sales at the expense of Cadillac. "These are LaSalle attributes which have won thousands to its ownership, through the unsuppressed enthusiasm of pioneer purchasers."

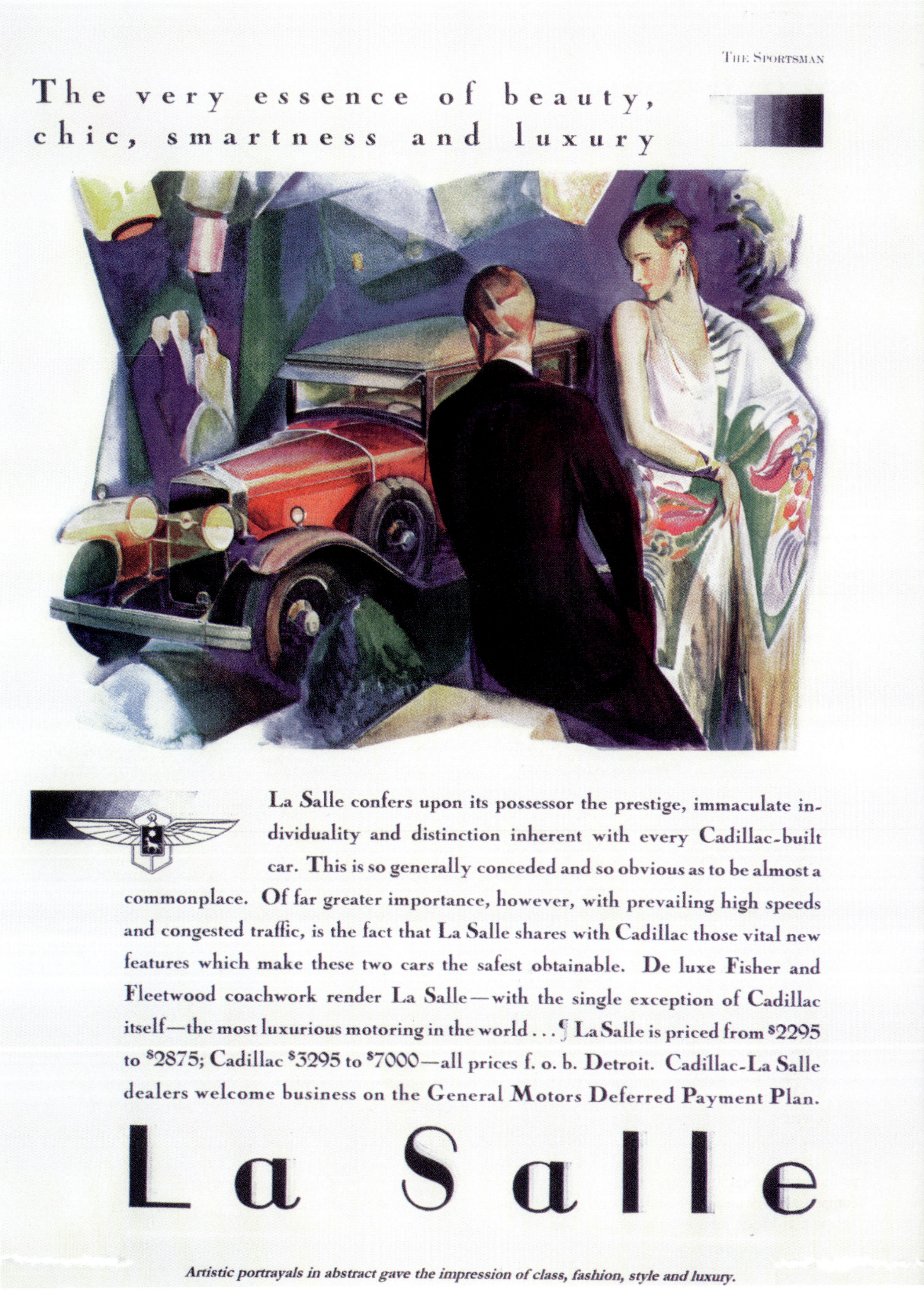
The Sportsman
The very essence of beauty, chic, smartness and luxury
La Salle confers upon its possessor the prestige, immaculate individuality and distinction inherent with every Cadillac-built car. This is so generally conceded and so obvious as to be almost a commonplace. Of far greater importance, however, with prevailing high speeds and congested traffic, is the fact that La Salle shares with Cadillac those vital new features which make these two cars the safest obtainable. De luxe Fisher and Fleetwood coachwork render La Salle—with the single exception of Cadillac itself—the most luxurious motoring in the world . . . ¶ La Salle is priced from $2295 to $2875; Cadillac $3295 to $7000—all prices f. o. b. Detroit. Cadillac-La Salle dealers welcome business on the General Motors Deferred Payment Plan.
La Salle

Artistic portrayals in abstract gave the impression of class, fashion, style and luxury.

FLEETWOOD TRANSFORMABLE TOWN CABRIOLET, No. 3751

Imposingly mounted on the 134-inch wheelbase, this exclusive custom car commands respect and admiration in any company. It expresses individuality and charm in every line and in all its appointments. It has the distinctive Fleetwood transformable feature.

Two Transformable Town Cabriolets by Fleetwood. One on a 134-inch wheelbase, the other on a 125-inch wheelbase. Note the speaking tube in the driver's compartment. Passengers gave instructions to the chauffeur through a speaker's tube almost touching the ear.

FLEETWOOD TRANSFORMABLE TOWN CABRIOLET, No. 3051

The perfected LaSalle mechanism in compact, 125-inch chassis, with coachcraft revealing a wealth of singular charm and exclusive styling. The driver's compartment is transformable from open to enclosed as occasions demand.

While visually the modifications were minor, the mechanical improvements were significant.

"High compression" heads were made available on domestic models. High compression meant an increase to 5.3:1, which provided about 105 pounds compression. A hand spark control on the instrument panel located directly in front of the steering column compensated for the higher compression and the various octane anti-knock fuels available during that era.

The Syncro-Mesh Silent-Shift transmission was introduced, which avoided the need for double clutching and eased the gear selection for the owner driven LaSalle. Brakes were improved, requiring less pedal pressure and all windows were fitted with shatterproof security plate glass. Driver seats became more fully adjustable. The ride was improved with hydraulic shock absorbers.

Wilson's artistic renderings continued to portray romantic international scenes. It was fashionable to have windows open and the driver's arm across the window sill. The European influence can be seen in each artistic advertisement. Therein lies the beauty of being able to suggest some new trends; i.e. European is stylish; European will help you stand out in a crowd; European will make dreams come true; and so will your LaSalle; etc. Each ad has a different emphasis in its heritage: small print connection to Cadillac; a product of General Motors; large print Cadillac Motor Car Company; and affiliation only as part of the text.

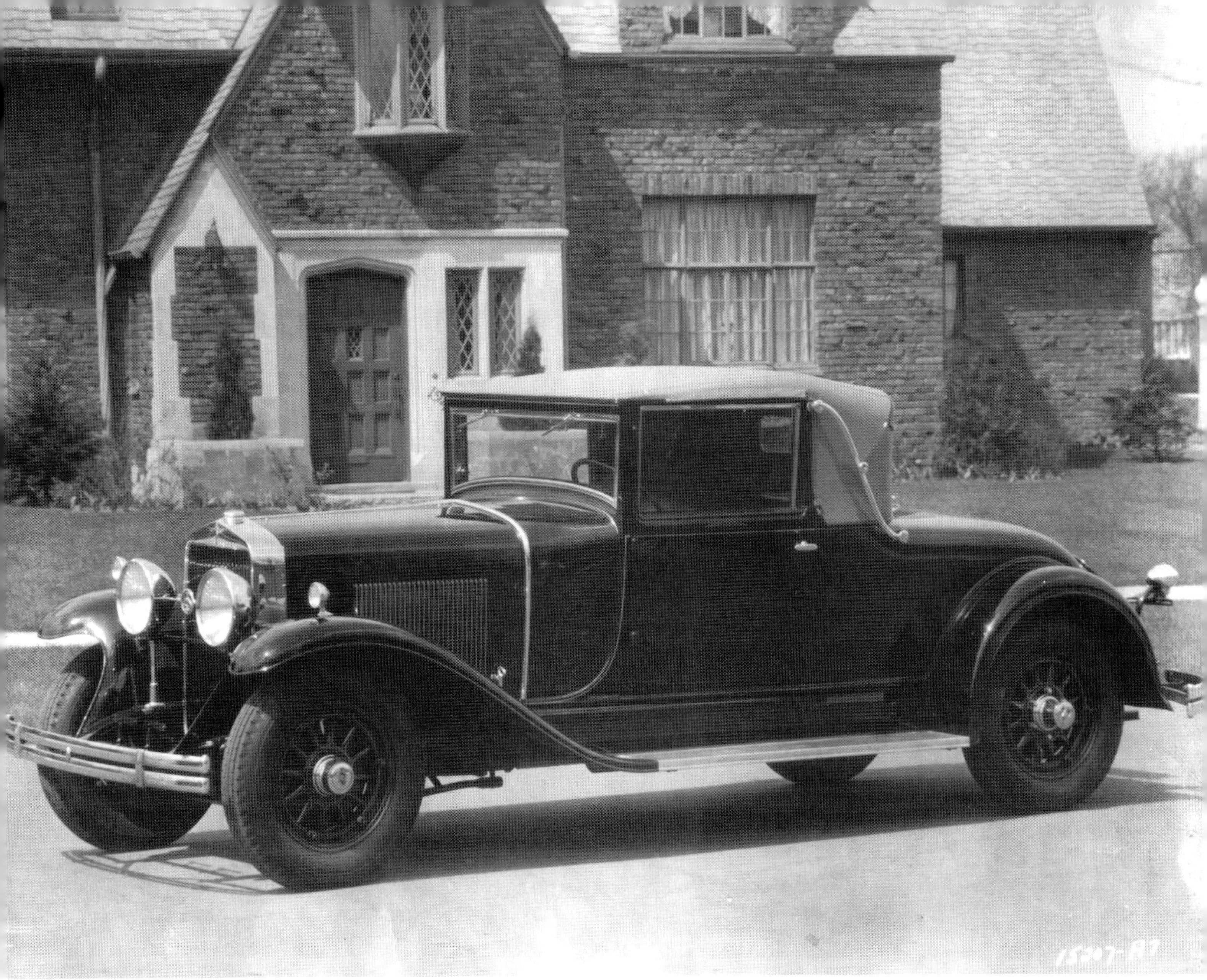

Top: This Series 328 Fisher-bodied Convertible Coupe stood on a 134-inch wheelbase chassis. Most noticeable is the absence of the spare tire in the fender and return to the reverse flow molding from the door port to the lower leading edge of the cowl, reminiscent of the carriage building days. Also absent are the battery and toolbox covers, a la Cadillac, above the running board step. Bottom left: A seven-passenger Sedan on 134-inch wheelbase weighed in at 4,555 lbs. Interiors were beautifully appointed and three-tone paint combinations were real attention-getters. Bottom right: A five-passenger Coupe Series 328 on a 134-inch wheelbase. Both closed cars on this page have a sun visor arrangement. All three have no fender mounted spare tire. Parking lights for 1929 were located on the fenders. Next page: Sales brochures for 1929 were illustrated in color. Some of them were unique and daring (lavender and green) or full of good taste (deep blue and beige).

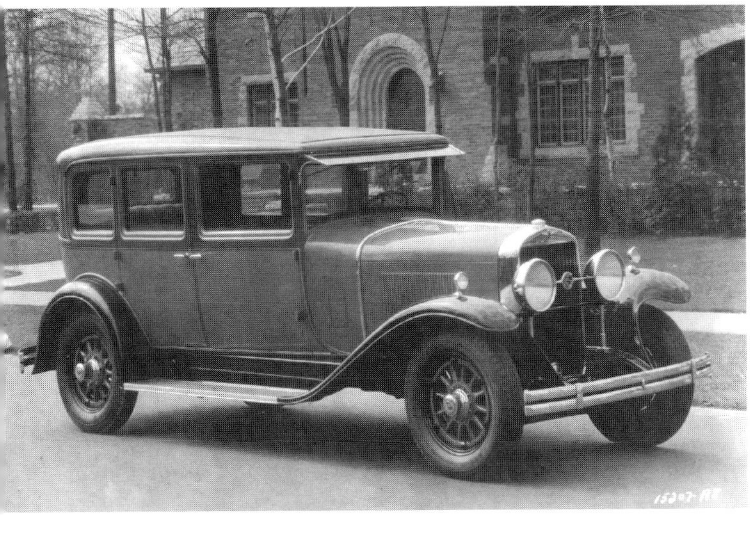

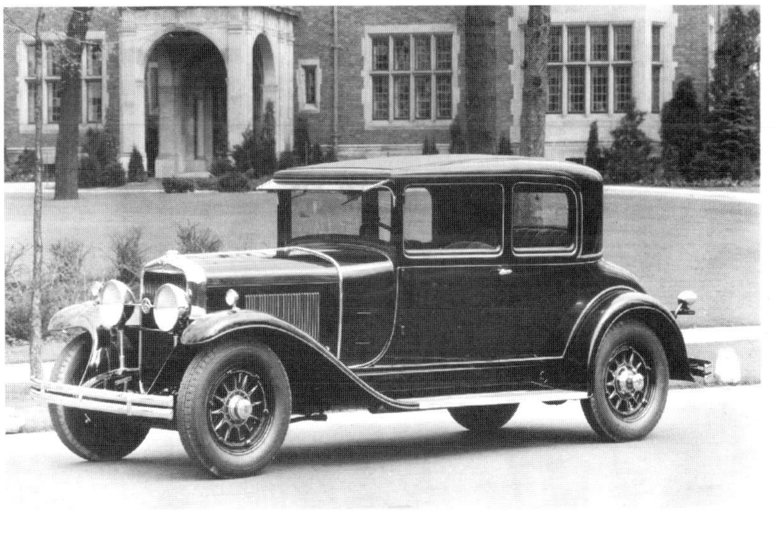

LASALLE TWO-PASSENGER CONVERTIBLE COUPE

A DASHING *model conceived and executed in full harmony with today's vogue. All bright parts are plated with costly chromium over polished nickel. Glass is Security-Plate glass. The deck seat is accessible, restful.*

LASALLE FOUR-PASSENGER SPORT PHAETON

REPLETE *with smart trappings, handsomely embellished with chromium plate, the Sport Phaeton is a striking LaSalle creation. The tonneau cowl carries a folding windshield of Security-Plate glass. Wheelbase is 125 inches.*

Exceptionally safeguarded against highway hazards

To travel in security and peace of mind is of the very essence of luxury. And the new LaSalle contributes to this feature of motoring in ways highly significant.

Abundance of power—a highly efficient braking system—exquisitely refined handling ease—all are features of the new LaSalle which, by inspiring confidence and a feeling of security, add still more to the pleasurable thrill of driving the LaSalle. The new LaSalle provides still another safety factor. It is fully equipped throughout—all windshields, all windows—with Security-Plate glass. This eliminates the remote hazard of flying glass.

This Security-Plate glass is also provided on the open cars, including the tonneau windshield of the Sport Phaeton.

LASALLE TWO-PASSENGER COUPE

This *handsome Two-passenger Coupe is especially designed for its specific functions. The seat is fully adjustable. The back window opens for easy communication with deck seat passengers. An ash receiver is fitted on the right door.*

LASALLE FOUR-PASSENGER PHAETON

Abundantly *powered by the enlarged 90-degree, V-type, eight-cylinder engine, and equipped with new Syncro-Mesh transmission and new Cadillac designed Duplex-Mechanical four-wheel brakes, the Phaeton asserts its right to first rank for performance and handling ease.*

So responsive to controls that it seems to drive itself

BRILLIANT performance, ever an essential La Salle attribute, is more highly than ever developed in the new La Salle. And with it is a refreshing, delightful ease of control that makes the car seem almost to drive itself. Gear shifting, so long an annoying feature to most drivers, is rendered simple and easy in these new La Salles, for the new Cadillac designed Syncro-Mesh transmission eliminates all necessity for deft skill in easing the gears into position, and enables even the inexperienced driver to make the necessary shifts quickly, smoothly, without clashing.

The new Cadillac designed Duplex-Mechanical four-wheel brakes are an important development that adds materially to the ease of operation. With this new Cadillac contribution to automotive engineering, braking becomes an easy, effortless operation. For the new brakes require surprisingly little pedal pressure and foot travel.

Steering with the easy grip, large diameter wheel, and the worm-and-sector gear is positive and soft.

All in all, driving ease is so highly developed in the new La Salle that driving the car entails neither exceptional skill nor physical prowess. As befits so luxurious a car, it drives luxuriously — is sensitively responsive to its driver, however light the touch upon the controls.

LASALLE FIVE-PASSENGER COUPE

A SHAPELY model, capitalizing to the full all the potentialities of the distinctive La Salle motif on the 134-inch wheelbase. Driver's seat is easily and quickly adjustable. Door panels are richly trimmed in broadlace. Outer hardware is plated in chromium.

LASALLE TWO-PASSENGER ROADSTER

SLIM in contour, asparkle with chromium plate, the Roadster accentuates the fleetness and vigor of La Salle design. The windshield is Security-Plate glass. There is a spacious deck seat. Wheelbase is 125 inches.

Already the outstanding leader, La Salle now claims new laurels

COURAGEOUS style leadership, proved mechanical worth—these have ever been outstanding attributes of the La Salle. It is acknowledged arbiter of fashion, brilliant exemplar of performance.

It won this high position by interpreting public preference sincerely and ably. And now, in the new La Salle, it supplies what motorists want today in cars of still more commanding presence, of still more impressive charm.

All standard closed models are mounted on a chassis of 134-inch wheelbase. They are noticeably wider inside than before and have an added inch of head room.

The power and liveliness that have made the La Salle such a joy to drive are increased in the new La Salle, for the famous Cadillac 90-degree, V-type, eight-cylinder engine has been refined, improved and enlarged, bringing its performance to new surpassing levels of brilliance.

The new La Salle bodies are even smarter than in the past. All exterior plating is in sparkling lustrous chromium over polished nickel. Parking lamps are mounted far forward on the fenders. Such items as the radiator cap, the sweep of the roof line above the visor, the moulding treatment upon rear quarter and back panels, reveal pleasing modifications.

LASALLE SEVEN-PASSENGER SEDAN

La Salle's *ultimate expression of travel luxury combined with the ample power and velvety performance of the Cadillac 90-degree, V-type eight. Doors are beautifully trimmed in costly broadlace. Upholstery is a rich mohair attractively tufted over luxury spring cushions. The front seat is fully adjustable. All external nickel is chromium-plated.*

LASALLE FIVE-PASSENGER LANDAU CABRIOLET

A wholly *new type of body design created by Cadillac engineers. Although it is extremely smart, it is also highly practical. The rear quarter of Burbank may be easily folded back to accord rear seat passengers the airiness and exhilaration of open car travel.*

A new spirited La Salle body type

THAT pleasing novelty and graceful symmetry, characteristic of La Salle design, find full expression in the new Five-passenger Landau Cabriolet. Developed along American lines, from an idea occasionally utilized in European models, it meets a wide range of motoring conditions.

Operated as a closed car, it has that full measure of luxurious comfort and rich appointment so closely associated with the La Salle name.

And at a touch, the rear quarter can be lowered to transform it into an open car. Windows lower into the doors, and the top swings snugly back into a compact fold. This new model is smart and modish, with a decided note of sophistication in its design. Revealing the full range of La Salle brilliance in performance, signalizing a broadened scope of utility in coachcraft, the Five-passenger Landau Cabriolet is a definite forward step in La Salle triumph.

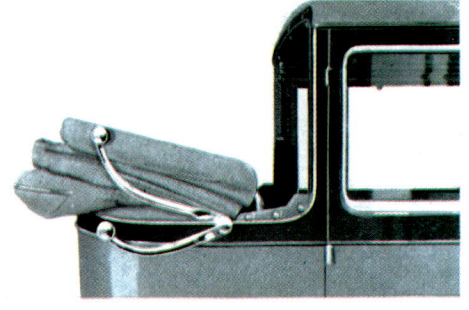

An inspiring spectacle of satisfaction

Only known photographic advertisement in color.

The contrary may have happened in some instances, but we have never heard of a case in which a Cadillac owner was induced to change in which disappointment did not ensue. The really significant thing however—in view of the tremendous pressure brought to bear upon them—is the amazingly small percentage of those who *do* change even in a five or ten year period. Cadillac owners are, of course, as they have always been, the focal-point of continuous competitive attack from a dozen aspiring and ambitious sources. But the solid phalanx of deep, abiding and immovable satisfaction remains substantially unbroken. The downright greater goodness of Cadillac in everything that makes a motor car a thing of beauty and a joy forever is too pronounced to be lightly forfeited.

CADILLAC
LA SALLE
FLEETWOOD

CADILLAC MOTOR CAR COMPANY · DIVISION OF GENERAL MOTORS

From any angle, the Series 328 two-passenger Convertible Coupe was handsome and carried its heritage with pride. This restored example has a rumble seat, luggage carrier and single Pilot Ray light. The Buffalo wire wheels add to the trendsetting European styling theme.

On the Series 328 there were many ways of saying LaSalle. Top left: A radiator ornament (optional) personifies the French nobleman and explorer . . . René Robert Cavalier, Sieur de la Salle. Bottom left: LaSalle, etched in amber glass was illuminated by the taillight assembly and was particularly bright when the brakes were applied. Top right: The LaS branding iron emblem was prominent on the tiebar between the headlights in front of the radiator screen. Middle right: LaSalle diagonally on the spare tire hub. Below right: The logo pressed into the running board rubber.

Top left: A view of the "deck seat" (rumble seat) has armrests built into the folding mechanism, providing passengers with additional support. Bottom left: The driver's compartment displays elegant taste for its time due to the lack of pattern, pleats or bolsters and the use of fine hides without blemishes. Top right: The steering wheel, instrument panel and foot controls are functional, robust and simple. Note pockets, door straps, map lights and single windshield wiper motor. Right center and bottom: Two views of the Convertible Coupe with the top down and canvas top cover in place. This assembly lays on top of the body, protected by four bumpers. 1929 was the first year for LaSalle to chrome plate over nickel.

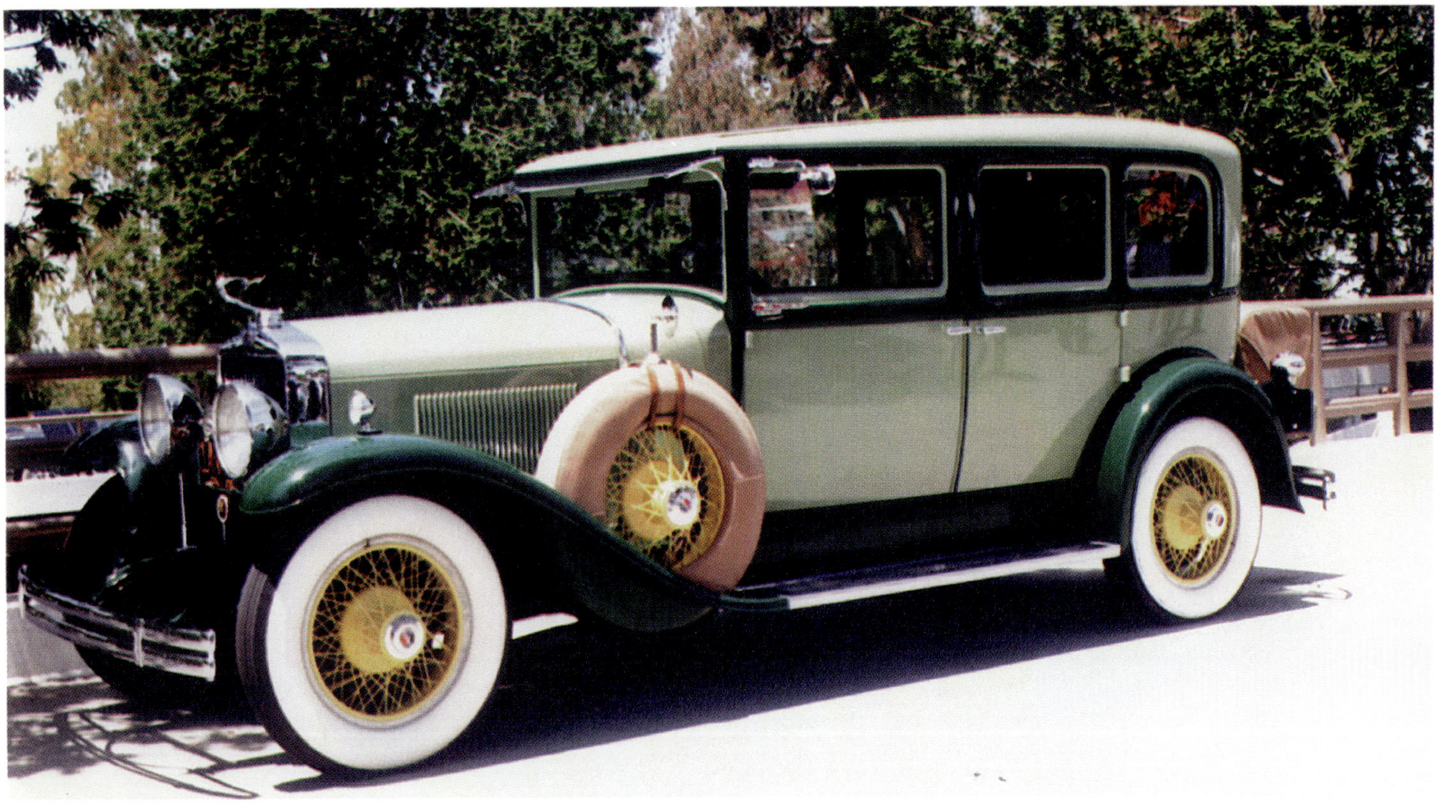

Top: A beautifully restored seven-passenger Sedan with optional Goddess radiator ornament, wire wheels and trunk on rear fold down luggage carrier. Bottom: The Series 328 two-passenger Coupe shown here, with whitewall tires, sidemounts, sidemounted mirrors and three-tone paint, stands proudly on a 134-inch wheelbase.

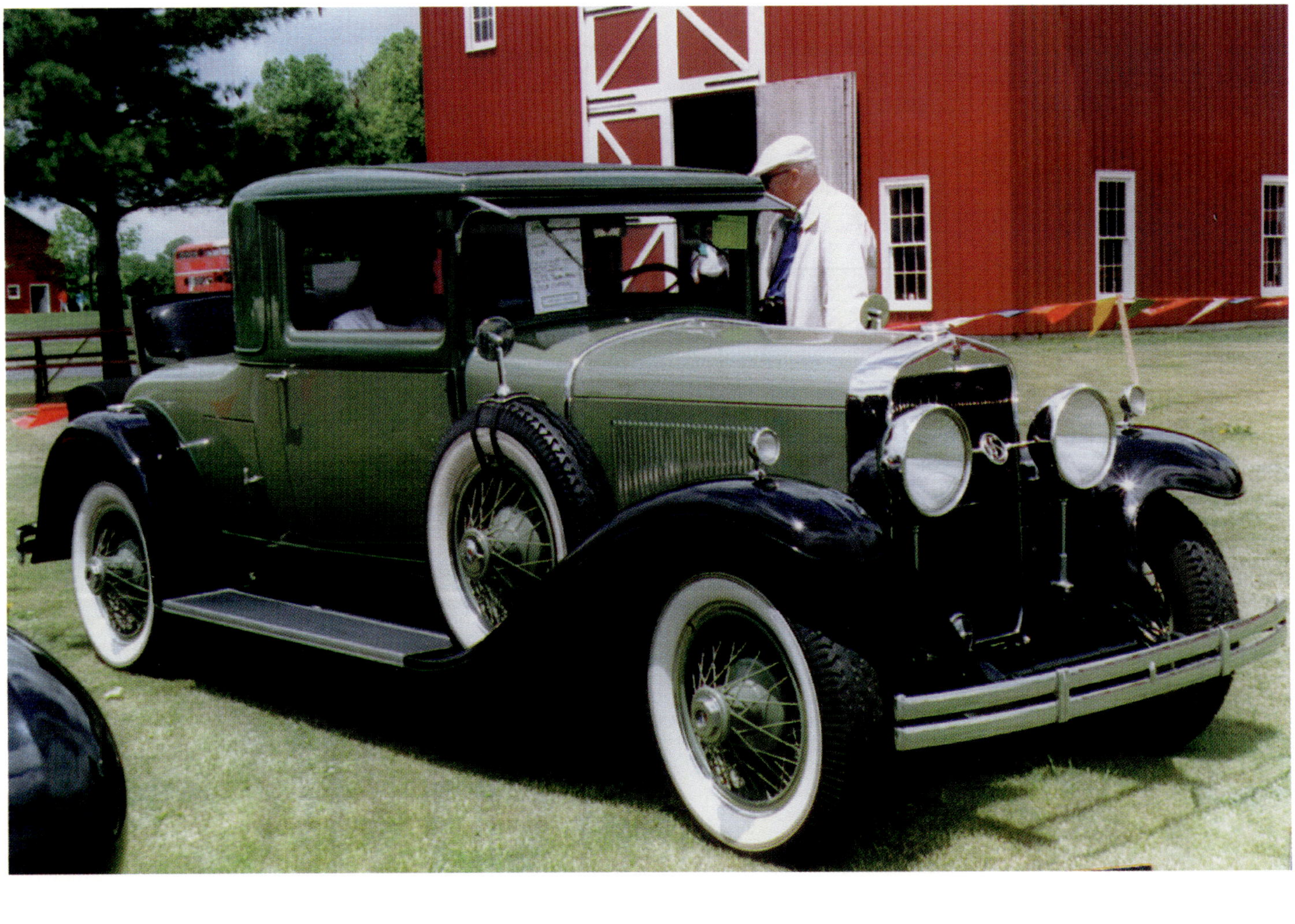

1929 LaSalle Production

<u>Total Production</u>: 22,961 automobiles and chassis.

<u>Serial Numbers</u>: 400001-422961. The Vehicle (engine) serial number is stamped "On the name plate on the front face of the left side of the dash and on the crankcase just below the water inlet on the right-hand side."

<u>Chassis Numbers</u>: Start with prefix "4 -" and increase from the first car, which has chassis number "4 -2." The numbers are not sequential. Location of chassis unit number is "on the upper surface of the right-hand side bar just in front of the oil filter."

<u>Body Plates</u>: Fisher job/style number (e.g., 1185) or Fleetwood job number (e.g., 3751) and body serial number are on the body plate attached "to the front face of the left side of the dash" (in the engine compartment).

Body Type and Style Numbers:		Wheelbase	List Price (Aug. 22, 1928)	Production
<u>Series 328 (LaSalle) Fisher Bodies</u>				
4-Pass. Phaeton	1185	125"	$2295.00	449
4-Pass. Sport Phaeton (dual cowl)	1185-B	125"	$2875.00	201
2-Pass. Roadster	1186	125"	$2345.00	351
7-Pass. Sedan	8530	134"	$2775.00	2629
7-Pass. Imperial Sedan	8540	134"	$2875.00	806
5-Pass. Sedan	8550	134"	$2595.00	5195
5-Pass. Family Sedan	8555	134"	$2450.00	4250
5-Pass. Coupe	8570	134"	$2625.00	2423
2-Pass. Convertible Coupe	8580	134"	$2595.00	1787
2-Pass. Coupe	8590	134"	$2495.00	1500
5-Pass. Convertible Landau Cabriolet	8600	134"	$2725.00	740
5-Pass. Imperial Conv. Landau Cabriolet	8605	134"	$2875.00	37
5-Pass. Town Sedan	8610	134"	$2675.00	2479
5-Pass. Imperial Town Sedan	8615	134"	$2825.00	17
Chassis		125"	$2200.00	57
Chassis		134"	$2250.00	3
LaSalle Hearse	Not listed	Not listed	Not listed	1
<u>Series 328 (LaSalle) Fleetwood Bodies</u>				
5-Pass. Transformable Town Cabriolet	3051	125"	$4800.00	7
5-Pass. Town Cabriolet (collapsible rear qtrs.)	3130	125"	$5200.00	1
5-Pass. Transformable Town Cabriolet	3751	134"	$4900.00	9
5-Pass. All-Weather Phaeton	3780	134"	Not listed	8
			Total	22,950

(Unexplained difference of 11 units)

LaSalle Color Policies

Fisher Line

The practice from previous years of introducing new standard colors throughout the model year was continued for 1929.

LaSalle Color Combinations - July/August 1928

<u>Closed Cars</u>	<u>Upper Panels</u>		<u>Lower Panels</u>	
Combination 101	Black		Calumet Blue	20235
Combination 102	Black		Thibetan Gray	20132
Combination 103	Millet Green	20336	Butternut Beige	20833
Combination 104	Kensington Green	20324	Sherwood Green	20325
<u>Open Cars</u>				
Combination 103			Butternut Beige	20833
Combination 104			Sherwood Green	20325
Unnumbered			Ching Blue	2441296
Unnumbered			Orinoco Green	20340

<u>Wheels</u>	Wood and Disc wheels match lower panels. Wire wheels are Black.
<u>Chassis</u>	Black.

Note: Paint combination numbers are not listed on the build sheets, only the paint names and manufacturers' paint numbers. Paint names and manufacturers' numbers released for production after August 1928 are not included above.

LaSalle Fleetwood

"The following have been selected by Fleetwood as attractive color combinations:
1. Duco Fleetwood Blue lower panels, Ivory striping.
2. Duco Fleetwood Maroon lower panels, Gold striping.
3. Duco Bon Soir Gray lower panels, Vermillion striping.
4. Duco Raleigh Green lower panels, Gold striping.
5. Duco Sable lower panels, Old Ivory striping.

All upper panels, mouldings, fenders and chassis are Black.

The Fleetwood Company will issue a color book, containing samples of suggested combinations which will be specified for cars in addition to the five colors shown..." Source: *The Book of Fleetwood* for 1929.

Trim Options

Standard closed bodies - job/style:
8530, 8540, 8550, 8570, 8590, 8600, 8605, 8610, 8615
  50 T 128 Gray Bedford Cord
  30 T 129 Silver Gray Mohair
  32 T 129 Taupe Mohair
  34 T 129 Greenish Gray Mohair
  38 T 129 Blue Mohair
  55 T 129 Taupe/Blue Pin Striped Broadcloth
  48 T 127 Plush (color not listed)
  30 T 129 Plush (color not listed)

Job/style 8555: 37 T 129 Gray cloth with Brown Stripe. Broadlace trimming around the doors and back of front seat is omitted on the style 8555 Family Sedan. The Family Sedan has individual type vanity case with leather cover, all other closed models have walnut cases.

Open bodies - job/style: 1185, 1185B, 1186, 8580
  22 T 1327 Dull Black Leather
  9 T 1328 Blue Leather Spanish Effect

Top: Drab Duck/Burbank standard,
  Black optional (6 T 1527)

Note: The Cadillac *Master Parts List* trim chart shows only the two above leather trim options for open body cars. The build sheets show that both Fisher Order and standard production open bodies through serial 403190 are trimmed in either 9 T 129 or 22 T 129. Descriptions of those trims numbers could not be located. Both are undoubtedly leather, probably Blue and Black, but in different finishes than the standard trims.

Exclusive Fleetwood:
"Fleetwood has developed nine upholstery materials of the highest grade which are available for all types of bodies. These consist of six doeskin suede Broadcloths and three special Venetian mohair velvets designed exclusively for Fleetwood. The broadcloths are manufactured in subdued colors that will harmonize with any paint selection.
Fleetwood Cloths (Seat Material):
    Wiese 2969 Green Gray   Wiese 2972 Silver Gray
    Wiese 2970 Maroon Taupe   Wiese 2973 Blue Gray
    Wiese 2971 Tan   Wiese 2974 Brown Taupe
The special Venetian mohair upholstery is of short nap and is available in the following colors: Fawn Gray - Drab Green - Taupe. " Source: *The Book of Fleetwood* for 1929.

Standard and Optional Equipment

Standard Equipment: Wood wheels, 6.50 X 19" U.S. Royal Cord tires only, rear spare tire carrier. Searchlight on right running board, Sport Phaeton only. Security plate glass throughout on all models with exception of rear curtains in open cars and Convertible 2-passenger Coupes. All lights and parts formerly nickel plated are chromium plated.

Optional Equipment: Five Wire wheels. Five Disc wheels. Six Wire, or Disc wheels, fenderwells, 2 spare tires and folding trunk rack.

Research Methodology: Microfiche copies of the individual Shipping Department records of the as-built configuration of each serial number were individually viewed. All record sheets were accounted for. All Fleetwood body styles were recorded by serial and body number to determine the quantity of each body style built. Fisher body styles 1185, 1185-B, 1186, 8540, 8580, 8600, 8605, 8615 and all chassis were recorded by serial number and body number to determine actual production. No attempt was made to construct cross reference lists of the other Fisher body numbers with corresponding engine numbers to account for the eleven unidentified vehicles and determine which body serial numbers were duplicated in production.

Notes on research findings:

1. The 1929 model year was the zenith of LaSalle production. On close inspection, the tidy looking vehicle record sheets hint at what was apparently a hectic year for the employees. Orders, production and shipments were at a record pace. The records are replete with recognizable errors, more so than any other year. There are many instances of body style names that do not match the listed style/job number. In some cases, it is impossible to determine which is correct without constructing a complete list of body numbers for each style.

2. Body Styles: Most of the body styles listed above need no explanation. "The new Convertible Landau Cabriolet (style 8600) is furnished in owner driven type only, with fully collapsible rear quarters. Standard trimming is 50 T 128 Bedford Cord but can be furnished on order in any of the optional mohairs for LaSalle." *Distributors Convention*, Aug. 1928. With an Imperial Partition added, style 8600 becomes style 8605. The 5-Pass. Fleetwood Transformable Town Cabriolets, available in two different wheelbases, are Town Cars with roll-up windows in the front doors and a removable soft top over the chauffeur's compartment. The Town Cabriolet is also an open front Town Car but features wind wings instead of roll-up windows for the front compartment and has a fully collapsible rear quarter roof section. Style 3780 is described in factory literature as a 5-Pass. Convertible Imperial Sedan but known in more common parlance as an All-Weather Phaeton and shown as such on the build sheets. The Cadillac *Master Parts List, First Edition, July 1931,* shows a 1929 LaSalle 5-Pass. Transformable Town Sedan, style 3751-C (collapsible rear quarters) on 134" wheelbase. None of the nine style 3751 cars built are identifiable from the build sheets as having the collapsible rear quarters.

3. Color: No listing of standard color combinations for the complete 1929 model year could be located. New standard colors were definitely introduced throughout the year. The Cadillac policy on paint durability was followed in 1929, rejecting orders received wherein the distributor specified colors not guaranteed for durability by the manufacturer. Such orders were accepted for shipment in primer finish, thus enabling the distributor to arrange locally to finish the car in any nondurable color. Thirty-four units encompassing eleven body styles were shipped to dealers in primer, "Rubbed out of rough stuff."

Paint names and manufacturer numbers were recorded to determine other probable standard combinations. Using the factory distinction of Upper Panel/Lower Panel color as a guide, a total of 543 combinations of color applications were recorded. Four-digit numbers listed below are Duco paint and probably prefixed by 244...., but not identified on the build sheets. Five-digit paint numbers are Rinshed & Mason, seven-digit numbers are Duco. Many paint combinations that are considered non-standard (not listed below) were applied as "Fisher Order" customer selections or on show cars. Some of the special order colors were used on as many as 46 cars. There are discrepancies in the paint numbers listed on the build sheets, with instances of as many as four different Duco numbers and one or two Rinshed & Mason numbers listed for the same paint name. Different paint names were found with the identical Duco paint number. These errors cannot be resolved from the LaSalle records without paint manufacturer records.

Probable other Standard Color Combinations

Upper Panels	Paint #	Lower Panels	Paint #
Arizona Brown	5906 (Duco)	Cashew Nut Tan	2447389 (Duco)
Avondale Blue	5574	Armada Blue	1751
Avondale Blue	5574	Balfour Blue	2445685
Beaver Brown, Light	1444	Beaver Brown, Dark	3024
Black	20460 (R & M)	Black	20460
Black		Bolling Green	2441331
Black		Boulevard Maroon	2444181
Black		Falmouth Gray	2441287
Black		Gettysburg Blue	2441205
Black		Madeira Maroon	5391 / 20624
Black		Matterhorn Gray	20162
Black		Naples Blue	5734
Black		Orriford Lake (Gray)	2443034
Black		Phantom Gray	2443356
Black		Sable	2445113
Black		Sherwood Green	2445762
Boulevard Maroon	2444181	Orriford Lake (Gray)	2443034
English Gray	2441774	Green Gray	2441775
Nevada Gray	7039 / 20128	Bardelys Gray	2443516
Pyramid Gray	2441314	Crystal Gray	2444738 or 3804 or 5209
Sea Fog Gray	2441454	Cape Smoke	2441482

4. Special Features: Both Fisher and Fleetwood body cars could be special ordered with virtually any body modifications to suit the purchaser. Cadillac General Manager Lawrence P. Fisher received a non-production body 7-Pass. Imperial Madame X Sedan with collapsible rear quarter. (In a tape recorded 1954 interview, Harley Earl indicated that this LaSalle was the first Madame X style car.) Louis A. Fisher received a non-production body Phaeton on a 134" wheelbase (vice the standard 125" wheelbase), fitted with six special Kelsey-type wire wheels and twin running board spotlights. Harley Earl received two Convertible Coupes; one with a non-production body, upper body molding in polished aluminum, chrome trunk rack and wire wheels with chromed hubs and spokes. A "Spec. 5/Sedan" style 8550 and a "non-production 5/Sedan" mounted on 125" wheelbase chassis were built for unnamed buyers. Two Fisher body 5-Pass. Sedans (style 8550) were built with "Imperial Partition." At least two 5-Pass. Family Sedans (style 8555) were built with "Imperial Partition." A known surviving Family Sedan with a factory installed Imperial Partition that is not indicated on the build sheet, is an indication of omissions that make it impossible to state with certainty what the total production of special feature cars really was. A 2-Pass. Convertible Coupe (style 8580) and two 2-Pass. Coupes (style 8590) were ordered with the rumble seat omitted and the deck lid hinges reversed to open from the bottom. Five cars were ordered with a single fenderwell to permit installation of a trunk rack. Numerous cars were done with special order interior trims.

5. The 1929 record sheets do not have the Purchaser block found in some other years. Only 101 vehicles indicated the name of the purchaser, including fifteen 7-Pass. Imperial Sedans that went to the U.S. Government for the War Department, U.S. Army, U.S. Navy and Marine Corps. Sixteen cars were listed to factory accounts of the Fisher brothers. Most of the others were for factory employees, including two to Eddie Rickenbacker, who was the LaSalle General Sales Manager at that time, and to Detroit area residents.

6. Canadian assembled cars: LaSalles were assembled in Oshawa in the 1929 model year, but the information in the Detroit factory records is very sketchy. Batches of as many as sixteen sequential serial numbers and as few as a single unit are identifiable. It is unclear whether or not the bodies were built in the U.S. and shipped to Oshawa with the chassis for final assembly. Of the 98 total units believed to constitute the Canadian production, 73 record sheets have no information other than the serial number and the date shipped. The record sheets do not give any indication of the distribution of completed vehicles. The sheets with data show that style 8530, 8540, 8550, 8555 and 8570 cars were assembled in Canada. Canadian cars are listed with Goodyear tires (only U.S. Royal tires were supplied on U.S. domestic units).

7. Chassis: Of the 60 indicated chassis sold, 44 (all on 134" wheelbase) were exports. Ten went to Paris, eight to Berlin, eight to London (R.H. drive) and seven to Antwerp. Five were shipped to Stockholm, three to Buenos Aires (right hand drive), two to Madrid and one to Warsaw, Poland. None of the records indicate who the intended body builders were nor the names of the purchasers. In addition to the chassis fitted with special bodies indicated in Note 4 above, three chassis went to New York City, two to Oshawa (Ontario), and one each to Baltimore, Bay City (Michigan), Brooklyn, Denver, Lima (Ohio) and Philadelphia. One of the chassis to New York and one to Oshawa were indicated as "Cut Open Chassis," of the type typically used for the auto shows to demonstrate the mechanical virtues and rugged construction of the marque.

8. <u>Export Cars</u>: In the 1929 model year, 1259 LaSalle automobiles and chassis were exported - five percent of total production. Exports included all Fisher body styles and two Fleetwood body styles. Vehicles built in the United States and shipped to Canada were not treated as exports, whereas vehicles shipped to Mexico were. Vehicles destined for the U.S. Territory of Hawaii were treated as exports. Right hand drive and low compression cylinder heads were common features for export cars destined for island nations plus Argentina, India and South Africa. Imperial Gallon fuel gauges were on vehicles destined for Canada and liter fuel dials on many cars entering Europe. Export totals by body style were:

Body Style	Style #	Qty.	Body Style	Style #	Qty.
4-Pass. Phaeton	1185	175	2-Pass. Coupe	8590	8
4-Pass. Sport Phaeton	1185-B	8	5-Pass. Conv. Landau Cabriolet	8600	69
2-Pass. Roadster	1186	26	5-Pass. Imperial Conv. Landau Cabriolet	8605	11
7-Pass. Sedan	8530	160	5-Pass. Town Sedan	8610	19
7-Pass. Imperial Sedan	8540	407	5-Pass. Imperial Town Sedan	8615	12
5-Pass. Sedan	8550	136	134" Chassis		44
5-Pass. Family Sedan	8555	43	5-Pass. Transformable Town Cabriolet	3051	1
5-Pass. Coupe	8570	13	5-Pass. Transformable Town Cabriolet	3751	3
2-Pass. Conv. Coupe	8580	124			

Where did the exports go? Destinations and associated number of units are listed below (destination not indicated on the records for four units):

City	Qty.	City	Qty.	City	Qty.
Antwerp, Belgium	179	Osaka, Japan	21	Cali, Columbia	3
Berlin, Germany	123	San Juan, Puerto Rico	21	Guadalajara, Mexico	3
Buenos Aires, Argentina	97	Manila, Philippine Islands	19	Monterrey, Mexico	3
Stockholm, Sweden	90	Melbourne, Australia	19	Recife, Brazil	3
Paris, France	85	Mexico City, Mexico	19	San Jose, Costa Rica	3
Madrid, Spain	80	Honolulu, Territory of Hawaii	18	Oruro, Bolivia	2
London, England	76	Port Elizabeth, South Africa	14	Calcutta, India	1
Sydney, Australia	46	Adelaide, Australia	13	Cuidad Obregon, Mexico	1
Copenhagen, Denmark	45	Batavia, Java	13	Guayaquil, Ecuador	1
São Paulo, Brazil	44	San Salvador, Central America	12	Lima, Peru	1
Alexandria, Egypt	41	Santiago, Chile	10	Port Au Prince, W. Indies	1
Havana, Cuba	35	Perth, Australia	8	Santo Domingo, Dominican Republic	1
Barranquilla, Columbia	33	Brisbane, Australia	7	St. Croix, Virgin Islands	1
Bombay, India	30	Montevideo, Uruguay	4	Tokyo, Japan	1
Caracas, Venezuela	21	Warsaw, Poland	4	Wellington, New Zealand	1

9. <u>Show Cars</u>: The Los Angeles show was marked by an enormous tent fire that destroyed many marque exhibits including LaSalle. Nine record sheets are annotated "Partially destroyed in Los Angeles Auto Show fire 3/5/29." Photos of the aftermath would lead anyone but an insurance company to conclude that the destruction was more than partial. The American Insurance Co. bought the remains. The records often do not identify specific show cars but one can guess from the paint schemes and other features. Cars painted and equipped identical to some of the Los Angeles fire cars (antique gold finish interior hardware, etc.) but shipped to Chicago, were undoubtedly show cars. Thirty-six 5-Pass. Sedans and Family Sedans were annotated "Special Display" in the chassis block of the build sheet and appear to have been displayed in Havana and cities across the U.S. with the fenders detached. Four cars were marked for display in the factory show room, three in the General Motors Building and one in the Book Cadillac (Detroit) Hotel.

10. <u>Factory installed accessories</u>: Very few cars had factory installed accessories other than the wire wheels, sidemounts and folding trunk rack option. Installed items were:

Bosch Horn	Special Export Windshield (some 1185, 1186, 8580 styles)
Cadillac two-way shock absorbers	Special Metal Trunk
Cadillac type steering wheel	Spotlight, running board mounted
Cadillac type foot rest	Spring Covers
Heavy Duty Springs	Tail & Stop light assembly, right side
Lorraine Spotlight	Tire Covers, Burbank/Black
Low Compression Cylinder Heads	Trunk with Burbank/Duck/Black cover
Mirror scopes	20" Wire wheels

11. None of the body styles were assembled in body number sequence. Fisher Order cars and non-standard paint color cars were generally substantially out of order due to the time required to make alterations.

<u>Fisher body styles.</u>

	First car built in each body series:	Last car built	Highest body number
1185	serial 400204, body 4	serial 421812, body 15	449
1185-B	serial 400304, body 1	serial 421878, body 201	201
1186	serial 400321, body 8	serial 422869, body 323	350
8530	serial 400001, body 3	serial 422958, body 2505	2629
8540	serial 400275, body 10	serial 421903, body 717	806
8550	serial 400010, body 28	serial 422961, body 4684	5195
8555	serial 400054, body 1	serial 422944, body 4237	4250
8570	serial 400011, body 43	serial 422321, body 2332	2423
8580	serial 400272, body 1	serial 422855, body 1798	1800
8590	serial 400270, body 6	serial 422879, body 1492	1500

8600	serial 400250, body 1	serial 422358, body 785	786
8605	serial 408983, body 274	serial 421991, body 783	783 See note
8610	serial 406592, body 2	serial 422960, body 2444	2496
8615	serial 409766, body 56	serial 422159, body 2380	2380 See note
chassis 125"	serial 415207	serial 420072	
chassis 134"	serial 400003	serial 422957	

Note: The style 8605 (Imperial division) cars are a subset of the style 8600 and share the same body number sequence. The style 8615 (Imperial division) cars are likewise a subset of the style 8610 and share the same body number sequence.

<u>Fleetwood body styles.</u> All of the Fleetwood bodies had serial numbers assigned by the bodyworks in Pennsylvania and do not have a unique set of body numbers associated with a specific body style, as is the case with Fisher bodies.

<u>First car built</u>: <u>Last car built</u>:
3051   serial 400006, body 10947   serial 412082, body10951
3130   serial 400005, body 10816
3751   serial 400007, body 10942   serial 416433, body 12996
3780   serial 409137, body 12007   serial 420915, body 12990

CONDENSED SPECIFICATIONS

POWER PLANT

ENGINE—Compensated, eight-cylinder, V-type; 90-degree angle between cylinder blocks. Engine and transmission in unit; 3-point suspension with improved rubber mountings on rear supports. Piston displacement 328 cubic inches. Bore $3\frac{1}{4}$ inches; stroke $4\frac{15}{16}$ inches. Horsepower S.A.E. rating 33.8; actually more than 86. Compression 5.3 to 1 standard; 4.8 to 1 optional.

CYLINDERS—Cast in blocks of 4, with detachable heads.

PISTONS—Nickel-iron, close grained and long wearing; 3 rings; lower ring special oil regulating type.

CONNECTING RODS—Drop-forged alloy steel, I-beam section, gun drilled, giving pressure lubrication to wrist pins; side by side, two on each pin. Bearings $2\frac{3}{8}$ inches x $1\frac{3}{8}$ inch. Babbitt in rods at lower ends.

VALVES—Inlet $1\frac{1}{2}$-inch clear, tungsten steel; exhaust $1\frac{1}{2}$-inch clear, silico-chrome steel, $\frac{21}{64}$-inch lift. Single spring. Exhaust automatically lubricated.

CRANKCASE—Special copper alloy aluminum; non-resonant.

CRANKSHAFT—Diameter $2\frac{3}{8}$ inches, length to outer ends of front and rear bearings $23\frac{25}{32}$ inches. Supported on 3 main bearings, bronze-backed Chadwick interchangeable. Crank throws 90 degrees apart, provided with compensators.

CAMSHAFT—Single hollow shaft, with 16 cams; shaft supported on 4 bearings. Driven from crankshaft by silent chain.

CLUTCH—Dry plate type with two discs, $9\frac{1}{2}$ inches in diameter. Positive release.

TRANSMISSION—Special Cadillac-La Salle Syncro-Mesh transmission giving noiseless, smooth gear shifting at all speeds. Selective type with 3 speeds forward and 1 reverse. Alloy steel, oil-hardened gears and shafts. Faces of gear teeth accurately ground.

GASOLINE SYSTEM

SUPPLY—20-gallon fuel tank located at rear of chassis. Feed is by vacuum to smaller tank on dash.

VACUUM PUMP—Special design, located at rear of crankcase and driven by eccentric on the camshaft, assists in preserving vacuum necessary to lift gasoline to vacuum tank under all conditions.

FUEL STRAINER—Straining device located between vacuum tank and the carburetor, cleans engine fuel before it enters the mixing chamber of the carburetor.

CARBURETOR—La Salle design and manufacture; maximum efficiency and economy. Air valve, single jet type. Automatic thermostatic mixture control. Intake header exhaust-heated. Valve in left exhaust manifold operated from instrument board; when closed deflects exhaust gases back from left cylinders through intake header jacket to the right manifold thus giving maximum heat for carburetor almost immediately. Manifold high turbulence type.

COOLING SYSTEM

RADIATOR—Copper with cellular core; casing is chromium-plated over polished nickel. Pump circulation.

WATER COOLING—Capacity $5\frac{1}{4}$ gallons. Centrifugal pump mounted on right side of engine and driven by silent chain from crankshaft. Cylinder blocks interconnected. One drain valve for entire system; necessary to disconnect only 3 hose couplings to remove radiator.

TEMPERATURE CONTROL—Thermostatically controlled by vertical balanced radiator shutter blades.

FAN—6 blades; driven at engine speed by a V-belt from camshaft. Hub carries gear oil pump and oil reservoir for its own lubrication.

LUBRICATING SYSTEM

ENGINE LUBRICATION—Pressure circulation system employing gear pump carried in oil pan and driven by extension of the distributor shaft. Supply in 8-quart capacity steel reservoir with screen for cleaning oil. Oil manifolds run length of crankcase, with leads connecting main bearings, the rear camshaft bearing, the pressure gauge and filter. Hollow camshaft carries oil from rear to other camshaft bearings. Connecting rods are gun drilled giving forced feed lubrication to wrist pins. Passages in the crankshaft conduct oil from main bearings to connecting rod bearings. Pressure is regulated by a piston valve, overflow from which lubricates chain mechanism. Exhaust valves are automatically lubricated by ports in cylinder walls. Oil level gauge on top of crankcase at rear of cylinder blocks.

CRANKCASE VENTILATION—An effective and unique system which prevents contamination of crankcase oil with water and unburned fuel.

OIL FILTER—An effective filtering device for removing impurities in solid form.

ELECTRICAL SYSTEM

IGNITION—Delco-Remy high-tension system; ignition timer with two sets of contact points, induction coil and condenser. Jump-gap type distributor.

IGNITION LOCK—Coincidental theft-proof ignition and transmission lock operated from instrument board.

GENERATOR—Two-pole Delco-Remy, mounted on right side of crankcase. Driven by same silent chain as water pump. Current regulated by automatic, thermostatic switch.

STARTING MOTOR—Four-pole Delco-Remy, mounted horizontally at the right side of transmission case. Has exceptionally high stalling torque.

BATTERY—La Salle-Exide, 100-ampere-hour, 6-volt, 3 cells. Carried on right-hand side of frame under front seat.

HORN—Delco-Remy high-frequency type, is mounted on left side of radiator. Concealed connections.

LIGHTING EQUIPMENT—Two headlamps; two parking lamps; new design, bullet type; tail lamp, controlled from new design switch at center of steering wheel. Parking lights mounted on front fenders. Stop signal lamp in unit with tail lamp, controlled by foot brake. Instrument board lighting controlled by separate switch on instrument board. Dome lamp in Two-passenger Coupe and Five-passenger Sedan.

WINDSHIELD WIPER—Electric windshield wiper, tandem type, controlled by switch on instrument board.

OPERATING CONTROLS

GEAR SHIFT—Center.

SERVICE BRAKES—Duplex-Mechanical brakes. Two independent braking systems of entirely new design. Completely enclosed, giving maximum efficiency in all weather. Mechanically operated, internal on both front and rear wheels. Division of pedal pull automatically proportioned between front and rear systems. Both front brakes operate when straight ahead, outer brake released on turn. All brakes 15 inches in diameter.

HAND BRAKE—Internal expanding on rear wheels and will not require adjustment during life of brake lining.

STEERING GEAR—La Salle design, worm-and-sector, completely adjustable; reduction 16 to 1. Steering wheel 19 inches in diameter, rubber composition with steel reinforcement; metal cast hub and spokes.

ENGINE CONTROL—Accelerator at right of brake pedal. Hand throttle lever built into central portion of steering wheel.

AUTOMATIC SPARK CONTROL—With manual lever located on instrument board directly in front of steering column.

INSTRUMENT BOARD—Special die cast panel with stamped moulding. Black finish standard. Coincidental transmission and ignition lock; ignition advance control; electric fuel gauge; ammeter; speedometer; oil pressure gauge; carburetor enriching button; electric windshield wiper switch; intake header heat control; clock; engine heat meter and cigar lighter; instrument lamps with separate switch.

MISCELLANEOUS

AXLES—Rear axle, La Salle design, three-quarter floating type with helical bevel gear and pinion. Shafts and pinion are alloy steel forgings. Front axle, reversed Elliott type; drop-forged special steel with inclined king bolts. Drop-forged steering spindles with ball thrust bearing at lower end.

DRIVE—Tubular steel propeller shaft 2 inches in diameter, turns in torque tube which completely seals assembly. Rear end rigidly connected to rear axle by splined sleeve; front end, to transmission shaft through universal joint. Torque tube is bolted to differential carrier at rear, and front end pivoted in ball-and-socket joint at rear of the transmission. Transmits drive of rear wheels to chassis and absorbs torque reactions due to acceleration and brakes.

FENDERS—One-piece metal; oval contour.

FENDER WELLS—Optional, at extra charge.

FRAME—Side bar channel section with wide top flange, carbon steel, maximum depth of side member $6\frac{1}{16}$ inches on the 134-inch chassis, $6\frac{1}{2}$ inches on the 125-inch chassis. Four channel cross-members and 2 tubular cross-members.

SPRINGS—Semi-elliptic suspension. Rear shackles of rear spring tension type provided with ball-and-socket joint. Delco-Remy Lovejoy shock absorbers are standard equipment. Front spring 39 inches x 2 inches; rear 58 inches x 2 inches.

TIRES—6.50—19 on all models. (Old designation 31 by 6.20.)

TIRE CARRIER—Rim type mounted at rear of chassis.

TOOLS—Complete set of tools in compartment under front seat.

WHEELBASE—134 inches and 125 inches.

GEAR RATIO—Standard 4.54 to 1; optional 4.91 to 1.

TURNING RADIUS—At tires, 19 feet 7 inches, right; 20 feet 8 inches, left.

WHEELS—Artillery type, 19 inches in diameter, 12 hickory spokes with steel felloe; demountable split type rim. Wire wheels, or disc wheels having rim integral, obtainable at extra charge.

SECURITY-PLATE GLASS—Is fitted for windshields and body windows in all models both open and closed.

Roomier - More power - Still easier to handle
THE NEW La Salles

On the basis of easily proved value the lowest priced of all truly fine cars

WHEN the new La Salles were introduced a few weeks ago a careful check-up of these latest models established to the satisfaction of their buyers that, by right of in-built worth, they were actually the lowest in price of all truly fine cars.

There was more of perfected performance, they found, more of the qualities that create mind-ease, pride of possession and motoring satisfaction per dollar investment than had ever been offered before.

This conviction can be easily reached by any one who takes the trouble to examine and drive the new La Salles and it is a conviction that leaves no room for doubt when other than La Salle cars are included in the investigation. Comparisons become deadly.

Tangible evidences of still greater superiority are quickly discernible in all that creates strictly modern motor car beauty. New Fisher-Fleetwood body designs abound in youthful grace. Their beauty is soundly conceived and free from glittering superficialities.

Best of all, it is a new beauty that is entirely practical—for these bodies are roomier and more comfortable than ever before, and so soundly constructed and so carefully protected against vibrations and other natural disturbances that maximum quietness is enjoyed under all conditions.

The new La Salles—as well as new Cadillacs and Fleetwoods—are presented as the most highly perfected of all motor cars.

You will especially appreciate this statement (and this is a point women in particular are advised to note) when you test the new La Salles for handling ease in parking, in traffic manipulations and in cross-country driving. For the new harmonized steering mechanism makes them easier to handle than ever before—just as easy, in fact, as the smallest, lightest runabout.

Then, too, gear shifting has been brought to a still higher degree of perfection in the refinements and improvements of the Syncro-Mesh Silent-Shift Transmission.

It is a great delight—enjoyed in no other car save Cadillac itself—to make a quick, silent shift almost unconsciously in an even, uniform motion and slip ahead of the procession when the traffic light flashes green. No effort, no time lost, no clashing.

Try also the exclusive Cadillac-La Salle Safety-Mechanical Four-Wheel Brakes—see if they are not, in truth, the most powerful as well as the easiest to operate of all braking systems. They have been materially simplified and improved. Together with the new harmonized steering system and improved transmission they assure complete mastery under all driving conditions.

These exclusive features, plus the protection of Security-Plate Glass (standard equipment in all windows, doors and windshields) add immeasurably to your peace of mind.

In no other cars, except Cadillac, can you find all these advantages and yet only a portion of what the La Salle owners enjoy has been enumerated. That is why you, too, will agree that in their lower and wider price range they exceed in value more strikingly than ever all other cars with which they can be legitimately compared.

CADILLAC MOTOR CAR COMPANY, DIVISION OF GENERAL MOTORS

This very matter-of-fact ad appeared two days after the stock market crash on October 24, 1929. Was the crash anticipated, or was it too late to cancel the ad?

THE NEW LA SALLE

The Cadillac Motor Car Company counsels you to confirm, by careful personal inspection and comparison, its statement that even a substantially greater investment will not bring you the exclusive ultra-fine car features and detailed refinements embodied in the new La Salles, introduced this autumn, and priced as low as $2285 f. o. b. Detroit.

The brilliant new La Salles, recently presented, retain all the elements of style and performance which made the first La Salle so instantly successful. In these new La Salles, however, there are embodied important new refinements, improvements and engineering developments; and still greater beauty, luxury, and grace.

These new La Salles are capable of even more thrilling and wholly satisfying performance. The new improved Cadillac-La Salle Syncro-Mesh Silent-Shift Transmission is today's highest development in transmissions for the *simplification* of control under all driving conditions. It has been deliberately designed to afford maximum freedom from either mental or physical strain in gear-shifting.

Use any speed, under any conceivable driving condition, and prove to your own satisfaction that this transmission is wholly adequate in every single respect and a decided advance over other existing methods. You cannot obtain the Syncro-Mesh Silent-Shift Transmission in any other car (excepting Cadillac) at any price.

One of the greatest contributions to safety, in the new La Salles, is the new Harmonized Steering System. This new Harmonized Steering System makes La Salle amazingly easy to handle in traffic congestion, in parking manipulations, and in cross-country driving.

The new improved Cadillac-La Salle Safety-Mechanical Four-Wheel Brakes are a revelation in smooth, responsive, powerful and positive control. These brakes assure more miles per hour with perfect safety.

All windows, doors and windshields in the new La Salles are equipped with non-shattering Security-Plate Glass. In the event of collision, this glass will not fly into fragments. Cadillac-La Salle owners who have actually experienced this protection would never again be without it.

In the new La Salles, the Cadillac-La Salle V-type 8-cylinder engine is larger, more powerful, and smoother than ever in operation. Remarkably eager responsiveness at low speeds. A superabundance of power for any and every emergency.

The new La Salle Fisher and Fleetwood bodies are lower, longer and racier in appearance than ever before. Luxurious new special fittings and appointments. Rear seats are roomier. Roomier front compartments. Adjustable front seats are even more easily adjusted than in the past.

The quiet elegance and quality of these exquisite Fisher and Fleetwood bodies add the crowning touch which makes the new La Salle models as perfect in appearance and appointment as they are in performance.

This ad appeared on November 23, 1929, just thirty days after the crash. It was unemotional and appealed to common sense while it also intended to exude confidence and calm.

NINETEEN THIRTY
Series 340

The outcome of success . . . that the new La Salle should thus so unquestionably continue its place as a leader in the fine car field is only natural. The developments which place it in the forefront of the buying cars of the day are the logical outcome of past success. Never before did any fine car so quickly and so thoroughly establish itself as La Salle. In every respect it was a car such as thousands had been waiting for—the car of today, for today; the car that brought fresh, appealing beauty to the motoring car along with performance standards based on principles proven by years of superiority.

—from the 1930 sales brochure

Supremely fine performance and surpassing charm are combined in the new La Salle.

Study the new La Salle from whatever point of view you choose—lines, color blending, luxury, roominess, safety, power, speed—and notable development is apparent. On a foundation of well established success, La Salle has built a still more significant motoring achievement.

Whether you inspect these new cars in the showroom or merely view them as they flash by on street or highway, their captivating beauty is equally apparent. There are no freakish lines or bazaar color effects that catch the eye; but there is, instead, the subtle charm of authentic styling and good taste.

The new La Salle body styles represent the supreme achievement of the world's greatest body builders— Fisher and Fleetwood—working in close association with Cadillac La Salle engineers and the Art and Colour section of General Motors. Refined, improved, given a newer, richer charm and beauty, they establish the new La Salle still more firmly as style arbiter in the field of fine motorcars.

NINETEEN THIRTY
Series 340

The 1930 LaSalle was introduced just a few weeks before the 1929 stock market crash on October 24. The ad in *The Saturday Evening Post* on October 26 was without illustration and stated: "When the new La Salles were introduced a few weeks ago, a careful check-up of these latest models established to the satisfaction of their buyers that, by right of in-built worth, they were actually the lowest in price of all truly fine cars. There was more of perfected performance, they found, more of the qualities that create mind ease, pride of possession and motoring satisfaction per dollar investment than had ever been offered before."

A month later, in November, an ad in *The Saturday Evening Post*, again without illustration, lauded the benefits of "more thrilling and wholly satisfying performance"; ". . . deliberately designed to afford maximum freedom from either mental or physical strain in gear shifting"; "amazingly easy to handle in traffic congestion, in parking manipulations, and in cross country driving."

In December, the ad read: "The quiet elegance and quality of the exquisite Fisher and Fleetwood bodies add a crowning touch which makes the new La Salle models as perfect in appearance and appointment as they are in performance."

It was as though nothing had happened. LaSalle was still pitching its prowess, in good taste, of course.

Actually, a very refined Series 340 LaSalle was introduced. All LaSalle models were on a 134-inch wheelbase, which was only six inches shorter than the more expensive Cadillacs. Styling-wise, the LaSalle and Cadillac were more alike. The Hispano-Suiza look was waning and a more distinctive Cadillac family style became evident. Listed in the catalog were seven Fisher bodies and eight custom-bodied Fleetwood models. These were referred to as the "LaSalle Fleetcliffe," "LaSalle Fleetlands," "LaSalle Fleetway," "LaSalle Fleetshire" or "LaSalle Fleetwind." Production records indicate that two more Fleetwood body styles were produced: one Transformable Cabriolet and one Brougham.

Styling of the closed cars was predominantly with one-piece, straight up and down windshields capped with a slight resemblance of a shallow outside sun visor. On some of the Fleetwood body styles the visor was eliminated.

An interesting body style was made available as part of the line-up. It was the Fleetwood-bodied Sedanette Cabriolet. This five-passenger, four-door Sedan had removable center pillars between the doors, giving it the open look of a Convertible, but the practicality of a closed four-door Sedan . . . in effect, a body style that later would be known as the "hardtop" introduced in 1949. LaSalle models also looked more fleeting because the battery and tool box doors prominently displayed on the Cadillac splash shield under the doors were nonexistent on the LaSalle, giving that panel a long smooth appearance.

Evident was the merging of Cadillac and LaSalle designs at the lower end of the Cadillac price spectrum. It had been only three years after the introduction of LaSalle and already LaSalle seemed to be moving away from the compact luxury car concept. Bigger, wider and longer was better.

LaSalle's price range remained fairly constant. Most LaSalles were longer than their predecessors, in some cases by as much as fifteen inches. Buyers were getting better, more spacious cars, without paying more money.

LA SALLE FIVE-PASSENGER TOWN SEDAN

La Salle–Fleetshire
FIVE-PASSENGER PHAETON BY FLEETWOOD

LA SALLE TWO-PASSENGER CONVERTIBLE COUPE

La Salle–Fleetcliffe
TWO-PASSENGER ROADSTER BY FLEETWOOD

La Salle–Fleetway
FOUR-PASSENGER ALL-WEATHER PHAETON BY FLEETWOOD

LA SALLE TWO-PASSENGER COUPE

LA SALLE FIVE-PASSENGER COUPE

LA SALLE FIVE-PASSENGER SEDAN

The LaSalle five-passenger Sedan was the epitome of conservative luxury. Its distinctive lines reveal the finest development of authoritatively styled coachcraft. This factory photo, in black and white, of a black Sedan with black tires and black wire wheels shows the purity of the overall design.

The engine was slightly more powerful. The bore was up to 3-5/16 inches while the stroke remained the same. It resulted in a new displacement of 340 cubic inches. Hence, the Series 340 designation. Horsepower was now 90, but when Cadillac introduced the immense 452 cubic inch V-16, LaSalle was overshadowed and was no longer in the limelight it had enjoyed since 1927. The stock market crash of 1929 had a tremendous effect on all U.S. automobile production. As the economy continued to decline, LaSalle production barely reached 15,000, which was slightly below Cadillac's production of nearly 20,000, augmented by the introduction of the V-16 and V-12 later that year.

Cadillac sponsored the LaSalle advertising and the word Cadillac appeared more often than the word LaSalle in LaSalle ads. Mechanical "advancements" were considered appropriate to advertise. "A new harmonized steering system makes it amazingly easy to handle a La Salle under all driving conditions; a larger, more powerful V-type, 8-cylinder engine—smoother than ever in operation"; "a quiet elegance and quality of the exquisite new La Salle." "The new La Salle Fisher and Fleetwood bodies are lower, longer and racier in appearance than ever before." Pictorially, it associated the automobile with the airplane. Most of the emphasis was on "true taste and elegance, but lenient on the purse strings." The prose was gone, the elegance barely perceptible. Two types of advertisements appeared. One that was artistic, yet realistic, while the other was more mechanical and art deco. They were all well done . . . subtle, classy and depicting aspiring lifestyles.

The black and white sales brochures lost some of the artsy overtones. Pictures of the models themselves were presented more precisely rather than romantically dramatized. A color sales brochure came later, which added beautiful color schemes to the cars depicted earlier in black and white, but still no background.

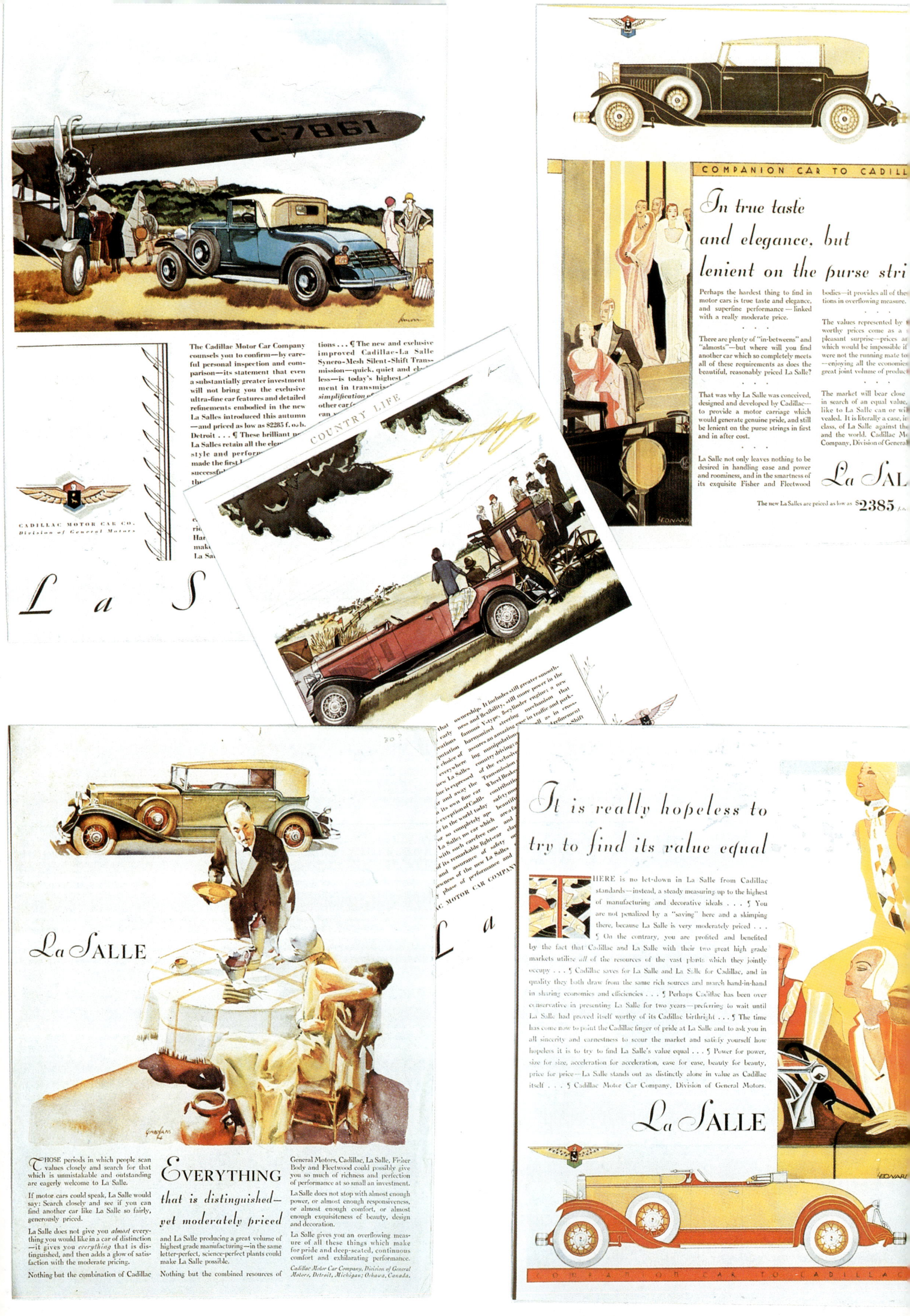
C-7861
The Cadillac Motor Car Company counsels you to confirm—by careful personal inspection and comparison—its statement that even a substantially greater investment will not bring you the exclusive ultra-fine car features and detailed refinements embodied in the new La Salles introduced this autumn—and priced as low as $2285 f. o. b. Detroit . . .
CADILLAC MOTOR CAR CO.
Division of General Motors
COUNTRY LIFE
COMPANION CAR TO CADILL
In true taste and elegance, but lenient on the purse stri
Perhaps the hardest thing to find in motor cars is true taste and elegance, and superfine performance — linked with a really moderate price.
There are plenty of "in-betweens" and "almosts"—but where will you find another car which so completely meets all of these requirements as does the beautiful, reasonably priced La Salle?
That was why La Salle was conceived, designed and developed by Cadillac—to provide a motor carriage which would generate genuine pride, and still be lenient on the purse strings in first and in after cost.
La Salle not only leaves nothing to be desired in handling ease and power and roominess, and in the smartness of its exquisite Fisher and Fleetwood
tions in overflowing measure.
The new La Salles are priced as low as $2385
La SALLE
EVERYTHING that is distinguished—yet moderately priced
THOSE periods in which people scan values closely and search for that which is unmistakable and outstanding are eagerly welcome to La Salle.
If motor cars could speak, La Salle would say: Search closely and see if you can find another car like La Salle so fairly, generously priced.
La Salle does not give you almost everything you would like in a car of distinction—it gives you everything that is distinguished, and then adds a glow of satisfaction with the moderate pricing.
Nothing but the combination of Cadillac and La Salle producing a great volume of highest grade manufacturing—in the same letter-perfect, science-perfect plants could make La Salle possible.
Nothing but the combined resources of General Motors, Cadillac, La Salle, Fisher Body and Fleetwood could possibly give you so much of richness and perfection of performance at so small an investment.
La Salle does not stop with almost enough power, or almost enough responsiveness, or almost enough comfort, or almost enough exquisiteness of beauty, design and decoration.
La Salle gives you an overflowing measure of all these things which make for pride and deep-seated, continuous comfort and exhilarating performance.
Cadillac Motor Car Company, Division of General Motors, Detroit, Michigan; Oshawa, Canada.
It is really hopeless to try to find its value equal
THERE is no let-down in La Salle from Cadillac standards—instead, a steady measuring-up to the highest of manufacturing and decorative ideals . . . ¶ You are not penalized by a "saving" here and a skimping there, because La Salle is very moderately priced . . . ¶ On the contrary, you are profited and benefited by the fact that Cadillac and La Salle with their two great high grade markets utilize all of the resources of the vast plants which they jointly occupy . . . ¶ Cadillac saves for La Salle and La Salle for Cadillac, and in quality they both draw from the same rich sources and march hand-in-hand in sharing economies and efficiencies . . . ¶ Perhaps Cadillac has been over conservative in presenting La Salle for two years—preferring to wait until La Salle had proved itself worthy of its Cadillac birthright . . . ¶ The time has come now to point the Cadillac finger of pride at La Salle and to ask you in all sincerity and earnestness to scour the market and satisfy yourself how hopeless it is to try to find La Salle's value equal . . . ¶ Power for power, size for size, acceleration for acceleration, ease for ease, beauty for beauty, price for price—La Salle stands out as distinctly alone in value as Cadillac itself . . . ¶ Cadillac Motor Car Company, Division of General Motors.
La SALLE

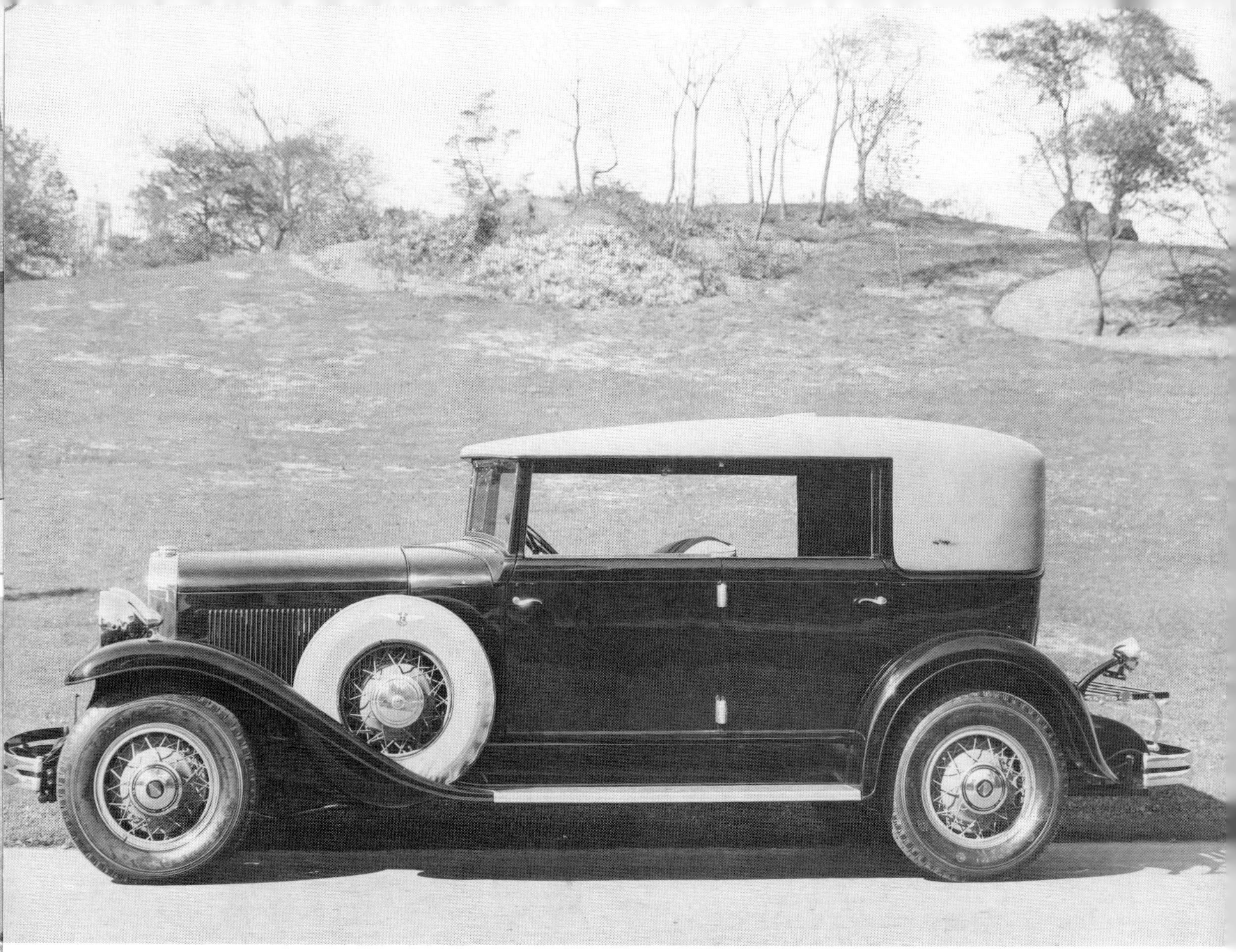

Top: The four-passenger Sedanette Cabriolet by Fleetwood had a slightly Vee'd windshield. With the side windows down, it resembles "hardtop" styling of the 1950s and 1960s. This top looks like a Convertible, but does not go down. Compare the belt molding of this car at the sail panel position with the All-Weather Phaeton on the next page. Bottom: The Fleetcliffe two-passenger Roadster by Fleetwood was on a 134-inch wheelbase. This factory photograph accentuates the length of the car with the absence of the tool and battery box covers and the light colored contrasting molding at the bottom of the body flowing over the rear fender. It was very sporty looking even though the wooden artillery wheels were beginning to look old fashioned. Note cowl louvers, a feature of all Fleetwood open models.

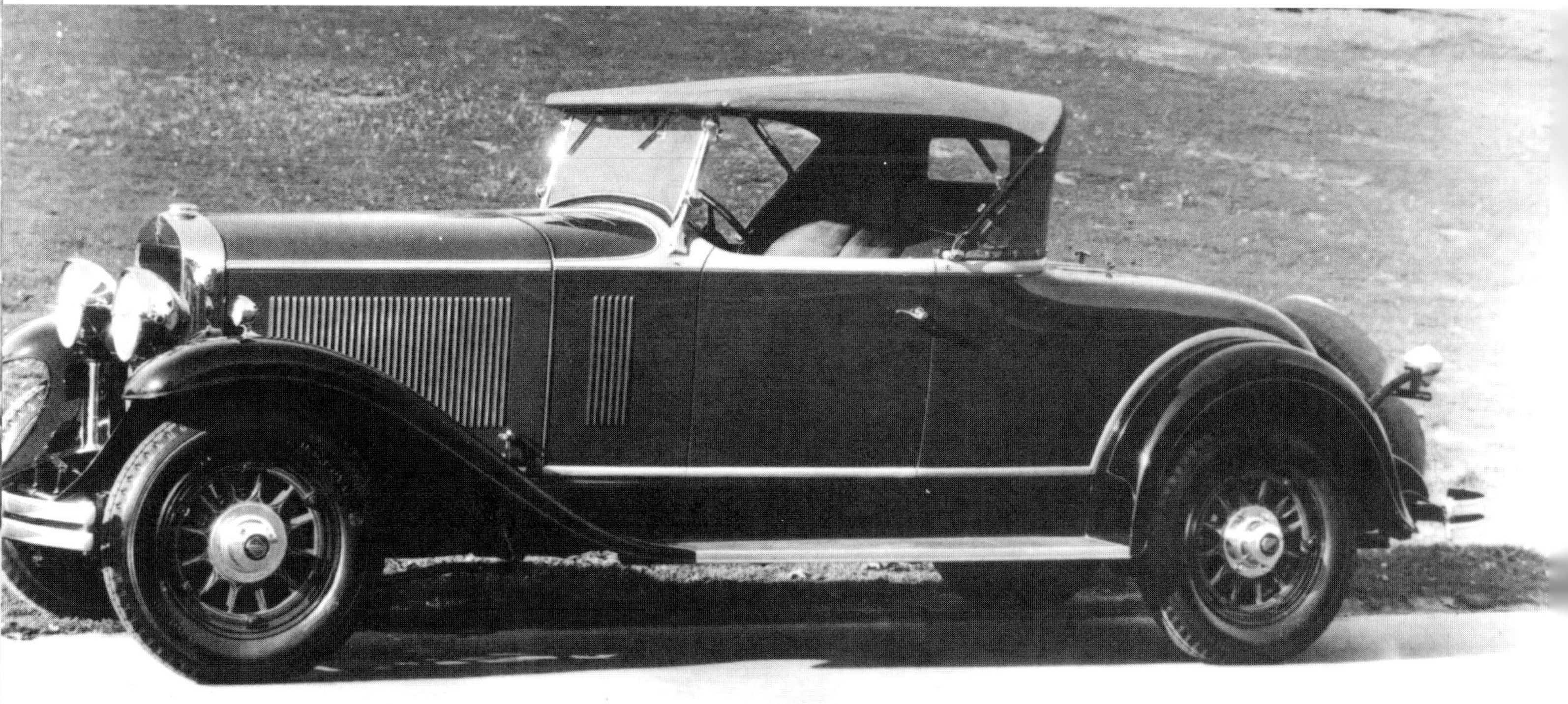

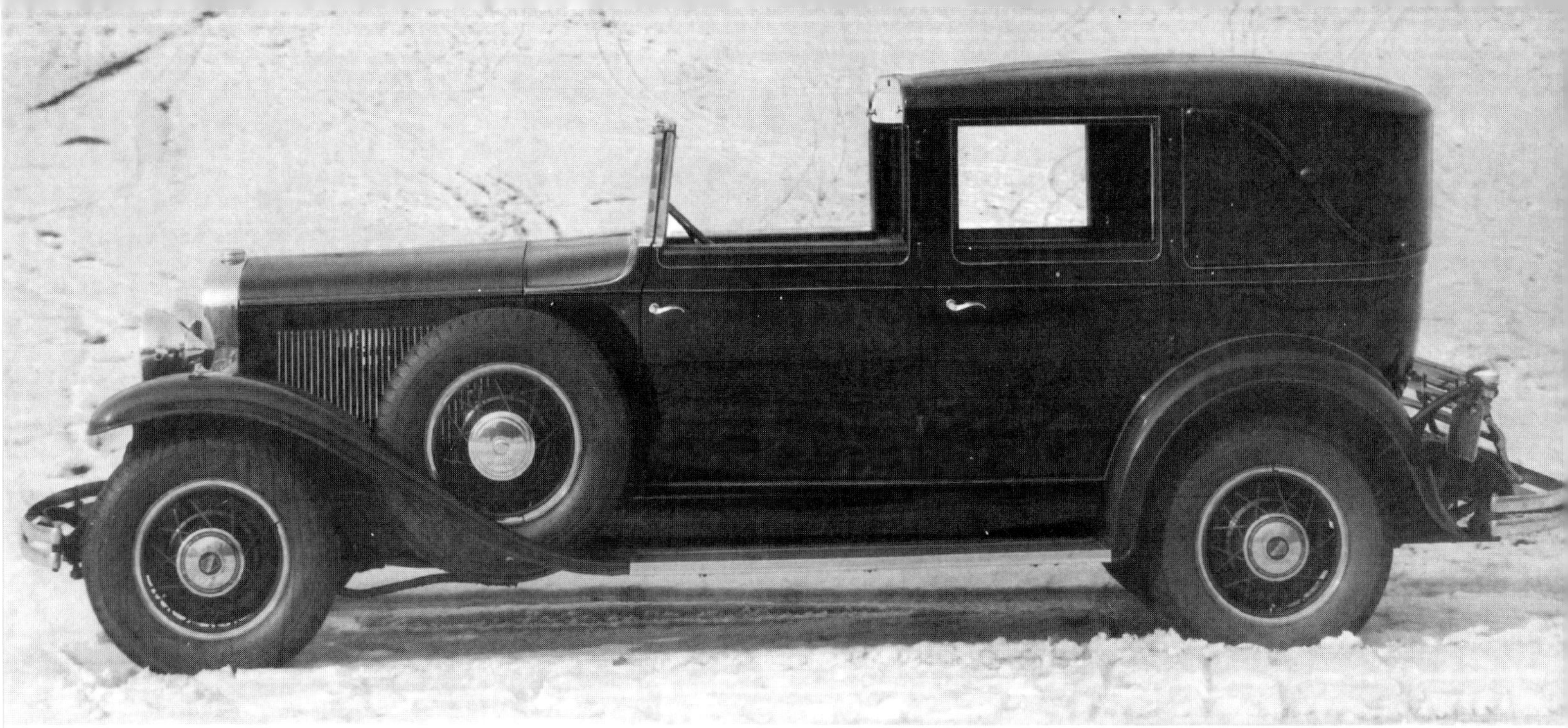

Top: Lines of this formal Fleetwood Transformable Cabriolet are well-proportioned and sleek. The chauffeur had little protection, especially on a cold snow-covered day when owners would demonstrate their station in life with the chauffeur exposed to the elements. Bottom: A five-passenger Town Sedan shows a paint scheme option which makes the windows look even larger on this very handsome body style.

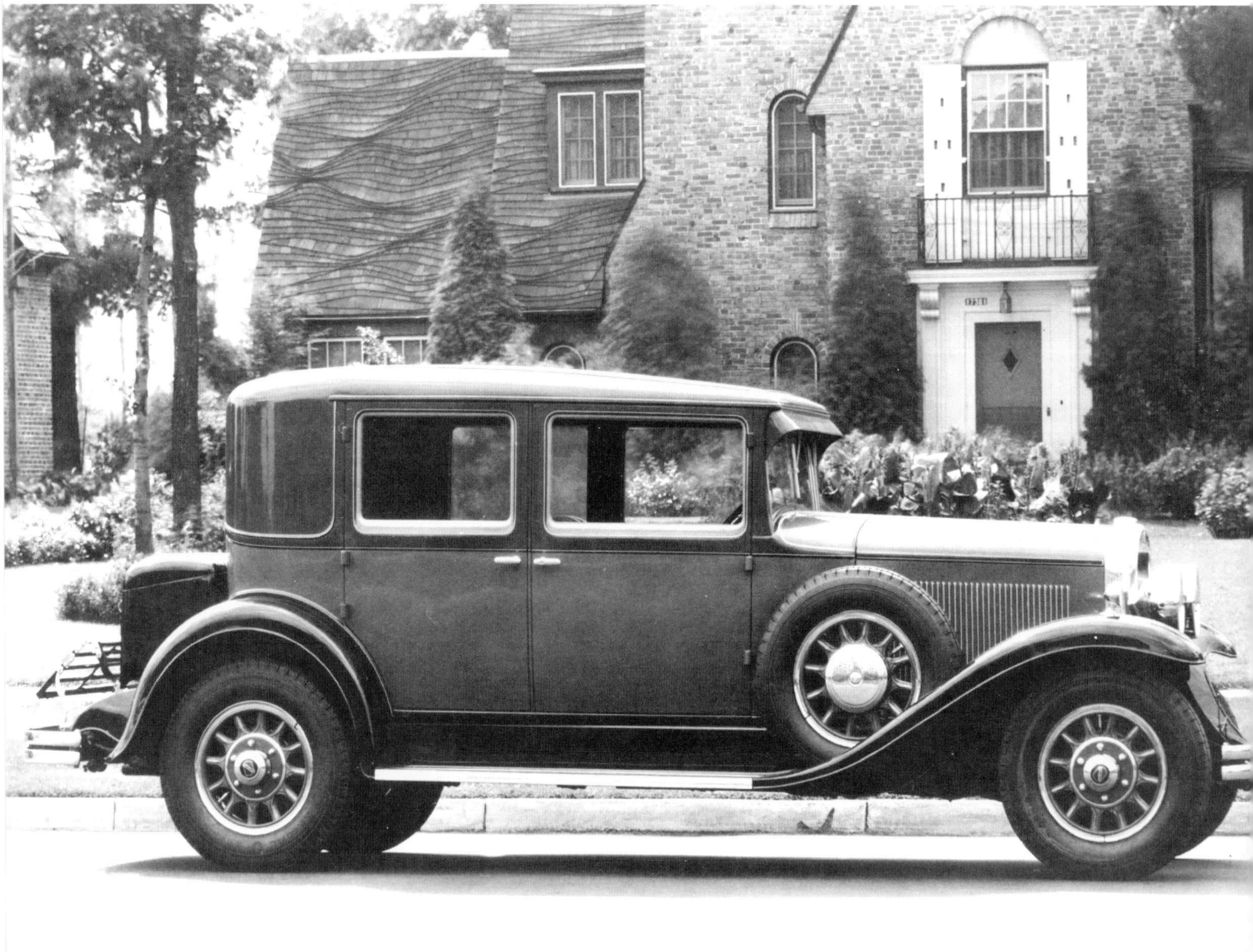

La SALLE

THE new La Salles, introduced this autumn, roomier and more powerful than ever, offer advantages unobtainable in any other car at any price—except Cadillac itself. These advantages are of vital importance because many of them have to do with greater driving ease and safety.... ¶ La Salle's improved Syncro-Mesh Silent-Shift Transmission is exclusively a Cadillac development—protected by basic patents. Even a new driver can shift these gears noiselessly, easily. The get-away is sure, quick, fast. ...¶ The new harmonized steering system, which makes the La Salle so easy to park and handle in traffic and the improved Safety-Mechanical Four-Wheel Brakes, the easiest to operate yet the most effective ever devised, are found only in Cadillac-built cars. Furthermore there is no extra cost for the protection of non-shatterable Security-Plate Glass. It is standard equipment in all windows, doors and windshields .... ¶ Test the La Salle as severely as you know how. Then compare it point by point with other than Cadillac-built cars—yes, regardless of price—and draw your own conclusions.

CADILLAC MOTOR CAR COMPANY, DIVISION OF GENERAL MOTORS

December 1929 Good Housekeeping

Top: An example of a surviving five-passenger Town Sedan with an almost convertible look due to the attractive paint scheme. Note the wooden spoked wheels. Bottom: A restored Series 340 Roadster with Fleetwood body has been staged to show off its lines from the rear. The rear bumper provides complete wrap--around protection.

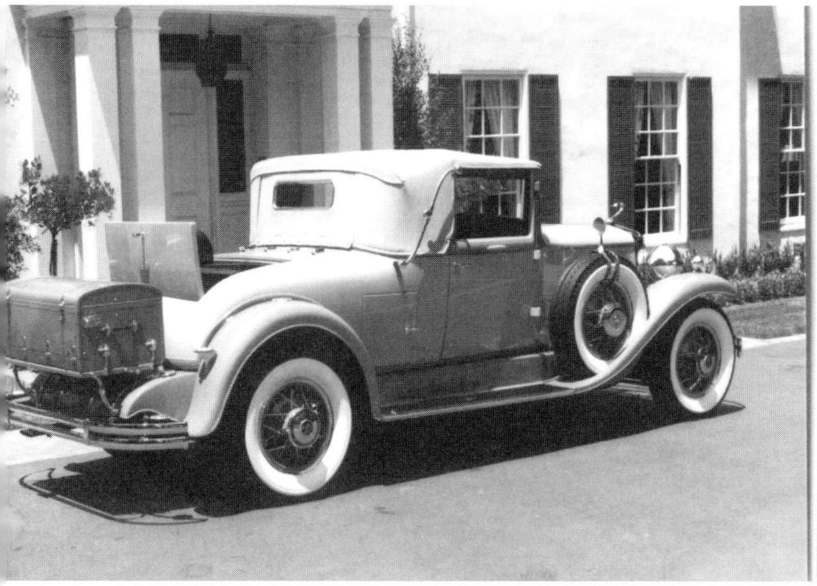

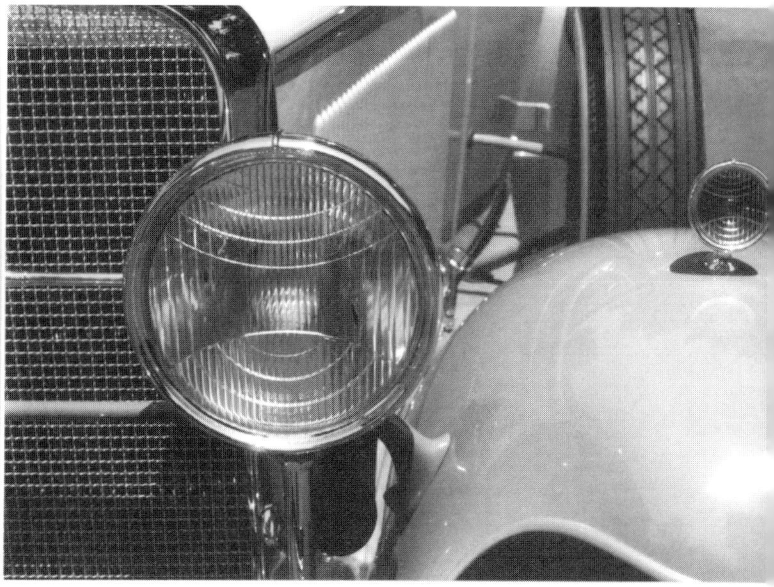

Top left: This Convertible Coupe has a rumble seat for two additional passengers and a luggage trunk on the rear. Top right: Headlights and parking lights have a matching theme. Middle left: A thoughtful rumble seat design incorporated armrests as part of the fold-down mechanism. Middle right: Golf club door provides access to rumble seat area for golf clubs or other occasional luggage. Running board has LaSalle emblem cast into the pattern. Bottom left: A closed trunk is fitted on the luggage rack extending over the rear bumper. Bottom right: Trunk on luggage rack demonstrates the ease of access for fitted luggage.

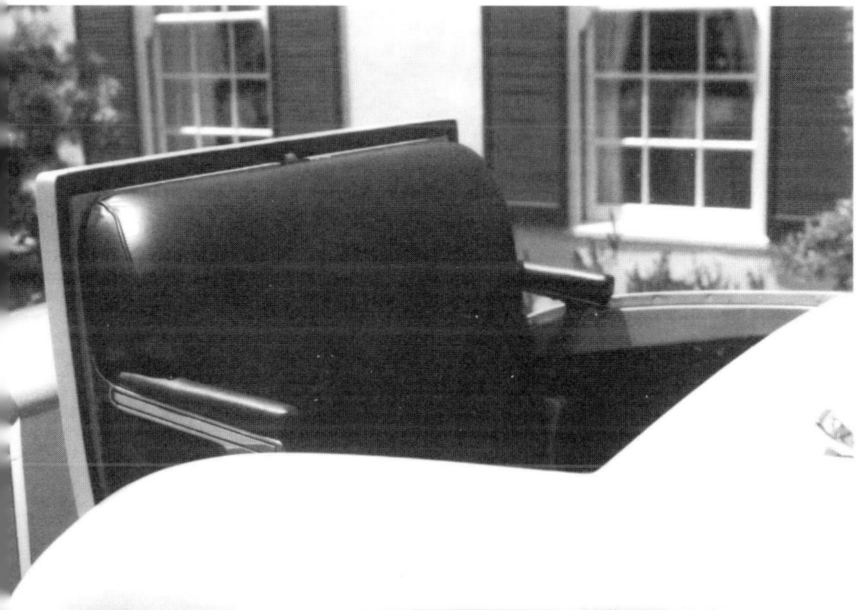

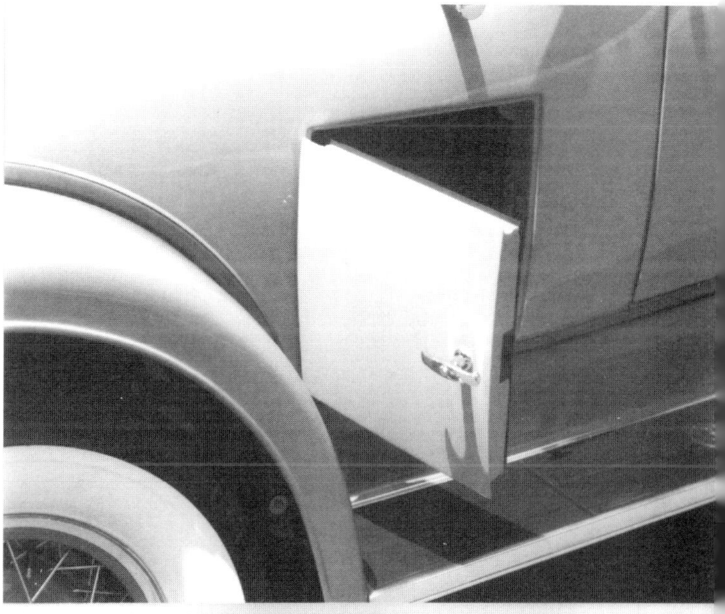

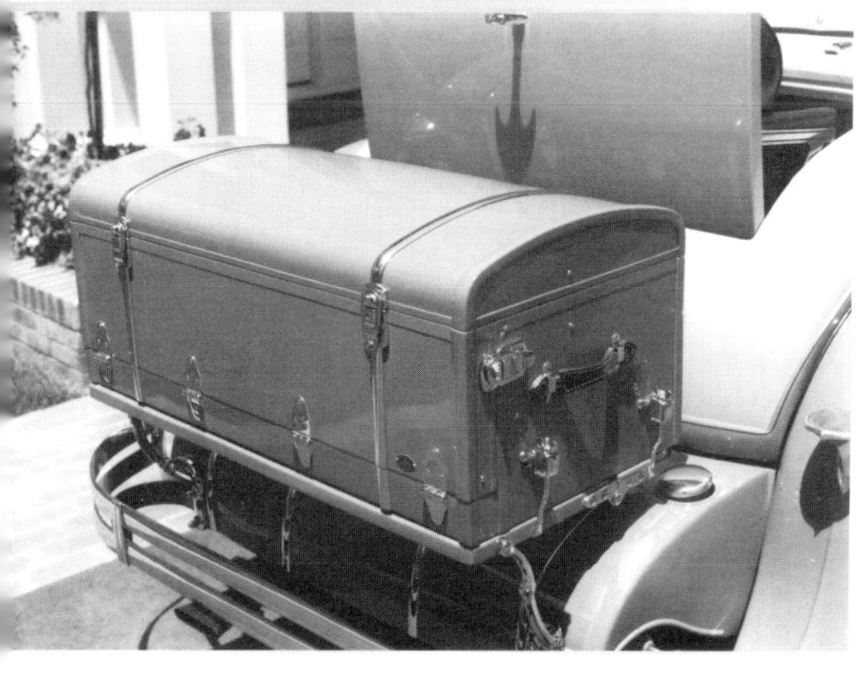

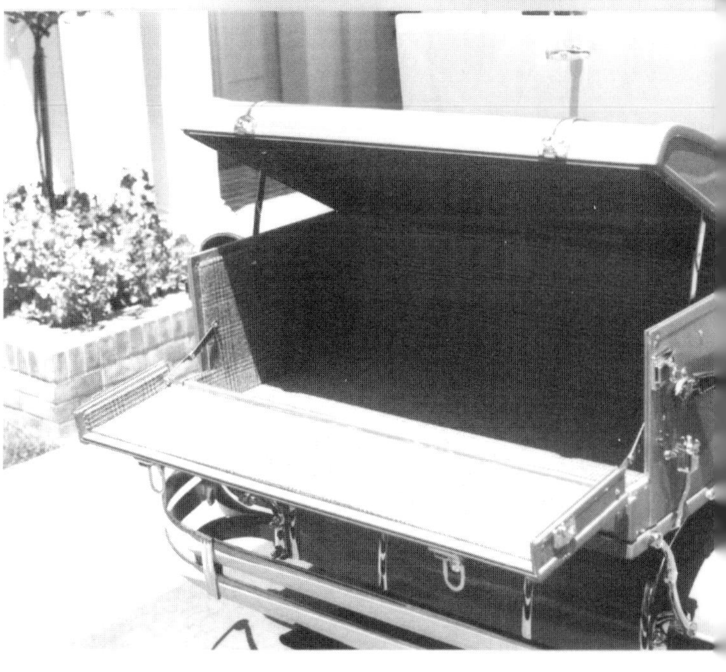

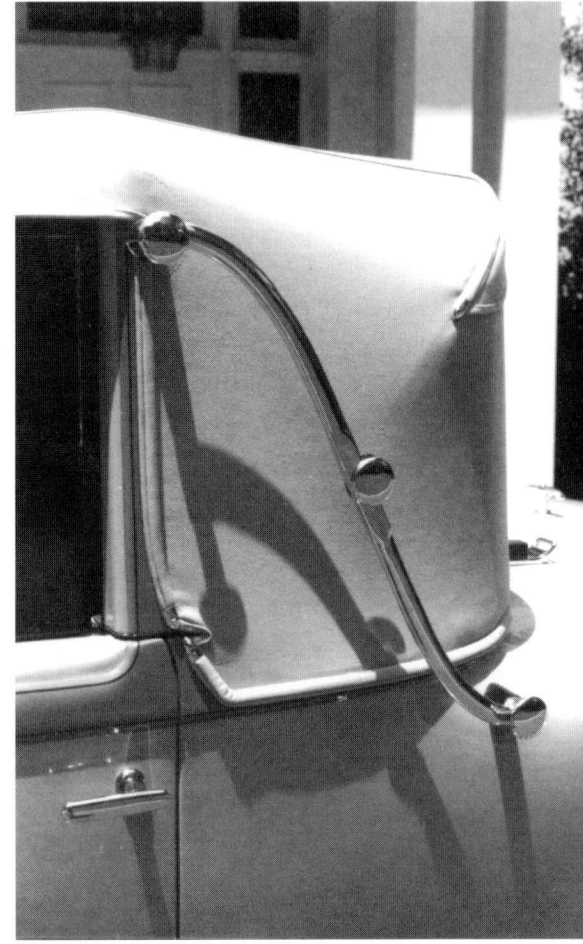

Top: Meticulous attention to detail and finish can be [seen] on the top supports and window contours. Middle [left]: This engine compartment has been restored to orig[inal] specifications. Every component has its place for g[ood] looks as well as function. Top right: These Landau i[rons] are functional and add to the Convertible's attractive [look]. Attention to detail makes this model a testimonial t[o the] designers and the engineers working together. Bot[tom:] The details above and on the previous page are a pa[rt of] this superb example of a two-passenger Conver[tible] Coupe with Fisher body.

NEW MODELS—NEW EASE NEW BEAUTY—NEW SAFETY

La SALLE

THE recent introduction of the new La Salles has enlivened the highways and boulevards this fall with the most beautiful and highly perfected motor cars that Cadillac has ever created —with the single exception of the latest Cadillacs themselves... ¶The newness of these new La Salles affects every phase of performance and ownership. It includes still greater smoothness and flexibility, still more power in the famous V-type, 8-cylinder engine—a new harmonized steering mechanism that assures an amazing ease in traffic and parking manipulations as well as in cross-country driving—a perfection and refinement of the exclusive Syncro-Mesh Silent-Shift Transmission and Safety Mechanical Four-Wheel Brakes that make these revolutionary contributions to greater handling ease, control and safety more valuable than ever—roomier, more beautiful, more luxurious Fisher bodies that are a fascinating realization of youthful dash and verve—and a wealth of other features that clamor for personal inspection and for a test on the road... ¶Nowhere in the world—save in Cadillac itself—can you find what these newest La Salles offer. In view of this fact, the price becomes the most impressive factor of all. In value and built-in worth, the market, beyond a doubt, has never seen their equal.

CADILLAC MOTOR CAR COMPANY, DETROIT, MICHIGAN

November 1929 Good Housekeeping

Combination 102   Upper Panels, Mouldings, Fenders, Chassis - Bellaire Gray 2445596
Lower Panels - Vista Gray, R-M 20163; Stripe - Cream Color, Light

Combination 103   Upper Panels, Mouldings, Fenders, Chassis - Black
Lower Panels - Boulevard Maroon, 2444181; Stripe - Rossmere Red

Combination 104   Entire Car - Alhambra Tan, R-M 20830; Stripe - Delmonte Brown

Combination 105   Upper Panels, Mouldings - Moonstone Gray, 2445118
Lower Panels - Cellini Green, 2443253
Fenders, Chassis - Black; Stripe - Cellini Green

Conservative Type Group

Combination 106   Roof, Rear Quarters, Lower Panels - Bolling Green, 2441331
Upper Panels, Mouldings - Ardsley Green, 2443038
Fenders, Chassis - Black; Stripe - Cream Color, Light

Combination 107   Upper Panels, Mouldings, Fenders, Chassis - Mississippi Brown, 2443558
Lower Panels - Roanoke Beige, 2445936; Stripe - Prairie Grass

Combination 108   Roof, Rear Quarters, Lower Panels - Boulevard Maroon, 2444181
Upper Panels, Mouldings - Harvard Maroon, 2444063
Fenders, Chassis - Black; Stripe - Rossmere Red

Combination 109   Upper Panels, Mouldings, Fenders, Chassis - Black
Lower Panels - State Blue, R-M 20291; Stripe - Cream Color, Light

Combination 110   Upper Panels, Mouldings, Fenders, Chassis - Black
Lower Panels - Marblehead Gray, 2445512; Stripe - Cream Color, Light

Note: Paint combination numbers are not listed on the build sheets, only the paint names and manufacturers' paint numbers. Paint names and manufacturers' numbers released for production after September 1929 are not included above.

Trim Options

Standard closed bodies - job/style:
30252, 30258, 30259, 30262, 30272
  17 T 130   Silver Gray Mohair
  19 T 130   Green Mohair
  21 T 130   Taupe Mohair
  37 T 130   Blue Mohair
  50 T 128   Gray Bedford Cord
  55 T 129   Taupe/Blue Pin Striped Broadcloth

Job/style 30263

  19 T 129   Blue Mohair
  24 T 129   Brown with darker brown Bellflower Pattern Broadcloth
  26 T 129   Gray with Blue Bellflower Pattern Broadcloth
  28 T 129   Tan with Green Bellflower Pattern Broadcloth
  50 T 128   Gray Bedford Cord
  51 T 128   Silver Gray Mohair
  53 T 128   Taupe Mohair
  57 T 128   Green Gray Mohair

Open bodies - job/style: 4002, 4057, 4060, 30268
  50 T 128   Gray Bedford Cord
  2 T 1330   Standard Tan Leather
  3 T 1330   Standard Blue Leather
  4 T 1330   Standard Green Leather
  5 T 1330   Standard Black Leather

Outside Top Material:
Job 4002, 4057, 4060	9 T 1528 Drab Duck
Job 4080, 4081, 4082	18 T 1528 Burbank
Job 30268 before body 536	18 T 1528 Burbank
Job 30268 after body 535	1 T 1530 Khaki Burbank

Top Lining   10 T 1528 (Not listed)

Exclusive Fleetwood Aero leathers by Radel:
   68   Blue (standard)
  451   Pearl Gray
  743   Tan (standard)
 2645   Black (standard)
 2646   Blue Gray
 4339   Green (standard)
 5875   Rich Maroon
 5885   Silver Gray

5897   Green Blue
6012   Dark Green
6016   Dark Blue
6019   Soft Green
9128   Light Brown
9131   Dark Brown
9205   Deep Maroon

Note: The domestic car records indicate only the upholstery number, not the type of material.

Standard and Optional Equipment

Standard Equipment: Wood wheels, 6.50 X 19" U. S. Royal Black Sidewall tires, rear spare tire carrier.

Optional Equipment:
   18" Wood, Wire or Disc wheels, 7.00 X 18" U. S. Royal tires, fenderwells.
   2-way Shock Absorbers
   Spring Covers

5 Wire wheels	$ 60.00
5 Demountable wood or Disc wheels	$ 50.00
6 Wire, Demountable wood or Disc wheels, fenderwells, 2 spare tires and trunk rack	$190.00
Delco-Remy Radio (all Fleetwood bodies are factory wired for radio)	$150.00

Research Methodology: Microfiche copies of the individual Shipping Department records of the as-built configuration of each serial number were viewed and Fleetwood body styles recorded by serial and body number to determine the quantity of each body style built. No attempt was made to construct cross reference lists of the Fisher body numbers with corresponding engine numbers to determine which body serial numbers were not used in actual production.

Notes on research findings:

1. Factory summary production records show a total of 14,986 cars and chassis built in the 1930 model year, which would indicate that nine serial numbers were not used. Record sheets for six of those serial numbers are found in the files with the notation "Open" and a date later than the end of production. Nine additional record sheets were found to be missing. Totalling the observed high body serial numbers for each style built results in nine more units than the factory indicated total production. Obviously, some Fisher body numbers were not used. Examination of the individual record sheets reveals that very near the end of 1930 production, thirty-one series 345 (1931) bodies were mounted on 1930 chassis and are recorded as 1930 models. Those bodies were added to production figures listed above: thirteen Town Sedans, sixteen 5-Pass. Sedans and two 7-Pass. Sedans. One of the 5-Pass. Sedan bodies replaced an All-Weather Phaeton body that was later installed by the factory on a 1931 chassis.

2. Body Styles: Most of the body styles listed above need no explanation. The Fleetwood style 3351 Transformable Cabriolet is an open front Town Car with division glass. The 5-Pass. Brougham, style 3364, is listed in the Cadillac Chart of Body Styles as a 1930 LaSalle offering only, without any body description. The Fleetwood style 4060 5-Pass. Phaeton is essentially the same car as the style 4057 7-Pass. Touring, but without the folding auxiliary seats for the extra two passengers. The style 4080 All-Weather Phaeton is a Convertible Sedan with a center division glass. The style 4081 5-Pass. Sedanette Cabriolet is a four-door, fixed-top Sedan with fully retractable windows and removable center pillars. Similar in appearance to the All-Weather Phaeton, the fixed top with blind rear quarters is covered in Burbank cloth, giving the very handsome look of a convertible car. The style 4082 5-Pass. Sedanette is a six-window fixed top Sedan with roll-up windows and removable window posts to make it a full four-door hardtop. The quarter windows only lower part way. The Sedanette top is covered with Burbank cloth.

3. Special Features: Both Fisher and Fleetwood body cars could be special ordered with virtually any body modifications to suit the purchaser. Numerous special order interior modifications were done in both ranges of cars including installation of upgraded upholstery, rear seat armrests, Fleetwood carpets, vanity cases, robe cords and window curtains in Fisher bodies, changes to seat heights, depth, seat angles, etc. Of a more substantial change nature, eleven Fisher body 5-Pass. Town Sedans (30-252) were ordered and built with an Imperial Partition behind the driver's seat. Seven were right hand drive units exported to Buenos Aires, Argentina, and one left hand drive to Warsaw, Poland. A single 2-Pass. Coupe (30-258) was ordered with the rumble seat omitted and the deck lid hinges reversed to open from the bottom. Two Fisher body 5-Pass. Sedans (330-259) were also built into "Imperial Sedans." One Convertible Coupe (30-268) was ordered without the standard feature golf bag door on the right side rear. On the Fleetwood bodies, one Touring car (4057) specified "Omit auxiliary seats and build tonneau compartment flush." A Phaeton (4060) order called for "Install special tonneau windshield & tonneau deck same as used on Sport Phaeton..." One All-Weather Phaeton (4080) had the standard partition glass eliminated and two Sedanette Cabriolets (4181) had the partition glass added during the body build. In keeping with the stated policy of rejecting orders for colors not guaranteed by the manufacturer for durability, four domestic units were shipped to dealers in primer, "Rubbed out of rough stuff." An additional seven unpainted "shell body" units, five 5-Pass. Sedans and two 7-Pass. Imperial Sedans, were among the exports to London, England.

4. The 1930 record sheets do not have a "Purchaser" block. However, nearly all of the special (Fisher and Fleetwood) order cars and hundreds of others are annotated with the buyer's name. An "F.O." is an indication of the application of a non-standard paint or upholstery selection, convertible top material, seat or body modifications, etc. A few of the cars were for auto industry personalities whom the public would recognize, including C. T. Fisher, Everall Fisher, Louis A. Fisher and W. A. Fisher. Other luminary purchasers were S. S. Kresge, Irwin Laughlin (U.S. Ambassador to Spain), Signor Martini (Italian Ambassador to the U.S.) and Rear Admiral Crosley of the Naval Training Station, Great Lakes, Illinois.

5. Canadian assembled cars: Batches of as many as twenty sequentially numbered chassis were shipped from Detroit to Oshawa, Ontario. It is unclear whether or not the bodies were built in the U.S. and shipped to Oshawa for final assembly. Unlike other years, all of the bodies on the Oshawa cars had serial numbers from the U.S. body number list for each style and the cars were painted and trimmed in U.S. colors and patterns, which suggests that complete bodies were also shipped to Oshawa, not built at Oshawa. The record sheets do not give any indication of the distribution of completed vehicles.

6. <u>Chassis</u>: Commercial chassis as such were not an offering in 1930. Of the 46 indicated units, 23 were exports. Two right hand drive units with closed car cowls went to London and three to Buenos Aires with no cowls indicated. Five units were shipped to Antwerp, with #607792 annotated "Locally built All-Weather Bodies." Chassis #607807 was similarly equipped and probably also received an All-Weather Phaeton body. Chassis #609820 was annotated "Locally built Convt. Coupe to be mounted at Antwerp." Three chassis went to Madrid, six to Paris and four to Stockholm. None of the records indicated who the intended body builder was nor the name of the purchaser.

Four domestic chassis remained on the factory account for display or show purposes. Two of those were "Cut Open" - one sent to the Grand Central Palace Exhibit in New York and the other to the Philadelphia Branch, tagged "Show Chassis." A third chassis was marked "For Show Opening Jan 11/30, Buffalo, N.Y." The remaining nineteen chassis were shipped to:

The A. J. Miller Company, Bellefountaine, Ohio	8 units
Cadillac Auto Company, Boston, Massachusetts	4 units
Knightstown Funeral Car Company, Knightstown, Indiana	2 units
Uppercu Cadillac Corp., Newark, New Jersey	2 units
Don Lee, Inc., San Francisco, California	1 unit
Fleetwood Body Company, Fleetwood, Pennsylvania	1 unit
Wescott Burlingame, Inc., Albany, New York	1 unit

The four chassis that went to Boston were tagged "Moxie Co." and became the basis for the 1930 version of their then widely-recognized Moxiemobiles. The Moxie soft drink advertising cars were full fendered LaSalles with bodies in the shape of a horse. The driver/rider operated the rolling advertisement from a saddle position astride the highly visible horse. Needless to say, the iron horses attracted a great deal of attention for the Moxie Co. At least one Moxie car still survives and is in operable condition.

7. <u>Export Cars</u>: In the 1930 model year, 540 automobiles and 23 chassis were exported, encompassing all Fisher body styles and four Fleetwood body styles. Vehicles built in the United States and shipped to Canada were not treated as exports; whereas vehicles shipped to Mexico were all assigned Export Control Order numbers. At the same time, vehicles destined for the U.S. Territory of Hawaii were labeled as exports. Right hand drive and low compression cylinder heads were common features for export cars, as were Imperial Gallon fuel gauges on vehicles destined for Canada and England. Buyers obviously regarded two body styles as particularly good value. Export sales accounted for 38% and 32% respectively of the total production of Fleetwood Touring cars and Fisher 7-Pass. Imperial Sedans. Export totals by body style were:

<u>Body Style</u>

5-Pass. Town Sedan	35	5-Pass. Coupe	10
2-Pass. Coupe	8	2-Pass. Roadster	23
5-Pass. Sedan	46	7-Pass. Touring	93
7-Pass. Sedan	56	5-Pass. Phaeton	45
7-Pass. Imperial Sedan	160	5-Pass. All-Weather Phaeton	14
2-Pass. Convertible Coupe	50	134" Chassis	23

Where did the exports go? Destinations and associated number of units are listed below:

Buenos Aires, Argentina	97	Berlin, Germany	14	Lima, Peru	2
Antwerp, Belgium	88	São Paulo, Brazil	12	Perth, Australia	2
Paris, France	38	Manila, Philippine Islands	8	San Juan, Puerto Rico	2
Caracas, Venezuela	29	Brisbane, Australia	7	Wellington, New Zealand	2
Stockholm, Sweden	27	Melbourne, Australia	7	Dakar, West Africa	1
Sydney, Australia	27	Adelaide, Australia	6	Guatemala	1
London, England	26	Alexandria, Egypt	6	Hong Kong	1
Havana, Cuba	25	Port Elizabeth, South Africa	6	International Railways of Central America	1
Mexico	23	Santiago, Chile	5	Panama	1
Honolulu, Hawaii	22	Osaka, Japan	4	Valetta, Malta	1
Copenhagen, Denmark	20	Batavia, Java	3	Warsaw, Poland	1
Bombay, India	18	Kingston, Jamaica	3	Destination not indicated	8
Madrid, Spain	17	Barranquilla, Columbia	2		

8. <u>Show Cars</u>: One hundred and thirty-three cars and chassis were noted as receiving special attention for shows in the 1930 model year. Seven were designated for the model Announcement Week in Detroit and thirteen for the Distributors Convention in Detroit. Eight were prepared for the GM Fall Salon in Chicago, Detroit, Los Angeles and New York; seven went to the Florida Exhibit. Six went to the GM Building Exhibit and three to GM of Canada for the Canadian National Exhibit. Throughout the year multiple cars went to the Chicago Branch, New York City, Boston, Atlanta, San Francisco, Los Angeles and the Philadelphia and Detroit Branch offices. Buffalo, Cleveland, Erie, London, Patterson (NJ) and Rochester (NY) each received a single show car.

9. <u>Factory installed accessories</u>:

Breeze Filter (under windshield)	Radio
Cadillac Duplex Pilot Ray (driving lights)	Rumble seat footrest
Cadillac Pilot Ray (single driving light)	Seat Covers
Chromium Plated Winter Front (radiator shutters)	Splash Shields
Double Type Rear Vision Mirror	Spotlights (Lorraine)
Dust Shields	Spotlights, running board
Fleetwood Metal Covered Trunk	Step Plates (running board)
Folding Trunk Rack, chromium plated	Tail & Stop light assembly, right side
Foot Hassocks	Tire Chains
Heavy duty rear springs	Tire Covers:
Hinge Mirror	Black Long Grain with Emblem
Hot Air Heater (Kelch) - single register	Burbank with Emblem
Hot Air Heater (Kelch) - dual register	Burbank, rim type
Hot Water Heater (Tropic Air)	Metal, spring type
Kool Kushions	Tire Mirrors
Low Compression cylinder heads	Tire Pump, hand
Metal Covered Trunk	Tire Pump, power (transmission mounted)
Onyx gear shift ball	Tonneau Windshield, chromium plated
Protectohood	Trunk Cover, Burbank cloth
Radiator Ornament	Windshield Wings - open cars

Seven different stock numbers for trunks were noted, representing trunks ordered without any luggage or with available combinations of long or standard suitcases and hat boxes in either pigskin or black Fabrikoid. The Fleetwood trunks are a low profile trunk specifically for open bodied cars, Convertible Coupes and Coupes.

10. None of the body styles were assembled in a straight body order sequence. Fisher Order cars and non-standard paint color cars were generally substantially out of order due to the time required to make alterations.

First car built in each body series:	Last car built:	Highest body number:
<u>Fisher body styles</u>		
30-252 serial 600462, body 8	serial 614856, body 3121	3125
30-258 serial 600261, body 47	serial 614709, body 974	1000
30-259 serial 600004, body 47	serial 614917, body 4653	4715
30-262 serial 600001, body 244	serial 614995, body 1426	1500
30-263 serial 600427, body 2	serial 614990, body 499	500
30-268 serial 600003, body 299	serial 614854, body 1392	1400
30-272 serial 600024, body 133	serial 614461, body 1395	1400
<u>Fleetwood body styles</u>		
3351 serial 602186, body 16655 (Pennsylvania built)		
3364 serial 602187, body 16656 (Pennsylvania built)		
4002 serial 600622, body 4	serial 614536, body 303	303
4057 serial 600628, body 3	serial 614898, body 234	248
4060 serial 600624, body 4	serial 614921, body 384	400
4080 serial 600630, body 2	serial 614958, body 27	257
4081 serial 600633, body 1	serial 614949, body 45	51
4082 serial 600631, body 1	serial 614905, body 44	50

CONDENSED SPECIFICATIONS — LA SALLE 340

POWER PLANT

Engine . . Compensated eight-cylinder, V-type. Ninety-degree angle between cylinder blocks. Engine and transmission in unit; three-point suspension with rubber-lined supports at rear. Piston displacement 340 cubic inches. Bore $3\frac{5}{16}''$. Stroke $4\frac{15}{16}''$. Horsepower N.A.C.C. rating 35.1, actually more than 90.

Crankcase . . Silicon-aluminum alloy, specially treated.

Crankshaft . . Diameter $2\frac{3}{8}''$; length to outer ends of front and rear bearings $23\frac{11}{16}''$. Supported on 3 main bearings. Crank throws 90 degrees apart, provided with compensators.

Cylinders . . Cast in blocks of four, with detachable heads. High-compression heads standard, low-compression optional.

Pistons . . Cast nickel-iron, special formula, annealed; 4 rings, 3 above wrist pin and 1 below; lower ring special oil regulating type.

Connecting Rods . . Drop-forged special formula steel. Side by side, two on each crank pin. Rods are gun-drilled for pressure lubrication of wrist pins. Bearings $2\frac{3}{8}'' \times 1\frac{5}{8}''$. Babbitt in rods at lower ends.

Camshaft . . Single, hollow shaft with 16 cams, supported on 4 bearings. Driven from crankshaft by silent chain.

Valves . . Intake $1\frac{5}{8}''$ clear, tungsten steel; exhaust $1\frac{7}{16}''$ silico-chrome steel, $\frac{11}{32}''$ lift. Mechanism enclosed. Valve stems automatically lubricated. Valves are unmasked.

GASOLINE SYSTEM

Carburetor . . Cadillac design and manufacture. Uniform distribution, with maximum efficiency and economy. Automatic thermostatic mixture control. Large accessible strainer. Overflow from carburetor drained to ground. Intake header exhaust-heated. Valve in left exhaust manifold automatically operated, when closed deflects exhaust gases back from left cylinders through intake header jacket to the right exhaust manifold, thus giving maximum heat for carburetor almost immediately after starting.

Supply . . Twenty-three gallon tank. Vacuum feed. Vacuum from intake manifold assisted by vacuum created by a special vacuum pump to insure positive feed under all conditions.

COOLING SYSTEM

Water Cooling . . Capacity 6 gallons. Forced circulation by one pump driven by a silent chain from the crankshaft. Cylinder blocks interconnected by a copper tube cast in crankcase. One drain plug for entire system.

Temperature Control . . Thermostatically controlled by radiator shutters with vertical balanced shutter blades.

Radiator . . Copper with cellular core. Casing chromium-plated on polished nickel.

Fan . . Diameter 21''; 6 blades; belt driven by pulley mounted on end of camshaft. Fan bearing automatically lubricated from main supply of engine.

LUBRICATING SYSTEM

Engine Lubrication . . Pressure system with gear pump conveys oil under pressure to all main bearings, connecting rod bearings, wrist pins, camshaft bearings, and fan. Pressure is controlled by an automatic pressure regulator. Oil level indicator is located on right-hand side of crankcase at rear.

Crankcase Ventilation . . An exclusive Cadillac system which prevents dilution of lubricating oil from unburned gasoline and from condensation of water vapors produced in combustion.

Oil Filter . . An effective filtering device which removes from the oil any impurities in solid form.

ELECTRICAL SYSTEM

Ignition . . LaSalle-Delco high-tension system with 2 timer contact arms actuated by 4-lobed cam. Jump-spark distributor.

Ignition Lock . . Coincidental theft-proof ignition and transmission lock operated from instrument board.

Generator . . Two-pole La Salle-Delco type, mounted on right side of engine. Positive drive by chain from crankshaft. Thermostatic and third brush control of charging current.

Starting Motor . . La Salle-Delco separate 4-pole unit; double reduction between motor and flywheel. Mounted along right side of transmission.

Battery . . Exide, 100-ampere hour, 6-volt, 3-cell.

Horn . . High-frequency vibrator horn of exceptional tone, carried on left headlamp bracket at side of radiator. Concealed connections.

Lighting Equipment . . Two headlamps with tiltable light beams controlled from steering wheel, fluted lenses, 21 c.p. double-filament bulbs and parking lamps with 3 c.p. bulbs. Parking lamps mounted on top of front fenders. Combination stop and tail light located on left rear fender.

OPERATING CONTROLS

Clutch . . Dry disc plate type. Two steel driven discs 10" in diameter, faced both sides with compressed asbestos fabric, driven by cast iron plates to which are attached all springs, levers, and other parts of clutch, with exception of clutch thrust bearing, which is supported by a sleeve bolted to the transmission case.

Transmission . . Special Cadillac-La Salle Syncro-Mesh transmission, giving noiseless, smooth gear shifting at all speeds. Selective type with three speeds forward and one reverse. Nickel-steel gears and shafts. Faces of gear teeth ground on special grinding machine to obtain silent operation. Mechanism contained in cast iron case.

Gear Shift . . Center gear shift.

Service Brakes . . Safety-mechanical brakes. Special design. Entirely enclosed, giving maximum efficiency in all weather. Mechanically operated, internal on both front and rear wheels. Division of pedal pull automatically proportioned between front and rear systems. Front brakes equalized when straight ahead, outer brake released on turn. All brakes are 15" in diameter.

Hand Brakes . . Internal, on rear wheels.

Steering Gear . . Cadillac design, worm and sector, completely adjustable. Reduction 14 to 1. Steering wheel 19" in diameter. Steering system completely harmonized by means of special modulator at the forward end of the left front spring completely eliminating all shimmy, front end tramp, and road shocks.

Engine Controls . . Accelerator at right of brake pedal. Hand throttle built into central portion of steering wheel.

MISCELLANEOUS

Axles . . Rear axle, Cadillac make, ¾ floating with special alloy steel axle shafts and gears. Spiral bevel gears mounted on large bearings. Front axle, reverse Elliott type, drop-forged steering spindles and arms; steering spindles have adjustable

The La Salle 7-passenger Sedan, illustrated below, is priced at $2475, f. o. b. Detroit—with slight additional cost for special equipment. All La Salle body types are available on G. M. A. C. terms.

When La Salle first made its appearance among the fine cars of the world, it occasioned extraordinary interest — for, up until that time, no one had anticipated a Cadillac-built car in the price range announced for La Salle. Today, five years after its introduction, LaSalle continues to hold the spotlight when the search is for fine-car value. For this distinguished creation has not only shared in every advancement that Cadillac has made, but its price has been lowered amazingly from that of five years ago. The LaSalle Two-Passenger Coupe, for instance, is now but $2195, f. o. b. Detroit.

LA SALLE V-8

NINETEEN THIRTY-ONE
Series 345

LaSalle emerged with very few styling changes over 1930. In fact, it was basically a 1930 model with a few subtle identifiers. New was a single bumper bar and the flat windshield was given a slight break within the corner pillar structure. Sales brochures at the time of introduction showed louvers on the hood side panels of all body styles. Later in the year, ventilator doors that could be opened and closed replaced the louvers.

Every previous body style was continued and could be obtained in a range of rich new colors. Both Fisher and Fleetwood bodies were low-slung and had a sweep of line that gave them an appearance of fleetness and power. In keeping with that theme, LaSalle promoted its V-8 engine as spirited.

Interiors were richly appointed and distinguished in appearance. They were finished in the best grade of mohair or in attractively colored broadcloth or whipcord. Interiors were wide and roomy, affording a maximum amount of space utilization. Seats in the Sedan models were like sofas on wheels. Pleasing visual highlights were afforded by the interior fittings and silver finish.

Non-shatterable security plateglass was installed in all doors and windows, as well as the windshield.

LaSalle's Roadster sported a top attractively lined with close-fitting side curtains and valance that theoretically sealed the car completely against drafts. Two extra passengers could be carried in the rumble seat. A smaller side door (popularly known as a golf club door) gave easy access to a spacious luggage compartment.

The Fleetwood All-Weather Phaeton had a glass division concealed in the rear of the front seat to give it an imperial effect for city driving or to serve as a tonneau windshield when the top was down. The side windows could be lowered and the center pillars could be folded completely out of sight.

While the two-door five-passenger Coupe by Fisher had a trunk built into the body, there was also a five-passenger Town Sedan that had a separate all-metal trunk positioned between the rear fenders, especially designed to blend with the lines and colors of the car.

A chrome-plated radiator screen and the Heron radiator ornament were popular options. However, in the sales brochures, all models were shown without these two extra-cost options.

Prices were lowered to meet the competition and also to overcome the deteriorated economic conditions. Production at the end of the model year was almost equal to Cadillac, both producing a little over 10,000 automobiles each.

All 1931 LaSalles were referred to as the Series 345. Sales brochures and all other factory literature published during the model year referred to the Series 345. It was not until the 1932 models were labeled as the Series 345-B that factory publications and others began referring to the 1931 LaSalle as the Series 345-A.

The engine was basically the same as 1930, except for a slight increase in horsepower due to a larger bore, hence the designation 345. The description of the engine, however, was elaborate and touted many of the features and their relationship to Cadillac. Both Cadillac and LaSalle expounded on the advantages of short and compact engines. LaSalle's Vee-type 8-cylinder engine was shorter than most other automobile engines of equal displacement. It was reasoned that it left a larger proportion of the wheelbase that could be used for passenger space, permitting roomier interiors.

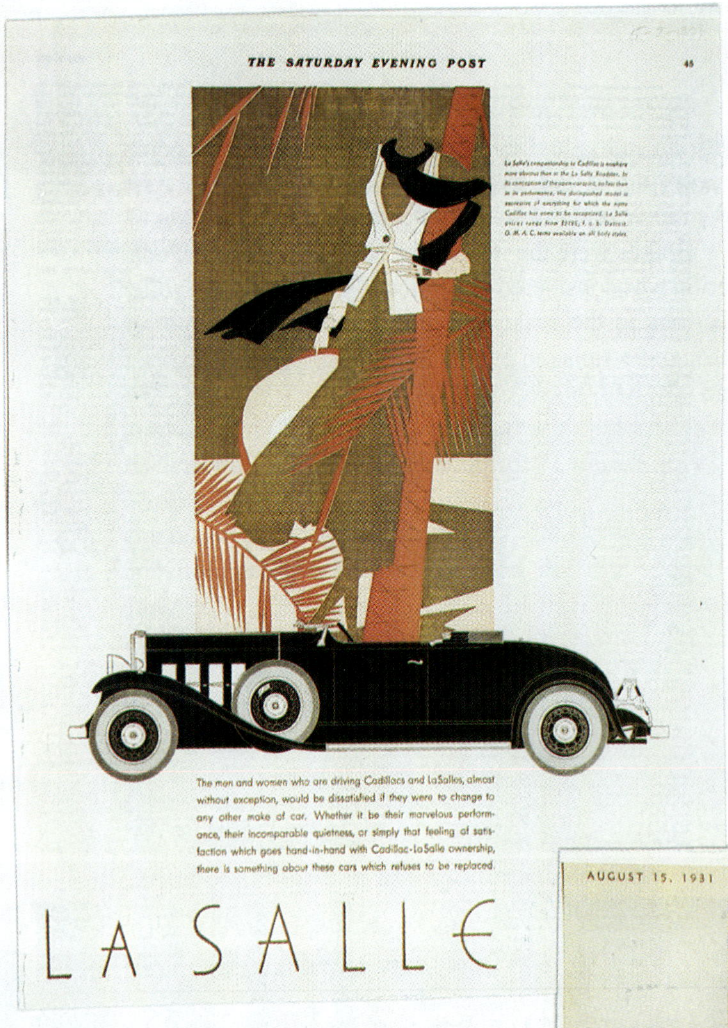
THE SATURDAY EVENING POST
45
The men and women who are driving Cadillacs and LaSalles, almost without exception, would be dissatisfied if they were to change to any other make of car. Whether it be their marvelous performance, their incomparable quietness, or simply that feeling of satisfaction which goes hand-in-hand with Cadillac-LaSalle ownership, there is something about these cars which refuses to be replaced.
LA SALLE

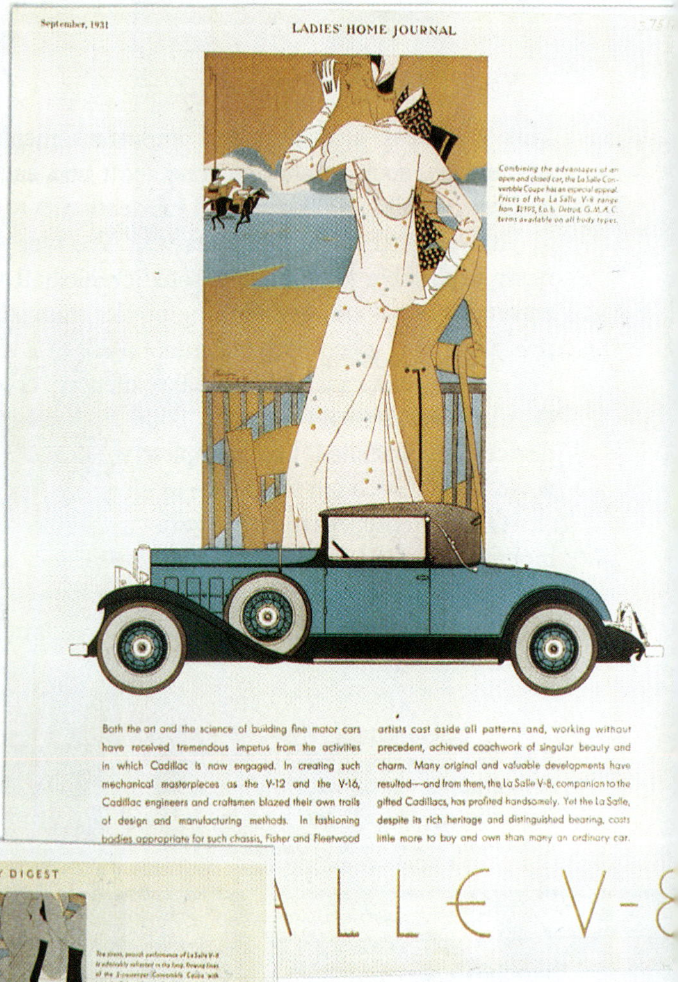
September, 1931
LADIES' HOME JOURNAL
Combining the advantages of an open and closed car, the La Salle Convertible Coupe has an especial appeal. Prices of the La Salle V-8 range from $2195, f.o.b. Detroit. G.M.A.C. terms available on all body types.
Both the art and the science of building fine motor cars have received tremendous impetus from the activities in which Cadillac is now engaged. In creating such mechanical masterpieces as the V-12 and the V-16, Cadillac engineers and craftsmen blazed their own trails of design and manufacturing methods. In fashioning bodies appropriate for such chassis, Fisher and Fleetwood artists cast aside all patterns and, working without precedent, achieved coachwork of singular beauty and charm. Many original and valuable developments have resulted—and from them, the La Salle V-8, companion to the gifted Cadillacs, has profited handsomely. Yet the La Salle, despite its rich heritage and distinguished bearing, costs little more to buy and own than many an ordinary car.
ALLE V-8

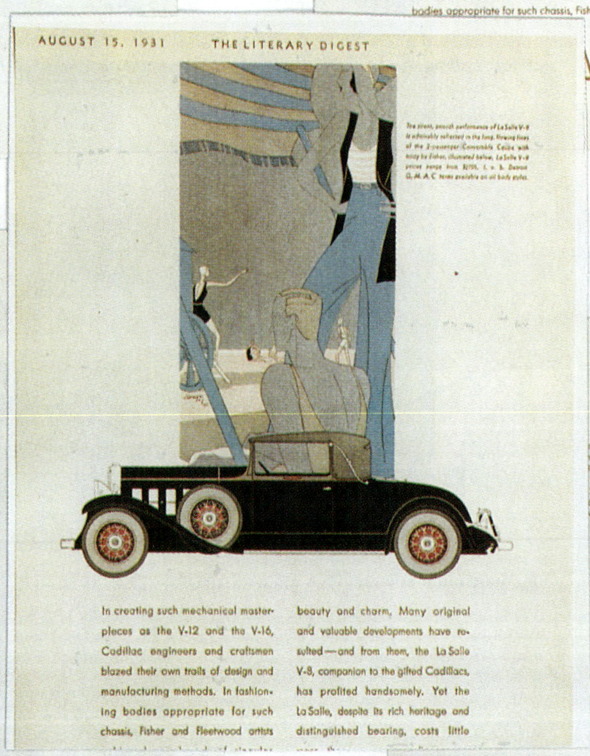
AUGUST 15, 1931
THE LITERARY DIGEST
In creating such mechanical masterpieces as the V-12 and the V-16, Cadillac engineers and craftsmen blazed their own trails of design and manufacturing methods. In fashioning bodies appropriate for such chassis, Fisher and Fleetwood artists
beauty and charm. Many original and valuable developments have resulted—and from them, the La Salle V-8, companion to the gifted Cadillacs, has profited handsomely. Yet the La Salle, despite its rich heritage and distinguished bearing, costs little

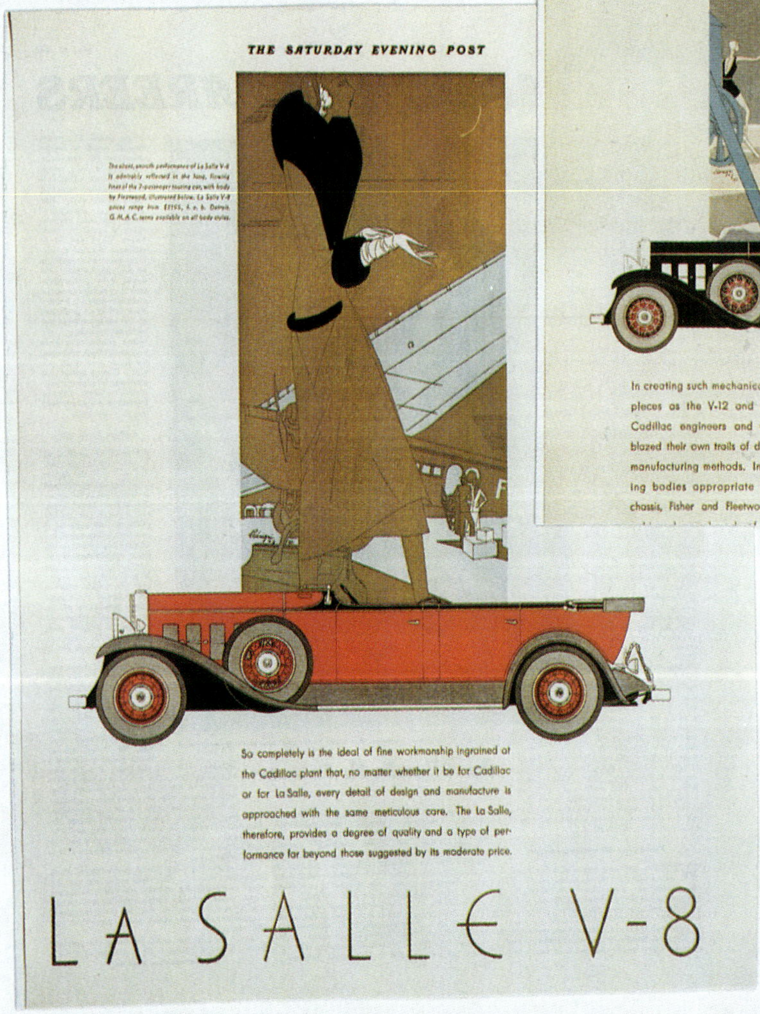
THE SATURDAY EVENING POST
So completely is the ideal of fine workmanship ingrained at the Cadillac plant that, no matter whether it be for Cadillac or for La Salle, every detail of design and manufacture is approached with the same meticulous care. The La Salle, therefore, provides a degree of quality and a type of performance far beyond those suggested by its moderate price.
LA SALLE V-8

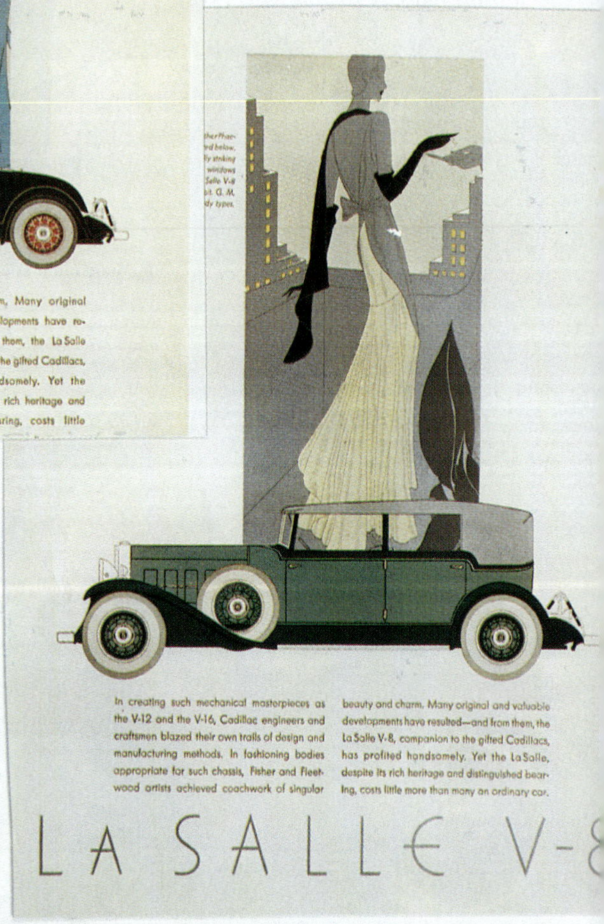
In creating such mechanical masterpieces as the V-12 and the V-16, Cadillac engineers and craftsmen blazed their own trails of design and manufacturing methods. In fashioning bodies appropriate for such chassis, Fisher and Fleetwood artists achieved coachwork of singular beauty and charm. Many original and valuable developments have resulted—and from them, the La Salle V-8, companion to the gifted Cadillacs, has profited handsomely. Yet the La Salle, despite its rich heritage and distinguished bearing, costs little more than many an ordinary car.
LA SALLE V-8

The front compartments of the LaSalles are carefully arranged for driving convenience

The LaSalle Five-Passenger Town Sedan
BODY BY FISHER

The LaSalle Seven-Passenger Sedan
BODY BY FISHER

THE ample passenger-carrying capacity of this LaSalle, combined with its graceful lines and dependable performance, makes it particularly desirable as a family car. Like all the La Salles, it has nonshatterable Security-Plate glass in all doors and windows as well as in the windshield, affording a priceless protection at no added cost.

located on the side of the hood panels. Factory photographs taken later also showed the ventilator doors. The master parts book clarifies this by referencing all models before engine No. 904745 to have vertical louvers while ventilator doors were used after engine No. 904744. All hood sides were interchangeable, except for model 4680. There was a caution of a mismatch possibility if ventilator door hood sides were to be placed on open body styles having vertical louvers on the cowl. No new sales brochures with the hood doors were printed.

The literature promised the LaSalle to last a lifetime, suggesting that LaSalle's purchase price would become of no consequence (would seem lower) and no deterrent. LaSalle's emphasis was, without question, on dependable service at reasonable cost so that its enduring qualities would give, according to the factory, a lifetime of service.

Contrary to the black and white representations in the sales brochure, most advertisements in *The Saturday Evening Post, Ladies' Home Journal,* and others were in striking colors with art deco background. These good looking ads are highly desirable and sought after by collectors today. It was as though new life had been blown into the public presentation of LaSalle by a newly-hired advertising agency.

Right: This two-passenger Roadster Series 345 is easily identified as an early 1931 because it has louvers on the side hood panels and the cowl. With the windshield folded forward and the top down, how could anyone not envy the owner of this LaSalle in their neighborhood? Below: This two-passenger Roadster with body by Fleetwood is shown with the top up. It is a later model with ventilator doors. Also shown is the optional radiator screen commonly referred to as a stone guard.

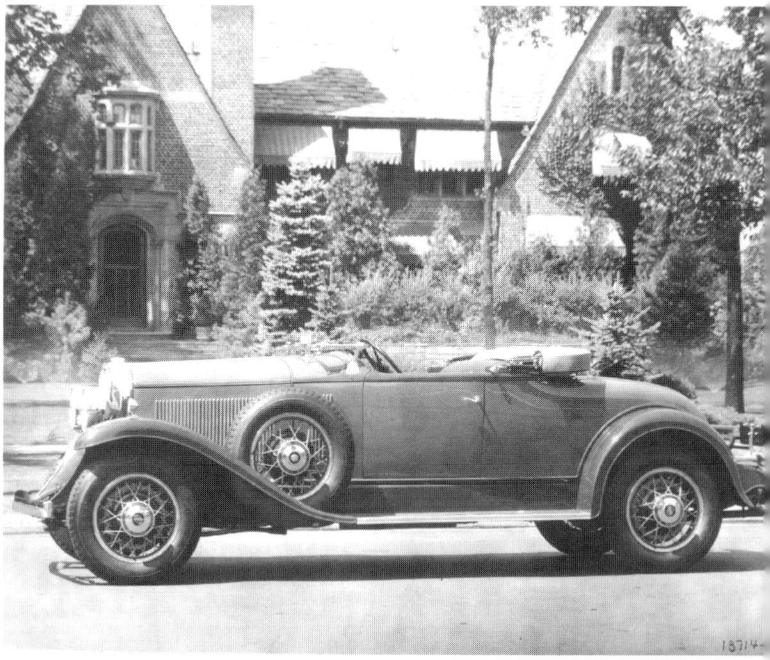

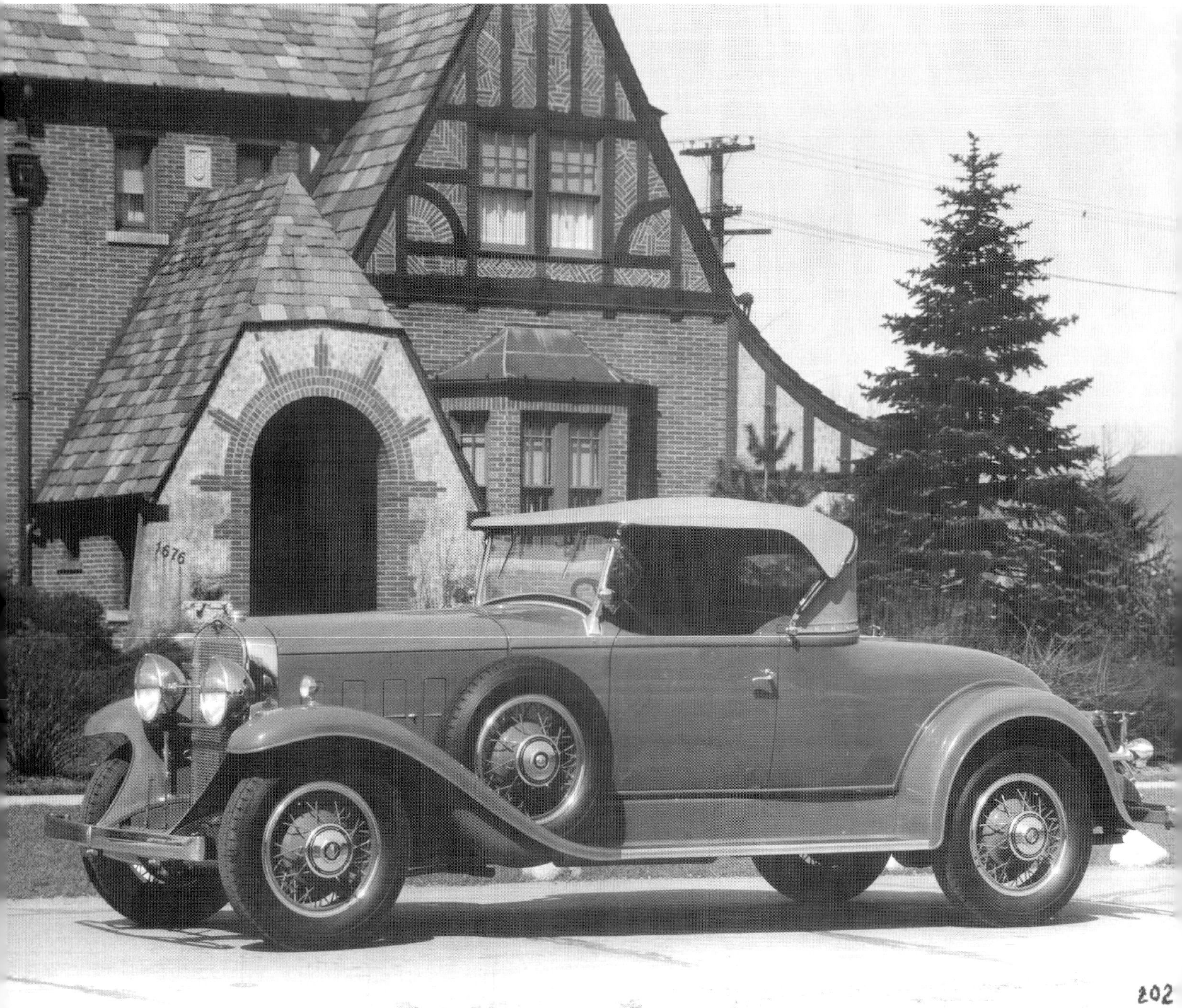
1676

Above: Here is a beautifully restored Series 345 two-passenger Roadster with body by Fleetwood. Two extra passengers can be carried in the spacious rumble seat. Posed in front of a contemporary Arizona home, this model seems very compatible with the weather conditions and lifestyles in that part of the country. Right: A frontal view with the top down at dusk shows an arsenal of lights aimed forward to illuminate dark roads. The duplex (twin) Pilot Ray driving lights turn with the wheels to preview turns at night for the driver. These were a $75 option. Also shown is the optional chromed radiator stone guard. Only the price and the LaS headlight connector bar distinguish the LaSalle from the Cadillac V-8.

Top: The instrument panel is symmetrical, simple and centered. Decorative wood veneer has been placed underneath the windshield frame. Right: A small turn-knob for the quarter window can be seen located just below the fancy ash receiver. A map pocket is located in each of the rear door panels. Mohair-like upholstery provides warmth and a couch-like elegance. Below: This all-original seven-passenger Sedan shows a beautiful combination of a deep two-tone green and black with wood spoke wheels. The spare is absent from the fenders. Its location at the rear gives an illusion of extra length. Note how the spare tire and rim are not affixed to a wheel.

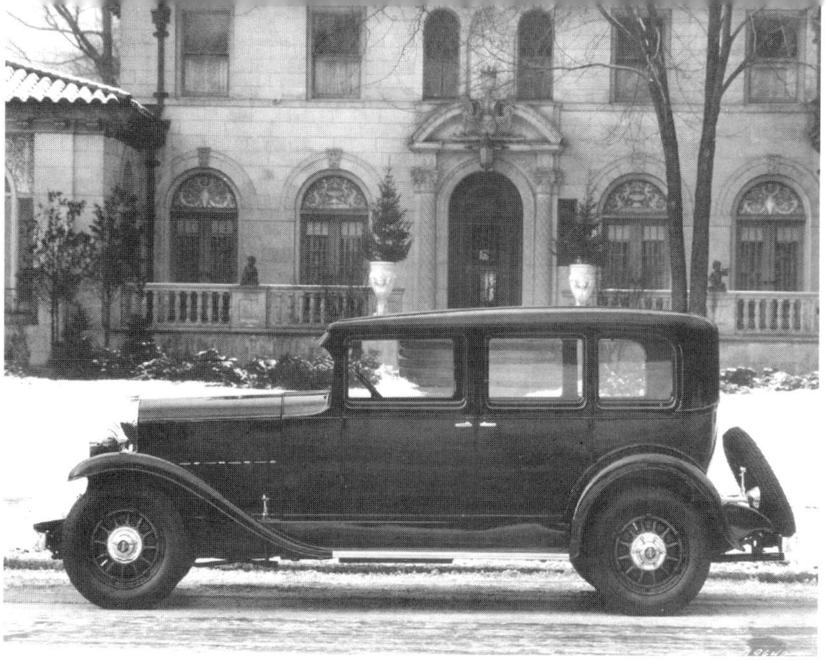

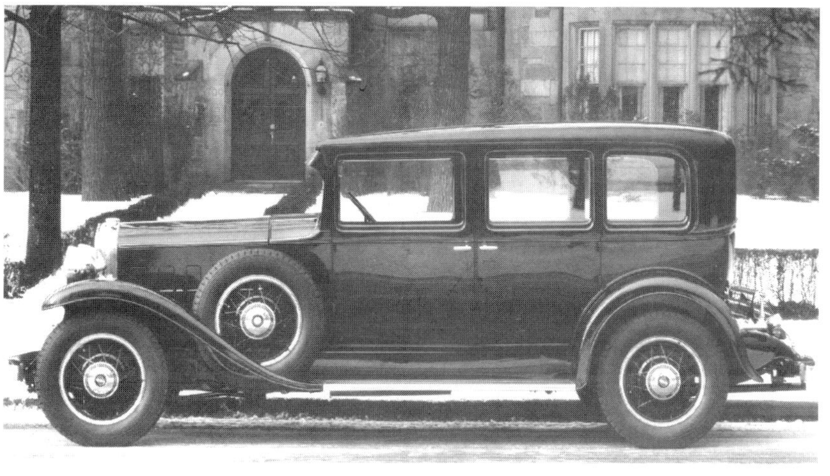

On streets covered with snow in one of Detroit's better neighborhoods, these elegant model 345 Sedans dramatically illustrate how changes in equipment can create contrasting configurations. Above: Here is a Sedan with wooden wheels and rear-mounted spare in profile. Middle: Wire wheels and fender-mounted spares set this same body style apart. Below: A revealing three-quarter view shows the wire mesh stone guard in front of the radiator.

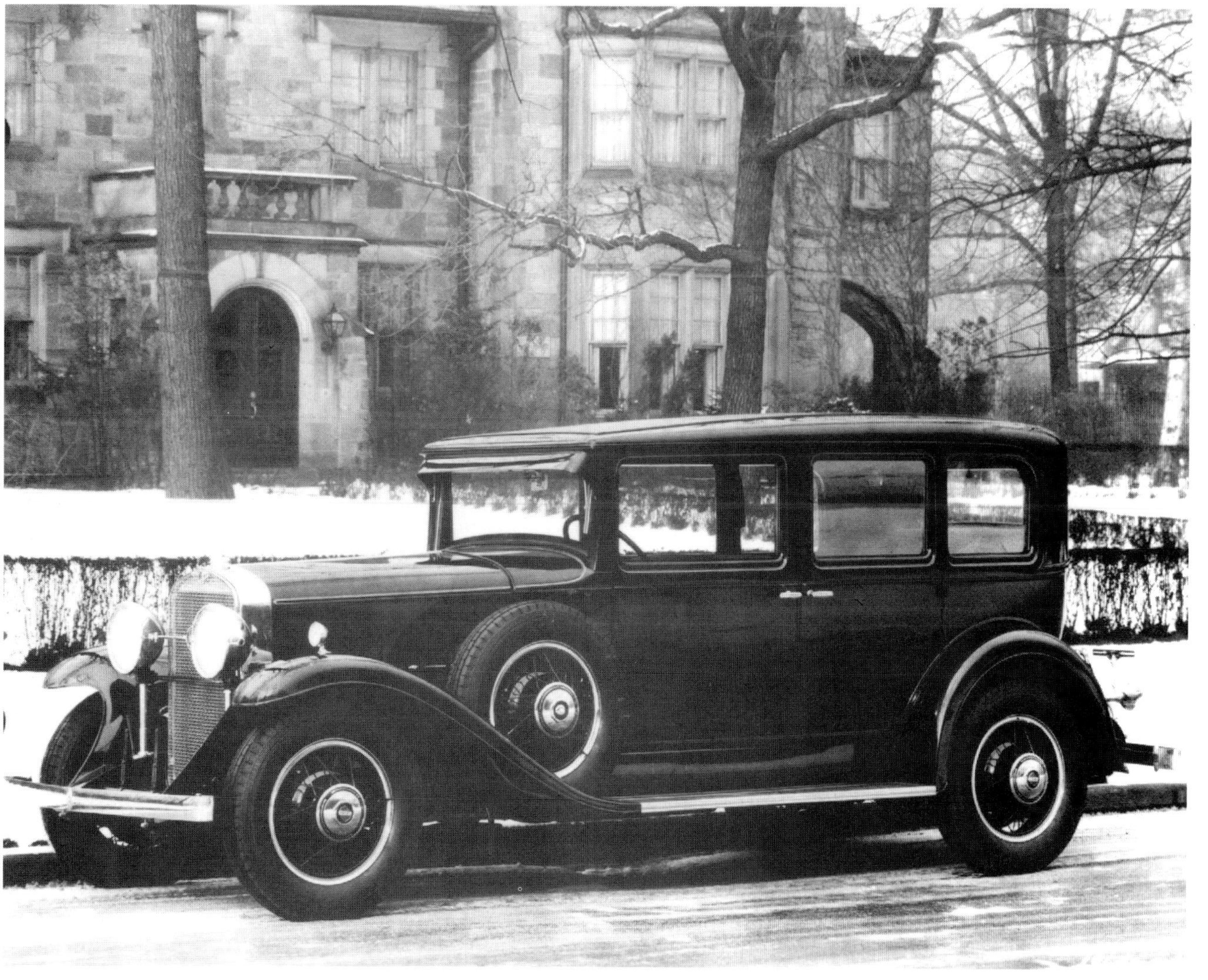

In addition to the rear deck compartment, there is a special luggage compartment with separate door

The La Salle Two-Passenger Convertible Coupe
BODY BY FISHER

NOTABLY smart and dashing in appearance, this La Salle model combines the advantages of closed and open cars. The top is smartly and trimly tailored and fully collapsible. Two extra passengers may be carried in the comfortable rumble seat which is fully trimmed and equipped with a foot rest and arm rests.

The windshields of the open model La Salles are trimmed with chromium plate and have an automatic wiper

The La Salle Seven-Passenger Touring
BODY BY FLEETWOOD

THE power and speed of the La Salle V-type, eight-cylinder engine can be enjoyed in fullest measure in this roomy open model, for the top folds down compactly and the windshield also can be folded. The upholstery is genuine top grain leather with plain trim, and all appointments are of special La Salle design.

A wide door gives easy access to a spacious luggage compartment

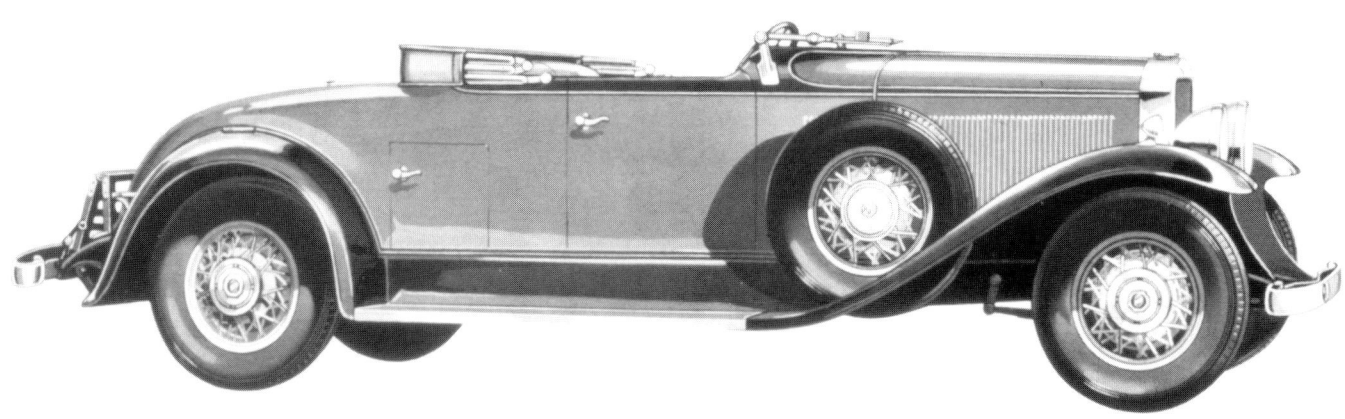

The LaSalle Two-Passenger Roadster
BODY BY FLEETWOOD

WITH windshield folded forward and top down, this smart La Salle Roadster permits full enjoyment of fine weather driving. The top is attractively lined, and close-fitting side curtains with a valance that completely seals the car against drafts are supplied. Two extra passengers can be carried in the spacious rumble seat.

If desired, radiator screen and heron ornament may be had on any model at slight extra cost

The LaSalle Five-Passenger All-Weather Phaeton
BODY BY FLEETWOOD

A GLASS division concealed in the rear of the front seat of this attractive La Salle can be raised to give the car an Imperial effect for city driving, or to serve as a tonneau windshield when the top is down. The side windows can be lowered and the center pillars can be folded completely out of sight.

Above: This 345 two-passenger Convertible Coupe was called "smart and dashing in appearance" in the factory literature. A metal, color-matched, all-weather trunk has been placed at the rear. Dual rear view mirrors have been mounted on the two spare tire covers. The single Pilot Ray driving light mounted on this LaSalle was listed as a $40 option. Ventilator doors on the hood side panels indicate this body to be produced later in the model year. Below: A seven-passenger Touring in profile gives a flavor of touring the great outdoors in grand style.

Above: A five-passenger Coupe has been tastefully restored. The rear deck provides ample space for luggage, especially with the spare tire mounted on the front fender. Often another trunk would be placed on the luggage rack as shown. Below: Another very fine 345 five-passenger Coupe is shown with a beautiful color combination and the spare tire mounted at the rear instead of on the front fender. This combination gives a totally different effect and eliminates any visual break of the body lines. The wooden spoke wheels shown on both cars are rare and were phased out by the end of the 1933 model year.

Combining the advantages of an open and closed car, the La Salle Convertible Coupe has an especial appeal. Prices of the La Salle V-8 range from $2195, f.o.b. Detroit. G. M. A. C. terms available on all body types.

Both the art and the science of building fine motor cars have received tremendous impetus from the activities in which Cadillac is now engaged. In creating such mechanical masterpieces as the V-12 and the V-16, Cadillac engineers and craftsmen blazed their own trails of design and manufacturing methods. In fashioning bodies appropriate for such chassis, Fisher and Fleetwood artists cast aside all patterns and, working without precedent, achieved coachwork of singular beauty and charm. Many original and valuable developments have resulted—and from them, the La Salle V-8, companion to the gifted Cadillacs, has profited handsomely. Yet the La Salle, despite its rich heritage and distinguished bearing, costs little more to buy and own than many an ordinary car.

LA SALLE V-8

1931 LaSalle Production

Total Production: 10,095 automobiles and chassis (8 serial numbers not used according to factory summary data).

Serial Numbers: 900001-910103. The Vehicle (engine) serial number is "stamped on the crankcase near the water inlet on the right-hand side."

Chassis Numbers: Start with prefix "9-" and increase from the first car, which has chassis number 9-6. The numbers are not sequential. Location of chassis unit number is "on the upper surface of the right-hand sidebar just in front of the oil filter."

Body Plates: Fisher job number (e.g., 31-652) or Fleetwood style number and body serial number are on the plate attached to passenger side of the cowl in the engine compartment.

Body Type and Style Numbers:		Wheelbase	List Price (Nov. 6, 1930)	Production
345-A (LaSalle) Fisher bodies				
5-Pass. Town Sedan	31-652	134"	$2345.00	2387
2-Pass. Coupe	31-658	134"	$2195.00	750
5-Pass. Sedan	31-659	134"	$2295.00	3828
7-Pass. Sedan	31-662	134"	$2475.00	698
7-Pass. Imperial Sedan	31-663	134"	$2595.00	250
2-Pass. Convertible Coupe	31-668	134"	$2295.00	1000
5-Pass. Coupe	31-672	134"	$2295.00	850
Chassis		134"	$1900.00	3
345-A (LaSalle) Fleetwood bodies				
5-Pass. Town Car	4151	134"	Not listed	1
2-Pass. Roadster	4602	134"	$2245.00	150
7-Pass. Touring	4657 (4057)	134"	$2345.00	59
5-Pass. All-Weather Phaeton	4680 (4080)	134"	$3245.00	107
5-Pass. Sedanette Cabriolet	4681 (4081)	134"	$3245.00	9
5-Pass. Sedanette	4682 (4082)	134"	$3245.00	4
			Total	10096 (Unexplained difference of one unit)

Standard Options

Standard closed bodies - job:
31652, 31658, 31659, 31662, 31663, 31672
- 3 T 131 Gray Mohair
- 5 T 131 Taupe Mohair
- 7 T 131 Taupe Broadcloth
- 16 T 131 Gray Whipcord
- 32 T 131 Taupe Whipcord
- 34 T 131 Blue Gray Broadcloth
- 99 T 131 Cloth

Open bodies - style/job: 4602, 4657, 4680, 31668
- 1 T 1331 Brown Leather
- 2 T 1331 Green Leather
- 3 T 1331 Black Leather
- 4 T 1331 Gray Leather
- 9 T 1331 Brown Leather
- 10 T 1331 Green Leather
- 11 T 1331 Black Leather
- 12 T 1331 Blue Gray Leather
- 16 T 131 Gray Whipcord
- 32 T 131 Taupe Whipcord
- Top: 2 T 1531 Khaki Burbank
- Top Lining: 3 T 1531

Note: There were apparently two different grades, finishes or types of leather used, hence the repeat leather colors. The domestic car records indicate only the upholstery number; some export cars show upholstery colors and descriptions.

Standard and Optional Equipment

Standard Equipment: Demountable wood wheels, 6.50 X 19" U.S. Royal Black Sidewall Tires, rear spare tire carrier.
Optional Equipment: Wire or disc wheels, fenderwells, trunk rack.

Accessories
Installed Price (April 15, 1931)

	Part No.			Part No.	
Breeze Filter (under windshield)	47219	$5.00	Folding Trunk Rack, chromium plated		Not listed
Cadillac Alpaca Robe		$52.50	Goddess Radiator Ornament	1098123	$20.00
Cadillac Cloth and Alpaca Robe		$55.00	Handy Kit:	A-592	$6.25
Cadillac Cloth and Plush Robe		$45.00	Tire Gauge		$1.50
Cadillac Fleetwood Foot Muff		$30.00	Bulb Kit		$1.25
Cadillac Fleetwood Pillow		$12.00	Metal Polish (pint)		$0.75
Cadillac Fleetwood Robe		$75.00	Body Polish (pint)		$1.00
Cadillac Plush Robe		$32.00	Fabric Cleaner (quart)		$1.25
Chromium Plated Spokes		Not listed	Dust Mit		$0.50
Deluxe Side Wings - open cars	47224	$47.50	Heron Radiator Ornament	A-586	$20.00
Draft Deflectors - closed car, pair		$25.00	Hinge Mirror	47060	$10.00
Duplex Pilot Ray driving lights		$75.00	Hood & Cowl Ports, chromium		Not listed
Fleetwood Metal Covered Trunk, (Convertible and Coupe body styles):			Hot Air Heater (single register)	A-617	$41.00
with two long Black Fabrikoid Suitcases		$100.00	Hot Air Heater (double register)	A-618	$55.00
with two Black Fabrikoid Suitcases and			License Frames		$7.00
one Black Fabrikoid Hat Box		$104.00	Lorraine Light (spotlight)		$37.50

	Part No.			Part No.	
Metal Covered Trunk:			Side Wings (Convertible Coupe), pair		$47.50
with three Black Fabrikoid Suitcases and			Slip-on Seat Covers:		
one Black Fabrikoid Hat Box		$119.00	Sea Breeze - Front or Rear Seat,		
with two Black Fabrikoid Suitcases and			Undivided	A-924/925	$9.75
one Black Fabrikoid Hat Box		$107.00	Jacquard Rayon - Front or Rear Seat,		
with three Black Fabrikoid long Suitcases		$115.00	Undivided	A-930/931	$12.25
Metal Covered Trunks can be had in colors to match car - extra		$10.00	Stainless Steel Spokes, per wheel		Not listed
Metal Tire Covers, pair (black)	885776 R.H.		Summer Cushions - Sea Breeze, set of two		$6.00
	885777 L.H.	$28.00	Sun Visors (pair)	A-645 or A-731	$14.00
in colors to match fender trim - extra, each		$2.50	Tire Chains	A-640 or A-641	$8.50
Metal Tire Covers, full chromium plated, pair		Not listed	Tire Cover - fabric, each:		
Metal Tire Cover Mirrors, pair	885767	$22.00	Burbank 2-T-1531 with Emblem	A-606	$9.00
Pilot Ray Light (single)		$40.00	(Black) Long Grain with Emblem	47177	$5.00
Radiator Screen	1098184	$33.00	Tire Mirrors (pair)	A-541	$32.00
Radio	A-916	$89.50	Town Sedan Case Assembly:		
Rumble Seat (Wind) Shield		$185.00	two Black Fabrikoid Suitcases, Hat Box, Auxiliary Floor		$37.00

<u>Research Methodology</u>: Microfiche copies of the individual Shipping Department records of the as-built configuration of each serial number were viewed and Fleetwood body styles recorded by serial and body number to determine the quantity of each body style built. No attempt was made to construct cross reference lists of the 9,797 Fisher body numbers with corresponding engine numbers to determine which body serial numbers were not used in actual production.

<u>Notes on research findings</u>:

1. Factory summary production records show a total of 10,095 cars and chassis built in the 1931 model year, which would indicate that eight serial numbers were not used. Blank record sheets for those serial numbers are found in the files, six with the notation "Will remain open" or "Open." Three additional record sheets were found to be blank. Totalling the high body serial numbers for each style built results in 10,332 units - 237 more units than the factory indicated total production. Obviously, some body numbers were not used. Examination of the records shows the excessive numbers are due primarily to the use of high serial number Fleetwood bodies that are carryover styles from the 1930 model year. Some of the build sheets list the 1930 Fleetwood style numbers (4057, 4080, 4081, 4082) with the high body serial numbers. Whether or not the body tags of the Fleetwood bodies all carried the 1931 style number is unknown. Examination of the individual 1930 record sheets reveals that very near the end of 1930 production, 29 series 345 (1931) bodies were mounted on 1930 chassis and are recorded as 1930 models. Those bodies were subtracted from production figures listed above.

2. <u>Body Styles</u>: Most of the body styles listed above need no explanation. The style 4681 5-Pass. Sedanette Cabriolet is a carryover from the 1930 model line and is a four-door, fixed-top sedan with fully retractable windows and removable center pillars. Similar in appearance to the All-Weather Phaeton, the fixed top with blind rear quarters is covered in Burbank cloth, giving the very handsome look of a convertible car. The style 4682 5-Pass. Sedanette is a six-window fixed top sedan with roll-up windows and removable window posts to make it a full four-door hardtop. The quarter windows only lower part way. The Sedanette top is covered with Burbank cloth. The Cadillac Master Parts List, First Edition, 1931, includes a LaSalle 5-Pass. Phaeton, Fleetwood style 4660 among the 1931 body styles. A sheet-by-sheet examination of the records fails to show any style 4660 cars produced in the 1931 model year.

Three Fisher body 5-Pass. Town Sedans (31-652) were ordered and built with an Imperial Partition behind the driver's seat. Three Fisher body 5-Pass. Sedans (31-659) were also built into "Imperial Cabriolets," with the addition of an Imperial Partition behind the driver's seat, rear quarter windows omitted, black leather cabriolet back and rear quarters and landau bars added for looks.

A recognizable body change was made shortly before the mid-point of 1931 production, which should make it easy to distinguish early from late 1931 cars. The early 1931 cars have louvre type hood sides as did all earlier model LaSalles. Late 1931 hood sides are equipped with ventilator covers (hood ports). The Cadillac Master Body Parts List identifies the change to the new hood type as occurring with serial #904745. Doubt is raised about this rigid demarkation point by notations on the build sheets for serials #904012 "New type hood ports, sure"; serial #905704 "Must have hood ports" and serial #907561 which indicates "Install hood ports instead of hood louvers."

3. <u>Color</u>: No written color policy or listing of standard color combinations for the entire 1931 model year could be located. The "LaSalle Series 345 V-8 Color Combinations, September - October 1930" pamphlet, however, confirms that the 1930 practice of introducing new colors throughout the year was continued:

Options

 Color combinations 7, 13, 22, 27 and Black are optional on all LaSalle body styles.
 Color combinations 8 and 12 are optional for open cars, Convertible Coupes, and 2-Passenger Coupes in addition
  to the five standard options.
 Combination 7 and 8 when specified for stationary top models, roof will be Black.
 Standard extra charges apply to the colored fenders supplied with combinations 7 and 8 but on request Black
  fenders will be furnished without charge.

Combination 7	Lower Panels, Window Reveals -	Beau Brummel Brown, Duco 2445912
	Rear Quarters, Upper Panels, Mouldings, Fenders, Chassis -	Hazelwood Brown Light, Duco 2446067
	Stripe -	Tokio Ivory, Duco 2885757

Combination 8	Lower Panels, Window Reveals, Rear Quarters -	Scaraba Green, Duco 2445679
	Upper Panels, Mouldings, Fenders, Chassis -	Arizona Gray, Duco 2446101
	Stripe -	Pastel Cream, Duco 2883853
Combination 12	Lower Panels, Window Reveals -	Sarasota Blue, R-M 20297
	Remainder Body -	Black
	Stripe -	Tokio Ivory, Duco 2885757
Combination 13	Lower Panels, Window Reveals -	Cambray Green, R-M 20391
	Remainder Body -	Black
	Stripe -	Tokio Ivory, Duco 2885757
Combination 22	Lower Panels, Window Reveals -	Afghan Maroon, Duco 2446172
	Remainder Body -	Black
	Stripe -	English Vermillion, Duco 2884182
Combination 27	Lower Panels, Window Reveals -	Jefferson Blue, Duco 2446125
	Remainder Body -	Black
	Stripe -	Avignon Blue, R-M 20267

Optional on all Body Styles - All Black;
        Stripe -   Tokio Ivory, 2885757

The 1930 policy on paint durability certainly was applied in 1931: "Specifications received wherein the distributor specifies colors not guaranteed for durability by the manufacturer will be rejected. We will, however, accept such orders for shipment in primer finish thus enabling the distributor to arrange locally to finish the car in any nondurable color for which he may receive orders." Thirteen domestic units were shipped to dealers in primer, "Rubbed out of rough stuff."

Combination numbers are not on the build sheets. Paint names were recorded to determine other probable standard combinations as opposed to the obviously special order colors requested by one or more customers. The predominant color combination was all Black, used on thousands of the cars built; Jefferson Blue was nearly as common, followed by Afghan Maroon and Cambray Green. A total of 292 distinct combinations of color applications were recorded.

Probable other Standard Color Combinations

Rear Quarters	Paint No.	Lower Panels	Paint No.	Fender Set/Chassis
Azure Blue, Dark	22312	Azure Blue	22313	Black or Azure Blue, Dark
Black		Classic Blue	22290	Black
Black		Viceroy Maroon	20623	Black
Daphnis Green	23403	English Gray	21167/2441774	Black or Daphnis Green
Highland Green	20338	Highland Green	20338	Black
Lama Gray	21155	Brewster Gray, Dark	21154	Black
Matisse Brown	28844	Ravenswood Brown	28845	Black or Matisse Brown
Ravenswood Brown	28845	Indiana Gray	20157	Black or Ravenswood Brown
Santa Rosa Gray	21162	Verona Gray	20160	Black or Santa Rosa Gray
Viceroy Maroon	20623	Maharajah Maroon	20653	Black or Viceroy Maroon

Many paint combinations that are considered non-standard were applied as "Fisher Order" customer selections. The listings below under "Cloth top" are not an indication that open body cars were painted only in those colors - those combinations are merely unique to the open cars and because of the cloth tops, did not have Rear Quarter colors indicated. Some of the special order colors were used on as many as 32 cars.

4. The 1931 record sheets do not have a "Purchaser" block. However, nearly all of the special (Fisher and Fleetwood) order cars are annotated with the buyer's name. An "F.O." is an indication of the application of a non-standard paint or upholstery selection, convertible top material, seat or body modifications, etc.

5. <u>Wheels</u>: In addition to the standard equipment wood wheels with 6.50 X 19" tires, the customer could order a car equipped with wire or disc wheels and 7.00 X 18" or 6.50 X 19" tires. Domestic sales were primarily cars equipped with five or six wood or wire wheels and 6.50 X 19" tires. Very few 18-inch disc wheels were fitted to domestic vehicles; no 19-inch disc wheels were noted on domestic cars, although they were fitted to 12 export units. Export sales were predominately wire wheel equipped cars with 7.00 X 18" tires. The tire chart in the Cadillac-LaSalle Shop Manual erroneously indicates that size 7.00 X 19" tires were an option for the Series 345 cars.

6. <u>Chassis</u>: Commercial chassis as such were not an offering in 1931. Only three 134" wheelbase chassis were sold in the 1931 model year:
    Serial 903746 - right hand drive, trunk rack, fenderwells, less tires - shipped to Melbourne, Australia
    Serial 904494 - left hand drive, disc wheels, fenderwells, fenders in primer - shipped to Stockholm, Sweden
    Serial 904749 - omit cowl, closed car type hood, 6 wire wheels, fenderwells, black fender set & chassis, uncut rear
        fenders, closed car instrument board - shipped to Uppercu Cadillac Corp., New York City

7. <u>Export Cars</u>: All Fisher body styles were exported outside of North America. Fleetwood body Roadster, Touring and All-Weather Phaeton cars were also exported. Right hand drive and low compression cylinder heads were common features for export cars. The very

Rear Quarters	**Paint No.**	**Lower Panels**	**Paint No.**	**Fender Set/Chassis**	**Paint No.**
Arga Green	2446043	Catskill Green	2441422	Black	
Arizona Gray	21143	Arizona Gray	21143	Scaraba Green	23341
Arizona Gray	21143	Scaraba Green	23341	Black	
Autumn Drab	28837	Chicle Drab	28838	Autumn Drab	
Autumn Drab	28837	Chicle Drab	28838	Black	
Azure Blue, Dark	22312	Azure Blue, Dark	22312	Black	
Beau Brun.mel Brown	2445912	Beau Brummel Brown	28824/2445912	Black	
Beau Brummel Brown	2445912	Tussing Red	1227	Black	
Billiard Green, Dark	2466924	Billiard Green	2466934	Billiard Green, Dark	
Billiard Green, Dark	2466924	Billiard Green, Dark	2466924	Billiard Green, Dark	
Black	Not listed	Almandine Maroon	5062	Black	
Black		Arizona Gray	21143	Black	
Black		Azure Blue, Dark	22312	Black	
Black		Bavarian Maroon	20651/2446216	Black	
Black		Beau Brummel Brown	28824/2445912	Black	
Black		Blue Hour	2441634	Black	
Black		Boatswain Blue	22260	Boatswain Blue	
Black		Boatswain Blue	22260	Black	
Black		Bolling Green	23396/2441331	Black	
Black		Bon Soir Gray	2463143	Black	
Black		Botticelli Blue	22272	Black	
Black		Brewster Gray, Dark	21154	Black	
Black		Brewster Green, Deep	Not listed	Black	
Black		Calumet Blue	20235	Black	
Black		Caramon Maroon	3338	Black	
Black		Carlysle Gray	6398	Black	
Black		Cashew Nut Tan	2447389	Black	
Black		Cellini Green	2883253	Black	
Black		Clare Purple, Dark	6158	Black	
Black		Cornice Gray	2446159	Black	
Black		Cracker Buff	28843	Black	
Black		Crockett Brown	2461486	Mt. Brown, Dark	2445155
Black		Dustproof Gray, Medium	2466427	Black	
Black		Eagle Brown	6609	Sioux Brown	7387
Black		Elizabethan Blue	20276	Black	
Black		Ember Gray	21156	Black	
Black		English Gray	21167/2441774	Black	
Black		Fleetwood Gray, Light	2466388	Black	
Black		Hessian Maroon	20654	Black	
Black		Garnet Maroon	20661	Black	
Black		Lama Gray	21155	Black	
Black		Larchmont Blue	2441273	Black	
Black		Laurel Green	2466423	Black	
Black		Locarno Maroon	2445346	Black	
Black		London Smoke	2441498	Black	
Black		Maharajah Maroon	20653	Black	
Black		Mallard Green	2443102	Black	
Black		Marblehead Gray	20198	Black	
Black		Matterhorn Gray	20162	Black	
Black		Minerva Blue	20256	Black	
Black		Moorish Brown	20823	Black	
Black		Mulberry Maroon	2445346	Black	
Black		Norse Gray	2441665	Black	
Black		Olive Drab	Not listed	Olive Drab	
Black		Pembroke Gray	21157/2445843	Black	
Black		Parketa Green	2465344	Black	
Black		Pinehurst Green	23320	Black	
Black		Ravenswood Brown	28845	Black	
Black		Regal Blue	2441654	Black	
Black		Regatta Blue, Light	22287	Black	
Black		Regent Maroon	20623	Black	
Black		Roncocas Beige	2445638	Thorne Brown	2445496
Black		Santa Rosa Gray	21162	Black	
Black		Saxon Gray	21160	Black	
Black		Scaraba Green	23341	Black	
Black		Seminole Blue	5397	Black	
Black		Sheffield Green	23392	Black	
Black		Soissons Gray	20167	Black	
Black		State Blue	20291/2445436	Black	
Black		Symbrite Maroon	5981	Black	
Black		Tampico Gray	20171	Black	
Black		Tonawanda Green	2445439	Black	
Black		Town Car Blue, Deep	222285	Black	
Black		Tunis Blue	2445568	Black	
Black		Valentines Dove Gray	3278	Black	
Blue Bell Blue	1332	Valli Blue	5617	Black	
Boatswain Blue	22260	Regatta Blue, Light	22287/2443537	Boatswain Blue	
Bois Green	23393/2445167	Bois Green	23393	Cambray Green	20391
Bolling Green	23396	Bolling Green	23396	Black	
Botticelli Blue	2447118	Botticelli Blue	2447118	Botticelli Blue	
Brazilian Brown	20835	Amazon Brown	2445523	Brazilian Brown	
Buckskin Brown	28864	Buckskin Brown	28864	Black	
Cairo Green	2445479	Merryweather Green	2466898	Cairo Green	
Cambray Green	20391	Bois Green	23393/2445167	Cambray Green	
Cambray Green	20391	Cambray Green	20391	Black	
Cambray Green	20391	Scaraba Green	23341	Black	
Cannes Gray	2443516	Samarkand Gray	2446224	Cannes Gray	
Chicle Drab	28838	Chicle Drab	28838	Autumn Drab	28837
Circe Blue	2447067	Indigo Blue	2441433	Black	
Cloth top		Academia Maroon	6171	Orriford Lake	4063
Cloth top		Alhambra Tan	20830	Alhambra Tan, Deep	20868
Cloth top		Alpenstock Green	2443005	Black	
Cloth top		Antibes Blue	2443537	Boatswain Blue	2443207
Cloth top		Armory Green	2461269	Black	
Cloth top		Balfour Blue	20229/2445685	Avondale Blue	20228
Cloth top		Bangor Beige	2466012	Black	
Cloth top		Batik Green	2466443	English Gray	21167
Cloth top		Bay Tree Green	2444036	Mimosa Green	2441638
Cloth top		Beau Brummel Brown	2445912	Orskany Gray	2447363
Cloth top		Beaver Brown, Light	2446392	Black	
Cloth top		Belgian Blue	2446262	Salamanca Blue	2446163
Cloth top		Besamere Blue	6207	Not listed	
Cloth top		Block Island Gray	244602	Hamilton Green	2444733
Cloth top		Bonaventure Green	2445941	Black	
Cloth top		Bourbon Brown	2441486	Black	
Cloth top		Cairo Gray	2441419	Black	
Cloth top		Cairo Green	2445479	Not listed	
Cloth top		Cannon Smoke Dull Fin.	2443357	Cannon Smoke Dull Finish	
Cloth top		Caramon Maroon	2443338	Briarcliff Beige	5915
Cloth top		Cattail Brown	20825	Black	
Cloth top		Cellini Green	2443253	Black	
Cloth top		Cierce Blue	2447067	Storm Cloud Blue	5818
Cloth top		Cigarette Cream	20749/2443181	Black	
Cloth top		Clenmont Green	23341	Black	
Cloth top		Colorado Gray	20129	Colorado Gray	
Cloth top		Cornice Gray	2446159	Cornice Gray	
Cloth top		C.P. Green, Dark	Not listed	Black	
Cloth top		Crescenda Green	2446174	Black	
Cloth top		Cromwell Blue	2445569	Black	
Cloth top		Crown Maroon	2446337	Caravan Maroon	2446921
Cloth top		Desdemona Blue, Dark	2446732	Black	
Cloth top		Dowager Gray	20159	Black	
Cloth top		Driftwood Smoke	2441312	Douglas Brown	2441279
Cloth top		Egyptian Gray	20143	Black	
Cloth top		Estrada Blue	20273	Dagestan Blue	20246
Cloth top		Everglades Blue	2441208	Black	
Cloth top		French Gray	2441418	Black	
Cloth top		Gazelle Brown	20855	Black	
Cloth top		Irving Gray	Not listed	Sampan Gray	Not listed
Cloth top		Jane Tan	2469851	Jane Tan, Dark	2469852
Cloth top		Laurel Green	2466423	Fennimore Green	2465942
Cloth top		Leaf Brown	Not listed	Uruguay Brown	Not listed
Cloth top		Lenglen Brown	1491	Black	
Cloth top		Mais	2445913	Black	

Rear Quarters	**Paint No.**	**Lower Panels**	**Paint No.**	**Fender Set/Chassis**	**Paint No.**
Cloth top		Marmora Gray	2885367	Pomarang Brown	2445591
Cloth top		Matterhorn Gray	20162	Soissons Gray	20167
Cloth top		Merrimac Beige	2441313	Black	
Cloth top		Mississippi Brown	2443558	Soudan Brown	
Cloth top		Moonstone	2445118	MoonstoneCelliniGreen	2443253
Cloth top		Motor Car Red, Light	3243	Black	
Cloth top		Napier Green	2443366	Black	
Cloth top		Napier Green	2443366	Napier Green	
Cloth top		Napoleon Gray	20134	Napoleon Gray	
Cloth top		Norge Gray	5924	Not listed	
Cloth top		Paris Gray	6517	Black	
Cloth top		Pemaquid Blue	2441658	Pemaquid Blue	
Cloth top		Pementa Green	2445334	Not listed	
Cloth top		Perugia Green	2443742	Black	
Cloth top		Perugia Green	2443742	Mimosa Green	2441638
Cloth top		Puritan Cream	2463251	Verdancia	2464802
Cloth top		Regalea Maroon	3553	Black	
Cloth top		Regal Blue	2441654	Regal Blue	
Cloth top		Rhapsody Green	2463038	Rhapsody Green	
Cloth top		Riviera Blue	5891	Black	
Cloth top		Robinhood Green	2441311	Chalet Green	2441308
Cloth top		Romany Red	20525	Black	
Cloth top		Rosewood	2441145	Topaz Tan	5208
Cloth top		Sabrina Gray	2444747	Black	
Cloth top		Sabrina Gray	2444747	Sabrina Gray	
Cloth top		Santa Fe Beige	2463949	Santa Fe Beige	
Cloth top		Sarasota Blue	20297	Boatswain Blue	22260
Cloth top		Sarasota Blue	20297	Sarasota Blue	
Cloth top		Scaraba Yellow	20723	Black	
Cloth top		Sheffield Green	23392	Ember Gray	21156
Cloth top		Soissons Gray	20167	Matterhorn Gray	20162
Cloth top		Stanford Brown	20845	Black	
Cloth top		Steel Gray	6255	Black	
Cloth top		Submarine Gray	2446406	Black	
Cloth top		Suburban Blue	2461206	Black	
Cloth top		Talina Brown	2461586	Talina Brown	
Cloth top		Thecla Brown	2444759	Beaver Brown, Dark	2443924
Cloth top		Tokio Ivory	20722	Black	
Cloth top		Tokio Ivory	20722	Tokio Ivory	
Cloth top		Van Winkle Green	2461259	Avenue Green	2465167
Cloth top		Verona Gray	20160	Marmora Gray	244536
Cloth top		Verdun Beige	2444739	Black	
Cloth top		Volga Gray	6612	Black	
Cloth top		Woodsmoke Brown	2441714	Black	
Cossack Brown	2441322	Cossack Brown	2441322	Czarina Beige	2443009
Cracker Buff	28843	Cracker Buff	28843	Black	
Cracker Buff	28843	Cracker Buff	28843	Cracker Buff	
Dauphine Gray	Not listed	English Gray	21167/2441774	Dauphine Gray	
Delphine Blue	2444095	Regatta Blue, Light	2443537	Black	
Dove Gray	2466426	Rolls Royce Blue	2463023	Black	
Dustproof Gray, Medium	2466427	Dustproof Gray, Medium	2466427	Dustproof Gray, Medium	
English Gray	2441774	Green Gray	2441775	Black	
Everglades Blue	1208	Halesite Blue	4005	Black	
Falcon Brown	2446885	Kaffa Brown, Dark	2446872	Falcon Brown	
Fenway Gray	21163	Fenway Gray	21163	Fenway Gray	
Fenway Gray	21163	Verona Gray	20160	Fenway Gray	
Fleetwood Gray	2443328	Fleetwood Gray, Light	2446388	Fleetwood Gray	
Gargoyle Gray	2446161	Cornice Gray	2446159	Gargoyle Gray	
Garnet Maroon	20661	Beau Brummel Brown	28824/2445912	Garnet Maroon	
Gettysburg Blue	5397	Seminole Blue	1584	Black	
Grisette Brown, Dark	Not listed	Mountain Brown, Light	2465156	Grisette Brown, Dark	
Hankow Brown	2466871	Cream Beige, Light	2466889	Hankow Brown	
Harbor Blue	5218	Portland Blue	2445219	Black	
Haverhill Brown	28836	Bangor Beige	2466012	Haverhill Brown	
Haverhill Brown	28836	Moorish Brown	20823	Black	
Haverhill Brown	28836	Moorish Brown	20823	Haverhill Brown	
Hawthorne Green	23355	Sherwood Green	23361	Hawthorne Green	
Heathcote Brown	2441771	Heathcote Brown	2441771	Bombay Brown	28829
Hempstead Green	23394	Hempstead Green	23394	Black	
Hessian Maroon	20654	Hessian Maroon	20654	Hession Maroon	
Ionian Blue	6052	Balfour Blue	2445685	Black	
Jane Tan, Dark	Dupont DE 701	Jane Tan	Dupont DE 700	Jane Tan, Dark	
Kaffa Brown	2446845	Cream Beige	2446859	Kaffa Brown	
King George Maroon	2449826	King George Maroon	2449826	King George Maroon	
Lady Mary Maroon	5939	Castor Gray	6335	Black	
Leicester Gray	2441774	Guilford Gray	2441775	Black	
Leicester Gray	2441774	Kensico Green	2445926	Leicester Gray	
Margot Maroon	2447446	Caravan Maroon	2466921	Margot Maroon	
Marine Blue	2441205	Field House Blue	2445475	Marine Blue	
Matisse Brown	28844	Indiana Gray	20157	Matisse Brown	
Maxfield Parrish Blue, Deep	2466774	Maxfield Parrish Blue	2466772	Maxfield Parrish Blue, Deep	
Metal Gray	21158	Desert Sand	28841	Black	
Metal Gray	21158	Desert Sand	28841	Metal Gray	
Metal Gray	21158	Metal Gray	21158	Black	
Milori Green	2463121	Avenue Green	2466054	Milori Green	
Mountain Brown, Light	2445156	Champagne Tan	2445563	Black	
Mountain Gray	6552	Volga Gray	6612	Not listed	
Mount Vernon Blue	2461555	Pemaquid Blue	2461658	Mount Vernon Blue	
Norse Gray	2441665	Helmet Gray	1642	Black	
Oakland Blue	2466325	Arno Blue	2466548	Oakland Blue	
Pembroke Gray	21157	Pembroke Gray	21157	Black	
Pembroke Gray	21157	Pembroke Gray	21157	San Remo Brown	28842
Pembrooke Gray	20131	Pembrooke Gray	20131	Pembrooke Gray	
Peter Pan Blue	22289	Peter Pan Blue	22289	Peter Pan Blue	
Phantom Gray	3356	St. James Gray	1315	Black	
Pine Manor Gray	2441635	Pine Manor Gray	2441635	Pine Manor Gray	
Racoon Gray	20137	Chinchilla Gray	20138	Black	
Radium Blue	22260	Manhasset Gray	20172	Radium Blue	
Ravenswood Brown	28845	Ravenswood Brown	28845	Ravenswood Brown	
Ravenswood Brown	28845	Saxon Gray	21160	Ravenswood Brown	
Regatta Blue, Light	2443537	Boatswain Blue	2443207	Regatta Blue, Light	
Rendezvous Gray	1475	Metropole Gray	7239	Rendezvous Gray	
Richland Green	23321	Bickland Green	20338	Black	
Riverhead Green	2465942	Bonaventure Green	2465941	Riverhead Green	
Roncocas Beige	2445738	Columbian RiverObsidianGray	2446535	Roncocas Beige	
Samarkand Gray	21159	Samarkand Gray	21159	Black	
San Remo Brown	28842	Bucknell Gray	21186	San Remo Brown	
San Remo Brown	28842	Pembroke Gray	21157	San Remo Brown	
San Remo Brown	28842	San Remo Brown	28842	San Remo Brown	
Santa Rosa Gray	21162	Santa Rosa Gray	21162	Andover Gray	21161
Santa Rosa Gray	21162	Santa Rosa Gray	21162	Black	
Saxon Gray	21160	Saxon Gray	21160	Black	
Scaraba Green	23341	Arizona Gray	21143	Scaraba Green	
Scaraba Green	23341	Scaraba Green	23341	Scaraba Green	
Seagate Blue	2466164	Bluet Blue	2446847	Seagate Blue	
Seagate Blue	2466164	Seagate Blue	2466164	Seagate Blue	
Sheffield Green	23392	Sheffield Green	23392	Black	
Sioux Brown	7387	Eagle Brown	6609	Black	
Soissons Gray	20167	Samarkand Gray	2466224	Soissons Gray	
Soissons Gray	20167	Soissons Gray	20167	Soissons Gray	
Sumatra Beige	20854	Pembroke Beige	2461345	Sumatra Beige	
Tilbury Blue	20269	Tilbury Blue	20269	Black	
Toga Maroon	2443954	Mulberry Maroon	2442346	Black	
Town Car Blue Deep	22085	Town Car Blue Deep	22085	Black	
Tryon Blue	20234	Azure Blue	22313	Tryon Blue	
Tunis Blue	20230	Tilbury Blue	20269	Tunis Blue	
Tunis Gray	2445454	Tunis Gray	2445454	Old Chester Gray	2445601
Turenne Gray	2466778	Virgilius Gray	2466779	Turenne Gray	
Typhoon Gray	2447033	Dowager Gray	20159	Typhoon Gray	
Uruguay Brown, Deep	2465829	Uruguay Brown, Deep	2465829	Uruguay Brow	Not listed
Verona Brown	28839	Van Dyke Brown	28835	Black	
Verona Brown	28839	Van Dyke Brown	28835	Verona Brown	
Viceroy Maroon	20623	Viceroy Maroon	20623	Black	

few cars shipped to Canada in 1931 were equipped with Imperial Gallon fuel gauges. One special body car, a style 652 configured as a 5-Pass. Imperial Sedan in right-hand drive, was shipped to Buenos Aires as one of the 157 cars exported. Three 5-Pass. Sedans (31-659) and three 7-Pass. Imperial Sedans (31-663) were shipped to London, England, annotated "Shell body as per deviation #380," which means - less trim, paint and tires.

8. <u>Show Cars</u>: Forty-nine cars were noted as receiving special attention for shows in the 1931 model year. An All-Weather Phaeton and a Convertible Coupe were showcased in the factory second floor exhibit. The Detroit Branch received four "Announcement Date" show cars and four other show cars. Ten went to the Chicago Branch: eight for the Hotel Stevens Ballroom Exhibit or Hotel Stevens Exhibition Hall Exhibit; one to the Chicago Coliseum Exhibit and one for the "Chicago Salon." Nine show cars went to the Cadillac Auto Co. of Boston. Uppercu Cadillac Corp. of New York City received six show cars, including a Town Sedan for the Grand Central Palace Exhibit and a 5-Pass. Coupe for the Hotel Astor Exhibit. Three cars went to Claude Nolan Cadillac in Jacksonville for the "Florida Salon." The other show cars went to Cleveland; Lima; Los Angeles; Philadelphia; Rochester, New York; and Washington, D.C.

9. None of the body styles were assembled in a straight body order sequence.

First car built in each standard body series:	Last car built:	Highest body number
31-652 serial 900001, body 1	serial 910025, body 1575	2400
31-658 serial 900005, body 1	serial 910103, body 733	750
31-659 serial 900002, body 1	serial 910030, body 3798	3844
31-662 serial 900008, body 1	serial 910053, body 363	700
31-663 serial 901377, body 13	serial 910087, body 150	250
31-668 serial 900007, body 1	serial 910100, body 616	1000
31-672 serial 900003, body 1	serial 909370, body 841	850
4602 serial 900006, body 1	serial 907996, body 150	150
4657 serial 900009, body 1	serial 908611, body 41	249
4680 serial 900004, body 1	serial 910088, body 286	375
4681 serial 902925, body 49	serial 908206, body 46	50
4682 serial 903862, body 41	serial 905604, body 42	48

CONDENSED SPECIFICATIONS—LA SALLE 345

POWER PLANT

Engine—Compensated eight-cylinder, V-type. Ninety-degree angle between cylinder blocks. Engine and transmission in unit. Three-point suspension with rubber-lined supports at rear. Piston displacement, 353 cubic inches. Bore, $3\frac{3}{8}$ inches. Stroke, $4\frac{15}{16}$ inches. Horsepower, N.A.C.C. rating, 36.45; actually more than 95.

Crankcase—Silicon aluminum alloy, specially treated.

Crankshaft—Diameter, $2\frac{3}{8}$ inches; length to outer ends of front and rear bearings, $23\frac{25}{32}$ inches. Supported on three main bearings. Crank throws 90 degrees apart, provided with compensators.

Cylinders—Cast in blocks of four, with detachable heads. High-compression heads standard, low-compression optional.

Pistons—Cast molybdenum iron, special formula, annealed; four rings, three above wrist pin and one below; lower ring, special oil-regulating type.

Connecting Rods—Drop-forged special formula steel; side by side, two on each crank pin. Rods are gun drilled for pressure lubrication of wrist pins. Bearings, $2\frac{3}{8}$ inches by $1\frac{3}{8}$ inches. Babbitt in rods at lower ends.

Camshaft—Single, hollow shaft with 16 cams, supported on four bearings. Driven from crankshaft by silent chain.

Valves—Intake, $1\frac{1}{2}$-inch clear diameter tungsten steel; exhaust, $1\frac{1}{2}$-inch clear diameter silichrome steel, $\frac{23}{64}$-inch lift. Mechanism enclosed. Valve stems automatically lubricated.

GASOLINE SYSTEM

Carburetor—Cadillac design and manufacture. Uniform distribution with maximum efficiency and economy. Automatic thermostatic mixture control. Large accessible strainer. Overflow from carburetor drained to ground. Intake header exhaust heated. Valve in left exhaust manifold automatically operated; when closed, deflects exhaust gases back from left cylinders through intake header jacket to the right exhaust manifold, thus giving maximum heat for carburetor almost immediately after starting.

Supply—Twenty-one-gallon tank. Vacuum feed. Vacuum from intake manifold assisted by vacuum created by a special vacuum pump to insure positive feed under all conditions.

COOLING SYSTEM

Water Cooling—Capacity, six gallons. Forced circulation by one pump driven by a silent chain from the crankshaft. Cylinder blocks independently fed. One drain plug for entire system.

Temperature Control—Thermostatically controlled by radiator shutters with vertical balanced shutter blades.

Radiator—Copper with cellular core. Casing chromium plated on polished nickel.

Fan—Diameter, 21 inches; six blades; belt driven by pulley mounted on end of camshaft. Fan bearing automatically lubricated from main supply of engine.

LUBRICATING SYSTEM

Engine Lubrication—Pressure system with gear pump conveys oil under pressure to all main bearings, connecting rod bearings, wrist pins, camshaft bearings, and fan; pressure is controlled by an automatic pressure regulator. Oil level indicator is located on right-hand side of crankcase at rear.

Crankcase Ventilation—An exclusive Cadillac system which prevents dilution of lubricating oil from unburned gasoline and from condensation of water vapors produced in combustion.

Oil Filter—An effective filtering device which removes from the oil any impurities in solid form.

ELECTRICAL SYSTEM

Ignition—La Salle-Delco high-tension system with two timer contact arms actuated by 4-lobed cam. Jump-spark distributor.

Ignition Lock—Coincidental theftproof ignition and transmission lock, operated from instrument board.

Generator—Two-pole La Salle-Delco type, mounted on right side of engine. Positive drive by chain from crankshaft. Thermostatic and third-brush control of charging current.

Starting Motor—La Salle-Delco separate 4-pole unit; double reduction between motor and flywheel. Mounted along right side of transmission.

Battery—Delco, 120-ampere hour, 6-volt, 3-cell.

Horn—High-frequency vibrator horn of exceptional tone carried on left head lamp bracket at side of radiator. Concealed connections.

Lighting Equipment—Two head lamps with tiltable light beams controlled from steering wheel, fluted lenses, 21-c.p. double-filament bulbs, and parking lamps with 3-c.p. bulbs. Parking lamps mounted on top of front fenders. Combination stop and tail light located on left rear fender.

OPERATING CONTROLS

Clutch—Dry disc plate type. Two steel driven discs, 10 inches in diameter, faced both sides with compressed asbestos fabric, driven by cast-iron plates to which are attached all springs, levers, and other parts of clutch, with exception of clutch thrust bearing, which is supported by a sleeve bolted to the transmission case.

Transmission—Special Cadillac-La Salle Syncro-Mesh transmission, giving noiseless, smooth gear shifting at all speeds. Selective type with three speeds forward and one reverse. Nickel steel gears and shafts. Faces of gear teeth ground on special grinding machine to obtain silent operation. Mechanism contained in cast-iron case.

Gear Shift—Center gear shift.

Service Brakes—Safety-mechanical brakes. Special design. Entirely enclosed, giving maximum efficiency in all weather. Mechanically operated, internal on both front and rear wheels. Division of pedal pull automatically proportioned between front and rear systems. Front brakes equalized when straight ahead, outer brake released on turn. All brakes are 15 inches in diameter.

Hand Brake—Internal on rear wheels.

Steering Gear—Cadillac design, worm-and-sector, completely adjustable. Reduction, 17 to 1. Steering wheel, 19 inches in diameter. Steering system completely harmonized by means of special modulator at the forward end of the left front spring, completely eliminating all shimmy, front end tramp, and road shocks.

Engine Controls—Accelerator at right of brake pedal. Hand throttle built into central portion of steering wheel.

MISCELLANEOUS

Axles—Rear axle: Cadillac make, three-quarter floating with special alloy steel axle shafts and gears; spiral bevel gears mounted on large bearings. Front axle: reverse Elliott type, drop-forged steering spindles and arms; steering spindles have adjustable bearings at both ends. Parallel rod has spring compensated ball-and-socket connections at end.

Drive—Hollow steel drive shaft, 2-inch diameter, turns in torque tube which completely seals assembly. Rear end of drive shaft rigidly connected to rear axle by splined sleeve, front end to transmission shaft through universal joint. Torque tube is bolted to differential carrier at rear, and front end pivoted in ball-and-socket joint at rear of the transmission. Transmits drive of rear wheels to chassis and absorbs torque reactions due to acceleration and brakes.

Frame—Side bar channel section with wide top flange, carbon steel; maximum depth, 8 inches; width, 29 inches in front, $44\frac{1}{4}$ inches in rear; flange width at top, 3 inches; at bottom, $2\frac{1}{4}$ inches.

Springs—Semielliptic system of suspension with rear springs underslung. Rear spring shackles of compression type. Front springs, 38 inches by 2 inches; rear, 58 inches by 2 inches. Double-action shock absorbers of hydraulic type, front and rear, with both upward and downward dampening action, give greatly improved riding qualities. Metal spring covers.

Gear Ratio—Standard, 4.75 to 1. Optional, 4.07 to 1 and 4.39 to 1.

Wheels—Artillery type, 12 hickory spokes with steel felloe. Adjustable ball bearings at front, demountable hot-rolled, split-type rim with six lugs. Large steel hub with 12 bolts. Disc, wire, or demountable wood wheels obtainable at additional cost.

Wheel Base—134 inches. Tread: rear, $59\frac{1}{2}$ inches; front, $57\frac{1}{4}$ inches.

Tires—6.50 x 19 on wood wheels.

Tools—Complete set of tools in special fabric holder.

Instrument Board—Instruments arranged in individual assembly. Fitted with windshield wiper control, spark control, oil-pressure gauge, button-controlling carburetor enriching device, switch for instrument board lighting independent of switch on steering column, speedometer, ammeter, electrically operated gasoline gauge, eight-day clock, coincidental transmission and ignition lock, engine temperature indicator, and cigar lighter.

Fenders—One-piece, full crown, wide type.

Security-Plate Glass—Is fitted in all models, both open and closed, for windshields and body windows.

Radiator screen extra charge.

Single-bar bumpers.

Curved tie rod between head lamps (452 type).

NINETEEN THIRTY-TWO
Series 345-B

Appearance, of course, is an outstanding factor in the new La Salle—for the very first car to bear its emblem set La Salle apart as a leading style creation. From the sleek, smart lines of its "air-foil" profile, to the harmonizing contours of its impressive rear valance, today's La Salle is a symphony of balance and color. The front ensemble of radiator shell, grille, headlamps and twin-mounted horns is done with the exquisite taste of a jeweler's setting. Many believe that no other front grouping has ever been so smart in its conception or so beautiful in its execution. The hood is longer, too, in the new La Salle, and flows back to the cowl in a line almost directly parallel to the ground. The effect, immediately recognizable, is a considerable emphasizing of length and lowness—those twin impressions so much sought after by designers who favor the Continental mode. In fact—whether the appraisal is made head-on, side-on, or from the rear—the La Salle is a smart *car, as distinctive in its appearance as any car that sits the curb.*

Upholstery fabrics have been chosen from the foremost looms of the nation—soft, rich, deep-textured materials of the rarest beauty. Wood paneling around the windows and doors is of the finest solid walnut. And all the accessory fitments—such as vanity sets, cigarette lighters and occasional lamps—are wrought with the skill of the master silversmith. Nor is the richness of La Salle interiors confined to upholstery and fitments alone. The instrument panel, for instance, has been made a work of art—and, coincidentally, more serviceable. The instruments, gleaming behind the finest watch crystal, have been grouped snugly about the steering column, immediately under the driver's eye—with the right side of the dash panel completely bare.

—from the 1932 sales brochure

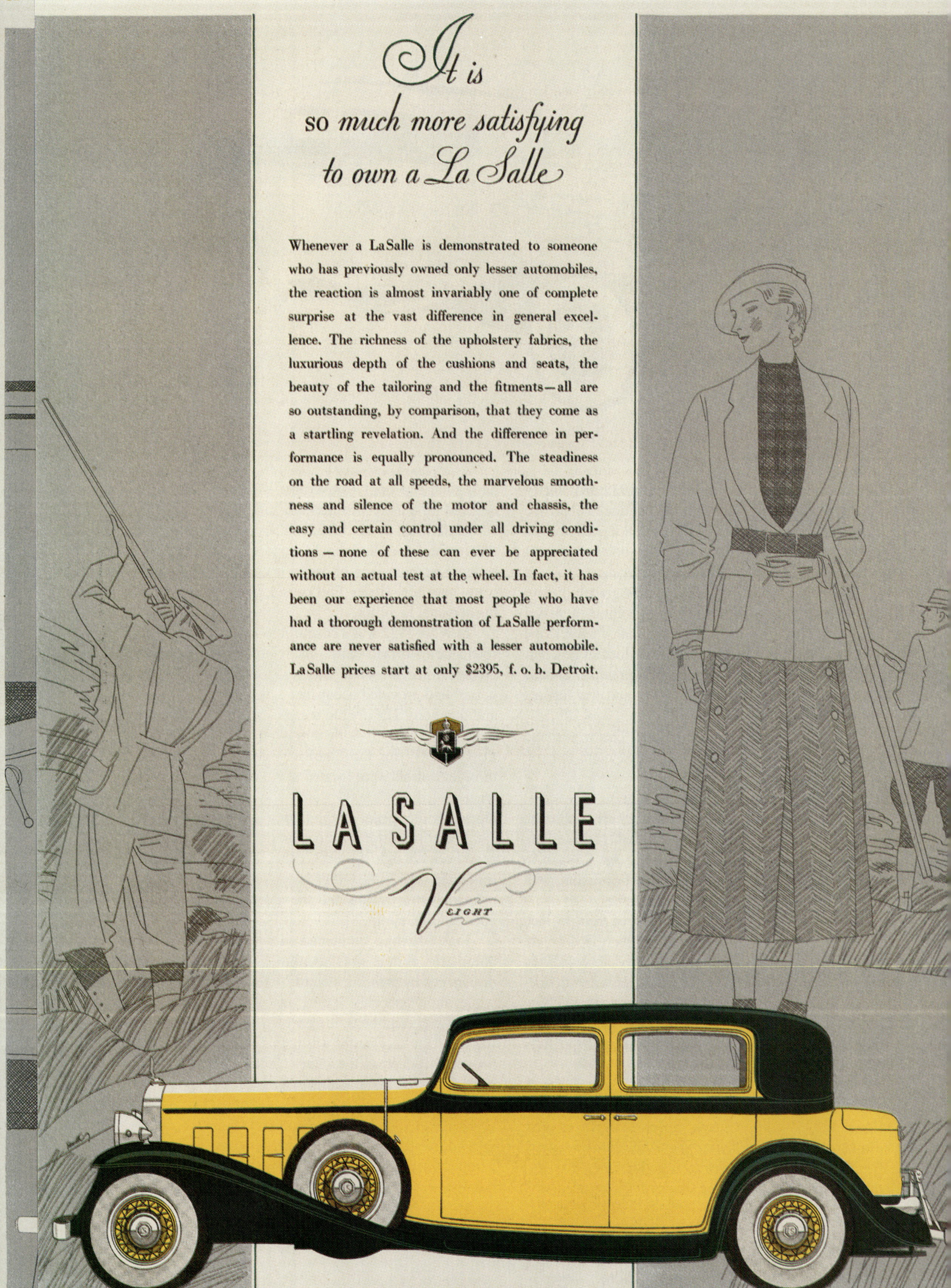
It is
so much more satisfying
to own a La Salle
Whenever a LaSalle is demonstrated to someone who has previously owned only lesser automobiles, the reaction is almost invariably one of complete surprise at the vast difference in general excellence. The richness of the upholstery fabrics, the luxurious depth of the cushions and seats, the beauty of the tailoring and the fitments—all are so outstanding, by comparison, that they come as a startling revelation. And the difference in performance is equally pronounced. The steadiness on the road at all speeds, the marvelous smoothness and silence of the motor and chassis, the easy and certain control under all driving conditions — none of these can ever be appreciated without an actual test at the wheel. In fact, it has been our experience that most people who have had a thorough demonstration of LaSalle performance are never satisfied with a lesser automobile. LaSalle prices start at only $2395, f. o. b. Detroit.
LA SALLE
V EIGHT

The La Salle V-8 Five-Passenger Town Sedan

NINETEEN THIRTY-TWO
Series 345-B

Appearance, of course, is an outstanding factor in the new La Salle—for the very first car to bear its emblem set La Salle apart as a leading style creation. From the sleek, smart lines of its "air-foil" profile, to the harmonizing contours of its impressive rear valance, today's La Salle is a symphony of balance and color. The front ensemble of radiator shell, grille, headlamps and twin-mounted horns is done with the exquisite taste of a jeweler's setting. Many believe that no other front grouping has ever been so smart in its conception or so beautiful in its execution. The hood is longer, too, in the new La Salle, and flows back to the cowl in a line almost directly parallel to the ground. The effect, immediately recognizable, is a considerable emphasizing of length and lowness—those twin impressions so much sought after by designers who favor the Continental mode. In fact—whether the appraisal is made head-on, side-on, or from the rear—the La Salle is a smart *car, as distinctive in its appearance as any car that sits the curb.*

Upholstery fabrics have been chosen from the foremost looms of the nation—soft, rich, deep-textured materials of the rarest beauty. Wood paneling around the windows and doors is of the finest solid walnut. And all the accessory fitments—such as vanity sets, cigarette lighters and occasional lamps—are wrought with the skill of the master silversmith. Nor is the richness of La Salle interiors confined to upholstery and fitments alone. The instrument panel, for instance, has been made a work of art—and, coincidentally, more serviceable. The instruments, gleaming behind the finest watch crystal, have been grouped snugly about the steering column, immediately under the driver's eye—with the right side of the dash panel completely bare.

—from the 1932 sales brochure

You'll drive for the Joy of driving when you own a new La Salle

Again, Cadillac has made motoring more completely delightful than it has ever been before. Starting with the beautiful new LaSalle, and ranging upward to the inimitable Cadillac V-16 —Cadillac offers, literally, a new *type* of performance. Actually, you seem to *float*, rather than ride. The motor is quiet almost to the point of absolute silence. The gears—low, second and high—are almost completely noiseless. You free wheel at the touch of a button—and shift without touching the clutch. You accelerate with incredible swiftness. You steer the car, and stop it, with the most delightful ease. In fact, it's the most entrancing performance since motor car history began. Will you confirm this with a LaSalle—today? LaSalle prices start at only $2395, f.o.b. Detroit.

LA SALLE
V Eight

The LaSalle Town Coupe with De Luxe Equipment

NINETEEN THIRTY-TWO
Series 345-B

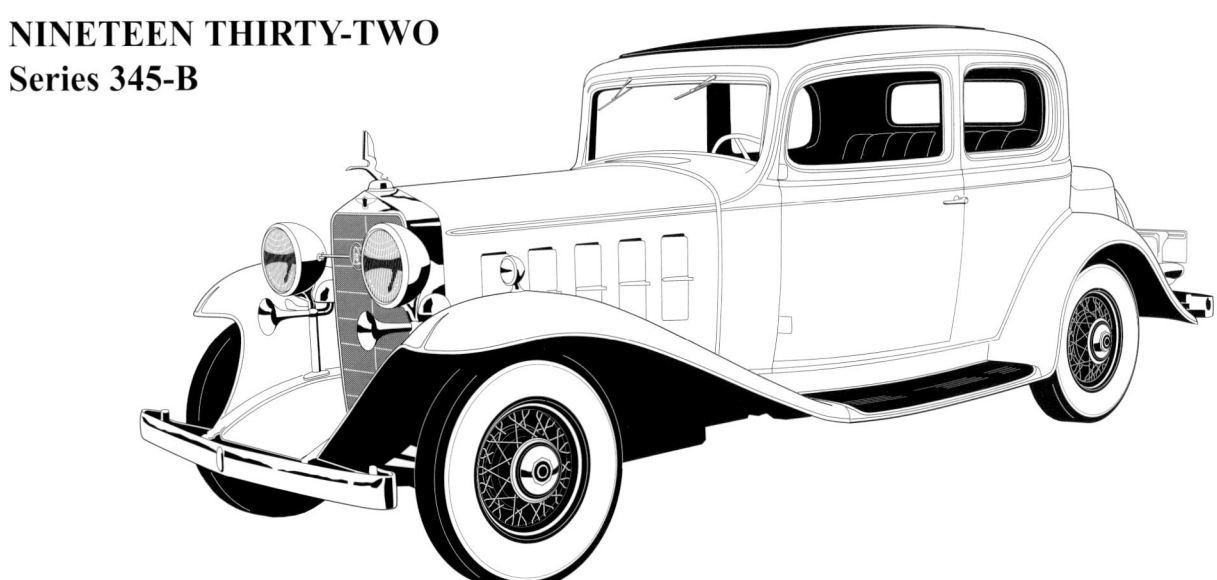

LaSalle was extensively restyled for 1932 and Harley Earl's influence was apparent. His continued objective was a longer, lower, wider, smoother-looking automobile with its own coherent personality. Every body component of the Series 345-B had been changed.

Sweeping new front fenders flowed gracefully into the running boards and continued without a visual break into the rear fenders, accented with a paint stripe all around the car. The running boards look to be a part of the fender structure as opposed to previous models where the running boards were flat and the fenders fastened to each end.

Body lines were more rounded. The windshield posts were more slanted, and appeared more integral with the flat glass.

Radiator shells were without shutters or screens. The waffle-patterned radiator was extremely handsome, accompanied on each side by the headlights and parking lights sporting windsplits. Unique to the LaSalle in 1932 was the tiebar between the two headlights, with LaS beautifully centered in a round frame.

Wheel sizes for LaSalle were reduced from 18-inch to 17-inch diameters. This and the decreased height dimension of the body substantially lowered the overall profile of the LaSalle. Models without side-mounted spare tires were particularly attractive. They provided an uninterrupted sweep of the clamshell fender on the top surface and accentuated the fully exposed length of the hood.

The bottom of the door sills was lowered, which also added to the grace of the body, complementing the flowing lines of the fenders. Seven body styles were available. All of them were Fisher bodied. Semi-custom Fleetwood bodied LaSalles were no longer ordered and the two-door Roadster was dropped in lieu of a very handsome two-door Convertible Coupe to fulfill the demand for a more weather-tight configuration.

Style-wise, it is considered by many to be the most refined and handsomely proportioned of the form-follows-function carriage design era. According to those who knew him, Harley Earl considered this year one of his personal favorites.

New for 1932 was a beautiful instrument panel with round, easy-to-read dials. Its symmetrical simplicity, chrome trim surrounds and wooden panel under the windshield provided occupants with a blend of luxury and function. The double breadloaf instrument cluster would be used by LaSalle through the 1934 model and through 1937 for the Cadillac V-16. Headlight and throttle controls were located at the hub of the steering wheel column, while the starter was just to the right of the accelerator pedal on the floor.

The horsepower was increased to 115 bhp at 3000 rpm even though the 353 cubic inch displacement remained the same. Other improvements were more refined carburization and the use of a mechanically operated fuel pump.

Free wheeling, combined with a vacuum operated automatic clutch, was available, which could be disengaged by pressing a button below the clutch pedal while simultaneously letting up on the accelerator. Under those conditions, there would be no compression felt when the accelerator was not used. There was also no need to depress the clutch pedal while changing gears when the car was underway.

An adjustable ride control was a standard feature that adjusted the hydraulic shock absorbers to provide a soft or firm ride in addition to its normal calibration. This could be controlled with a handle underneath the dash and monitored by a special gauge on the instrument panel.

Top: A beautiful ensemble posed atop the photographic roof at Cadillac. In this factory photo, a LaSalle script, not used in production, can be seen in the upper segment of the radiator shell. A crank cover is located at the bottom of the radiator. It covers the opening in the event a crank start would be necessary in case of an emergency. It was a practical but clever design element. It would be the last year for the tiebar between the headlights. The windshield frame outline hints at a repeat theme of the radiator shell. Middle: This rear view shows a very stylish trunk rack with LaS emblazoned in the center and dual taillights. A single spring steel bumper protected the car in one piece from side to side on the six-wheel models. Bottom: The rounding of windows, the body, the belt molding, the fenders, and the running board flowing into the fender marked the beginning of more stylish automobile designs and divorcing the styling from the carriage coachwork design of the past. A fifth wheel mounted on the rear of this model necessitated a two-piece bumper for protection.

1932 advertisements in *The Saturday Evening Post, Ladies' Home Journal,* and others were elegant and accentuated the restyled long and flowing lines. Most ads showed the LaSalle in profile views with beautiful paint color combinations. Perpendicular to the horizontal grace of the car in the ads were art deco, highly stylish depictions of ladies in evening gowns and men in tuxedos, emanating class and high fashion. Subdued grays and silver in the background were contrasted by LaSalles in vivid colors. All of them had an art deco flavor. Themes at the height of the Depression were carefully chosen: "Wise, indeed, is the buyer who chooses the La Salle." "Do you know for what a moderate sum you can own a New La Salle?" "*It is so much more satisfying to own a La Salle.*"

Sales brochures were beautifully rendered, with artistic grace and beautiful color combinations. Practically every model was shown in a two-tone color combination with the fenders having the darker color, the body the lighter color, and the moldings and the tops in darker hues. Wheel colors were either complementary or contrasting.

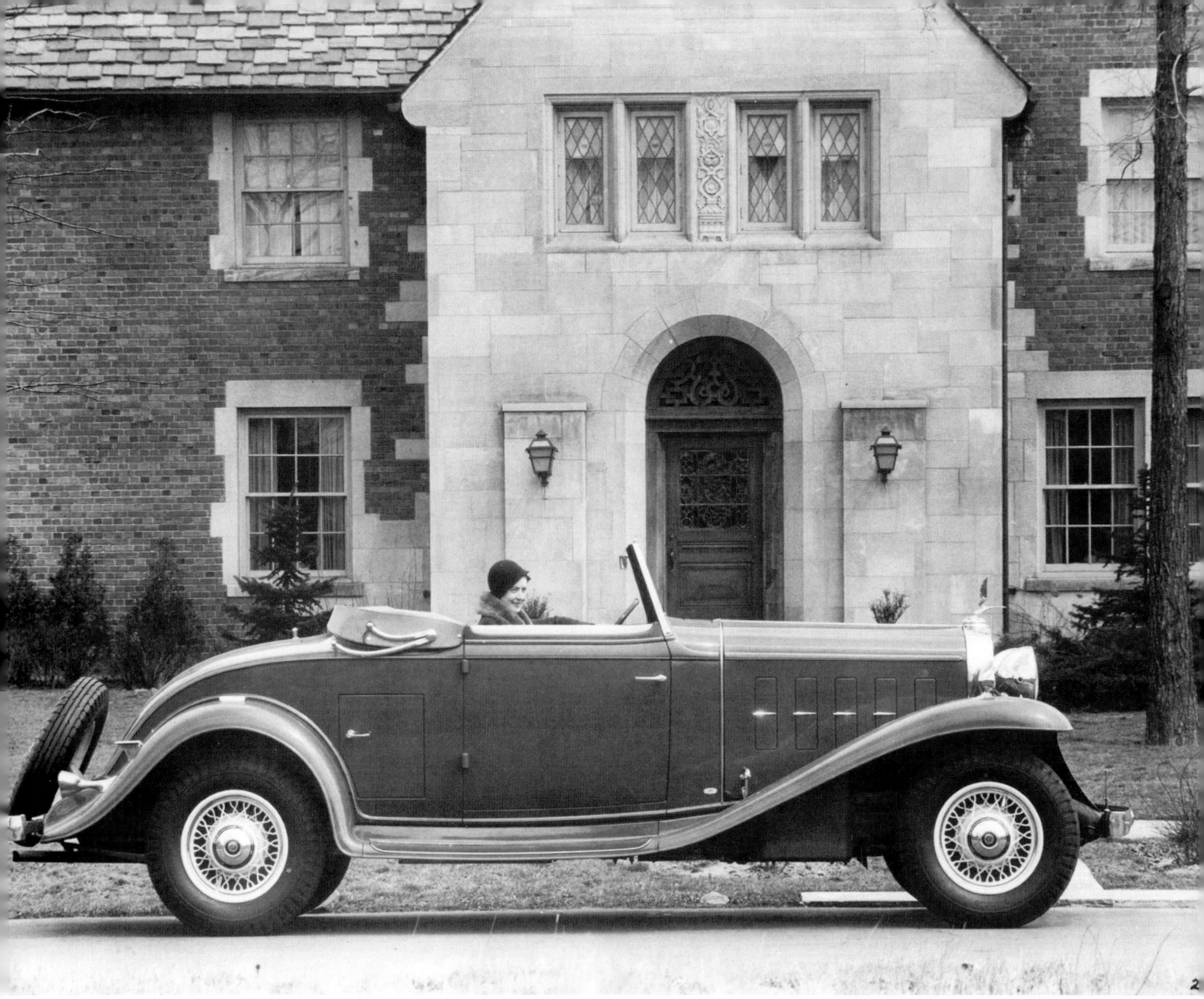

Above: In another factory photograph, the five-wheel Convertible Coupe, with the top down, is shown in front of a better-than-middle-class home, also with a young lady at the wheel. Both pictures show off the elegant, uninterrupted flow of the fenders and body. Below: The sporty attire of the lady model, no doubt, was intended to reflect the sportiness of the Series 345-B LaSalle Convertible Coupe.

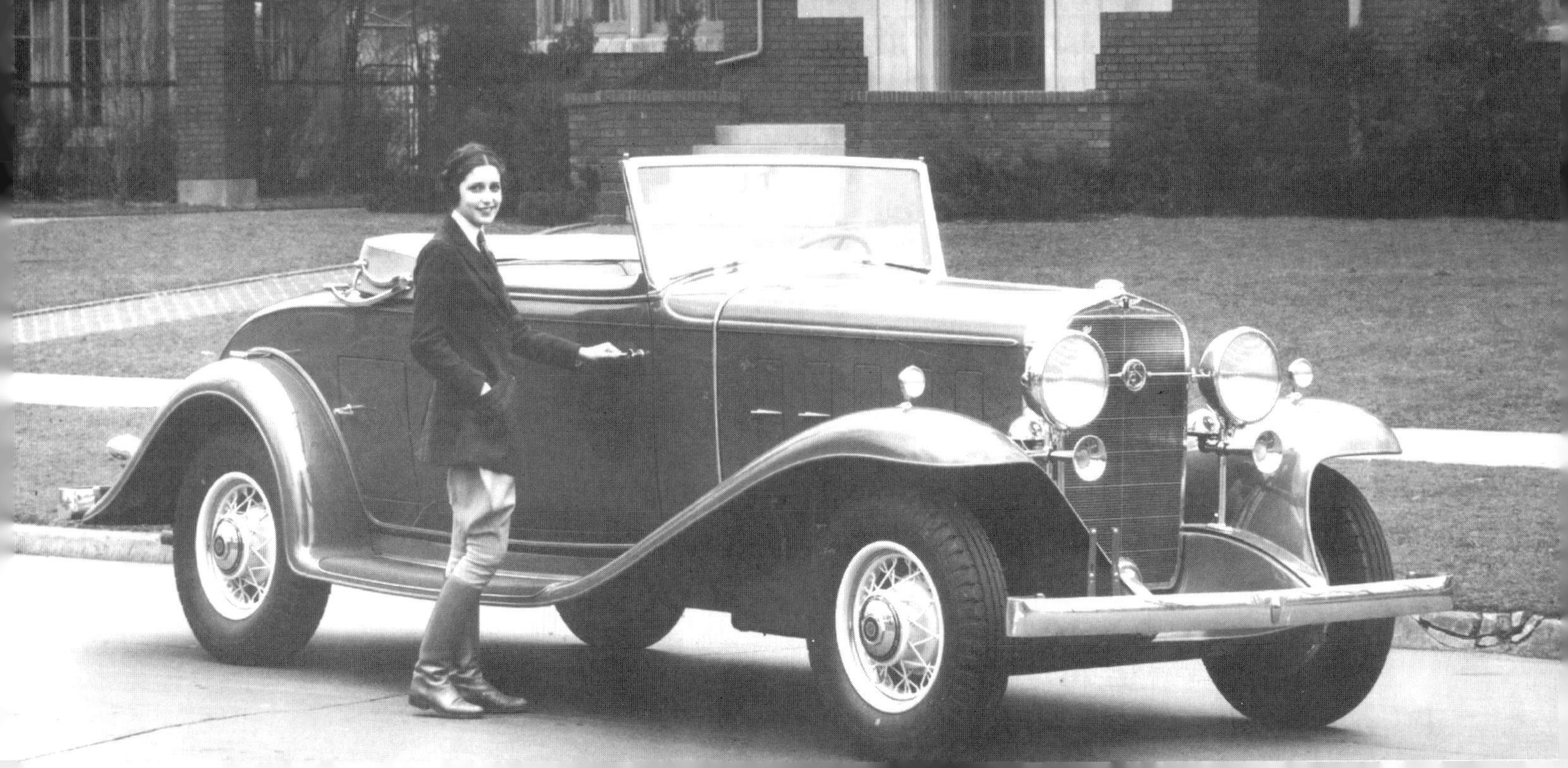

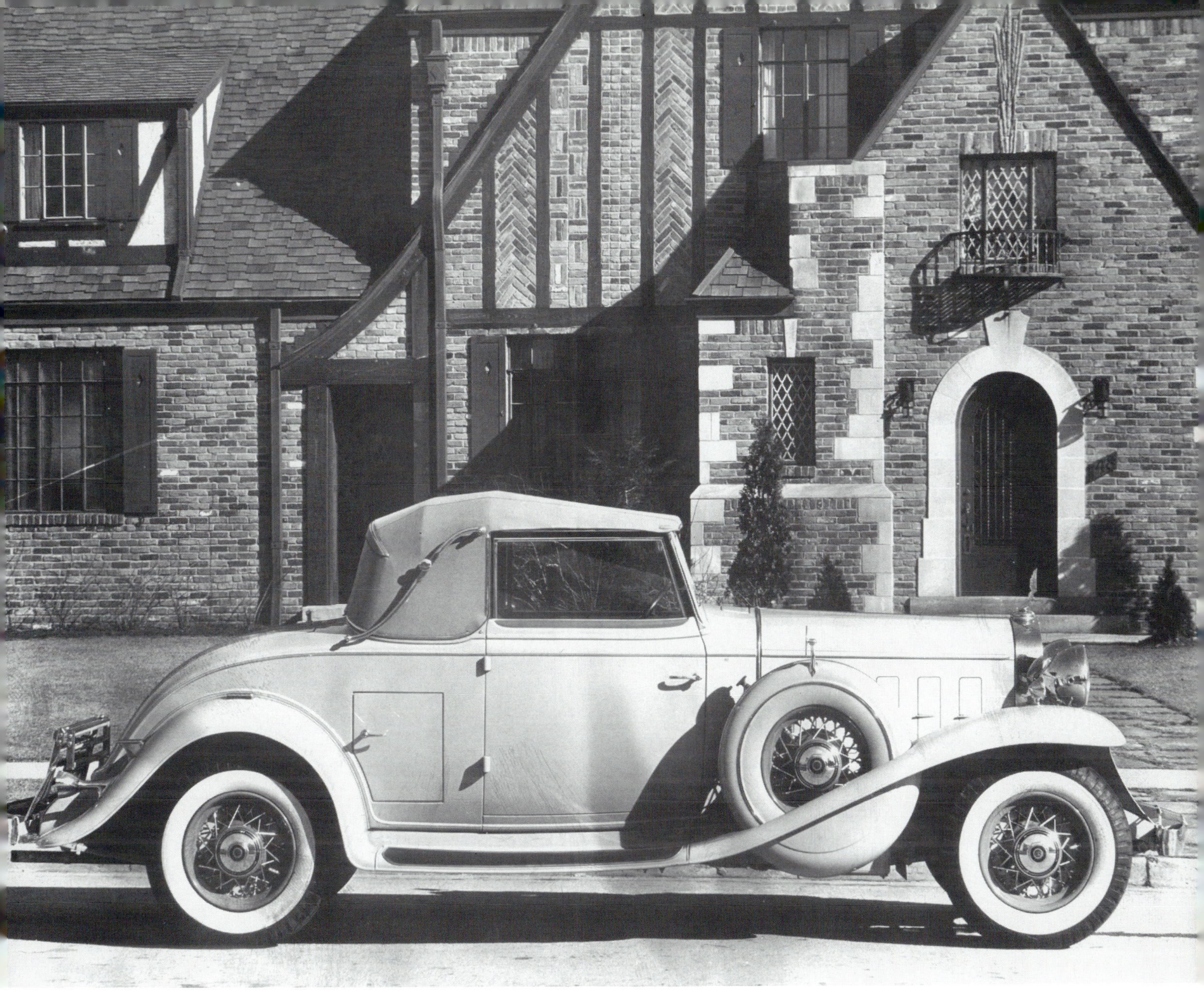

This factory photograph shows another Convertible Coupe, this time with the top up. The six-wheel accessory equipment creates a much more formal and luxurious image, especially when outfitted with a metal spare tire cover. The rumble seat has a golf club door pass-through from the passenger side. Whitewall tires and light-colored paint change the perception of length.

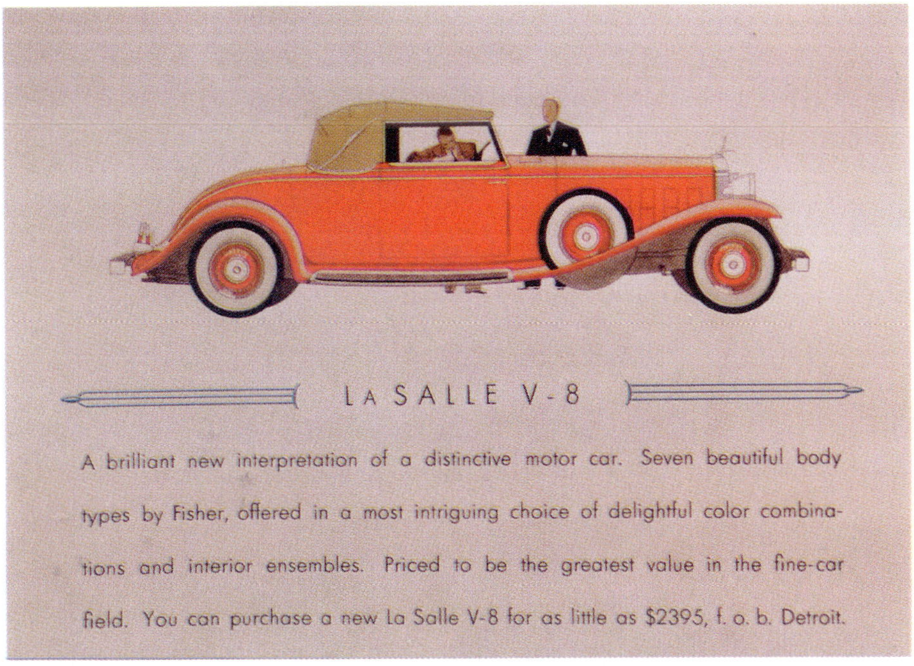
LA SALLE V-8
A brilliant new interpretation of a distinctive motor car. Seven beautiful body types by Fisher, offered in a most intriguing choice of delightful color combinations and interior ensembles. Priced to be the greatest value in the fine-car field. You can purchase a new La Salle V-8 for as little as $2395, f. o. b. Detroit.

A WIDELY popular La Salle creation is the 2-passenger Convertible Coupe—which offers, at the driver's pleasure, the snug comfort of a closed car, or the dashing smartness of the Roadster. The rumble seat is lighted from a conveniently-located switch. Design, construction and complete interior appointments by Fisher. Five wire wheels standard equipment at no extra cost. Shown here on the 130-inch La Salle chassis.

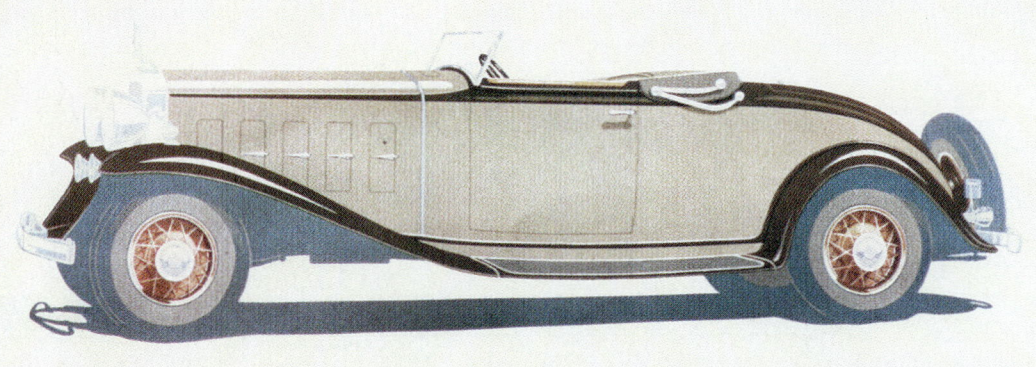

*B*ECAUSE of its fleet performance and its unusually smart appearance, La Salle has always been a favorite among those who prefer the smaller, more intimate body types. Illustrated below is Fisher's conception of the two-passenger Coupe, with rumble seat—mounted on the 130-inch La Salle chassis. The driver's half of the seat is adjustable, forward and back. Five wire wheels standard equipment at no extra cost.

*I*N THE La Salle 5-passenger Town Sedan, Fisher has achieved an unusual combination of the practical and beautiful. Amply roomy for five passengers, with the added utility of a large luggage trunk—it is also one of the most distinctive cars on the highway. A new rake to the windshield increases the driver's visibility a full thirty per cent. Available on the 136-inch chassis. Five wire wheels are standard equipment.

Illustrations from the sales brochure emphasize length and the pastel characteristics of the beautiful paint combinations. Note the wooden artillery wheels on the Town Sedan.

Right: A Convertible Coupe painted dark blue and orange is dramatically depicted on gold paper in a combined Cadillac LaSalle sales brochure foldout entitled, "Let's Go Adventuring." Below: Chrome wheel discs, introduced as an accessory, are shown on a close coupled Town Coupe. Few chrome discs have survived, but add a touch of stylistic beauty to an otherwise mundane color combination.

COMBINING the close-coupled seating intimacy of the Coupe, with the generous passenger comfort of a 5-passenger Sedan—the La Salle Town Coupe is an unusually smart and desirable creation. Oversize trunk permits an exceptional complement of baggage. Adjustable four-position inside visor for the driver's comfort. Five wire wheels standard equipment at no additional cost. Illustrated on the 130-inch chassis.

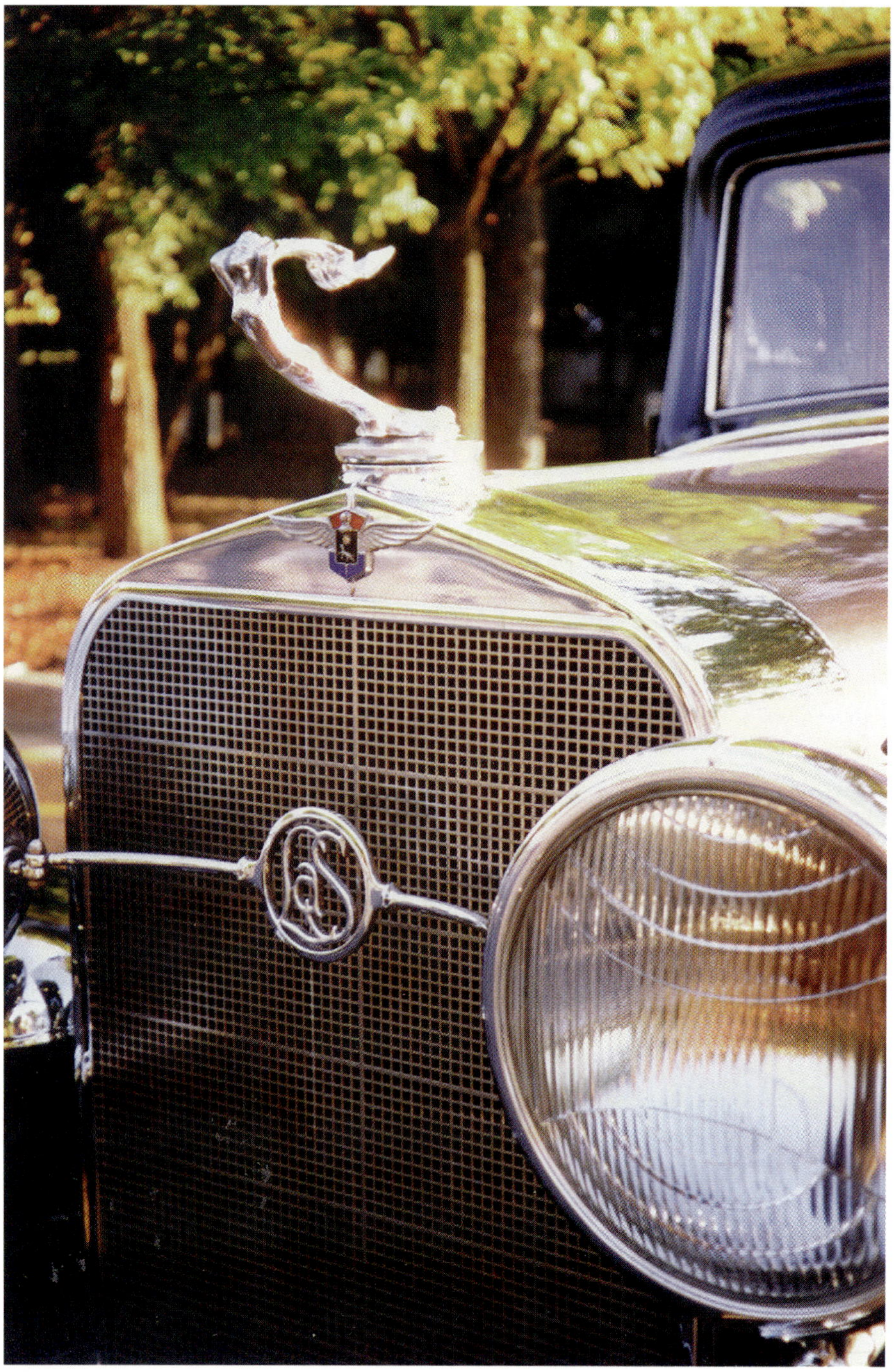

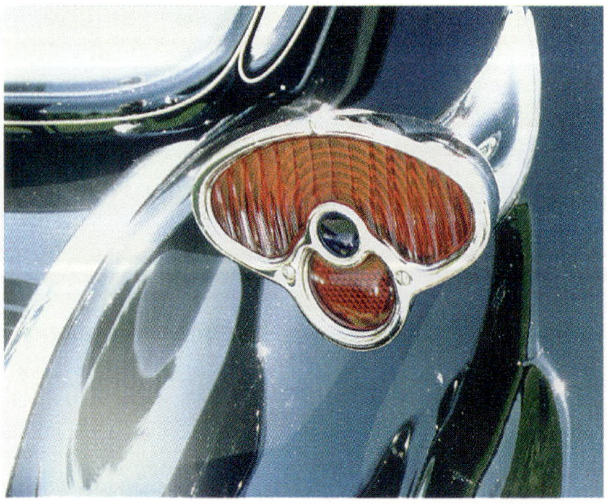

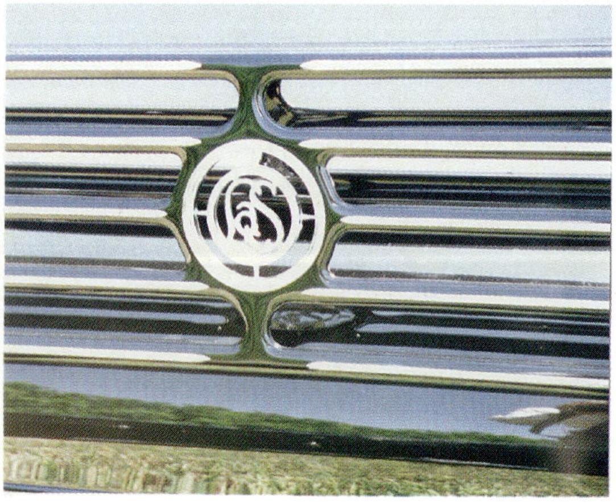

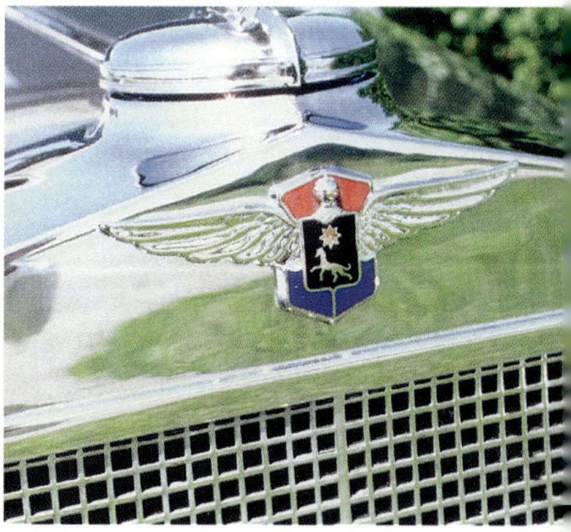

Top: A close-up of a 1932 LaSalle front ensemble shows the classic radiator, beautiful LaSalle insignia on the peaked radiator shell and the optional Goddess radiator cap ornament. Bottom left: A close-up of the LaSalle stop-taillight assembly. Middle: The scripted LaS branding iron emblem was used on the rear trunk rack. Bottom right: The beautiful winged LaSalle crest is proudly mounted at the top of the radiator shell.

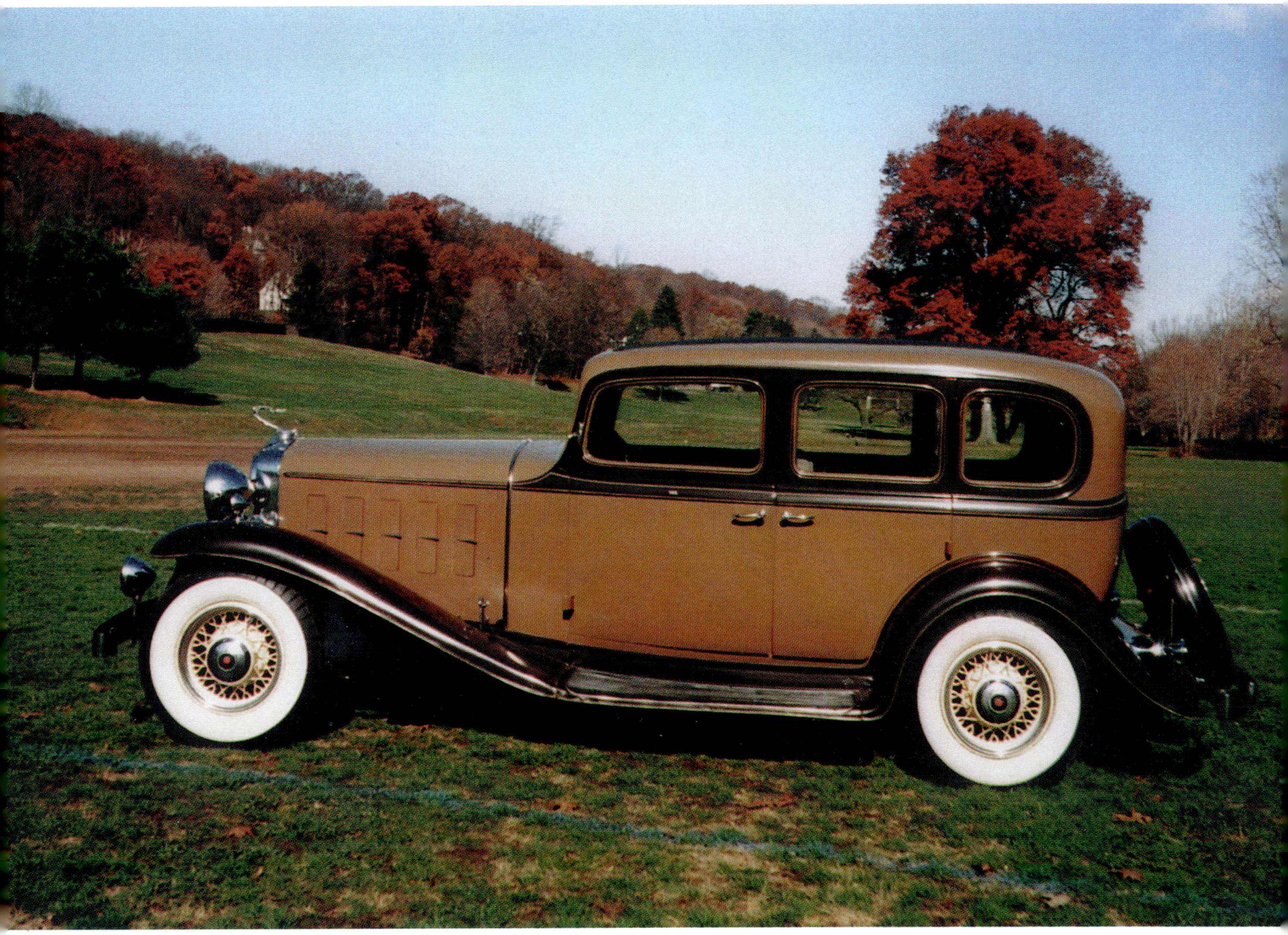

Above: Nothing could be finer than a LaSalle in 1932, or today, amid a beautiful New England Fall while the leaves are turning. This restored five-passenger Sedan harmonizes the environment with its interesting paint scheme. Below: Of note is the absence of fender mounted spare tires. Instead, the rear mounted, metal covered, painted spare adds length, abetted by the optional rear bumper Protection Bar.

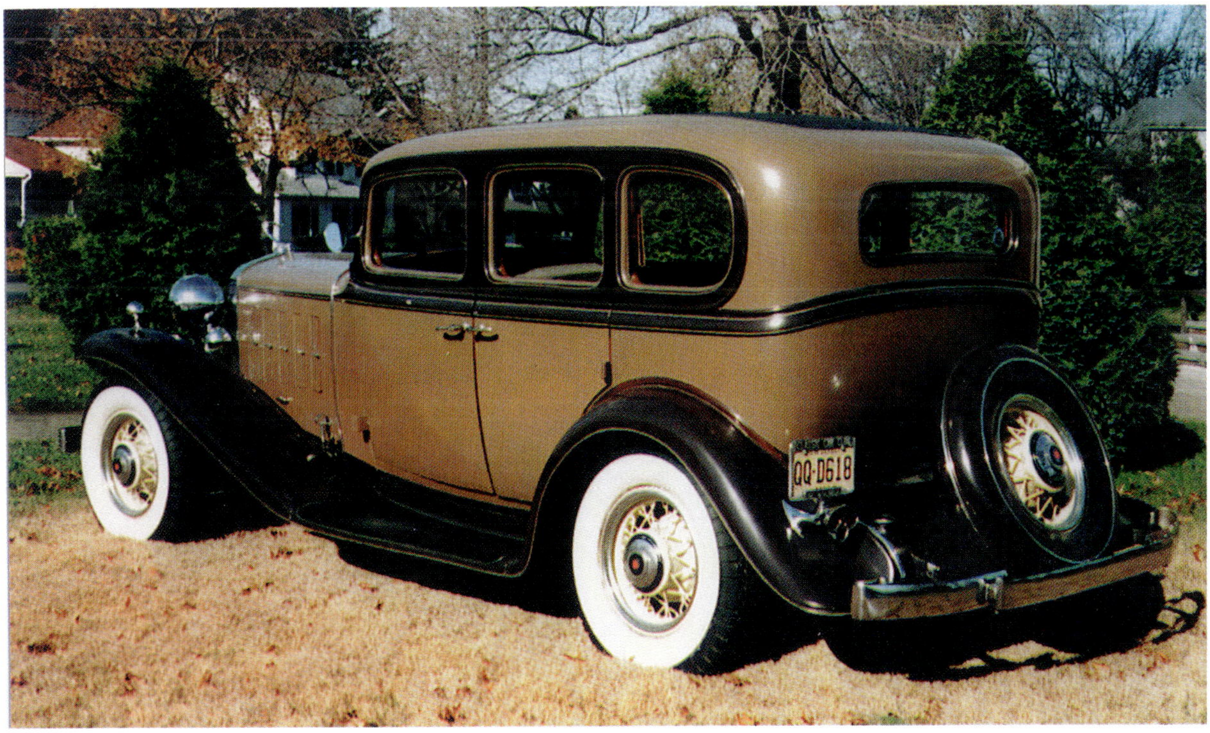
QQ-D618

Above: A brand new two-passenger Coupe with rumble seat and six-wheel equipment shows off its pleasing profile in front of a swanky Detroit neighborhood house. Below: The two-door five-passenger Town Coupe in this factory photograph images the beautifully rounded lines of the windows in harmony with the entire style theme for 1932.

Top: A five-passenger Sedan looks demure in the shade. Middle: A beautiful color even on a rainy day transported this owner to a recent Cadillac LaSalle owners meet in grand style. Bottom: An original six-wheel Town Coupe with an unusual three-tone paint combination, giving the rounded windows a masked effect. Compare the side-mounted fender lines with the five-wheel offering shown in the middle. Seventeen-inch wheels on all 1932 LaSalle models lengthened and lowered the overall appearance.

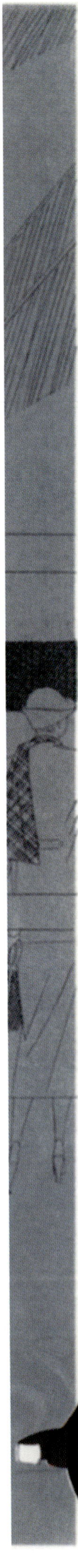

Do you know for what a moderate sum you can own a New La Salle?

Because of their deep regard for La Salle's high place among the fine cars of the world, many people do not realize that La Salle is *not* a costly car to own. The initial expenditure is very little more than the price of many automobiles of less distinguished character. As a result of the thorough quality Cadillac creates with its fine design and precise craftsmanship, the expense for La Salle's operation and maintenance is surprisingly small. And, finally, La Salle's faultless style and faithful performance inspire an unusual span of ownership. One is happy to keep a La Salle over a much greater length of time and drive it a great deal farther than a lesser automobile. In fact, the actual figures often prove that many who are now driving lower-priced cars might very *profitably* be enjoying the prestige and satisfaction of owning a LaSalle. Why not get the facts from your Cadillac-LaSalle dealer today? LaSalle prices from $2395, Cadillac from $2795, f.o.b. Detroit.

LASALLE

V EIGHT

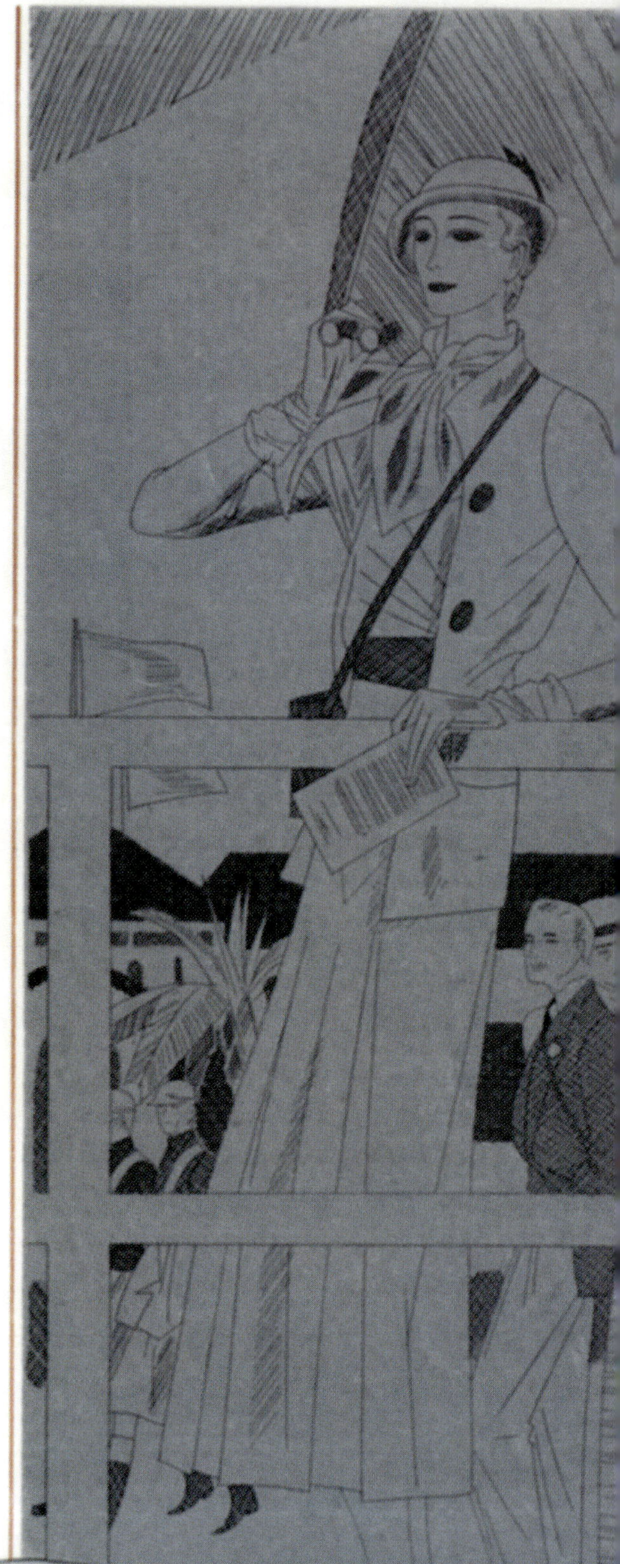

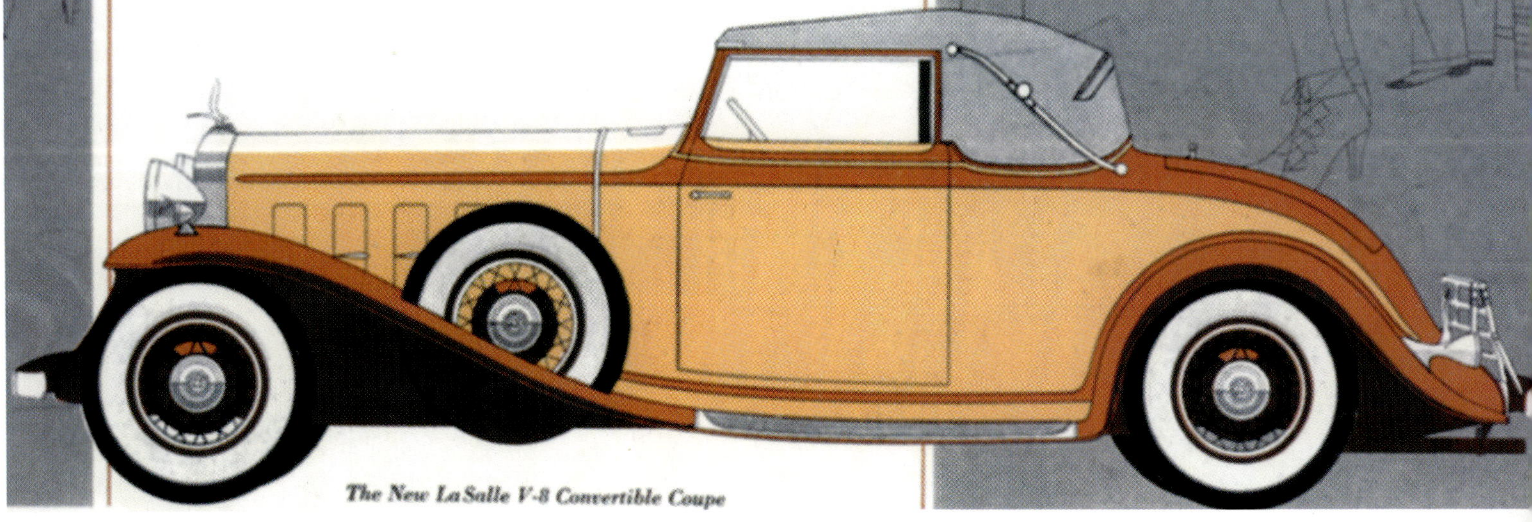

The New La Salle V-8 Convertible Coupe

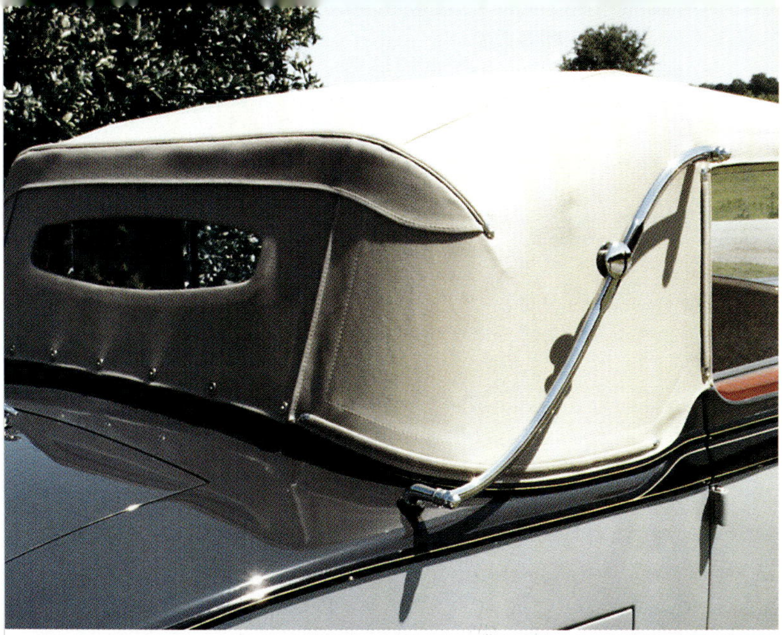

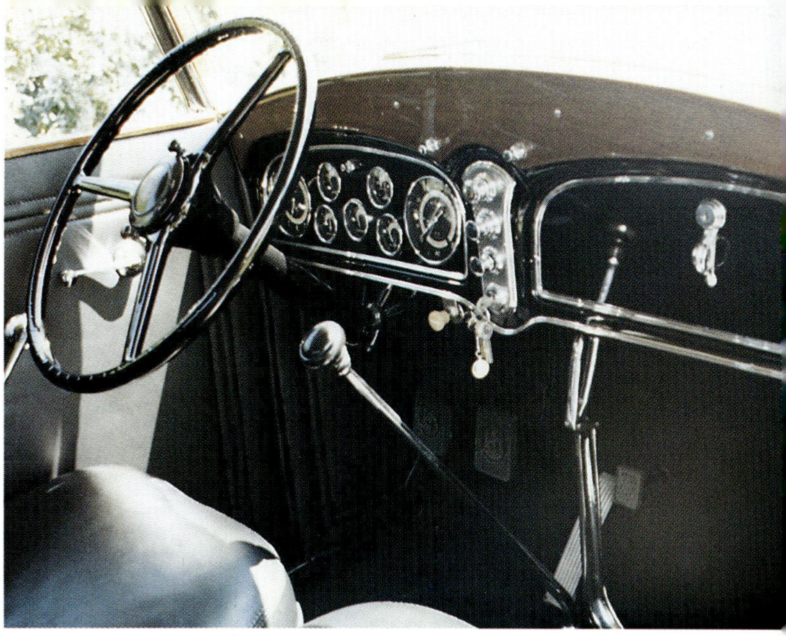

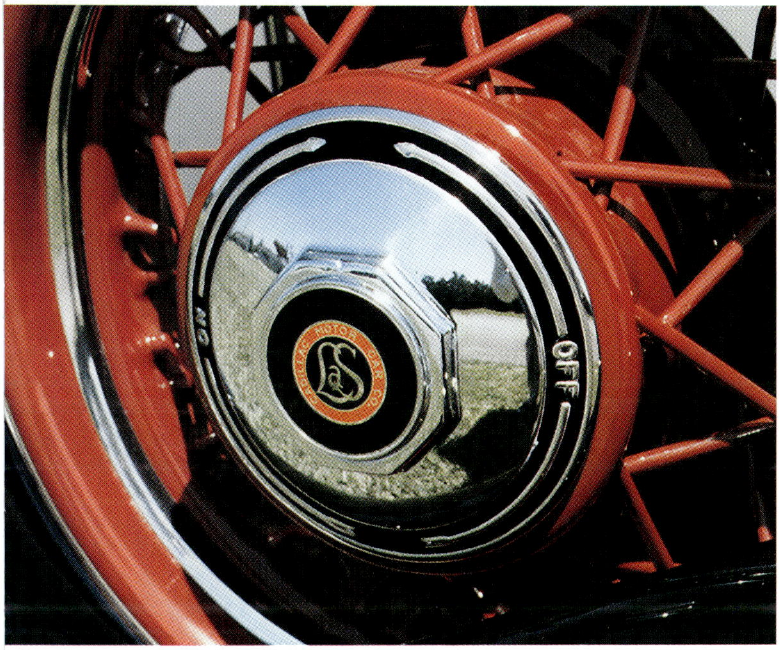
ON
OFF

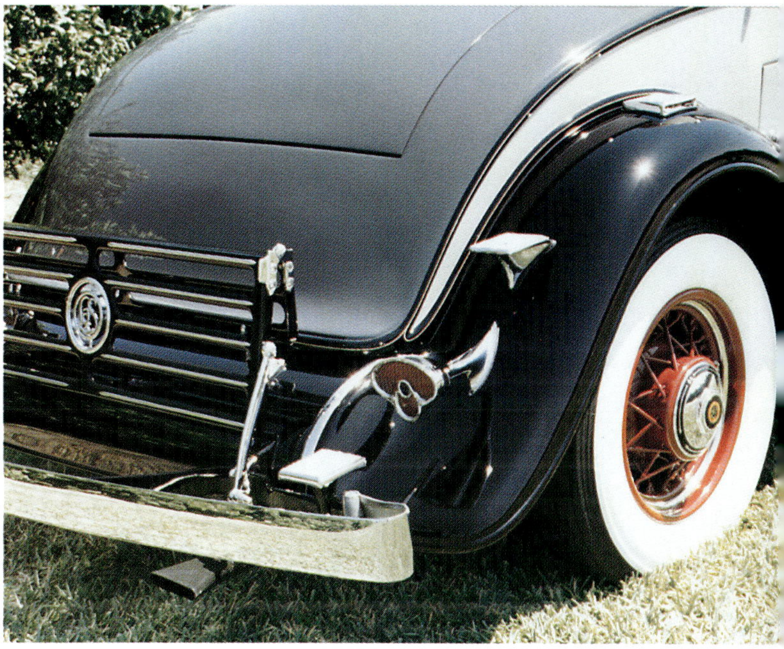

Top left: This restored 345-B Convertible Coupe has the correct oval rear window, flat snaps and landau iron. Top right: Instrument cluster was new for 1932 as part of a simple symmetrical, yet elegant, dash panel. Locating the gauges to the driver position made monitoring easier. Middle left: Spare tire hubcap displays a beautiful rounded LaS emblem. Middle right: Conspicuous are the lines flowing from the rear deck (no trunk on this car) and the body in harmony with the fenders. Step plates are provided to transport passengers into the rumble seat. Bottom left: Shown here is a proud Heron radiator ornament on top of a LaSalle radiator cap. The optional rear view mirrors have been mounted on top of the metal spare tire covers. Bottom right: A meticulously detailed 353 cubic inch LaSalle engine for 1932.

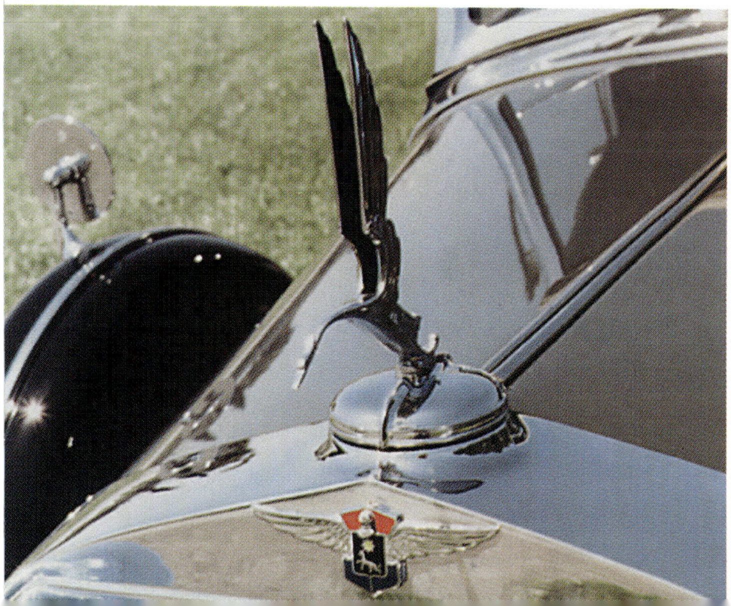

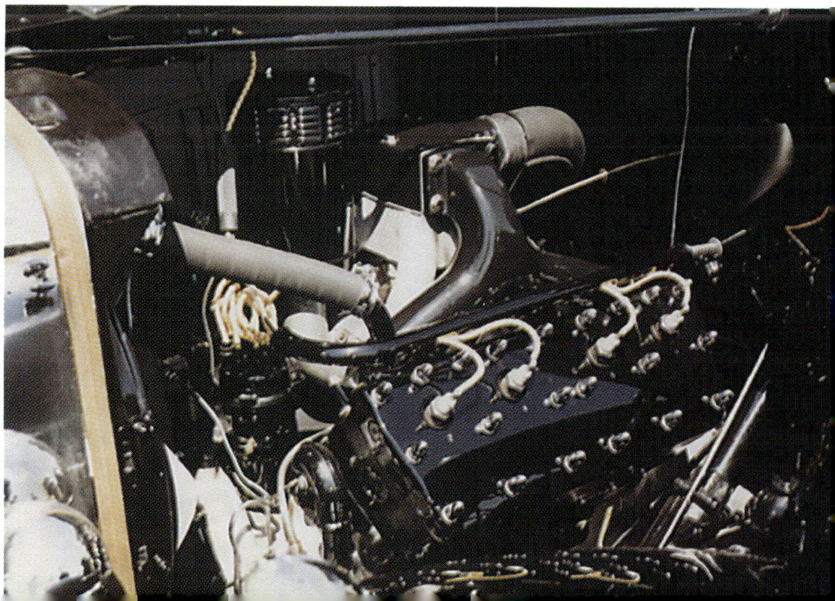

INTERIOR OF THE LA SALLE V-8 FIVE-PASSENGER SEDAN

The exquisite interior of the La Salle 5-passenger Sedan, illustrated here, furnishes eloquent evidence of the thorough custom quality of La Salle's coachwork. The tailored upholstery, offered in three fabric selections, bespeaks luxury. The tasteful appointments gleam like jewels against the silken textiles. Elbow recesses beside broad arm rests, the unusual width of the rear seat, and increased leg room make this a pleasant and restful traveling compartment — no matter how arduous the journey. Other exceptional features are noted in the tapestried arm slings, Fisher No-Draft Individually Controlled Ventilators, door operated dome lights, carpet covered foot rail, and deep pile carpet

In the La Salle Town Coupe, Fisher has contrived a most pleasing union of coupe companionship and sedan capacity. The right front seat tilts forward, permitting easy access to the rear compartment. The trunk — weather-tight and fitted with locks — is exceptionally commodious. Five wire wheels are standard equipment at no additional cost. Illustrated on the 130-inch chassis.

NINETEEN THIRTY-THREE
Series 345-C

The Series 345-C was the recipient of several new styling concepts. While the basic body configurations were 1932, the grille, fenders and hood appeared to be more integrated with the rest of the body. There was a flow and more protective aura surrounding the entire design. A beauty with certain sophistication. Significantly evolutionary to look different, but not radical or revolutionary, which could have turned its loyal traditional customer base off.

A "false" grille totally surrounded the outside of the actual radiator without being tied to the shape of the radiator. This radiator shell concept opened up a whole new vista of front ensemble styling possibilities. For 1933, it incorporated a painted body color with a chrome outline, or it could be ordered completely chromed. The V-type windsplit radiator shell flowed smoothly into the tapered hood. Gone was the LaSalle tiebar arrangement between the headlights, but the headlights were still on stanchions with trumpet horns attached.

Fenders were "skirted." They were intended to help contain any debris thrown out from under the tires. This repeat theme on all four fenders provided a strong image. The flair of the leading edge on each of the front fenders curving gracefully up from the frame was particularly handsome.

Ventilator doors on the side of the hood were horizontal in motif as opposed to the vertical doors in 1932. Headlights were mounted on vertical stanchions to which the horns were attractively attached. It would be the last year for the exterior mounting of the horn trumpets. While a new Goddess and a refined Heron were available for LaSalle in 1933, it was the modernistic Torpedo radiator ornament that was brand new. It would serve LaSalle exclusively through 1940. Its location on the top of the radiator shell instead of the radiator made it non-functional for the first time. It had become an ornament and a symbol. Now the radiator filler neck was hidden under the hood. The hood had to be opened first to gain access for adding fluid. It would also be the last year until 1940 for positioning the parking lights as stand-alones on the top of the front fenders.

Windows were fitted with ventilator panes to control the flow of fresh air through the car, promoted as the "Fisher No-Draft Ventilation." Such ventilator windows were also located in the rear door or the rear window in the sail panel and, for the first time, the windshield did not open.

The double-molded beltline, as in 1932, gave numerous color options in conjunction with the top and fenders. Sidemounted spare tires with covers were available. A five-wheel arrangement with rear-mounted spare was standard. Cadillacs and LaSalles were difficult to distinguish from each other and the family resemblance had merged even more. Seven Fisher-bodied models were available on 130-inch and 136-inch wheelbases, depending upon the body style. Also built were four Fleetwood Town Coupes, one Phaeton and two All-Weather Phaetons.

Sadly, LaSalle experienced the lowest production run in its history or, if 101 export models are counted, its second lowest production run. Economic times were bad and the demand for luxury was almost non-existent, because being rich and having a fine car were not popular images in 1933.

The 1933 sales brochures were fine artistry with exotic color schemes depicted on each model.

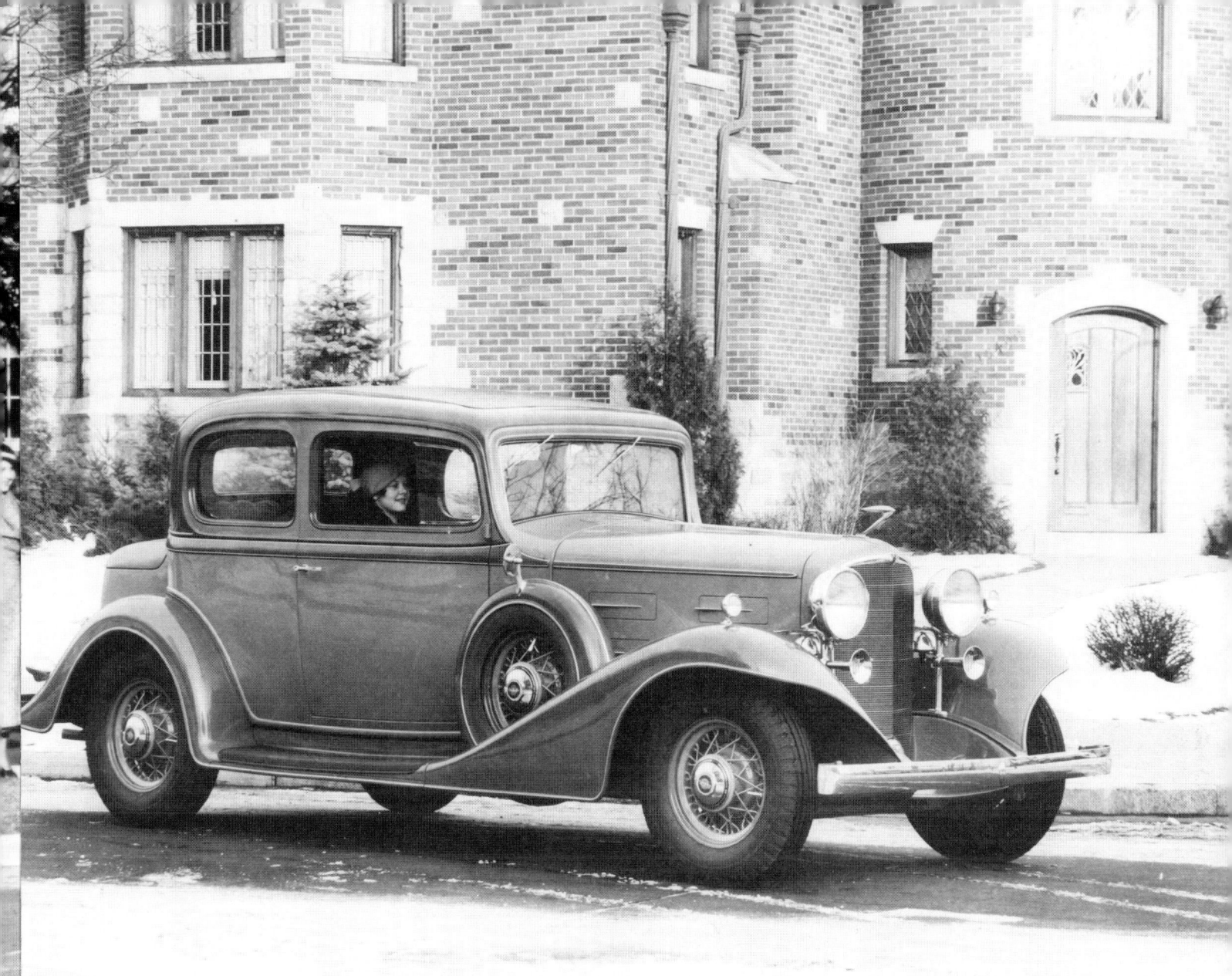

The Series 345-C Town Coupe was graceful with good looks. The outline of the sweeping skirted fenders was tied into the overall design motif with a bright stripe that went completely around the car including the front splash shield, the leading edge of the front fenders, running boards and the rear gasoline tank cover. Five wire wheels and an integral, lockable and weather-tight trunk were attractive features of the often referred to "Victoria Coupe" style. The snow scene outside and the comfort depicted inside the LaSalle were befitting to the new appearance of the 1933 LaSalle.

The 1933 V-8 engine was the same as the one for 1932. The improved Synchro-Mesh transmission continued to provide silent operation in second and third gears.

Other mechanical features were the hydraulic shocks, which were adjustable from the instrument panel by the driver. This feature was called the Full Range Ride Regulator. According to the factory, "This device gives the driver full control over the type of ride, literally transforming all roads into boulevards, regardless of car speed."

A brake assister for the mechanical units was installed similar to the principle used on Cadillac, although not interchangeable. For LaSalle, this would be the only year for the assisters. Hydraulic brakes replaced the mechanical units in 1934.

Controlled free-wheeling was not carried over from 1932, but remained available on order and was fitted to several 1933 cars.

For LaSalle advertising, Cadillac hired the well-known commercial artist, Edwin Wilson. His illustrations graced many of the 1927 advertisements in *The Saturday Evening Post, Ladies' Home Journal,* and others. For 1933, Wilson depicted each automobile as part of the American dream: luxurious, refined, fun, but within reach. Colors were vivid and attractive. Coupled with advertising agency prose, LaSalle was depicted with grace under titles of "THERE'S LOGIC BEHIND YOUR PURCHASE"; "A FINER AND FAR MORE DISTINGUISHED LA SALLE"; "A REAL EXPERIENCE AWAITS YOU *at the Wheel of a New*

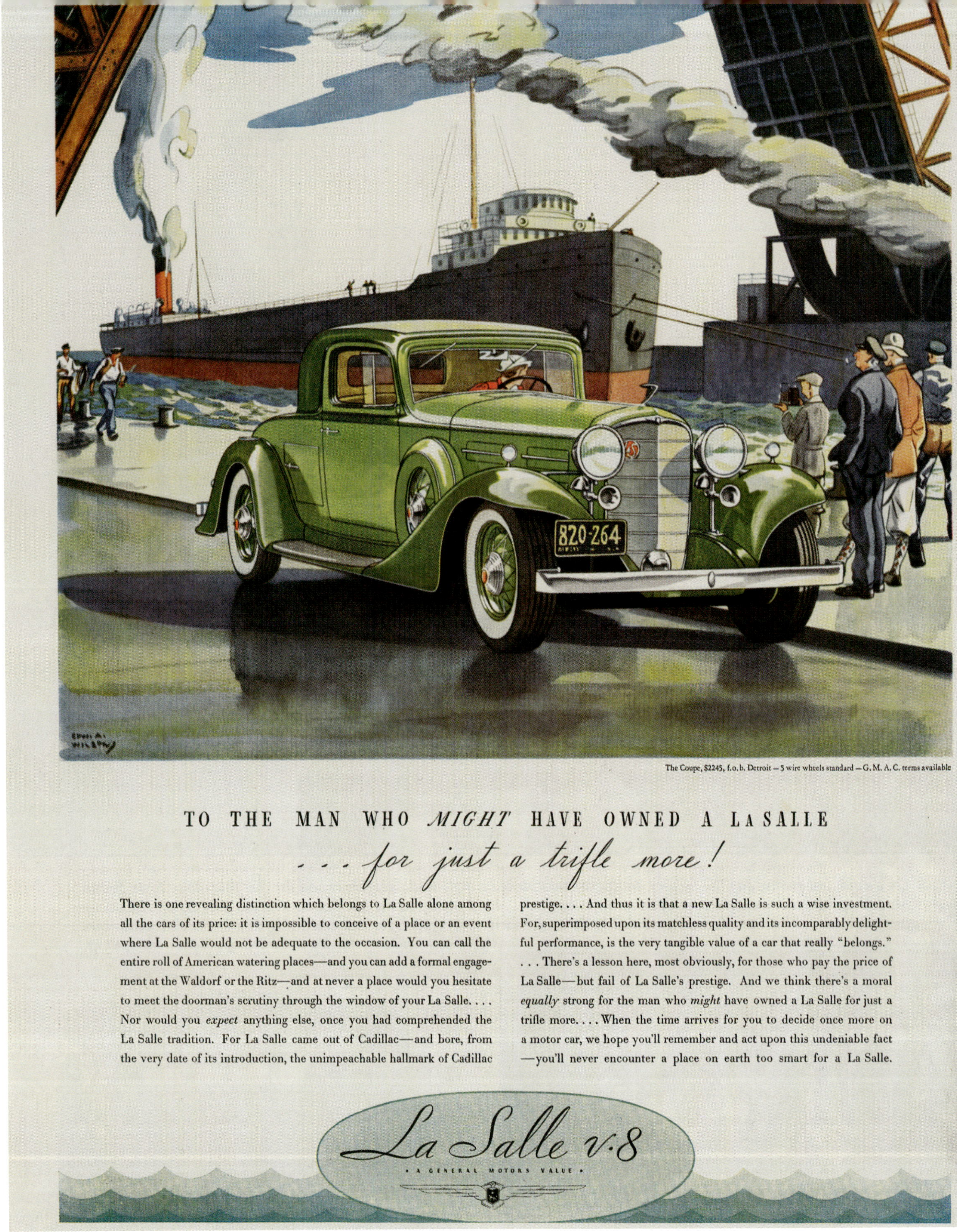
820-264
The Coupe, $2245, f.o.b. Detroit — 5 wire wheels standard — G. M. A. C. terms available
TO THE MAN WHO *MIGHT* HAVE OWNED A LA SALLE
. . . for just a trifle more!
There is one revealing distinction which belongs to La Salle alone among all the cars of its price: it is impossible to conceive of a place or an event where La Salle would not be adequate to the occasion. You can call the entire roll of American watering places—and you can add a formal engagement at the Waldorf or the Ritz—and at never a place would you hesitate to meet the doorman's scrutiny through the window of your La Salle. . . . Nor would you *expect* anything else, once you had comprehended the La Salle tradition. For La Salle came out of Cadillac—and bore, from the very date of its introduction, the unimpeachable hallmark of Cadillac prestige. . . . And thus it is that a new La Salle is such a wise investment. For, superimposed upon its matchless quality and its incomparably delightful performance, is the very tangible value of a car that really "belongs." . . . There's a lesson here, most obviously, for those who pay the price of La Salle—but fail of La Salle's prestige. And we think there's a moral *equally* strong for the man who *might* have owned a La Salle for just a trifle more. . . . When the time arrives for you to decide once more on a motor car, we hope you'll remember and act upon this undeniable fact —you'll never encounter a place on earth too smart for a La Salle.
La Salle V·8
A GENERAL MOTORS VALUE

Above: This artistic representation is typical of the 1933 advertisement series . . . colorful, with presence. Opposite p
top left: The gorgeous Vee'd front ensemble was made possible by a shroud around the radiator. Of note is the new
branding iron badge and that 1933 was the last model for the headlights and the trumpet horns to be mounted on stanch
Top right: The exquisite winged LaSalle crest became more dominant by crowning the contour of the radiator shell ou
Middle: A meticulously restored two-door Coupe with rumble seat is shown with the paint scheme typical of the er

ld be the last time the body was designed to accommodate painting the raised body moldings. Bottom left: A new
lle center hubcap emblem is shown on the last one-sixth turn-on type hubcap. In 1934, LaSalle would use clamp-on
. Bottom right: An early 1933 Fisher no-draft ventilation front vent window. It is unique because the large window
ains the guide for the vent window. This required lowering the big window before the vent window position could be
sted. Later in the year, this was changed to a vertical, permanently stationary receiver for both windows.

THE SATURDAY EVENING POST

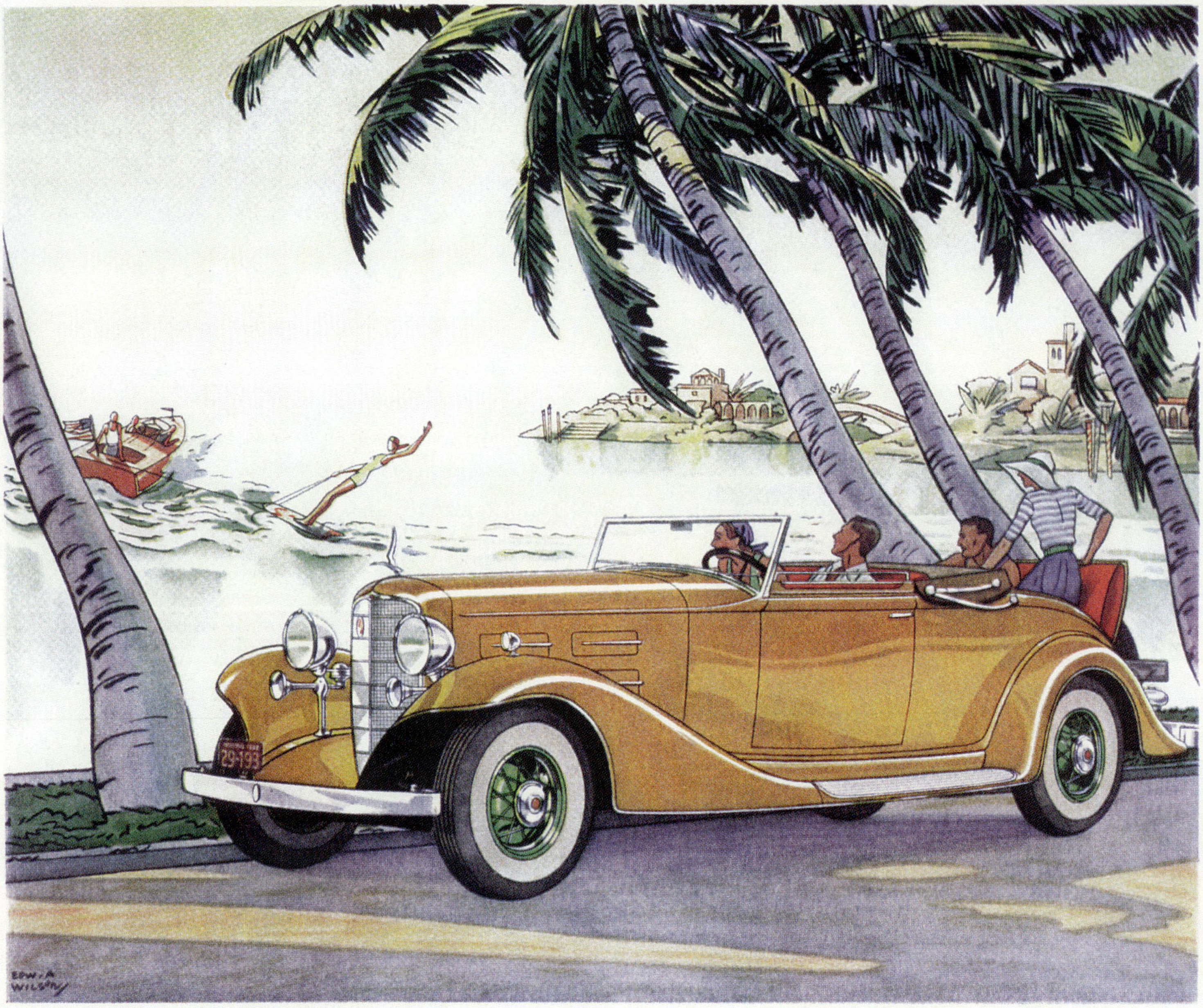
EDW. A WILSON

La Salle Convertible Coupe

THERE'S LOGIC BEHIND YOUR PURCHASE

. . . when you choose a New La Salle

It is certainly difficult to question a man's judgment when he buys a new La Salle, for it is doubtful whether the purchase of *any* commodity can be justified more completely. . . . First of all, La Salle is a reasonably-priced car—with the 5-passenger Sedan now retailing at $2,245 at the factory. Yet, despite this moderate price, La Salle is built by Cadillac, and comes by the full tradition of Cadillac craftsmanship. It is built by the self-same workmen who fashion the Cadillacs. It is designed by the self-same engineers. And it is held to identical limits of precision—and to the same metallurgical specifications. Certainly, to have such a car by Cadillac, at a cost within the immediate range of an ordinary car, is to have one of the biggest values in the modern commercial world. . . . Consider, too, that La Salle is a *prestige* car, in the strictest sense of the word—a car that can take you *anywhere* in a manner befitting the occasion. And, finally, remember that a La Salle retains its youthful appearance and its brilliant performance over such an expanse of time that one is happy to keep it far longer than the average automobile. . . . The sum of these facts makes a reason for ownership so sound that no one can seriously question it. So, when you purchase your next motor car, put *logic* behind your selection—and choose a La Salle.

LA SALLE V·8

A General Motors Value

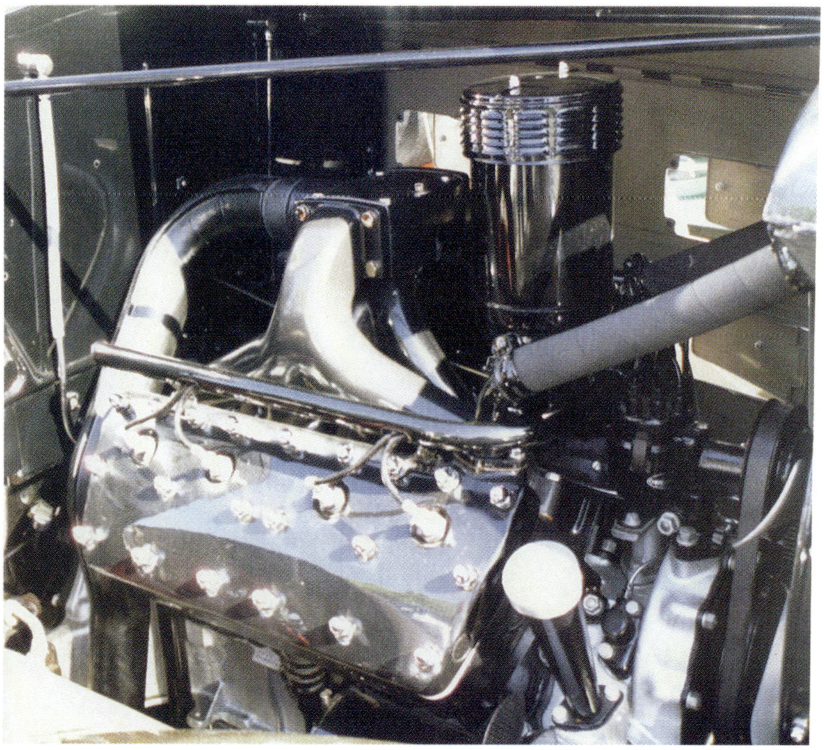

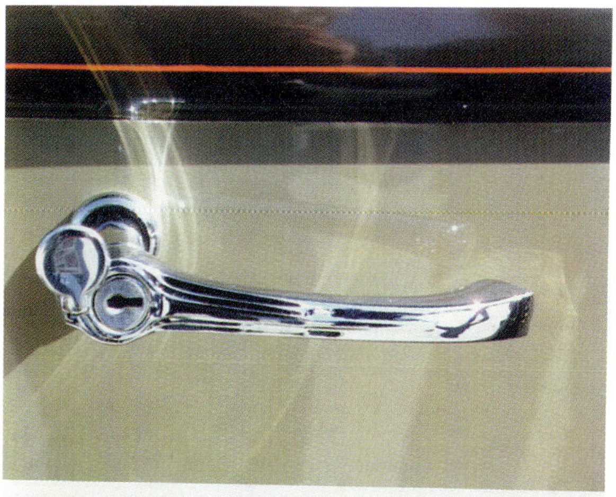

Top left: 1933 would be the last year for the use of a V-8 engine by LaSalle until 1937. Top right: The beautifully-styled door handle on the passenger side boasts its lock cover to keep the dirt and grime out. Middle: This was also the last year for the flat trunk rack. New were the modern straight-line letters for the LaS branding iron design. Below: A restored 345-C Convertible Coupe with the new Torpedo hood ornament, sidemounted spare tires and mirrors, and metal trunk on top of the luggage carrier, shows off its well-proportioned design.

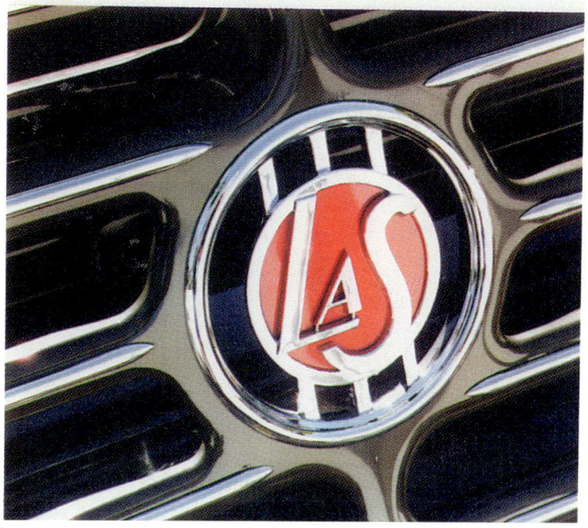

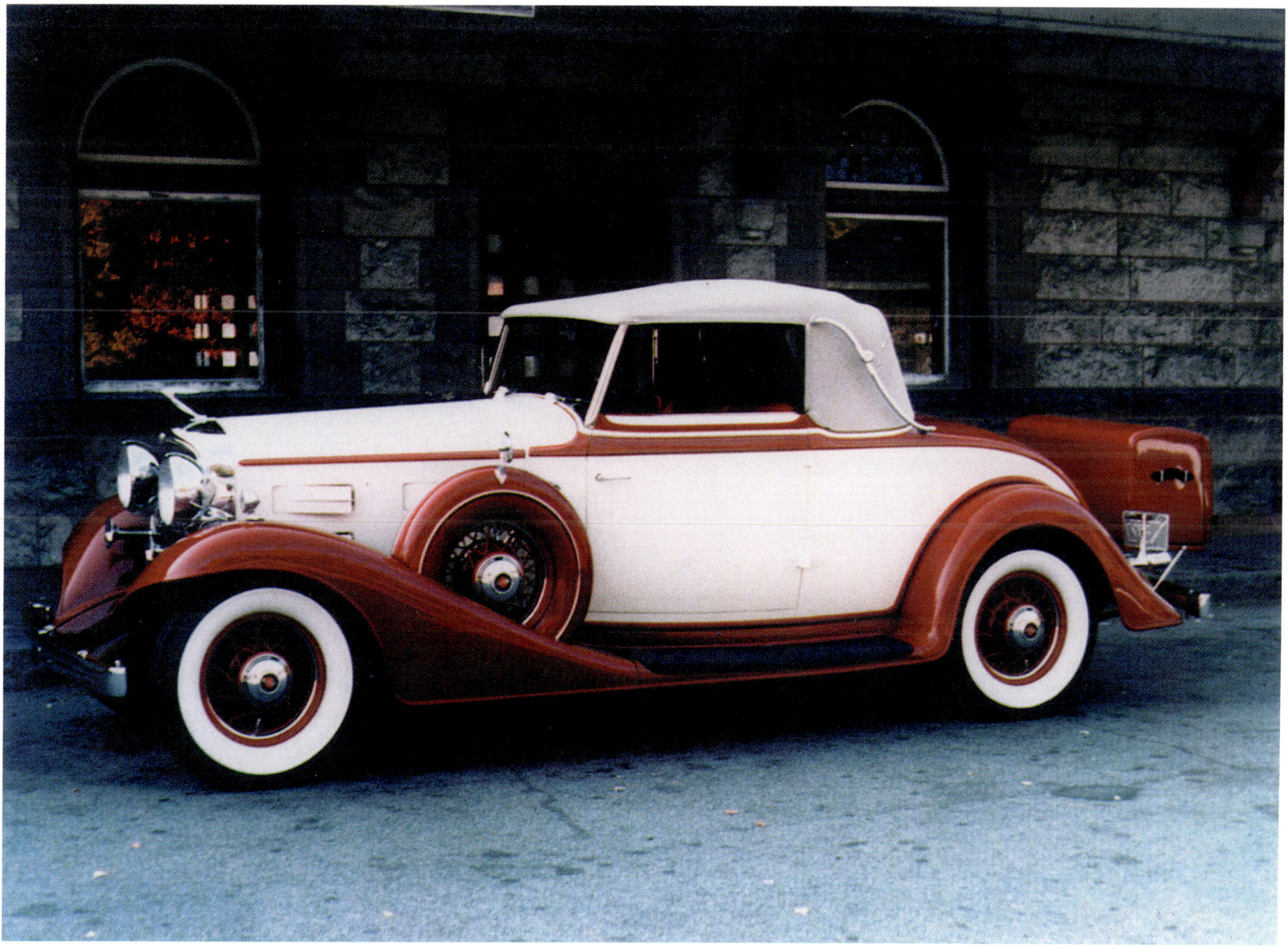

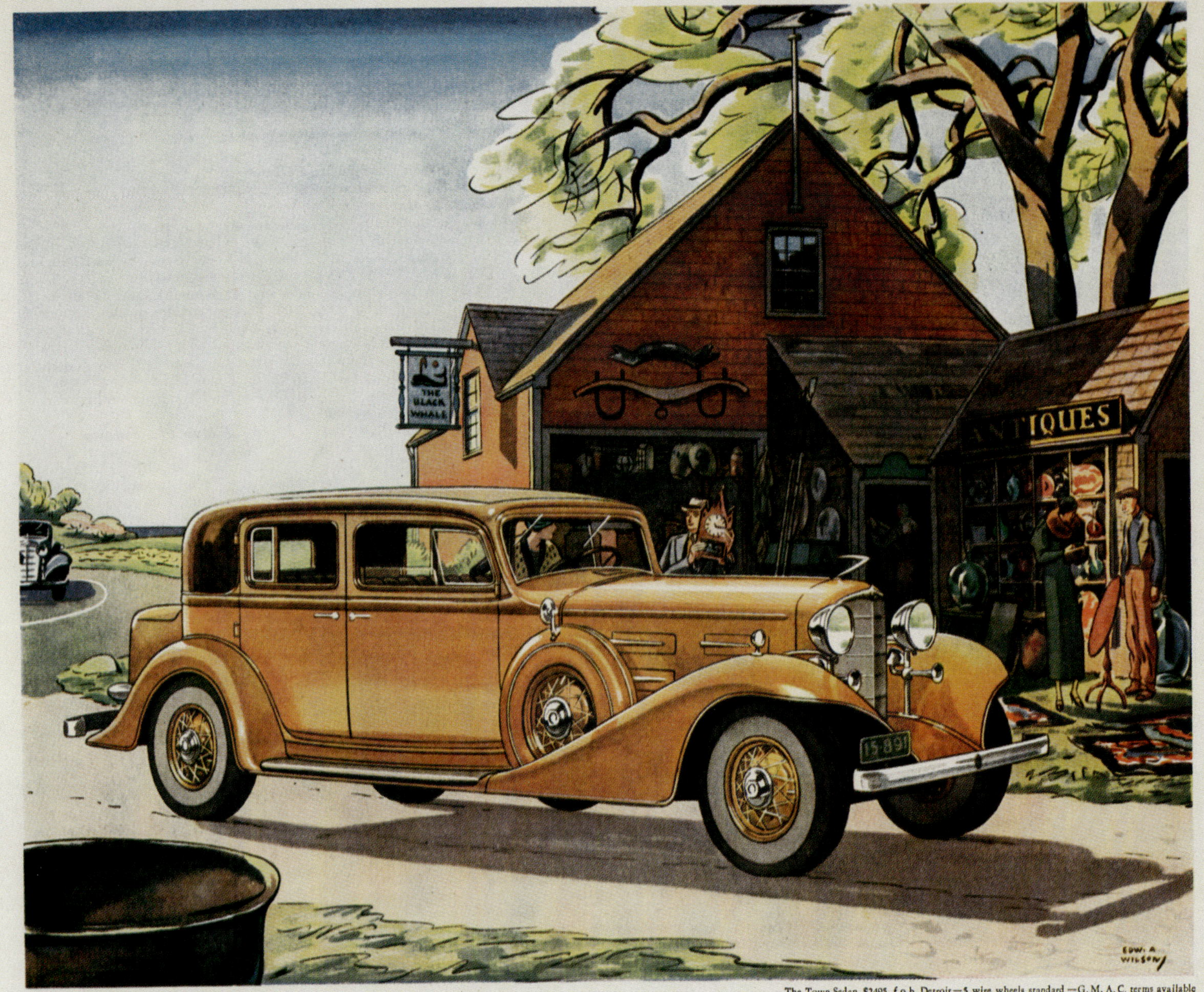
THE BLACK WHALE
15-891
EDW. A. WILSON

The Town Sedan, $2495, f.o.b. Detroit—5 wire wheels standard—G. M. A. C. terms available

A REAL EXPERIENCE AWAITS YOU
at the Wheel of a New La Salle

It is doubtful whether any "first owner" among motorists enjoys quite the same degree of exhilaration as the man who moves up to La Salle. . . . Regardless of the car or cars to which he may have been accustomed, his introduction to La Salle performance is certain to prove a most unusual experience. He will never before have known that an engine could be so smooth—so alertly responsive to the throttle—or so steady in its output of power. He will never have known that a car could be so quiet, in both the body and chassis—so perfectly balanced on the road—so easy to handle—or so completely obedient to its brakes. And he will certainly never have known how *comfortable* a car can be! . . . This, of course, might be expected. For La Salle is built by Cadillac, to the Cadillac ideal—and this makes it a different *kind* of car from anything else around it. . . . If you have been driving lesser cars in the belief you were satisfied, your dealer will surely be glad to arrange to have you drive a La Salle. After thirty minutes behind the wheel, we'll leave the decision to you! . . . La Salle list prices now begin at $2245, f. o. b. Detroit—for the 5-passenger Sedan.

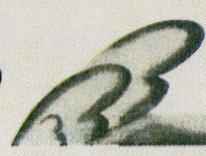

LA SALLE V·8
A General Motors Value

1933 LaSalle Production

<u>Total Production</u>: 3482 automobiles, chassis and commercial chassis.

<u>Serial Numbers</u>: 2000001-2003381 and 3010001-3010103 The Vehicle (engine) serial number is "stamped on the crankcase near the water inlet on the right-hand side."

<u>Chassis Numbers</u>: Start with prefix "20-" and increase from number 20-1. The numbers are not sequential, not consecutive and, for unknown reasons, run as high as 20-3659. Location of chassis unit number is "rear of L.H. side of radiator cross member."

<u>Body Plates</u>: Fisher or Fleetwood job number (e.g., 33-659) and body serial number are on the plate attached to passenger side of the cowl in the engine compartment.

<u>Body Type and Style Numbers</u>:

Body Type	Style No.	Wheelbase	List Price	Production
345-C (LaSalle) Fisher bodies				
2-Pass. Coupe	33-678	130"	$2245.00	154
2-Pass. Convertible Coupe	33-668	130"	$2395.00	146
5-Pass. Town Coupe	33-672	130"	$2395.00	271
5-Pass. Sedan	33-659	130"	$2245.00	1491
5-Pass. Town Sedan	33-652	136"	$2495.00	752
7-Pass. Sedan	33-662	136"	$2495.00	467
7 Pass. Imperial Sedan	33-663	136"	$2645.00	190
Phaeton (Cadillac body)	8-256	136"	$2695.00	1
5-Pass. Coupe (Cadillac body)	8-272	136"	$2695.00	2
All-Weather Phaeton (Cadillac body)	8-273	136"	$3195.00	2
Chassis		130"	$1850.00	1
Chassis		136"	$1900.00	1
345-C (LaSalle) Fleetwood bodies				
5-Pass. Town Coupe	8-222	136"	Not listed	4
			Total	3482

Standard Color Options

Cadillac-LaSalle 1933 Features of Construction indicates that the cars would be offered in thirteen standard colors. No list of standard colors could be located. Only eleven apparently standard (not special order) colors are obvious from examination of the build sheets.

Color name	Dupont #	Color name	Dupont #
Black	20488	Black/Radium Blue	22260
Black Classic Blue	22290	Arlington Gray/Quebec Gray	20175/20179
Black/Glenbrook Green	23455	Bedell Green/Carolina Green	20385/20361
Black/Labrador Grey	20195	English Gray/Ludington Green	21167/23459
Black/Marshall Maroon	20693	Ravenswood Brown/Riviera Beige	28845/28898
Black/Maylene Maroon	20637		

Two-tone cars were typically painted with the top, rear quarter panels, moulding, window offsets or door saddles, fender set and chassis in the first color listed; upper and lower body panels in the second color.

Trim Options

<u>Closed Bodies</u>:
22 T 132 Gray Whipcord
24 T 132 Taupe (Blue Tan) Striped Broadcloth
26 T 132 Tan Plain Broadcloth

<u>Convertible Bodies</u>:
9 T 1331 Brown Leather
10 T 1331 Green Leather
11 T 1331 Black Leather
12 T 1331 Blue Gray Leather

Convertible top: 1 T 1532, Tan with tan lining (standard); 7 T 1533 Blue Gray (optional)
"Special upholstery material may be specified at extra charge."

Accessories

<u>Group Equipment and Extras</u>:
Group No. 1 - (for cars with 5 wheels) - Black metal tire cover and protection bar, hinge mirror, moto-pack,
  cowl ventilator screen $ 40.00
Group No. 1A - Same as Group No. 1 with metal tire cover in color to match fender set $ 42.50
Group No. 2 - (for cars with 6 wheels) - 2 black metal tire covers and mirrors, moto-pack, cowl ventilator screen $ 66.50
Group No. 2A - same as Group No. 2 with tire covers in color to match fender set $ 71.50
Colored fender set and chassis $ 25.00
Standard Service Contract $110.00

<u>Suggested Minimum Equipment - Factory Installation</u>:

For Cars with 5 Wire Wheels
  Spare tire and tube (Distributor installation)
  Torpedo radiator ornament $20.00
  License frames $ 7.00

For Cars with 6 Wire Wheels
  Fenderwells, 2 spare wheels and tires and
    folding trunk rack $110.00
  Torpedo radiator ornament $ 20.00
  License frames $ 7.00

Accessories (All prices include installation):

Electric curtain control	$ 13.50	
Radio	$ 89.50	
Hot air heater (single register)	$ 31.50	
Hot air heater (double register)	$ 34.50	
Chromium wheel discs, each	$ 9.50	
Spot light	$ 37.50	
Trunks	$100.00 to 180.00	
Robe	$ 45.00	

Standard Equipment:
Five wire wheels; tire size 7.00 X 17"
U.S. Royal black sidewall tires
U.S. Royal white sidewall tires $3.00 extra per tire
High Compression cylinder heads

Research Methodology: Microfiche copies of the individual Shipping Department records of the as-built configuration of each serial number were viewed, starting at the highest serial number and working backwards, to determine the highest body serial number of each body style. Each serial number record sheet was viewed and recorded with body style and body number. No attempt was made to construct cross reference lists of body numbers with corresponding engine numbers to verify that all body numbers were used in actual production.

Notes on research findings:

1. The standard body style and job number offerings for 1933 were listed in the *Cadillac-LaSalle 1933 Features of Construction* book (undated) and subsequently in the August 1933 supplement to the 1932 Cadillac-LaSalle Shop Manual. *Features of Construction* also notes that "Fleetwood Bodies are available on the LaSalle chassis. Prices on application." Factory records indicate that the 1933 LaSalle was introduced on January 3, 1933. A notebook in the Cadillac Historical Collection archives, titled "Fleetwood Extra Charges," contains a carbon copy of a single sheet dated January 25, 1933, that is labeled "Miscellaneous Prices." The sheet includes the following LaSalle special body offerings:

345-C LaSalle

130" W.B.	Roadster	(8-155)	$2545	136" W.B.	5-Pass. Coupe	(8-272)	$2695
	Conv. 5-P. Coupe	(5285)	3900		Phaeton	(8-256)	2695
					Special Phaeton	(8-280)	2795
					Sport Phaeton	(8-279)	2945
					A.W. Phaeton	(8-273)	3195

These special offerings are particularly interesting - all of them were Cadillac body styles. The "Conv. 5-P. Coupe (5285)" style number is thought to be a typographical error. A style 5585 Fleetwood 5-pass. Convertible Coupe was offered on the 149" W.B 1933 V-16 chassis. The others listed above were Fisher bodies offered as follows:

Style	Year	Application
8-155	1932/33	134" W.B. V-8, V-12; 143" W.B. V-16
8-272	1932/32	140" W.B. V-8, V-12
8-256	1932/33	140" W.B. V-8, V-12; 149" W.B. V-16
8-280	1932	140" W.B. V-8, V-12; 149" W.B. V-16
8-279	1932	140" W.B. V-8, V-12; 149" W.B. V-16
8-273	1932/33	140" W.B. V-8, V-12; 149" W.B. V-16

In addition to the cars in the "Miscellaneous Prices" list, a sheet-by-sheet examination reveals that four "LaSalle 345-C 136" Fleetwood Town Coupe" (5-Pass.) cars were built with the style 8-222 bodies offered only in 1932 on the 140" W.B. V-8, V-12 and 149" W.B. V-16 Cadillacs. One of the bodies was subsequently "Dismounted" and a LaSalle style 652 Fisher Town Sedan body fitted to the chassis.

The LaSalle offerings listed above do not appear in any known sales literature nor in the Master Parts List "Chart of body types, style or job numbers and wheelbase." There is no indication on any of the sheets as to what body modifications were done to harmonize the Cadillac bodies with LaSalle hoods, adapt to the LaSalle wheelbases, etc. The sheets do indicate body numbers from the stock Cadillac sequence.

2. Early in the production run (serial #2000394, 0419 and 0449), three 136" chassis were shipped to General Motors of Canada, Ltd., at Oshawa, Ontario. These records were annotated "Use chassis built for 662 #45," etc. Notes indicated "Job 662 chassis parts, include all instruments, fenderwells, black metal tire covers," etc. They are assumed to have been assembled into complete cars, as was the case in other production years. The cars are included in the domestic production numbers with the respective body numbers. There is no indication of the distribution of the Canadian cars.

3. All cars shipped from the factory to California were equipped with "Ruby Centered Taillights" as opposed to the standard blue dot taillights. Blue dot taillights were illegal in California.

4. Demountable wood (often referred to as artillery) wheels were last offered as an option on LaSalles in the 1933 model year. A mere 15 cars were equipped with the wood wheels. An era had passed - the wood wheels were out of style with the new skirted fenders and the beginning of streamlining.

5. The 1933 record sheets do not have a "Purchaser" block. A very small number, principally "Fisher Order" cars, are annotated with the buyer's name.

6. Commercial Chassis: Distinctly commercial chassis were yet to become an important part of the LaSalle production. A single 130" wheelbase chassis (serial 2001615) was shipped to the A. J. Miller Co., Bellefontaine, Ohio, charged to Cadillac Providence Co., Providence, Rhode Island, and tagged "Morrone Brothers." This chassis was equipped with a closed car cowl, fenderwells and six wire wheels.

7. <u>Passenger Car Chassis</u>: A single 136" wheelbase chassis (serial 301003) equipped with fenders in prime, fenderwells and wire wheels, low compression heads and a power clutch was shipped to General Motors Export in Berlin, Germany. There is no indication of the ultimate body style and body builder.

8. <u>Export Cars</u>: General Motors Export, General Sales Department, sold LaSalle cars around the world as the Series 355-CX Cadillac-LaSalle (see section titled The Mystery Cars). For some inexplicable reason, five additional standard LaSalles were exported as follows:

    Style 663 7-Pass. Imperial Sedan - two cars to Antwerp, Belgium
    Style 663 7-Pass. Imperial Sedan - two cars to Osaka, Japan
    Style 652 5-Pass. Town Sedan - one car to São Paulo, Brazil

9. <u>World's Fair Cars</u>: LaSalle was represented at the 1933 World's Fair in Chicago by six specially prepared closed body cars, all done in non-standard paint schemes:

    5-Pass. Town Sedan - Cinnebar Red (24650798) with six Nasturtium (28950433) wire wheels
    5-Pass. Town Sedan - Peasant Blue (24650654) with six Alpine Blue (24650284) wire wheels
    5-Pass. Sedan - Hawthorne Green (23355) with five Rhapsody Green (23461) wire wheels
    5-Pass. Town Coupe - Brainard Blue (24650487) with five Brainard Blue Lt. (24650631) wire wheels
    5-Pass. Town Coupe - Storm Cloud Blue (22368) with six stainless steel spoke wire wheels
    2-Pass. Coupe - India Green Deep (23375) with five Tokio Ivory (20722) wire wheels

10. <u>Factory Installed Accessories</u>: The following accessories were installed by the factory on one or more cars. Part/Accessory numbers are listed where they could be determined:

Accessory	Number	Accessory	Number
Automatic Clutch Control	2001389	Lorraine Spotlight (closed car)	891531
Black Metal Tire Covers	A-875,6	L.C. Cylinder Heads (Low Compression)	
Black Metal Tire Cover (rear spare)	A-877	Moto Pack	A-945
Black Metal Tire Covers (w/mirrors)	A-981,2	Protection Bar (rear spare tire)	891697
Bumper Fender Guards		Radio	M10/26
Cadillac Hot Air Heater, single register	877641	Ring Shroud on fan	
Cadillac Hot Air Heater, dual register	877642	Ruby Centered Taillights (California cars)	1844987
Cadillac Radio	A-916	Sea Breeze Seat Covers	
Chrome Radiator Shell		Seat Covers, Laidlaw	A-100
Chrome Trim Rings		Stainless Steel Wire Wheels	890980
Chromium Hood Ports		Standard Radio	A-1035
Chromium Wheel Discs	891728	Tire Chains	A-641
Cowl Screen	892404	Tire Pump, transmission mounted	891925
Duplex Pilot Rays	A-976	Tires	
Electric Clock		Firestone whitewalls	
Electric (rear) curtain control	A-984	Goodyear blackwalls	
Heron Ornament	A-965	Royal whitewalls	
H.H.C. Cylinder Heads (High High Compression)		Torpedo Ornament	A-975
Hinge Mirror	891623	Town Sedan Case Assembly	
Hot Water Heater		2 suitcases, 1 hat box	A-854
Imperial Radio	A-1032	Trunk	85059 and 892356
Interior Sun Visor (R.H. side)	027064	Trunk	1098280
Jacques Rayon Slip On Seat Covers		Trunk (2 suitcases and hat box)	A-912
License Frames	A-974	Trunk (3 cases and hat box)	1098279

Note: It is unclear that any production cars were actually equipped with the electric rear curtain control. Many early build sheets indicate "Curtain Control." The build sheets, however, were typed before the car was assembled. The production "Checkers" made hand written notes and check marks on the sheets and entered component serial numbers by hand. Most are hand annotated "B.O." (back ordered). After serial 2000766, the sheets indicate "Cancelled." The archive copy of the Dealer's Accessory Price List issued December 15, 1932, is annotated "Discontinued."

11. None of the body styles were assembled in a straight body order sequence. Fisher Order cars and non-standard paint color cars were generally substantially out of order due to the time required to make alterations.

First car built in each standard body series:	Last car built:
33-678 serial 2000002, body 1	serial 2003070, body 153
33-668 serial 2000085, body 1	serial 2003071, body 146
33-672 serial 2000041, body 3	serial 2003305, body 238
33-659 serial 2000001, body 4	serial 2003374, body 1471
33-652 serial 2000073, body 9	serial 2003381, body 748
33-662 serial 2000036, body 3	serial 2003379, body 458
33-663 serial 2000067, body 2	serial 2003310, body 186

The Mystery Cars

During the fourteen years of LaSalle production, Cadillac and LaSalle cars were identified by distinctive serial number groups that differentiated between each model year and car series. Thus, a 1933 Cadillac Series 355-C V-8 had a serial number beginning with 300----. A 1933 LaSalle Series 345-C V-8 had a serial number beginning with 200----. Both the Cadillac and the LaSalle shared the same 353 cubic inch engine and mechanicals. The Cadillac was offered in 134" and 140" wheelbases. The LaSalle is listed in factory literature as available only in 130" and 136" wheelbases.

A very small group of 103 cars was designated as Series 355-CX and assigned serial numbers 3010001 through 3010103. The 355-C series number and 301---- serial number would seem to indicate that these cars were Cadillacs. The X means that these were export cars. This group of cars has long been listed as Cadillacs in the Cadillac-LaSalle Club, Inc., listing of vehicle production.

What was different about these cars that caused them to have a unique series number and a distinct set of serial numbers? Were they Cadillacs or were they really LaSalles? Carl L. Steig, past president of the Cadillac-LaSalle Club, Inc., had briefly studied the build sheets, determined that the cars had LaSalle bodies and classified them as Cadillacs with LaSalle bodies. That would satisfy the apparent Cadillac series and serial number assignments.

However, original factory "Model Year Production By Series" summaries list a total of 3,482 LaSalle cars built in the 1933 model year. The highest serial number for an apparently regular production LaSalle is 20003381; a total of 3381 cars was built. The production difference of 101 units would seem to indicate that Cadillac Motor Car Company considered the 355-CX cars to be LaSalles. Other than the individual car record sheets, there is nothing in the Cadillac Motor Car Company archives about the Series 355-CX cars.

A sheet-by-sheet analysis of the mystery car records revealed some clues about these cars:

1. The records are not build sheets in the usual sense. They are all hand written in the same penmanship seen on export sheets in 1933 and other years. All are on export control order forms and are missing the check marks found on a regular build sheet. Typical production build sheets were typed before the cars were assembled. The "Checkers" made hand written notes and check marks on the sheets and entered the component serial numbers by hand. The mystery car sheets do not have the "Checked" and "Double Checked" signatures nor the "Month/Period/Number" information at the top of the sheet. Very few of the mystery sheets have the paint number descriptions, only the paint color name - another sure sign that the sheets are not build sheets.

2. Unit Assembly Numbers. Various components, including the engines, were serial numbered at the time of manufacture. During vehicle assembly, the engine was also stamped with the vehicle serial number. Both Cadillac and LaSalle in 1933 had unit engine numbers beginning with "30-." LaSalle chassis numbers began with "20-"; Cadillac chassis began with "30-." LaSalle steering gear numbers began with "11-"; Cadillac steering gear began with "12-."
   Serial 3010001 is shown as a "355-C.X. Special." The 7-Pass. Imperial Sedan style #663, steering gear 11-3883 and chassis 20-444 are all clearly LaSalle identifiers.
   Serial 3010003 is shown as a "355-C.X.," but is a 136" chassis with fender set that was shipped to Berlin. It can only be a LaSalle; Cadillac chassis were 134" and 140" wheelbase. The chassis number, 20-722, is also a LaSalle number.
   Listing the chassis numbers reveals that 89 have a LaSalle number and 12 have a Cadillac number. Multiple sheets have the number changed from "30-" to "20-." The steering gear numbers are LaSalle. All export sheets for 1933 Cadillac and LaSalle cars are in the same handwriting. Presumably the writer was accustomed to writing the more frequent Cadillac numbers and made transcription errors. Four successive vehicle numbers illustrate the point: chassis 20-3167, 30-3168, 30-3166 and 20-3183. All are from the LaSalle number sequence. Two are recorded as Cadillac chassis (different wheelbase).

3. Destination. If they were LaSalles, did they have special serial numbers because these were the only 1933 LaSalles that were exported? No, there were five regular LaSalle cars exported: Two to Antwerp, Belgium; two to Osaka, Japan; and one to São Paulo, Brazil. Were these cars special because they were right hand drive exports? No, only nine were right hand drive. Of the 103 mystery serial numbers, two record sheets are missing. The other units were shipped as follows:

Antwerp, Belgium	78	Osaka, Japan	3
Barcelona, Spain	2	Port Elizabeth, South Africa	3
Batavia, Java	1	San Juan, Puerto Rico	1
Bombay, India	1	Shanghai, China	7
Berlin, Germany	2	Stockholm, Sweden	1
Caracas, Venezuela	2		

4. Body Styles. Was there something special about the bodies? If so, the record sheets do not show it. Only four of the seven standard body styles were included: 652 5-Pass. Town Sedan, 659 5-Pass. Sedan, 662 7-Pass. Sedan, 663 7-Pass. Imperial Sedan. Interestingly, 89 of the units indicated a "Heron" hood ornament which is a normal Cadillac item but an available LaSalle option.

The true identity of the mystery cars was finally resolved quite by accident in July of 1998. Cadillac-LaSalle Club, Inc., member Paul Ayres of Farmington Hills, Michigan, purchased a selection of original literature for reference in restoring a newly-acquired 1933 Cadillac Convertible Coupe. Included was a piece dated March 8, 1933, issued by General Motors Export, General Sales Department, Service Division, entitled "1933 Cadillac Specifications." The bottom of the front page tells it all: "Cadillac-LaSalle V-8, Series 355-CX is available for Export only - known as LaSalle in the United States."

For forty years, members of the Cadillac-LaSalle Club, Inc., have patiently corrected people for referring to a particular car as a "Cadillac LaSalle," explaining that the car was made by Cadillac but is distinctly a LaSalle! It turns out that the marketers actually linked the two names to enhance export sales during the 1933 model year.

GENERAL MOTORS EXPORT
GENERAL SALES DEPARTMENT
SERVICE DIVISION

To be filed in Service Dept.

1933 CADILLAC SPECIFICATIONS

- V-8 Cadillac-LaSalle – Series 355-CX
- V-8 Cadillac – Series 355-C
- V-12 Cadillac – Series 370-C
- V-16 Cadillac – Series 452-C

General Motors Export reserves the right to make changes in Specifications and Equipment or add improvements at any time without incurring any obligation to install the same on cars previously dispatched.

Dispatched from DETROIT, Michigan. Left hand drive standard. Right hand drive available at extra charge except as covered by note under "Chassis Available" page #3.

MODELS AVAILABLE – V-8 and V-12
(As indicated by "X")

BODY BY FISHER	355-CX V-8 130" W.B.	355-C V-8 134" W.B.	370-C V-12 134" W.B.
2 Pass. Roadster (Dickey Seat)	-		
2 Pass. Convertible Coupe (Dickey Seat)	x	x	x
2 Pass. Coupe (Dickey Seat)	x	x	x
5 Pass. Town Coupe	x	x	x
5 Pass. Sedan	x	x	x
	136" W.B.	140" W.B.	140" W.B.
5 Pass. Coupe	-	-	-
5 Pass. Sedan	x	x	x
5 Pass. Town Sedan	x	x	x
7 Pass. Sedan	-	x	x
7 Pass. Imperial Sedan	-	x.	x
5 Pass. Phaeton	-	x	x
5 Pass. All Weather Phaeton			x
BODY BY FLEETWOOD			
5 Pass. Sedan	-	x	x
7 Pass. Sedan	-	x	x
7 Pass. Limousine	-	x	x
5 Pass. Town Cabriolet (Leather Back-Opera Seats)		x	x
7 Pass. Town Cabriolet (Leather Back)		x	x
7 Pass. Limousine Brougham (Metal Back)		x	x

Cadillac-LaSalle V-8, Series 355-CX is available for Export only – known as LaSalle in the United States.

Issued: March 8, 1933.

CADILLAC-LASALLE 355-CX
Passenger Chassis – 130" and 136" Wheelbase.

CADILLAC 355-C and 370-C
Passenger Chassis – 134" and 140" Wheelbase.
Commercial Chassis – 156" Wheelbase.

CADILLAC 452-C
Passenger Chassis – 149" Wheelbase

Note:- The following wheelbases are not available in Right Hand Drive, either as Chassis or complete cars.

- 130" Series 355-CX
- 134" Series 370-C
- 156" Series 355-C and 370-C

NO EXTRA CHARGE (UNLESS OTHERWISE SPECIFIED)

Fuel Gauge – Calibrated Imperial Gallons or Litres.

Rear Axle Ratio –

All 5 and 7 Passenger Closed Cars and All Weather Phaetons.

	355-CX and 355-C	370-C	452-C
Standard	4.60 to 1	4.80 to 1	4.64 to 1
Optional	4.36 to 1	4.60 to 1	4.31 to 1

All other models except Commercial Chassis.

	355-CX and 355-C	370-C	452-C
Standard	4.36 to 1	4.60 to 1	4.31 to 1
Optional	4.60 to 1	4.80 to 1	4.64 to 1

Commercial 156" Chassis – 355-C and 370-C
Standard   4.64 to 1   – no option.

452-C Series only.

ACCESSORY FACTS

Published in the interest of Accessory Sales
by Cadillac Motor Car Company, Detroit, Michigan

Volume 3   NOVEMBER-DECEMBER, 1932   Numbers 11 and 12

NEW ORNAMENTS—A NEW ORNAMENT POLICY FOR 1933

WITH the showing of the new Cadillacs and LaSalles for 1933 three new and distinctive radiator ornaments will be announced. They are a new Goddess, a refined Heron, and a new Torpedo ornament—distinctively styled in pace with the distinguished beauty of the new cars.

The new Goddess is one of the most, if not the most, beautiful ornaments ever created for a motor car—and as expected—is created for the exclusive adornment of the new custom Cadillac V-Sixteen. Its rare beauty and heavy gold plate finish will identify the new V-Sixteen to the most casual observer.

The revised Heron ornament is executed in the modernistic trend of styling. Its smooth, gently curved surfaces finished in bright chromium make it symbolic of all that Cadillac stands for. It was developed especially for the new Cadillac V-Eight and V-Twelve.

The new Torpedo—an addition to the line—is quite frankly modernistic. When seen in motion on the car its rugged, powerful form

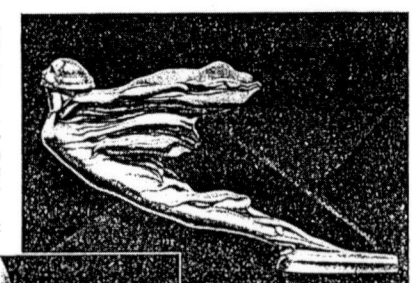

THE GODDESS

seems to sharply cleave the air. As the new LaSalle is styled to appeal to the younger smart set—so is this ornament designed to accentuate that appeal. It was conceived to match those characteristics of this outstanding new LaSalle.

It is the belief of the management that creating an ornament specifically for a particular model and con-

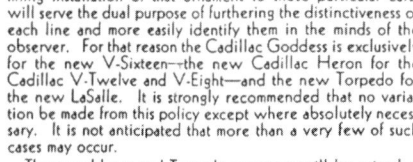

THE HERON

fining installation of that ornament to those particular cars, will serve the dual purpose of furthering the distinctiveness of each line and more easily identify them in the minds of the observer. For that reason the Cadillac Goddess is exclusively for the new V-Sixteen—the new Cadillac Heron for the Cadillac V-Twelve and V-Eight—and the new Torpedo for the new LaSalle. It is strongly recommended that no variation be made from this policy except where absolutely necessary. It is not anticipated that more than a very few of such cases may occur.

The new Heron and Torpedo ornament will be priced at $20.00 the same as before.

THE TORPEDO

EDITORIAL

Within a few days the year 1932 will be a matter of history and 1933 will begin with a clean sheet but a bad handicap.

Four times at this season we have turned our faces forward with optimism, anticipating a return of business volume which would mean prosperity. At this period in 1929 we were certain that in the year 1930 we would recuperate the losses of 1929. At the end of that year we confidently looked to 1931 to change the downward trend which had continued unchecked all through 1930. At the beginning of 1932 we once again turned a sober but still confident front to the future and said that the coming year would mark the beginning of a new era of progress greater than ever before. But 1932 as we now know, continued to reflect the declining trend of business begun those three and a half weary years before.

Some of us no doubt find it hard today to look forward again to a new year with a feeling of security. But sober reflection makes us realize that something did happen in 1932 which justifies our hopes for 1933. The lowest ebb of business was reached in August this year. Since that time a leveling off of the business curve has occurred with an ever so slight upward turn, but nevertheless a definite upward trend. It is not practical for us in our every day life to sift the mass of printed matter and varying public opinion on the subject and feel the true pulse of the business world. Statistics however have evidenced that such a change has occurred.

The second justification for confidence in 1933 is the result of the national election recently completed. Whether you be Republican or Democrat—happy over the results of that election or not—one fact remains that must be soberly considered. The most important element in a return to more normal business in the markets of the nation is the confidence of the people that compose that market. In November of 1932 the people in no doubtful manner voiced their will for a change in governing party. Shortly after 1933 is under way that change will actually be accomplished, and it must of necessity mean a more confident attitude of the people—because that change was their desire and they have achieved their desire.

So let us bear these two great facts in mind and realize that while 1933 cannot miraculously return to us the volume of business received in the peak years, still it seemingly must mark the beginning of a return to a profitable and more stable business. That we will go forward and not still farther downward—that with sincere hard work and straight thinking—we can make our personal 1933 a year of progress—and one which we will enjoy remembering.

Above left: Brand new for 1933 was the Torpedo radiator ornament, a motif continued for the next seven model years. The Goddess and Heron were also available. What a choice for only $20. Above right: This editorial is worth reading as it reflects the era fraught with the effects of the 1929 stock market crash . . . no one at Cadillac used the word Depression. The next four pages are from the large deluxe sales brochure and depict the accessories available and mechanical features in handsome black and white illustrations.

1933 CADILLAC SPECIFICATIONS
SERIES 355-CX AND 355-C

CONDENSED SPECIFICATIONS

Wheelbase		
Cadillac 355-CX	130" and 136"	(3.302 m. & 3.454 m.)
Cadillac 355-C	134" and 140"	(3.404 m. & 3.556 m.)
Number of Cylinders	8	
Bore	3-3/8"	(85.72 m/m.)
Stroke	4-15/16"	(125.41 m/m.)
Piston Displacement	353 Cu. In.	(5.78 Lts.)
S.A.E. or R.A.C. Rating	36.4 H.P.	
Brake Horse Power	115 H.P. at 3000 R.P.M.	
Compression Ratio -	See page #6	
Fuel Tank Capacity	30 Gals.	(113.55 Lts.)
Oil System Capacity Refill	8 Qts.	(7.57 Lts.)
Transmission Lubricant Capacity	2-1/4 Qts.	(2.13 Lts.)
Rear Axle Lubricant Capacity	3 Qts.	(2.84 Lts.)
Cooling System Capacity	6-1/2 Gals.	(24.60 Lts.)
Wheels Diameter	17"	(.432 m.)
Rim Size	17 X 4.15	
Tires	7.00-17 - 6 Ply	
Tire Pressure - Front and Rear	40 Lbs. per Sq. In.	(2.81 Kgs. per Sq.Cm.)
Total Braking Area	238 Sq. In.	(1536 Sq.Cm.)
Tread - Front	59-7/8"	(1.52 m.)
Tread - Rear	61"	(1.55 m.)
Road Clearance Front Axle	8-1/8"	(.206 m.)
Road Clearance Rear Axle	7-5/8"	(.194 m.)
Rear Axle Ratio	See page #5	

Issued: March 8, 1933.

AUXILIARY EQUIPMENT

Typical Cadillac Auxiliary Equipment available to fulfill every individual preference

RADIO—brings the world to your finger tips—tone, distance, and volume comparable to the finest home radio performance. Compact, all electric. Factory installed when specified on order.

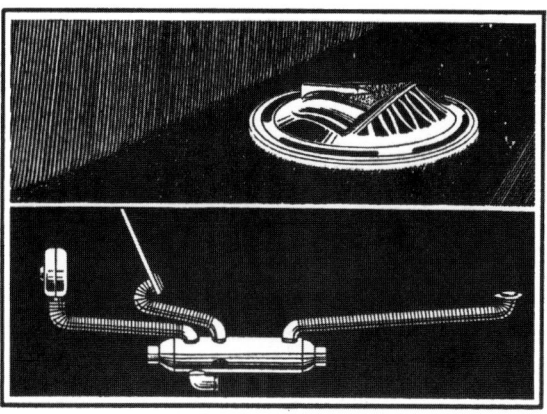

HEATER—only this new hot air type is engineered to co-ordinate with the new Fisher Ventilating System. A quiet power blower forces fresh, odorless, heated air to every corner of the car.

WHEEL DISCS—bright chrome steel shells snugly fitted to standard wire wheels—add dash to the smartest sport car—distinction to the most luxurious limousine. Removable at will.

TRUNKS—a touring necessity splendidly engineered. Steel outer construction, lined with wood. Dust and water-proof. Cases of various sizes and leathers to meet personal requirements.

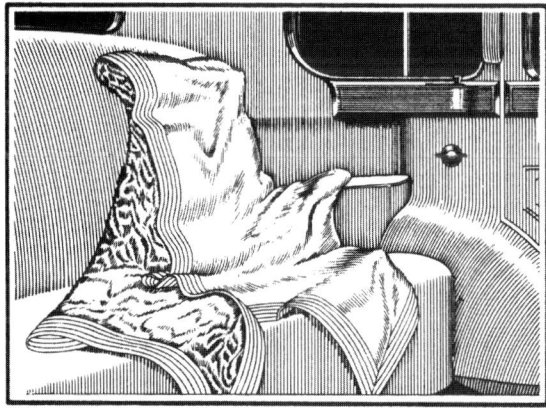

ROBES—a cold weather comfort of exceptional beauty. Custom tailored for Cadillac of the exact fabric with which the interior is upholstered. Linings of luxurious silk plush or soft, warm alpaca.

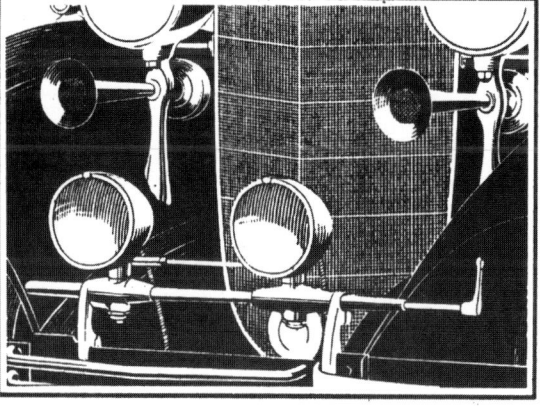

DRIVING LIGHTS—steering controlled to direct broad twin light beams in the pathway of the car or powerful hand directed spot lights—exactly matching Cadillac headlights.

These are but a few of the select group which your Cadillac dealer has ready to demonstrate for your consideration

MECHANICAL FEATURES

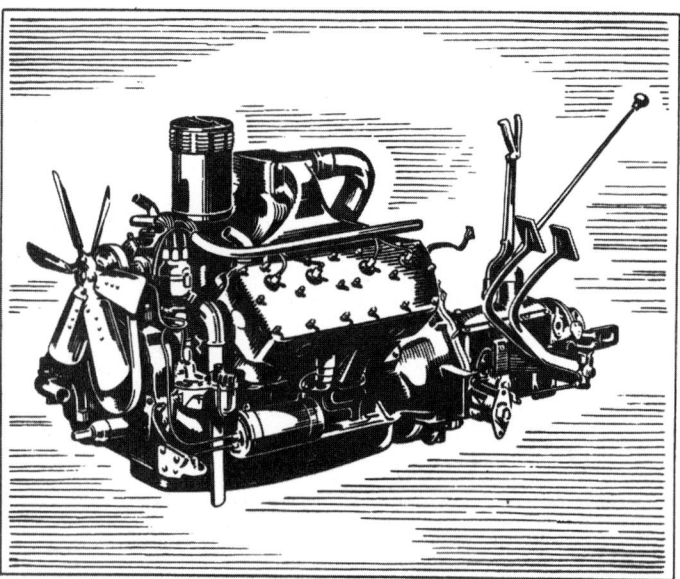
The V-Type Eight-Cylinder La Salle Engine

The Triple-Silent Syncro-Mesh Transmission

The Attractive La Salle Front Ensemble

In the belief that a brief account of La Salle chassis units, and a more detailed description of the coachwork will be of interest, the story of La Salle features is continued here.

POWER PLANT

For nineteen years, the Cadillac Motor Car Company has held to the V-type principle of engine design.

The V-type engine of La Salle is, basically, exceedingly simple. Because the cylinders can be placed side by side in two banks of equal number, a V-type engine is shorter. This permits a shorter crankshaft—with resulting reduction of vibration. It permits shorter and more direct fuel passages; a less complex cooling system within the engine; shorter and less circuitous oil lines; a more efficient crankcase ventilating system. The result is economy in maintenance, as well as high efficiency and extremely long life.

The La Salle engine is suspended at six points. This type of suspension aids materially in securing the exceptional freedom from vibration which characterizes La Salle. Furthermore, it constitutes the most satisfactory manner of mounting the engine which Cadillac has yet devised.

As a result of this advanced design, the power plant of La Salle provides greater brilliance in performance, and higher economy of operation than have ever before been attained in a La Salle engine.

TRANSMISSION

Cadillac and La Salle automobiles presented, in 1928, a notable contribution to driving pleasure and control in the Syncro-Mesh transmission. Cadillac engineers later added to this non-clashing transmission another improvement—*complete quiet in all forward speeds.*

Actually, transmission noise in low and second, as well as high, has been reduced to a degree which is scarcely audible.

FULL RANGE RIDE REGULATOR

The Full Range Ride Regulator constitutes another decided improvement in the safety and comfort of motoring. Briefly, it is a mechanism which enables the driver to adjust the action of the hydraulic shock absorbers at will.

Hydraulic shock absorbers employ a "liquid cushion" to absorb road shock before it reaches car occupants. Hitherto, the degree of "softness" has been established by a fixed adjustment or restricted control. With this Ride Regulator, it can be instantly modified over an extremely wide range to accommodate the car ride to the road surface and the speed of travel.

Unlike other systems of shock absorber control, La Salle's Full Range Ride Regulator is effective to the minutest degree at all times. This sensitivity is

MECHANICAL FEATURES

The La Salle Cast Molybdenum Brakes

The Exclusive La Salle Instrument Panel

Showing the Graceful Rear Treatment

due to the use of spring loaded check valves in each absorber unit, distinctly different from the conventional, varying-orifice type of valve.

CAST MOLYBDENUM SAFETY BRAKES

Three years ago, Cadillac presented new-type Safety Brakes, featuring roller bearings in the linkage, an aluminum alloy shoe, a self-centering cam, and an articulated link. This design reduced pedal pressure; eliminated brake failure caused by excessive drum expansion under continuous brake application; minimized the possibility of unequal braking effect; and assured *full surface action* throughout the life of the facing.

Cast molybdenum drums—pioneered in the Cadillac V-16, and used on all Cadillacs and La Salles—provide another decided improvement. Made of duplex electric furnace iron, these new-type drums completely eliminate scoring and render a period of service far beyond the expectancy of conventional drum materials.

To make braking a mere matter of control, and virtually eliminate physical exertion, all La Salle models are now equipped with a Vacuum Brake Assister—a new device which compounds the pressure of the driver's foot with mechanical power derived from the vacuum in the manifolding system.

RADIATOR AND COOLING SYSTEM

A new radiator of ultra-modern, smart contour and improved construction gives more effective cooling at all car speeds. There is no exterior radiator cap—the opening through which water is poured into the radiator being under the hood and on the same side as the oil funnel. The air channels through the core have louvres and the radiating fins are bonded to the water passages with solder. An adjustable ring shroud, on the rear face of the core, increases effective fan suction and prevents re-circulation of air around the engine.

NEW FENDER TIE-ROD

Another feature which owners are certain to appreciate in the La Salle V-8 is a new fender tie-rod. Running from the fenders to the radiator, and securely anchored at each terminal, this rod makes the entire front body assembly a rigid unit—and eliminates the tendency to vibrate which fenders have previously evidenced in driving on rough roads. This new front-end stability adds greatly to the driver's sense of security and is really a vital contribution to the pleasure of motoring.

COACHWORK BY FISHER

Seven luxurious body styles of distinctly custom manner are provided by Fisher for this La Salle V-8. The styles provide a model and a passenger capacity to fit every motoring requirement. A definite note of modern air-

MECHANICAL FEATURES

At top, the detail of the exclusive Ride Regulator valving. The diagrams illustrate the even comfort possible, with the five adjustments, on various road surfaces.

foil design is instantly apparent. This is intensified by the new fenders, new hood doors, new radiator design, gracefully arched windows, and sweeping moldings. The artistic treatment of the rear ensemble, blending fenders and gas tank valance into a trim, neat composition, puts a pleasing finish to a most attractive design.

All glass is non-shattering Security-Plate—first used by Cadillac. Insulation on the dash, floors, floor pans, and side panels protects occupants from engine and exhaust heat and assures a restful quiet within the car.

In addition to the Fisher No-Draft *Individually Controlled* Ventilation system, La Salle has a new, more efficient cowl ventilator. It can be open in rain or snow without allowing any moisture to enter the body interior. Therefore, even with the windows closed, there is always a plentiful supply of cool, fresh, washed air—and there never is any tendency for the windows or windshield to "steam."

La Salle's instrument panel represents a pleasing departure from the conventional. All dials are grouped at the left, immediately in front of the driver, beneath polished watch crystals. The right half of the panel serves as a door to a convenient and lockable package compartment. Between dials and locker, an ingenious compartment lamp, the cigar lighter, and the ignition lock are located.

La Salle bodies are fitted with door locks of improved construction—easier to operate, and so designed that it is virtually impossible to lock oneself out. Turning the remote control handle automatically locks and unlocks the door. Attempting to turn the outer handle does not affect the security of the lock in any way.

All doors incorporate four advanced features of design. Bottoms overlap the floor, made draft-tight by a wind bead which is compressed when the door is shut. Tops are fitted with a rubber dam, making a joint as water-tight as that of a refrigerator. A gutter, lengthwise of the door top, drains off condensation, and doubly assures absence of moisture inside the car. Windshields are set in steel and rubber—absolutely draft-and-water-tight.

Windshield wipers, in tandem, are concealed except for the blade and the control pin. The driver's half of the front seat is adjustable four inches. Wider arm rests of sponge rubber, in rear seats, are made even more comfortable by an elbow recess—which utilizes the space formerly required to accommodate the rear window when lowered.

Like all Fisher coachwork, that for La Salle surpasses in strength and durability because of the fundamental Fisher principle of composite wood-and-steel construction. With this construction, great flexibility is secured without compromise on the all-important factor of safety for passengers.

NINETEEN THIRTY-FOUR
Series 350

Cadillac has styled, designed and built the newest car in all the world—LaSalle. So newly smart, so exclusive with its Fleetwood bodies, so different—so completely captivating is this new LaSalle that it puts years between yesterday and today. None but an artist could have conceived and carried out the daring new aerodynamic design which removes this new LaSalle so far from the usual and the commonplace.

Sleek, smooth, powerful and aristocratic—the new LaSalle has character and individuality; smartness with distinction; beauty with strength.

None but the superb craftsmanship of Fleetwood custom builders could transform expressionless wood and metal into this masterpiece.

It would be difficult for you to imagine the satisfaction of owning this youthful aristocrat of motordom, so pronounced is the contrast between LaSalle and all else that has gone before.

—from the 1934 sales brochure

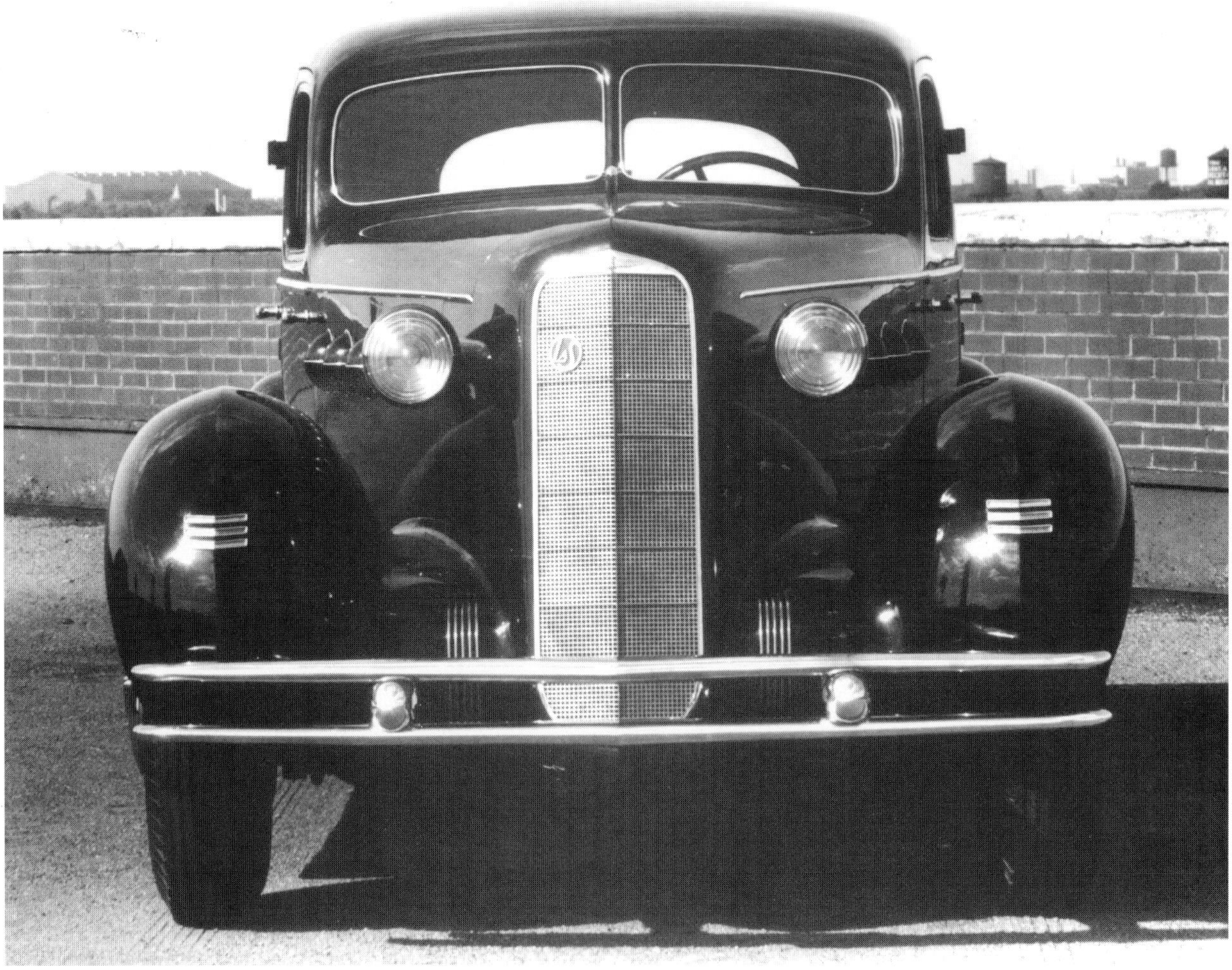

Above: The new proposal had a radically narrow grille, headlights on the radiator shroud, a low rakish two-piece windshield and chevrons on each front fender. Below: The initial proposal was a very traditional concept with a wide grille, flared fenders, headlights on vertical stanchions and boxed body. Note an interesting hint of things to come . . . those beautiful biplane bumpers.

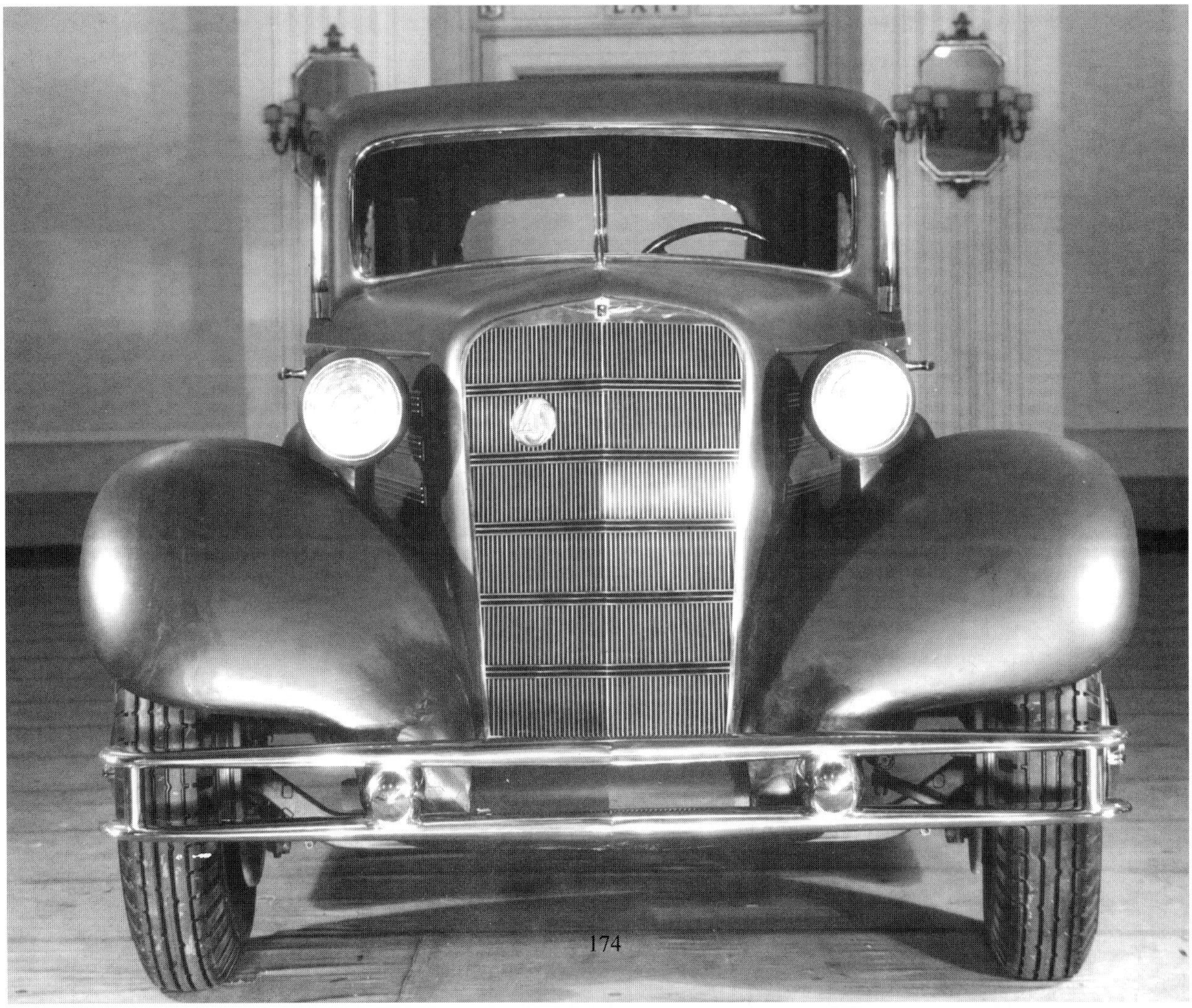

DECISION TO DROP LaSALLE FOR 1934 - REVERSED

A factory photo of the 1934 LaSalle mock-up in profile illustrates how streamlining was based upon aerodynamic principles. Barely noticeable are the two windsplits on each of the fenders and a single windsplit on each of the five round ventilation pods. Even the hubcaps were in keeping with this theme. Would management buy this concept or drop LaSalle as a companion car?

By 1932, the companion car concept had all but disappeared. Buick had dropped the Marquette, Oldsmobile had dropped the Viking and Oakland was dropped in favor of Pontiac. There was also talk about scuttling the LaSalle. This bothered Harley Earl tremendously inasmuch as the 1927 phenomenon had been his baby. LaSalle sales had plummeted to a low of 3,386 in 1932 and 3,482 in 1933. This added fuel to that argument and GM's financial staff recommended its discontinuance. It is generally accepted by historians that Cadillac would drop LaSalle for 1934.

Harley Earl had asked for new and fresh ideas for the 1934 LaSalle that could resuscitate the decision to discontinue. In the autumn of 1932, Harley Earl sailed for Europe to make his usual rounds of the Paris salons. Left behind were Tom Hibbard, head of the Cadillac design group; Jules Agramonte, heading up the LaSalle group; and Harry Shaw, as overall coordinator.

While Harley Earl was gone, Jules Agramonte, who had come over from Fleetwood, decided to try a totally different approach apart from the group. Having been influenced by the narrow-fronted English beach racers, Agramonte utilized some of those concepts in his designs. The grille was slender and tall, the nose and hood were narrow and tapered, the headlights were attached to the radiator shroud with short stubby wings, the catwalk was very low and there were fender skirts over the front wheels similar to the pontoon landing gear of racing airplanes.

Agramonte showed his proposal, an airbrush rendering on black paper, to Harry Shaw. He suggested that this might make a good LaSalle, but Shaw disregarded the proposal and told Agramonte to put it away. However, when Harley Earl returned from his Paris visit, Shaw left on vacation and Agramonte took the occasion to leave his LaSalle drawings laying around for Harley Earl to see when he made his rounds, often late at night. According to accounts, Harley Earl became terribly excited about what he saw and told Agramonte to develop the concept further and make clay models. That went so well that a sample body was ordered to be made from scrimmed wood and metal completely trimmed. It was accurate in every detail, including the round hood ports, the biplane bumpers, the three chevrons on the leading edge of each front fender and the five chromed hash marks resembling fins of inboard drum brakes on racing cars. What to do next?

The initial proposal for the 1934 LaSalle was very traditional, with a similar-to-Cadillac wide grille, skirted fenders as in 1933, headlights on vertical stanchions, dual 1933 taillights and an exposed rear-mounted spare tire. The hood ornament was a Heron. Could it be that Cadillac took this design over for its 1934 models?

What a difference between these proposals by Jules Agramonte and the traditional on the previous page. It became a trendsetter with the rakish two-piece windshield, beavertail rear trunk, concealed spare tire, art deco taillights, streamlined fenders and flowing body lines covering all chassis components. Management was stunned when this mock-up was shown to them by Harley Earl. It was a risky decision, but it took them less than five minutes to reverse their position. LaSalle received a reprieve for 1934 and stayed in production six more model years.

SUPPLEMENT

The CADILLAC-LASALLE

February 1934
No. 2

Salesmen's Monthly Delivery Record

PRODUCTION STARTED ON THE 1934 LA SALLE

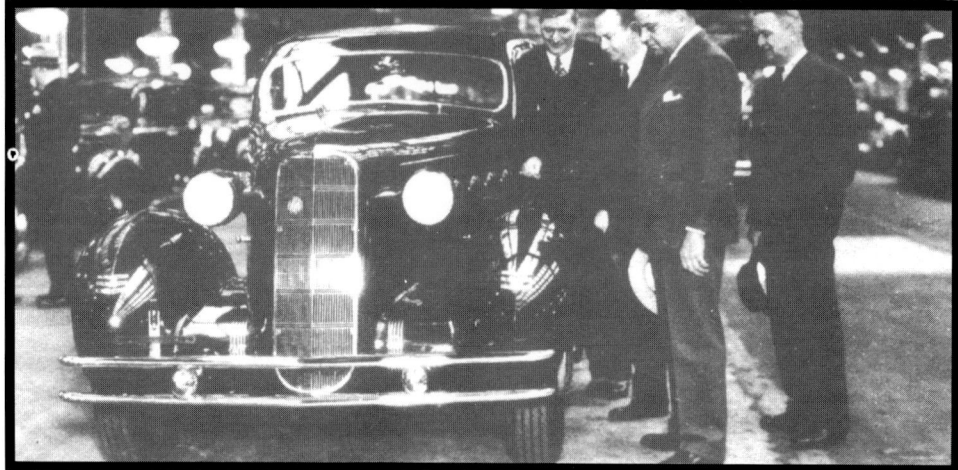

This car—the first 1934 La Salle marked the beginning of production. Mayor Frank Couzens, of Detroit, and William S. Knudsen, executive Vice-President of General Motors Corp., were among the guests of President L. P. Fisher and Sales Manager J. C. Chick to witness completion of the first La Salle.

March 15, 1934

It will be welcome news to all Cadillac Distributors, Dealers and Salesmen to hear that the new 1934 La Salle production lines have been put into operation following several months of intensive activity on the part of our Engineering and Manufacturing Divisions.

I wish it were possible for every member of the Cadillac Selling Organization to know and appreciate the great response from the public following the introduction and announcement of the new La Salle at the automobile shows.

At the factory we have been literally swamped with wires, letters and 'phone calls requesting information as to date of delivery on these new cars and it seems to me that this definitely indicates the large waiting market for this new La Salle when it is available for delivery in all of our outlets.

We confidently believe the new La Salle will quickly dominate the Upper Medium Price Group in which market there has been delivered nearly 450,000 cars in the past four years and now that the new La Salle is in production I want to urge every one in Cadillac to make the most of the opportunity which is in front of us.

The kind of a selling job that we do in the next six months will have much to do with our place in this new market hereafter and with the distinct advantage that the new La Salle has in style, price, performance and prestige when compared with other cars being sold in this market, I am confident the new La Salle will be the most talked of car as soon as it appears on the streets and highways of the country.

One of the greatest thrills afforded those of our Selling Organization who have visited the factory in the past few days has been the sight of La Salle and Cadillac coming down the same production lines together and being given the same care and thought that has made Cadillac Craftsmanship a Creed and Accuracy a Law in the Cadillac factory for so many years.

Inasmuch as it is physically impossible for so many of our Dealers and Salesmen to come to the factory, I am sending you this folder which shows some of the many interesting manufacturing operations on the new La Salle.

It is now the definite responsibility of the Selling Organization to get the new La Salle before the public quickly and impressively and I hope every man will do his part in making this new La Salle the leader in its market just as Cadillac is in the High Price Group.

Very truly yours,

J. C. Chick
General Sales Manager

NINETEEN THIRTY-FOUR
Series 350

LaSalle was the big news from the Cadillac Motor Car Division in 1934. In fact, it was big news for the entire automobile world. It sent shock waves to the design departments of every GM division, to every domestic carmaker and to many international companies. LaSalle had turned the tables on the design world. Instead of America looking to Europe for design inspiration, now Europe and the rest of the world were looking with envy to America and the beautiful new LaSalle. Until 1936, when Cord and Lincoln Zephyr designs stirred the automobile world, every carmaker had the 1934 LaSalle in his sights . . . to copy, to use as a point of design departure and to make sure that their transition would also be in vogue. It was as if LaSalle had thrown down the gauntlet.

The narrow grille, the low catwalks, the pontoon fenders and the overall smooth flowing effect were elements most influential. The LaSalle looked lithe, youthful and streamlined. Art deco ornamentation was tastefully applied . . . those beautiful protruding pressed glass taillights, the five round ventilators on each side of the hood, the three chevrons on the leading edge of each front fender, five vertical chromed brake fin speed hashes on each side of the grille at the leading edge of the catwalk and, of course, the Torpedo hood ornament with three stabilizers nosing into the wind. The finishing touch was the effect of the biplane bumpers. They gave a see-through view to the beautiful front grille, enhancing its narrow vertical motif. Every bodyline flowed smoothly without interruption. All elements were integrated.

Everything gave the appearance of streamlining and speed; even the windshield of the closed models was low and racy looking. The car looked longer, even though the wheelbase had been reduced. The car looked fast, even when standing still.

To further preserve the streamlined effect, the factory discouraged two-tone paint schemes and discouraged fender mounted spare tires. The approved LaSalle design for 1934 made a provision for a spare tire to be concealed inside the rear luggage compartment of the four-door Sedans and in a special compartment below the rumble seat on the two-door models. Unfortunately, fender mounted spares had to be made available anyway for the more conservative customer, but the factory discouraged their use by making them an added cost option.

Production of this modern look in 1934, however, was fraught with many manufacturing complications. It required a great deal of hand fitting, welding and finishing because the presses were not yet capable of the complex sheet metal configurations, such as the pontoon fenders and the deep dish headlight and taillight housings. None of the body panels were interchangeable with Cadillac. Out of necessity, due to the short time from design approval to production, and with these manufacturing limitations, it was logical to use Fleetwood craftsmen. They were skilled and accustomed to hand finishing. Cadillac did not want to lose these craftsmen while the demand for the expensive Fleetwood-bodied Cadillacs had been waning due to America's economic conditions. It is also ironic that the body with such a modern look was fitted over old fashioned hardwood framing, albeit the best available. Nineteen thirty-four would be the last year for such coach building construction.

Top right: The two 1934 Tootsy Toy models are very rare. They are standing on the 1934 LaSalle sales catalog showing the five-passenger four-door Sedan. Below right: The three-fold, three-model color flyer was often mailed as well as given away in showrooms. Bottom left: The greenish brochure describes a walk through the plant where LaSalles are built, in order to impress potential clientele with Cadillac kinship and Body by Fleetwood.

The beautiful new narrow grille and radiator shroud with the dramatically narrow long engine compartment became the hallmark of future LaSalles. Note the five chrome hash marks and telescopic spring-loaded bumper supports.

Club Sedan with a blind rear quarter. A four-door Convertible was also listed, but none were built.

Inside and out, the 1934 LaSalle exuded Fleetwood. Even some of the chrome exterior trim was stamped with the LaSalle style and body numbers to match the model inasmuch as all of the doors were of different dimensions. This was a typical Fleetwood-only practice used to identify custom-fitted parts.

Factory build invoices also confirmed the Fleetwood heritage of LaSalle for 1934. All Series 350 models were first designated with a four-digit Fleetwood number; e.g., 6376 was the number designation for the two-door Coupe. The four digits were crossed out later when shipped and replaced with the three-digit 178 LaSalle number.

Early on, it was rumored that LaSalle consisted of numerous Oldsmobile parts because both makes had a 119-inch wheelbase, chassis components resembled each other and both had a Straight-8 engine. Interchange manuals of that era also suggested the interchangeability of numerous parts; however, as it turned out, very few were identical. It should be noted now that just a visual comparison of body design and construction makes it obvious even to the most casual observer that there was no interchangeability with other GM makes for the 1934 model year. The 1934 LaSalle was a unique, stand-out-by-itself design.

Only four LaSalle body styles were offered: a two-door Convertible with rumble seat, a two-door Coupe with rumble seat, a four-door Sedan and a four-door

Note the Torpedo hood ornament and elongated teardrop headlight containers. Unique to the LaSalle were the art deco ventilation pods and three chevrons on leading edge of new front fenders at the crease. All elements depicted speed and streamlining.

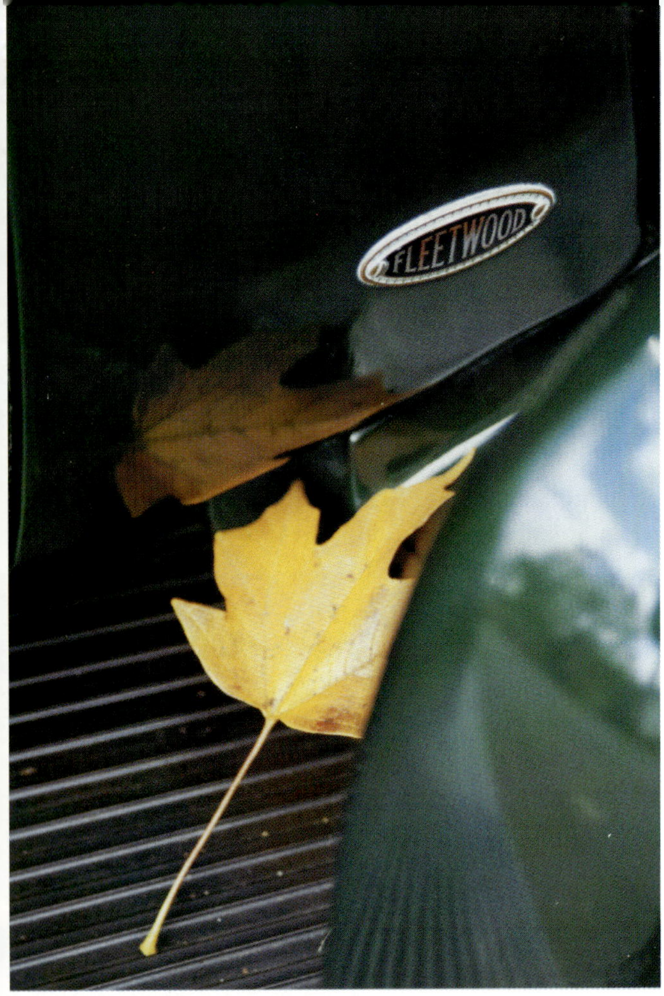
FLEETWOOD

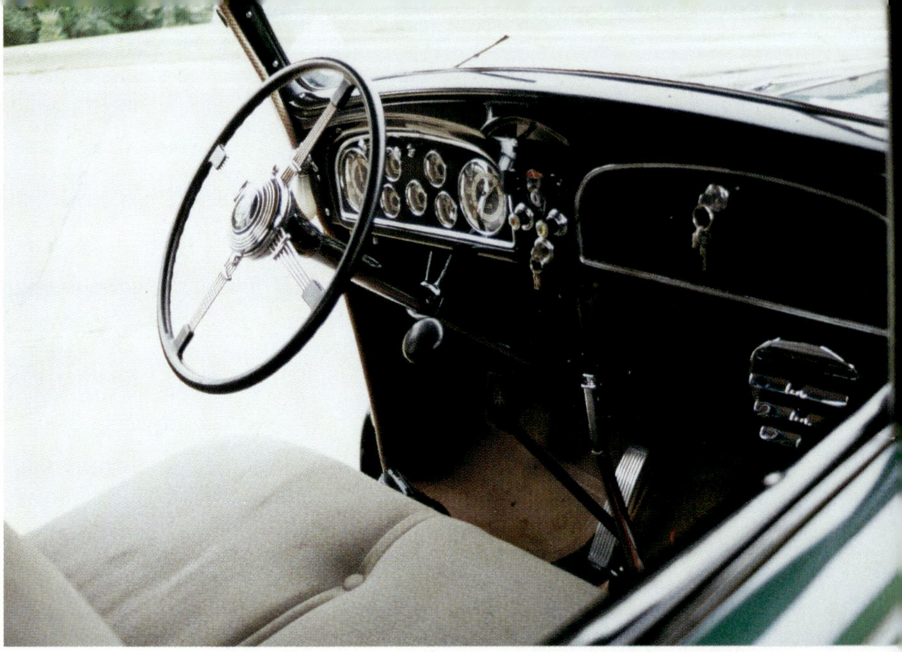

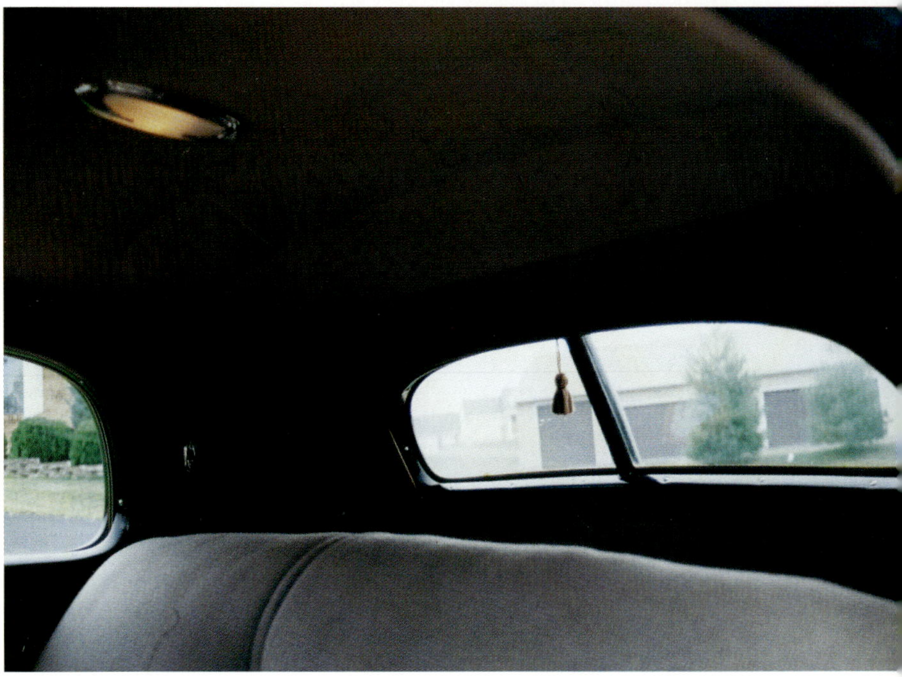

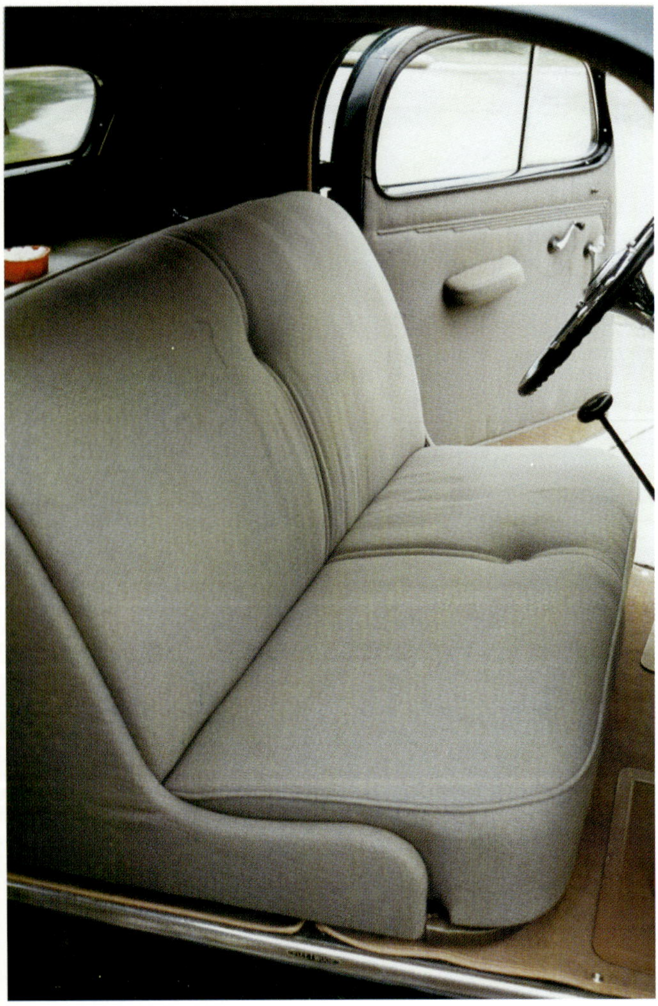

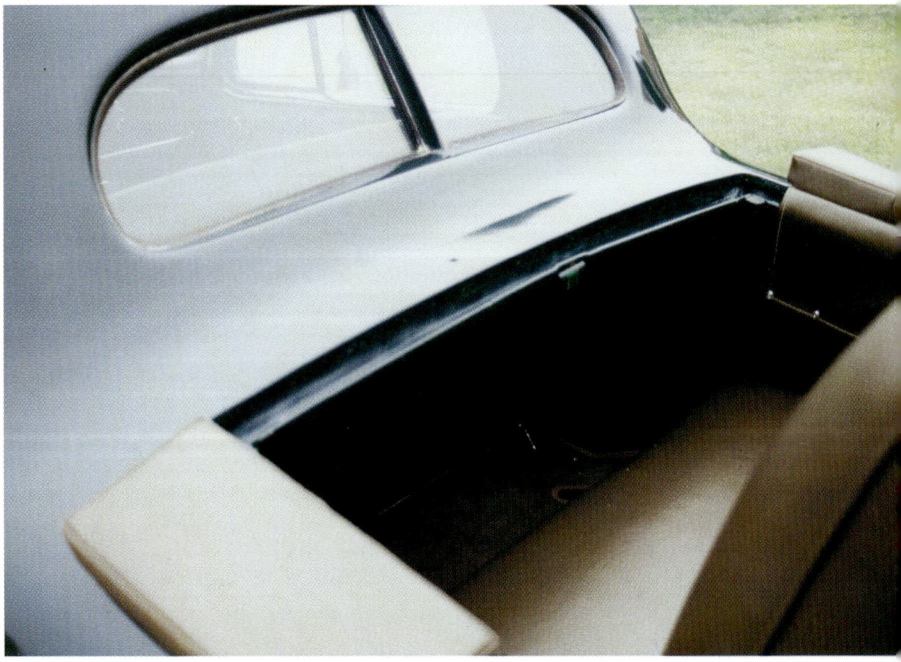

Above: This beautifully staged factory photograph shows the LaSalle Series 350 two-door rumble seat Coupe with Fleetwood number 6376 and LaSalle number 178. Previous page, top left clockwise: The 1934 LaSalle proudly wears the Fleetwood badge on its cowl. Interior instrumentation was borrowed from 1933. The optional deluxe four-spoke banjo steering wheel is shown with the light controls at the horn button hub. Cadillac made the accessory heater. There is a window shade that pulls down to cover the single split rear window. The dome light has Fleetwood art deco cover. The leather rumble seat was made as comfortable as possible. Inside, the upholstery trim, pattern and workmanship by Fleetwood employees was simple, but elegant. Craftsmanship is obvious.

In November of 1934, Cadillac changed its number designation to reflect the new 1935 model introduction. Strangely enough, LaSalle changed its model designation on the body plate also, but continued to build and supply the 1934 body configuration in its entirety until March of 1935. It is presumed that this was done to obtain maximum use of the leftover inventory and spread the high production costs of this custom Fleetwood approach to building fine automobiles. There was also a need for more time to work the kinks out of the all steel "turret" top to be introduced on the new 1935 models to be built on the Fisher body production line. It is likely that both reasons were responsible for this unusual extension of a previous body style well into the new model year.

A few items were carried over from 1933, such as the Torpedo hood ornament, the beautiful double breadloaf instrument panel and the art deco dome light bezel used by other Fleetwood-bodied cars. Everything else was new and radically different from the 1933 model.

All 1934 LaSalle bodies were manufactured by Fleetwood craftsmen in the Fleetwood plant at West Fort Street and West End Avenue in Detroit. This was proudly indicated on every LaSalle built that year with a Fleetwood body plate affixed to the lower-outside right-side cowl.

Artists' renderings in advertisements of the 1934 LaSalle were stretched out and exaggerated to emphasize the narrow vertical motif and its streamlined features. It was headlined as "the newest car in the world," Cadillac designed and built. An opportunity was never

LADIES' HOME JOURNAL

Lucky Lady!

Priced at $1495 and $1595 F.O.B. DETROIT

We call this lady lucky because she has, for her very own, the most beautifully streamlined car in the world—La Salle! And, too, there is no *anywhere*, another motor car so ideally suited to a woman's personal use. ✱ With all the earnestness of which we are capable, we say to yo this: if anybody *ever* offers to buy you a motor car—or if you *ever* decide to buy one for yourself—by all means, choose a La Salle. ✱ It's t easiest to handle, the thrillingest to drive, and the most beautiful to look at of all the cars anywhere. ✱ And, of course, it's a *Cadill* product in the fullest meaning of the word—and *all* its bodies are by Fleetwood, the foremost builder of custom bodies in the worl

DESIGNED AND BUILT BY THE CADILLAC MOTOR CAR COMPAN

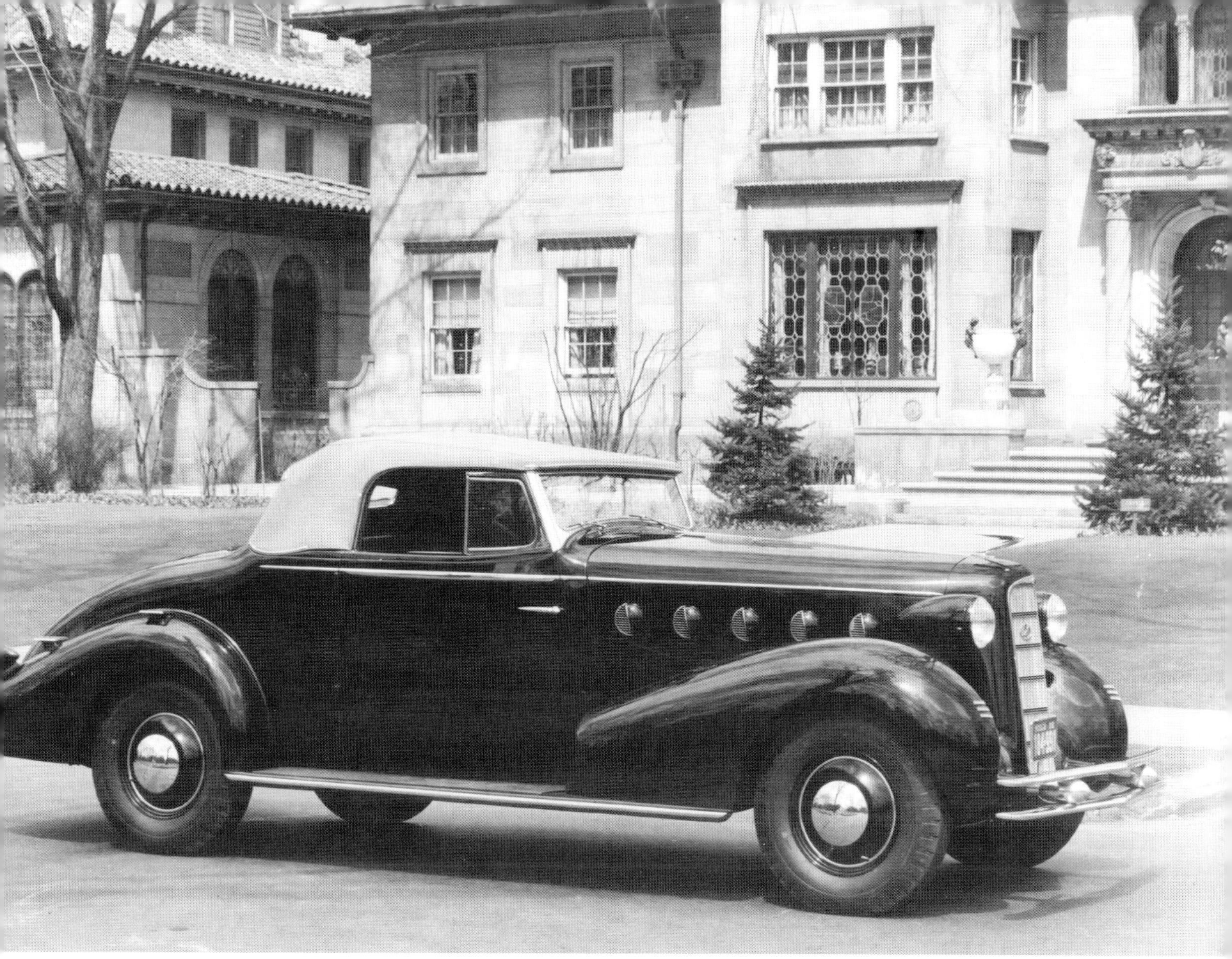

The low slanted windshield of the Convertible gives the LaSalle a racy look. Factory photos of the 1934 two-door Convertible with rumble seat and concealed spare, Model 6335/168, demonstrate appearance changes with light paint color, light wheel covers and dark wheel covers with black wall tires.

missed to link LaSalle to Cadillac. "America, you—above all other nations—know how priceless is style . . . for nothing can be desirable that is anywise out of date. Cadillac presents La Salle . . . supreme and streamline design . . . so smart, so different, so captivating that it puts years between yesterday and today . . . as final assurance of its style and elegance and quality—remember that all bodies for the La Salle are built by Fleetwood, the foremost custom builder in the world."

A special appeal was made to women. An ad in the *Ladies' Home Journal* was headlined, "Lucky Lady!" It further explained, "We call this lady lucky because she has, for her very own, the most beautifully streamlined car in the world—La Salle! And, too, there is not, *anywhere*, another motor car so ideally suited to a woman's personal use."

One of the most interesting advertisements in *The Saturday Evening Post* was a two-page feature on April 14, 1934, illustrated by Count Alexis de Sakhnoffsky. These artistic renderings dramatized the unique LaSalle styling features. "To look upon these impressions by Count Alexis de Sakhnoffsky . . . or to

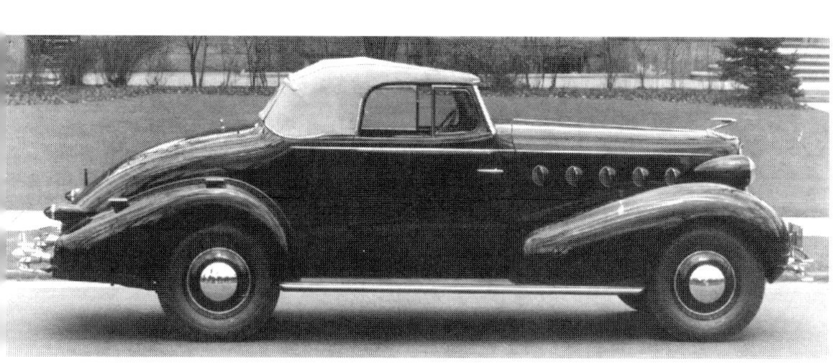

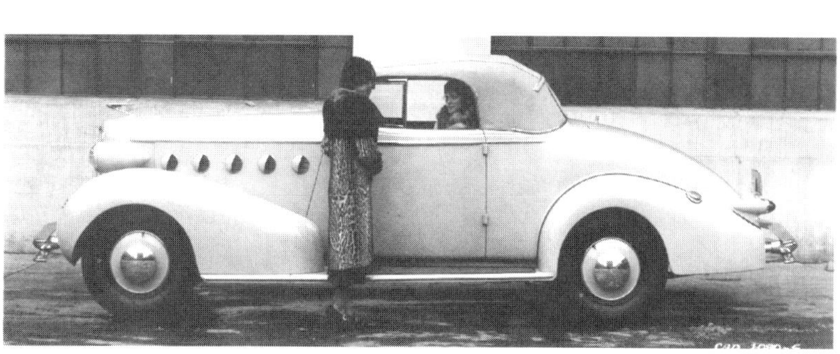

Top: Another important feature of the new 1934 LaSalle body styling is the elimination of protruding parts at the rear by the concealment of the spare wheel and tire in order to complete the air streamlining from the front to the rear of the car. They are carried with the rear of the body in a special compartment, above which is space for luggage. Middle: The new narrow radiator grille—the streamlining of the headlamps and supports—the filleting of fender and radiator casing—all contribute to the beauty of the new 1934 LaSalle. These details have a practical side, too—as their scientific aerodynamic design assists free passage of air currents. Bottom: This right hand drive Club Sedan from South Africa has been slightly customized with the belt molding dipping to complement the contour of the streamlined deck.

The five-passenger Club Sedan with solid rear quarters, Model 182/6333-S, had a very formal look.

examine the new La Salle personally . . . is to know that it is the supreme expression of streamline styling, as well as the most *beautiful* car of the year." The *Ladies' Home Journal* illustrated the inside of a LaSalle with a mother looking over her shoulder at her child asleep on the back seat headlined, "Hush-a-bye, my baby . . . close your little eyes and sleep." And, "ever so gently, like a lilac spray in the zephyrs, your new-found couch will rock you to the heart of slumberland . . ." Tugging away at mother's heartstrings, how could one resist? Very few ads featured actual photographs with realistic settings. They were in black and white.

Sales brochures were artists' renditions with each model presented very simply with no background setting. There was also a three-fold color brochure which could be mailed in a number ten envelope. It showed only three models.

The big news for 1934 was LaSalle's departure from the practice of providing a V-8 engine. Instead, a Straight-8 powered the Series 350. It delivered 95 bhp at 3700 rpm from 240 cubic inch displacement with a compression ratio of 6.5 to 1.

All domestic cars were supplied with 16-inch all-steel disc wheels with a for-one-year-only 1934 wheel disc cover available in a variety of matching or harmonizing paint colors or chrome.

New with LaSalle was the adoption of hydraulic brakes, two years ahead of Cadillac.

Another big news item was the new "knee action" independent, coil spring suspension. Knee action utilized wishbone links, permitting the wheel to move up and down in an almost vertical plane, which helped to absorb side thrusts and brake torque reaction. Coil springs were used with rubber bumpers installed on the inside of the coil to guard against bottoming. Over expansion was prevented by a rubber bumper placed on the frame. A unique torsional stabilizer bar was used at the rear to help prevent side sway as resistance to the softer coil springs up front.

One of the through-the-year transitional improvements was the adoption of Hotchkiss drive, replacing the torque tube construction used by Cadillac for so many years. There were also several mid-year changes in the transmission, primarily in the gate and the size of the gearbox.

This gorgeous full-page ad ran only once in June of 1934.

Pictured here are examples of two restored Fleetwood-bodied LaSalles—a two-passenger Coupe and a two-passenger Convertible. The low windshield and long narrow hood on both the open and closed models accentuated the streamlined flow of the new design. Both models have a rumble seat for two more passengers desiring to experience the exhilaration of the great windblown outdoors.

LADIES' HOME JOURNAL   May, 1934

"Hush-a-bye, my baby..."

"Hush-a-bye, my baby... close your little eyes and sleep." And, ever so gently, like a lilac spray in the zephyrs, your new-found couch will rock you to the heart of slumberland.... For the bad, bad seats that pitched and tossed, and made it so very bothersome for little folks to sleep, have gone away for a year and a day—and they'll *never* come back any more.... For *Cadillac* built some new-type springs for the new streamlined La Salle. And La Salle *now* rides, on *any* road, like a down-filled trundle-bed. There's never a jounce, and there's never a bump—no matter *where* you may drive. The very *meanest* and *roughest* roads smooth out like a boulevard.... So, mother, don't worry—and, mother, don't fret—for when you arrive, he'll be slumbering *yet*.

LA SALLE
FROM **$1495** F.O.B. DETROIT

Designed by Cadillac   *Built by Cadillac*

Above: Two factory photographs of the most purchased model . . . the five-passenger Sedan. A long hood, low rakish windshield, biplane bumpers and five hood side ventilators made the streamlined appearance of LaSalle a radical departure from most other 1934 models and makes. Below: In 1934, this LaSalle styling was very unfamiliar, but it was soon realized that streamlining helped the engine perform, to the delight of its owners.

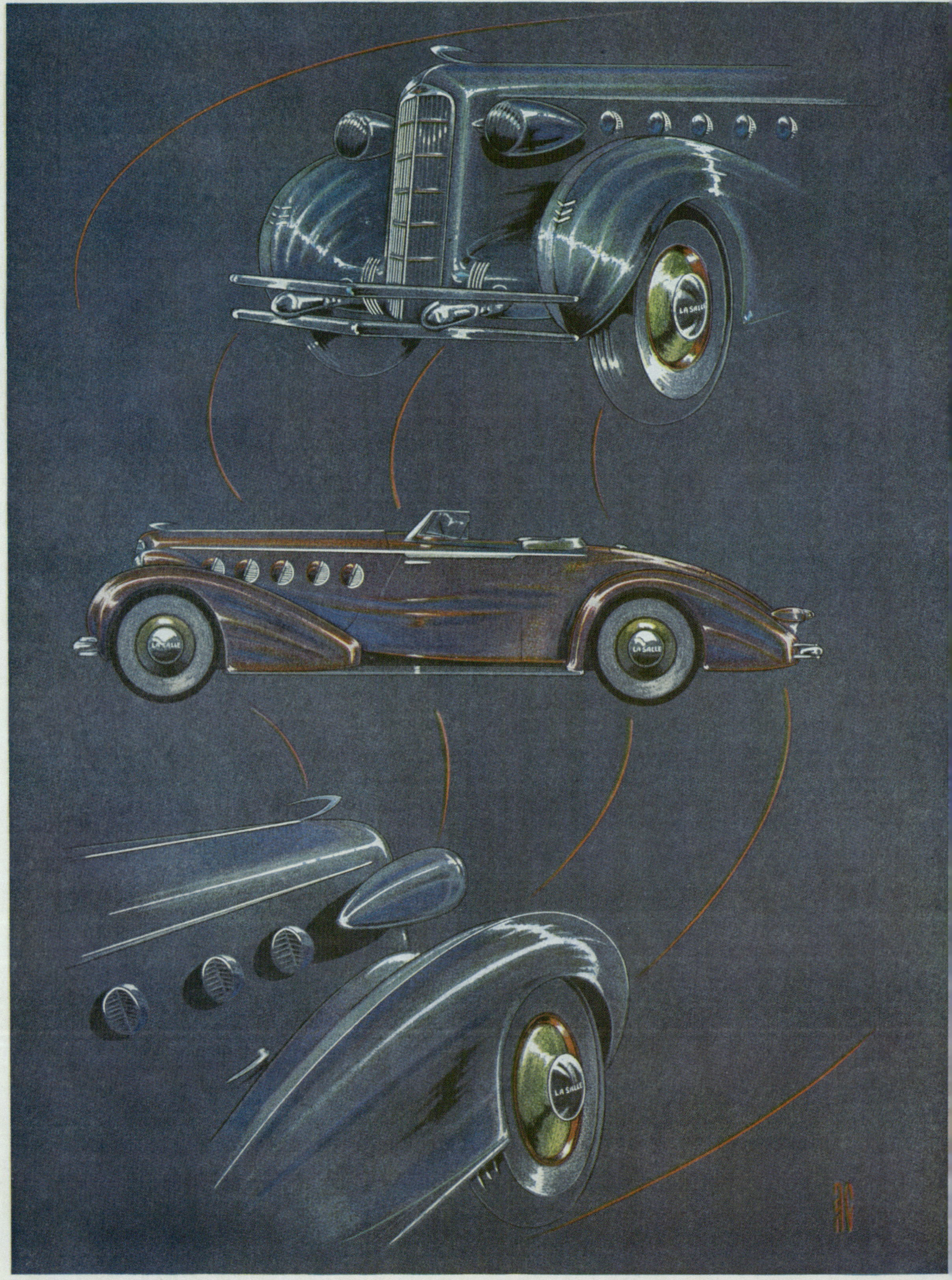
LA SALLE
LA SALLE
LA SALLE
LA SALLE

THE SATURDAY EVENING POST

The New STREAMLINE
La Salle

illustrated by
COUNT ALEXIS de SAKHNOFFSKY

❧

What can we say about the new streamlined La Salle to equal what *you*, and thousands of other men and women, have been saying about it ever since the first hour it appeared? We can only repeat this thought, which doubtless has been growing in your own mind: If you want the most *thrilling* new motor car of 1934, then most certainly you want this new Cadillac-built La Salle! To look upon these impressions by Count Alexis de Sakhnoffsky... or to examine the new La Salle personally... is to know that it is the supreme expression of streamline styling, as well as the most *beautiful* car of the year. To drive it is to know comfort, agility and safety such as you have never experienced before. The bodies are *special bodies* by Fleetwood. The chassis is a *precision chassis* by Cadillac. The net effect is the *new style*, the *new vogue*, in motor car performance and appearance, exactly as was the original La Salle of a few years ago. But perhaps you do not fully realize this further point, which, to many people, is the most amazing of all. The new La Salle lists as low as $1495, f. o. b. Detroit—almost *one thousand dollars* below last year's price! With this fact in mind, does it not become comparatively easy to gratify your desire to *own* a new La Salle?

from $1495
F.O.B. DETROIT

(Equipment other than standard at slight extra cost.)

LA SALLE
Cadillac designed Cadillac built

This array of Convertibles and their trendsetting design features have used different paint schemes and other optional equipment. Top left: The sleek streamlined Torpedo hood ornament was unique to LaSalle and the only one available. Middle left: This front view dramatically shows the influence of racing on the design; e.g., the extremely low windshield, the low catwalk, center creased fenders and the very narrow grille peaking through the twin-bladed biplane bumpers. Headlights appear to be mounted on short airfoils. Bottom left: The grille shell surrounded thirty-nine separate pieces, plus the winged LaSalle red and blue crest. All horizontal crossbars were inlaid with red paint matching the LaS logo. Top, middle and bottom: These three Convertibles speak for themselves and their individuality, including an export right hand drive model. Opposite page top: One tone paint schemes were recommended by the factory to emphasize the new-for-1934 streamlined effect. Chrome wheel discs mated to the chrome hubcaps were precursors to the full size hubcaps of the future. Middle left: A comparison study of the Convertible Coupe and the two-door Coupe with the same Diana Cream color scheme points out their own individuality and smooth flow of the basic body lines. Even the upper body structure of the Coupe looks racy with its low windshield and smooth roof drop-off at the rear. Painted wheel discs, as separate bolt-on items, were unique to 1934 only. Middle top right: Streamlining was an integral part of all functional items such as the deep, elongated taillight assembly from which the pinched glass lens emerges. Middle bottom right: LaSalle's new branding iron LaS logo was jewel-like. Bottom left: Design-wise, spare tires were not to be seen, so a special compartment was created behind the rumble seat of all two-door models. Note the double handles on the lid. Step plates on the bumper and fenders were entry to the rumble seat. Below right: Ventilation ports on the hood sides were special art deco design elements.

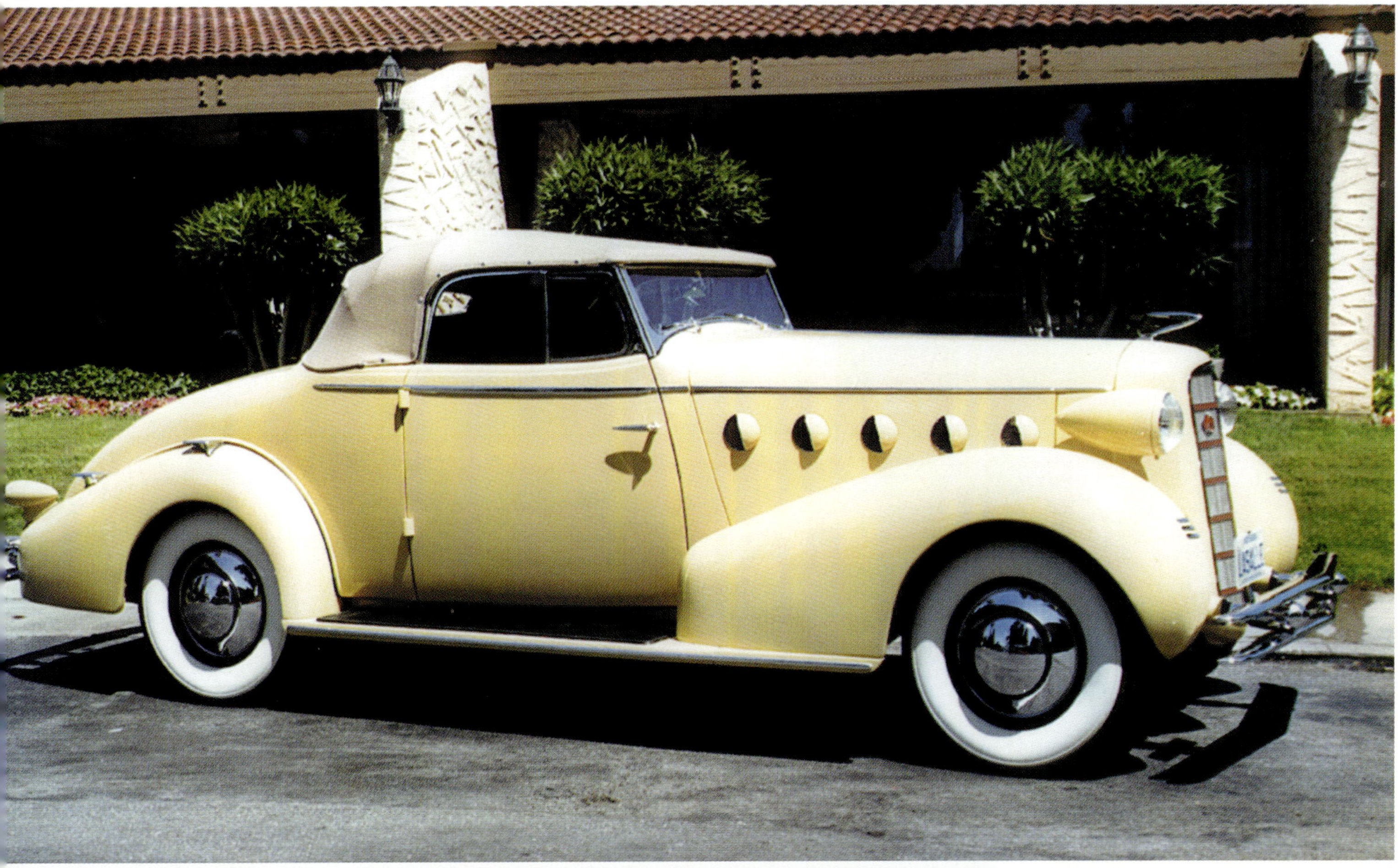

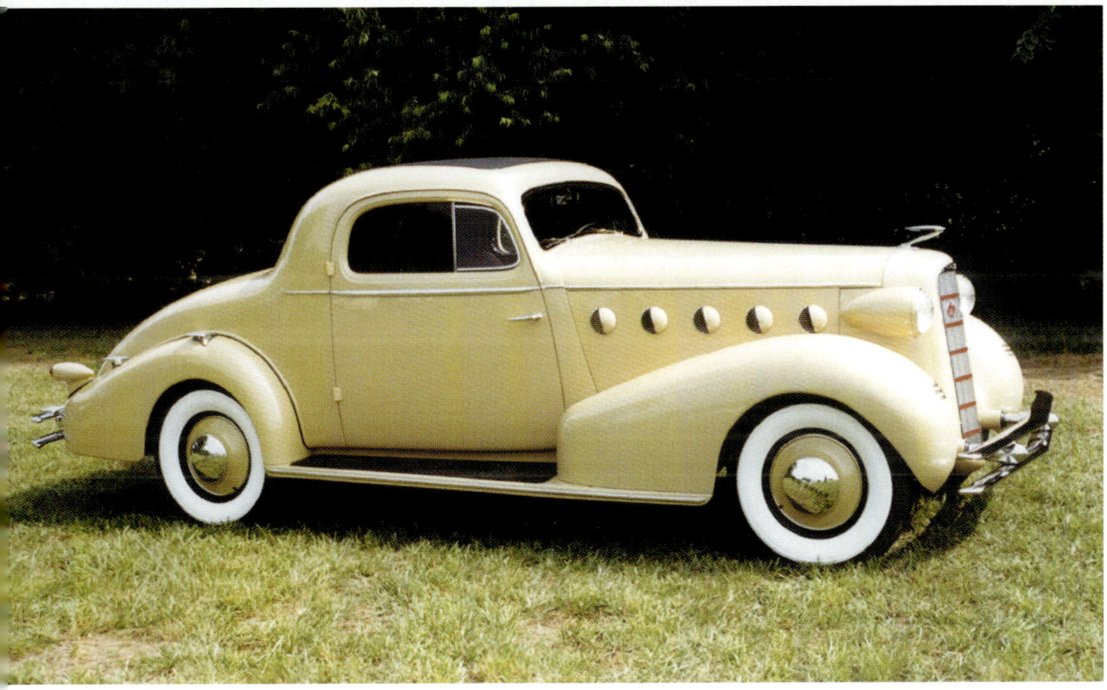

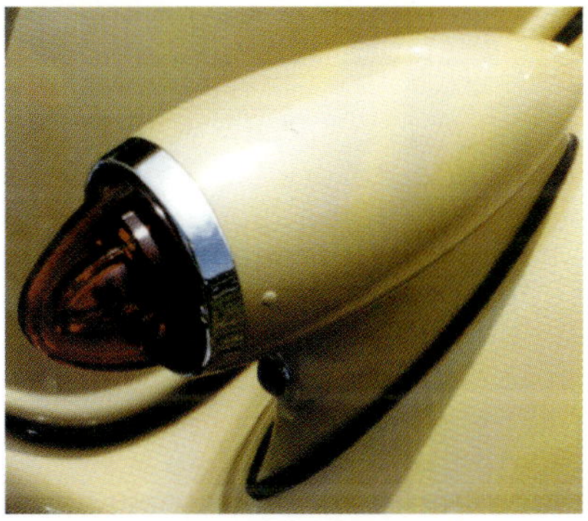

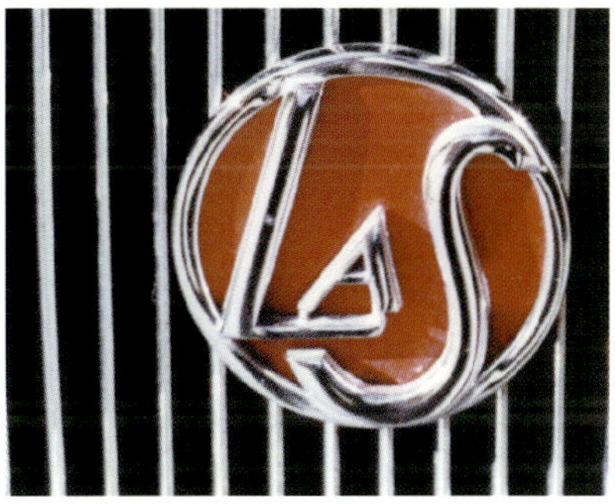

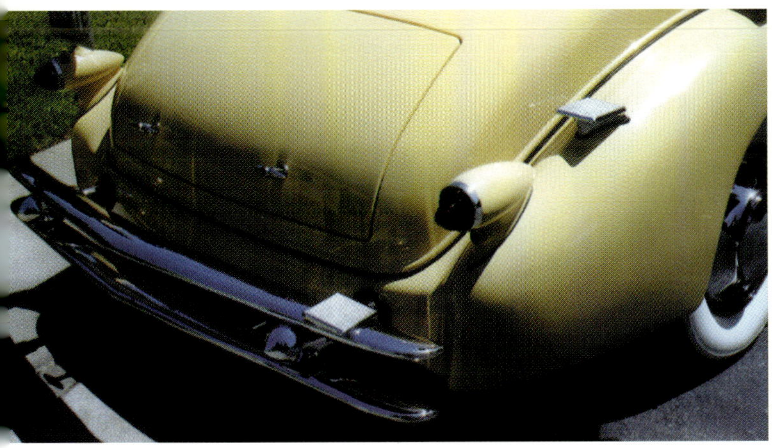

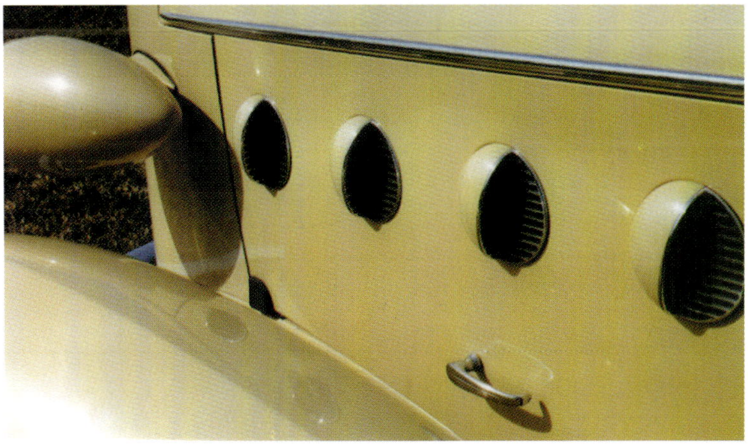

WHY THE LaSALLE - Straight-8 - ENGINE

The new LaSalle design required some innovative measures under the hood. The slender radiator shroud, long tapered hood, and narrow engine compartment could not accommodate any of Cadillac's existing V-type engines, as had been the practice heretofore. Economic conditions and competition dictated lowering the FOB price. That, in turn, demanded greater cost efficiency. To create a brand new engine from scratch would be very expensive and time-consuming. After a thorough search, a design that came the closest to meeting the Cadillac specifications was one used by Oldsmobile. Due to these factors and the short lead time, it was decided that the LaSalle engine block would be subcontracted to a foundry already supplying General Motors. This led to the perception that the LaSalle engine was an Oldsmobile engine. In many respects, the two engines had a similar outward appearance except for different carburetors, air cleaners, fuel pumps, manifolds and cylinder heads.

The fact is that when the engine block casting was received from the foundry, Cadillac workmen did all of the machining, three cylinder boring operations, reaming, honing, decking and fitting. Even though the bore, stroke and other dimensions were similar to the 1934 Oldsmobile 8, the LaSalle used a different bell housing, aluminum pistons and different main bearing widths. Different cylinder head configuration provided a higher compression ratio of 6.5 to 1 for the LaSalle. External engine accessories were also very different; i.e., the distributor, the manifolds, dual down draft carburetion and location of the coil.

Anyone who has tried to restore a LaSalle engine will attest to its uniqueness and the frustrating lack of interchangeability. A review of the interchange manuals, used by wrecking yards in those days, provides a confusing picture. Some parts appear interchangeable, but overall they demonstrate the lack of interchangeability unless a complete ready-to-run engine or transmission were to be interchanged, but that would be non-authentic.

Cadillac, in the 1934 LaSalle salesman's handbook and *1934 Features of Construction*, asked the question, "Is the rumor true that LaSalle is an assembled automobile with either a Buick or an

LaSalle was awarded the honor at the Indianapolis 500 Mile Sweepstakes as the Official 1934 Pacemaker. This was a real public relations coup.

Streamlining and racing were linked in those days as were aerodynamics and flying. Harley Earl loved racing, which he did as a youngster. No wonder he was attracted to the streamlining elements of Fleetwood designer Jules Agramonte's proposal for the 1934 LaSalle. It had been inspired by the racing world. Agramonte had taken the basic shapes used by the beach race cars designed to set land speed records in the 1930s. Bodies were streamlined by making them as narrow as possible and completely enveloping the chassis to reduce the effects of wind resistance. He was also influenced by racing planes that often enclosed the landing gear with fully skirted pontoon fenders. These concepts were beautifully transformed into the design of the trendsetting 1934 LaSalle.

In 1927, Bill Rader had driven a LaSalle on the General Motors Proving Grounds at high speeds, proving its reliability. Now, Bill Rader was the driver of a 1934 LaSalle Convertible Coupe as pace car for the Indianapolis 500. Its streamlined design heritage from the racing world became obvious to all who watched, heard or read about the race.

In the publicity photo, Eddie Rickenbacker is at the wheel.

Oldsmobile 8 chassis?" This was answered by, "That is not true. The LaSalle was designed and developed by Cadillac engineers and measures up to the Cadillac standards in every respect. The LaSalle engine, transmission, rear axle . . . are all built in the Cadillac factory to Cadillac standards ."

In retrospect, it probably would not have been cost effective for LaSalle to have shared the V-8 engine with Cadillac in 1934. It was heavy, an older design and expensive. LaSalle's new hood design had to have a narrow engine. Was it less expensive to go with the Straight-8? Yes. Did it save engine design and development time? Yes. Did it perform well? Yes. Was it different from Oldsmobile? Definitely. LaSalle had the right to call this engine "its own make." Objective analysis of the facts verifies this claim and lays to rest the long time erroneous perception of LaSalle using an Oldsmobile engine. LaSalle indeed had its own Cadillac factory built engine.

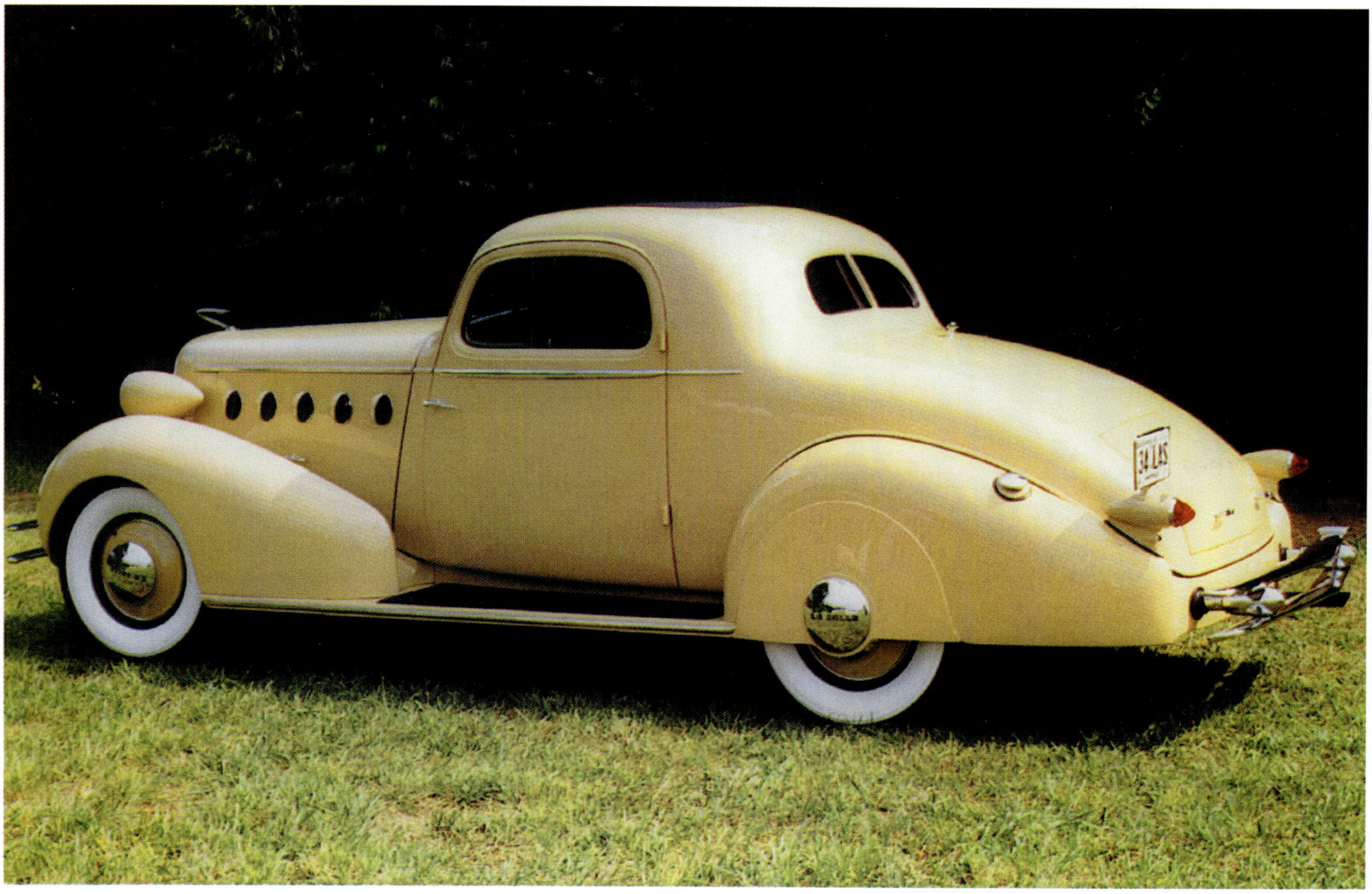

34 LAS

In June of 1934, "The Cadillac Accelerator" distributed a supplementary notice to announce the availability of wheel shields which dealers could order from the factory, painted to match the owner's car for $25 per pair installed. These fender skirts were promoted as "completely concealing the running gear" and "fully in keeping with the surface contours of the individually streamlined fenders and body."

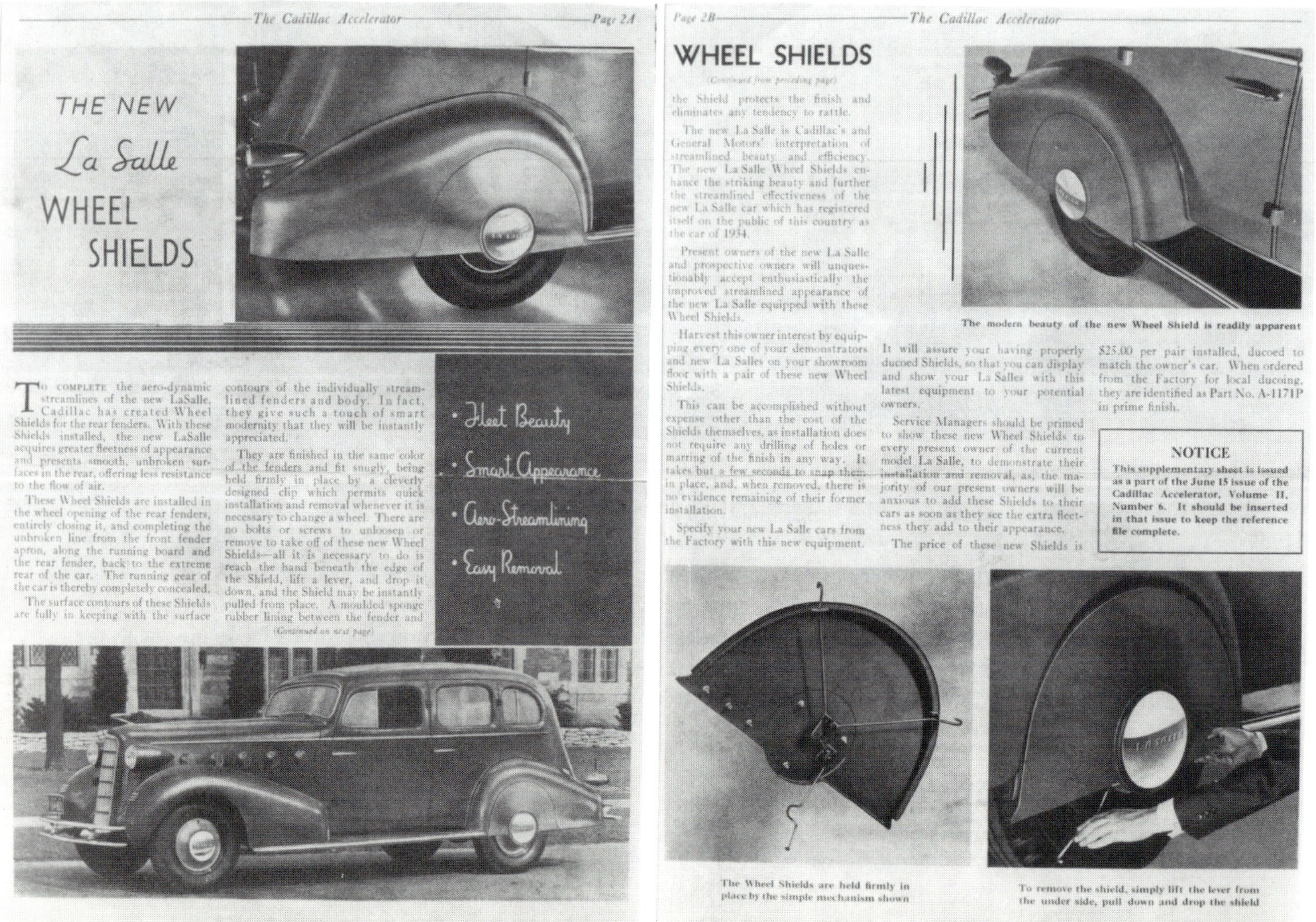

The Cadillac Accelerator — *Page 2A*

THE NEW *La Salle* WHEEL SHIELDS

To complete the aero-dynamic streamlines of the new LaSalle, Cadillac has created Wheel Shields for the rear fenders. With these Shields installed, the new LaSalle acquires greater fleetness of appearance and presents smooth, unbroken surfaces in the rear, offering less resistance to the flow of air.

These Wheel Shields are installed in the wheel opening of the rear fenders, entirely closing it, and completing the unbroken line from the front fender apron, along the running board and the rear fender, back to the extreme rear of the car. The running gear of the car is thereby completely concealed.

The surface contours of these Shields are fully in keeping with the surface contours of the individually streamlined fenders and body. In fact, they give such a touch of smart modernity that they will be instantly appreciated.

They are finished in the same color of the fenders and fit snugly, being held firmly in place by a cleverly designed clip which permits quick installation and removal whenever it is necessary to change a wheel. There are no bolts or screws to unloosen or remove to take off of these new Wheel Shields—all it is necessary to do is reach the hand beneath the edge of the Shield, lift a lever, and drop it down, and the Shield may be instantly pulled from place. A moulded sponge rubber lining between the fender and

(Continued on next page)

· Fleet Beauty
· Smart Appearance
· Aero-Streamlining
· Easy Removal

Page 2B — *The Cadillac Accelerator*

WHEEL SHIELDS

(Continued from preceding page)

the Shield protects the finish and eliminates any tendency to rattle.

The new La Salle is Cadillac's and General Motors' interpretation of streamlined beauty and efficiency. The new La Salle Wheel Shields enhance the striking beauty and further the streamlined effectiveness of the new La Salle car which has registered itself on the public of this country as the car of 1934.

Present owners of the new La Salle and prospective owners will unquestionably accept enthusiastically the improved streamlined appearance of the new La Salle equipped with these Wheel Shields.

Harvest this owner interest by equipping every one of your demonstrators and new La Salles on your showroom floor with a pair of these new Wheel Shields.

This can be accomplished without expense other than the cost of the Shields themselves, as installation does not require any drilling of holes or marring of the finish in any way. It takes but a few seconds to snap them in place, and, when removed, there is no evidence remaining of their former installation.

Specify your new La Salle cars from the Factory with this new equipment.

The modern beauty of the new Wheel Shield is readily apparent

It will assure your having properly ducoed Shields, so that you can display and show your La Salles with this latest equipment to your potential owners.

Service Managers should be primed to show these new Wheel Shields to every present owner of the current model La Salle, to demonstrate their installation and removal, as, the majority of our present owners will be anxious to add these Shields to their cars as soon as they see the extra fleetness they add to their appearance.

The price of these new Shields is $25.00 per pair installed, ducoed to match the owner's car. When ordered from the Factory for local ducoing, they are identified as Part No. A-1171P in prime finish.

NOTICE

This supplementary sheet is issued as a part of the June 15 issue of the Cadillac Accelerator, Volume II, Number 6. It should be inserted in that issue to keep the reference file complete.

The Wheel Shields are held firmly in place by the simple mechanism shown

To remove the shield, simply lift the lever from the under side, pull down and drop the shield

1934 LaSalle Production

<u>Total Production</u>: 7,232 automobiles, chassis and commercial chassis.

<u>Serial Numbers</u>: 2100001-2107232. The Vehicle (engine) serial number is on the "Left side of cylinder block at front, just below the cylinder head."

<u>Chassis Numbers</u>: 21-1 through 21-7232. Location of chassis number is "Top surface of frame side bar, left side, just ahead of dash."

<u>Body Plates</u>: "Body and style number - Left side of cowl just under hood."

Body Type and Style Numbers:		U.S. Production	List Prices - FOB Detroit (April 4, 1934)	Canadian (Oshawa)
350 Series 50 (119" Wheelbase) -	Fleetwood Bodies			
5-Pass. Sedan	34-159 (6330-S)	4074	$1695.00	101
2-Pass. Convertible Coupe	34-168 (6335)	600	$1695.00	18
2-Pass. Coupe	34-178 (6376)	786	$1595.00	12
5-Pass. Club Sedan (solid quarters)	34-182 (6333-S)	658	$1695.00	11
5-Pass. Sedan	35-159	962		
2-Pass. Convertible Coupe	35-168	34		
2-Pass. Coupe	35-178	19		
5-Pass. Club Sedan (solid quarters)	35-182	6		
Series 350 passenger car chassis		32		
LaSalle "50" 119" commercial chassis		10		
	Total	7181 (51 units unaccounted for)		142

The unaccounted for cars include 41 missing second series record sheets, at the end of production, that likely understate the highest second series Sedan body number, plus 10 unknown units.

Note: All U.S. produced 1934 LaSalle build sheets indicate Fleetwood bodies. There are three distinct body style numbers for each body type of 1934 LaSalle. In the first series of cars (ended at serial #2106169), the "34-..." number is used interchangeably with the associated "63.." number, depending on who typed the build sheet. The second series of cars (started at serial #2106170) has a separate set of body serial numbers for each body type. Thus, there are two U.S. built 1934 LaSalle 5-Pass. Sedans with body #1, etc. In addition, the Canadian built cars have a separate set of body serial numbers for each body type, starting with body #1. Consequently, there were actually three 1934 LaSalles in each body type with body #1, etc. Although assigned a "35-..." style number, the second series cars have 1934 serial numbers and are distinctly identified on export control order record sheets as "LaSalle 1934 Series 50" cars.

The 1935 models use the same "35-..." style numbers but have a different set of serial numbers and are designated Series "35-50-B" on the record sheets.

Color Options, U.S.

Code	Body and Fenders	Dupont #	Wheels	Dupont #
31	Black	20488	Black (standard)	20488
			Vincennes Red	20527
			Ski Green	20308
32	Admiral Blue	20211	Freedom Blue	20212
33	Richmond Maroon	26635	Vincennes Red	20527
34	Ardsley Green	23387	Ski Green	20308
35	Brazilian Brown	20835	Malay Brown Light	28938
36	Cranbrook Gray	21230	Ski Green	20308
37	Sheridan Blue	20210	Italian Cream	20734
38	Lamar Tan	28937	Sealing Wax Red	20558
39	Diana Cream	20768	Diana Cream	20768

"Any single durable color may be had without extra cost. Opalescent finish available at extra charge. Standard practice is to finish fenders in same color as body panels. Black fenders may be specified without extra charge."

The standard color combinations above are from a listing in the Cadillac Motor Car Company publication "1934 LaSalle Features of Construction." Examination of the build sheets reveals that nearly all of the cars had black wheels and the wheel discs were painted in the specified "Wheels" color. The two-digit paint codes do not appear on the build sheets, except for the export cars. The paint name and paint numbers for body panels, fenders and chassis, wheels and wheel discs are listed on each build sheet.

Trim Options, U.S.

Closed Bodies:		Convertible Bodies:	
Tan Heather Mixture Cloth	63 T 134	Black Leather	1 T 1334
Gray Heather Mixture Cloth	65 T 134	Tan Leather	2 T 1334
Tan Highland Twist Cord	69 T 134	Tan Highland Twist Cord	69 T 134
Gray Highland Twist Cord	70 T 134	Gray Highland Twist Cord	70 T 134

Convertible top: Tan with tan lining (1 T 1533)
"Special upholstery material may be specified at extra charge."

Colors used on Canadian built cars

Amber White Pale	24650916	Hemlock Green	24650454
Biarritz Blue	24650322	Lamar Tan	28937
Black	20488	Laurel Green	2466423
Burgundy Maroon	24650507	Malay Brown Light	28939
Chessylite Blue	2465322	McLaughlin Blue	2468187
Circassian Brown	24650588	Ormond Brown	24650589
Diana Cream	20768	Oshawa Blue	2468188
Donado Blue	24650659	Pocono Gray	24650944
Dozar Blue	24659765	Pueblo Brown	24650278
Fern Green	24650751	Regent Maroon	24650721
Gettysburg Blue	20247	Richmond Maroon	26635
Glyndon Green	24650569	Venetian Blue	24650616
Harbour Mist Gray	24650312		

Trim Options, Canadian

126	Brown Leather, Cloth Headlining
127	Taupe Broadcloth, Blue Welts
128	Taupe Broadcloth, Green Leather Welts
129	Taupe Broadcloth, Taupe Welts
131	Brown Leather
132	Blue Leather
135	Taupe (Broadcloth), Black Welts
	Green Leather
	Red Leather

Accessories
(April 4, 1934)
(Prices include complete installation and Federal Excise Taxes)

Cadillac Metal Tire Covers for LaSalle (pair)	$ 35.00	A-981, 982 and A-1096, 1097
Cadillac Metal Cover Mirrors (pair)	$ 20.00	
Cadillac Auxiliary Mirror (hinge)	$ 8.00	A-1125
Cadillac License Frames (pair)	$ 7.00	Various part numbers, by size
LaSalle Moto-Pack	$ 5.65	A-1078
Cadillac Master Radio	$ 89.50	A-1115
Cadillac Standard Radio	$ 59.50	A-1188
Cadillac Steam Heater (front compartment)	$ 44.50	A-1110
Cadillac Trunks and Cases -		
Standard trunk only	$ 85.00	1408724
Equipped with 3 standard cases	$122.00	
Equipped with 4 standard cases	$134.00	
Equipped with genuine cowhide cases	$195.00	
Equipped with aerotype linen cases	$175.00	
Cadillac Fleetwood Trunk and Cases -		
Fleetwood trunk only	$ 95.00	
Equipped with 3 standard cases	$132.00	1098280
Equipped with 4 standard cases	$144.00	
Equipped with 3 standard long cases	$140.00	
Equipped with genuine cowhide cases	$205.00	
Equipped with aerotype linen cases	$185.00	
Cadillac Lorraine Driving Light	$ 24.50	1409332
Cadillac Fleetwood Robe	$ 45.00	
Cadillac Double Alpaca Robe	$ 20.00	
Cadillac Alpaca and Plush Robe	$ 20.00	
LaSalle Steel Tire Chains	$ 8.00	

(Prices below include complete installation but Excise Taxes to be added)

LaSalle Torpedo Ornament	$ 20.00	A-1100
Flexible Spoke Steering Wheel	$ 15.00	1096288
Cadillac Fleetwood Trunk Rack	$ 35.00	1098538
Cadillac Fleetwood Trunk Rack Platform	$ 15.00	A-1146

Recommended Minimum Equipment

Torpedo Radiator Ornament	$20.00
License Frames	$ 7.00
For cars with 5 wheels	
Spare tire and tube	Not listed
For cars with 6 wheels	
Fenderwells, 2 disc covered spare wheels with tires	$90.00

Five disc covered steel wheels standard equipment. U.S. Royal 7.00 X 16" black sidewall tires standard equipment.

Research Methodology: Microfiche copies of the individual Shipping Department records of the as-built configuration of each serial number were viewed, starting at the highest serial number and working backwards, to determine the highest body serial number of each body style. No attempt was made to record all engine and body numbers of production cars and to construct cross reference lists of body numbers with corresponding engine numbers to verify that all body numbers were used in actual production.

Notes on research findings:

1. "The New LaSalle 1934 Features of Construction" (undated) lists a Fleetwood Body Style 6380, 5-Pass Conv. Sedan. A sheet-by-sheet examination of the individual build sheets indicates that no production Convertible Sedans were built.

The standard configuration for all styles of 1934 LaSalle was with the spare wheel and tire concealed in a rear body compartment. Disc wheels were standard equipment. Features of Construction states "Wood or wire wheels not available." Most of the Canadian built cars, however, were equipped with wire wheels (colors not specified.) Only one U.S. built passenger car and one commercial chassis were found to be fitted with wire wheels.

The Canadian cars are thought to have been built on complete runable chassis shipped from Detroit to Oshawa. The records list only the style (job) number, body number, car type (e.g., 5-Pass. Sedan), upholstery number and type, body panel color, wire wheels when so equipped and ignition key number. There is no indication of the distribution of the Canadian cars.

All body styles were produced in both left and right hand drive and with the optional six wheel dual-sidemount configuration. A single passenger car (Coupe) was built with a left side fenderwell only.

Numerous special order cars were built with custom features including: special upholstery and top materials, chrome garnish mouldings, graining on the instrument panel, folding armrest in the rear seat back, front seat center armrest (Conv. Coupe), individual bucket-type front seats, curved glass Imperial division (two cars), raised steering wheel, leather rim steering wheels, rumble seat omitted with reversed deck lid made longer to include tire compartment, "Catalin" and "Tenite" dash knobs in various colors, special radiator ornaments, no radiator ornament, roller curtains on rear windows, chrome head and tail lamps, full metal roof, carpet covered bar-type foot rail, robe rail instead of robe cord, etc. Fender skirts were not yet a listed accessory but were furnished by the Art & Colour studio for a World's Fair Convertible and multiple special orders.

2. The 1934 buying public took full advantage of "...the custom-car option of nine carefully harmonized color schemes for finish; with an unlimited choice, at no extra charge, when deferred delivery is satisfactory to the buyer." A virtual panoply of colors was ordered. Some combinations became nearly as common as the standard offerings. Nearly all of the non-standard colors were used on more than one vehicle. Studying the export record sheets indicates that some of the non-standard colors were actually assigned two-digit paint codes to simplify record keeping. An amazing total of 208 different body colors and 163 different wheel disc colors were indicated on the U.S. and Canadian build sheets! The 1934 LaSalle received true custom color treatment when most other makes were offered in a handful of color options.

Special Order and no charge color combinations on U.S. built cars included:

Body Color		Wheel Discs		Body Color		Wheel Discs	
Admiral Blue	20211	Prairie Grass	20890	Cierce Blue	(22330) 2447067	Cierce Blue	22330
Aiken Gray	21133	Aiken Gray	21133			Horton Blue	20242
Alvarado Ivory	20737	Seashore Tan	20838	Classic Blue	22290	Classic Blue	22290
Ambassador Maroon	5891418	Ambassador Maroon	5891418			Freedom Blue	20212
American Green	24650748	Ski Green	20308	Clio Brown, Dark	28878	Lamar Tan	28937
Angelus Green (or Gray)	24650926	Angelus Green	24650926	Confederate Gray	24651055	Chrome plated	
		Danube Green, Light	24650747	Crown Point Tan	2465909	Crown Point Tan	2465909
Argentine Orange	2441447	Argentine Orange	2441447	Czarina Beige	2443009	Czarina Beige	2443009
Avon Blue	2445669	Avon Blue	2445669	Dagistan Blue	24650661	Chrome plated	
Avon Blue Pearlite	P.E.201	Sagamore Red, Light	20555	Dawn Gray, Light	24651064	Dawn Gray, Light	24651064
Azure Blue Deep Pearlite	P.E. 2312	Chrome plated		Deauville Blue	24650286	Folla Blue	24622634
Banderlog Brown	2441304	Premet Dark Tan	2444544	Deauville Grey	21123	Deauville Grey	21123
Bangkok Brown, Light	N.L.	Scarab Yellow	2105207			Grattan Grey	20168
Barcelona Blue	24650875	Barcelona Blue	24650875	Deep River Blue	2445827	Italian Cream	20734
Bay Tree Green (20306)	2444036	Bay Tree Green	20306	Desert Sand	20870	Chrome plated	
Beau Brumell	2445912	Carnival Red	24451071	Driftwood Smoke	(28942) 2441312	Driftwood Smoke	28942
Bellaire Gray	21254	Chrome plated				Flax Green	24650985
Bellevue Beige	24650094	Bellevue Beige	24650094			Motmot Green	24650532
Berkley Green, Light	28951412	Berkley Green, Light	28951412			Pomarang Brown	2445591
Black	20488	Argent	2463735	Dush Rose	2447238	Dush Rose	2447238
		Italian Cream	20734	Dustproof Grey, Light	21139	Dust Proof Grey, Light	21139
		Matador Orange	2441335			Vincennes Red	20527
		Tokio Ivory	20722	Dusty Gray	24651073	Chrome plated	
Blue Devil Blue	22378	Blue Devil Blue	22378	Eton Blue	24650634	Eton Blue	24650634
Blue Moss	2444566	Blue Moss	2444566			Mountain Ash Scarlet	20545
Bonaventure Green (23480)	2465941	Bonaventure Green	23480			Vincennes Red	20527
		Ski Green	20308	Elder Green	20394	Elder Green	20394
Bonita Blue	20217	Bonita Blue	20217	Elizabethan Blue	20276	Elizabethan Blue	20276
Bonita Gray	24650955	Bonita Gray	24650955	Empire Blue, Dark	24651128	Empire Blue, Dark	24651128
Bosphorus Green	24650562	Bosphorus Green	24650562	Faience Blue	22367	Storm Cloud Blue	22368
Briarcliff Beige	2445915	Briarcliff Beige	2445915	Fallon Brown, Light	2465044	Fallon Brown, Light	2465044
Brookside Gray	24650984	Brookside Gray	24650984			Pimpernel Scarlet	24651151
Bucknell Grey	21186	Kildare Green, Light	24650701	Freedom Blue	24650633	Freedom Blue	24650633
Cadet Blue, Light	24650663	Cadet Blue, Light	24650663			Vincennes Red	20527
Cadillac Special Gray	21238	Cataract Green	2445863	Galion Green Pearlite	P.E. 308	Chrome plated	
Canton Blue	20229	Canton Blue	20229	Garland Green	24650671	Bolivia Green	24650888
Canyon Gray	20136	Canyon Gray	20136	Garnet Maroon	20661	Sagamore Red, Light.	20555
		Pomerang Brown	2445591			Roslyn Red	20551
Carlisle Beige, Light	28897	Carlisle Beige, Light	28897	Gering Green Pearlite	P.E. 314	Chrome plated	
Carolina Green	20361	Carolina Green	20361	Gettysburg Blue	20247	Blue Devil Blue	22378
Caromel Brown, Light	24650575	Caromel Brown, Light	24650575			Italian Cream	20734
Castleton Ivory	20771	Chrome plate				Satsuma Beige	24650254
Cathedral Gray	21125	Vincennes Red	20527			Tokio Ivory	20722
		Burnt Orange	2461295	Glacier Metallic	20251571	Glacier Metallic	20251571
Chantilly Green	23420	Chantilly Green	23420	Gobelin Blue	24650364	Gobelin Blue	24650364
Chateau Gray	(21215) 24650947	Chateau Gray	24650947	Golden Tan Pearlite	P.E. 805	Clifton Orange	20745
Cheruit Blue	22357	Cheruit Vermillion	20559	Grattan Gray	20168	Deauville Green	23458

These ads demonstrate the unique positioning of the 1934 model. Top left: A trendsetting comparison introduced the thought of design leadership by comparing LaSalle streamlining to other forms of transportation. Top right: The use of photographic reality matches LaSalle to lifestyles. Above left: Placed in February 1935, this ad still shows the 1934 model LaSalle, while Cadillac showed its 1935 model. Note the LaSalle biplane bumpers and Cadillac's new re-designed safety bumper bar. Above right: Finally, the new 1935 LaSalle model is shown in the April 27 issue of The Saturday Evening Post.

NINETEEN THIRTY-FIVE
Series 50

In appearance, the new La Salle is smarter than the style setting La Salle of last year—the car that established the streamlined trend for the entire industry.

In performance, the new La Salle seems actually inspired. It whisks its way through traffic with alert and resourceful ease. It meets the challenge of the open road with hour after hour of swift unlabored speed. It takes the longest hills in flashing, effortless stride.

Designed and built by Cadillac, the La Salle is a genuine tribute to fine car ideals. Its quality construction, finish, and appointments are instantly apparent.

Equally important with its excellence of materials, however, is the quality reflected in La Salle's brilliant new styling, its flashing new performance, and its new measure of dependability and safety.

The new La Salle has been called the extra value La Salle.

–from the 1935 sales brochure

La Salle Two Door Touring Sedan

La Salle Four Door Touring Sedan

—*from the 1935 sales brochure*

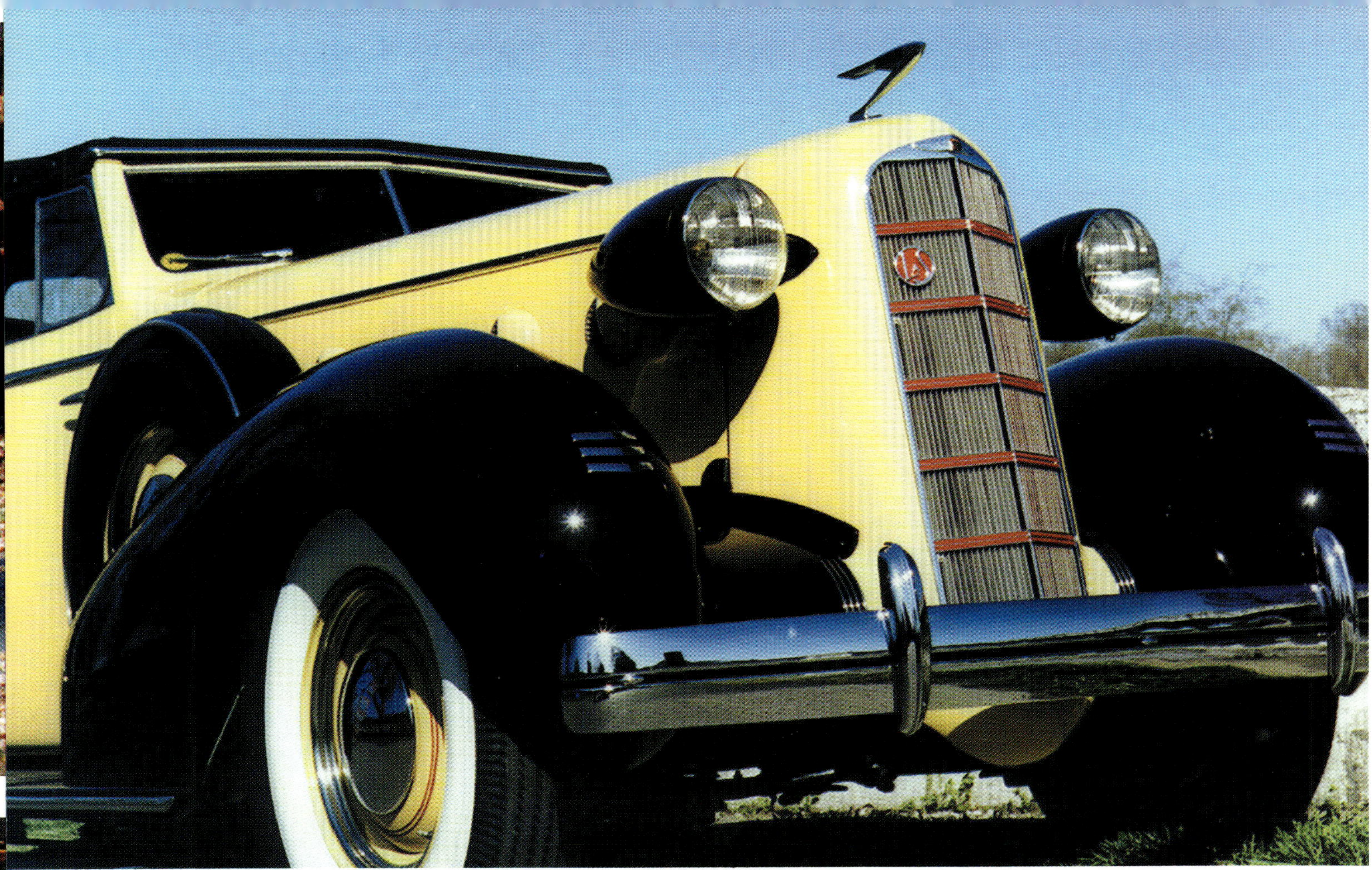

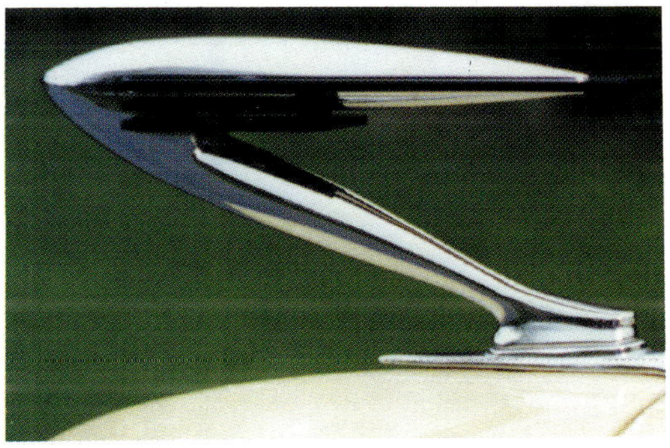

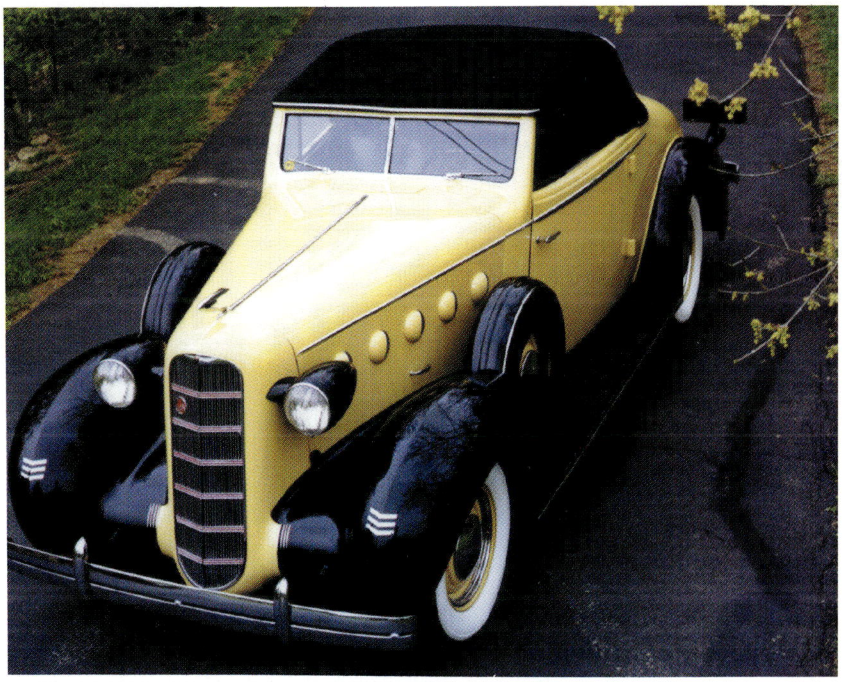

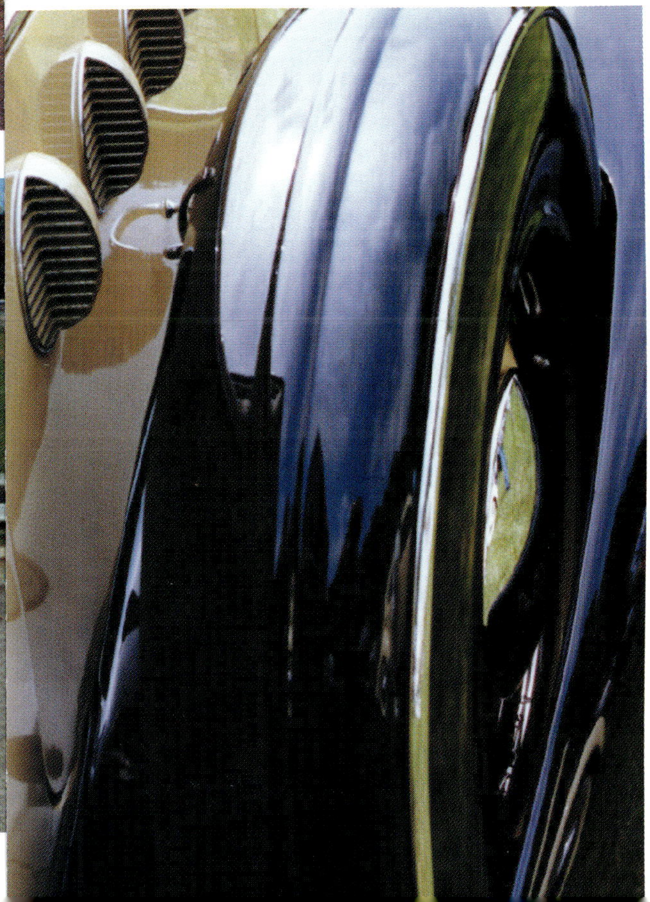

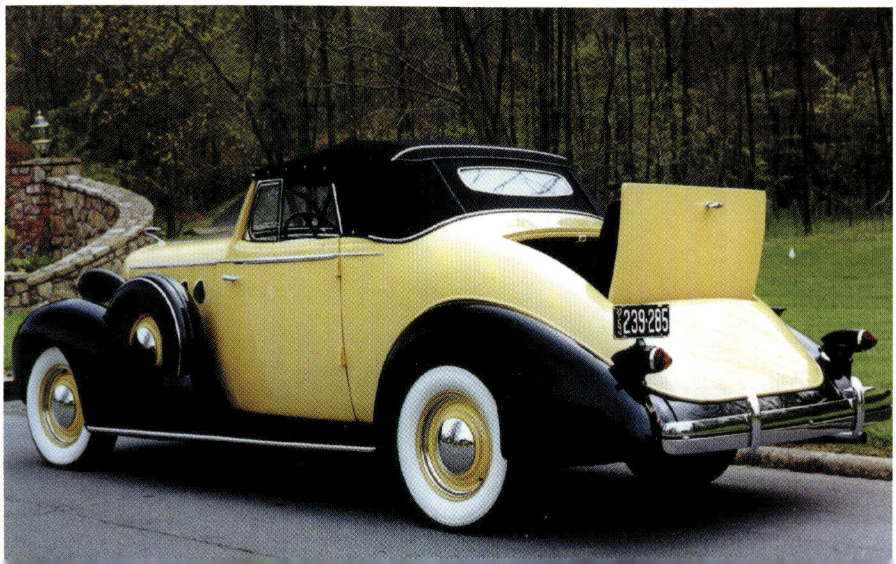
239-285

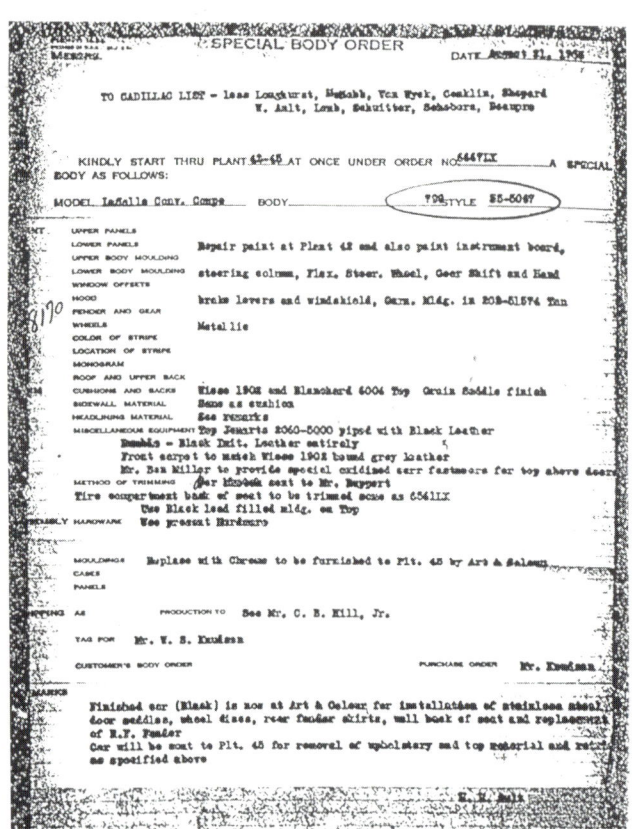

Top: Cadillac and LaSalle owners interested in quality customizing at reasonable prices often commissioned Derham of Rosemont, Pennsylvania, to do the work. One such project was this 1935 LaSalle Sedan with trunk customized into a handsome Town Car with padded top, open chauffeur's compartment and rear doors rounded at the top. The long hood gave this model a very formal and expensive look. Above left: There were also factory custom built LaSalles. Not to be confused with options available to the public, these were often done to personal cars of GM executives to suit their taste or to test market reaction. A close look at this factory Special Body Order reveals a very much customized LaSalle Convertible Coupe for W. S. Knudsen. Numerous items were changed, such as paint, leather, trim, fender skirts, oxidized fasteners, etc. Middle right: The pressed glass taillight lens was a carryover from 1934, but the gas tank cap and funnel were relocated from the outside left rear fender to the inside right rear fender panel. Above right: Typical driver's view of the new-for-1935 instrument panel. A derivative of the 1932-1934 double breadloaf design, it moved the clock to the glove box and increased the size of the speedometer.

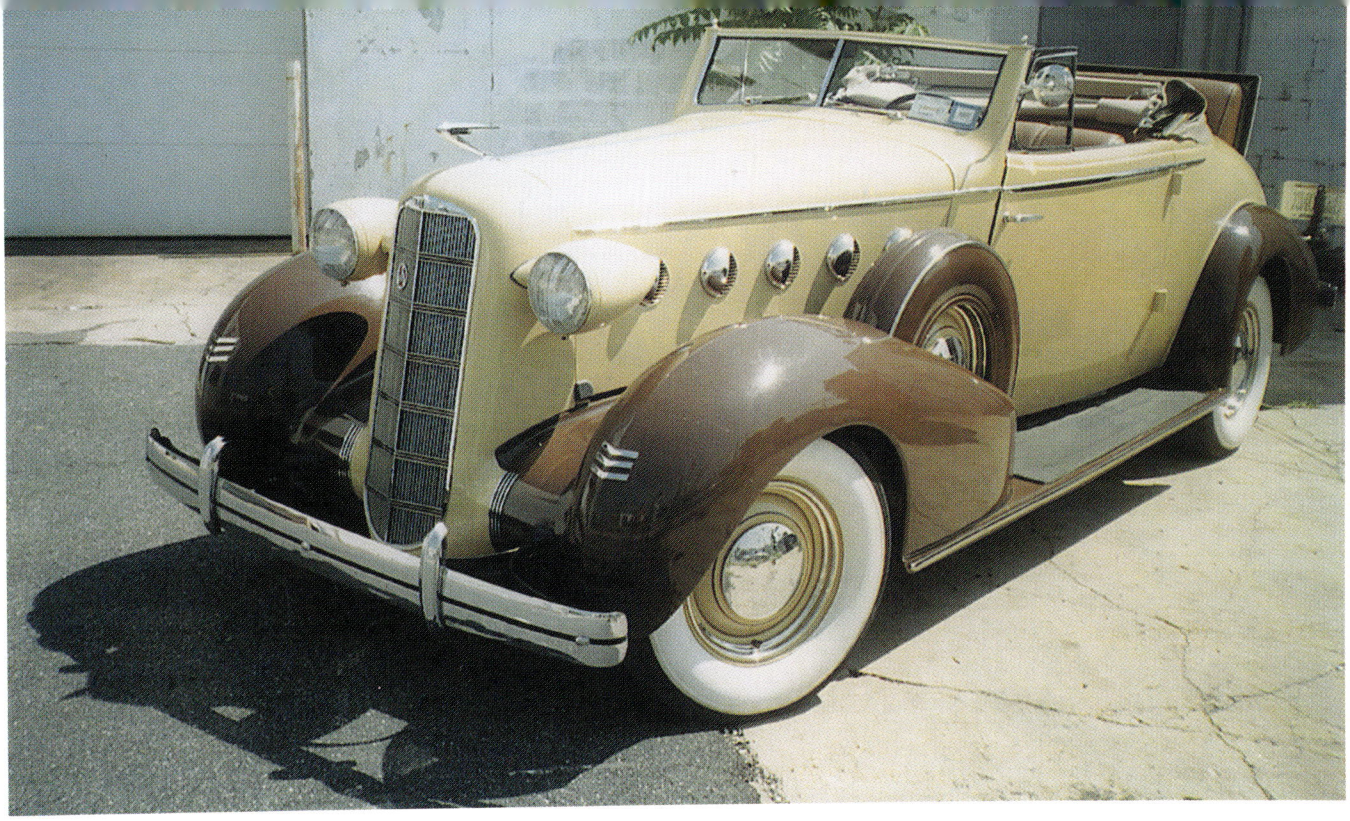

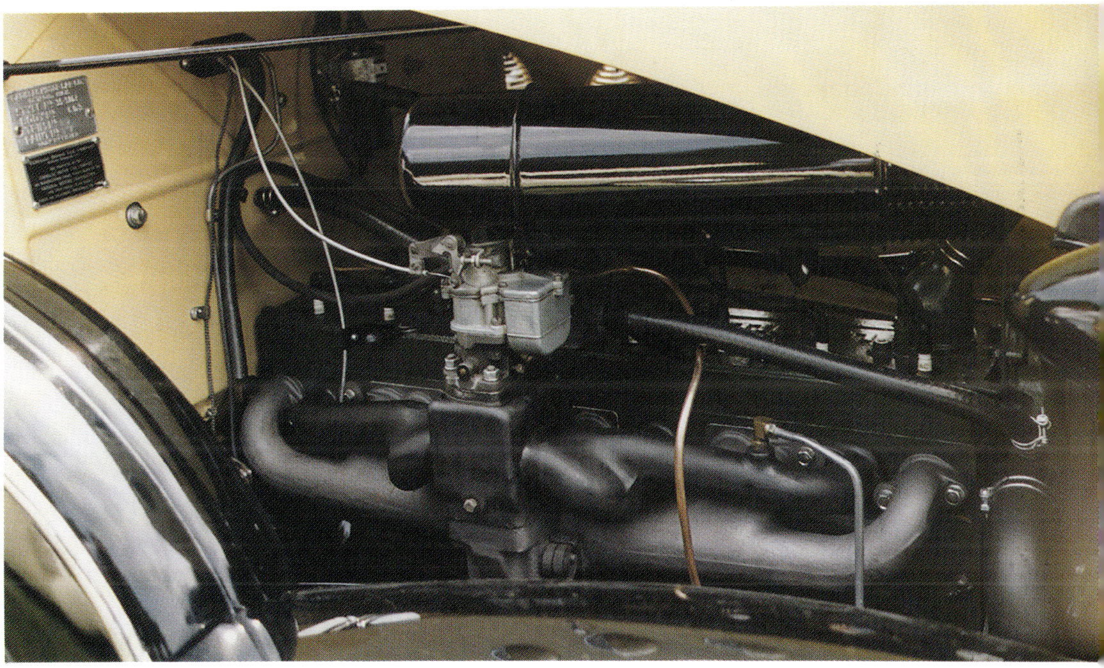

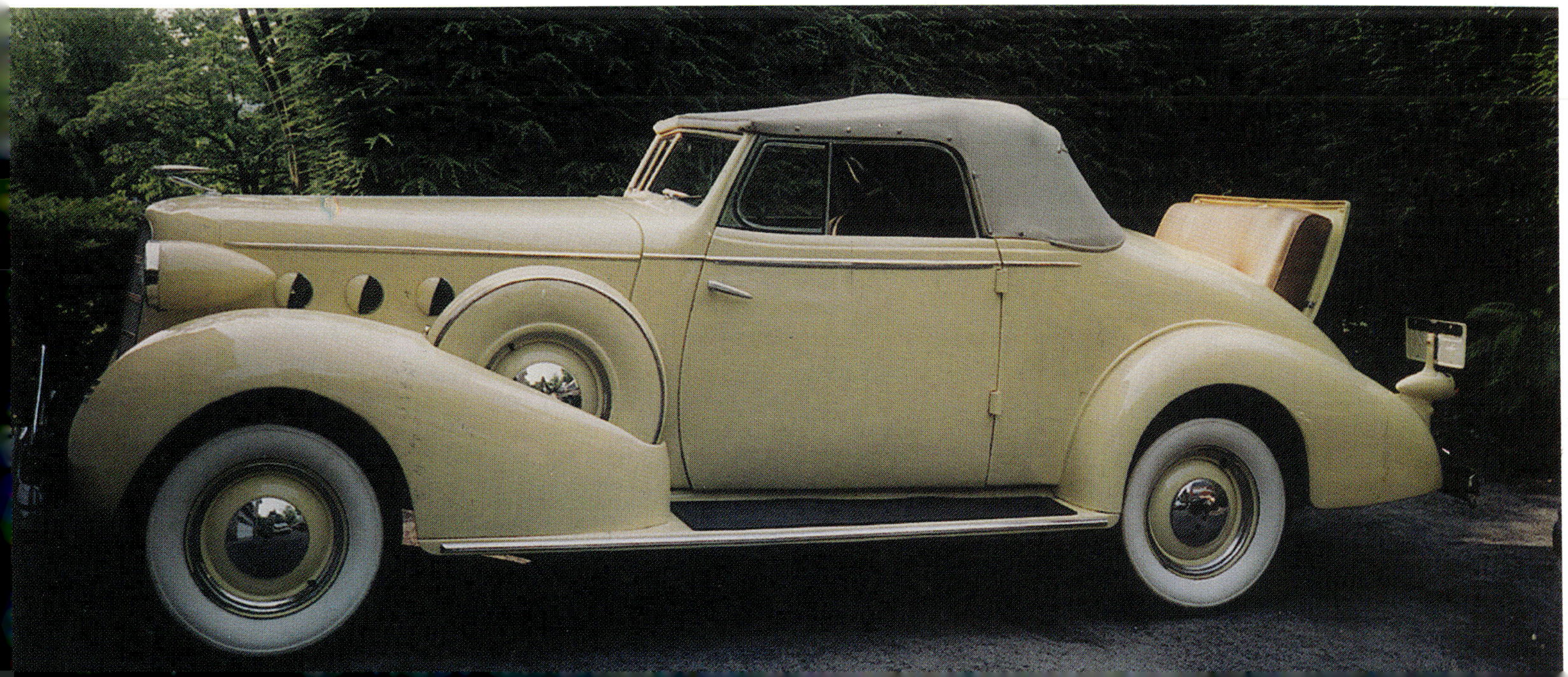

1935 LaSalle Production

Total Production: 8653 automobiles and chassis.

Serial Numbers: 2200001-2208653. The Vehicle (engine) serial number is "On the left side of the cylinder block at the forward end just below the cylinder head."

Chassis Numbers: 22-1 through 22-8653. Location of chassis number is "On top surface of frame side bar left side just ahead of dash."

Body Plates: "Body identification plate indicating style number, body number, trim and paint combination code number, will be found on front of dash panel under hood on right hand side."

Body Type and Style Numbers:		U.S. Production	Canada	Standard Configuration
Series 35-50-B (120" Wheelbase) -	Fisher Bodies			
5-Pass. Standard Sedan	35-5009	100		Spare tire at rear concealed
5-Pass. Touring Coupe	35-5011	1133	17	Trunk, concealed spare tire
5-Pass. Touring Sedan	35-5019	5602	148	Trunk, concealed spare tire
2-Pass. Convertible Coupe	35-5067	800	20	Rumble, R.H. Fenderwell.
2-Pass. Coupe	35-5077	756	18	No rumble, spare tire under deck.
Commercial Chassis (121" W.B.)	35-50	53		
Passenger car chassis		5		
		Subtotal	203	
		Total	8652	(1 unit unaccounted for)

Note: The Touring Coupe was also referred to as a "2-Door Touring Sedan" in factory literature.
Note: The factory records list the Canadian built style 5067 as a "4-Pass. Conv. Coupe," vice 2-Pass. The Canadian style 5011 was also shown as a "5-Pass. coach."
The Canadian built cars do NOT share the body number sequence with the U.S. built cars. Each Canadian built body style has a body #1, etc.

List Prices - FOB Detroit: (March 11, 1935)

5-Wheel Cars: (Extra charge for right hand fenderwell on styles 5011, 5019 or 5077 $23.00)

		6-Wheel Cars:	
5009 5-Pass. Sedan	Not listed	5009 5-Pass. Sedan	Not listed
5011 5-Pass. Touring Coupe	$1255.00	5011 5-Pass. Touring Coupe	$1320.00
5019 5-Pass. Touring Sedan	$1295.00	5019 5-Pass. Touring Sedan	$1360.00
5067 2-Pass. Convertible Coupe	$1325.00	5067 2-Pass. Convertible Coupe	$1370.00
5077 2-Pass. Coupe	$1225.00	5077 2-Pass. Coupe	$1290.00
Commercial Chassis	Not listed		
Passenger car chassis	Not listed		

Standard Color Options, U.S.

Body and Fenders	Dupont #	Wheels	Dupont #
75 Black	2462048	Black	
		Vincennes Red	20527
		Ski Green	20308
76 Admiral Blue	24650534	Admiral Blue	24650534
77 Richmond Maroon	2445179	Romany Red	20525
78 Meadowgrass Green	24650745	Kildare Green - Dark	24650723
79 Shirley Green	24650662	Scarab Green	24650537
80 Canyon Gray	24651788	Indiana Gray	20157
81 Purvis Gray	24650989	Como Blue	24650876
82 Canton Blue	24650661	Marquis Blue	943219
83 Diana Cream	24651466	Diana Cream	24651466
84 Samarkand Gray	2446224	Ski Green	20308
		Vincennes Red	20527
85 Army Blue	24650469	Eton Blue	24650634
86 Regal Maroon	24450721	Romany Red Dulux	20525

Note: "Extra Charges for Special Colors will be furnished upon request."

Painting in a non-standard color combination or changes to the standard upholstery options were recorded as Special Body Orders (S.B.O.).

Standard Trim Options, U.S.

Closed Bodies:

Tan Heather Mixture Cloth	63 T 134	Taupe Plush	13 T 134
Gray Heather Mixture Cloth	65 T 134	Black Leather	1 T 1334
Tan Highland Twist Cord	69 T 134	Tan Leather	2 T 1334
Gray Highland Twist Cord	70 T 134		

Convertible Bodies:
Black Leather	1 T 1334
Tan Leather	2 T 1334
Tan Highland Twist Cord	69 T 134
Gray Highland Twist Cord	70 T 134

Convertible top: Tan outside (1 T 1533) with tan (2 T 1533) lining.
Special upholstery material may be specified at extra charge.

Note: A large proportion of the Convertible Coupes were built with cloth interiors.

Color Options, Canadian

590 Black		595 Madrid Maroon
591 Oshawa Blue	2468188	596 Hanson Brown
592 Turrenne Gray		597 Willow Green
593 Harbormist Gray		598 Moritz Green
594 Ontario Maroon		

Note: Additional non-standard colors were used, including Antibes, Beaver Tan, Elizabethan Blue (20276), McLaughlin Blue, Navarre, "prime" and "Special." No paint manufacturer or other paint codes are listed.

Accessory Groups

Basic Equipment Group "X" $60.00
Torpedo Ornament, Bumpers, Security Plate Glass, Extra Tire and Tube.

A (5 wheel) $25.00	B (5 Wheel) $48.00	C (6 Wheel) $60.00	D (6 Wheel) $83.00
Clock	Clock	Clock	Clock
R.H. Sun Visor	R.H. Sun Visor	R.H. Sun Visor	R. H. Sun Visor
Wheel Trim Rings	Wheel Trim Rings	Wheel Trim Rings	Wheel Trim Rings
	Flexible (Steering) Wheel	Metal Tire Covers	Metal Tire Covers
	License Frames		Flexible (Steering) Wheel
			License Frames

Note: Although Basic Group "X" is listed as an extra charge item, all vehicles were built with that equipment.

Standard Equipment:
5 disc covered steel wheels. U.S. Royal 7.00 X 16" Black sidewall tires.

Accessories
(March 11, 1935)

Master Radio	$89.50	Moto-pack	$ 5.85
Standard Radio	$54.50	Luggage Compartment Rug (5 wheel)	$ 4.75
Radio Antenna	Not listed	Luggage Compartment Rug (6 wheel)	$ 6.25
Electric Clock	$14.50	Steam Heater	$35.00
Right Hand Sun Visor	$ 3.50	Visor Mirror	$ 1.85
Wheel Discs (Chrome)	Not listed	Fleetwood Robe (made of identical	
Wheel Trim Rings (each)	$ 1.50	upholstery cloth)	$45.00
Flexible Steering Wheel	$16.00	Double Alpaca Robe	$20.00
License Frames (pair)	$ 7.00	Alpaca and Plush Robe	$20.00
Ash Trays (each)	$ 1.90	Tire Chains	$ 8.00
Metal Tire Covers (pair)	$35.00	Custom Control Knobs	$ 5.00
Luggage - Tan Duck or Black Duckoid Finish		Seat Covers	Not listed
Wardrolette	$47.50	Lorraine Spot Light	$27.50
Ladies' Aviatrix	$35.00		
Gentlemen's Aviator	$35.00		

ALL PRICES INCLUDE INSTALLATION

Note: The Cadillac Serviceman Bulletins of March 1, 1934, and March 1, 1935, give warning of the too delicate nature of the Steam Heater introduced in 1934. "Since a loss of only 1/4 ounce of water is sufficient to render the heater inoperative, tightening the connections to the limit is of the utmost importance." "The Steam Heater operating instructions call for the use of clean battery water in the reservoir. This means clean and clear distilled water, free from all foreign particles and solutions. The water and steam lines of the steam heater are so fine that even a slight amount of rust, scale or dirt may clog them." "Do not use the battery filler syringe for filling the heater cup. The slight amount of battery electrolyte that might remain in the syringe would react with the metals in the system to form substances that would clog the system and might result in serious deterioration of the lines." The Steam Heater apparently quickly gained a bad reputation. A scant 27 LaSalles were equipped with the Steam Heater by the factory in 1935. One car shipped on August 23, 1935, is annotated "New type hot water heater - heater loose in car." The Steam Heater was to disappear from the market.

Notes on research findings:

1. The 1935 cars are designated "35-50-B" on the record sheets. The "B" distinguishes the 1935 cars from the "35-50" bodies produced late in the 1934 production run and included in the 1934 numbering sequence (210-----). None of the vehicle record sheets for 1935

show the price of the vehicle, price of accessories or additional charges for special orders or transportation. The sheets are considered to be actual build sheets, with the exception of the sheets for the Canadian built cars.

As in prior years, the Canadian cars are thought to have been built on complete runable chassis shipped from Detroit to Oshawa. The records list only the style (job) number, body number, car type (e.g., 5-Pass. Sedan), upholstery number, body panel color, number of wheels and ignition key number. Four upholstery code numbers (161 thru 164) are shown without any indication of the upholstery type. There is no indication of the distribution of the Canadian cars.

2. The standard configuration for each body style is indicated with the production numbers above. Factory built deviations by body style include:

      5009 6-wheels with dual fenderwells
      5011 Right hand fenderwell; 6-wheels with dual fenderwells
      5019 Right hand fenderwell; Left hand fenderwell; 6-wheels with dual fenderwells
      5067 6-wheels with dual fenderwells; one S.B.O. with instructions to "Reverse deck lid & omit rumble seat," three S.B.O. with instructions to "Omit FW, place extra wheel & tire loose in rumble seat," "Spare tire back of front seat"
      5077 Fourteen S.B.O. with instructions to "Reverse deck lid & install rumble seat"; RH fenderwell; 6 wheels with dual fenderwells

3. A small number of cars are shown with the name of the purchaser, principally the Special Body Order cars. Celebrity buyers included: Miss Kresge, Miss Mary Louise Maytag, Mr. Oscar Hammerstein, Mr. Fields - Hollywood, C. T. Fisher and A. J. Fisher (Fisher brothers), Ernest Seaholm (Cadillac Chief Engineer), W. S. Knudsen (GM Executive V.P.), and Alfred P. Sloan, Jr. (GM Chairman). The Sloan Convertible was, of course, an S.B.O. unit and included chrome door garnish mouldings, center top bow, steering column, brake and shift levers, wheel discs and fender skirts. The Convertible for Mr. Knudsen, serial 2208170, presents a rare opportunity to read an actual Special Body Order. The S.B.O. sheets went to the body plants and are infrequently included in the Cadillac files.

4. <u>Factory Installed Accessories</u>: A large portion of production in most model years consisted of cars built for inventory, based on sales projections by body style, color, etc. Dealer orders for cars to put on the sales floor were filled from stock. Current owners naturally want to know the history of their particular car. Factory records do not exist to identify the original purchaser of most cars. Dealership records may survive. A careful study of the build sheets will at least provide evidence that a particular car was ordered by an individual. The Special Body Order (S.B.O.) cars are obvious, all of those were individual orders. So, too, were the cars with specific accessories other than the above indicated Accessory Groups. The dealer profit margin on accessories was always substantial and they were eager to load up a car with options. All of the following individual accessories (including some not listed in the published accessory lists) were installed by the factory on one or more cars. Part numbers are listed where they could be determined:

Master Radio	1413290
Standard Radio	1413292
Radio Antenna (Running Board Aerial)	1096466
Radio (installation) kit	1413583
Electric Clock	1561361
Right Hand Sun Visor	Various, by upholstery type and color
Wheel Discs (Chrome)	1096495
Wheel Trim Rings (Chrome)	1413248
Flexible Steering Wheel	1096448
License Frames	Various, by size used in individual states
Ash Trays	1413902
Metal Tire Covers	1096480(R), 1096481 (Early Cars); 1096505(R), 1096506(L)
Luggage	
Wardrolette	1413832 (Black); Tan-not listed
Ladies' Aviatrix	1413834 (Tan)
Gentlemen's Aviator	1413833 (Tan)
Small Suitcases For Trunk	1413830 (Black), 1413831 (Black)
Moto-pack	A-1078
Luggage Compartment Rug	1413747
Luggage Compartment Board	1096474
Steam Heater	1413932
Visor Mirror	1411361
Alpaca and Plush Robe (Grey)	Not listed
Seat Covers (Seabreeze)	1414603 (front); 1414605 (rear)
Lorrainne Spot Light	1415659
Lorrainne Lights (fog)	1409332
Chrome Hood Ports	Not listed
Fender Lamps (export cars only)	Not listed
Fender Skirts	Not listed
Grease Gun	Not listed
Hassock (rear seat)	Not listed
Low Compression Head	1096424
Oil Bath Air Cleaner	Not listed

5. As with other years, a number of cars in various body styles received special preparation for the show circuit and were tagged for the "General Motors Spring Show." One 5019 Sedan was tagged "Statler Hotel Display." Two 5019 Sedans and a 5011 2-door were marked "Special Show Job" and shipped to General Motors Argentina at Buenos Aires.

6. <u>Special Features</u>: One style 5011 and one 5019 were special ordered with a "folding center armrest in rear seatback."

Two style 5019 Sedans, serial 2206617 and 2206620, were special built with "Quarter windows omitted, solid metal rear quarter panels, brown silk curtains on rear doors and rear window." Both cars were painted and trimmed identically and shipped to General Motors, Ltd., Bombay, India.

7. <u>Commercial Chassis</u>: Commercial chassis and engines are numbered the same as the automobiles, in the sequence in which they came down the assembly line. No distinctly commercial chassis were built until serial 2206066. That chassis and all subsequent chassis were listed as 121" wheelbase. Commercial chassis were shipped to:

	Units:
A. J. Miller Company, Bellefontaine, Ohio	2
Meteor Motor Car Company, Piqua, Ohio	50
Knightstown Body Company, Knightstown, Indiana	1
	53

8. <u>Domestic Chassis</u>: A single Touring Sedan chassis, serial 2201669, was assigned to the Engineering Department Experimental Garage and subsequently sold to Mr. N. A. Zannoth of Dept. V-21 on January 9, 1936.

The first two 1935 chassis sold, serial 2201706 and 2201861, are shown on the records as 120" chassis. These chassis went to traditional commercial vehicle builders, Knightstown and Eureka, and may in fact be passenger car chassis for custom bodies; there is no way to determine that, short of finding a surviving unit with the corresponding serial number.

9. <u>Export Chassis</u>: Two passenger car chassis were shipped to GM Continental, Antwerp, Belgium: Serial 2204037 with 5 wheels, chrome trim rings, dummy cowl and primered fenders and Serial 2204215 with 6 wheels, chrome trim rings, closed car cowl complete with instrument panel toe and floor boards (less windshield), primered fenders and metal tire covers. The body builders were not specified.

10. <u>Convertible Frames</u>: There was obviously a problem with the frame of the 1935 Convertible Coupe. There are numerous record sheets that are annotated "Special Conv. Coupe frame #148736 with all attaching parts shipped......." Many were shipped/installed as late as August 1936.

11. All models of the standard production cars were exported outside of the U.S./Canada. Numerous export cars are indicated with combinations of right hand drive, kilometer speedometers and low compression heads.

12. As with other years, none of the body styles were built in a straight body order sequence. S.B.O. (Special Body Order) cars were generally substantially out of order due to the time required to make alterations.

First car built in each body style:	Last car built in each body style:
5009 body #1, serial 2202558	body #75, serial 2208633
5011 body #1, serial 2200005	body #1119, serial 2208631
5019 body #399, serial 2200001	body #5595, serial 2208626
5067 body #4, serial 2200007	body #663, serial 2208585
5077 body #1, serial 2200003	body #752, serial 2208616
120" chassis, serial 2201706	121" chassis, serial 2208653

CONDENSED SPECIFICATIONS

ENGINE—Cadillac precision built; 8 cylinders in line; L head; bore 3"; stroke 4⅜"; displacement 248 cu. in.; taxable horsepower 28.8; brake horsepower 105 at 3600 R. P. M.; engine mounted in rubber at three points.

MAIN BEARINGS—Five—bronze backed babbitt.

CRANKSHAFT—Statically and dynamically balanced with eight counterweights forged integral; harmonic balancer to give maximum smoothness.

CONNECTING RODS—Drop-forged and matched in sets to precision limits; gun drilled to allow for pressure lubrication to piston pins, which are carefully fitted and locked in the piston.

PISTONS—Trans-slot design aluminum alloy for uniform expansion; special anodizing process hardens wearing surface to prevent scuffing and scoring, fitted with two compression rings and two oil rings.

LUBRICATION SYSTEM—Full pressure feed to mains, connecting rods, wrist pins and camshaft bearings; connecting rods have bleed hole for lubrication to inside of cylinders.

COOLING SYSTEM—Harrison radiator. Forced circulation by centrifugal pump. Thermostatic control.

CARBURETION—Stromberg dual down-draft with equalized manifolding, redesigned fuel pump, air cleaner, intake silencer. Entirely new Triple Range manual and electric choke—found on no other car at any price. Automatic heat control and 18-gal. gas tank.

GENERATOR—The Delco-Remy Peak Load generator maintains full charging rate, even while headlamps, radio and heater and other electrical accessories are all being used simultaneously. It is a new, exclusive feature on La Salle, offered on no other car at any price, and eliminates all worry concerning battery condition.

STARTER—Conveniently located button on instrument panel connects with solenoid switch on starter that gives positive pre-engagement of starter pinion with flywheel before starter operates, thus relieving starter gears of shock loads.

CLUTCH—10" x 6" single plate dry disc type with 100.6 sq. inches of facing area. Gives gradual and smooth application of power. Requires uniform pedal pressure of only 28 pounds at all engine speeds.

TRANSMISSION—Cadillac built Syncro-Mesh with three forward speeds and reverse gears. Reverse gears as well as low and second speed gears are helical for extreme quietness. All gears are both ground and lapped, an expensive process in quality manufacturing not used in any other car at any price. All gears fully carburized for hard use and long life.

BATTERY—17 plate Delco-Remy, 110 amp. hour capacity.

LIGHTING—Multi-beam headlights with double filament 32 c.p. lamps. Foot dimmer switch changes beam from country driving to country passing. Light rays from right headlamp are deflected to left side of road. Rays from left headlamp are deflected to right side of road. Control switch on instrument panel provides selection of four beams— one for city driving, parking, and two for country driving. Visible headlamp beam indicator dials on the instrument panel show which of four beams is being used. Parking lights are mounted in headlamps. Double tail lights with reflecting buttons also contain stop warning lamps actuated by brake pedal action.

FRONT WHEELS—Independent "Knee Action" front wheels, with large, resilient coil springs for smoother riding comfort and effortless driving control. Thoroughly proven by a year of use and millions of miles of testing.

BRAKES—Bendix Duo-Servo Super-Hydraulic brakes operate in centrifuse brake drums. Self-energizing, fully enclosed, internal expanding type in 12" brake drums. Total braking area front and rear 207 sq. in. Mechanical hand brake operates independently of the hydraulic system and can be used for parking or emergency purposes.

REAR SPRINGS—Semi-elliptic, 54¼" long, 2" wide, packed in graphite lubricant with metal spring covers. Front and upper rear spring bushings are rubber mounted; lower rear spring shackle is threaded.

DRIVE SHAFT—Hotchkiss drive with torque taken through rear springs. Three universal joints mounted on needle roller bearings packed with lubricant.

REAR AXLE—Cadillac design and manufacture. Semi-floating type with spiral bevel gears, insuring quiet, dependable performance without friction or need for special lubricants. Exceptionally sturdy and rugged.

STEERING GEAR—Sturdy worm and double roller type. The steering link operates a bell crank supported by the massive front cross member. Attached to it are two steering rods, each of which controls one front wheel. The steering ratio is 20 to 1. Can be turned or parked in much smaller space than many cars of the same wheelbase.

FRAME—The chassis has a low frame that reduces the overall height of car. Lower center of gravity and wide tread gives unusual stability and roadability. The strong rigid center X-member extends forward and to the rear within the main frame, forming a sturdy box member construction, which prevents twisting and distortion. The frame is 6" deep, ₇⁄₃₂" thick and has a flange width of 2".

RIDE STABILIZER—A spring steel shaft carried by the shock absorber arms behind the rear axle to prevent body roll and side sway at high speeds when making turns.

TIRES AND WHEELS—Low pressure, 7.00 x 16, carrying 26 lbs. air pressure. Large section tires cushion road shock; new tread design. 5 steel disc wheels with large chrome disc hub covers. 6 wheel equipment with fenderwells at extra cost.

SHOCK ABSORBERS—Double-action, hydraulic type front and rear.

FENDERS—Fenders, splash apron, and other chassis sheet metal parts, which are exposed to weather, are bonderized to prevent rust.

NINETEEN THIRTY-SIX
Series 50

New beauties of design grace the new LaSalle . . . no more than a glance at LaSalle's handsome new models is required to establish their fresh grace of line and beauty of contour.

The difference is more marked than ever . . . the whole industry has moved forward—mostly in the direction of mass demand and sprightly appearance and performance, but of course Cadillac has been, as always, in the forefront of that forward movement . . . in fact, the difference in distinction in Cadillac and LaSalle has become more marked than ever, for Cadillac has deliberately planned its 1936 creations to widen the gap between the Royal Family of Motordom and all other cars in the world.

Those who revel in the special ease and elegance in the pronounced distinction which Cadillac and LaSalle provide for their owners simply cannot satisfy themselves with anything else.

The satisfaction of rising above the rank and file of the best of motorcars is yours now at figures which make the Royal Family of Motordom the paramount value of the time and year.

—from the 1936 sales brochure

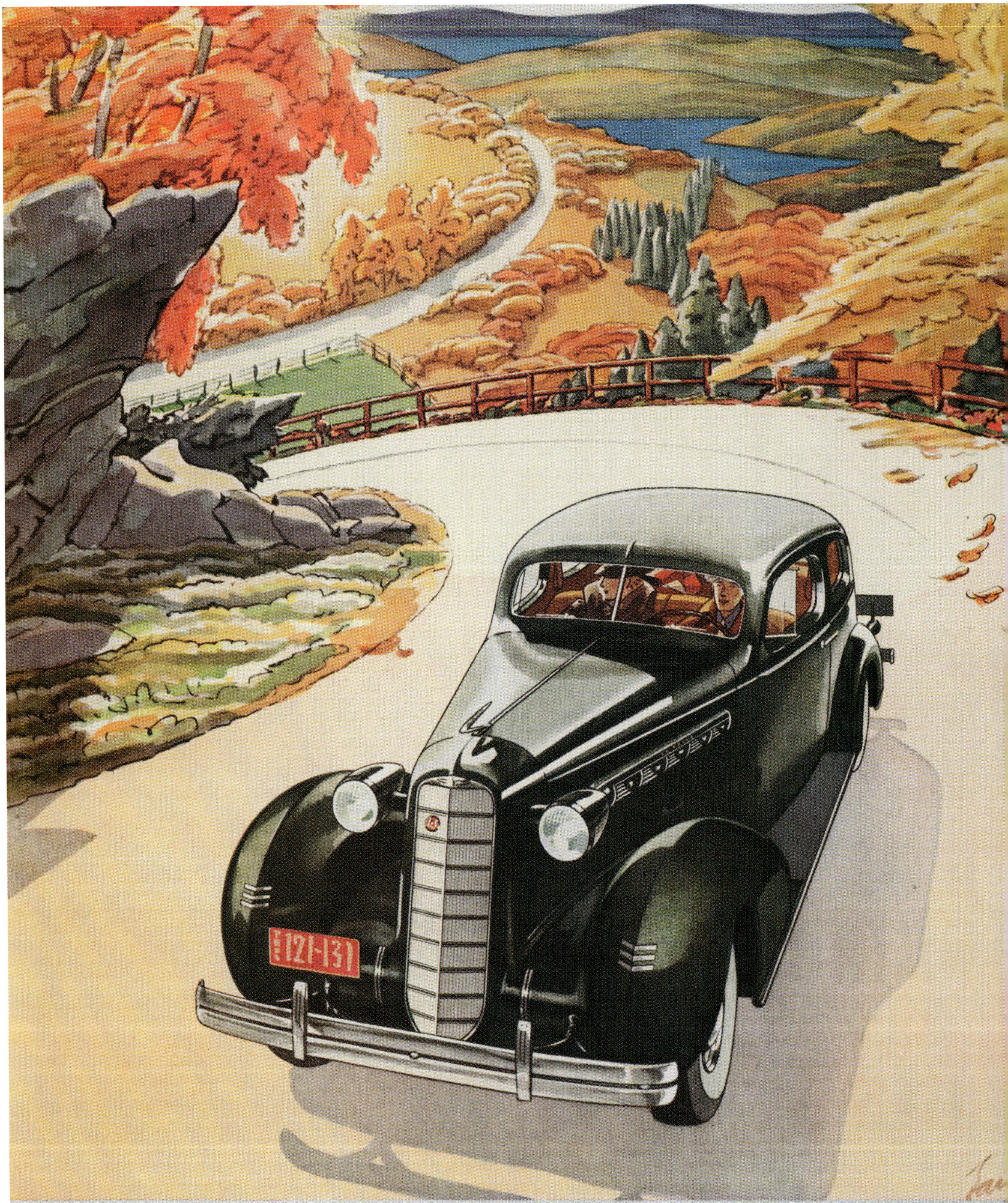
121-131

La Salle Two-Door Touring Sedan—$11

THE NEW

LA SALLE

Illustrated above is the beautiful new La Salle, captivating member of the Royal Family of Motordom. La Salle is really one of the marvels of this great manufacturing age. It is endowed with Cadillac engineering and Cadillac manufacturing throughout, and offers the priceless advantage of Cadillac prestige—yet it is priced so low that it is a prudent choice for even the modest budget. W believe sincerely that there is no other car like La Salle- none other that offers so much of luxury and elegan and distinction, at a price so remarkably low. You Cadillac-La Salle dealer would welcome an oppo tunity to demonstrate its exceptional performance—toda

NINETEEN THIRTY-SIX
Series 50

LaSalle for 1936 entered with little change. It was still riding on the basic style established by the 1934 trendsetter: "the new LaSalle is acclaimed everywhere as a style leader." All four models offered were essentially 1935, except for some small details.

New were horizontal louvers covered by an eyebrow-like panel that ran the length of the hood. Gone were the five porthole hood ventilators. Also gone were the suicide doors. For safety's sake, all doors except for the rear doors on the four-door Sedan were hinged at the front and opened at the rear.

The radiator grille, while the same dimensionally as the 1935 and 1934 models, now was cast in one piece with nine, instead of six, horizontals.

Only two chromed hashes were placed at the leading edge of the catwalks. The hood ornament, headlights, chevrons at the leading edge of the front fenders and two splits in the rear window were a carryover from 1935.

LaSalle's brand new simple and symmetrical instrument panel was very similar to Cadillac of this year.

1936 was the year of tremendous competition from the Packard 120 and Lincoln Zephyr. LaSalle also had competition from inside the Division. Cadillac introduced a new model: the Series 60. It boasted one more inch in the wheelbase, 121 inches, and styling that was almost identical to the Series 50 LaSalle on a 120-inch wheelbase. With all that competition, LaSalle was still able to produce 13,000, and that was nearly twice the number produced in 1934 . . . no small accomplishment.

The same Straight-8 engine was used for the third and last year. It did its job well with 105 bhp at 3600 rpm. A vacuum advance was added to the distributor.

The advertising theme for 1936 was "the Royal Family of Motordom." All models—LaSalle, Cadillac and Fleetwood—were promoted simultaneously as "family." It was an all for one and one for all approach, as in previous brochures and advertisements, but even more so in 1936. They did go so far as to say that "LaSalle is really one of the marvels of this great manufacturing age." Some ads headlined "there can be no difference of opinion" . . . "the difference is more marked than ever." That difference being "deliberately planned in its 1936 creation to widen the gap between the Royal Family of Motordom and all other cars in the world . . ." Sales brochures were beautifully illustrated with an impressionistic flair.

The La Salle Coupe

WHAT *Money* CAN AND CANNOT BUY

When it comes to motor cars, there are some things that money *can* and *cannot* buy. ᛫᛫ Money can buy size and horsepower and fitments and trimmings—but it cannot, alone and unaided, procure a reputation. ᛫᛫ That is inherent in the product itself—and only time and effort and attainment can put it there. ᛫᛫ Cadillac's relation to the motor car industry has long since established it as the accepted standard for those who desire to go beyond the conventionally good. ᛫᛫ So firm is this Cadillac reputation—so faultlessly buttressed by more than thirty years of progression—that none other can bestow quite the same degree of superiority. ᛫᛫ Whichever car you choose from the Royal Family of Motordom— whether the new La Salle, the new Cadillac or the new Cadillac-Fleetwood—you can drive it with the definite knowledge that it deserves the highest respect a motor car can receive. ᛫᛫ For Cadillac has endeavored more earnestly than ever, in its current creations, to widen the gap between the Royal Family of Motordom and all other cars in the world.

La SALLE $1175 ᛫ CADILLAC $1645 ᛫ *Cadillac* FLEETWOOD $2445

Prices list at Detroit, subject to change without notice. Special equipment extra. Monthly payments to suit your purse on the G. M. Installment Plan.

THE ROYAL FAMILY OF MOTORDOM

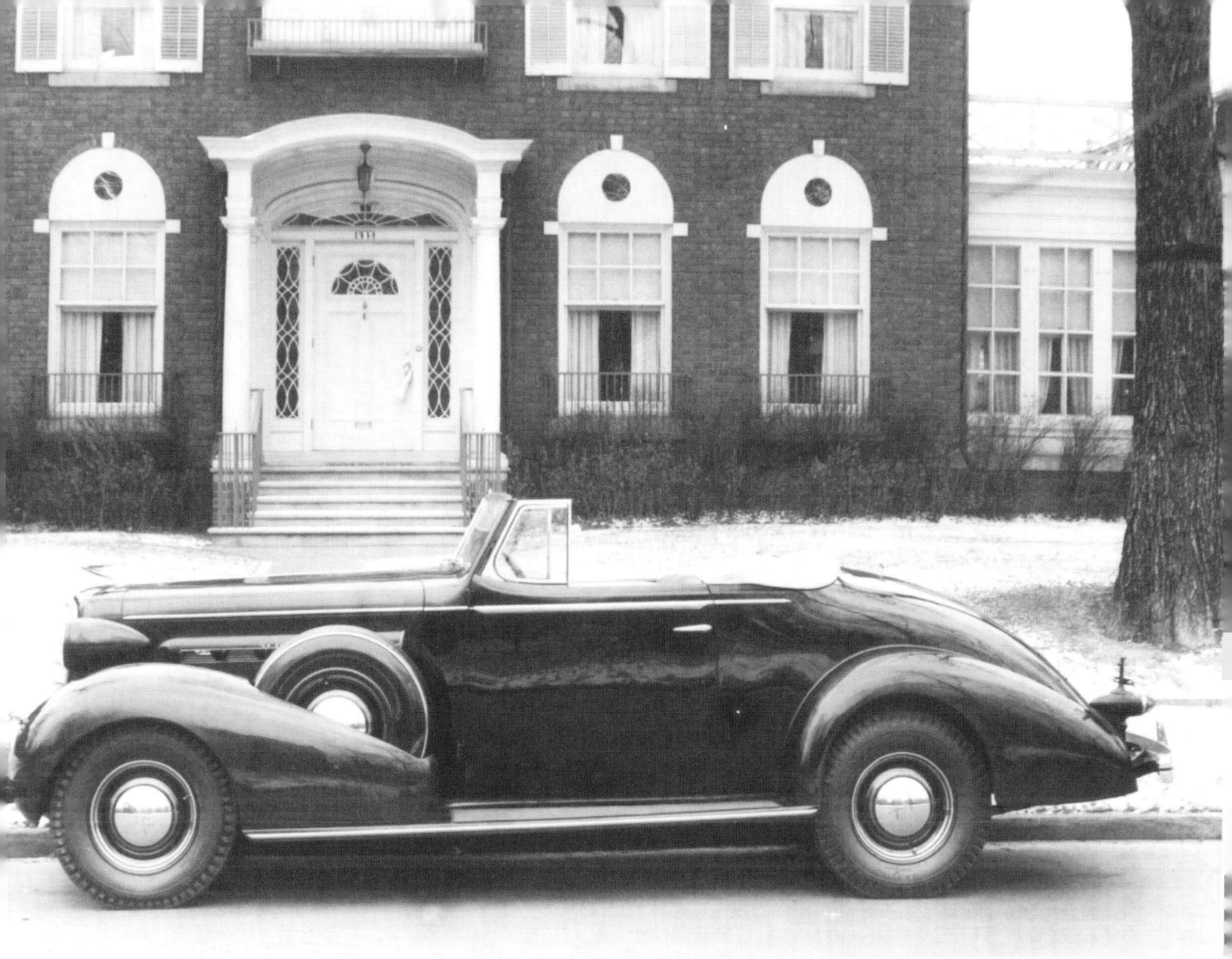

Above: A Series 50 Convertible Coupe could seat two or four passengers. Its profile was the same as 1935 but a number of improvements had been initiated. The optional fender mounted spare tire covers were outlined with a polished stainless steel molding, while the very handsome horizontal line of the ventilator eyebrow lid was allowed to peek from behind the cover on either side. Only small hubcaps with beauty rings were available. LaSalle on the hubcaps was in scripted letters instead of the block letters used in 1934 and 1935. Below: A Series 50 Coupe was attractive from any angle. It was sold as a two- or four-passenger model, depending on whether the trunk or rumble seat version was ordered.

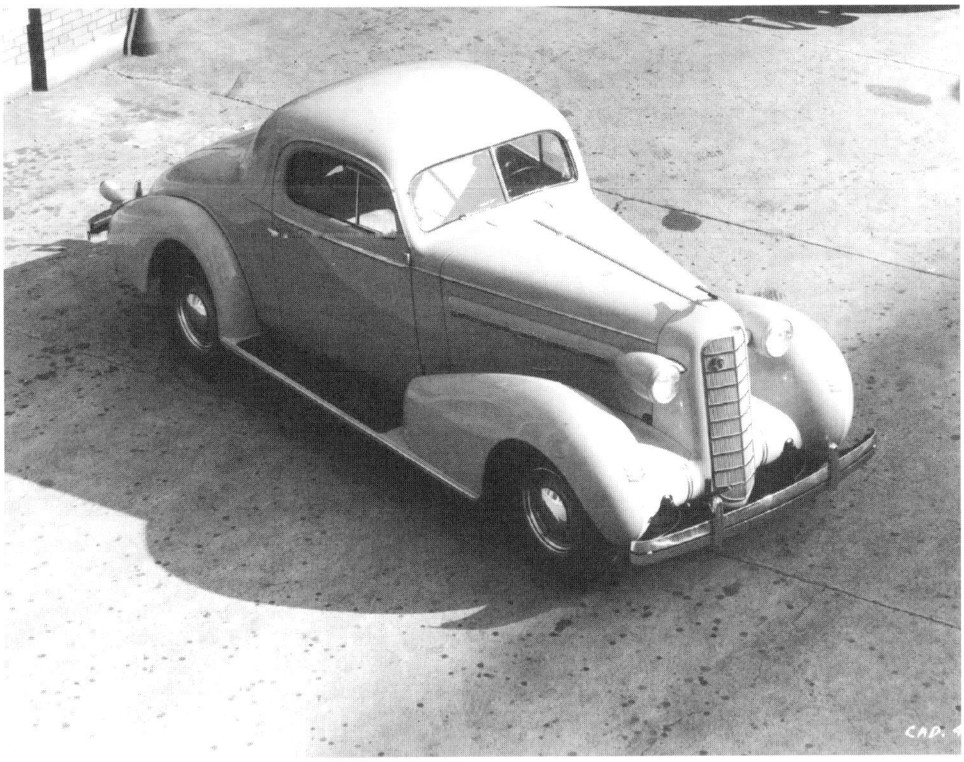

LA SALLE CONVERTIBLE COUPE

LA SALLE COUPE

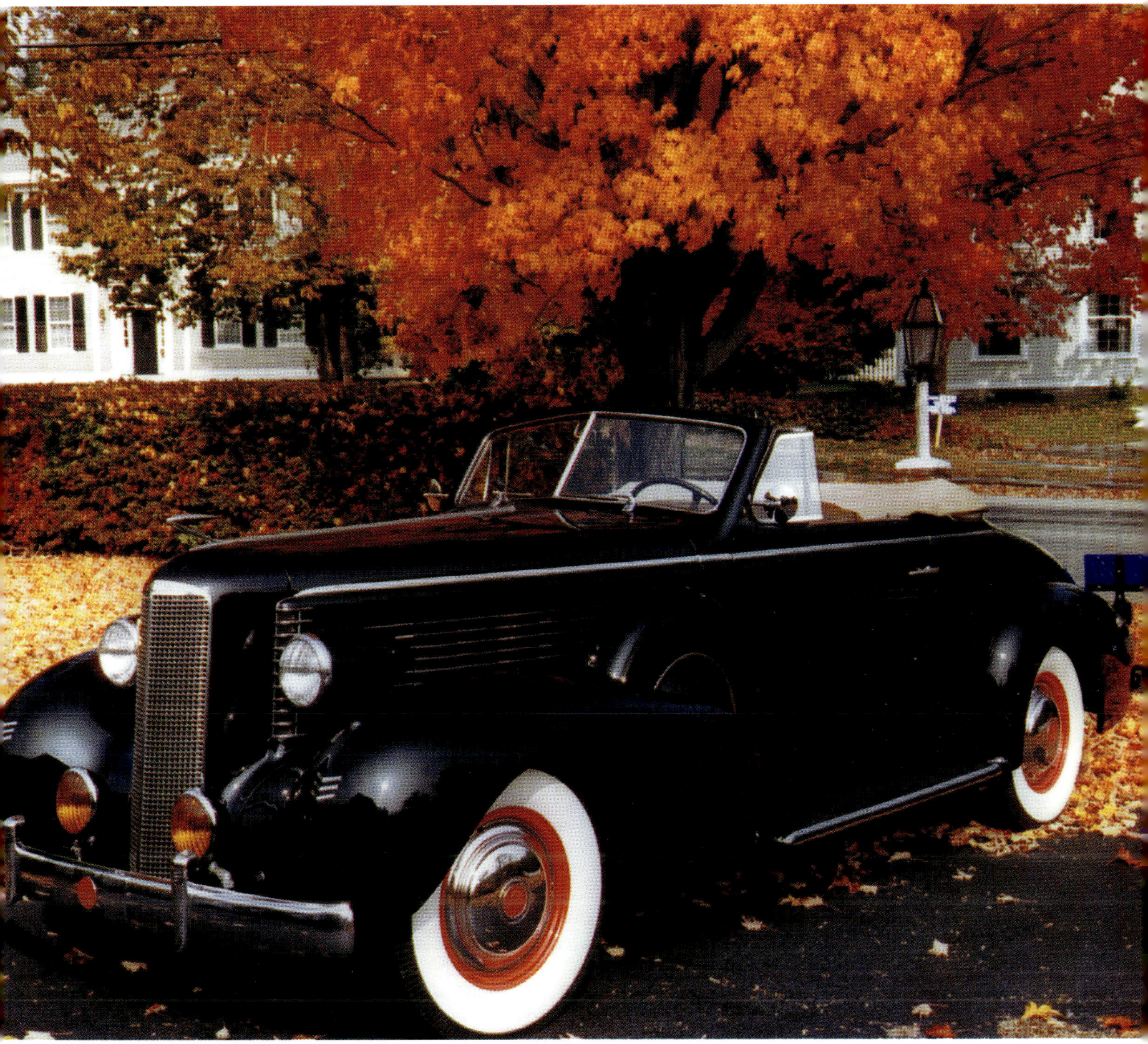

NINETEEN THIRTY-SEVEN

Look at LaSalle!

FINER THAN EVER— AT THE LOWEST PRICE!

It is doubtful whether the motoring public has ever had a greater surprise than when it first heard the price of the new La Salle V-8.

Here is the finest La Salle ever built— powered by a 125-horsepower V-8 Cadillac engine—increased in wheelbase, size, comfort and beauty... yet priced at only $1095*.

And that is the *delivered* price, at Detroit —including all standard accessories!

The result is precisely what might have been expected. There has been such a swing to the new La Salle as the fine-car field has not witnessed in years. Within six weeks after its introduction, almost ten thousand people placed their orders for this extraordinary car!

If you are contemplating the purchase of a motor car anywhere above the very lowest in price—we ask that you, too, *look at La Salle!*

Its low price—its low operating costs—and its unmistakable Cadillac quality—make it an extremely logical choice.

V-8 BUILT BY CADILLAC FOR THE FAMILY OF MODEST INCOME

$1095* AND UP

*Delivered price at Detroit, Mich., $1095 and up, subject to change without notice. This price includes all standard accessories. Transportation, State and Local Sales Taxes, Optional Accessories and Equipment—Extra. Car shown has white sidewall tires at slight extra cost.

1937 LaSalle Production

<u>Total Production</u>: 1937 marked the high point in production of the fourteen years that LaSalle automobiles were built; 32,005 automobiles and chassis.

<u>Serial Numbers</u>: 2230001-2262005. The Vehicle (engine) serial number is "On the crankcase just behind the left cylinder group, parallel to the dash."

<u>Chassis Numbers</u>: 2-B-1 through 2-B-32005. Location of chassis number is "Top surface of frame side bar, just ahead of dash."

<u>Body Plates</u>: "The body style number, job number and paint and trim numbers are stamped on a plate attached to the front of the dash under the hood on the left side on LaSalle 37-50."

<u>Body Type and Style Numbers:</u>		<u>Production</u>	<u>Standard configuration</u>
Series 37-50 (124" Wheelbase) -	Fisher Bodies		
5-Pass. Touring Sedan - 2-Door	37-5011	1801	Trunk, concealed spare
5-Pass. Touring Sedan - 4-Door	37-5019	21514	Trunk, concealed spare
5-Pass. Touring Sedan - 4-Door, CKD (Export)		314	
5-Pass. Touring Sedan Chassis (Export)		64	
2-Pass. Sport Coupe	37-5027	5801	Two opera seats, spare under deck
			Rumble seat when ordered
5-Pass. Convertible Sedan	37-5049	530	Plain back, R.H. fenderwell
2-Pass. Convertible Coupe	37-5067	995	Rumble seat, spare under deck
2-Pass. Convertible Coupe, CKD (Export)		24	
Flower Car	37-5067F	6	Note: Included in 5067 total above
124" W.B. Chassis (w/closed car cowl)		1	
Commercial Chassis (160 3/8" W.B.)	37-50	949	
	Total	31,993	(Unexplained difference of 12 units)

Note: Style 5011 is listed on numerous record sheets within the first 7000 cars built as "LaSalle Touring Coupe." That designation is not used in the Data Book, Shop Manual, sales literature or Master Parts List.

<u>List Prices - FOB Detroit: (October 20, 1936)</u>
5011 2-Door Touring Sedan	$1105.00
5019 5-Pass. Touring Sedan	$1145.00
5027 2-Pass. Coupe	$ 995.00
5049 5-Pass. Convertible Sedan	$1485.00
5067 2-Pass. Convertible Coupe	$1175.00
124" W.B. Chassis	$ 850.00
160" Commercial Chassis	$ 925.00

Standard Color Options

<u>Body and Fenders</u>	<u>Dupont #</u>	<u>Wheels</u>	<u>Dupont #:</u>
20 Black	242-2101	Black (standard)	242-2101
		Flare Red, Clearwater Green (optional)	
21 Admiral Blue	242-50534	Admiral Blue	242-50534
22 Ricardo Maroon	242-5238	Flare Red	943549
23 Douglas Green	242-50618	Clearwater Green	242-50567
24 Peruvian Gray	242-52337	Flare Red	943549
25 Briarcliff Blue	242-50878	Lullwater Blue	242-50951
26 Springdale Green Metallic	202-52276	Springdale Green Metallic	202-52276
27 Golden Beige Metallic	202-51626	Ormond Brown	242-50589
28 Rockledge Gray	242-51015	Clearwater Green	242-50567
29 Santaupe Metallic	202-51485	Kashan Blue	242-50686

<u>Instrument Panel & Garnish Mouldings</u>
Center section - early type	Kasha Beige, 246-50308
Center section - later type	Andes Sand, 243-2007
Sides & top	Shadow Metallic, 202-51575
Garnish Mouldings	Shadow Metallic, 202-51575

Trim Options

<u>Closed Bodies:</u>	<u>Convertible Bodies:</u>
80 Tan Bedford Cord	86 Black Leather
81 Tan Plain Broadcloth	87 Tan Leather
82 Gray Bedford Cord	88 Gray Leather
83 Gray Plain Broadcloth	89 Green Leather

Accessory Groups
Basic Group "X" Equipment $55.00
Ornament, Extra tire and tube, Bumpers, Guards, Electric Clock, Air Cleaner

A 5 (5 Wheel) $36.50	A 6 (6 Wheel) $66.50	B 5 (5 Wheel) $22.50	B 6 (6 Wheel) $54.00
4 Wheel Discs	4 Wheel Discs	5 Trim Rings	6 Trim Rings
Flexible (Steering) Wheel	Flexible (Steering) Wheel	Flexible (Steering) Wheel	Flexible (Steering) Wheel
License Frames	License Frames		2 Metal Tire Covers
	2 Metal Tire Covers		

Note: Although Basic Group "X" is listed as an extra charge item, all vehicles were built with that equipment.

Additional Charges

6 Wheels and fenderwells (Except Convertible Sedan)	$65.00
6 Wheels and fenderwells, Convertible Sedan	$45.00
Right Hand Fenderwell on all Body Styles except Convertible Sedan	$23.00
White Sidewall tires, 6 ply, each	$ 3.60

Accessories

Flexible Steering Wheel	$15.00		Master Radio - Complete With Aerial	$79.50
Heater-Defroster (Hot Water)	$24.50		Standard Radio - Complete With Aerial	$59.50
Hinge Mirror	$ 8.00		Robes:	
Hot Water Heater	$19.50		Fleetwood Cloth and crushed Plush or Alpaca	$45.00
License Frames (pair)	$ 5.50		Pillow to Match	$ 8.00
Luggage Compartment Carpets			Monogram	$ 5.50
5 wheel	$ 5.00		Double Alpaca Robe in Brown or Gray	$20.00
6 wheel	$ 7.50		Alpaca and Plush Robe	$20.00
Luggage - Tan Duck or Black Duckoid Finish			Seat Covers - Sea Breeze (per seat)	$ 7.50
Gentlemen's Aviator	$35.00		Spotlight (closed cars)	$22.00
Ladies' Aviatrix	$35.00		Tire Chains (7.00 X 16")	$ 8.50
Wardrolette	$47.50		Tire Covers - Metal (each)	$15.00
Miscellaneous			Ventilating - Defrosting Fan	$ 6.50
Blue Coral	$ 2.50		Water - Cooled Cushion	$ 7.50
Body Polish (pint)	$ .60		Wheel Discs - Chrome (each)	$ 4.00
Bulb Kit	$ 1.25		Wheel Trim Rings (each)	$ 1.50
Dust Mitt	$ .50			
Fabric Cleaner (pint)	$ .60			
Flashlight	$ 1.50			
Glass Cleaner	$ .65			
Handy Brush	$ 2.00			
Metal Polish (pint)	$ .60			
Moto-Pack	$ 6.25			
Tire Gauge	$ 1.50			

ALL PRICES INCLUDE INSTALLATION

Research Methodology: Microfiche copies of the individual Shipping Department records of the as-built configuration of each serial number were viewed, starting at the highest serial number and working backwards, to determine the highest body serial number of each body style. Commercial chassis numbers were individually recorded to determine actual production. No attempt was made to record all engine and body numbers of production cars and to construct cross reference lists of body numbers with corresponding engine numbers to verify that all body numbers were used in actual production. Serial numbers of completely-knocked-down (CKD) cars and export chassis were recorded to verify actual numbers produced and list the destinations.

Notes on research findings:

1. Cars built before serial 2256712 are recorded on Cadillac Form 3800A, which has a block titled "Purchaser." Although only a small fraction of total production, a surprisingly large number of sheets indicate the name of the actual purchaser in addition to the usual dealership destination. Owner information is very seldom seen in other year record sheets.

2. Convertible Coupe record sheets were carefully scrutinized, in an attempt to identify the actual Pace Car for the 1937 Indianapolis 500 race. Cadillac-LaSalle Club member Bob Murphy of Norwich, Connecticut, provided a copy of an American Automobile Association "Certificate of Performance" that identifies the Pace Car as serial #2248164. The certificate is part of a fold-out brochure that touts the performance of the LaSalle in setting a new production car speed record at Indianapolis. The build sheet indicates serial 2248164 was assigned to the Engineering Department and charged to "Cars in company use (Eng. Dept)" on 4/30/37. Absent any other indication, serial #2248164 is believed to be the Pace Car.

3. The 5067F Flower Cars are not listed in any other known production data. There is no reference in the Master Parts Lists, etc. By recording Convertible Coupe body numbers, it was possible to absolutely establish that the Flower Cars were custom conversions of production Convertible Coupes. The Convertibles were sent to Meteor Motor Car Co., Piqua, Ohio, under individual Cadillac purchase order numbers for "reconstruction" or "re-operation." Specified modifications were: "Flower Compartment must be at least 54" X 54". Specify black Burbank top over driver's seat and also for dummy rear top. Spare tire to be stored in rear compt. Flower compartment to have trap door to allow for cleaning of floor. Flower compartment to have scuppers to allow drainage of rain water." The completed cars were returned to Cadillac Motor Car Company and all were subsequently shipped to "Randall-Donaldson Cad. Corp, Brooklyn, N.Y." or

"New York Branch, New York, N.Y." Three photos of these units are shown in the "Cadillac LaSalle Commercial Cars" brochure for 1938, produced by the Cadillac and LaSalle Commercial Division. Two photos show two units with dual sidemounts and the tops down, wearing 1937 New York license plates. The third photo shows three units, two with sidemounts, all with the tops up and no license plates. The three-car photo clearly shows an extension to the standard running boards, indicating a chassis extension. Based on the known running board length of 59" for a 1937 Coupe, the chassis extension scales out to be 21", or a wheel base of 145". Flower car serial numbers are 2242020 (body 355), 2242025 (body 354), 2243973 (body 406), 2244128 (body 405) and 2255672 (body 875).

4. Commercial Chassis: The commercial chassis and engines are numbered the same as the automobiles, in the sequence in which they came down the assembly line. Thus commercial chassis 2B-25537 with engine #2255537 comes after the style 5027 Coupe with chassis 2B-25536, engine #2255536. Some commercial chassis sheets indicate "closed cowl," others state "cowl, instruments and wiring shipped separate." No chassis indicated open cowl. Commercial chassis were shipped to:

	Units
A. J. Miller Co., Bellefontaine, Ohio	400
American Trailer & Mfg. Co., Los Angeles, California (serial 2237434, 2237447)	2
Meteor Motor Car Company, Piqua, Ohio	478
The Eureka Co., Rock Falls, Illinois	37
Knightstown Funeral Car Co., Knightstown, Indiana	13
Canada Body & Carriage Co., Brantsford, Ontario (via GM Oshawa Branch)	13
GM Oshawa Branch, no destination indicated (serial 2239459, 2258722, 2260415)	3
Henny Motor Car Company, Freeport, Illinois (serial 2233201, 2243862)	2
Ingersoll Mitchell Hearse Co. Ltd. (Canada), via GM Oshawa Branch (serial 2233952)	1
	949

5. All models of the standard production cars were exported outside of the U.S./Canada. Numerous cars were sent to the Oshawa branch.

6. As with other years, none of the body styles were built in a straight body order sequence. S.B.O. (Special Body Order) cars were generally substantially out of order with a notation "engine no. 224----reserved."

First car built in each body style:
5011 body #1, serial 2230014
5019 body #9229, serial 2230005
5027 body #1, serial 2230016
5049 body #1, serial 2230015
5067 body #7, serial 2230055
commercial chassis, serial 2230001

Last car built in each body style:
body #1799, serial 2260391
body #21389, serial 2262005
body #5749, serial 2260207
body #520, serial 2256364
body #977, serial 2259960 (export to Buenos Aires)
serial 2260459

7. Export Chassis: GM Holden Division in Australia received a total of 64 right hand drive chassis for 5019 Sedans. Chassis were shipped to Adelaide, Melbourne and Sydney.

8. Domestic Chassis: A single 124" W.B. chassis, serial 2233393, with a closed car cowl, fender set with RH fenderwell and metal cover in primer was shipped to the Brown and Thomas Auto Co., New Haven, Connecticut.

9. Completely-Knocked-Down (CKD) Exports: It is not clear whether all of the chassis exported (other than to Australia) were complete boxed kits to assemble cars or whether some units sent to Antwerp and Japan were, in fact, chassis only. They are thought to be CKD and listed as such.

GM South African Ltd., Port Elizabeth	27 style 5019 Sedans
GM India Ltd., Bombay	36 style 5019 Sedans
GM Japan, Osaka	24 style 5019 Sedans
GM Do Brasil, São Paulo	11 style 5019 Sedans
GM Brasil, Santos	12 style 5019 Sedans
GM Continental S.A., Antwerp	204 style 5019 Sedans
GM Continental S.A., Antwerp	24 style 5067 Convertible Coupes

Note: These cars did not have body numbers assigned and are, therefore, not included in the domestic production numbers (e.g., 995 U.S. assembled Convertible Coupes).

Most of the CKD units were shipped in increments of 12. The discrepancy of 12 vehicles between known total production of 32,005 and the 31,993 accounted for in the production table is likely to be a missing CKD export record sheet.

SPECIFICATIONS

Engine—Cadillac precision built; 8 cylinders V-type; "L" head; bore 3⅜"; stroke 4½"; displacement 322 cu. in.; taxable horsepower 36.45; brake horsepower 125 at 3400 r.p.m.; engine mounted in rubber at three points.

Pistons—T-slot design aluminum alloy for uniform expansion; special anodizing process hardens surface to prevent scuffing and scoring; fitting with two compression rings and two oil rings.

Cooling System—Harrison Radiator, simplified water circulation system; automatically adjusted water pump packing, thermostatic radiator shutters.

Carburetion—Stromberg or Carter dual down-draft with equalized manifolding, fuel pump, air cleaner, intake silencer. Automatic choke, 22 gallon gas tank.

Generator—The Delco-Remy Peak Load generator maintains charging rate, even while headlamps, radio and heater are being used. It eliminates worry concerning battery condition.

Clutch—10½" x 6½" single plate dry disc type with 107 square inches of facing area; semi-centrifugal. Gives gradual and smooth application of power.

Transmission—Cadillac-built Syncro-Mesh with three forward speeds and reverse. Reverse gears as well as low and second speed gears are helical for extreme quietness. All gears fully carburized for hard use and long life. Pin type synchronizers assure easy shifting.

Lighting—Visible headlamp beam indicator in the speedometer shows which of three headlamp beams is being used. Controls rearranged to give added safety.

Front Wheels—Independent "Knee-Action" front wheels, strong and simple with large, resilient coil springs for smoother riding comfort and effortless driving control. Thoroughly proven by three years use and millions of miles of testing.

Brakes—Bendix Duo-Servo Super-Hydraulic brakes operate in centrifuse brake drums. Mechanical hand brake operates independently of the hydraulic system.

Drive Shaft—Hotchkiss drive. Two universal joints mounted on needle roller bearings permanently packed with lubricant requiring no service attention.

Rear Axle—Cadillac design and manufacture. Semi-floating type with hypoid gears, insuring quiet, dependable performance. Ratio 3.92 to 1.

Steering Gear—Sturdy worm and double roller type, with straddle mounted roller. The cross-mounted steering link operates a lever supported by the massive front cross member. Attached to it are two steering rods, each of which controls one front wheel. The steering ratio is 23.2 to 1. Can be turned or parked in much smaller space than many cars of the same wheelbase.

Frame—The chassis has a more rigid frame that improves stability and riding comfort. The frame is 8 11/16" deep, ⅛" thick and has a flange width of 2⅜".

Ride Stabilizer—Two stabilizers, one front and one rear for better roadability and to keep car on even keel.

Tires and Wheels—Low pressure, 4-ply tires, 7.00 x 16 carrying 26

Transmission—Cadillac-built Syncro-Mesh with three forward speeds and reverse. Reverse gears as well as low and second speed gears are helical for extreme quietness. All gears fully carburized for hard use and long life. Pin type synchronizers assure easy shifting.

Lighting—Visible headlamp beam indicator in the speedometer shows which of three headlamp beams is being used. Controls rearranged to give added safety.

Front Wheels—Independent "Knee-Action" front wheels, strong and simple with large, resilient coil springs for smoother riding comfort and effortless driving control. Thoroughly proven by three years use and millions of miles of testing.

Brakes—Bendix Duo-Servo Super-Hydraulic brakes operate in centrifuse brake drums. Mechanical hand brake operates independently of the hydraulic system.

Drive Shaft—Hotchkiss drive. Two universal joints mounted on needle roller bearings permanently packed with lubricant requiring no service attention.

Rear Axle—Cadillac design and manufacture. Semi-floating type with hypoid gears, insuring quiet, dependable performance. Ratio 3.92 to 1.

Steering Gear—Sturdy worm and double roller type, with straddle mounted roller. The cross-mounted steering link operates a lever supported by the massive front cross member. Attached to it are two steering rods, each of which controls one front wheel. The steering ratio is 23.2 to 1. Can be turned or parked in much smaller space than many cars of the same wheelbase.

Frame—The chassis has a more rigid frame that improves stability and riding comfort. The frame is 8 11/16" deep, ⅛" thick and has a flange width of 2⅜".

Ride Stabilizer—Two stabilizers, one front and one rear for better roadability and to keep car on even keel.

Tires and Wheels—Low pressure, 4-ply tires, 7.00 x 16 carrying 26 lbs. air pressure. Five steel disc wheels with large chrome disc hub caps.

Fenders—Fenders, and other sheet metal parts are bonderized to prevent rust.

Turning Radius—Right 20 feet, Left 20 feet.

Body Types—Fisher all-steel bodies with No-Draft ventilation and Turret-Top roofs. Optional selection from Bedford Cord or Broadcloth upholstery and several body colors at no extra charge. Trunks standard equipment on 2- and 4-door touring sedans. Large trunk storage space.

• • •

The right is reserved to change specifications, colors, prices or equipment at any time without incurring any responsibility with regard to cars previously sold.

NINETEEN THIRTY-EIGHT

Every line and contour of this smart, new LaSalle V-8 will win your immediate admiration. Its styling is authentic—graceful and dignified, yet charmingly fresh and distinctive. Viewed from the front, the new LaSalle is strikingly smarter and more beautiful. The characteristic LaSalle radiator grille is more deeply curved and two inches wider—giving a more massive appearance.

The new Syncromatic Gear Shift is standard. There is nothing to learn, nothing to forget. But there is a wholly new and delightful experience to enjoy. Located out of the way, on the steering column . . . you drive with complete relaxation.

Built with the experience of age . . . the new LaSalle is styled with the vision of youth. Its smart, new lines will immediately capture your admiration. They are lines of exquisite beauty and authentic grace . . . style ofttimes copied, but never duplicated.

—from the 1938 sales brochure

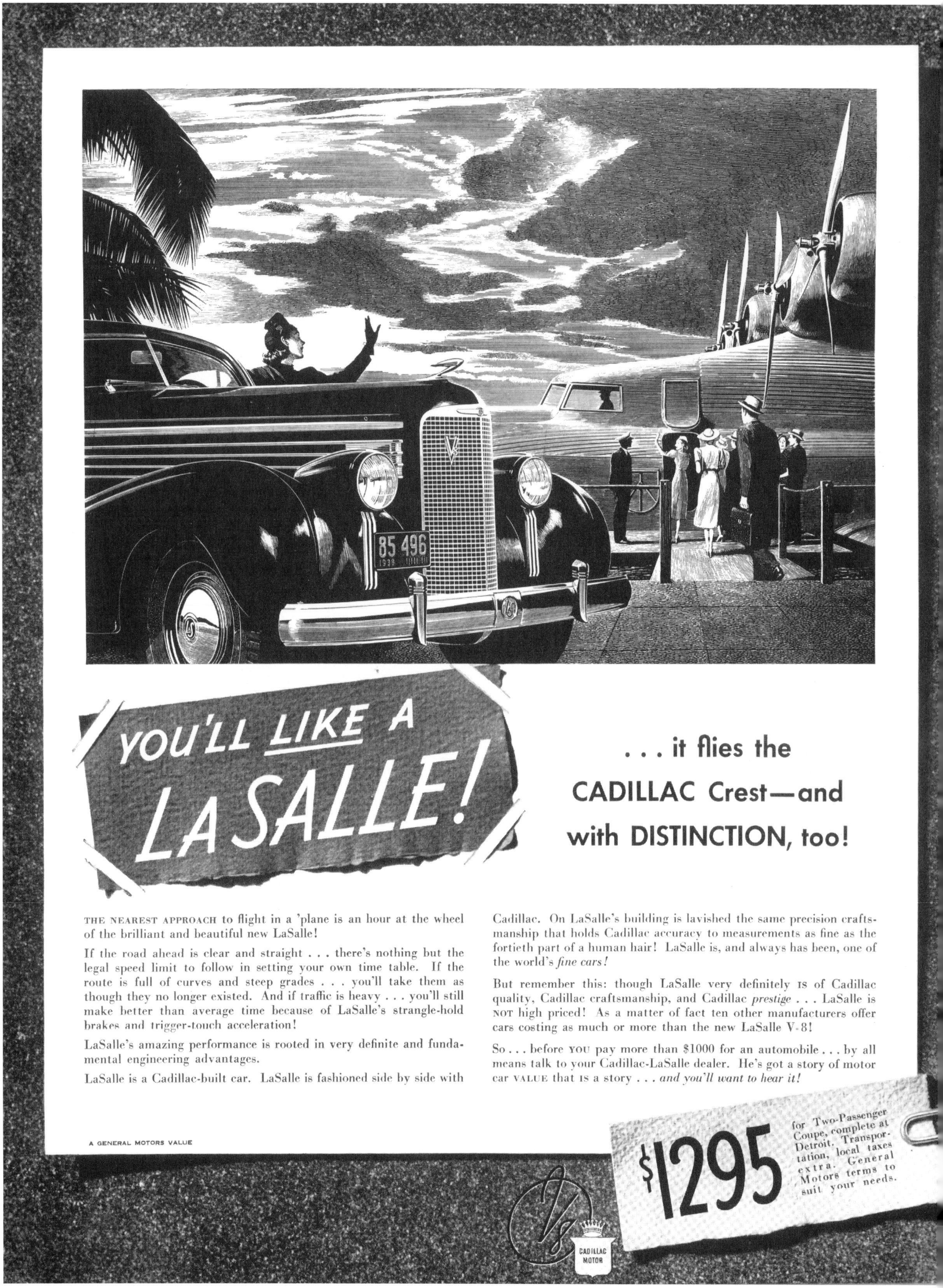
85 496
1938
YOU'LL LIKE A LASALLE!
. . . it flies the CADILLAC Crest—and with DISTINCTION, too!
THE NEAREST APPROACH to flight in a 'plane is an hour at the wheel of the brilliant and beautiful new LaSalle!
If the road ahead is clear and straight . . . there's nothing but the legal speed limit to follow in setting your own time table. If the route is full of curves and steep grades . . . you'll take them as though they no longer existed. And if traffic is heavy . . . you'll still make better than average time because of LaSalle's strangle-hold brakes and trigger-touch acceleration!
LaSalle's amazing performance is rooted in very definite and fundamental engineering advantages.
LaSalle is a Cadillac-built car. LaSalle is fashioned side by side with Cadillac. On LaSalle's building is lavished the same precision craftsmanship that holds Cadillac accuracy to measurements as fine as the fortieth part of a human hair! LaSalle is, and always has been, one of the world's fine cars!
But remember this: though LaSalle very definitely IS of Cadillac quality, Cadillac craftsmanship, and Cadillac prestige . . . LaSalle is NOT high priced! As a matter of fact ten other manufacturers offer cars costing as much or more than the new LaSalle V-8!
So . . . before YOU pay more than $1000 for an automobile . . . by all means talk to your Cadillac-LaSalle dealer. He's got a story of motor car VALUE that IS a story . . . and you'll want to hear it!
A GENERAL MOTORS VALUE
$1295
for Two-Passenger Coupe, complete at Detroit. Transportation, local taxes extra. General Motors terms to suit your needs.
CADILLAC MOTOR

NINETEEN THIRTY-EIGHT
Series 50

The 1938 Series 50 LaSalle received a number of styling changes from 1937. They were mostly facelift cosmetics which enhanced its good looks. A slightly larger, Vee'd, diecast grille continued to emphasize the vertical theme while the horizontal length was emphasized by slimmer side hood ventilator panels that extended the entire length of the hood.

All the fenders looked longer and were more squared-off. The headlights were even longer and nestled low in the catwalk on decorative, fluted, vertical stanchions. The traditional chevrons that immediately identified every LaSalle, located on the leading edge of the front fenders, had now been eliminated, after four years running. Arguably, this put greater visual emphasis on the grille. The more likely explanation had to do with the overall cost reduction effort. All General Motors Divisions had a cost reduction program in place. Competition was fierce and the U.S. was facing an economic recession.

The big news for 1938 was the relocation of the gearshift lever from the floor to the steering column just below the steering wheel. Ease of shifting gears and seating three on the front seat were the benefits.

It would be the last year for the rumble seat, available in the two-door Convertible and two-door Coupe models only. While sidemounted tires were not a part of the original design, LaSalle did follow Cadillac styling in providing a very smooth, hinged sidemount cover.

Interiors on the Series 50 were also modernized. A new exotic material was introduced that could be inexpensively cast and gave a jewel-like appearance . . . plastic. The steering wheel, gearshift knob, radio center console grille and numerous other parts were made of this new material. Its translucent coloring was rich and had a beautiful smooth finish when new. Unfortunately, through the years, these early plastics reacted unfavorably under extreme temperature conditions and the ultraviolet rays of the sun. Cracking and warping were common.

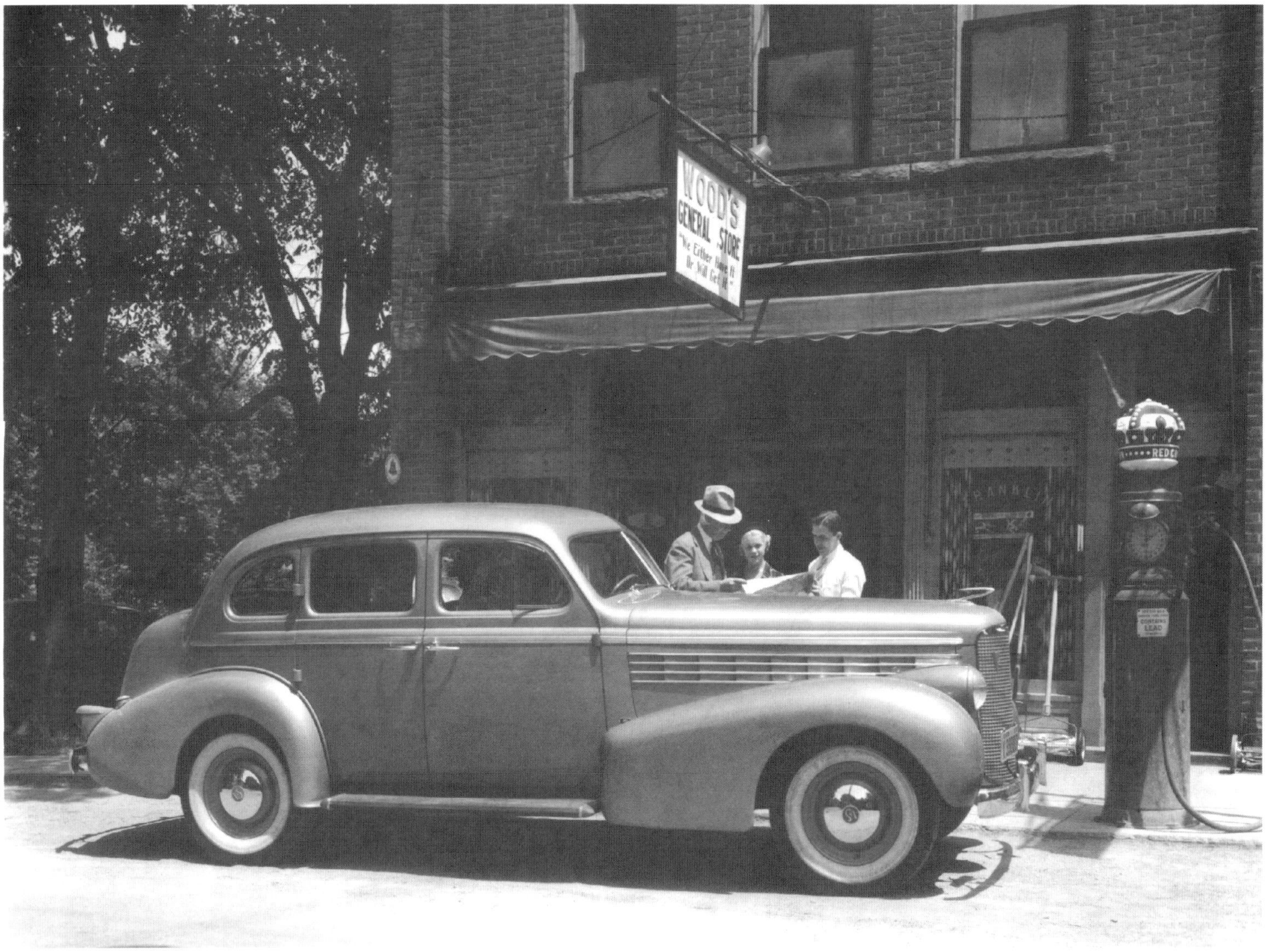
WOOD'S
GENERAL STORE

Above: This factory photo depicts traveling with the five-passenger, four-door Touring Sedan model 5019. It was the best selling model, usually purchased without sidemounts and with small hubcaps. Signs of the times are evident with the public telephone sign and Red Crown gasoline pump at Wood's General Store. Below: A two-door, five-passenger Touring Sedan model 5011 was shown with the door open on the factory's rooftop. Accessibility to the rear compartment was generous, even before the front seatbacks are folded forward.

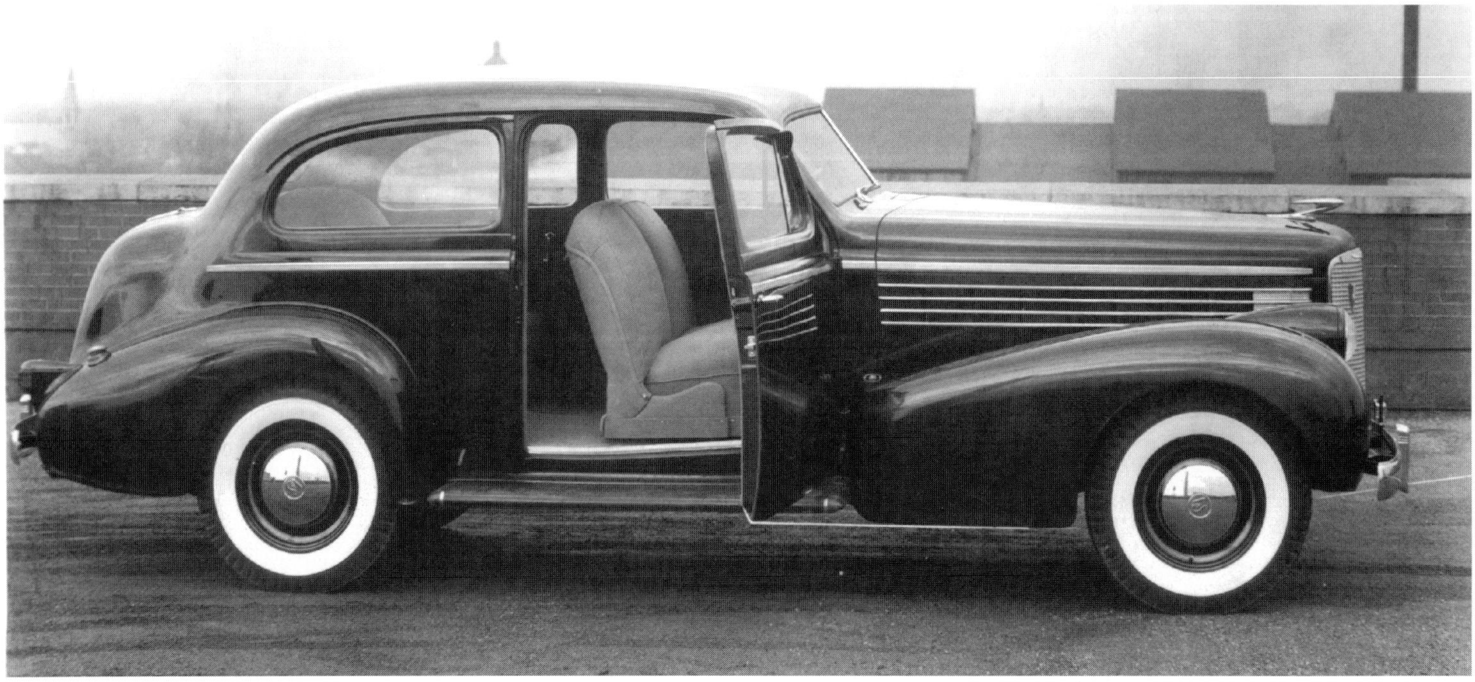

This factory photo of a two-door Coupe model 5027 in profile dramatizes the long nose and clean, unobstructed lines. The very contemporary residence as a backdrop was meant to attract the younger generation. There was abundant room for luggage as well as convenient storage of the spare tire in the large trunk compartment.

LaSalle continued to use the 125 horsepower 322 cubic inch V-8 engine. It was quiet, with hydraulic valve silencers, and powerful with a high ratio of power to weight. Crankcase breathing was considered necessary and was very simply executed with a tube between the air cleaner and the valley cover at the rear of the engine.

A new alligator-type hood opening was adopted. It opened by lifting the hood ornament. Mechanics found it less convenient because the side panels, while separate units that could be removed, usually stayed in place, making access less convenient. Once the hood ornament opening became familiar and more often used, there were many 1937 non-movable, permanent hood ornaments mistakenly broken by service station attendants. But, it did become a trend and the other automakers did the same.

The sales brochures had full color renderings of the five models. They were beautifully done with crisp detail and with only slight exaggerations.

LaSalle was a superb value in 1938. It had refined styling, mechanical V-8 powered dependability and was easier to drive. Without a doubt, more LaSalles would have been sold in 1938 had there not been an economic recession affecting all car sales.

Full page ads had more written content than usual, leaving artist illustrations of the car no more than one-fourth of the page. For the second year in a row, all LaSalle advertisements were in black and white only, except in conjunction with Cadillac color ads. "Want..." seemed to be a theme throughout: "Want something different?" "Want to go somewhere?" "Want a lot for a little?" This transitioned into "<u>Now</u> look at LaSalle!" Most ads also made reference to the new shift lever location. "Learn the amazing ease and simplicity of Cadillac's Syncromatic Gear Shift!" ". . . there is almost miraculous new ease of control to enjoy!"

Now LOOK AT LaSALLE!

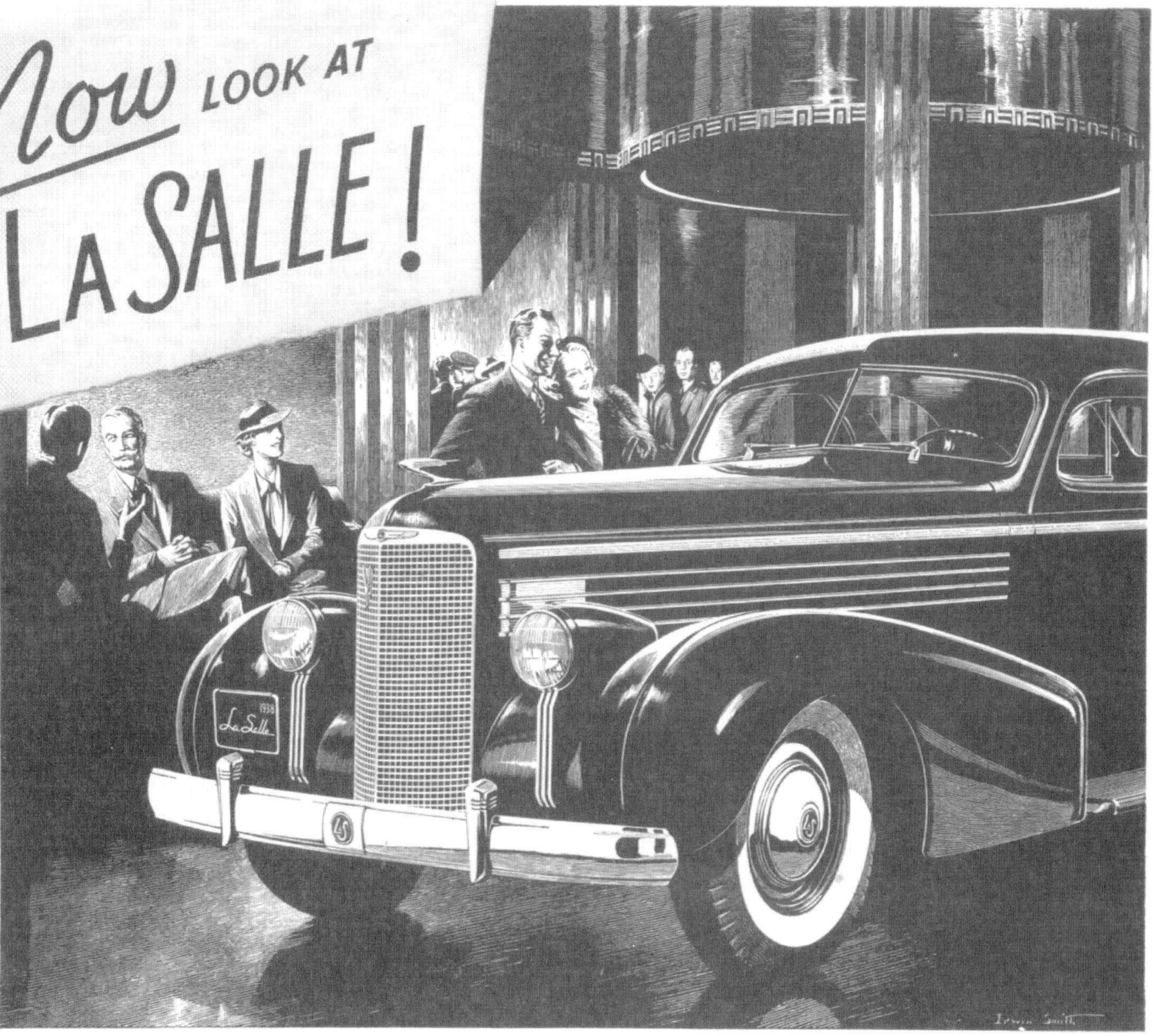

IT OFFERS NEW SMARTNESS AND LUXURY AND THRILLING NEW EASE OF CONTROL

You have always known LaSalle as the embodiment of *style*—a fleet, luxurious, fine-performing car, designed and built by Cadillac. But wait till you see and drive the *new* LaSalle!

The smart, new lines of this great V-8 are a revelation in beauty. Its inherent luxury is apparent in the smallest detail. Its performance is simply unduplicated in any car near it in price. And it offers the latest in a long line of Cadillac engineering advancements—the Syncromatic Gear Shift!

The Syncromatic Shift is *standard*. There's nothing to learn, nothing to forget. But it literally revolutionizes driving—makes it far easier and simpler and safer.

All through this new LaSalle V-8 you will find just what you would expect to find in every Cadillac-built car—Cadillac quality and craftsmanship in every major and minor detail.

And remember—LaSalle is *still* the world's *most economical* fine car! Not only is it amazingly low in price—but it is almost as easy on gasoline and oil as *any* car you could buy.

Why not see and drive the new LaSalle V-8 today?

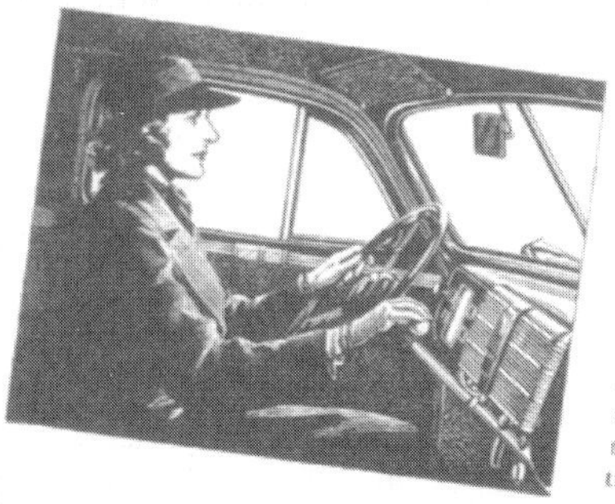

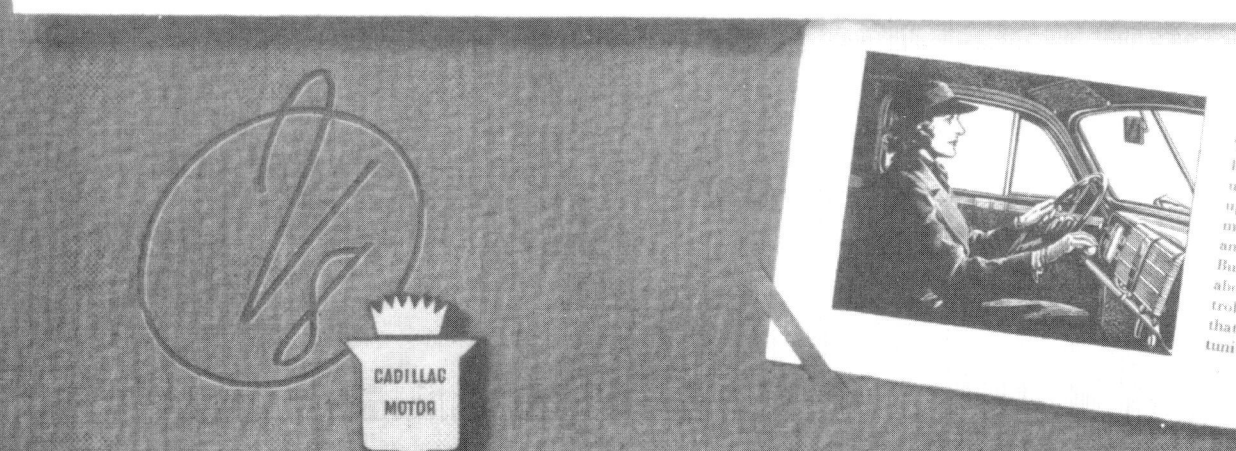

A FINER, EASIER CONTRO
A NEW AND SMARTER

The lever of the new Syncromatic G
located at your fingertips on the ste
umn, operates exactly as the old lever
up so much floor-room in the front c
ment. You move it up and back for *firs*
and forward for *second*; straight back f
But you can never appreciate, just by
about it, the almost miraculous new ease
trol this new shift provides. We hope, the
that you will actually *try it*, at your first
tunity. It will prove a delightful exper

A GENERAL MOTORS VALUE

CADILLAC MOTOR

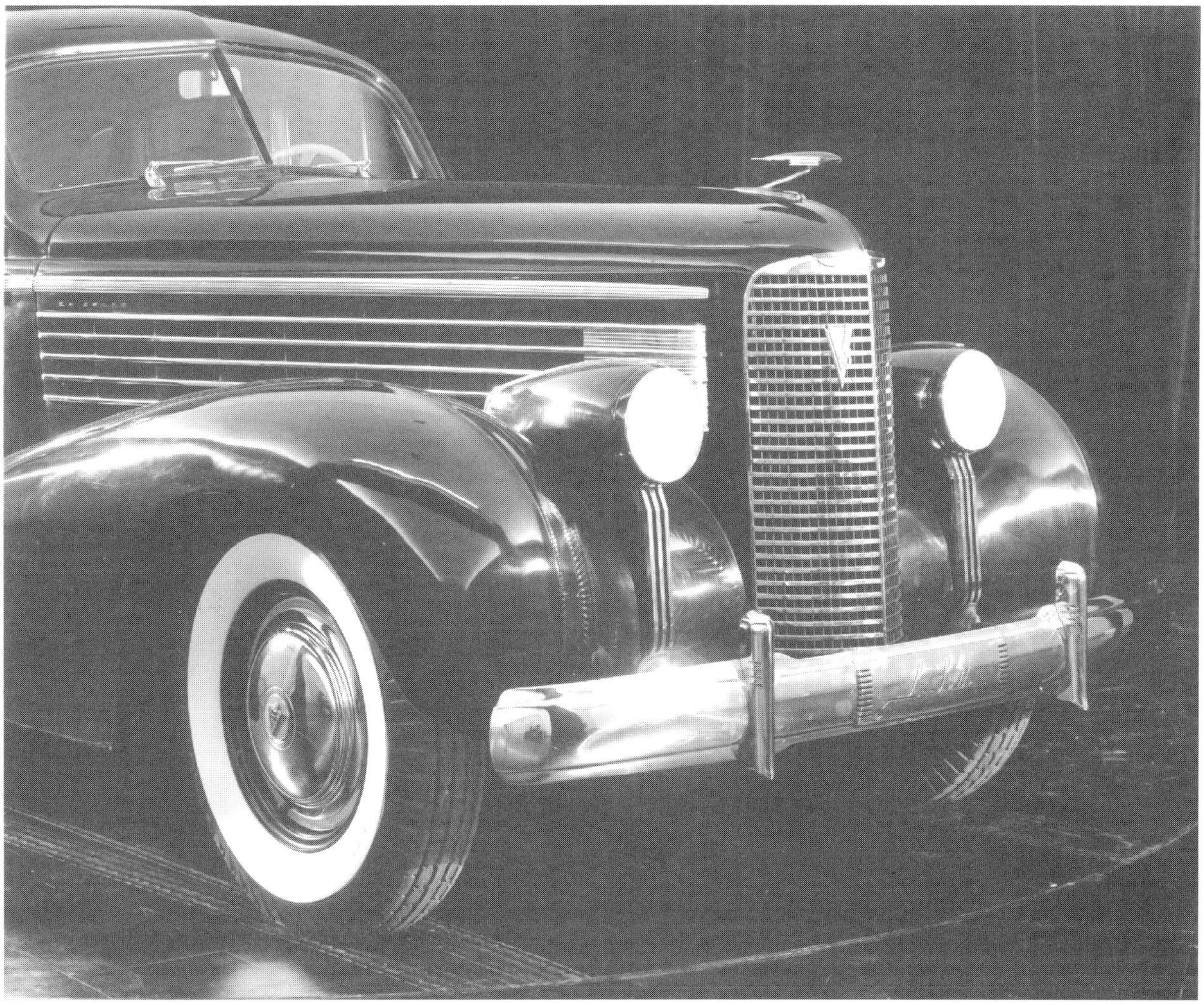

Above: In this factory photograph, a few last minute details are being evaluated. The bumper badge has LaSalle in script and the wheel covers have the protruding V-8 similar to the V-16. The location of the V-8 emblem on the grille is not centered. Below: A simpler bumper badge and accessory foglights are featured in this photo.

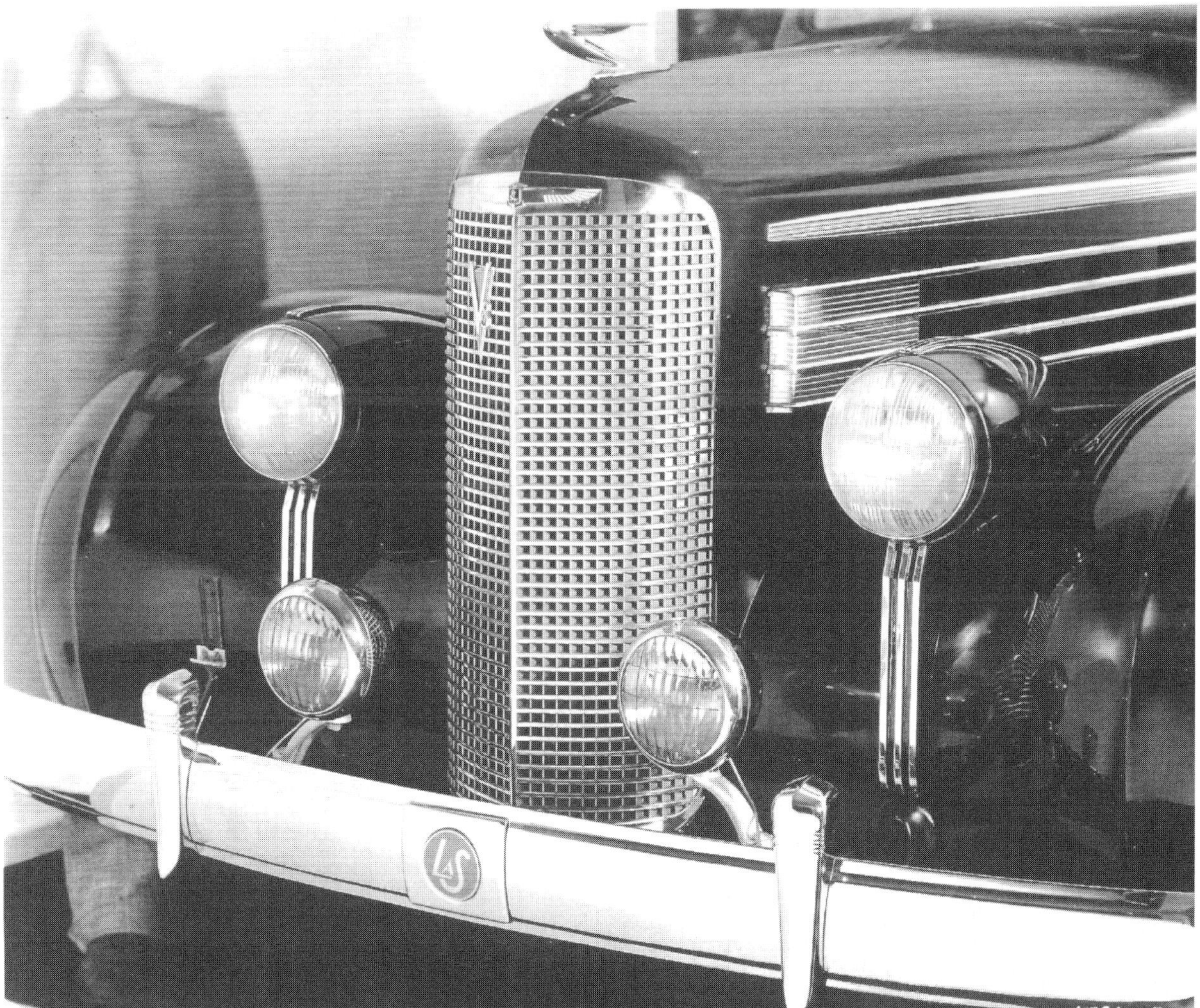
4796-47

LaSalle's Convertible Coupe is an exceptionally distinguished "all-weather" car. Its smart, expertly tailored and tight-fitting top is practically invisible when lowered. A comfortable rumble seat, upholstered in leather, accommodates two or even three additional passengers.

Convertible Coupe

This new LaSalle gives you the freedom of an open car when days are fair, the comfort and security of a sedan in inclement weather. Its lines are strikingly beautiful... its performance most brilliant, and its fine utility particularly satisfying.

Convertible Sedan

Two-Passenger Coupe

Two luxuriously upholstered opera seats, located inside the body, permit four passengers to ride comfortably in the new LaSalle Coupe. There is abundant room for plenty of luggage, and for the convenient storage of the concealed spare tire, in the gracefully sloping rear compartment.

There is abundant room in the Five-Passenger Touring Coupe. Three passengers may easily ride in comfort in the front seat. Exceptionally wide doors afford easy entrance. The spacious, built-in trunk, which also conceals the spare tire, makes this car particularly ideal for long tours.

Five-Passenger Touring Coupe

You'll like La Salle's New Smartness and Modernity

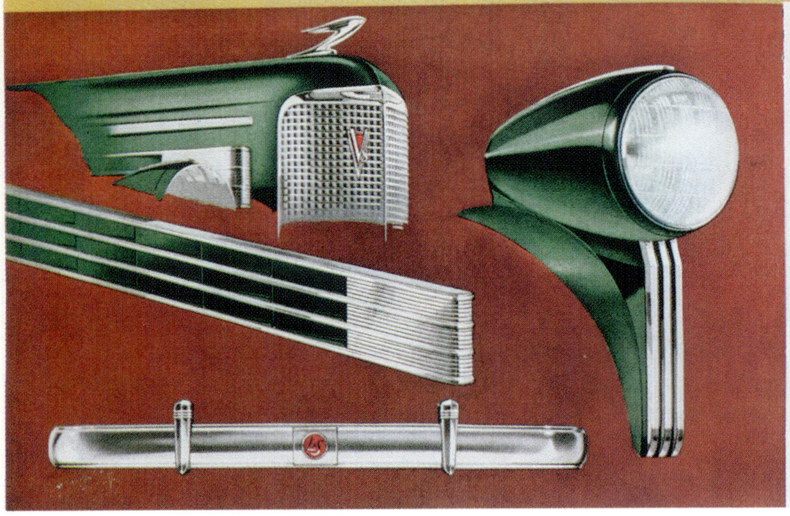

Cadillac has styled the new LaSalle in the most modern vogue with low, fleet lines and a massive overall appearance suggestive of its great power and sturdiness.

The gracefully rounded radiator grille is sharply veed of rugged die-cast construction—graceful hood louvres accentuate its low, fleet lines. Long, streamlined headlamps appear submerged within huge sweeping fenders—beneath each lamp a modernistic pillar adds a distinctive touch.

Bumpers are wide and heavy for protection, chromed for beauty—the clear vision instrument panel grille is fashioned from a beautiful and costly plastic, colored to match interior trim.

Chrome door handles modeled from heavy material, gracefully curve for safety—running boards are separated from fenders and neatly striped with chrome.

Uniquely designed tail lamps appear an integral part of rear fenders and the rear view of the new LaSalle presents a perfect blend of smooth, flowing, harmonious lines.

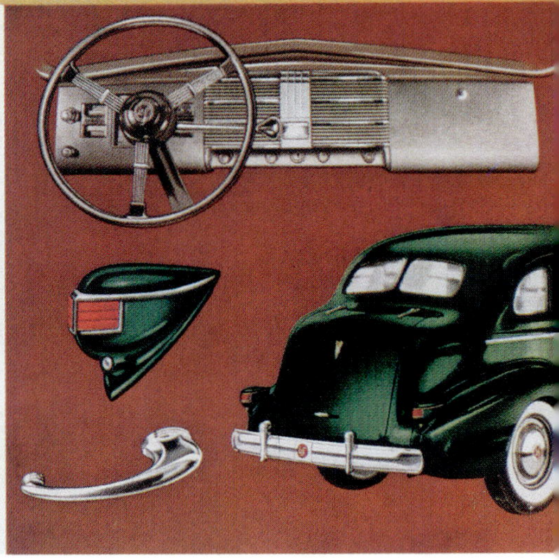

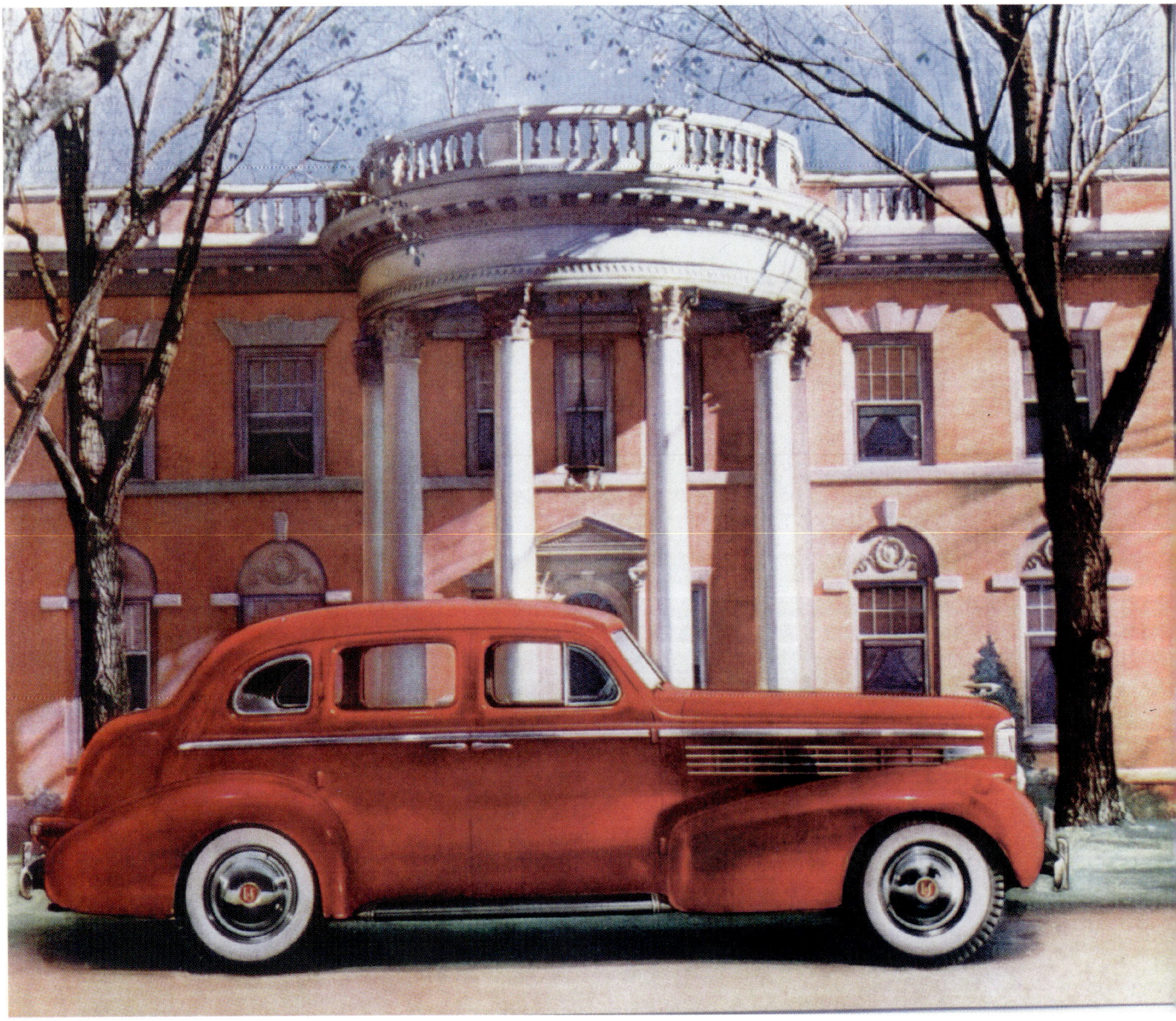

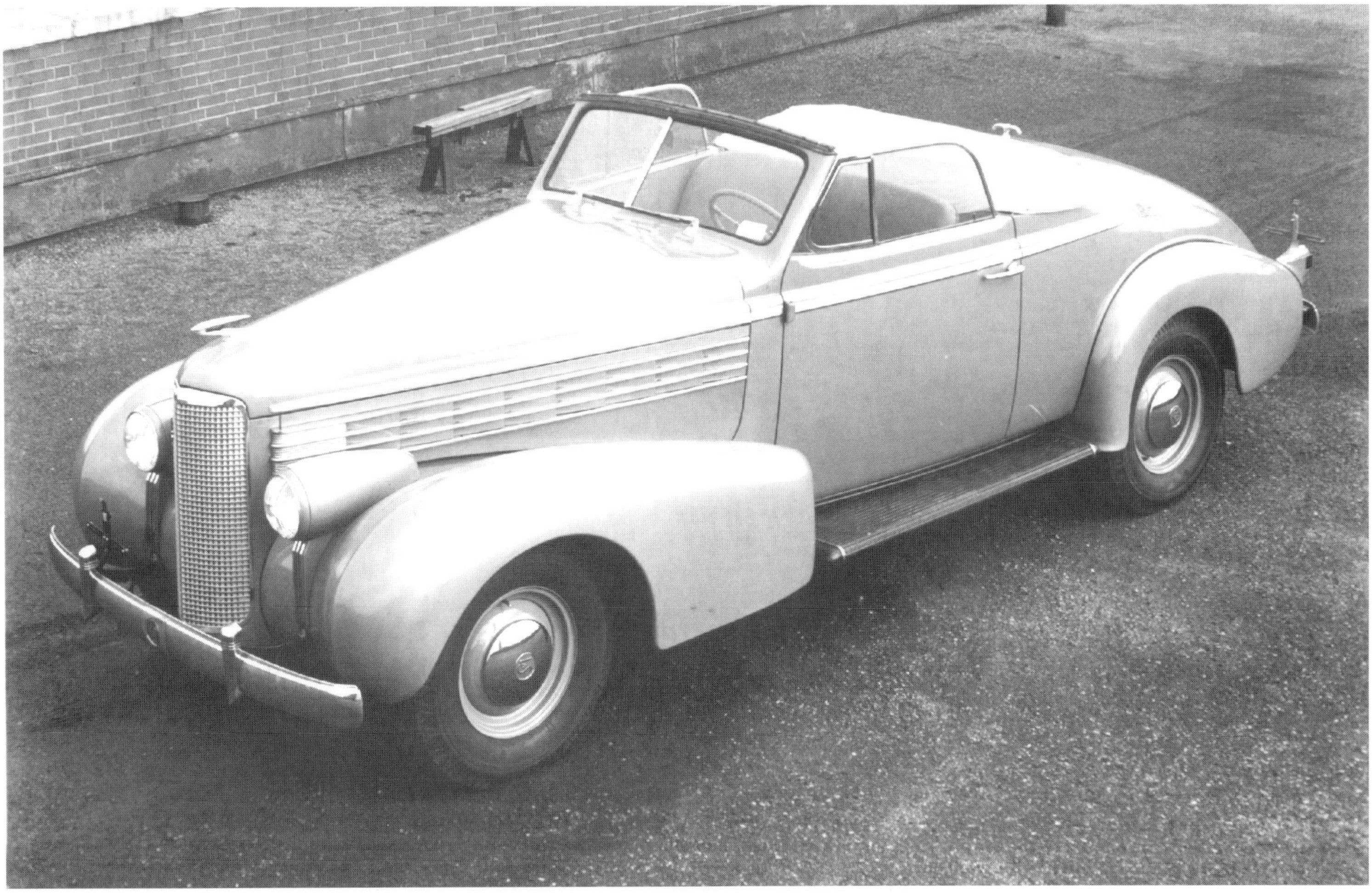

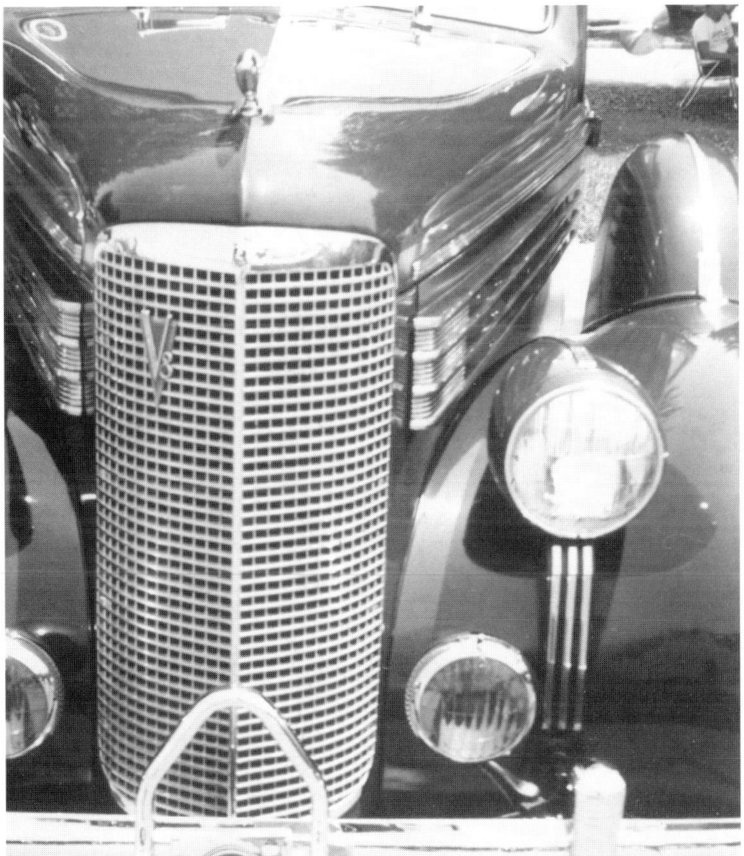

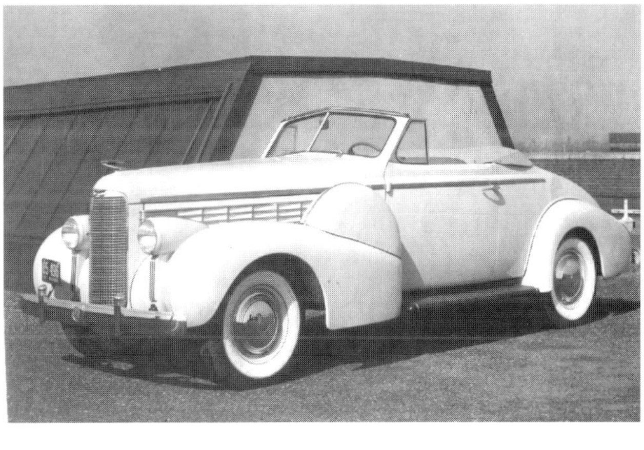

Top: A conservatively accessorized model 5067 two-door Convertible was photographed with blackwall tires and small hubcaps. Above: In contrast, this deluxe model was shown with large wheel covers, whitewall tires and the smooth fender mounted spare tire covers. Bottom left: Shown here is the very rare grille guard and genuine amber foglight factory accessories. Opposite page: These artist renditions came from the 1938 LaSalle sales brochure.

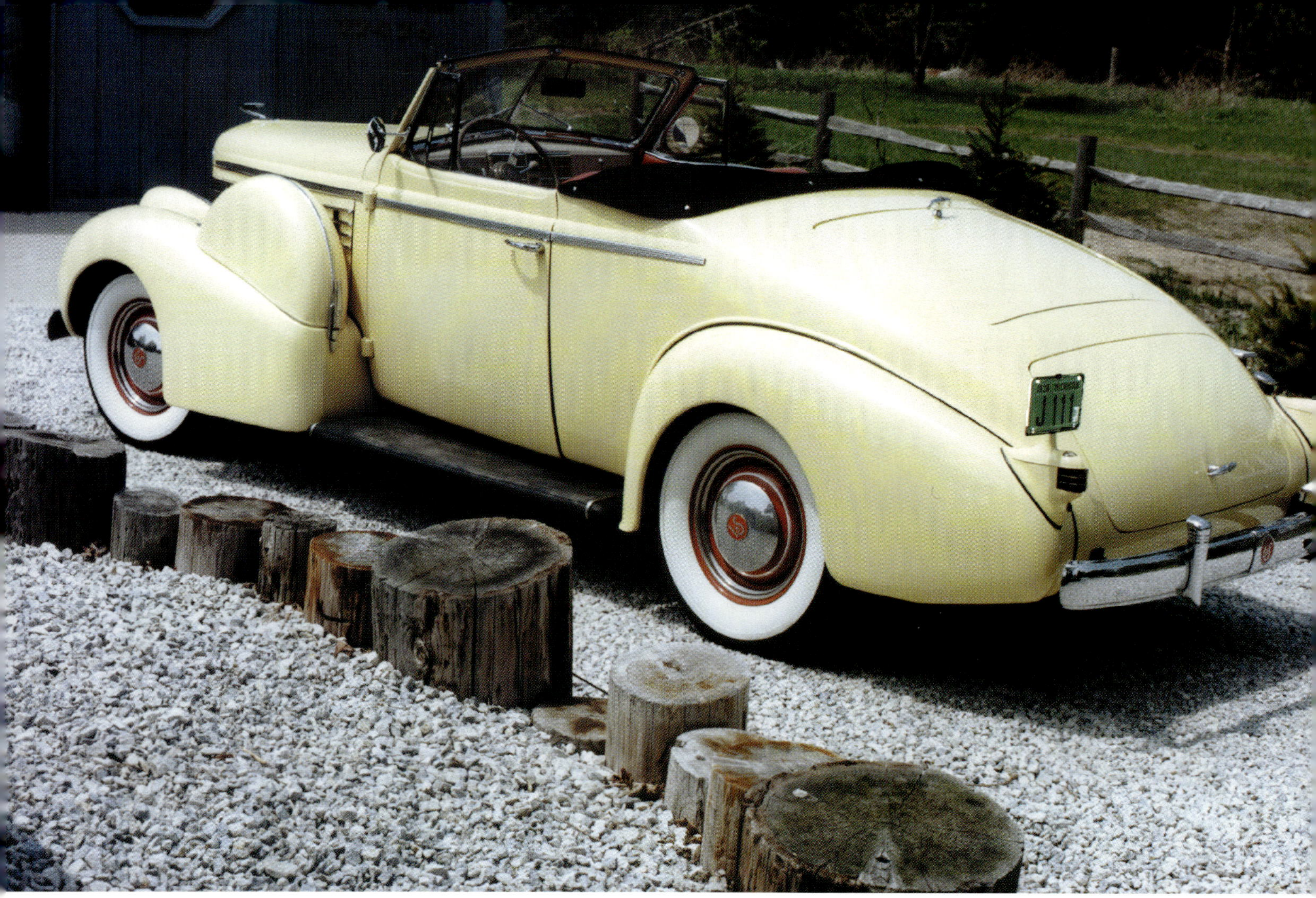

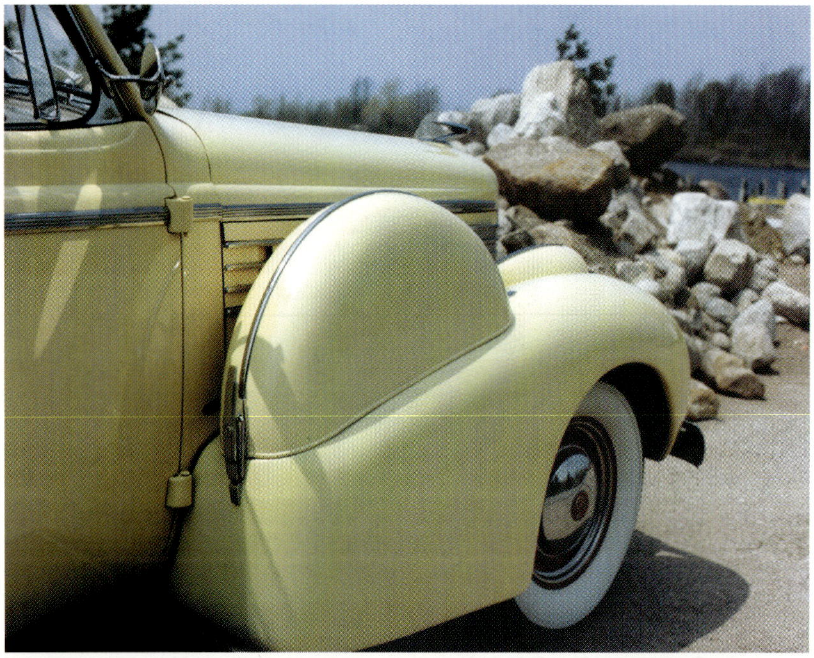

Top: A beautiful view from the rear of a two-door Convertible Coupe with rumble seat. The contrasting red wheels with small hubcaps add to the beauty of this restored example. Middle left: An artistically staged close-up view of the new smooth sidemount cover. Bottom: On the left is a LaSalle two-door Convertible Coupe standing beside a 1938 Cadillac two-door Convertible Coupe. Both cars were identically accessorized, but note how much longer the hood appears on the LaSalle, due to the very narrow grille and long horizontal ventilator strips, assisted by a chrome belt molding the full length of the car from the hood to the rear deck.

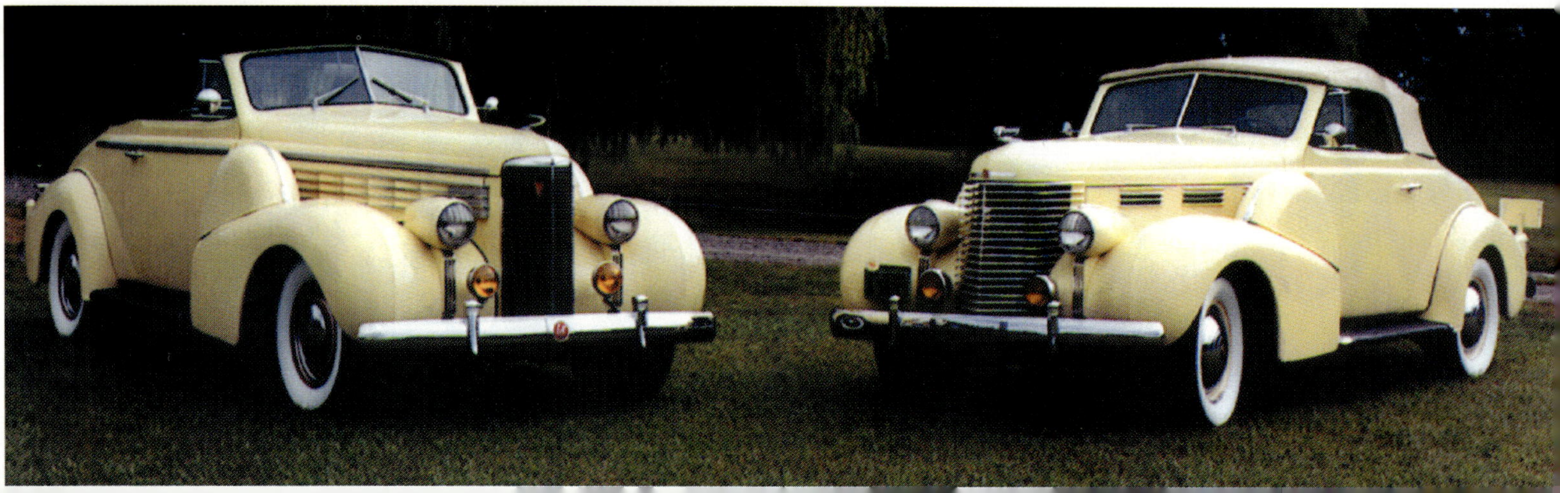

Two handsome survivors. Above: This two-door Convertible Coupe has no sidemounted spare. The spare tire is concealed in the rear compartment. Non-sidemounted cars allowed the stainless steel strips on the side of the hood to be fully exposed. Below: A beautifully restored model 5027 two-passenger Coupe was equipped with smooth fender mounted spare tire covers. Factory photographs and sales catalogs often show the Cadillac taillight and Cadillac running board ends. It has the correct black LaSalle running board caps.

Above: This particularly handsome front ensemble features no hood ornament, a 1937 LaSalle grille, low catwalks and flush fender mounted headlights. Below: The trunk and integrated rear deck ensemble modernizes the three chevrons on the lid and glass taillights flush with the fenders.

Above: An appearance lengthening side panel grille and the lack of a belt molding dramatizes the streamlined body. Below: A good side view illustrates the two crease "suitcase" fenders and the convertible window frame elegance of this initial and quickly produced proposal for the Sixty Special.

1938 LaSalle Production

Total Production: 15,501 automobiles and chassis.

Serial Numbers: 2270001-2285501. The Vehicle (engine) serial number is "On rough flat surface on rear portion of crankcase in bell housing back of L.H. block."

Chassis Numbers: Same as engine serial numbers. Location of chassis number is "Top surface of frame side bar, just ahead of dash and opposite steering gear."

Body Plates: "Body and style number on plate on left side of dash." (under the hood)

Body Type and Style Numbers:

Series 38-50 (124" Wheelbase) -	Fisher Bodies	Production	Standard configuration
5-Pass. Touring Coupe	38-5011	700	Trunk, concealed spare
5-Pass. Touring Sedan	38-5019	9768	Trunk, concealed spare
5-Pass. Sedan, CKD (Export)	38-5019	229	
2-Pass. Coupe	38-5027	2711	Two opera seats, spare under deck
5-Pass. Convertible Sedan	38-5049	265	Plain back, R.H. fenderwell
2-Pass. Convertible Coupe	38-5067	819	Rumble seat, spare under deck
2-Pass. Conv. Coupe, CKD (Export)	38-5067	36	
124" W.B. Chassis (Export)		7	
124" W.B. Chassis, CKD (Australian)		74	
Commercial Chassis (160" W.B.)	38-50	900	
	Total	15,509	(Unexplained difference of 8 units)

List Prices - FOB Detroit: (November 22, 1937)

5011 5-Pass. Touring Coupe	$1345.00
5019 5-Pass. Touring Sedan	$1385.00
5027 2 Pass. Coupe	$1295.00
5049 5-Pass. Convertible Sedan	$1825.00
5067 2-Pass. Convertible Coupe	$1420.00
124" W.B. Chassis	$1050.00
160" Commercial Chassis	$1082.75

Standard Color Options

Body, Fenders, Tire Cover	R & M #	Wheels	
1 Black	20498	Black (standard)	94-005
		Flare Red (optional)	94-3549R
		Clearwater Green (optional)	94-5245
2 Antoinette Blue	22290	Antoinette Blue	9420506
3 Patillo Maroon	26655	Patillo Maroon	9420501
4 St. Regis Green	020364	Atlantis Green	9420505
5 Moleskin Gray	20181	Flare Red Dulux	94-3549R
6 Pelham Gray	020155	Desert Sand	9420499
7 Manchu Beige Iridescent	P.S. 816	Laquedoc Orange	9420504
8 Chantel Blue	020219	Chantel Blue	9420511
9 Deauville Beige Iridescent	P.S. 815	Deauville Beige Iridescent	9420502
10 Cloudmist Green Iridescent	P.S. 308	Cloudmist Green Iridescent	9420500
11 Fairhaven Blue Iridescent	P.S. 202	Fairhaven Blue Iridescent	9420507
12 Cruiser Gray Iridescent	P.S. 108	Nimbus Gray Iridescent	942663
13 Edgewood Green Iridescent	P.S.340	Edgewood Green Iridescent	9420503
14 Italian Cream	20734	Italian Cream	9420498
15 Carolina Green	20361	Carolina Green	20361
16 Sea Gull Gray	21271	Carolina Green	20361
17 Oxblood Iridescent Maroon	P.S. 608	Oxblood Iridescent Maroon	P.S. 608
18 Barcelona Blue	022224	Cascion Beige	24251737

Instrument Panel & Garnish Mouldings

Center section	Tenite, 4157
Top, sides, compartment door	Light Beige, 202-51942 (Dupont)
Steering wheel, steering column	Light Beige, 202-51942
Garnish Mouldings	Light Beige, 202-51942
Hand Brake Lever	Light Beige, 202-51942

Trim Options

Code No.		Trim No.	Convertible Tops
30	Tan Pattern Cloth	60T138	Tan (standard
31	Tan Ribbed Cloth	61T138	Blue (Special)
32	Gray Pattern Cloth	64T138	Black (Special)
33	Gray Ribbed Cloth	65T138	
35	Tan Plush (Export)	41T138	Convertible Top Lining
36	Black Leather	1T1338	Tan used with all colors
37	Tan Leather	2T1338	
38	Gray Leather	3T1338	
39	Green Leather	4T1338	
50	Blue Leather	5T1338	
51	Red Leather	6T1338	
	Gray Plush (Export)	54T138	

Accessory Groups
(September 28, 1937)

B $27.50	AD $49.00	AR 5 (5 Wheel) $40.50	AR 6 (6 Wheel) $42.00
Clock	Clock	Clock	Clock
Flexible (Steering) Wheel	Discs (4)	Trim Rings (5)	Trim Rings (6)
	Flexible (Steering) Wheel	Flexible (Steering) Wheel	Flexible (Steering) Wheel
	License Frames	License Frames	License Frames

Additional Charges
6 Wheels, fenderwells, tire covers — $95.00
    Except Convertible Sedan — $60.00
Right Hand fenderwell on all body styles except Convertible Sedan — $40.00
White Sidewall tires, each — $ 3.60
(7.00 X 16" Royal or Firestone 4-ply black tires are standard equipment)

Accessories

Master Radio (installed complete	$79.50	Moto-Pack	$ 6.85
Standard Radio (installed complete)	$65.00	Hot Water Heater-Defroster	$26.50
Wheel Discs (each)	$ 4.00	Fleetwood Robe (made of identical cloth)	$50.00
Wheel Trim Rings (each)	$ 1.50	Double Alpaca Robe	$30.00
Flexible Steering Wheel	$15.00	Alpaca and Plush Robe	$30.00
License Frames (pair)	$ 5.50	Seat Covers (each seat)	$ 7.50
Adverse Weather Lights	$17.50	Luggage - Brown and White Striped Duckoid Finish -	
Spotlight	$18.50	Wardrolette	$42.50
Hinge Mirror	$ 4.50	Ladies' Aviatrix	$35.00
Automatic Battery Filler	$ 7.50	Gentlemen's Aviator	$35.00

Research Methodology: Microfiche copies of the individual Shipping Department records of the as-built configuration of 15,003 vehicles and chassis were examined to determine configurations built, accessories installed by the factory, paint and upholstery combinations actually used, etc. Serial numbers of completely-knocked-down (CKD) cars, export chassis and commercial chassis were recorded to verify actual numbers produced and list the destinations. Records for 500 vehicles are not on microfiche and not readily available for review. The total numbers of some styles may, therefore, not be accurate.

Notes on research findings: A small number (less than 1%) of the record sheets indicate the name of the original purchaser. The cars that indicate the purchaser are generally Special Body Orders (S.B.O.).

1. How to read the build sheet: In 1938, build sheets were simplified. The individual blocks to identify the paint code, upholstery code, number and color of wheels were eliminated. With the exception of Special Body Order (S.B.O.) cars, a single line immediately below the style and body number now identified all of those items.
    Example: 1-31-5 Flare Red 20539
        First number (1) is the paint code – Black
        Second number (31) is the upholstery code – Tan Ribbed Cloth
        Third number (5) is the number of wheels – will either be 5 or 6
        Color of wheels (Flare Red) is indicated, because wheel color is optional with black

In the case of S.B.O. cars, an X will appear in place of the paint or upholstery number (e.g., X-31-5). Farther down the sheet, an explanation of the Special Order will appear (eg., COLOR - SILVER GRAY GREEN 202-52194).

The standard configuration for each body style is indicated with the production numbers above. Factory built deviations by body style include:
    5011   Right hand fenderwell; 6 wheels with dual fenderwells
    5019   Right hand fenderwell; left hand fenderwell; 6 wheels with dual fenderwells
    5027   Right hand fenderwell; left hand fenderwell; 6 wheels with dual fenderwells
    5049   Standard front fenders, spare wheel in rear compartment; 6 wheels with dual fenderwells
    5067   6 wheels with dual fenderwells; omit rumble seat

2. <u>Flower Cars</u>: Two style 5067 Convertible Coupes (2282252, 2282333) and two 5027 Coupes (2283762, 2283774) were sent to The Eureka Co., Rock Falls, Illinois, with the annotation "To be built into Flower Car." Unlike the 1937 units, the cars were not returned to Cadillac Motor Car Company and did not have a factory build sheet designation as a Flower Car (5067F).

3. <u>Combination Ambulance</u>: Following the practice used in producing the 1937 Flower Cars, a style 5011 Touring Coupe (serial 2280495) was consigned by the factory to The Eureka Co. "To be re-operated to Combination Ambulance, as per Commercial Catalogue." The finished unit was returned to the factory for credit and subsequently shipped to Randall Cad. Corp., Brooklyn, NY. The Combination Ambulance featured a single seat for the driver with an elongated right door that allowed a gurney with patient to be loaded in the right side of the car.

4. <u>Show Cars</u>: Style 5019, 5027, 5049 and 5067 cars tagged "For Paris Show" were shipped to Antwerp. Special preparation was given to vehicles assigned "For use of GM Parade of Progress" and to various branch offices (Chicago, Cleveland, Detroit, New York) and individual dealers marked "Show Car."

5. <u>Factory Installed Accessories</u>: Factory records do not exist to identify the original purchaser of most cars. A careful study of the build sheets will at least provide evidence that a particular car was ordered by an individual. The Special Body Order (S.B.O.) cars are obvious; all of those were individual orders. So, too, were the cars with specific accessories other than the above indicated Accessory Groups. All of the following individual accessories (including some not listed in the published accessory lists) were installed by the factory on one or more cars. Part numbers are listed where indicated on the build sheets:

Adverse Weather Lights (Fog Lights)	
Automatic Battery Filler	
Double Alpaca Robe to match interior	
Electric Clock	1096916
Export Clock	X-101
Electric fan on steering column	1422311
Fender Lamps (export cars only)	
Flexible Steering Wheel	1426169
Gravel Deflectors	1425250
Grease Gun	
Heater-Defroster	
Hinge Mirror	
Illuminated Vanity Mirror	
Insect Screen	
Kilo Speedometer	
License Frames	Various, by size used in individual states
Low Compression Heads	
Luggage Compartment Carpet	
Master Radio	
Standard Radio	
Cowl type aerial	
Running Board aerial	
Roof aerial	7233281
Moto-Pack	1426435
Seat Covers (Sea Breeze), front and rear	
Set of Tools	
Spot Light (Lorraine)	
Tire Chains	1418448
Triangle Grille Guard	
Wheel Discs (Chrome)	
Wheel Trim Rings (Chrome)	1413248

6. <u>Commercial Chassis</u>: The commercial chassis and engines are numbered the same as the automobiles, in the sequence in which they came down the assembly line. Some commercial chassis sheets indicate "closed cowl," others state "cowl, instruments and wiring shipped separate." No chassis indicated open cowl. Commercial chassis noted in the records examined were shipped to:

	Units
A. J. Miller Co., Bellefontaine, Ohio	184
Canada Body & Carriage Co., Brantsford, Ontario	13
Flixble Co., Loudonville, Ohio	81
GM Car Div, GM Sales Corp, Oshawa, Ontario	1
Henny Motor Co., Freeport, Illinois (#2277917)	1
Ingersoll Mitchell Hearse Co. Ltd. (Canada)	1
Knightstown Body Co., Knightstown, Indiana	36
Meteor Motor Car Company, Piqua, Ohio	191
Sayers & Scovill, Cincinatti, Ohio	222
Shaw Motor Co., Minneapolis, Minnesota	1
Superior Body Co., Lima, Ohio	102
The Eureka Co., Rock Falls, Illinois	48
Total	881

Note: 500 records not researched

7. All models of the standard production cars were exported outside of the U.S./Canada. Export cars were equipped with combinations of right-hand drive, low compression cylinder heads, kilo speedometers, fender lamps, export clocks and special headlight configurations

for left side driving. Numerous cars were sent to the Oshawa branch. Unlike previous years, there were no cars found to have been assembled in Canada.

8. As with other years, none of the body styles were built in a straight body order sequence. S.B.O. (Special Body Order) cars were generally substantially out of order with a notation "no. 227----reserved."

First car built in each body series:	Last car built in each body series:
5011 body #11, serial 2270038	body #697, serial 2285338
5019 body #31, serial 2270018	body #9768, serial 2285501
5027 body #12, serial 2270039	body #2703, serial 2285447
5049 body #1, serial 2270221	body #262, serial 2285311
5067 body #1, serial 2270216	body #794, serial 2285411
124" chassis, serial 2270023	
commercial chassis, serial 2270001	serial 2285500

9. <u>Export Chassis</u>: GM Holden Division in Australia received two "Engineering Sample" Sedan chassis and 72 right hand drive CKD "Australian Chassis" with "Deletions and additions as per Australian specifications." Sent in six-unit packs, the kits each contained a Motor case, Axle case, Frame case, Sheet Metal case and a Hood case. The bodies were designed and built by Holden. Chassis were shipped to Melbourne.

Three 5019 Sedan chassis, 2272637, 38 and 39, were sent to General Motors Argentina S/A in Buenos Aires.

Sedan chassis 2272643 went to GM Continental at Antwerp. Sedan chassis 2281126 was also sent to GM Continental, annotated "Supply convertible short sill cowl." The custom body builders were not identified for either car.

Chassis 2277848 and 2277858 were sent to General Motors France at Paris, annotated "Equip w/Convertible frame, convertible cowl in prime." The custom body builder was not identified.

10. <u>Domestic Chassis</u>: None noted in the records examined.

11. <u>Completely-Knocked-Down (CKD) Exports</u>: Of the examined cars, 265 CKD units were shipped as indicated. Previously published statistics have listed 72 CKD Sun-roof Sedans. No record of such cars was found.

GM Argentina, Buenos Aires	48	style 5019 Sedans
GM Do Brasil, São Paulo	24	style 5019 Sedans
GM Continental S.A., Antwerp	133	style 5019 Sedans
GM Continental S.A., Antwerp	36	style 5067 Convertible Coupes
GM Java Ltd., Batavia	12	style 5019 Sedans
GM South African Ltd., Port Elizabeth	<u>12</u>	style 5019 Sedans
Total	265	

Note: These cars did not have body numbers assigned and are, therefore, not included in the domestic production numbers (e.g., 9768 U.S. assembled 5019 Sedans).

SPECIFICATIONS

ENGINE—Cadillac precision built 90° Vee 8 design, L-head, bore $3\frac{3}{8}''$, stroke $4\frac{1}{2}''$, displacement 322 cu. in., taxable horsepower 36.45, brake horsepower 125 at 3400 r.p.m. Engine mounted in rubber at three points.

PISTONS—T-slot design Lo-Ex aluminum alloy for uniform expansion, special anodizing process hardens wearing surface to prevent scuffing and scoring, fitted with two compression rings and two oil rings.

CARBURETION—Dual down-draft with equalized manifolding, mechanical fuel pump, oil bath type air cleaner, intake silencer, fully automatic choke.

GASOLINE TANK—Capacity 22 gallons.

GENERATOR—The Delco-Remy peak load generator maintains charging rate, even when headlamps, radio, and heater are being used. It eliminates worry concerning battery condition.

CLUTCH—$10\frac{1}{2}''$ semi-centrifugal single plate disc of 107 square inch facing area. Permanently lubricated ball throwout bearing reduces service expense.

TRANSMISSION—Cadillac pioneered and built Syncro-Mesh with the pin type synchronizers, sliding low and reverse gears, constant mesh second gear. Syncromatic control clears front compartment. Transmission gears helical and fully carburized for hard use and long life.

LIGHTING—Three-beam asymmetrical system, double filament bulbs, instrument board and foot switch control. Headlamp beam indicator in speedometer face.

FRONT SUSPENSION—Independent "Knee-Action" front wheels, simple and sturdy with large, helical coil springs and forged forked arms for smoother riding comfort and effortless driving control. Thoroughly proven by four years' use and millions of miles of testing.

SPRINGS—Front suspension independent helical type, rear springs semi-elliptic type $54\frac{1}{2}''$ long, $2''$ wide, spring leaves lubricated by wax impregnated liners.

BRAKES—Bendix super-hydraulic brakes operate in composite drums with 220 square inches braking area. Mechanical hand brake operates independently.

DRIVE SHAFT—Hotchkiss drive. Two universal joints of the needle roller bearing type permanently packed with lubricant requiring no service attention.

REAR AXLE—Hypoid rear axle, Cadillac design and manufacture. Semi-floating type, insuring quiet, dependable performance. Gear ratio 3.92 to 1.

STEERING GEAR—Sturdy worm and double roller type. Center-point steering provides steering accuracy at all times. Can be turned or parked in much smaller space than many shorter cars.

FRAME—Tread: front $58''$, rear $59''$. Rigid frame, X-type, with very deep X-member junction and reinforced side members. Maximum depth $8\frac{11}{16}''$, flange width $2\frac{3}{8}''$, thickness $\frac{1}{8}''$.

RIDE STABILIZER—Double ride stabilizers hold car to level position and promote high speed roadability and safety, torsion bar type front, cross link type rear.

TIRES AND WHEELS—Low pressure, 4 ply tires, 7.00x16, steel disc wheels with large chrome disc hub caps.

FENDERS—Fenders and other sheet metal parts are bonderized to prevent rust.

WHEELBASE—$124''$. Over-all length with bumpers $201''$.

BODY TYPES—5 body types with Fisher No-Draft Ventilation and Turret Top roofs. Nuvo Cord or Ribbed Broadcloth upholstery and several body colors optional at no extra charge. Roomy luggage compartments in all models.

PRINTED IN U. S. A. SEPTEMBER, 1937

NINETEEN THIRTY-NINE
Series 50

Your first glimpse of the new La Salle V-8 will tell you that here is a car of unusual distinction—for it was styled by the same designers who created the custom Cadillac-Fleetwoods. Relying for its beauty upon correct proportions and harmony of line—rather than upon trick decorations and radical departures in form—La Salle is, nonetheless, one of the most individual cars of the year.

No other car looks even remotely like the new La Salle. The striking new radiator, narrowed almost to the span of a man's hand, identifies the La Salle from a point as far as the eye can see.

At the rear, the new La Salle presents an unusually smart ground-gripping appearance.

Distinctive appointments and authentic trimming styles lend fine-car atmosphere to the new interiors. The higher, wider doors greatly improve the ease of entrance or exit. The softly upholstered rear seat armrest, a standard appointment, quickly converts the rear compartment seat into two spacious lounge chairs.

Admiring glances will confirm your good judgement . . .

—from the 1939 sales brochure

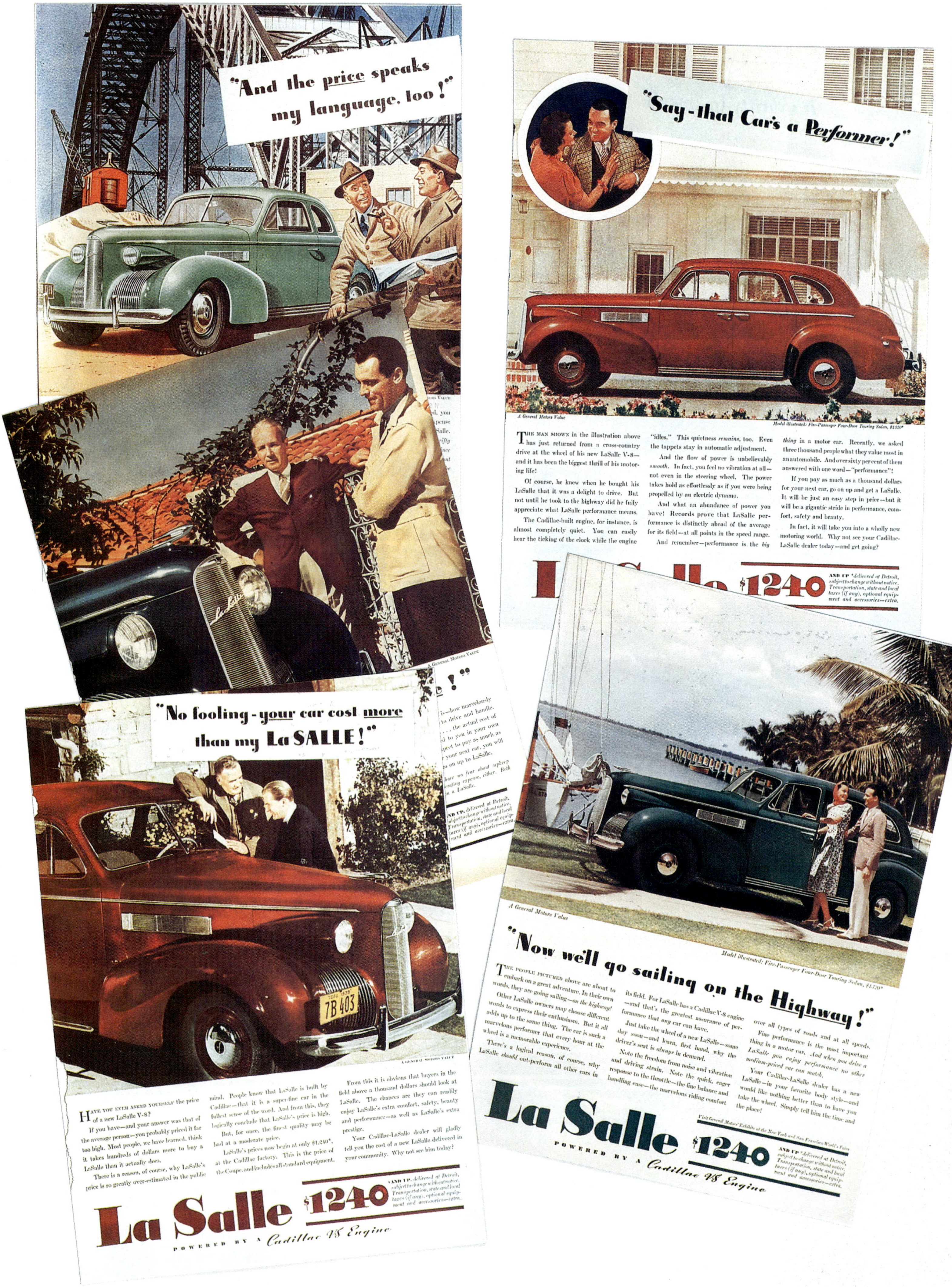
"And the price speaks my language, too!"
"Say-that Car's a Performer!"
A General Motors Value
Model illustrated: Five-Passenger Four-Door Touring Sedan, $1320*
THE MAN SHOWN in the illustration above has just returned from a cross-country drive at the wheel of his new LaSalle V-8—and it has been the biggest thrill of his motoring life!
Of course, he knew when he bought his LaSalle that it was a delight to drive. But not until he took to the highway did he fully appreciate what LaSalle performance means.
The Cadillac-built engine, for instance, is almost completely quiet. You can easily hear the ticking of the clock while the engine "idles." This quietness remains, too. Even the tappets stay in automatic adjustment.
And the flow of power is unbelievably smooth. In fact, you feel no vibration at all—not even in the steering wheel. The power takes hold as effortlessly as if you were being propelled by an electric dynamo.
And what an abundance of power you have! Records prove that LaSalle performance is distinctly ahead of the average for its field—at all points in the speed range.
And remember—performance is the big thing in a motor car. Recently, we asked three thousand people what they value most in an automobile. And over sixty per cent of them answered with one word—"performance"!
If you pay as much as a thousand dollars for your next car, go on up and get a LaSalle. It will be just an easy step in price—but it will be a gigantic stride in performance, comfort, safety and beauty.
In fact, it will take you into a wholly new motoring world. Why not see your Cadillac-LaSalle dealer today—and get going?
$1240
AND UP *delivered at Detroit, subject to change without notice. Transportation, state and local taxes (if any), optional equipment and accessories—extra.
"No fooling-your car cost more than my La SALLE!"
7B 403
A GENERAL MOTORS VALUE
HAVE YOU EVER ASKED YOURSELF the price of a new LaSalle V-8?
If you have—and your answer was that of the average person—you probably priced it far too high. Most people, we have learned, think it takes hundreds of dollars more to buy a LaSalle than it actually does.
There is a reason, of course, why LaSalle's price is so greatly over-estimated in the public mind. People know that LaSalle is built by Cadillac—that it is a super-fine car in the fullest sense of the word. And from this, they logically conclude that LaSalle's price is high.
But, for once, the finest quality may be had at a moderate price.
LaSalle's prices now begin at only $1,240*, at the Cadillac factory. This is the price of the Coupe, and includes all standard equipment.
From this it is obvious that buyers in the field above a thousand dollars should look at LaSalle. The chances are they can readily enjoy LaSalle's extra comfort, safety, beauty and performance—as well as LaSalle's extra prestige.
Your Cadillac-LaSalle dealer will gladly tell you the cost of a new LaSalle delivered in your community. Why not see him today?
La Salle $1240
*AND UP, delivered at Detroit, subject to change without notice. Transportation, state and local taxes (if any), optional equipment and accessories—extra.
POWERED BY A Cadillac V8 Engine
A General Motors Value
"Now we'll go sailing on the Highway!"
Model illustrated: Five-Passenger Four-Door Touring Sedan, $1320*
THE PEOPLE PICTURED above are about to embark on a great adventure. In their own words, they are going sailing—on the highway!
Other LaSalle owners may choose different words to express their enthusiasm. But it all adds up to the same thing. The car is such a marvelous performer that every hour at the wheel is a memorable experience.
There's a logical reason, of course, why LaSalle should out-perform all other cars in its field. For LaSalle has a Cadillac V-8 engine—and that's the greatest assurance of performance that any car can have.
Just take the wheel of a new LaSalle—some day soon—and learn, first hand, why the driver's seat is always in demand.
Note the freedom from noise and vibration and driving strain. Note the quick, eager response to the throttle—the fine balance and handling ease—the marvelous riding comfort over all types of roads and at all speeds.
Fine performance is the most important thing in a motor car. And when you drive a LaSalle you enjoy performance no other medium-priced car can match.
Your Cadillac-LaSalle dealer has a new LaSalle—in your favorite body style—and would like nothing better than to have you take the wheel. Simply tell him the time and the place!
La Salle $1240
Visit General Motors' Exhibits at the New York and San Francisco World's Fairs
AND UP *delivered at Detroit, subject to change without notice. Transportation, state and local taxes (if any), optional equipment and accessories—extra.
POWERED BY A Cadillac V8 Engine

NINETEEN THIRTY-NINE
Series 50

LaSalle was dramatically restyled for 1939. The design for the Series 50, now on a reduced wheelbase of 120 inches, was challenged to make it look long, low and luxurious. This was successfully executed by an extremely narrow one-piece diecast vertical grille. An added styling feature helped this effort with the placement of a grille in front of the catwalk on each side of the center radiator grille. Headlights were positioned to the side of the radiator and hood in a forward lurching position with windsplits on the side (instead of the top). Every line seemed to flow toward the front and center.

Glass area had been increased significantly. This gave the overall appearance of the LaSalle a more squared and sculptured effect. Inspired, no doubt, by the 1938 Cadillac 60 Special convertible-like windows, LaSalle cleverly put stainless steel trim around each window opening as if there was no further support. It was a very handsome treatment.

The V-8 grille emblem was moved to each hood side ventilator grille. On the grille, LaSalle was attached in script. The round branding iron LaS emblem remained on the hubcaps only. The 1939 hubcaps were the only ones with a black, instead of red, field on the emblem. The instrument panel was new for 1939 with a narrow horizontal, rectangular and symmetrical motif. It had slightly convex, rounded glass over the speedometer, radio and clock dials.

Sidemounted spare tires were no longer in vogue. They were available as an option, only. They were positioned high atop the fenders and were unusual and seldom seen.

Rumble seats on Coupes and Convertible Coupes were no longer available. It was an era gone by. Instead, fold up seats were mounted inside.

Overall, the car looked very modern, was perceived to be lower and, for the first time, was offered without running boards, as well as with.

Interior accoutrements were mostly made from plastic, except for the diecast chromed radio grille located at the center of the dashboard.

Five body styles were again available. Of particular interest was a new "Sunshine Turret-Top" roof available on the two- and four-door Sedans.

The 1939 models were introduced in late Fall of 1938. The United States was experiencing an economic recession. This, no doubt, affected the theme of LaSalle's advertising. "No, I didn't get rich—I just got wise!" "And the price speaks my language, too!" LaSalle was presented very conservatively with blackwall tires and lack of accessories. Most of the ads were in color. Some were color photographs while others were enhanced artists' renderings.

The 1939 sales brochure accurately captured in profile the stylish lines of the yellow Convertible Coupe and the green four-door Convertible Sedan. Running boards and sidemounted spare tires in the front fenders were not illustrated in the sales literature anymore even though they were still available. Also not shown was the very popular grille guard mounted on the front bumper nor the deluxe heater air inlet on the passenger side cowl. Yet, all models were shown with whitewall tires and large hubcaps. Those who prepared the promotional material made sure that the models shown were at their visual best. Illustrations shown in a three-quarter view were drawn slightly out of proportion, particularly the roof lines. Sales brochures were often prepared before the production models were manufactured, so some artist liberties were acceptable, if not desirable.

Top: A handsomely restored four-door Convertible is showing its prize-winning condition with the top up. Above: A factory photo shows the four-door Convertible Sedan model 5029 with four smiling young ladies, in an attempt to capture the growing young ladies' market.

LaSalle sales brochures were artistically done and quite appealing, except for the color finish on the cars. They were dull and did not represent the actual colors to their best advantage. Notable exceptions in the same brochure were the style and beauty drawings. They were superb.

LaSalle continued to be powered by the same 322 cubic inch, 125 horsepower, V-8 engine introduced in 1937. Dependability and whisper-quiet performance confirmed its growing reputation for reliability and desirability.

Cadillac design makes *LaSalle* both STYLE

Your first glimpse of the new LaSalle V-8 will tell you that here is a car of unusual distinction—for it was styled by the same designers who created the custom Cadillac-Fleetwoods. ¶ Relying for its beauty upon correct proportions and harmony of line—rather than upon trick decorations and radical departures in form—LaSalle is, nonetheless, one of the most individual cars of the year. No other car looks even remotely like the new LaSalle. ¶ The striking new radiator, narrowed almost to the span of a man's hand, identifies the LaSalle from a point as far as the eye can see. Across the front of the grille appears the LaSalle name in white and gold script. The new

Here are a few of the features that recommend it

leader of the medium-price field in and BEAUTY

headlamps are long and streamlined, flowing into the hood side panels. All models have chrome window reveals and are available with or without running boards, at no extra charge. The lower turret top, streamlined hood, forwardly inclined rear quarter pillar, and the new trunk into which the body lines flow, all contribute to an appearance of extraordinary agility and fleetness. ⁋ At the rear, the new LaSalle presents an unusually smart ground-gripping appearance. A new rear bumper carries the name "LaSalle" in script. ⁋ The new 1939 LaSalle is now completely identified as a beautiful quality-built car—a worthy product of Cadillac's master craftsmen.

Here are some of the special things it offers

And here are some of its many advantages

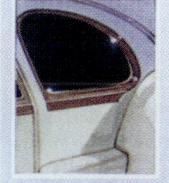

Left: An extremely rare five-passenger two-door Touring Sedan model 5011-A is shown with the "Sunshine Turret-Top" roof. Only twenty-three were built. This extra cost option provided increased ventilation and an upward view while retaining the structural strength of a closed car. It was sturdy and tamperproof. It consisted of a sliding steel panel, easily operated and locked with one hand, in any desired position. When kept clean, the unit provided a good seal to prevent air or water leaks.

Middle right: A nicely restored two-door five-passenger Touring Sedan model 5011 is shown without running boards, a no-cost option, and small hubcaps with beauty rings. Two-door Sedans were becoming a very popular configuration. They had a sportiness about them yet provided ample room equal to a four-door family Sedan. Below left: A two-passenger Convertible Coupe model 5067 dons an unusual two-tone paint scheme rarely found on cars from the late 1930s. Below right: A two-passenger Coupe model 5027, in a one-tone paint scheme without running boards. The Coupe had a cavernous trunk with additional storage behind the front seat when the auxiliary seats were folded up.

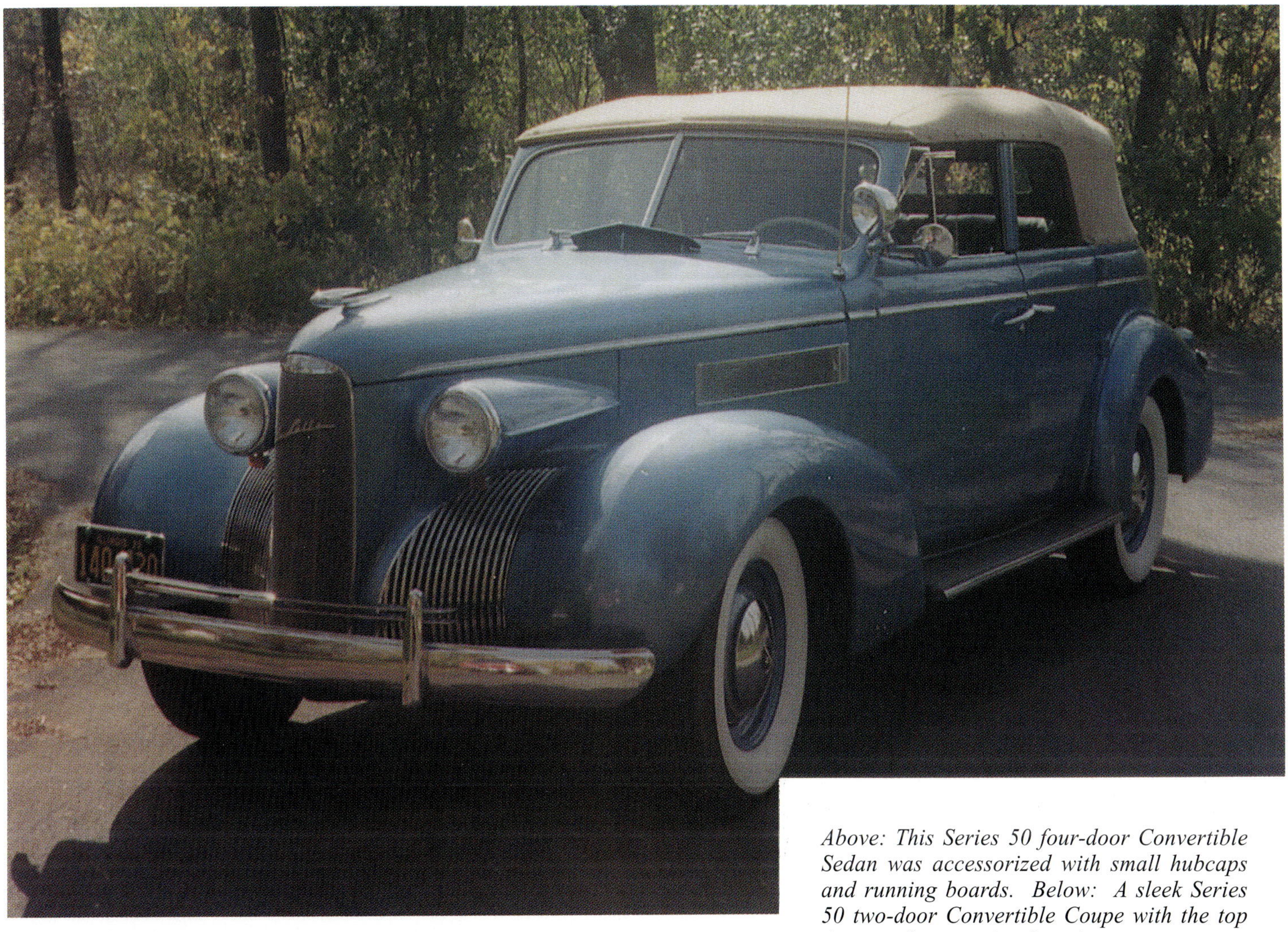

Above: This Series 50 four-door Convertible Sedan was accessorized with small hubcaps and running boards. Below: A sleek Series 50 two-door Convertible Coupe with the top down and no running boards.

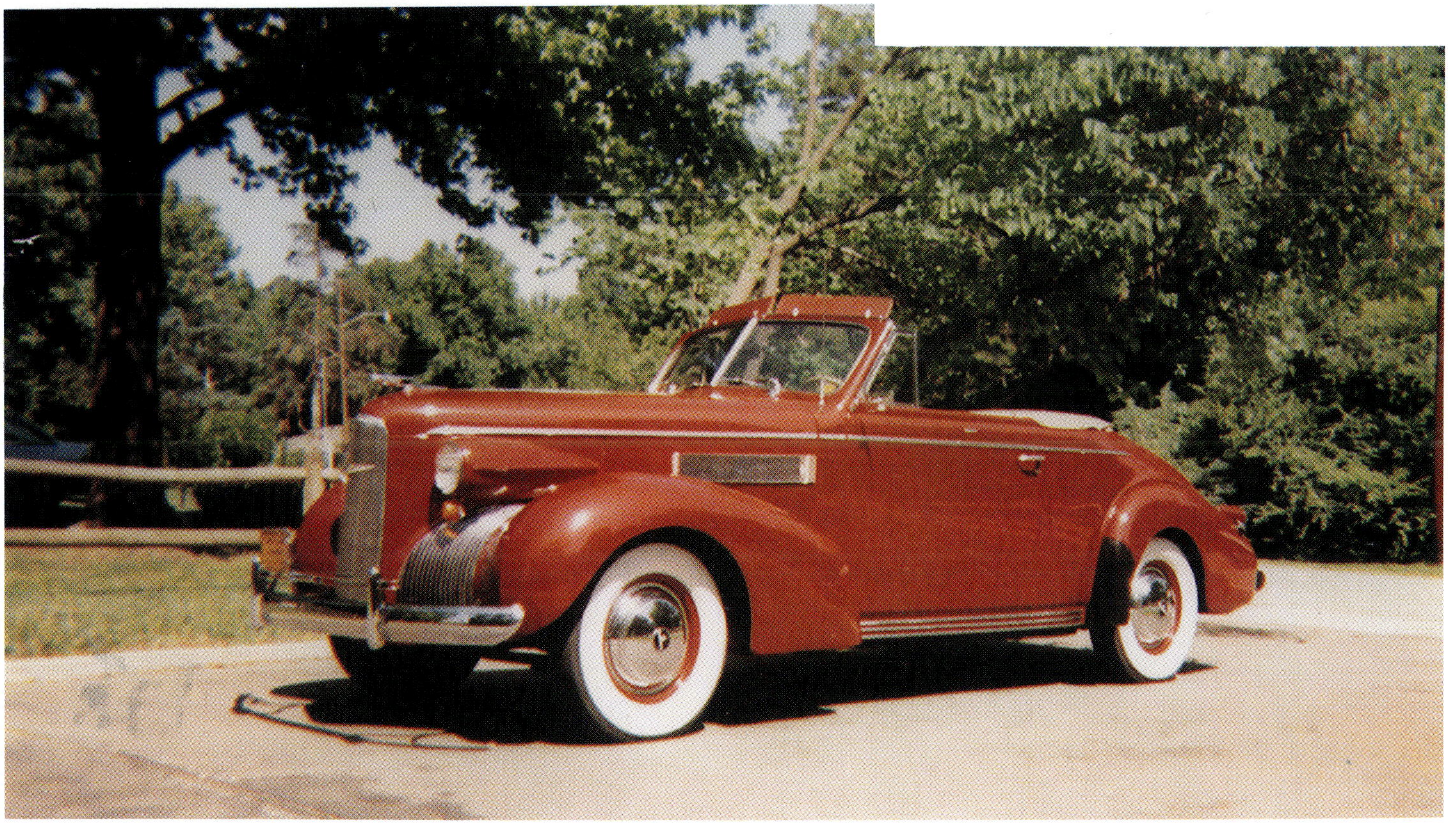

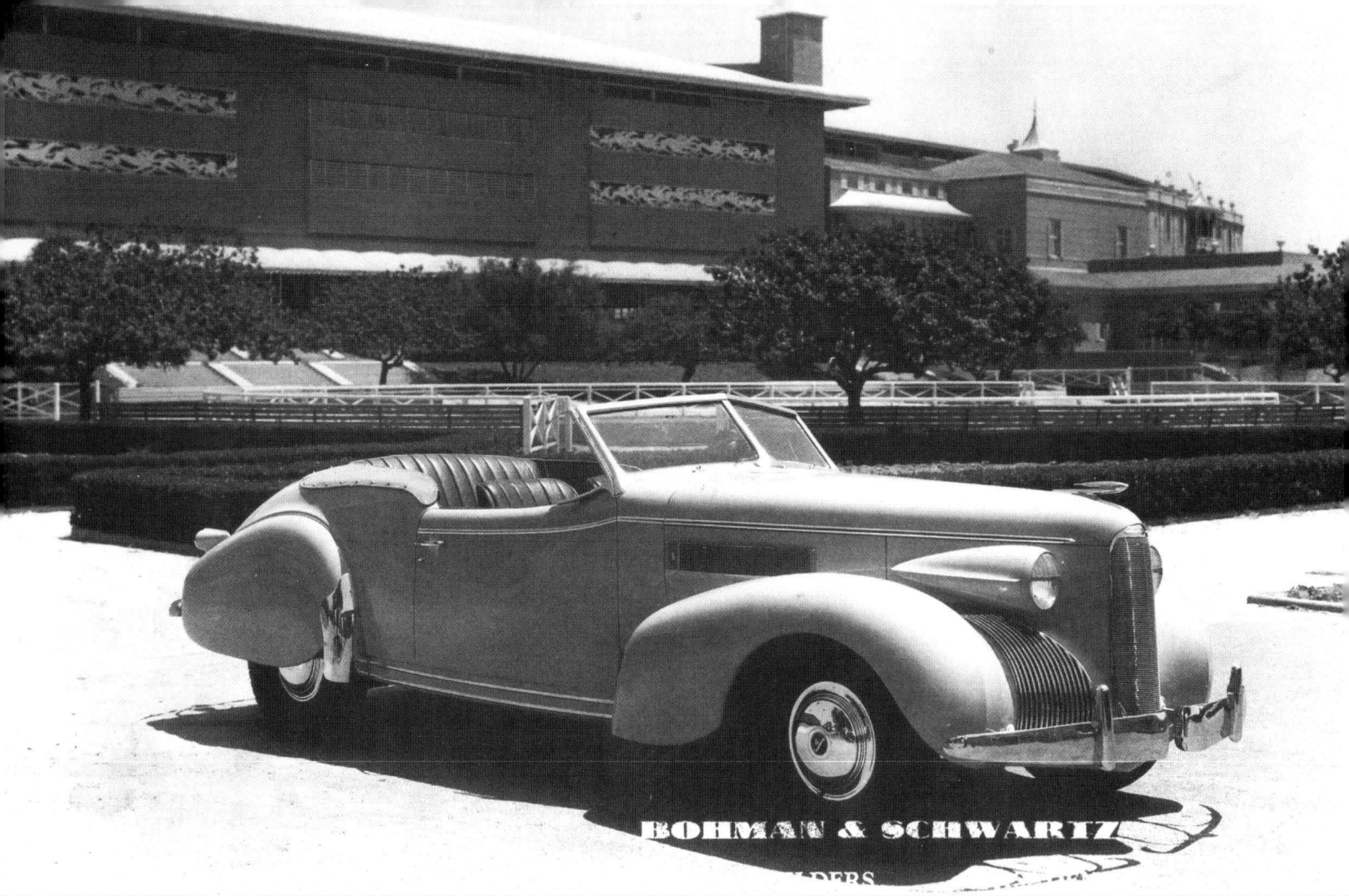
BOHMAN & SCHWARTZ

THE BOHMAN AND SCHWARTZ LaSALLE

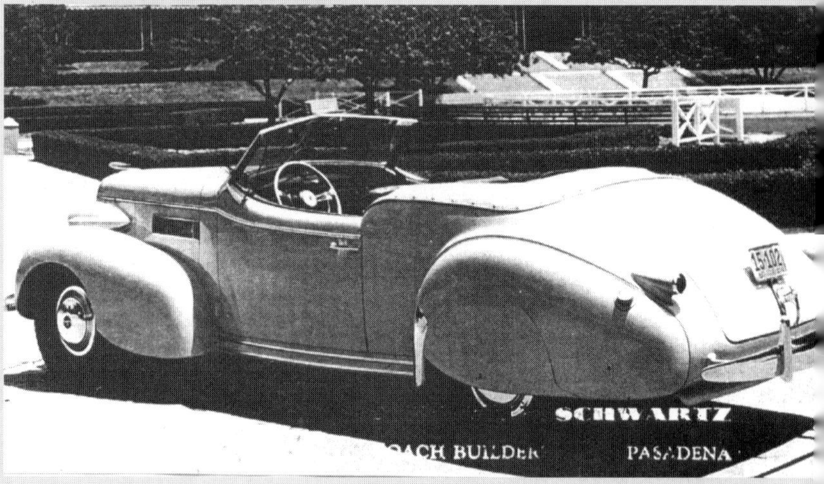
SCHWARTZ
PASADENA

Bohman and Schwartz was a well-known custom body shop in Pasadena, California. Cars driven by the rich and famous, who wanted something different, were gracefully transformed by this firm, as was the case of this 1939 LaSalle.

During the late 1930s, Packard contracted with Darrin, another custom design shop, to build special Convertibles. One of Darrin's trademarks was the dip in the door, lengthening the cowl and a Vee'd windshield frame.

Apparently Darrin was so busy that when a customer of Don Lee Cadillac in San Francisco wanted a Darrin body, the availability was non-existent. So, he placed an order for a Bohman and Schwartz instead, for a custom-bodied LaSalle with similar design elements. But, Bohman and Schwartz incorporated some fascinating styling features of their own. The door line was dipped à la Darrin; a chrome belt molding paralleling the dip stopped at the door opening without the customary flow-through to the rear body panel; two sill strips, instead of three, connected the flow line between the front and rear fenders; a chromed rock shield was placed at the leading edge of the rear fender while the fender skirts had an upturn echoing the dip line of the door; the rear wheels appeared to be peeking out from behind the fender skirts; and that same dip was repeated at the bottom edge of the front fender. This repeat dip theme created a very stylish effect.

The interior had pleated and rolled upholstery with two bucket seats up front and a rolled pad effect atop the dash. Both the front and rear bumpers were customized to create the illusion of greater length. The front bumper was split in the middle, providing an unobstructed view of the tall narrow LaSalle grille à la 1934.

Two similar Convertibles were built on 1940 Cadillac chassis. It is believed that only one LaSalle of this design was built.

Top and Middle: Until recently, it was hypothesized that there was only one 1939 LaSalle Convertible customized by Bohman and Schwartz. However, two photographs have surfaced, sent by Chris Bohman to a Cadillac LaSalle enthusiast. These lead us to the conclusion that there were at least two built, very similar, but not exactly the same. The split front bumpers appear the same, as do the windshield frame, the dip in the door, the chrome belt molding stopping at the door edge and the upturn on the rear fender skirts. What appears different is the lack of upturn at the bottom of the front fenders and the rear deck configuration. The trunk lid is shorter and has a spare tire bulge. The rear passenger compartment also looks longer and takes more of the body sheet metal away where the top fastens across the rear deck. All-in-all, a very attractive but curious custom LaSalle.

Bottom left: Shown here are some unusual accessories on a model 5027 two-door Coupe. Very unusual are the twin side-mounted metal-covered spare tire covers, particularly with the running board deletion. Their profile extended slightly above the hood and cut into the fender contour. Also available were these fender skirts as an after-market accessory. The bottom edge, changing elevation at the midpoint around the medallion base, adds to their sleekness. Their design is somewhat reminiscent of the 1934 factory wheel shields. A manufacturer's number, 84557, has been stamped on the inside mechanism, but the name of the manufacturer is unknown. *Bottom right:* All of these unusual features are shown in combination on this two-door Coupe.

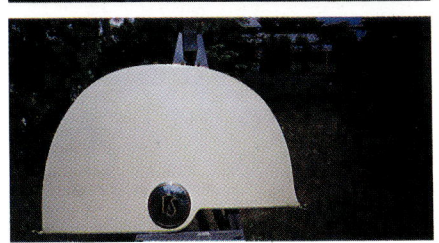

1939 LaSalle Production

Total Production: 23,002 automobiles and chassis.

Serial Numbers: 2290001-2313002. The Vehicle (engine) serial number is "On rough flat surface on rear portion of crankcase back of L.H. block, numbered at right angle with the crankshaft. Numbering to start from the top."

Chassis Numbers: Same as engine serial numbers. Location of chassis number is "Top surface of frame side bar, just ahead of dash, opposite steering gear."

Body Plates: "Body and style number on plate on left side of dash." (under the hood)

Body Type and Style Numbers:	Fisher Bodies	Production	List Price (October 18, 1938)
Series 39-50 (120" Wheelbase) -			
5-Pass. 2-Door Touring Sedan	39-5011	977	$1280.00
5-Pass. 2-Door Touring Sedan (Sunshine Turret-Top Roof)	39-5011A	23	$1317.50
5-Pass. 4-Door Touring Sedan	39-5019	15683	$1320.00
5-Pass. 4-Door Touring Sedan, (Sunshine Turret-Top Roof)	39-5019A	380	$1357.50
5-Pass. 4-Door Touring Sedan - CKD (Export)	39-5019	252	
5-Pass. 4-Door Touring Sedan - CKD (Export)	39-5019A	24	
2-Pass. Coupe	39-5027	3531	$1240.00
5-Pass. Convertible Sedan	39-5029	185	$1800.00
2-Pass. Convertible Coupe	39-5067	1020	$1395.00
2-Pass. Convertible Coupe - CKD (Export)	39-5067	24	
Chassis (120" W.B.)		5	$ 985.00
Commercial Chassis (156" W.B.)	39-50	874	$1020.00
Chassis CKD (Export)		24	
	Total	23002	

Color Options

Body, Fenders, Tire Cover	R & M #	Wheels	
51 Black	20498	Black (standard)	94-005
		Triton Green (optional)	94-20957
		Corsican Red (optional)	94-20940
52 Antoinette Blue	22290	Antoinette Blue	94-20871
53 Cavern Green	023355	Triton Green	94-20957
54 Marblehead Gray	20198	Corsican Red	94-20940
55 Dragoon Blue Iridescent	P.S. 261	Kashan Blue	94-3888
56 Piedmont Green Iridescent	P.S. 371	Piedmont Green Iridescent	182-20948
57 Franconia Beige Iridescent	P.S.875	Franconia Beige Iridescent	182-20951
58 Oxblood Maroon	P.S. 608	Oxblood Maroon Iridescent	182-20955
59 Monterey Blue Iridescent	P.S. 258	Monterey Blue Iridescent	182-20947
60 Trinidad Gray Iridescent	P.S. 183	Corsican Red	92-20940
61 Empire Green	023354	Empire Green	92-20929
62 Kingston Gray	020161	Kingston Gray	92-20894
63 Ludington Green	23459	Ludington Green	94 20952
English Gray	21147		
64 Silver French Gray Iridescent	P.S. 106	Monterey Blue Iridescent	182-20947
Monterey Blue Iridescent	P.S. 258		

Note: Two-tone color splits are Belt Molding and above/below Belt Molding and Fenders. Although the color chart indicates that colors 63 and 64 are for the Cadillac 6019S sedan only, production LaSalles were painted in those colors.

Standardized Colors - All Cars:
Radiator Grille - Center	White Dulux and Chrome	94-20850
Radiator Grille - Side	Black Dulux and Chrome	94-005
Hood Ventilator	White Dulux and Chrome	94-20850
Steering Gear Housing Tube, Wheel Hub, Bracket and Gear Shift Housing Tube, Lever and Hand Brake	Cocoa Brown	242-53199
Wheel Stripe	Pale Gold Bronze	
Garnish Moulding Above Belt Line	Light Beige	202-53093
Instrument Panel	Transfer Type Finish	

Trim Options

Code No.		Trim No.	Convertible Tops	Trim No.
30	Tan Pattern Cloth	51T139	Tan (standard)	
31	Tan Ribbed Cloth (Broadcloth)	52T139	Blue Grey (Special)	9T1539
32	Gray Pattern Cloth	55T139	Black (Special)	11T1539
33	Gray Ribbed Cloth (Broadcloth)	56T139		
34	Blue Leather	5T1339		
35	Red Leather	6T1339	Convertible Top Lining	
36	Black Leather	1T1339	Tan used with all colors	
38	Gray Leather	3T1339		
39	Green Leather	4T1339		
40	Brown Leather	2T1339		

Accessory Groups
(December 1, 1938)

B $20.25	BG $29.50	AR6 (6-wheel) $29.25	ARG6 $38.50
Flexible (Steering) Wheel	Flexible Wheel	Flexible Wheel	Flexible Wheel
Automatic Lighter	Automatic Lighter	Automatic Lighter	Automatic Lighter
License Frames	License Frames	License Frames	License Frames
	Grille Guard	6 Trim Rings	6 Trim Rings
			Grille Guard

AR5 (5-wheel) $27.75	ARG5 $37.00	AD $36.25	ADG $45.50
Flexible Wheel	Flexible Wheel	Flexible Wheel	Flexible Wheel
Automatic Lighter	Automatic Lighter	Automatic Lighter	Automatic Lighter
License Frames	License Frames	License Frames	License Frames
5 Trim Rings	5 Trim Rings	4 Wheel Discs	4 Wheel Discs
	Grille Guard		Grille Guard

Running Boards are standard equipment, deletion is optional at no charge.
Clock is standard equipment.

Additional Charges

6 Wheels, fenderwells, tire covers	$95.00	White Sidewall tires, $4.00 per tire
Single right side fenderwell	$40.00	(7.00 X 16" Royal or Firestone 4-ply black tires are standard
Sunshine Turret-Top on Touring Sedans	$37.50	equipment)

Accessories
(All prices include installation but are less local taxes)

Name		Part No.	Name		Part No.
Automatic Cigarette Lighter	$ 2.25	1097019	Miscellaneous (continued)		
Cool Cushion	$ 2.95		Handy Brush	$ 2.00	
Flexible Steering Wheel	$15.00		Moto-Pack	$ 6.85	1426435
Fog and Adverse Weather Lights (pair)	$14.50	1434057	Radiator Inhibitor	$ .75	
Glare Shield	$ 1.50		Tire Gauge	$ 1.00	
Heater-Defrosters (Ventilating)	$31.50	1428483	White Sidewall Cleaner (pint)	$ .60	
Heater-Defrosters (Non-Ventilating)	Not listed	1434509	NO-ROL (hill holder)	$11.00	1434434
Hinge Mirror	$ 4.50	1425809	Radiator Insect Screen	$ 2.25	
Illuminated Vanity Mirror	$ 6.50	1434615	Radio, Automatic with Vacuum		
License Frames (pair)	$ 3.00	1433702	or Running Board Aerial	$69.50	1433970
Luggage			Rear Compartment Radio	$79.50	
Gentlemen's Aviator	$35.00		(does not include body preparation		
Ladies' Aviatrix	$35.00		fee averaging $30.00)		
Wardrolette	$42.50		Robes - Fleetwood cloth and		
Sport Bag	$15.00		crushed plush or alpaca	$50.00	
Aerolite Case	$18.50		Pillow to match	$ 8.00	
Miscellaneous			Monograms	$ 5.50	
Blue Corral	$ 2.50		Double alpaca robe, brown or gray	$30.00	
Blue Corral Sealer	$ 1.00		Alpaca and plush robe, brown or gray	$30.00	
Blue Corral Prophylactic	$ 1.00		Scuff Pads (door)	$ 1.50	1427663
Dust Mit	$ .65		Seat Covers (per seat)	$ 8.25	
Body Polish (pint)	$ .60		Spotlight (Right hand)	$18.50	1434066
Bulb Kit	$ 1.10		Spotlight (Left hand)	$18.50	1434067
Chrome Cleaner (pint)	$ .60		Wheel Discs (Chrome, each)	$ 4.00	3504855
Fabric Cleaner (pint)	$ .60		Wheel Trim Rings (each)	$ 1.50	1413248
Flashlight	$ 1.50		Windshield Washer	$ 5.75	1434464
Glass Cleaner	$ .45		Windshield Washer Winter Solution	$ .25	

Research Methodology: Microfiche copies of the individual Shipping Department records of the as-built configuration of each serial number were viewed, starting at the highest serial number and working backwards, to determine the highest body serial number of each body style, special features, etc. Commercial chassis, CKD units, Convertibles and Sunshine Turret-Top car numbers were individually recorded to verify actual production.

Notes on research findings:

1. Each LaSalle body style has a distinct body number series, starting with number one, through the highest number of bodies built. In the case of the 1939 Sunshine Turret-Top cars (5011A and 5019A), the style is not shown as a distinct series on the build sheet - the "A" suffix does not appear. On those two body styles, the build sheets are annotated "SUNSHINE ROOF" in the area where factory installed accessories are listed.

The Cadillac Historical Collection archives contain machine printouts for three of the 1939 body styles (5011, 5019, 5027) in body number sequence, cross referenced to engine number. Studying the lists reveals:

Style 5011 2-Door Sedan. The highest body number is 980; 24 duplicate body numbers are listed (includes 23 Sunshine Turret-Top cars); 4 body numbers were not used, therefore total production is 1000 cars.

Style 5019 4-Door Sedan. The highest body number is 15696; 394 duplicate body numbers are listed (includes 380 Sunshine Turret-Top cars); 3 triplicate body numbers are listed; 33 body numbers were not used, therefore total production is 16063 cars.

Style 5027 2-Pass. Coupe. The highest body number is 3544; 2 duplicate body numbers are listed; 10 bodies were used for Flower Cars; 5 body numbers were not used, therefore total production is 3531 cars. The Coupe production number is significant in that it is verifiable by serial number and represents 1006 more cars than the previously published summary production data found in *Cadillac—The Complete History* by Maurice Hendry and *80 Years of Cadillac LaSalle* by Walter M. P. McCall. The previously published data is from incorrect summary data found in the Cadillac factory records.

2. Domestic Cars: Unlike previous years, the standard configuration of all body styles was with five wheels and the spare tire concealed in the trunk. Body styles and buyers' tastes had changed, roads and tires were improved and the sidemounted fender was rapidly disappearing from the automotive scene. Of the 21,799 factory built production cars, only two had a single right hand sidemount and 226 were equipped with dual sidemounts. Additional commercial chassis and CKD export Sedans were equipped with sidemounts.

A diminishing number of Special Body Order (S.B.O.) cars continued to be built. Nearly all of the orders were in the nature of special trim or paint. Two-tone paint was found on Coupes and a Convertible Coupe with black fenders and Kingston Gray body. Multiple closed cars were done with full or partial leather interiors. The build sheets for 1939 do not have a block for the name of the purchaser. A very few S.B.O. sheets list the purchaser, notably, GM officials such as W. S. Knudsen, A. J. Fisher, E. F. Fisher and Ernest Seaholm.

Special requests were also filled for mechanical features. At least three cars were fitted with "Series 61 engine and other parts." The Cadillac series 61 engine at 346 cubic inches, vice the 322 cubic inch LaSalle engine, boosted horsepower from 125 to 135. The engines carried a Cadillac engine unit number and the LaSalle vehicle serial number. High compression cylinder heads were fitted to several cars, electric fuel pumps were furnished on export and domestic orders and directional indicators were shipped loose with a Sedan sent to Shanghai, China. An export special order Convertible Coupe sent to London was equipped with "One single window in each door, eliminating draft windows."

All models of the standard production cars, except the 5011A 2-Door Touring Sedan with Sunshine Turret-Top Roof, were exported outside of the U.S. Export cars were equipped with combinations of right hand drive, low compression cylinder heads, kilo speedometers, fender lamps, export clocks and special headlight configurations for left side driving. Numerous cars were sent to the GM Car Div., GM Sales Corp., Oshawa, Ontario. There were no 1939 LaSalles found to have been assembled in Canada.

3. Completely-Knocked-Down (CKD) Exports: Factory production summary data indicates a total of 300 CKD LaSalles shipped for overseas assembly; 240 style 5019 Sedans, 24 style 5019A Sunshine Turret-Top Sedans and 36 style 5067 Convertible Coupes. Shipping records exist for all 300 units. Examination reveals only 24 Convertible Coupes shipped (there was a $6.50 additional charge per chassis, listed for "5067 Convertible Frame"). Identification of the 24 Sunshine Turret-Top units is based on the additional charge of $1.75 per unit for "Crating of Bonnets," the only discernible difference in the records. The CKD cars did not have body numbers assigned and are, therefore, not included in domestic production numbers (e.g., 1020 U.S. assembled Convertible Coupes). CKD distribution was:

GM Argentina, Buenos Aires	24	style 5019 Sedans
GM Brazil, Sao Paulo (shipped to Santos)	48	style 5019 Sedans
GM Continental, Antwerp	144	style 5019 Sedans
GM Continental, Antwerp	24	style 5067 Convertible Coupes
GM India, Ltd., Bombay	12	style 5019A Sunshine Turret-Top Sedans
GM Java, Batavia	12	style 5019A Sunshine Turret-Top Sedans
GM S. African, Ltd., Port Elizabeth	36	style 5019 Sedans
Total	300	

4. Chassis, CKD Export: GM Holden in Australia received 24 right hand drive CKD chassis, with credits for unspecified deletions. Holden built distinctly different bodies on their LaSalles and the credits would be for body components not used in their production. Six units were shipped to the Holden headquarters in Melbourne and eighteen units to Sydney.

5. Chassis (120" W.B.): Five units were shipped, with no indication of the intended custom bodies that were to be installed:

Serial 2292049, 2292062 and 2292076, shipped to GM Holden, Adelaide, Australia, were Convertible chassis fitted with closed car cowls.

Serial 2299400, shipped to Central Cadillac Co., Milwaukee, Wisconsin, was fitted with closed car cowl, dual sidemounts, hood panels and fenders painted black.

Serial 2311203, shipped to The Eureka Company, Rock Falls, Illinois, marked "Charge to Mid Town Motor Sales, Ltd., Montreal" was fitted with closed car cowl, 5 wheels, hood panels and fenders painted black.

6. <u>Commercial Chassis</u>: The commercial chassis and engines are numbered the same as the automobiles, in the sequence in which they came down the assembly line. Some commercial chassis sheets indicate "closed cowl"; others state "cowl, instruments and wiring shipped separate." No chassis indicated open cowl. Commercial chassis were shipped to:

A. J. Miller Company, Bellefontaine, Ohio	152	Meteor Motor Car Company, Piqua, Ohio	223
Canada Body & Carriage Co, Brantsford, Ontario	9	Sayers & Scovill, Cincinnati, Ohio	169
Flxible Co., Loudonville, Ohio	73	Superior Body Co., Lima, Ohio	152
GM Car Div, GM Sales Corp, Oshawa, Ontario	1	The Bender Body Co., Cleveland, Ohio	32
Ingersoll Mitchell Hearse Co. Ltd. (Canada)	2	The Eureka Company, Rock Falls, Illinois	38
Knightstown Body Co., Knightstown, Indiana	23	Total	874

7. <u>Flower Cars</u>: Flower cars built from the 1937 and 1938 LaSalles were commercial conversions of production Coupes or Convertible Coupes, with chassis extended by the coach builders. A single 1939 production Coupe, serial 2310494, body #3207, was shipped to The Eureka Company "To be converted to Flower Car." Presumably, it was converted into a relatively short wheelbase Flower Car. An additional eleven 1939 units were built on the 156" wheel base commercial chassis, with production car bodies either mounted at the factory or trucked to the coach builders:

2290174 Meteor, Coupe body #2 shipped separate	2306401 Bender, Coupe body #2521 mounted
2290188 Miller, Coupe body #1 shipped separate	2306830 Eureka, Coupe body #2617 mounted
2302936 Meteor, Coupe body #1881 mounted	2308181 Knightstown, Coupe body #2822 mounted
2302960 Meteor, Coupe body #1883 mounted	2308156 Knightstown, Coupe body #2828 mounted
2304335 Meteor, Coupe body #2153 mounted	2309138 Eureka, Convertible Coupe, body #899 mounted
2304928 Miller, Coupe body #2314 mounted	

8. <u>Show Cars</u>: The World's Fair was held in New York in 1939. At least three LaSalles were done in special livery for the show: a Croyden Cream (R&M 242-51389) Convertible Coupe with Black leather, a Silver Gray (EX 42-142) Convertible Sedan with Pearl leather and a Silver Gray (EX 42-142) 5019 Sedan with special Wiese cloth interior. A second Convertible Sedan painted "Special Crystal Green" with all white Eagle Ottawa leather was sent to New York as the "Grand Palace - Show Car." The Waldorf Astoria show cars were a Kingston Gray Convertible Coupe and a Trinidad Gray Iridescent Convertible Sedan. Specially prepared "Show" cars were done for the Branch Offices in Chicago, Detroit, New York, and Oshawa, plus the GM Building lobby in Detroit and the GM Parade of Progress.

9. As with other years, none of the body styles were built in a straight body order sequence:

First unit built in each body series:	Last unit built in each body series:
5011 body #5, serial 2290191	body #954, serial 2312823
5011A body #4, serial 2296740	body #22, serial 2309742
5019 body #1, serial 2290001	body #14993, serial 2312822
5019A body #1, serial 2291131	body #375, serial 2312721
5027 body #138, serial 2290035	body #3537, serial 2312801
5029 body #1, serial 2290857	body #182, serial 2312404
5067 body #1, serial 2290072	body #1010, serial 2311898
commercial chassis, serial 2200047	serial 2313002

CONDENSED SPECIFICATIONS

ENGINE—Cadillac precision built 90° Vee 8 design—L-head, bore 3⅜", stroke 4½", displacement 322 cu. in. Taxable horsepower 36.45 with brake horsepower 125 at 3400 r.p.m. Engine mounted in rubber at three points.

PISTONS—T-slot design LO-Ex aluminum alloy for uniform expansion. Special anodizing process hardens wearing surface to prevent scuffing and scoring. Fitted with two compression rings and two oil rings all with ferrox coating.

CARBURETION—Dual down-draft with equalized manifolding, mechanical fuel pump, oil bath type air cleaner, intake silencer and fully automatic choke.

GASOLINE TANK—Capacity 22 gallons.

GENERATOR—The Delco-Remy peak load generator maintains charging rate even when headlamps, radio, and heater are being used. It eliminates worry concerning battery condition.

CLUTCH—10" semi-centrifugal single plate disc. Permanently lubricated ball throwout bearing reduces service expense.

TRANSMISSION—Cadillac pioneered and built Syncro-Mesh with pin type synchronizers, sliding low and reverse gears, constant mesh second gear. Syncromatic control clears front compartment. Transmission gears helical and fully carburized for hard use and long life.

LIGHTING—Three-beam asymmetrical system with double filament bulbs, instrument board and foot switch control. Headlamp beam indicator in speedometer face.

FRONT SUSPENSION—Independent Knee-Action front wheels, simple and sturdy with large, helical coil springs for smoother riding comfort and effortless driving control. Thoroughly proven by five years' use and millions of miles of testing.

REAR SUSPENSION—Cadillac Controlled-Action Ride gives both velvety riding qualities and excellent roadability. This system includes variable rate leaf springs lubricated by wax-impregnated liners, rubber bushings at all points. No lubrication or other service attention required.

DRIVE SHAFT—Hi-Plane Hotchkiss drive. Two universal joints of the needle roller bearing type permanently packed with lubricant requiring no service attention.

BRAKES—Bendix super-hydraulic brakes operate in composite drums with 196 square inches braking area. Mechanical hand brake operates independently.

REAR AXLE—Hypoid rear axle of Cadillac design and manufacture. Semi-floating type, insuring quiet, dependable performance. Gear ratio 3.92 to 1.

STEERING GEAR—Sturdy worm and double roller type. Parallel cross steering provides steering accuracy at all times. Can be turned or parked in much smaller space than many shorter cars.

FRAME—Tread: front 58", rear 59". Rigid frame, X-type, with very deep X-member junction and reinforced side members. Maximum depth 8 5/16", flange width 2⅜", thickness ⅛".

RIDE STABILIZER—Torsion ride stabilizer holds car to level position and promotes high speed roadability and safety.

TIRES AND WHEELS—Low pressure, 4 ply tires, 7.00 x 16. Steel disc wheels with large chrome disc hub caps.

FENDERS—Fenders and other sheet metal parts are bonderized to prevent rust.

WHEELBASE—Over-all length with bumpers 202½"

BODY TYPES—5 body types with Fisher No-Draft Ventilation and Turret-Top roof construction on closed models. Nuvo Cord or Ribbed Broadcloth upholstery and a wide selection of body colors optional at no extra charge. Roomy luggage compartments in all models.

NINETEEN FORTY
Series 50

LaSalle 50. The greatest fine car value ever offered—incorporates the major features of last year's popular LaSalle body with the new modern frontal design streamlined in every detail.

LaSalle is built by Cadillac . . . and that's the finest recommendation a motorcar could have.

Briefly speaking, built by Cadillac means so much that you could safely choose a new LaSalle without knowing one more thing about it. You could actually buy it sight unseen and still be absolutely sure that you were getting the best car in LaSalle's priced group.

The most obvious way in which LaSalle excels other cars in its field is in the distinction of its styling—for LaSalle was styled by the same designers who created the regal Cadillac-Fleetwoods. As usual, LaSalle has its characteristic narrow radiator. But the rest of the front end ensemble has been altered until it presents much the same strong, graceful appearance as the head-on view of a modern transport plane. These, with other refinements, make LaSalle's appearance not only smarter and richer, but different from that of any other car in the world.

—from the 1940 sales brochure

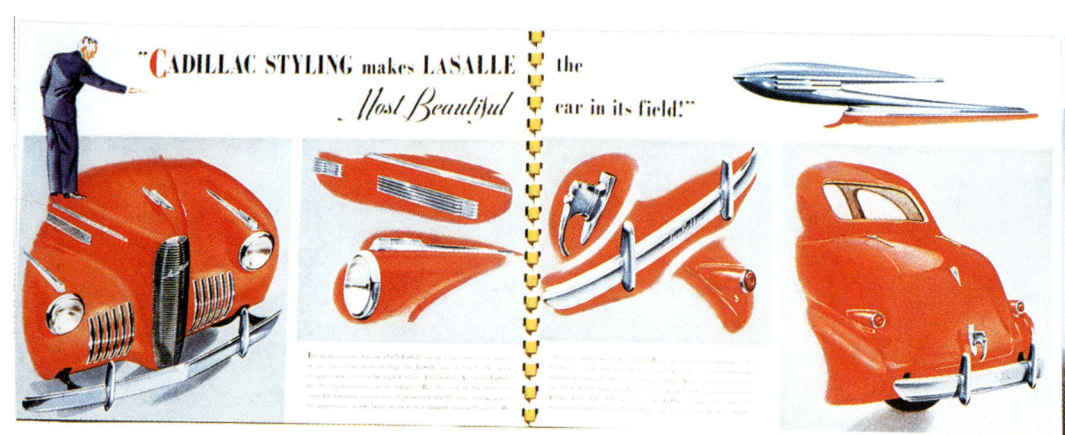
"**CADILLAC STYLING** makes LASALLE the *Most Beautiful* car in its field!"

"Here is the TWO-PASSENGER COUPE...

"Here is the LASALLE SPECIAL COUPE...

"Here is the CONVERTIBLE SEDAN... and these are a few of its *Special* points" "Here is the LASALLE SPECIAL SEDAN... an

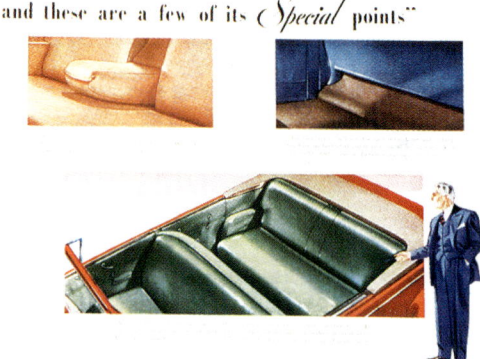

"Here is the CONVERTIBLE COUPE... and these are a few of its *Features*" "Here is the TWO-DOOR SEDAN... an

NINETEEN FORTY
Series 50

Series 52 "Special"

For 1940, LaSalle produced two series: the Series 50 and the Series 52 "Special." These were two distinctly different styles. Two totally different concepts with dazzling looks of their own.

The Series 50 was a carryover of the basic 1939 body with a 1940 hood, grille and front fenders update.

The front grille was beautifully refined with the perception that it was taller and narrower than the 1939. At the leading edge of the front fenders on each side of the grille were six narrow vertical air intakes with chrome surrounds replacing the one piece catwalk grille of the previous year.

The hood seemed extra long on the Series 50 because of a belt molding that ran from the leading edge of the hood through the door to the rear. The narrow shape of the hood was unique to the Series 50, which added to the length perception.

Running boards were not part of the original design intent, but were available on all models as a delete option. In their place on the Series 50 were three stainless steel horizontal moldings.

The basic design intended to have the spare tire stowed in the trunk and out of sight. However, fender mounted spare tires were available as an option on the Series 50 only. Very few were so fitted.

Unique to the Series 50 were the 1939 carryover round taillights mounted on the body close to each side of the trunk and a "Sunshine Roof" offered on the four-door and two-door Sedans only.

Five Series 50 body styles were available: a two-door Coupe, a two-door Sedan, a four-door Sedan, a two-door Convertible Coupe and a four-door Convertible Sedan. Production of the two Convertibles was very low, 599 for the Coupe and 125 for the Sedan. The slab-sided Series 50 was more conservative and served its purpose well. It was a beautiful carryover.

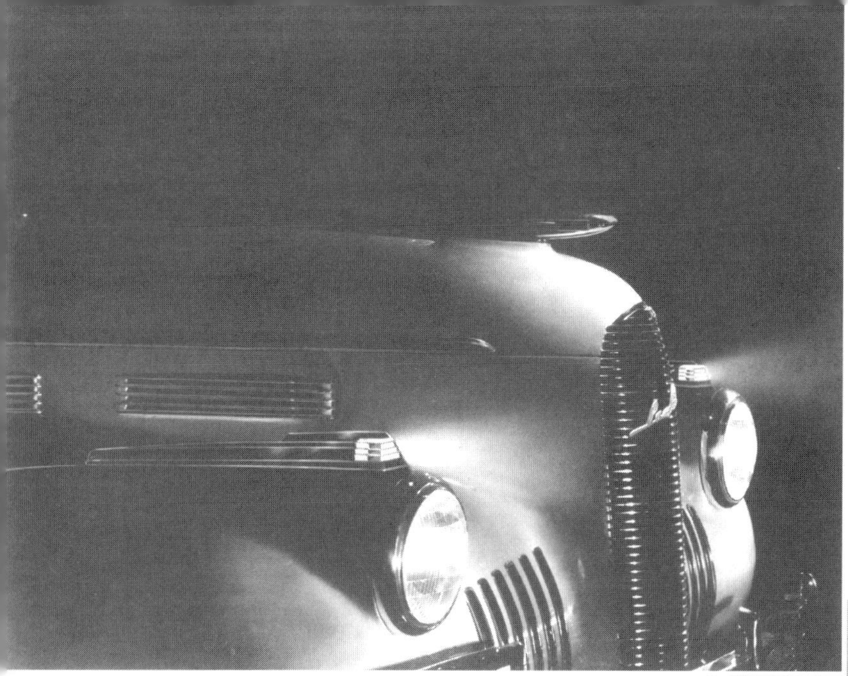

Above: A very artistically lighted picture taken for the factory of the front ensemble of the Series 50. Right: This picture of a 1940 Series 50 Convertible Coupe, taken on top of the factory roof, has an unusual combination of accessories. It has the grille guards, but no full wheel discs, no side rear view mirror and no whitewall tires. Below: The same Convertible with the top down.

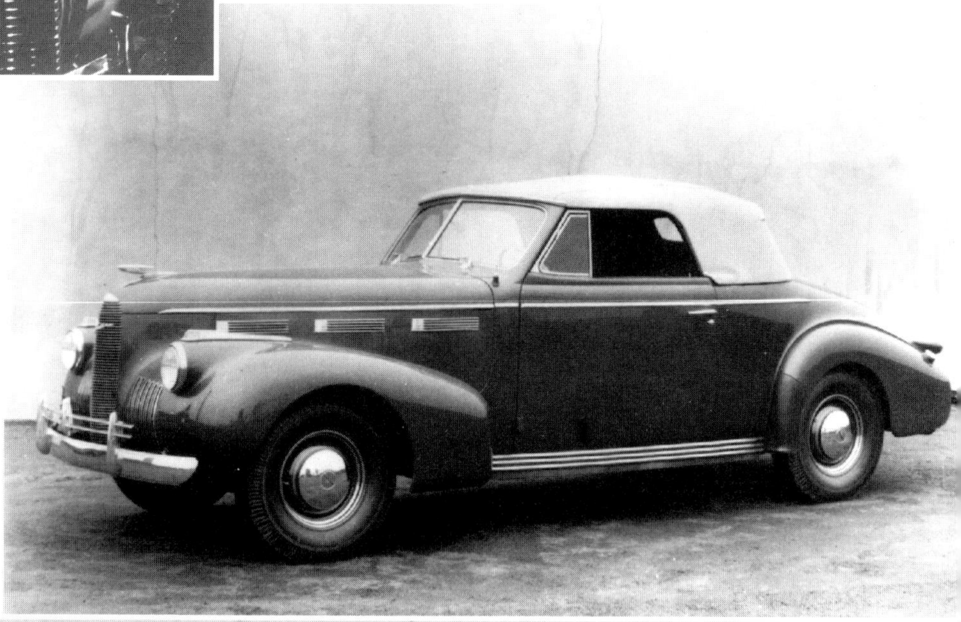

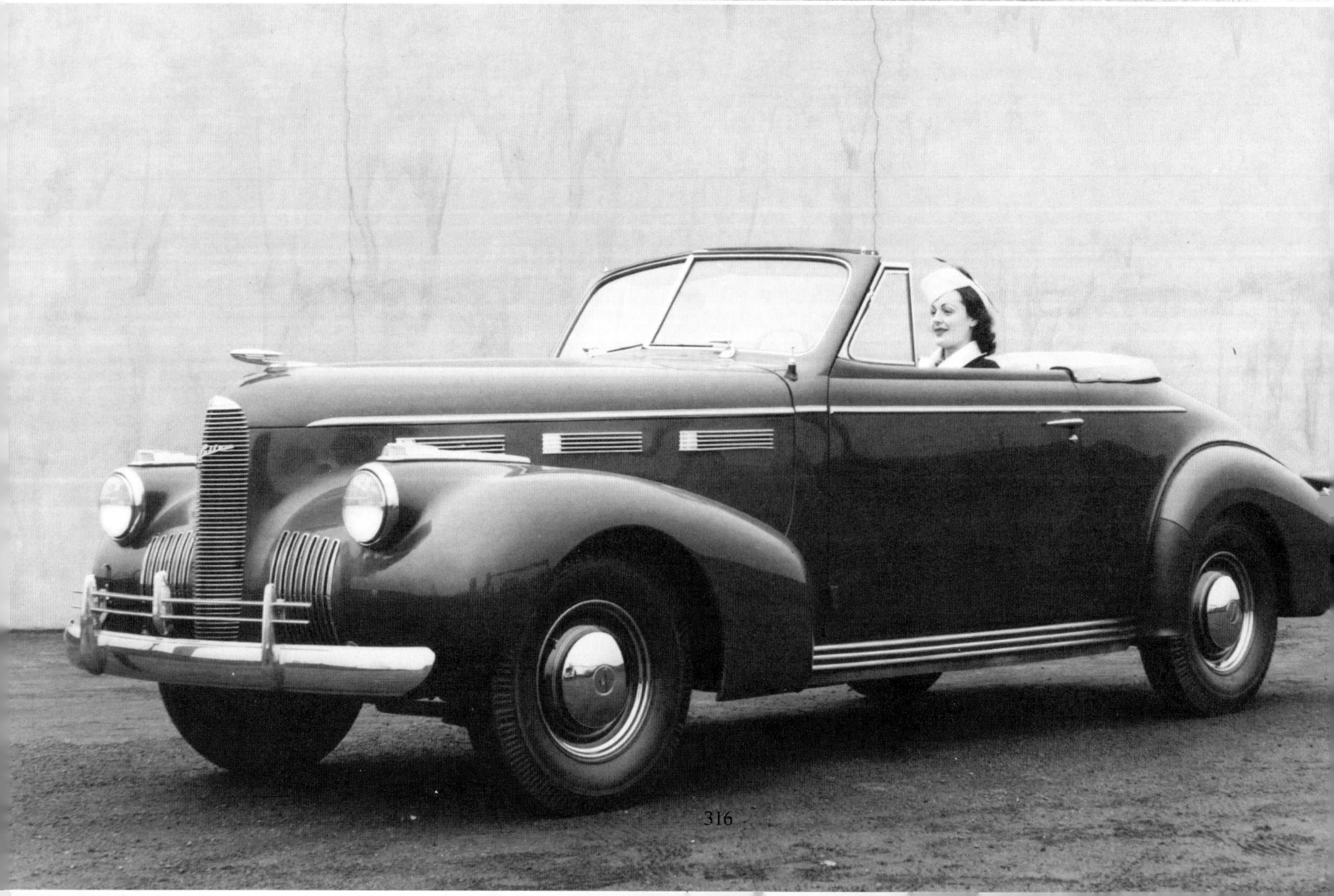

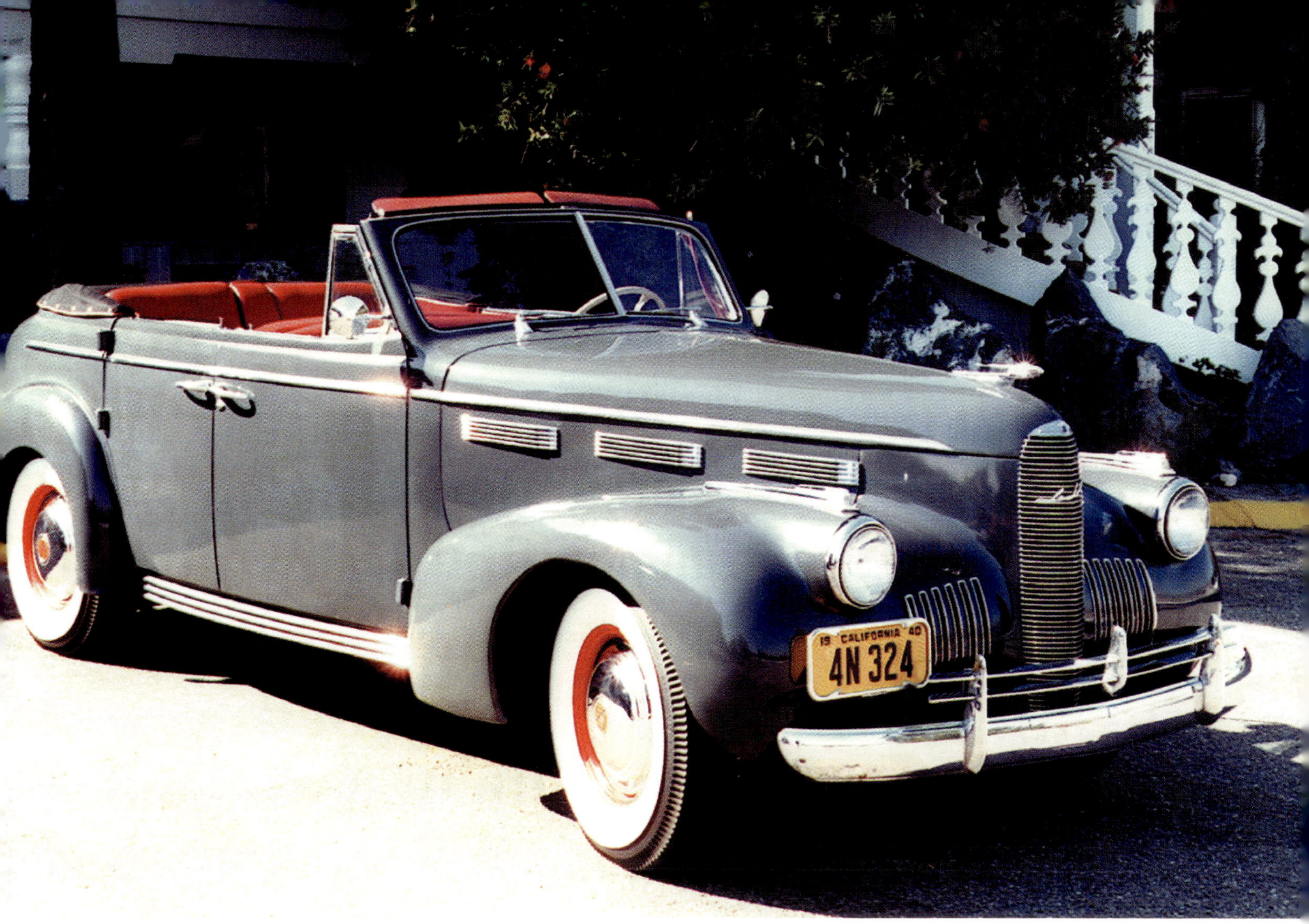
19 CALIFORNIA 40
4N 324

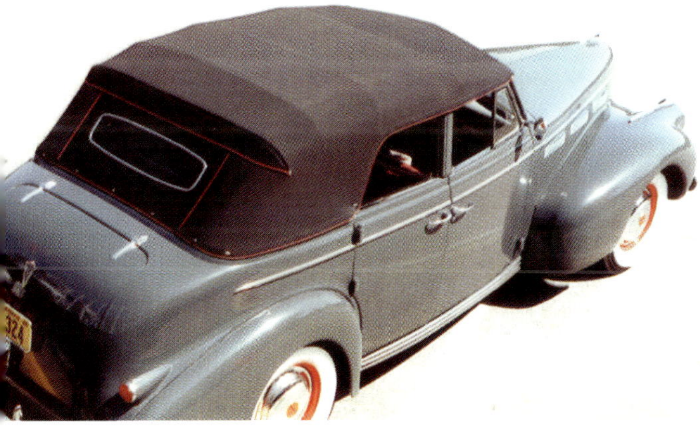

Above: A gorgeous 1940 Series 50 four-door Convertible Sedan with the top down is a stunning sight. Red interior includes sun visors located on windshield frame. Red wheels complemented the interior. Middle: From a very high angle, the top with the correct oval rear window glass can be seen. Below: A four-door Sedan has running boards, small hubcaps and beauty rings. The long belt molding from the front of the hood to the rear gives it length and continuity.

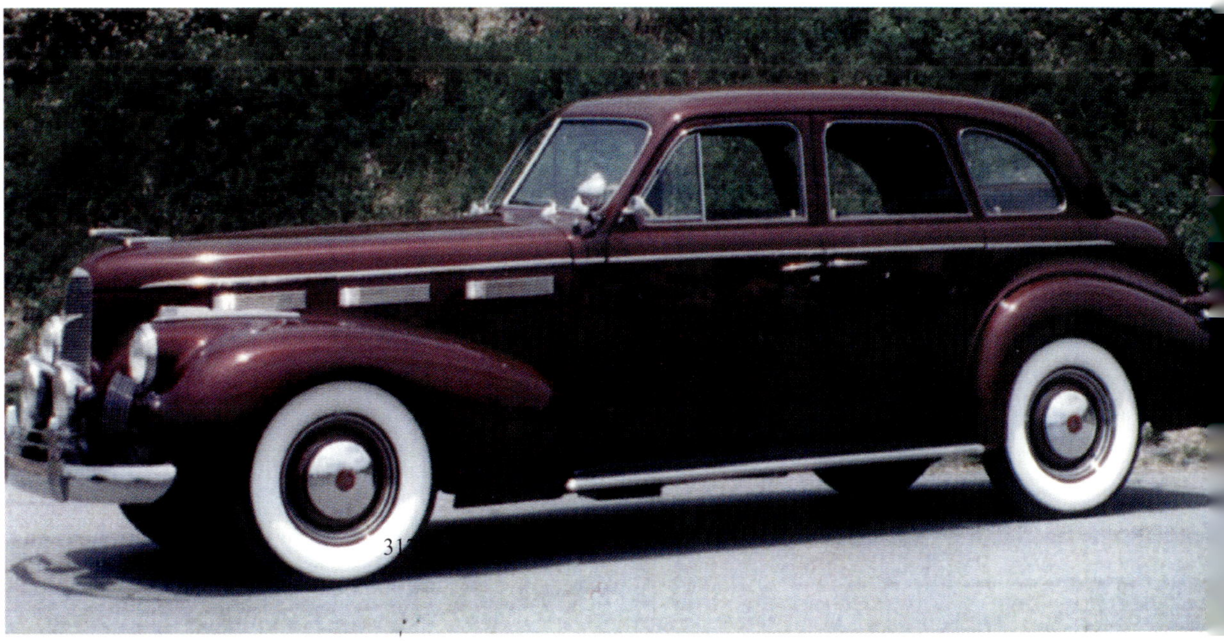

Left: A Series 50 Sedan is superimposed on a skyline. Models are leaning forward in front of the windshield to be seen smiling. Middle: This 5019 was a prototype. Note LaSalle 52 and Cadillac 62 Series taillights instead of the 1939 carryover style actually used. Bottom left: An unusual "give away" LaSalle. Bottom right: Front ensemble factory photo shows the more angular lines of the windshield, the appearance of a taller grille (not really) and the location of the headlights and parking lights on the front fenders.

DRIVE A LaSalle!

For Performance, Comfort and Economy

When it comes to motor cars—performance is the watchword! Performance makes or mars your satisfaction. And that's reason Number One why you should buy a LaSalle. It has *Cadillac* performance!

The minute you take the wheel, you'll sense what this means. There's a smooth feel to that big V-8 engine that you get nowhere else. But don't let its soft voice fool you—for it speaks with authority. You'll go farther and faster on a touch of throttle than you've ever gone before. And you'll do it so *easily!* You just make up your mind what you want to do—and your LaSalle follows suit. Never before was there such an *obedient* car.

And it's *so* restful to ride in. LaSalle provides the *Cadillac* standard of comfort. Your LaSalle ride is actually levelized. Not even on the roughest roads do you feel like holding onto yourself. You sit without effort, completely relaxed. Truly, to ride in the new LaSalle is to rest.

You'll ride more *thriftily*, too. Among the many fine advancements introduced by LaSalle for 1940 is *new economy*. LaSalle's more powerful Cadillac engine now gives as much as 10% greater gasoline economy.

But you can't *read* yourself a LaSalle ride! You'll actually have to sit at the wheel to get the whole magnificent story. Why not do it today—while you're in the mood? Your dealer will be glad to prove everything we have said with a LaSalle demonstration.

If performance comes first with you, then so will LaSalle—because, underneath its shapely hood is a Cadillac V-8 engine, more powerful than ever, and even more economical!

A GENERAL MOTORS VALUE

V-8

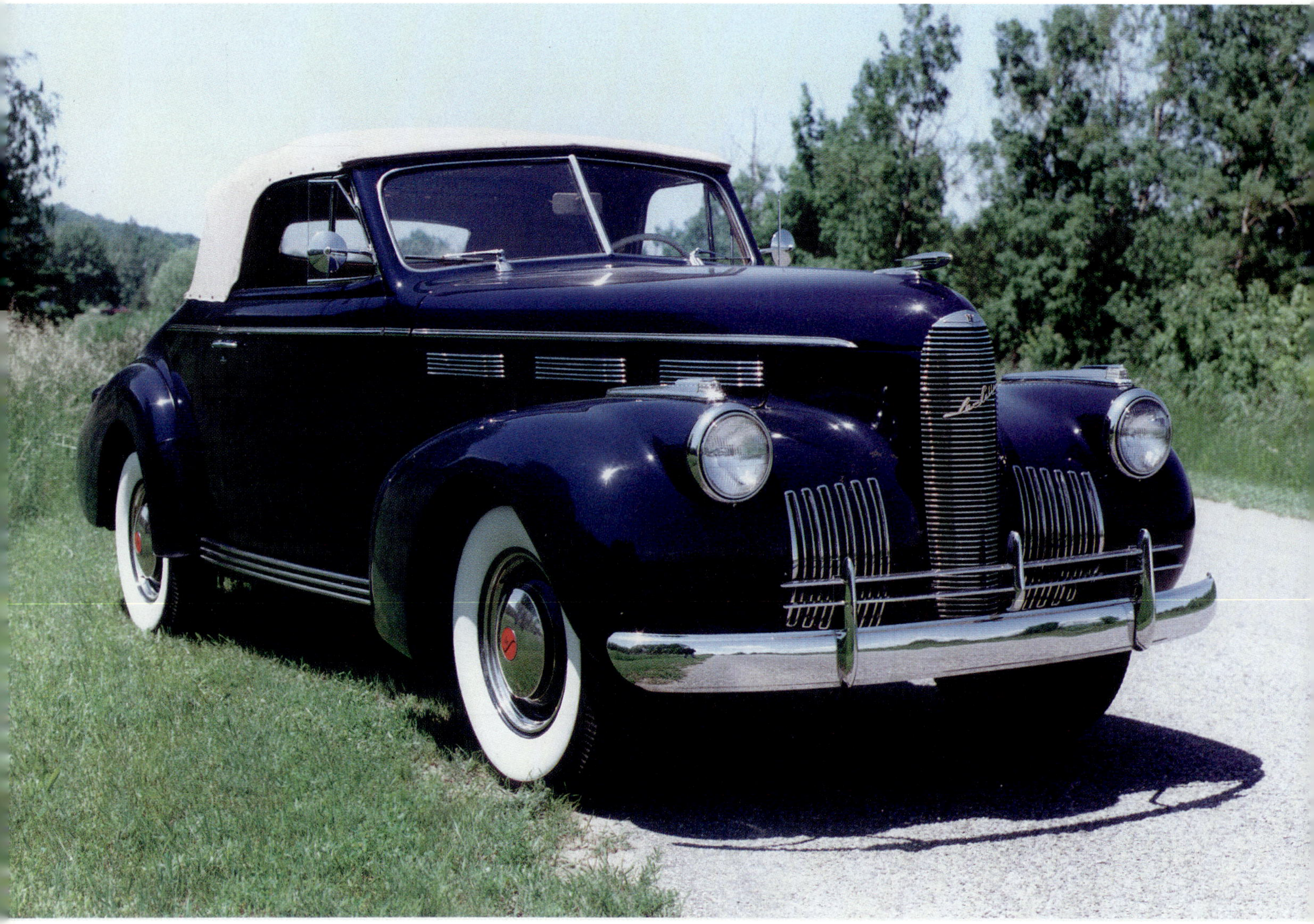

Above: A handsome example of a Series 50 two-door Convertible Coupe with grille protector and no running boards. The absence of running boards put a rubber rock shield on the leading edge of the rear fender and three decorative stainless steel trim strips under the door sill. Below: A 5029 with the exceptionally rare optional spare tire mounted into the fender with cover, small hubcaps and beauty rings.

LaSALLE'S LIFETIME WARRANTY

When Cadillac decided to discontinue using the LaSalle name at the end of the 1940 model year, there were an estimated 32,000-35,000 LaSalles still on the road. How does a car company maintain the confidence and trust of those loyal owners who would be driving an orphan automobile?

In the 1930s, when a car brand was discontinued, and there were many, the surviving examples became difficult to repair because of problems in obtaining parts. They became undesirable trade-ins and their resale value dropped dramatically because of their orphan status.

Cadillac did not want this to happen to LaSalle owners, because Cadillac was hoping to motivate

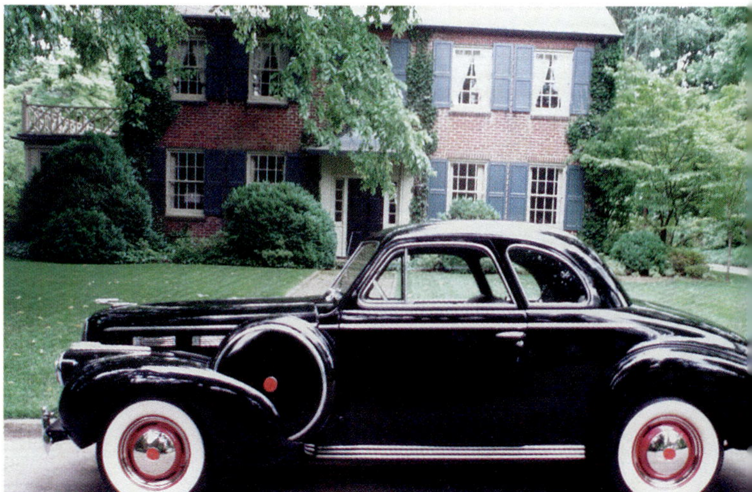

LaSalle owners to become Cadillac owners. In an effort to avoid such a stigma, Cadillac gave a certificate to owners of a LaSalle, purchased new, that they would have no problem obtaining service and parts for repair as long as they owned the car.

Recently, such a certificate was found for a 1940 LaSalle Series 50 Convertible Coupe originally owned by the daughter of Admiral Frank Berrien, USN, in May 1940. Through a series of coincidences, the certificate and the current owner of the LaSalle have been reunited. Current policy for most manufacturers requires parts to be available from seven to ten years at best. What would Cadillac have done had it still been in the hands of the original owner?

Top right: A reduced size copy of the certificate issued by Cadillac to LaSalle purchasers. Below: This 1940 Series 50 Convertible Coupe was covered by the lifetime warranty, but was restored before the certificate was found. The current owner now owns the certificate.

The Chassis Comes First!

LaSalle is invariably the choice of the man who looks under the hood when buying a car.

He buys LaSalle because LaSalle's superiority is so readily discernible in its chassis construction; because Cadillac's standards of craftsmanship and materials are so evident in every part of the LaSalle chassis.

And, as you know, on the chassis are almost entirely dependent the essential qualities of performance, of economy, and of riding comfort. In fact, the very life of the car is built in its chassis.

That is why it is *important* for you to know the LaSalle chassis is designed and built by Cadillac engineers and craftsmen—the same men who build the magnificent Cadillac-Fleetwood.

That is why you should know that LaSalle is powered with a Cadillac V-8 engine, and that the same exacting standards are applied equally to Cadillac and LaSalle chassis construction and materials.

It is no wonder that LaSalle buyers remain enthusiastic LaSalle owners through the years—for they *enjoy* the advantages of driving a medium-priced car built on a Cadillac foundation.

Your nearest Cadillac-LaSalle dealer would be pleased to have you drive this exceptional car. Then you can prove to your own satisfaction that no other car in its price class equals LaSalle.

Cadillac Motor Car Division—builder of LaSalle, Cadillac and Cadillac-Fleetwood cars.

LaSalle
A GENERAL MOTORS VALUE

CADILLAC V8 ENGINE

$1240 for the Series Fifty Coupe, delivered at Detroit, Mich. Sedan prices start at $1280. Transportation based on rail rates, state and local taxes (if any), optional equipment and accessories—extra. Prices subject to change without notice.

Top and Middle: A Series 5227-C two-door Coupe nicely restored speaks for itself in support of those who find the 1940 torpedo style one of the most beautiful LaSalles ever made. Bottom: A view from the rear shows the graceful lines of the trunk lid, rounded rear window and fender flow, but with conservative running boards and small hubcaps.

Some snapshots taken when the cars were in daily use. Top left: A beautiful 5227-C two-door Coupe. Top right: An unusual station wagon on a 7-inch stretched frame (now being restored). Middle left: 5267 with top down and original owner are basking in the 1940 sun. Middle right: 5267 with Carson top. Bottom left: 5267s were always a good photo shoot. Bottom right: LaSalles were popular subjects for customizing with 15-inch wheels, sombrero hubcaps, lowering blocks, skirts and dual exhausts—Wow!

Some LaSalle enthusiasts have generated rosters of a particular model. One such example is the 1940 Series 52 two-door Convertible Coupe. Often added to a roster is additional information pertinent to the model listed. Having contact with owners of similar cars can be rewarding as additional sources of information and parts.

ANSWERS TO OFTEN ASKED QUESTIONS
1940-5267

Original factory records: Fortunately, factory build order or shipping invoices for nearly all LaSalles are still in existence and have been recorded on microfiche. Shipping invoices contain trim, paint, accessories and other information unique to that specific car. Copies are available and worth obtaining from Cadillac Historical Services for a nominal fee. (Names of original owners were not listed.)

Production: A total of 425 "special" LaSalle two-door Convertible Coupes was built. About four or five 5267s were built per working day. Body #3 (still in existence) was shipped on March 5, 1940, and the last body, #425, was shipped June 20, 1940. That is only seventeen weeks of production. A very short run.

Promotional items: The only reference to the Series 52 Convertible was made in the third revision of the Sales Data book on March 7, 1940. Other sales literature or advertisements of these Convertibles seems to be non-existent.

Survivors: A total of twenty-three 40-5267 LaSalles has been found and documented. That is about 5%. Trivia: #212, #213 and #214 are sequentially still in existence as are #291 and #292 and #359 and #360. The lowest surviving body number is #3 and the highest is #360.

VIN numbers: All Series 52 LaSalles, regardless of body style, have VIN numbers from 4320001-4333751. Shipping dates are not necessarily in sequence with VIN numbers, nor with body numbers . . . e.g., body #226 has VIN number 4329999, while a higher body, #236, has a lower VIN number of 4329960. Body #3 (4327670) has a lower VIN number than body #2 (4327712). The last body, #425, has VIN number 4332905, while an earlier body, #420, has a higher VIN number (4333050). Generally speaking, however, most body and VIN numbers were in ascending order.

Upholstery pattern: Interior upholstery patterns are the same for both the Series 52 LaSalle and Series 62 Cadillac, single and two-tone combinations. Those newly-introduced torpedo series were the first to use two-tone leather combinations. However, the Series 52 patterns have nothing in common with the Series 50 LaSalle Convertibles.

Special Order trim: There are eight surviving cars with S.O. trim numbers and ten with the number "7" added to the trim number on the body plate. Records indicate that the interior upholstery patterns, whether S.O. or not, were all the same without deviation. The number "7" added to the trim number still remains a mystery. The "7" does not appear anywhere on the factory shipping invoices.

Top colors: Tan (GM Part No. 4103432) was standard with blue-gray (4103433) or black (4110966) available at additional charge. Tan lining (4103435) was used with all top colors. Binding around the canvas top was colored to harmonize with interior leather trim colors . . . red, blue or green (see March 7, 1940, revised Data Book pages). All tops are black on the surviving cars with listed S.O. trim numbers . . . bodies #287, #291, #331 and #359. Only body #111 does not indicate a top color.

Power top: All Series 52 LaSalle and Series 62 Cadillac Convertible Coupes (only) have the "All-Weather Power Top," which is vacuum-operated. The canvas top does not have a zipper or flap opening around the rear window. This was unique to the 40-52 series (40-62 series) only. Whether the top is in the up or the down position, the rear window stays in place at all times.

Paint colors: By 1940, Cadillac Motor Car Company had a long history of painting a new automobile virtually any durable color upon request and usually at a small additional charge. Ten surviving 40-5267 Convertible Coupes have the paint number blank on the body plate. One has a completely custom color and three have LaSalle colors listed from one of the two-tone combinations available for closed cars. The most frequently listed color of the survivor cars is oxblood (#11).

Instrument panel color: The dash and the floor carpet are a blending shade of the upholstery colors . . . maroon with red leather, blue with blue leather, green with green leather combinations, etc. In the case of S.O. non-LaSalle exterior paint, the dash and steering column could be painted the same color upon request.

Rear bumper LaSalle script color: It is a very light beige, the same as the grille name badge. However, it has legitimately been argued that the rear bumper color could also be black because the factory sales literature shows both. Factory photographs indicate the white beige for LaSalle and black for Cadillac.

LaSalle grille bar badge location: The top of the last "e" should be nine spaces from the top, even though some promotional literature shows eight spaces.

Left exterior rear view mirror location: This was standard equipment. On the early models, it was mounted at the top of the vent pane frame (I.C.V. frame) on the driver's side. Soon it was moved to the mid-position, and finally it was mounted at the bottom of the vent pane bar. Only at the latter position was it possible for the driver to have a decent view toward the rear. The factory did not offer a right side rear view mirror.

Windshield washer: It is located on the passenger side firewall under the hood and the two spray nozzles are located individually on top of the cowl (not as part of the windshield wiper tower as in earlier model years).

Interchangeability of the body parts: From the cowl rearward, the basic body shell, trunk lid, doors, windows, top mechanism and top configuration are identical to the 1940 Cadillac Series 62 Convertible Coupe. Bumpers, fenders, hood, grille and other trim features are unique to LaSalle. Interior upholstery, instrument panel, floor mats, steering wheel, heaters, radios and steering column are also identical to the Series 62 Cadillac of that year. No sheet metal parts are interchangeable with the Series 50 LaSalle.

Running boards: All Series 52 LaSalles and Series 62 Cadillacs were available with running boards. If they were not desired, it was so noted as a no-charge option on the shipping invoice "less running boards . . . NC."

Engine: The LaSalle engine is identical to the V-8 Cadillac engine, except for a 1/8-inch smaller cylinder bore, reducing the bhp by just 5 and the use of a Carter carburetor.

Prices: Shipping invoices indicate wholesale prices to the distributor or dealer. Dealers, in turn, published their own "delivered prices," including accessory and service package options.

NOTE: Rosters of this kind will also list names of current owners and the specifics of the cars they own. Some rosters will even collect pictures and other interesting statistics. The statistics on these pages are dated and not necessarily current.

EXPLANATION OF THE CODES

What do the numbers mean? Most of the numbers are well defined, but some still elude an explanation. What we know is based upon 1940 Data Book information, shipping invoices, original factory literature and parts books. Located on the firewall under the hood is an identification plate with code numbers unique to each car:

<u>STYLE NO.</u>: All 1940 Series 52 two-door "special" Convertibles are designated as 40-5267.

<u>BODY NO.</u>: These numbers apply to the "special" Convertible Coupe and are sequenced 1 through 425. Other LaSalle models and body styles had their own body number sequence beginning with 1.

<u>TRIM NO.</u>: **These numbers specifically relate to interior colors, combinations and materials used. Two-tone leather combinations are designated with an "A" such as 28A, which stands for red and buff leather. Single tones are two digit numbers only, such as 23 for blue and 28 for red leather. Special order ("S.O.") numbers reference customer requests or deviations from factory announced specifications. These same S.O. numbers appear in the S.B.O. block on the factory shipping invoice. The meaning of trim numbers with a suffix of "7" is still a mystery, because there is no reference to a "7" on any of the shipping invoices.

<u>PAINT NO.</u>: **Paint color numbers listed on the firewall identification plate refer to standard available colors. Whenever the paint number appears blank on the plate, the applied color could be totally custom or a standard color not necessarily recommended by the factory for a Convertible. If blank, the factory shipping invoice will list the exterior color.

<u>VIN NO.</u>: At the factory, the vehicle identification number stamped on the frame and the number stamped on the engine were the same. The engine sequence was shared with all Series 52 LaSalle body styles and is not unique to the 5267. Engines arrived at the assembly line one after another, were installed in whatever body style was next, and were not necessarily in body number sequence due to other production line factors and/or irregularities.

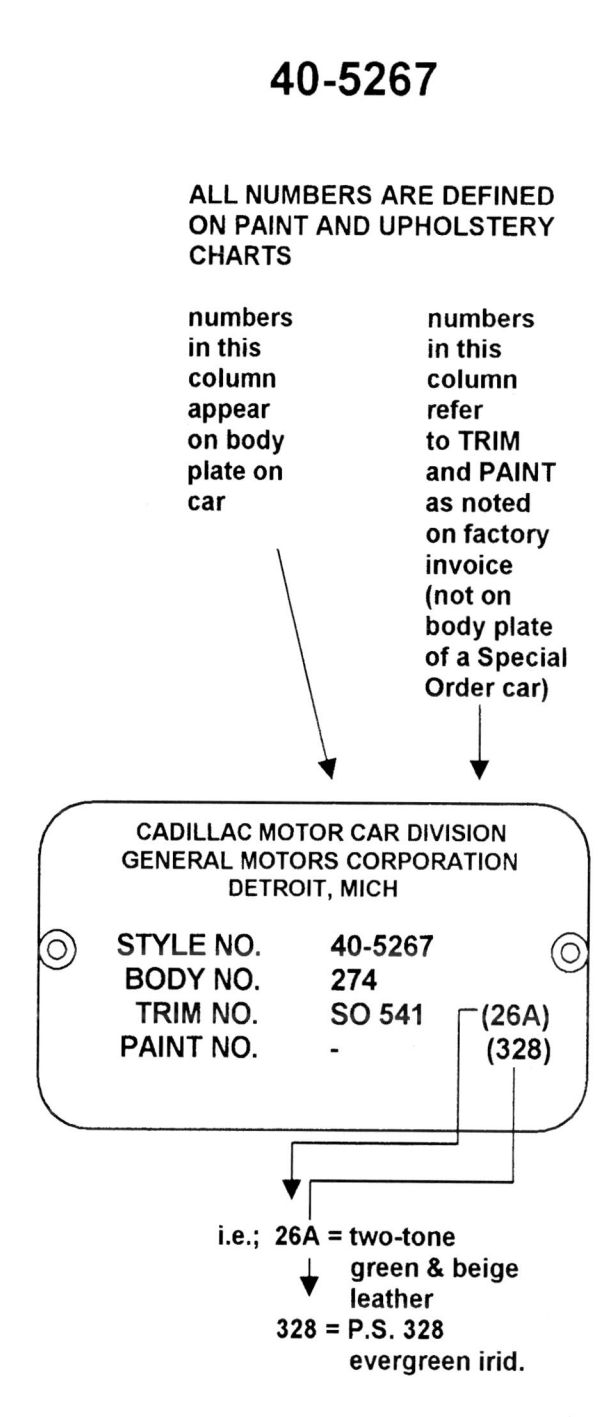

**Note: Standard trim and paint numbers are defined on upholstery and paint charts.

1940 LaSalle Production

Total Production: 24,130 automobiles and chassis.

Serial Numbers: Series 50 are 2320001-2330382 (two numbers not assigned).
Series 52 are 4320001-4333751 (one number not assigned).
The Vehicle (engine) serial number is "On rough flat surface on rear portion of crankcase back of L.H. block, numbered at right angle with the crankshaft. Numbering to start from the top."

Chassis Numbers: Same as engine serial numbers. Location of chassis number is "On top surface of frame side bar, just ahead of dash, opposite steering gear."

Body Plates: "Body and style number on plate on left side of dash." (under the hood)

Body Type and Style Numbers:		Production	List Price
Series 40-50 (123" Wheelbase) -	Fisher Bodies		(Feb 15, 1940)
5-Pass. 2-Door Touring Sedan	40-5011	366	$1220.00
5-Pass. 2-Door Touring Sedan (Sunshine Turret-Top Roof)	40-5011A	9	$1305.00
5-Pass. 4-Door Touring Sedan	40-5019	6558	$1260.00
5-Pass. 4-Door Touring Sedan (Sunshine Turret-Top Roof)	40-5019A	140	$1345.00
2-Pass. Coupe	40-5027	1525	$1180.00
5-Pass. Convertible Sedan	40-5029	125	$1730.00
2-Pass. Convertible Coupe	40-5067	598	$1335.00
Chassis (123" Wheelbase)		2	$ 935.00
Commercial Chassis (159" Wheelbase)	39-50	1030	$ 980.00
Chassis CKD (Export)		24	
	Total	10377 (Difference of 3 units)	
Series 40-52 (123" Wheelbase) -	Fisher Bodies		
5-Pass. 4-Door Touring Sedan	40-5219	10181	$1380.00
5-Pass. 4-Door Touring Sedan - CKD (Export)	40-2519	132	Not listed
2-Pass. Coupe	40-5227C	3000	$1320.00
5-Pass. Convertible Sedan	40-5229	75	$1825.00
2-Pass. Convertible Coupe	40-5267	425	$1475.00
	Total	13750	

Standard Color Options

Body, fenders, tire cover	R&M#	Wheels	
1 Black	2532122 (Duco)	Black (standard)	94-005
		Triton Green (optional)	94-20957
		Vincennes Red (optional)	94-3618
2 Antoinette Blue	22290	Antoinette Blue	94-20871
3 Cavern Green	023355	Triton Green	94-20957
4 Knickerbocker Gray	020185	Vincennes Red	94-3618
5 Marquette Gray	020182	Vincennes Red	94-3618
6 Long Key Green Iridescent	P.S. 389	Long Key Green	182-21341
7 Beaver Brown Iridescent	P.S. 860	Beaver Brown	182-21340
9 Corlear Blue Iridescent	P.S. 297	Corlear Blue	182-21339
10 Homer Gray Iridescent	P.S. 170	Vincennes Red	94-3618
11 Oxblood Maroon Iridescent	P.S. 608	Oxblood Maroon	182-20955
13 Chicory Green Iridescent	P.S. 367	Chicory Green	182-21336
Evergreen Iridescent	P.S. 328		
14 Harbormist Gray Iridescent	P.S. 1123	Submarine Gray	182-21338
Submarine Gray Iridescent	P.S. 1124		
15 Beaumont Blue Iridescent	P.S. 262	Beaumont Blue	182-21342
Pilot Blue Iridescent	P.S. 233		
16 Silver French Gray Iridescent	P.S. 195	Luzon Green	182-21337
Luzon Green Iridescent	P.S. 391		

Note: Two-tone color splits are Belt Moulding and above/below Belt Moulding. Paint code number is on the body cowl tag.

Standardized Colors: The interior fittings and controls on Series 40-50 and 40-52 cars are toned to match the upholstery in the body. Parts made of plastic and certain painted parts are identified in the listing as gray and tan. Below is a chart indicating the color of parts used with the various trim combinations. Two shades of Gray and Tan are used on Instrument Panel and Belt Panel portion of the Garnish Mouldings.

Series 40-50 and 40-52 **except** Styles 40-5229 and 40-5267:
To match trim combination 21, 24, 26, 26A, 28, 28A, 29, 31, 41, 46, 51, 51-4, 51-8, 52, 55, 56, 56A-Tan
To match trim combination 22, 23, 25, 27, 27A, 30, 44, 53, 53-7, 54 - Gray

First Type	Dexter Gray	242-9989	Canterbury Beige	202-53095
Second Type	Hermes Gray	202-32563	Seaforth Beige	202-53098

Series 40-52, Styles 40-5229 and 40-5267:

	To match trim combination	Instrument Panel Color
23	Hermes Gray	R&M P.S. 1129
26, 26A	Evergreen	R&M P.S. 328
27, 27A, 53-7	Corlear Blue	R&M P.S. 297
28, 28A, 51-8	Oxblood Maroon	R&M P.S. 608
24, 51-4	Seaforth Beige	R&M P.S. 8829

Garnish Mouldings without belt panels and portions excluding belt panel section are painted the following colors:

To match color tone Tan	Brompton Beige	202-53071
To match color tone Gray	Nassack Diamond Gray	242-6518

Standard Trim Options

Code No.		Trim No.	Convertible Tops	Trim No.
21	Tan Ribbed Broadcloth - Series 50	31T140	Tan (standard)	
22	Gray Ribbed Broadcloth - Series 50	34T140	Blue Grey (Special)	9T1540
23	Black Leather - Series 50, 52	1T1340	Black (Special)	15T1540
24	Tan Leather - Series 50, 52	2T1340		
25	Gray Leather - Series 50, 52	3T1340	Convertible Top Lining	
26	Green Leather - Series 50, 52	4T1340	Tan used with all colors	
26A	Two-tone Beige and Green Leather - Series 52	40T1340 (Light Beige), 4T1340 (Green)		
27	Blue Leather - Series 50, 52	5T1340		
27A	Two-tone Beige and Blue Leather - Series 52	40T1340 (Light Beige), 5T1340 (Blue)		
28	Red Leather - Series 50, 52	6T1340		
28A	Two-tone Beige and Red Leather - Series 52	40T1340 (Light Beige), 6T1340 (Red)		
29	Tan Bedford - Series 50	16T140		
30	Gray Bedford - Series 50	81T140		
51	Tan Bedford Cord - Two-tone - Series 50, 52	40T140		
51-4	Tan Bedford Cord with Tan Leather - Series 52	40T140, 2T1340 (Tan)		
51-8	Tan Bedford Cord with Red Leather - Series 52	40T140, 6T1340 (Red)		
52	Tan Herringbone - Series 52	51T140		
53	Gray-Green Bedford Cord - Two-tone - Series 50, 52	37T140		
53-7	Gray Bedford Cord with Blue Leather - Series 52	37T140, 5T1340 (Blue)		
54	Gray Herringbone - Series 52	53T140		
55	Tan Bedford Cord - Series 52	22T140		
56	Tan Plain Cloth - Series 52	46T140		

Accessory Groups
(February 15, 1940)
Prices include cost of installation. State and local taxes extra.

B (5 wheel) $27.75
Flexible (Steering) Wheel
Automatic Lighter
License Frames
Trim Rings (5)

B6 (6 wheel) $29.25
Flexible Wheel
Automatic Lighter
License Frames
Trim Rings (6)

C (5 wheel) $37.75
Flexible Wheel
Automatic Lighter
License Frames
Trim Rings (5)
Grille Guard

C6 (6 wheel) $39.25
Flexible Wheel
Automatic Lighter
License Frames
Trim Rings (6)
Grille Guard

D (5 or 6 wheel) $36.25
Flexible Wheel
Automatic Lighter
License Frames
Wheel Discs (4)

E (5 or 6 wheel) $46.25
Flexible Wheel
Automatic Lighter
License Frames
Wheel Discs (4)
Grille Guard

Running Boards are optional.

Additional Charges (February 15, 1940)

6 Wheels, fenderwells, tire covers	$100.00
Right hand fenderwell	$ 42.00
Sunshine Turret-Top Roof	$ 85.00
White sidewall tires,	$ 6.55 per tire

(7.00 x 16" Royal or Firestone 4-ply black sidewall tires are standard equipment)

Accessories

Prices include installation. State and local taxes are extra.

Name	Price	Part No.
Automatic Battery Filler	$ 7.50	1438450
Automatic Cigarette Lighter	$ 2.25	1437246
Automatic Radio	$69.50	7238650
Cool Cushion	$ 2.95	
Defrosting Heater	$26.50	1437350
Defrosting Heater (Ventilating)	$31.50	1437701/1097190
Dual Ventilating Defrosting Heater	$48.50	
Fire Extinguisher - Pint	$10.00	
Fire Extinguisher - Quart	$12.50	
Flexible Steering Wheel	$15.00	1437260/1437992
Fog and Adverse Weather Lights (pair)	$14.50	14336322/1436323
Glare Shield	$ 1.50	1427683
Grille Guard	$10.00	1438171
Grease Gun	$ 0.50	
Hinge Mirror	$ 4.50	1425809
Illuminated Vanity Mirror	Not listed	1434615
Lamp Kit	$ 1.00	
License Frames (pair)	$ 3.00	14337063
Luggage - Sport Bag	$15.00	
Luggage - Aerolite Case	$18.50	
Locking Gas Cap	$ 1.50	985076
Moto-Pack	$ 6.85	1437257
NO-ROL (hill holder)	$11.00	14338271
Radiator Insect Screen	$ 2.25	
Robes - Fleetwood	$50.00	
Robe monograms	$ 5.50	
Double alpaca	$30.00	
Alpaca and plush	$30.00	
Scuff Pads (door)	$ 4.50	1438356/1438357
Seat Covers (per seat)	$ 8.25	
Sheepskin Rug	$45.00	
Spotlight (Right hand)	$18.50	1437356
Spotlight (Left hand)	$18.50	1437357
Underseat Heater	$48.50	3113807
Wheel Discs (Chrome, each)	$ 4.00	
Wheel Trim Rings (each)	$ 1.50	
Windshield Washer	$ 6.50	1434464

1940 Series 50

Research Methodology: Microfiche copies of the individual Shipping Department records of the as-built configuration of each serial number were individually viewed. Commercial chassis, CKD units, Coupes, Convertibles, two-door Sedans and all Sunshine Turret-Top car serial numbers were individually recorded to verify actual Series 50 production and to resolve body serial number discrepancies with factory summary production data.

Notes on research findings:
1. Each LaSalle Series 50 body style has a distinct body number series, starting with number one, through the highest number of bodies built. In the case of the 1940 Sunshine Turret-Top cars (5011A and 5019A), the style is not shown as a distinct series on the build sheet - the "A" suffix does not appear. On those two body styles, the build sheets are annotated "SUNSHINE ROOF" in the area where factory installed accessories are listed.

A diminishing number of Special Body Order (S.B.O.) cars continued to be built. Nearly all of the orders were in the nature of special trim or paint. Multiple closed cars were done with full or partial leather interiors. The build sheets for 1940 do not have a block for the name of the purchaser. Only a very few S.B.O. sheets list the purchaser in the shipping instructions block.

All models of the Series 50 standard production cars, except the 5011A two-door Touring Sedan with Sunshine Turret-Top Roof, were exported outside of the U.S. Export cars were equipped with combinations of right hand drive, low compression cylinder heads, kilo speedometers, export clocks and electric fuel pumps. Numerous cars were sent to the GM Car Div., GM Sales Corp., Oshawa, Ontario, for distribution throughout Canada.

2. Imperial Sedans: The *1940 Cadillac - LaSalle series Chassis Parts List* includes a "Style No.40-5019F 5-Pass. Imperial Sedan." That designation does not appear in the sales literature or data book, nor in the salesman's or factory price lists. Four such units were built (serial #2333794, 2326989, 2328870, 2329126). The individual record sheets do not show 5019F, only the notation "Imperial Division" in the area where factory installed accessories are listed.

3. Chassis (123" W.B.): Two chassis not classified by Cadillac as Completely-Knocked-Down (CKD) units were shipped to GM Holden,

Ltd., in Australia. Both were very low serial number right hand drive sedan chassis, (serial #232014 shipped to Fisherman's Bend and #2320349 to Adelaide), with dummy cowls and sheet metal in primer. There is no indication of the bodies to be built on the chassis. An additional chassis, serial 2326066, was sent to General Motors Institute in Flint, Michigan, for the engineering students to study. Subsequently, it was returned to the factory, a 5019 body mounted and the car sold to a dealership.

4. Chassis, CKD Export: GM Holden, Ltd., in Australia received 24 right hand drive CKD chassis, with credits for unspecified deletions. Holden built distinctly different bodies on their LaSalles and the credits would be for body components not used in their production. Twelve units were shipped to the Holden plant in Sydney and twelve to Fisherman's Bend, Australia.

5. Commercial Chassis: The commercial chassis and engines are numbered the same as the automobiles, in the sequence in which they came down the assembly line. Some commercial chassis sheets indicate "closed cowl"; others state "cowl, instruments and wiring shipped separate." No chassis indicated open cowl. Commercial chassis were shipped to:

A. J. Miller Co., Bellefontaine, Ohio	235	Jones Motor Car Co., Richmond, Virginia	1
Flxible Co., Loudonville, Ohio	80	Knightstown Body Co., Knightstown, Indiana	45
GM Car Div., GM Sales Corp, Oshawa, Ontario	2	Meteor Motor Car Company, Piqua, Ohio	234
(for the Canadian National Railroad)		Sayers & Scovill, Cincinnati, Ohio	160
GM Sales Corp., Detroit Branch	1	Superior Body Co., Lima, Ohio	210
GM Suisse, Bienne, Switzerland	1	The Eureka Company, Rock Falls, Illinois	60
Ingersoll Mitchell Hearse Co., Ltd.. (Canada)	1	Total	1030

7. Flower Cars: Two 159" wheelbase commercial chassis were identified in the record sheets as being purchased with "coupe body shipped separate," to be built into flower cars. Meteor Motor Car Company received chassis #2320366. The Eureka Body Company received chassis #2325807. In general, the records of Cadillac Motor Car Company do not identify the bodies built on their commercial chassis.

8. Tires: Cadillac Motor Car Company enjoyed a reputation for anticipating demand for cars that were factory equipped to the customer's specification. A November 1, 1939, listing that informed dealers of the 1940 LaSalle tire and tube options, with additional charges per tire, is illustrative:

Tires	7.00 X 16" 4-ply B.S.W.	4-ply W.S.W.	6-ply B.S.W.	6-ply W.S.W.
U.S. Royal Deluxe	standard	$ 4.00	$ 4.00	$ 8.00
Firestone Champion	standard	$ 4.00	$ 4.00	$ 8.00
Goodyear G100	$ 2.00	$ 6.00	$ 6.00	$10.00
Goodyear Silvertown Non-Skid	$ 2.00	$ 6.00	$ 6.00	$10.00
U.S. Royal Master	$13.15	$20.20	$19.50	$27.99
Firestone Imperial RAYODIPT	$14.95	$22.35		
Goodyear Double Eagle	$13.45	$20.30		

7.00 X 16" Premium Inner Tubes	
U.S. Master	$ 1.00
Firestone Life Protector	$10.20
Goodyear Life Guard	$10.10

9. Sidemount Fenders: It was the last year of sidemount fenders as an option on Cadillac motorcars. Of the 9321 Series 50 LaSalle passenger cars built, only 161 were ordered with sidemounts - their time had passed. There were none on the series 5011/5011A; 147 on the 5019; one 5019A; three 5027; four 5029 and six 5067 cars shipped with sidemounts.

10. Show Cars: At least 66 Series 50 cars and one commercial chassis received special factory attention and were designated on the build sheets as "Show Cars." A Long Key Green Iridescent Convertible Coupe and a Marquette Gray Convertible Sedan were very early cars labeled for the World's Fair. The Waldorf Astoria Hotel foyer show cars for 1940 were a Barranca Yellow Convertible Coupe and a Garland Green 5019 Sedan. Specially prepared cars were done for the Branch Offices in Chicago, Detroit, New York, and Oshawa, plus the GM Building lobby in Detroit. The Toronto Auto Show visitors got an eyeful with an Oyster White Pale Convertible Coupe (Pimpernell Scarlet underside of fenders and rocker sills), an Oxblood Maroon Iridescent 5019 Sedan and a Luzon Green 5019 Sedan. Dealerships in Washington, DC; Syracuse; Los Angeles; Baltimore; Milwaukee; Boston; Philadelphia; Brooklyn; Hartford; Philadelphia; Pittsburgh; Portland, Maine; Rochester, New York; Newark; Worcester, Massachusetts; St. Louis; San Francisco; Indianapolis and Erie, Pennsylvania, all received at least one "Show Car." Commercial chassis sales had become a significant market for the LaSalle. For the National Funeral Directors Conference in Oklahoma City, a commercial chassis was done with hood, radiator casing, front fenders and cowl painted in Oyster White Pale and the entire chassis metal finished prior to painting. A "Special Yellow" 5019 Sedan was done to grace the stage of the Masonic Temple Theater in Detroit for the Cadillac Distributors Convention. A car of each body style (no sunroofs) plus a 5019 "Accessory Display Car" were done for the factory "Engineering Building Display."

11. As with other years, the 1940 Series 50 body styles were not generally built in a straight body order sequence. Only the nine Style 5011A two-door Sunshine Turret-Top Roof Sedans were numbered in body sequence, with a spread of 8065 cars from the first to the last.

First unit built in each body series:	Last unit built in each body series:
5011 body #3, serial 2320179	body #360, serial 2330092
5011A body #1, serial 2321625	body #9, serial 2329690
5019 body #9, serial 2320001	body #6530, serial 2330145
5019A body #1, serial 2320391	body #132, serial 2330142
5027 body #5, serial 2320004	body #1551, serial 2330056
5029 body #4, serial 2320149	body #119, serial 2330147
5067 body #1, serial 2320027	body #599, serial 2329851
commercial chassis, serial 2320007	serial 2330382

1940 LaSalle
Series 52 "Special"

<u>Research Methodology</u>: Microfiche copies of the individual Shipping Department records of the as-built configuration of each Series 52 serial number were individually viewed. CKD units and convertible car serial numbers were individually recorded to verify actual production. No attempt was made to record and verify Coupe and Sedan serial numbers. Two serial number record sheets are missing.

<u>Notes on research findings:</u>

1. Each LaSalle Series 52 body style has a distinct body number series, starting with number one, through the highest number of bodies built. In the case of the 1940 Series 5227C 2-Passenger Coupe, the "C" suffix does not appear on the build sheets. Factory summary production data indicate 10,181 Sedans were built. The highest recorded Sedan body number is 10,115, which indicates that duplicate body numbers were used.

All body styles of the Series 52 were shipped to Canada and all except the Convertible Sedan were exported outside of North America. Export cars were built in left or right hand drive and equipped variously with low compression cylinder heads and electric fuel pumps.

The Convertible cars, style 5229 and 5267, were introduced quite late in the model year and had a short production run. The first Convertible Sedan was shipped on February 15, 1940; the first Convertible Coupe was shipped on March 5, 1940. Convertible production had ceased and all were shipped to dealers by June 28, 1940.

2. <u>Special Body Orders</u>: A significant number of Series 52 S.B.O. cars were built. All of the orders were in the nature of special trim or paint. There were no factory custom bodies. Multiple closed cars were done with full or partial leather interiors. The build sheets for 1940 do not have a block for the name of the purchaser. Only a few S.B.O. sheets, primarily sales to factory personnel, list the purchaser in the shipping instructions block.

The styling of the Series 52 cars was very conducive to two-tone paint treatment. Sixteen standard color options, including only four two-tone options, had been selected by the company. The buying public was in a different mood and created their own two-tone combinations; reversing the color sequences, adding colors from years gone by and the unusual step of painting the fenders in other than the lower body panel color. Convertible Coupes and Convertible Sedans were also treated to many non-standard color selections, including selecting a single color from the standard two-tone offerings. In total, 361 cars were done in non-standard paint schemes. All cars that were ordered in a non-standard color are shown on the build sheet with an S.B.O. number and on the body cowl tag as an S.O. All Convertibles that were ordered with the optional Black or Blue Gray top are also shown with an S.O. number on the build sheet.

Closed Car Special Order Colors

<u>Upper Panels</u>		<u>Lower Panels</u>		<u>Fenders</u>		# Built
Adobe Red	241-53291	Marquette Gray	020182	Adobe Red		1
Afghan Green	20330	Ganges Green	20331			1
Antoinette Blue	22290	Corlear Blue Iridescent	PS 297			2
Aurora Blue	202-36593	Fellmore Blue	202-36607			2
Bandera Blue	202-36312					1
Beaumont Blue Iridescent	PS 262					7
Beaumont Blue Iridescent	PS 262			Corlear Blue Iridescent		1
Beaumont Blue Iridescent	PS 262	Corlear Blue Iridescent	PS 297			5
Beauregard Beige	020830					1
Beaver Brown Iridescent	PS 860	Oxblood Maroon Iridescent	PS 608			8
Beaver Brown Iridescent	PS 860	Long Key Green Iridescent	PS 389			1
Belden Blue	PS 219					3
Black	253-2122	Brewster Green	23482			1
Black	20498	Italian Cream	20734			3
Black	20498	Italian Cream	20734	Black		1
Black	253-2122	Marquette Gray	020182			3
Black	253-2122	Oxblood Maroon Iridescent	PS 608			10
Black	253-2122	Oyster White Pale	21235			1
Black	253-2122	Special Yellow	27751			1
Black	20498	Submarine Gray Iridescent	PS 1124			1
Black Iridescent	202-52473	Oxblood Maroon Iridescent	PS 608			2
Black Iridescent	202-52473	Silver French Gray Iridescent	PS 195	Black Iridescent		2
Brompton Beige	202-53071	Adobe Red	242-53291			13
Brompton Beige	202-53071	Black	253-2122			2
Brompton Beige	202-53071	Carolina Green	20361			1
Brompton Beige	202-53071	Kashan Blue	023347			1
Brompton Beige	202-53071	Transport Red	246-6469			4
Carolina Green	20361					4
Casino Beige	242-51737					1
Cavern Green	023355	Luzon Green Iridescent	PS 391			2
Cellini Green	244-3253					1
Cezanne Beige	210-53007	Maple Brown	202-53255			3
Chessylite Blue	246-50666	Trianon Blue	242-3167			1
Chicory Green Iridescent	PS 367					1
Corlear Blue Iridescent	PS 297	Antoinette Blue	22290			1
Corlear Blue Iridescent	PS 297	Beaumont Blue Iridescent	PS 262	Corlear Blue Iridescent		1
Corsican Red	20526					1
Diana Cream	20768					2
Evergreen Iridescent	PS 328					12

Upper Panels		Lower Panels		Fenders	# Built
Evergreen Iridescent	PS 328	Cavern Green	023355		1
Evergreen Iridescent	PS 328	Chicory Green Iridescent	PS 367		2
Evergreen Iridescent	PS 328	Chicory Green Iridescent	PS 367	Evergreen Iridescent	4
Folkstone Beige	202-53094				6
Franconia Beige	PS 875	Oxblood Maroon Iridescent	PS 608		4
Frisco Beige	PS 8843	Rossmer Green	PS 3317		1
Gunmetal Light	PS 101	Gunmetal Deep	PS104		1
Harbormist Gray Iridescent	PS 1132				4
Harbormist Gray Iridescent	PS 1132	Black	20498 & 253-2122		3
Harbormist Gray Iridescent	PS 1132	Corlear Blue Iridescent	PS 297		1
Hollywood Green	020357				1
Homer Gray	PS 170	Antoinette Blue	22290		2
Homer Gray	PS 170	Corlear Blue Iridescent	PS 297		1
Homer Gray	PS 170	Marquette Gray	020182		1
Homer Gray	PS 170	Sherwood Gray	213-36253		1
Italian Cream	20734				3
Kashan Blue	023347				1
Kingston Gray	020161	Antoinette Blue	22290		1
Knickerbocker Gray	020185	Beaver Brown	PS 860		3
Knickerbocker Gray	020185	Marquette Gray	020182		6
Liberty Blue	202-36586	Charles Blue	202-36589		1
Lindhurst Green	202-36196	Maticoke Green	202-36154		1
Luzon Green Iridescent	PS 391				6
Luzon Green Iridescent	PS 391	Silver French Gray Iridescent	PS 1123	Luzon Green Iridescent	6
Macquarie Blue Iridescent	PS 258				1
Marquette Gray	020182	Beaver Brown Iridescent	PS 860		2
Marquette Gray	020182	Black	253-2122		1
Marquette Gray	020182	Corlear Blue Iridescent	PS 297		2
Marquette Gray	020182	Chicory Green	PS 367		2
Marquette Gray	020182	Homer Gray Iridescent	PS 170		3
Marquette Gray	020182	Knickerbocker Gray	020185		6
Marquette Gray	020182	Long Key Green Iridescent	PS 389		1
Marquette Gray	020182	Oxblood Maroon Iridescent	PS 608		6
Nassau Gray Light	2446518				1
Oxblood Maroon Iridescent	PS 608	Beaver Brown Iridescent	PS 860	Oxblood Maroon Iridescent	1
Oxblood Maroon Iridescent	PS 608	Black	235-2122		1
Oxblood Maroon Iridescent	PS 608	Santone Beige Iridescent	PS 8824	Oxblood Maroon Iridescent	1
Palm Green Iridescent	PS 348				1
Piedmont Green Iridescent	PS 371				1
Pilot Blue Iridescent	PS 233				10
Pilot Blue Iridescent	PS 233	Beaumont Blue Iridescent	PS 262		2
Pilot Blue Iridescent	PS 233	Corlear Blue Iridescent	PS 297		1
Plastic Beige	202-53263				1
Rainmist Gray	246-50316	Dusty Gray	21259		1
Riverhead Green	020310	Verdancia Green	23451	Riverhead Green	3
Santa Anita Beige	202-53007	Maple Brown	202-53255		7
Santone Beige Iridescent	PS 8824	Oxblood Maroon Iridescent	PS 608		20
Santone Beige Iridescent	PS 8824	Cherokee Red	20585		3
Silver French Gray Iridescent	PS 1123	Antoinette Blue	22290		1
Silver French Gray Iridescent	PS 1123	Beaumont Blue Iridescent	PS 262		2
Silver French Gray Iridescent	PS 1123	Black	20498		2
Silver French Gray Iridescent	PS 1123	Chicory Green	PS 195		1
Silver French Gray Iridescent	PS 1123	Corlear Blue Iridescent	PS 297		13
Silver French Gray Iridescent	PS 1123	Homer Gray	PS 170		1
Silver French Gray Iridescent	PS 1123	Long Key Green Iridescent	PS 389		2
Silver French Gray Iridescent	PS 1123	Luzon Green Iridescent	PS 391		4
Silver French Gray Iridescent	PS 1123	Monterey Blue Iridescent	PS 258		3
Silver French Gray Iridescent	PS 1123	Oxblood Maroon Iridescent	PS 608		5
Silver French Gray Iridescent	PS 1123	Parma Wine	202-33039		1
Silver French Gray Iridescent	PS 1123	Pilot Blue Iridescent	PS 233		2
Silver French Gray Iridescent	PS 1123	Submarine Gray Iridescent	PS 1124		1
Silver French Gray Iridescent	PS 1123	Tamarack Green	PS 301		2
Silver French Gray Iridescent	PS 1123	Triton Green	23486		1
Silvermist Gray	246-50314	Mountainmist Gray	246-50315		1
Special Yellow	27751				1
Special Yellow Green (per sample)					1
Submarine Gray Iridescent	PS 1124				3
Submarine Gray Iridescent	PS 1124	Black	20498		1
Submarine Gray Iridescent	PS 1124	Harbormist Gray Iridescent	PS 1123		3
Submarine Gray Iridescent	PS 1124	Harbormist Gray Iridescent	PS 1123	Submarine Gray Iridescent	4
Submarine Gray Iridescent	PS 1124	Marquette Gray	020182		2
Sunset Rose	2447237				1
Surf Green	202-52595	Long Key Green Iridescent	PS 389		1
Tacoma Cream	Not listed	Pale Gold Bronze	Not listed		1
Toast Tan Pearl	EX 42-181	Ginger Brown Pearl	EX 42-180		1
Transport Red	246-6469				1
Vera Cruz Gray	PS 186	Augsburg Gray	PS 1117		1
Verdancia Green	23451	Riverhead Green	020310		3
				Total	314

THE LAST LaSALLE SURVIVES ! ! !

The last LaSalle to roll off the production line still exists today in its original condition. It is a Series 52 "Special" Sedan, serial number 4333751, body number 9986. It is a remarkable testimonial to the affection, respect and care owners and hobbyists have demonstrated over the years for LaSalle.

NINETEEN FORTY-ONE

motivated to move up into a Cadillac, and have Cadillac reign supreme as the "Standard of the World."

Cadillac learned that, during hard times, even Cadillac owners were reluctant to drive a Cadillac. Driving a LaSalle gave them all the advantages of a Cadillac without being ostentatious. LaSalle was a Cadillac without the name. However, LaSalle was often thought to be its own make instead of a Cadillac product.

Consumers had also demonstrated that they really preferred a car with a prestige name if several price levels were available (i.e., Packard 110 and 120; Lincoln Zephyr, etc.). Which was it going to be for LaSalle? At some point, GM and Cadillac management concluded that this duplicity was costly and counterproductive. All cars built by Cadillac should carry the name Cadillac.

To be considered expendable was not new for LaSalle. Cadillac decided to drop LaSalle in 1934, but an extremely daring design proposal by designer Jules Agramonte, and presented by Harley Earl, persuaded GM management to reverse its decision, and to continue building the LaSalle. LaSalle was Harley Earl's first love. No doubt, it was his idea to put the LaSalle front ensemble on several very attractive body styles for 1941. It may have been another attempt to dissuade GM management from dropping the LaSalle name. Whatever the initial intent, it was to no avail. This time management was serious, and its decision was final.

In the past, LaSalle had served its purpose by helping Cadillac overcome some very difficult economic times and without tarnishing Cadillac's reputation. Now, the time had come for LaSalle to be called what it really was . . . a Cadillac. The rest is history.

In 1941, the entire lineup of automobiles was Cadillac and the LaSalle name, indeed, had been dropped. Cadillac established itself as the "Standard of the World" with the most comprehensive model offering ever . . . six in all: the Series 61, 62, 63, 67, 75 and 60 Special.

Factory photograph provides a clear view of the Series 52 LaSalle ornamentation and the 1941 Cadillac instrument panel.

LaSalle taillights, bumpers and trunk handle assembly similar to Cadillac, but a newly-designed LaSalle trunk emblem.

LaSalle had been a success in every way. It survived fluctuating economic conditions, withstood competition from inside the Cadillac division and forged an envious reputation in the marketplace. LaSalle had been a superb value and, without a doubt, in some years Cadillac lost money on building those LaSalles, but it kept Cadillac in the game. One thing is for sure, LaSalle was a car with a name that was synonymous with styling excellence that is recognized even today as deserving a place among the great trendsetters.

Common to ALL proposals . . .

* The bullet hood ornament, slightly more streamlined at a lower angle than the 1940.
* The hood side ventilation grille with LaSalle crest.
* The fender spears, three wrap around each fender with painted stripe inside elongated chrome surround.
* Individual block letters LaSALLE above front fender spears.
* Taillight assembly with fin and plastic jewel.
* Glass taillight, more flat than Cadillac, with five line slits in the upper portion.
* New design LaSalle trunk emblem with crest and three chevrons.
* Door handles.
* Windshield wiper assemblies.
* Windsplits on fenders, including headlight rims.

Three quarter views:

* Series 50 parking lights under front windsplit. (Series 51 and Series 52 are on the windsplit.)
* License plate on Series 50 has 41-50.
* Front bumper guards connected with almost stock tiebar design from 1941 Cadillac.
* Series 50 grille has LaSalle script name across front à la 1940. (Series 52 and Series 51 do not have an emblem.)
* Series 50 has stainless molding tying all windows together and serves as belt molding all along the rear notch. (Series 52 has molding around each window individually; Series 51 has one tying strip binding all windows together, but no belt molding.)
* Two-tone color combinations on Series 52 and Series 50.
* Series 50 stainless steel sill plate same as Series 51, but different from Series 52.
* Series 50 chrome headlight rims, Series 51 and Series 52 are painted.
* Chrome reveals around six vertical ventilation slits all appear the same.
* Full wheel discs are 1941 Cadillac production with LaS emblem. (Series 51, which has the LaSalle crest in the center and three spinners, is an exception.)

Series 51: The brand new fastback body was well executed with quarter window in sail panel. It looks balanced front and back, sits very low to the ground, appears long and streamlined, and has horizontal parking lights below the horizontal crease in frontal area.

Series 50: Profile and three-quarter rear views show unique notchback Series 50 body style with stainless steel belt molding all around and connected to the molding which visually ties the windows together. This style was considered to be the most eligible for the 1941 LaSalle. It ultimately became the Series 63 Cadillac in 1941. This photograph of the notchback was the only one taken outside on the factory roof. All others were taken inside.

Series 52: Except for trim, this handsome body style was inaugurated in 1940 as the Series 52 "Special" and also as the Cadillac Series 62. It had the wider Torpedo body, notchback and no quarter window in the sail panel.

Frontal Views, opposite page:

* Shape of horizontal cross bars on grille is different, as is the overall curvature of the grille outline.
* Location of parking lights differ. Only the Series 52 has LaSalle script across the grille.
* Round driving light covers are different: the Series 51 has three sections with three chevrons in the center, the Series 52 had four sections with LaS in the center.
* Bumpers differ in a center license plate bracket.
* The tiebar in the Series 51 has a LaSalle crest in round frame.
* Different windshield frame shape.
* Chrome headlight frame on Series 52. Painted on Series 51.
* Series 51 and Series 50 had no rain drips over front vent window. Series 52 did have them.

Below: A brand new Series 51 fastback sits extra low to emphasize streamlined effects, a trick also used by dealers from time to time to have the car look lower and longer while on display. The fender skirt carries a LaSalle crest. Opposite page, top: The grille on the Series 52 is very slightly different from the Series 51 shown in the lower picture.

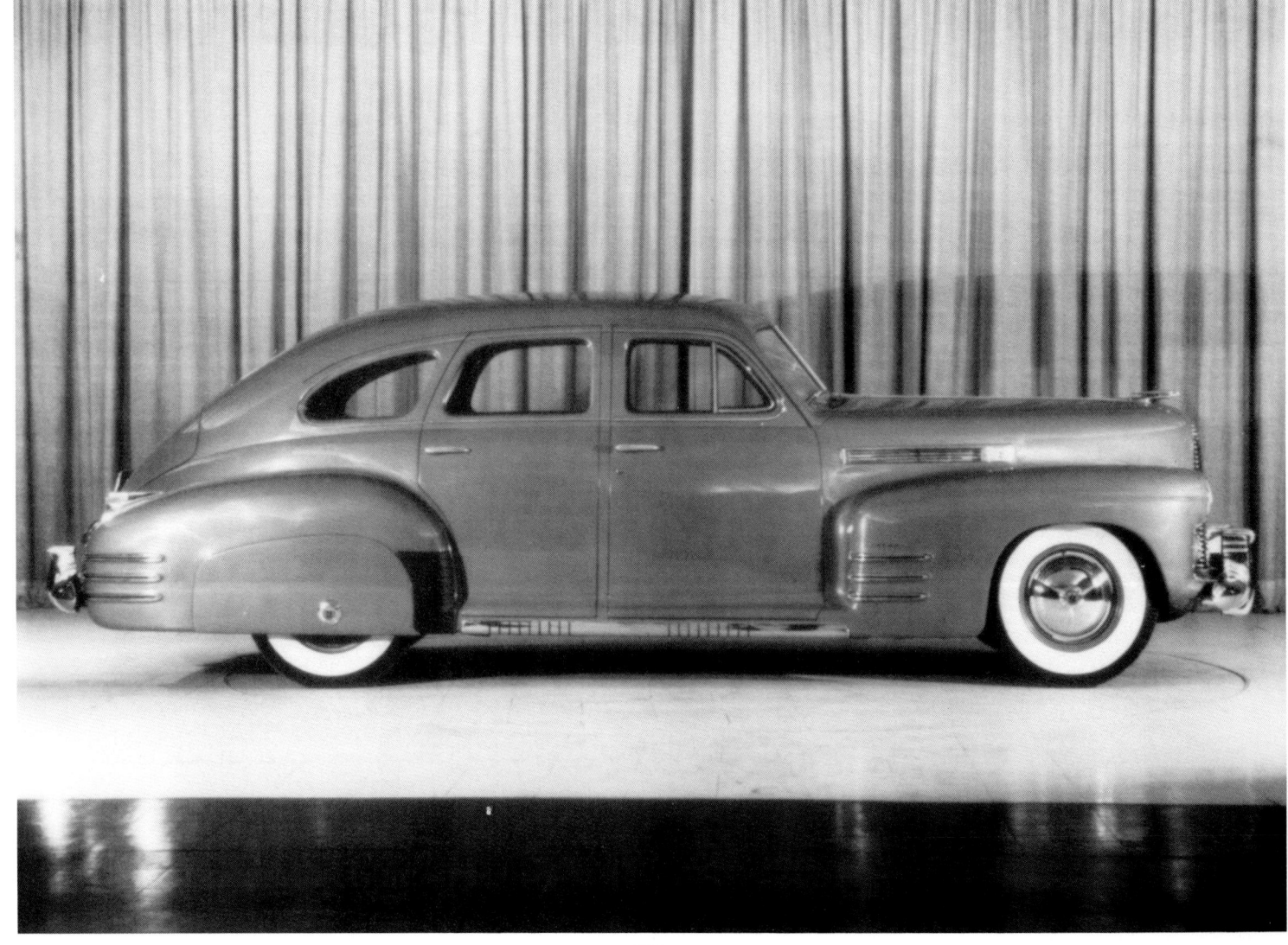

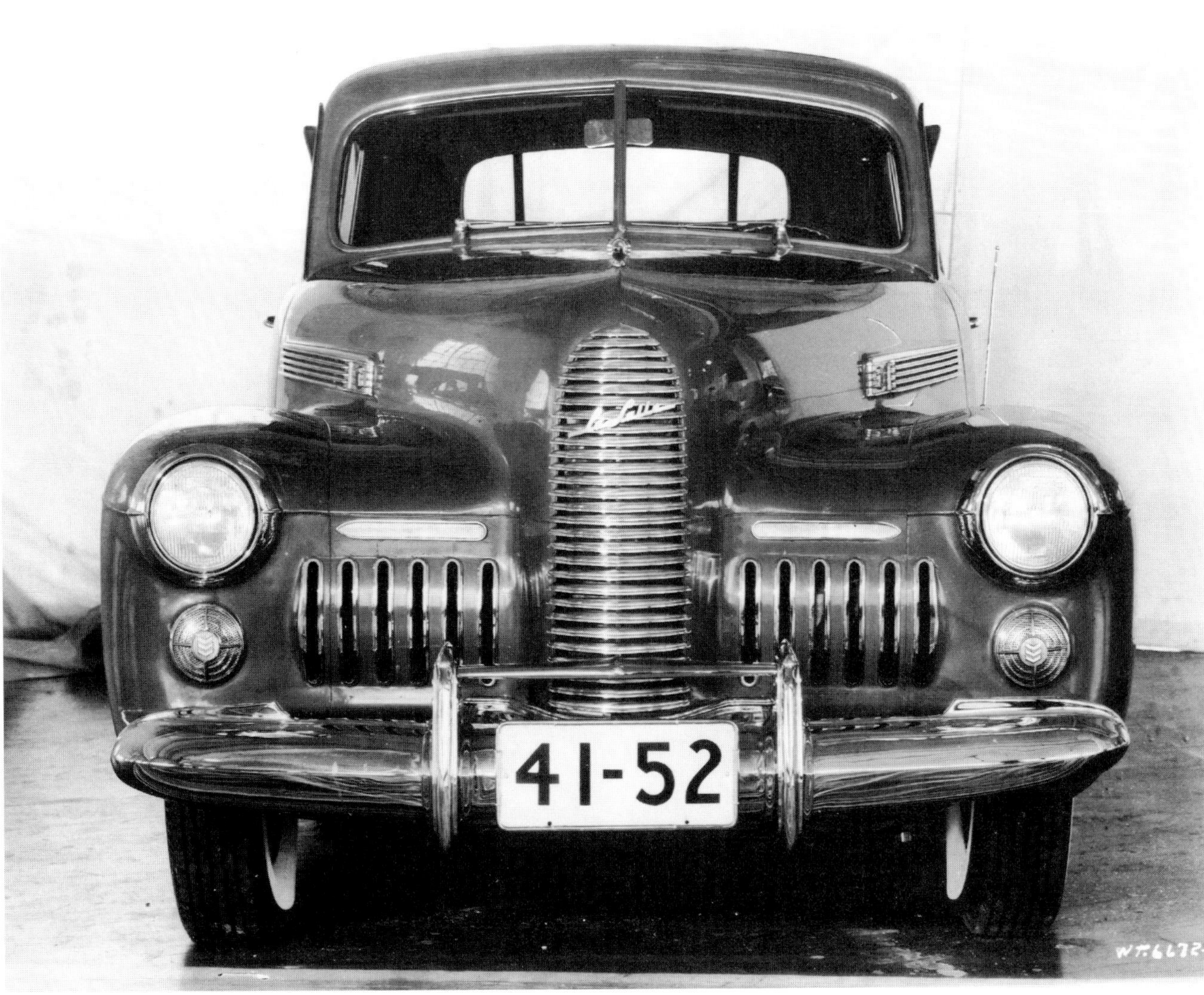
41-52
WT6672-3.

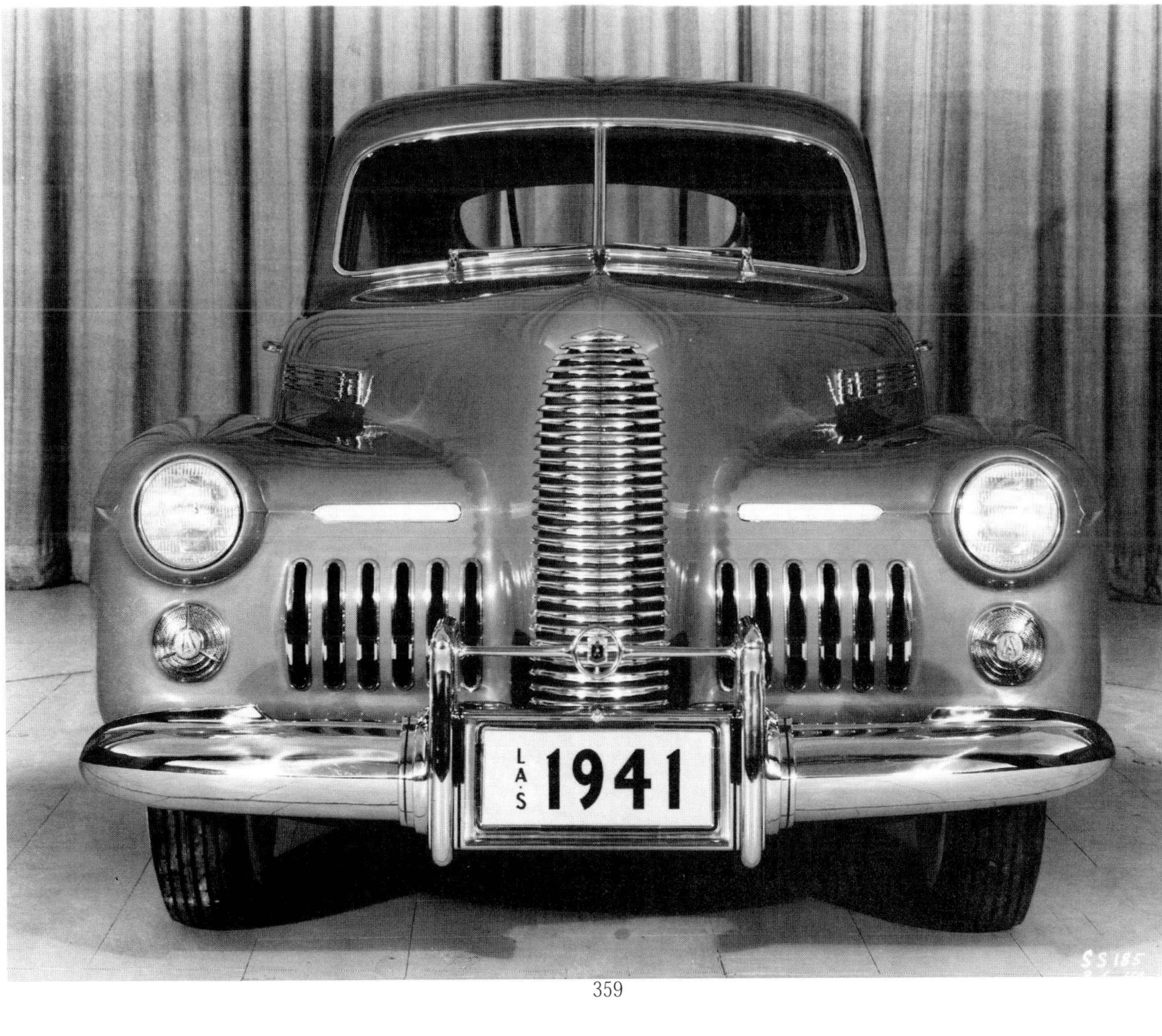
LAS 1941

Rear views:

* Narrow taillight jewel same on all proposals.
* All three rear window shapes are different, but all have typical Cadillac dividers. (LaSalle in 1940 had no dividers.)
* All trunk emblems are the same - three chevrons with LaSalle crest.
* Series 50 has wider license plate bracket than Series 51 and Series 52 which are stubbier.
* Bumpers are the same, but the three sets of guards are different.
  Series 50 has a high and low wrap around bracket; Series 52 has a wide outside bracket. Series 51 has very wide outside bracket with two painted rings and a tiebar. (Will it allow the trunk lid to clear?)
* All three trunk lid openings are different, as are the shapes of the body that flow into the trunk area.
* See 1940 LaSalle dash through rear window of Series 52. (Series 52 on previous page shows typical 1941 Cadillac instruments.)

Below: Series 50. Opposite page top: Series 51. Opposite page bottom: Series 52.

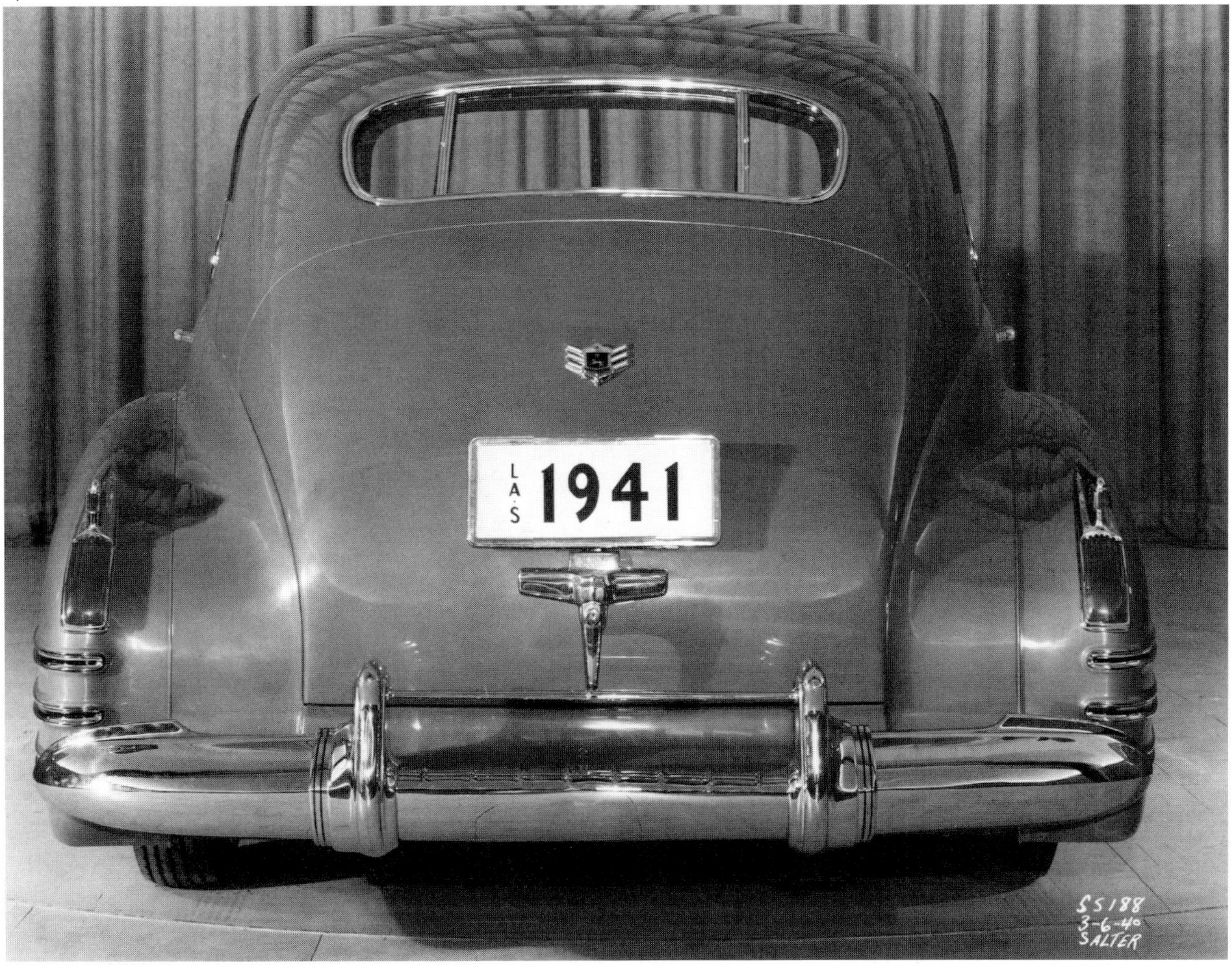
L A S 1941
SS188
3-6-40
SALTER

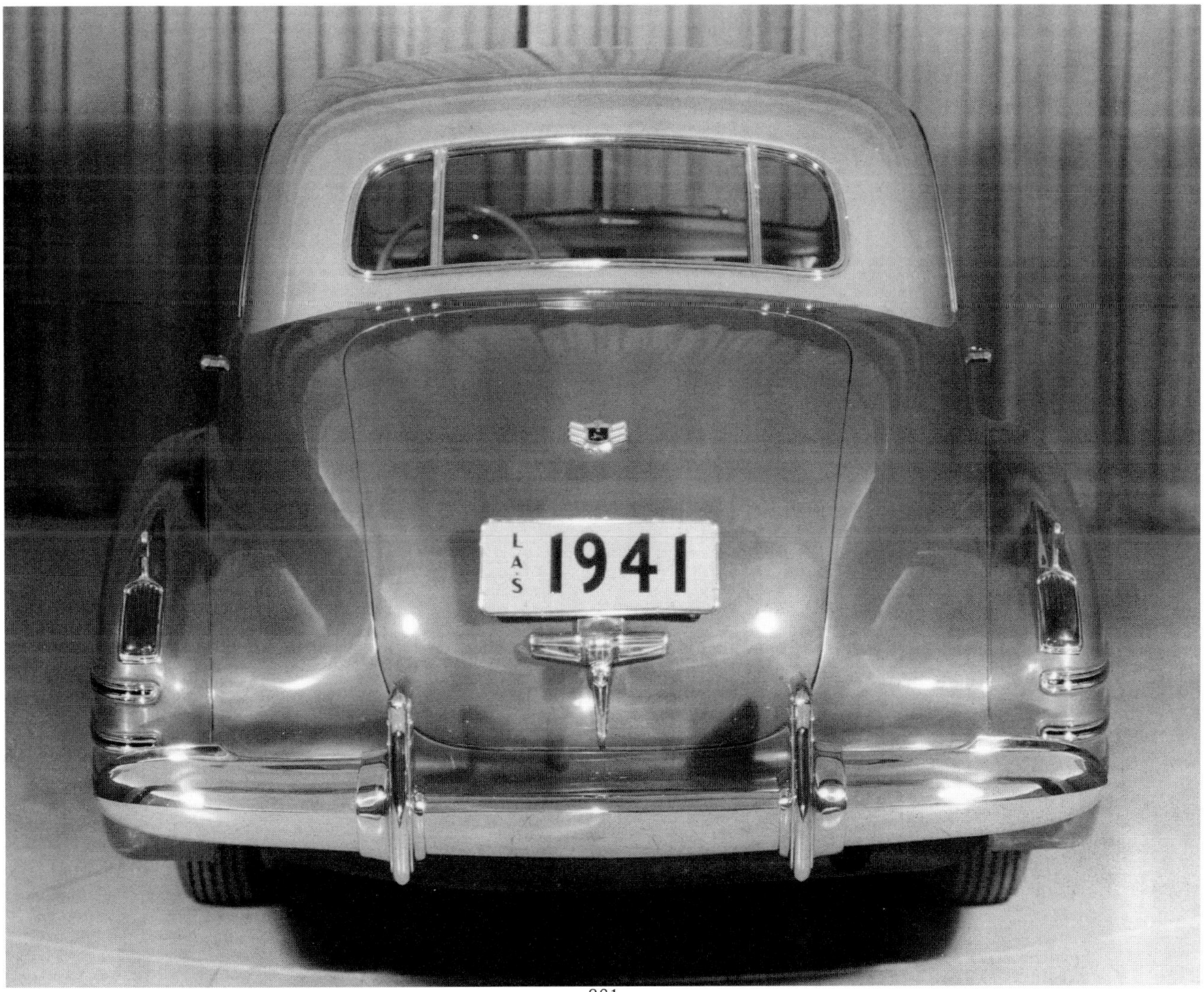
L A S 1941

It was Harley Earl's intent to have this model 50 mock-up become the LaSalle for 1941. There would have been no sharing with other GM divisions. It was unique and handsome in its own right with the stainless steel belt molding all around and connected to the molding which visually ties the windows together. GM management in Cadillac decided to keep this design in the lineup . . . but, as a Cadillac Series 63. It was the end of an era.

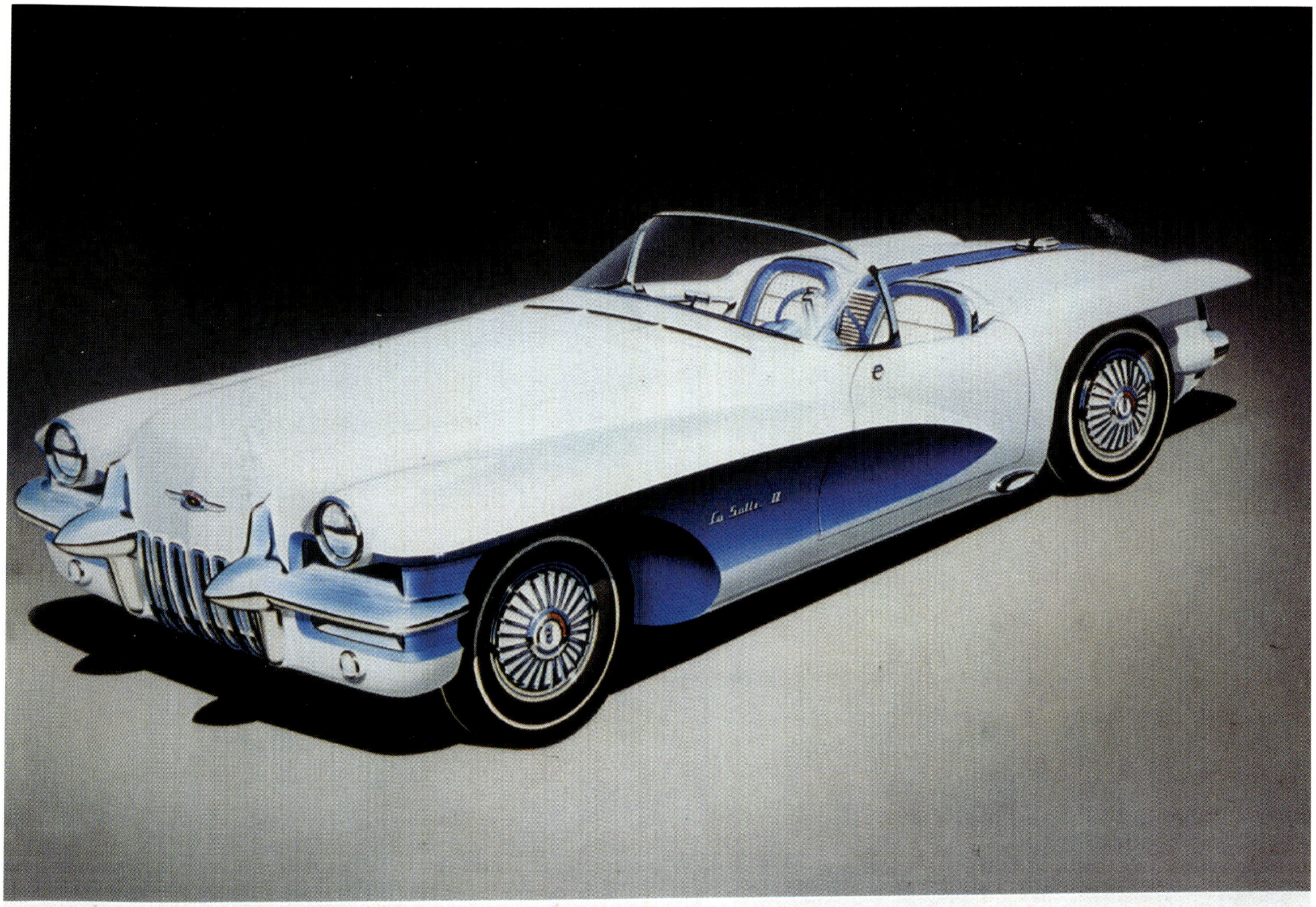

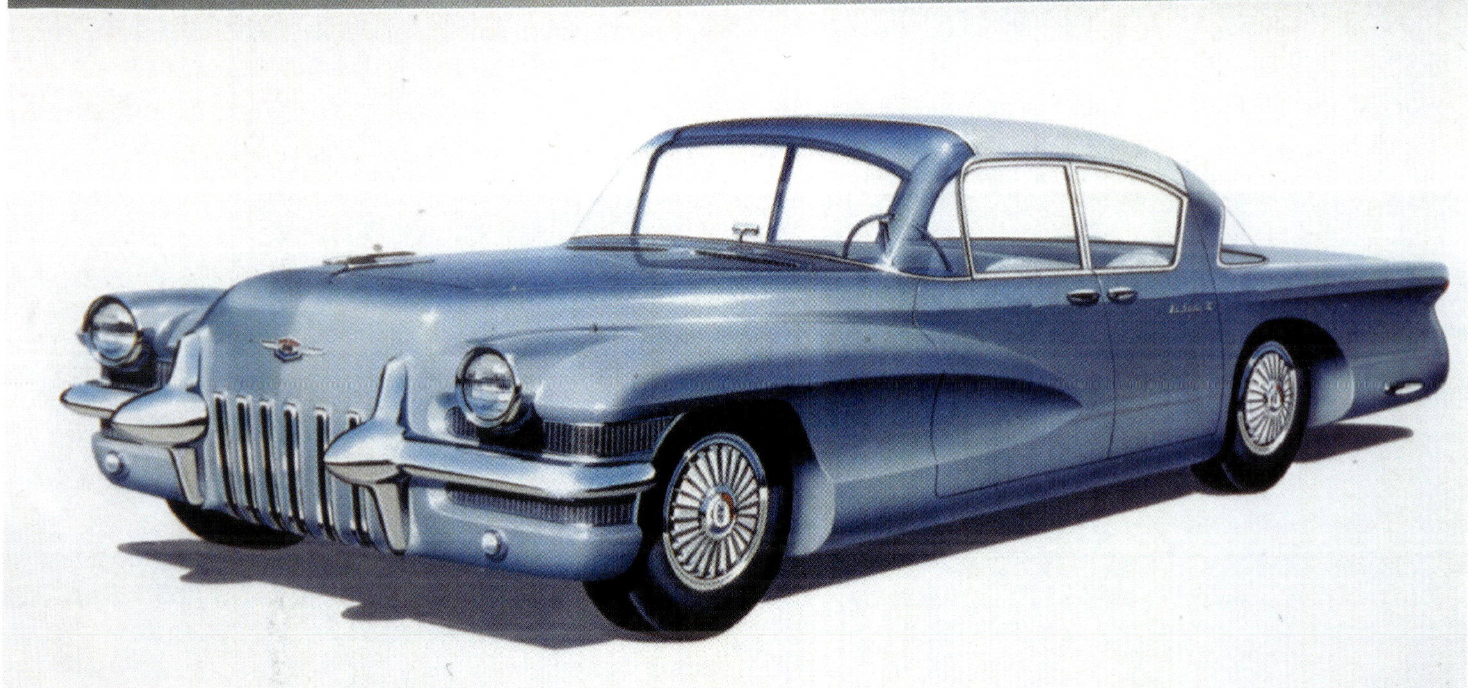

NINETEEN FIFTY-FIVE

Above: A gorgeous 1939 Convertible Coupe with right hand drive and upside down and backwards column shift pattern fitted right into a great Australian lifestyle. Below: A 1940 Series 50 LaSalle with Holden body seems similar to the U.S. configuration but is uniquely different with dual rear window, more rounded trunk area, a sloping stainless steel belt molding and different window configuration.

Above: A Holden body plate is proudly displayed on the passenger's side cowl. Right: A 1938 LaSalle with a Holden's Buick shared body stands shyly in a very private location. Below: Holden installed mostly leather seats and door panels for LaSalle. Note the rear window configuration on the car pictured at the right.

In 1931, General Motors purchased Holden Enterprises and formed General Motors-Holden's, Ltd., for the specific purpose of fitting a complete Australian body and interior on American chassis.

After 1935 LaSalles were fitted with four-door Sedan bodies built entirely by Holden in Adelaide. At a glance, the bodies looked similar to the U.S. version but were very different with the use of a two-piece rear window, no exterior window moldings, different door hinging, etc. Australian leathers were used for the interiors; unique hardware was used, including different bumpers, bumper ornamentation and door handles. Other modifications were made to make LaSalle street legal. Chassis were shipped from Detroit modified to suit right hand drive, to accommodate the steering drag link, pedal assembly, bell housing and steering box. When the gear shift was relocated on the steering column, the bell housing was changed to carry the rod action of the left side shift linkages to cross over to the steering column on the right side. This resulted in an entirely different shift pattern as compared with left hand steering wheel versions.

For the five years that Holden fitted bodies to LaSalles, there was a total of 302 Sedans produced, according to the factory. The survival rate approaches 30 percent.

All three pictures are of a more conservatively painted Nordberg custom-bodied 1930 LaSalle Cabriolet. It is elegant looking with the body lines setting the mood, handsomely matched to the LaSalle fenders, radiator, hood and windshield. A metal trunk was fitted to the traditional Victoria body. Presumed to have been commissioned by H.K.H. Prince Gustaf Adolf of Sweden, it reflected the Prince's passion for good looking and fast automobiles. A touch of the unique was a bronze sculpture, specifically designed for the Prince by Maud von Rosen, which served as the radiator ornament. The sculptress was the daughter of Compte Clarence von Rosen, who founded the Swedish Automobile Club in 1903.

Above: Captured in 1951, this 1937 LaSalle Convertible Coupe travels boldly on a cold December day through Kensington, London, England. Note what appears to be the original rear window and rumble seat with concealed spare tire trunk, even though it has dual sidemounts. Uniquely European are the turn signal indicators mounted on the cowl and the back-up light on the driver's side underneath the license plate. Below: A 1938 LaSalle Cabriolet with custom coachwork by Carrosserie Sodomka in Czechoslovakia is shown with sweeping European fenders front and back, parking lights on the front fender, European driving lenses on headlights, huge suicide doors on heavy hinges permitting easier entry to the rear and door glass without chrome frame. LaSalle's long hood helps to balance the overall design. The car was built for H.R.M. King George VI of the U.K. Was it for his use? Note the steering wheel on the left side.

LaSALLE IN EUROPE

There were more LaSalles exported to Europe than any other continent. They were production models usually sent to a GM assembly plant or authorized dealer. However, a few were shipped to customers for customization.

Custom body builders in Europe such as Van den Plas and Gläser of Switzerland provided beautiful coachwork for LaSalle during the mid-Thirties. Custom coachwork on LaSalle was an exception rather than the rule because the fundamental streamlined flow of the production body was so well done that LaSalle owners worldwide found little reason to attempt an improvement on existing designs.

LaSALLE WORLDWIDE

South America, South Africa and the Pacific Rim were additional export markets where LaSalles were sold, but to a more limited extent.

While the international market was not very lucrative for LaSalle and relatively few were exported as a percent of domestic production, today there are dedicated enthusiasts all over the world who cherish their LaSalles.

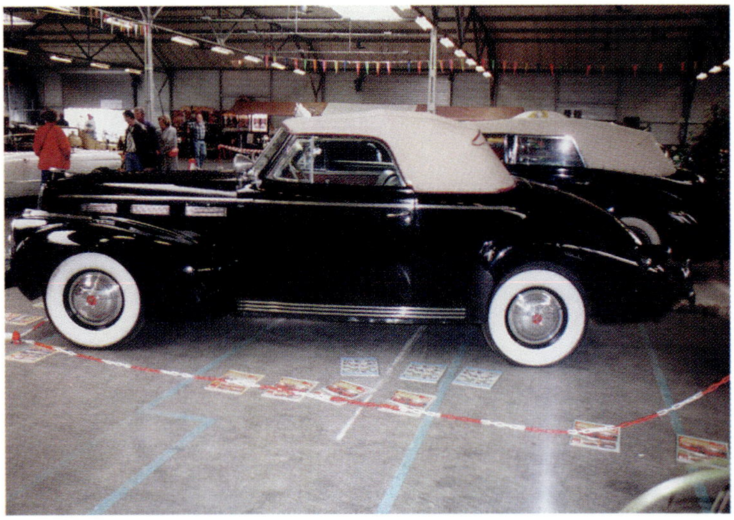

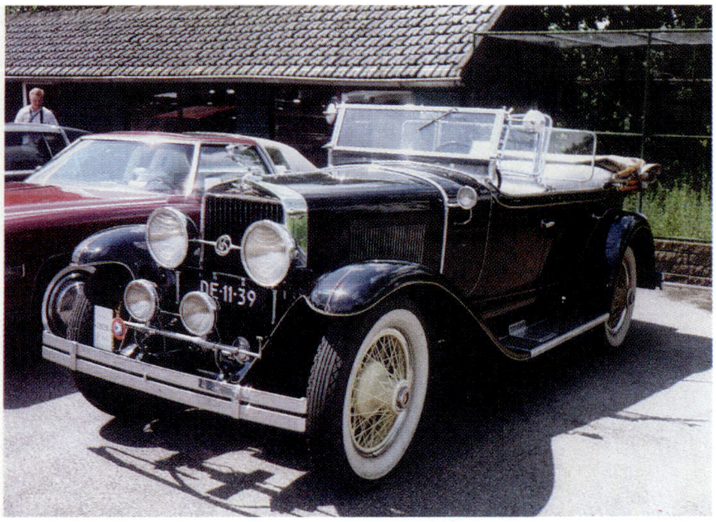
DE-11-39

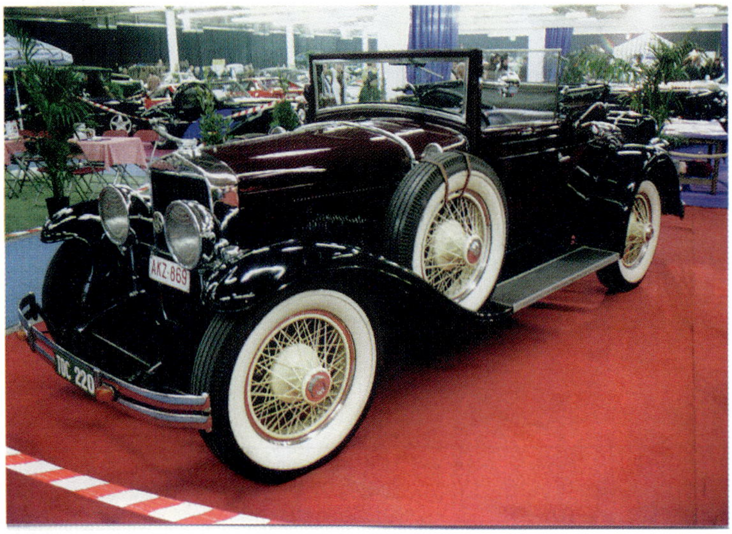

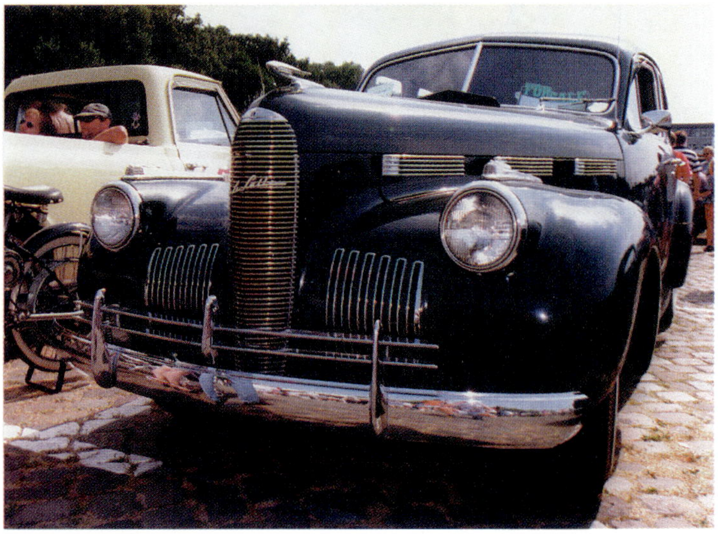

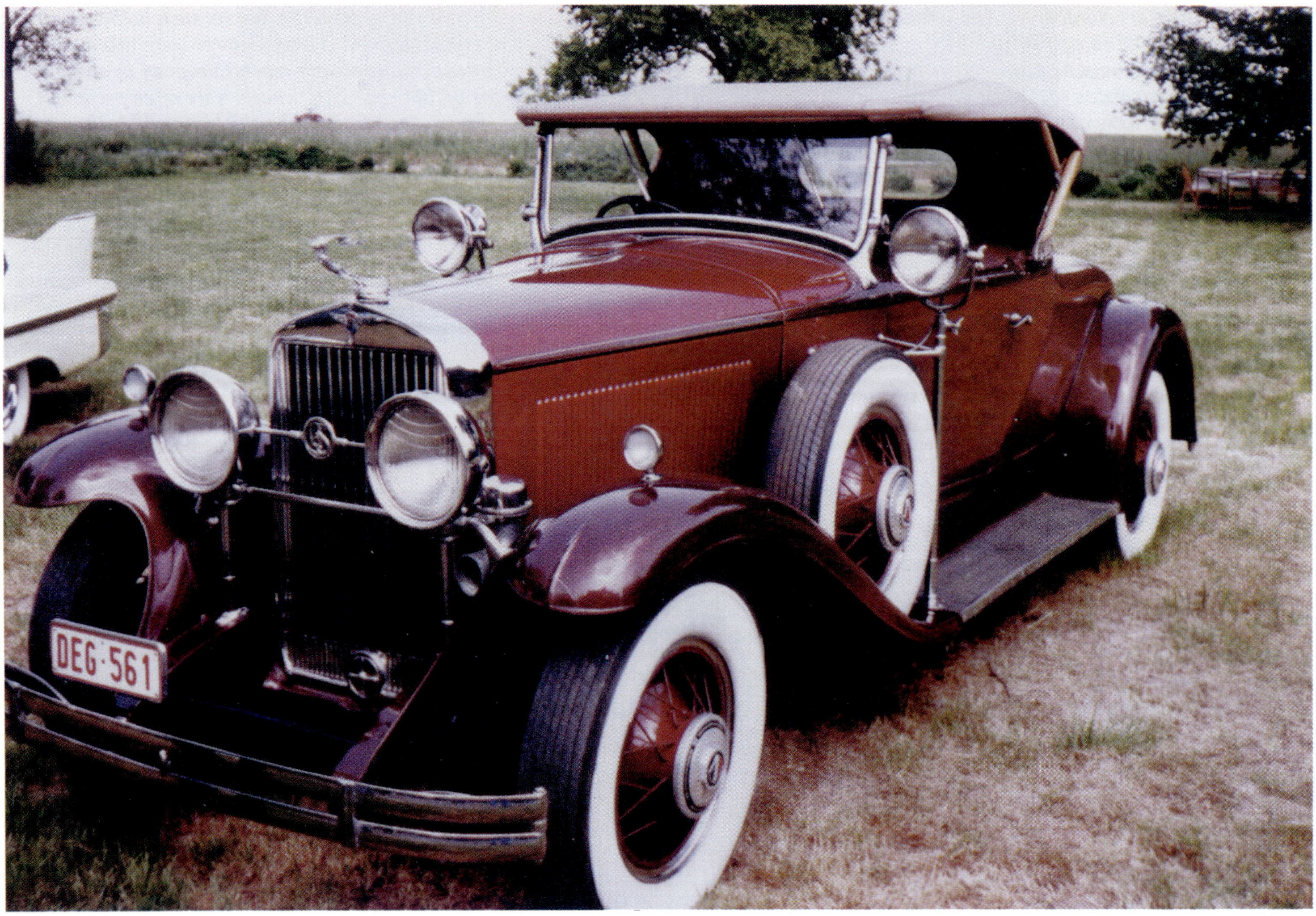
DEG·561

Above: A very rare 1934 Club Sedan resides in South Africa, where a number of LaSalles were imported from the United States. Note the unique hood ornament, chromed headlights, chromed pods and sloping to the rear belt molding. Opposite page: Belgium and Holland are the residences of these LaSalles: a 1940 Series 50 Convertible Coupe, a 1928 LaSalle Phaeton, a 1928 Convertible Coupe, a 1940 Series 51 Special Sedan and a 1930 LaSalle Roadster.

CKD and partially assembled units were, more often than not, shipped to GM assembly plants located overseas for further disposition.

GM plants predominantly assembled four-door Sedans. Such plants would assemble more than one GM product. It was not uncommon that a LaSalle would be going down the same assembly line as a Buick or Oldsmobile or Pontiac.

American made automobiles were not sought after on a large scale because Europe was considered the style center of the world. A few LaSalles went to custom body shops and very few custom-bodied LaSalles are known to have survived. Factory photographs of those rare cars appear to be almost nonexistent.

There are also very few exported LaSalles known to exist in the country to which they were originally exported. Internationally, many LaSalles have more recently been exported by enthusiasts.

The General Motors assembly plants operational overseas during the LaSalle years are listed chronologically as follows:

GM International - Copenhagen, Denmark
GM Limited - Dunstable, United Kingdom
GM Continental - Antwerp, Belgium
GM Argentina - Buenos Aires, Argentina
GM Do Brasília - São Paulo, Brazil
GM France - Gennevilliers, France
GM South Africa - Port Elizabeth, South Africa
GM New Zealand - Petone/Wellington, New Zealand
GM Uruguay - Montevideo, Uruguay
GM Australia - Adelaide, Australia
GM GmbH - Berlin, Germany
GM Japan - Osaka, Japan
GM Java - Java, Batavia (Indonesia)
GM Norway - Oslo, Norway
GM Nordiska - Stockholm, Sweden
GM India - Bombay, India
GM Polsce - Warsaw, Poland
GM Holden - Melbourne, Australia
GM Peninsular - Madrid, Spain
GM Suisse - Bienne, Switzerland
GM Near East - Alexandria, Egypt
GM De Mexico - Mexico City, Mexico

General Motors & Holden's Formed by Merger of the Two Australian Companies

WITH the unanimous ratification by the stockholders of Holden's Motor Body Builders Ltd. in Adelaide on March 5, arrangements for the proposed merger of that company with General Motors Australia Pty. Ltd. were completed. The new company, which is to be known as General Motors & Holden's Limited, will have as Chairman of the Board and operating head,

Complete Affiliation with Body Builders Effected in Order to Identify General Motors as Native Industry and Thus Strengthen Position in the Australian Market

E. W. Holden, formerly Chairman and Managing Director of the Holden company. A. N. Lawrence continues in his capacity as Managing Director and a member of the Board.

James R. Holden, who has been in charge of body development and sales at Holden's, will be Manager of the Body Building Division of the new company and a member of the Board.

New Availability Plan Hailed As Powerful Sales Weapon in Sweden

Sees New Financing Plan as Removal [of] Barrier to Effective Distribution Job

General Motors WORLD

Published in New York by
GENERAL MOTORS EXPORT DIVISION
1775 Broadway, New York City

HELEN L. WRIGHT, Editor

MAY, 1935
Vol. XIV

Miss Sarah Leander, Sweden's most popular musical comedy star, and the LaSalle she purchased a few months ago

General Motors Products Stage Encouraging Come-Back in Poland

D. F. Ladin, Managing Director of General Motors International, on a recent trip to Poland—Wherever the LaSalle stopped, it was the immediate object of inspection for interested bystanders

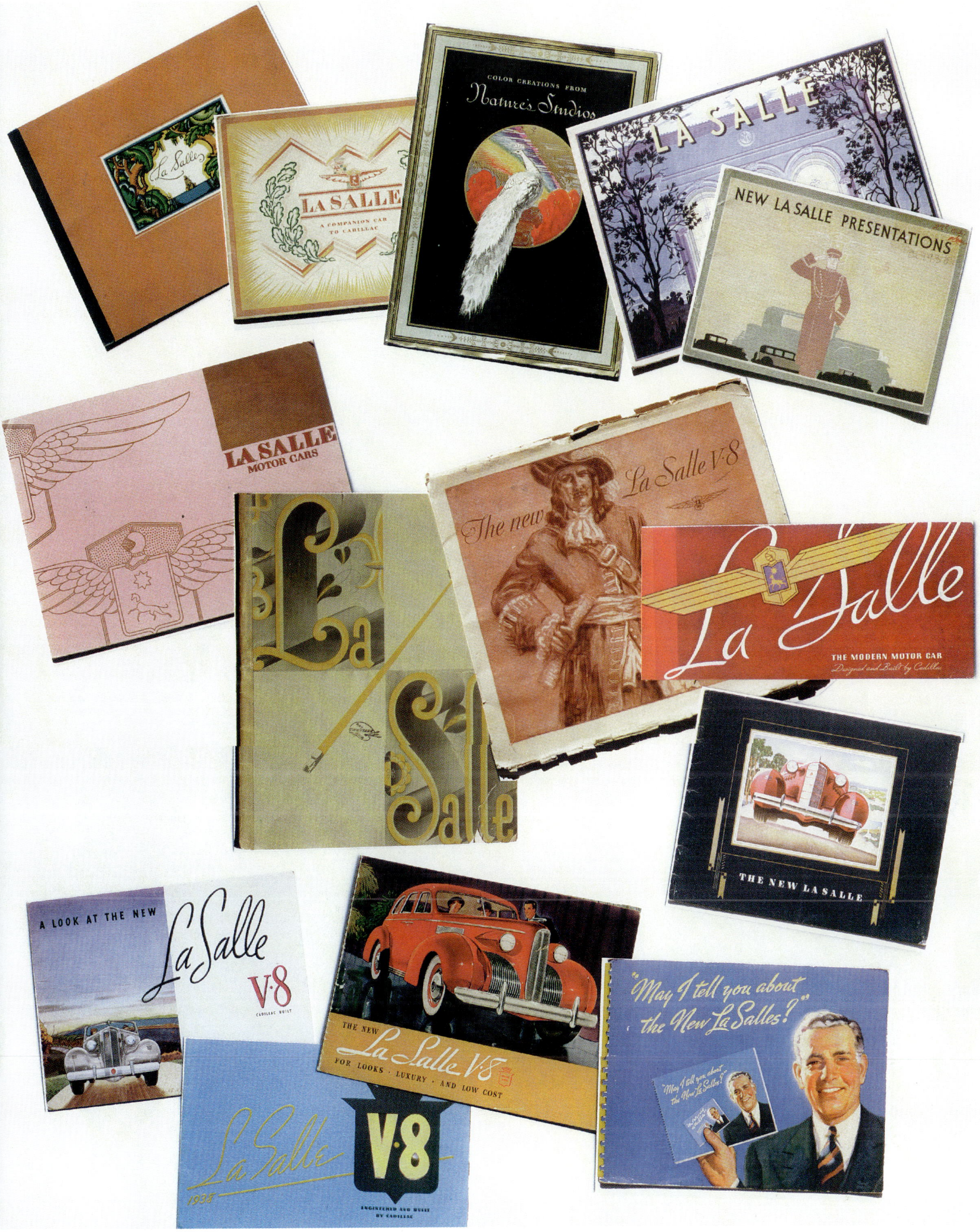
La Salle
LA SALLE
A COMPANION CAR TO CADILLAC
COLOR CREATIONS FROM
Nature's Studios
LA SALLE
NEW LA SALLE PRESENTATIONS
LA SALLE
MOTOR CARS
The new La Salle V-8
La Salle
La Salle
THE MODERN MOTOR CAR
Designed and Built by Cadillac
THE NEW LA SALLE
A LOOK AT THE NEW
La Salle
V-8
CADILLAC BUILT
THE NEW
La Salle V-8
FOR LOOKS · LUXURY · AND LOW COST
"May I tell you about the New La Salles?"
La Salle
1938
V-8
ENGINEERED AND BUILT BY CADILLAC

FACTORY LITERATURE

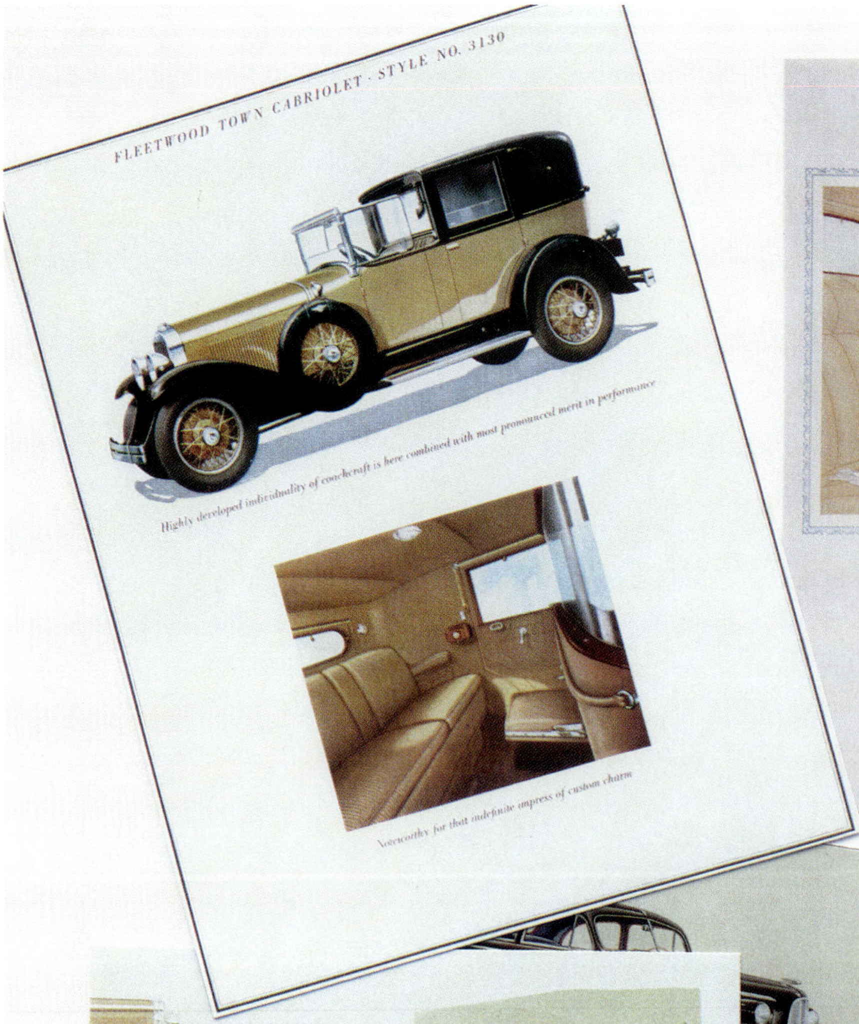
FLEETWOOD TOWN CABRIOLET · STYLE NO. 3130
Highly developed individuality of coachcraft is here combined with most pronounced merit in performance
Noteworthy for that indefinite impress of custom charm

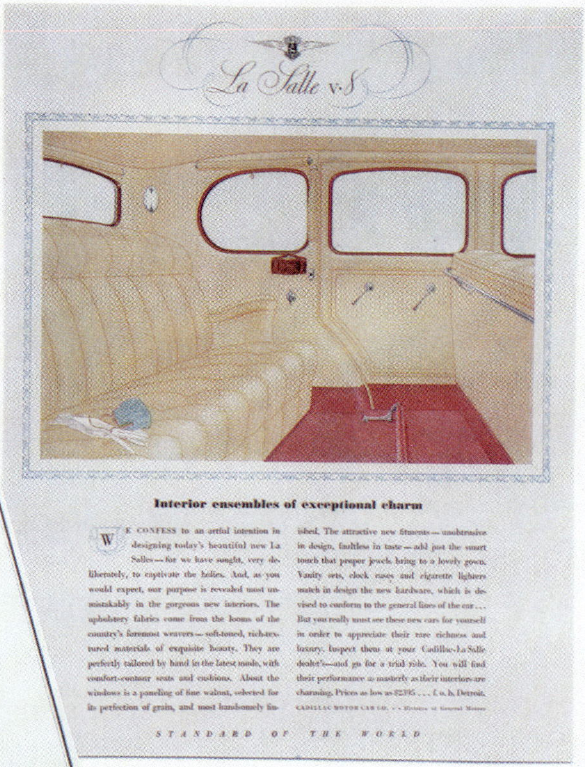
La Salle V-8
Interior ensembles of exceptional charm
WE CONFESS to an artful intention in designing today's beautiful new La Salles—for we have sought, very deliberately, to captivate the ladies. And, as you would expect, our purpose is revealed most unmistakably in the gorgeous new interiors. The upholstery fabrics come from the looms of the country's foremost weavers—soft-toned, rich-textured materials of exquisite beauty. They are perfectly tailored by hand in the latest mode, with comfort-contour seats and cushions. About the windows is a paneling of fine walnut, selected for its perfection of grain, and most handsomely finished. The attractive new fitments—unobtrusive in design, faultless in taste—add just the smart touch that proper jewels bring to a lovely gown. Vanity sets, clock cases and cigarette lighters match in design the new hardware, which is devised to conform to the general lines of the car . . . But you really must see these new cars for yourself in order to appreciate their rare richness and luxury. Inspect them at your Cadillac-La Salle dealer's—and go for a trial ride. You will find their performance as masterly as their interiors are charming. Prices as low as $2395 . . . f. o. b. Detroit.
CADILLAC MOTOR CAR CO. · · Division of General Motors
STANDARD OF THE WORLD

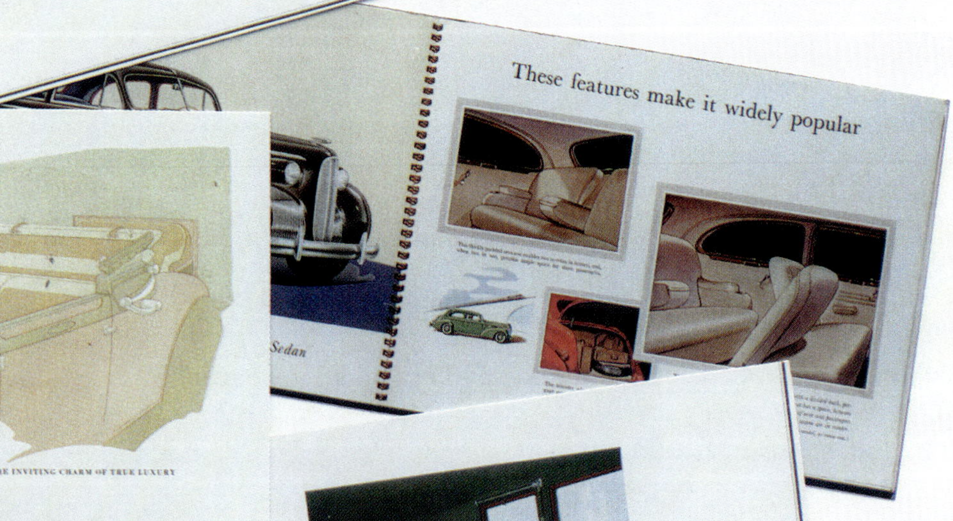
These features make it widely popular
Sedan

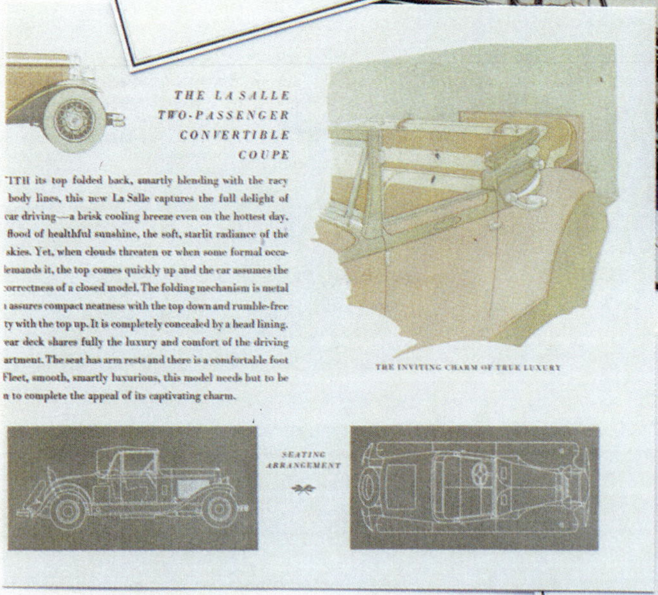
THE LA SALLE
TWO-PASSENGER
CONVERTIBLE
COUPE
TTH its top folded back, smartly blending with the racy body lines, this new La Salle captures the full delight of car driving—a brisk cooling breeze even on the hottest day, flood of healthful sunshine, the soft, starlit radiance of the skies. Yet, when clouds threaten or when some formal occa- lemands it, the top comes quickly up and the car assumes the correctness of a closed model. The folding mechanism is metal assures compact neatness with the top down and rumble-free ty with the top up. It is completely concealed by a head lining. ear deck shares fully the luxury and comfort of the driving artment. The seat has arm rests and there is a comfortable foot Fleet, smooth, smartly luxurious, this model needs but to be n to complete the appeal of its captivating charm.
THE INVITING CHARM OF TRUE LUXURY
SEATING ARRANGEMENT

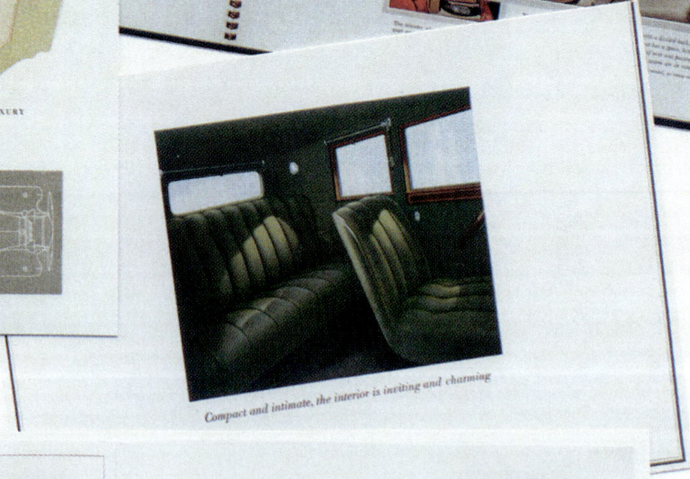
Compact and intimate, the interior is inviting and charming

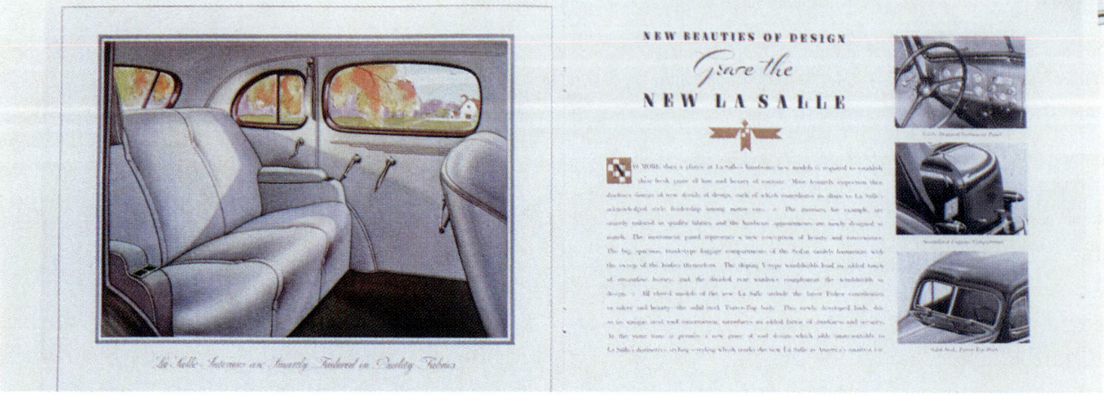
NEW BEAUTIES OF DESIGN
Grace the
NEW LA SALLE
La Salle Interiors are Smartly Tailored in Quality Fabrics

FACTORY LITERATURE

To market, sell and service LaSalles, a variety of publications were produced, for a variety of users. Sales brochures, special features pamphlets, value comparisons and special occasion literature were intended for the prospective buyer. Sales data books, paint chips, upholstery fabrics and sales and marketing updates were intended for the salesperson. Shop manuals, announcement bulletins and troubleshooting leaflets were for the service department.

LaSalle sales literature was presented in elaborate, self-contained brochures separate and apart from those featuring Cadillac, even though its kinship was always mentioned, be it in small print or by conspicuous reference. Cadillac literature, on the other hand, would contain only a sampling of LaSalle models to show the full range of automobiles offered by the Cadillac Division.

There was at least one LaSalle sales brochure in color for each model year—sometimes two, a small one and a larger, more elaborate one. Several years had black and white brochures in addition to the color brochures. Most illustrations in the color brochures were artist renditions. They were beautiful, but the body lines were often exaggerated to make them look longer and more streamlined. Only in 1927, 1928 and 1929 did the black and white brochures closely resemble photographic quality proportions of each body style.

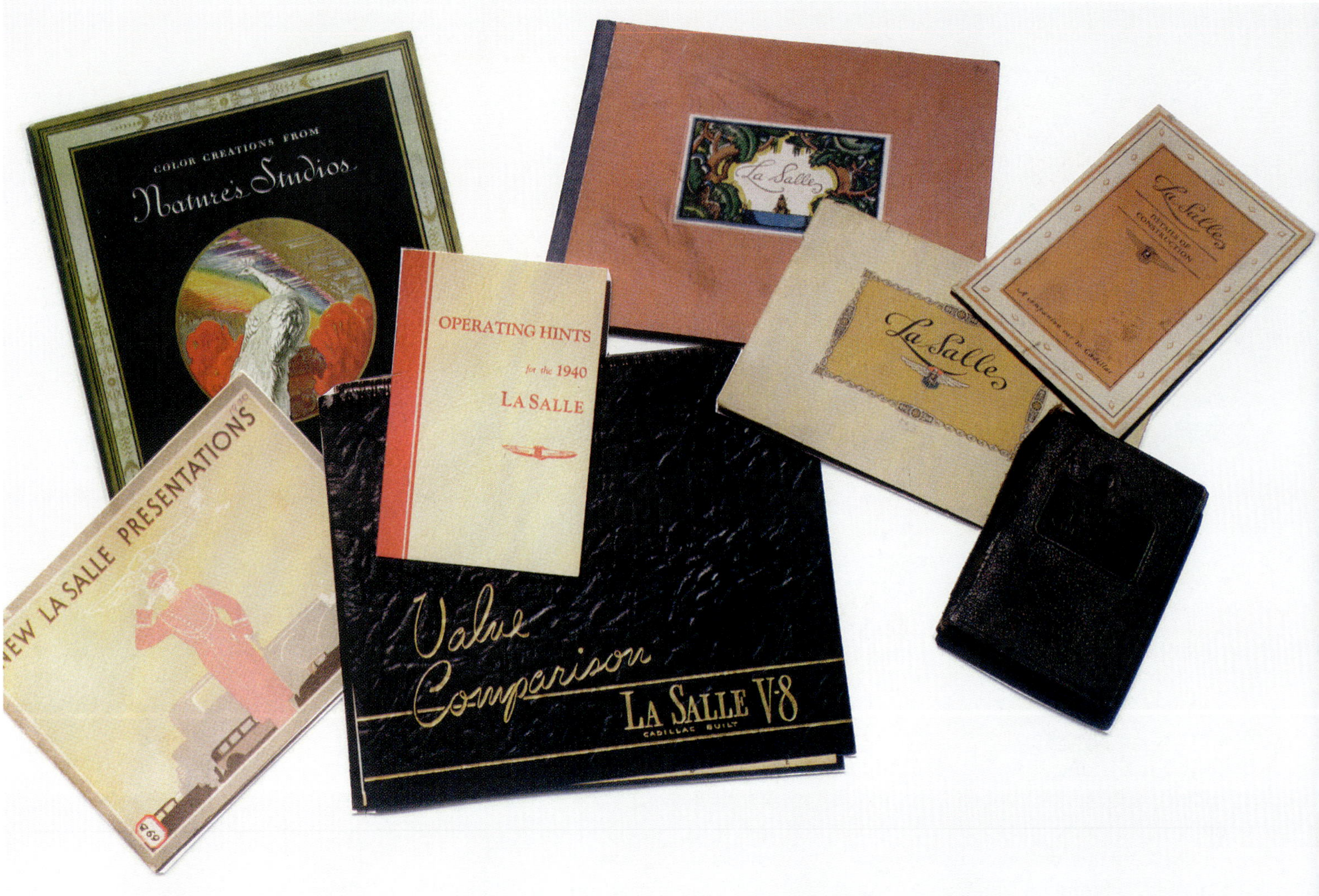
COLOR CREATIONS FROM
Nature's Studios
NEW LASALLE PRESENTATIONS
OPERATING HINTS
for the 1940
LA SALLE
Value Comparison
LA SALLE V-8
CADILLAC BUILT
La Salle
La Salle
La Salle

Sales brochures for each year depicted all body styles intended for production at the beginning of the model year. Body styles added during the year were not included in reprints and did not have a separate brochure. Some, not all, semi-custom models were listed or illustrated. Full custom coachwork was usually not printed in factory literature, but LaSalle sales literature was often augmented by separate brochures illustrating special features, custom body offerings, accessories or mid-year introductions.

From 1927 through 1933, LaSalle made available special brochures depicting semi-custom bodies by Fleetwood on the LaSalle chassis.

At delivery time, each LaSalle came with an owner's manual which contained instructions to guide the owner with the operation and functioning of the car. It included lubrication schedules, operation of the instruments, tire changing procedures, capacities and licensing data.

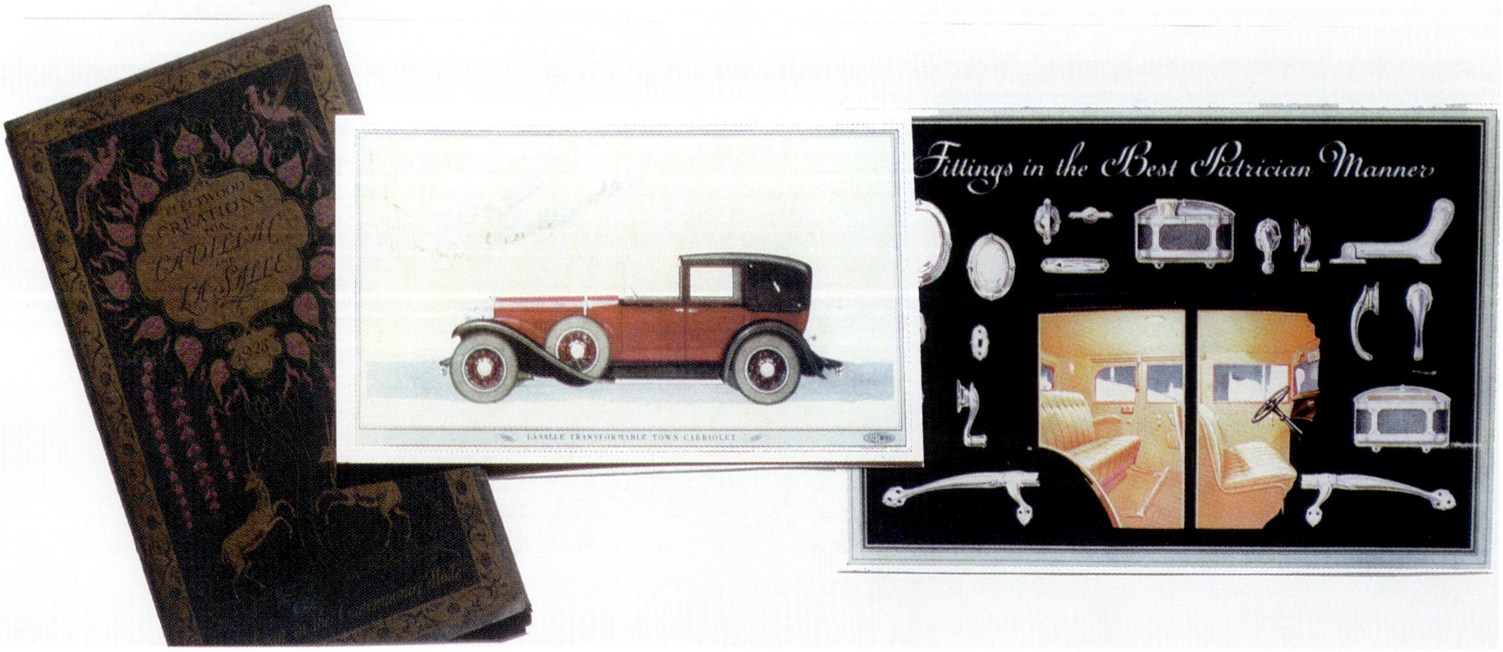
Fittings in the Best Patrician Manner

Features of Construction books in the early years through 1934 and the sales data books thereafter were used by showroom sales personnel to help them understand how to sell LaSalle. Dimensions, specifications, features and value comparisons with other makes were all factually presented.

No attempt was made to sell LaSalle instead of Cadillac. Throughout LaSalle's production run, it was represented as a companion car to Cadillac, not as a replacement for Cadillac. LaSalle was assumed to be a stepping stone toward owning a Cadillac. Data books were indexed, pocket size and in black and white.

Color option chips and upholstery samples were available in separate brochures or in *Features of Construction* books. Today, these are rare and extremely difficult to find for the early years.

Numerous publications were produced to help service the cars. Technical manuals were very important. In some years there were two versions of the shop manual—a preliminary manual to help familiarize mechanics with new introductions, and a comprehensive Cadillac-LaSalle shop manual for the repair or replacement of all components for each year's model. These manuals treated LaSalle, along with Cadillac, as a total and complete reference. Some shop manuals were leather-bound, to which pages with subsequent changes could be added from time to time as they were produced. Those bound in leather or leather-like material had greater longevity despite heavy use in the garage. They were well done and easily understood.

Literature was produced for automobile shows around the country and other similar occasions, such as special brochures to introduce the *Nature Studios* colors in 1928, Pacemaker car write-ups for 1934 and 1937, the reintroduction of the V-8 engine in 1937 and *Value Comparisons* pamphlets explaining LaSalle's market niche.

In-house communications were very important. Internally, LaSalle was a part of Cadillac and not separated by exclusive LaSalle-only literature. LaSalle was covered by a number of Cadillac bulletins such as *Clearing House, The Cadillac Craftsman* and *Service Man*. These would update sales personnel on recent developments and motivate them to sell with new arguments. Many of these bulletins were also directed to service department personnel. Their frequency ranged from weekly to monthly or when needed.

Bulletins were sent out with updated procedures experienced by or reported from the field. The factory would respond with recommendations back to the field in memo form. These memos are priceless because some of the vital repair information cannot be found elsewhere.

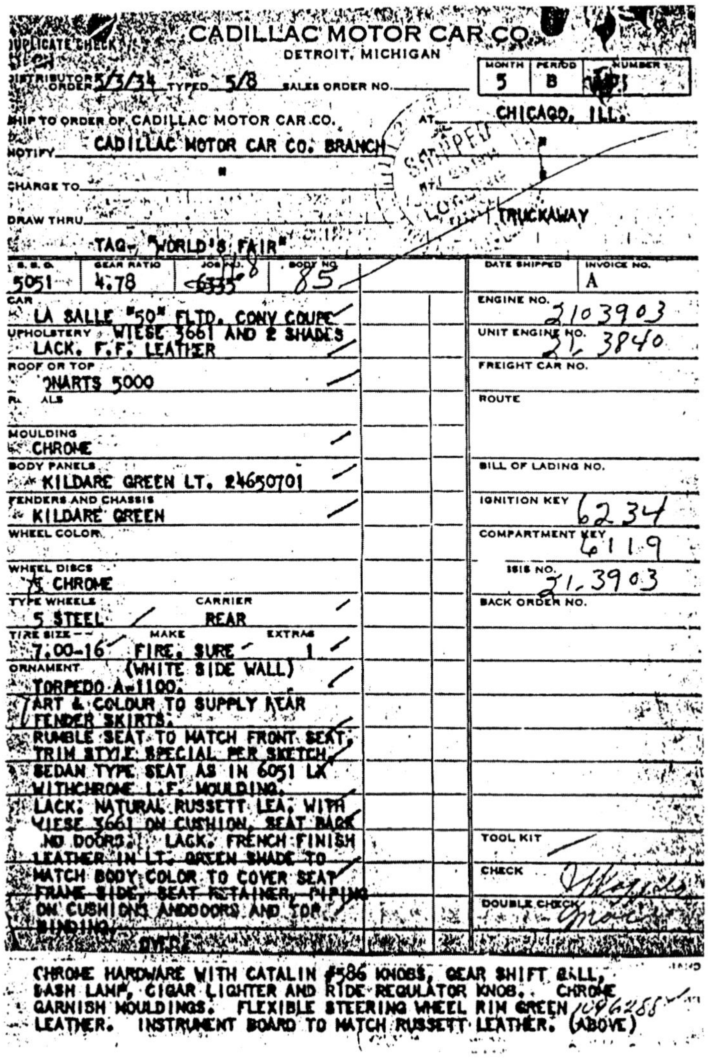

CADILLAC MOTOR CAR CO.
DETROIT, MICHIGAN

DISTRIBUTOR ORDER 5/3/34 TYPED 5/8 SALES ORDER NO.

MONTH	PERIOD	NUMBER
5	B	

SHIP TO ORDER OF CADILLAC MOTOR CAR CO. AT CHICAGO, ILL.
NOTIFY CADILLAC MOTOR CAR CO. BRANCH
CHARGE TO
DRAW THRU TRUCKAWAY
TAG - "WORLD'S FAIR"

S. O.	GEAR RATIO	JOB NO.	BODY NO.	DATE SHIPPED	INVOICE NO.
5051	4.78	6335	85		A

CAR: LA SALLE "50" FLTD. CONV COUPE
UPHOLSTERY: WIESE 3661 AND 2 SHADES LACK. F.F. LEATHER
ROOF OR TOP: 2NARTS 5000
MOULDING: CHROME
BODY PANELS: KILDARE GREEN LT. 24650701
FENDERS AND CHASSIS: KILDARE GREEN
WHEEL COLOR
WHEEL DISCS: CHROME
TYPE WHEELS: 5 STEEL — CARRIER: REAR
TIRE SIZE: 7.00-16 — MAKE: FIRE. SURE — EXTRAS: 1
ORNAMENT: (WHITE SIDE WALL) TORPEDO A-1100.
ART & COLOUR TO SUPPLY REAR FENDER SKIRTS.
RUMBLE SEAT TO MATCH FRONT SEAT. TRIM STYLE SPECIAL PER SKETCH. SEDAN TYPE SEAT AS IN 6051 LX WITH CHROME L.F. MOULDING.
LACK. NATURAL RUSSETT LEA. WITH WIESE 3661 ON CUSHION, SEAT BACK AND DOORS. LACK. FRENCH FINISH LEATHER IN LT. GREEN SHADE TO MATCH BODY COLOR TO COVER SEAT FRAME SIDE, SEAT RETAINER, PIPING ON CUSHIONS AND DOORS AND TOP BINDING.

ENGINE NO. 2103903
UNIT ENGINE NO. 21 3840
FREIGHT CAR NO.
ROUTE
BILL OF LADING NO.
IGNITION KEY 6234
COMPARTMENT KEY 6119
S/S NO. 21 3903
BACK ORDER NO.
TOOL KIT
CHECK
DOUBLE CHECK

CHROME HARDWARE WITH CATALIN #586 KNOBS, GEAR SHIFT BALL, DASH LAMP, CIGAR LIGHTER AND RIDE REGULATOR KNOB. CHROME GARNISH MOULDINGS. FLEXIBLE STEERING WHEEL RIM GREEN LEATHER. INSTRUMENT BOARD TO MATCH RUSSETT LEATHER. (ABOVE)

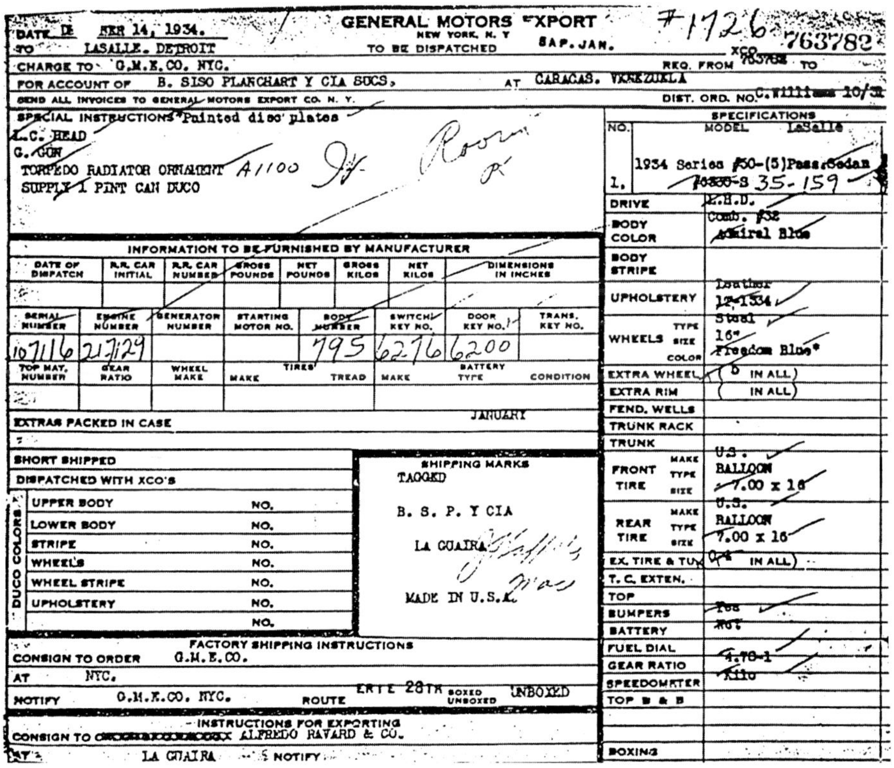

GENERAL MOTORS EXPORT
NEW YORK, N. Y.

DATE NOV 14, 1934. #1726 763782
TO LASALLE. DETROIT — TO BE DISPATCHED SAP. JAN.
CHARGE TO G.M.E.CO. NYC. — REQ. FROM 763782 XCO TO
FOR ACCOUNT OF B. SISO PLANCHART Y CIA SUCS, AT CARACAS. VENEZUELA
SEND ALL INVOICES TO GENERAL MOTORS EXPORT CO. N. Y. — DIST. ORD. NO. C. Williams 10/31
SPECIAL INSTRUCTIONS Painted disc plates
L.C. HEAD
G. GUN
TORPEDO RADIATOR ORNAMENT A1100
SUPPLY 1 PINT CAN DUCO

INFORMATION TO BE FURNISHED BY MANUFACTURER

SERIAL NUMBER	ENGINE NUMBER	GENERATOR NUMBER	STARTING MOTOR NO.	BODY NUMBER	SWITCH KEY NO.	DOOR KEY NO.	TRANS. KEY NO.
107116	217129			795	6276	6200	

SPECIFICATIONS

MODEL	LaSalle
1.	1934 Series 50-(5) Pass. Sedan 35-159
DRIVE	L.H.D.
BODY COLOR	Comb. #32 Admiral Blue
BODY STRIPE	
UPHOLSTERY	Leather 12-1534
WHEELS TYPE / SIZE / COLOR	Steel 16" Freedom Blue
EXTRA WHEEL	6 IN ALL
EXTRA RIM	IN ALL
FEND. WELLS	
TRUNK RACK	
TRUNK	
FRONT TIRE MAKE / TYPE / SIZE	U.S. BALLOON 7.00 x 16
REAR TIRE MAKE / TYPE / SIZE	U.S. BALLOON 7.00 x 16
EX. TIRE & TUBE	6 IN ALL
T. C. EXTEN.	
TOP	
BUMPERS	Yes
BATTERY	
FUEL DIAL	
GEAR RATIO	4.78-1
SPEEDOMETER	Kilo
TOP B & B	
BOXING	

SHIPPING MARKS
TAGGED
B. S. P. Y CIA
LA GUAIRA
MADE IN U.S.A.

FACTORY SHIPPING INSTRUCTIONS
CONSIGN TO ORDER G.M.E.CO.
AT NYC.
NOTIFY G.M.E.CO. NYC. ROUTE ERIE 28TH UNBOXED
INSTRUCTIONS FOR EXPORTING
CONSIGN TO ALFREDO RAVARD & CO.
AT LA GUAIRA

Today, the LaSalle owner can find specific information about his or her car's original color, original upholstery, accessories, special features, etc. Cadillac Motor Car Company has kept a file of records for every automobile it has built since 1902. These build sheets and order invoices now reside on microfiche at the Cadillac Historical Collection for the complete fourteen-year LaSalle production run. Some exceptions exist. A copy of that information can be obtained for a small service fee. Requests must include the year and vehicle identification number, which is the engine number. Quality of the microfiche reproduction is fair at best, but it does provide the necessary information.

The Cadillac-LaSalle Club (CLC), founded in 1958, consists of a membership that serves as a source for cars and parts, service and publications specific to LaSalle. The CLC provides an interchange of information between members through a monthly magazine, which lists LaSalle literature for sale. The Club also publishes an annual membership directory where LaSalle owners and their cars are listed by state and country.

1927 La Salle

Series 27C

Ad characteristics: initially black & white, later in color; drawings of cars in French settings with short captions in French.

1927 La Salles have 12 large louvres on the hood sides while 1928 La Salles have 28 narrow hood louvres. Both cars have cowl lights.

Ads appearing in *The Saturday Evening Post*			
Date	Page	Car, caption	Same/similar ad appeared
4-30-27	35	B&W Roadster, "Ah, Madame!"	*IS*, 5-27, p. 7
5-14-27	39	B&W Touring, airplane, "Pour Londres"	*IS*, 6-27, 7; *NG*, 6-27
5-28-27	63	B&W 5-pass. Sedan, "A la Campagne"	*A&D*, 6-27
		Same ad: green & black Sedan, "A la Campagne"	
6-11-27	37	B&W Conv. Cou— Le Coeur de P—	
		Conv. Coupe, "La beauté et l'utilité"	—, 9-27, p. 95 (b&w); *HB*, 9-27; *H&G*, 9-27; *WWA*, ? (b&w); *HIC*, 9-27, p. 117
		& black Roadster, "Le Lievre et La Tortue"	
	46	Green Close-coupled Sedan, "Le Souvenir"	
11-5-27	44	Maroon Victoria Coupe, "La Nouvelle Arrivee"	*HB*, 12-27

LaSalle Ad Types: 27A, 27B, 27C, 28A, 28B

LaSalle advertisements are fascinating and unique to their era. Different approaches to different audiences were evident in a variety of magazines, such as *The Saturday Evening Post* versus *Vanity Fair*. Interest in collecting these magazine ads appears to be growing, but finding the right one can be difficult. Not knowing what to look for and not knowing where to find a particular advertisement can lead to endless searches. Fortunately, today's technology can be of help to the search collector. In its infancy, and by no means complete, a web page on the Internet lists advertisements by name and date of the appearance with a computer picture, its slogan or caption. Some ads are grouped by common artistic and graphic features while others are chronologically listed by model and magazine title.

From 1934 to 1940, LaSalle made postcards available to sales personnel that they could send to prospects with a message on the back . . . often a testimonial from a satisfied customer. These postcards were colorful and attempted to place the LaSalle in everyday settings.

The PENALTY OF LEADERSHIP

IN every field of human endeavor, he that is first must perpetually live in the white light of publicity. ¶Whether the leadership be vested in a man or in a manufactured product, emulation and envy are ever at work. ¶In art, in literature, in music, in industry, the reward and the punishment are always the same. ¶The reward is widespread recognition; the punishment, fierce denial and detraction. ¶When a man's work becomes a standard for the whole world, it also becomes a target for the shafts of the envious few. ¶If his work be merely mediocre, he will be left severely alone—if he achieve a masterpiece, it will set a million tongues a-wagging. ¶Jealousy does not protrude its forked tongue at the artist who produces a commonplace painting. ¶Whatsoever you write, or paint, or play, or sing, or build, no one will strive to surpass, or to slander you, unless your work be stamped with the seal of genius. ¶Long, long after a great work or a good work has been done, those who are disappointed or envious continue to cry out that it can not be done. ¶Spiteful little voices in the domain of art were raised against our own Whistler as a mountebank, long after the big world had acclaimed him its greatest artistic genius. ¶Multitudes flocked to Bayreuth to worship at the musical shrine of Wagner, while the little group of those whom he had dethroned and displaced argued angrily that he was no musician at all. ¶The little world continued to protest that Fulton could never build a steamboat, while the big world flocked to the river banks to see his boat steam by. ¶The leader is assailed because he is a leader, and the effort to equal him is merely added proof of that leadership. ¶Failing to equal or to excel, the follower seeks to depreciate and to destroy—but only confirms once more the superiority of that which he strives to supplant. ¶There is nothing new in this. ¶It is as old as the world and as old as the human passions—envy, fear, greed, ambition, and the desire to surpass. ¶And it all avails nothing. ¶If the leader truly leads, he remains—the leader. ¶Master-poet, master-painter, master-workman, each in his turn is assailed, and each holds his laurels through the ages. ¶That which is good or great makes itself known, no matter how loud the clamor of denial. ¶That which deserves to live—lives.

Cadillac Motor Car Co. Detroit, Mich.

Cadillac... LaSalle's Parent Company

Cadillac has risen from its humble beginnings in 1902 to become a recognized symbol of excellence throughout the world. Then the Cadillac Automobile Company, and later the Cadillac Motor Car Division of the General Motors Corporation, has manufactured distinguished automobiles in each succeeding year up to the present. It hasn't always been easy. Conditions, circumstances and opportunities have often dictated direction. Such was the case with Cadillac in the early days when the combustion engine for the automobile was still in its very formative stages and dependability was always a question mark. Cadillac was uniquely qualified to meet that challenge.

Henry M. Leland, in his untitled capacity as Cadillac's first manager, had an engineering fetish for precision, accuracy and quality. "Craftsmanship a Creed; Accuracy a Law" was his motto, and he required his employees to implement accordingly. He demanded manufacturing tolerances within a thousandth of an inch or less. This was music to the market at that time and the thrust for excellence paid off when, in 1908, Cadillac was awarded the coveted Dewar Trophy for close manufacturing tolerances and interchangeability of parts. Almost simultaneously with the award, Cadillac began representing itself with the slogan: "Standard of the World."

A final look. Cadillac executives compare the design features of the 1940 LaSalle torpedo body Series 52 Special and the 1940 Cadillac Series Sixty Special.

Continuing the pursuit of excellence, Cadillac has since introduced a long list of automobile mechanical "firsts," such as the electric self-starter, one of three elements for which it was awarded another Dewar Trophy in 1913; the first mass produced V-8 engine in 1914; and many others. Cadillac's automotive leadership was personified in one of the most famous advertisements ever written, "The Penalty of Leadership."

Aside from all the mechanical firsts, Cadillac also introduced a new concept of designing the looks of production automobiles. The 1927 LaSalle was designed by Harley Earl, a professional stylist. This exercise was so successful that GM established a completely separate styling section, comprised of professional designers instead of engineers.

It was Cadillac that gave LaSalle a running start when it was introduced as Cadillac's companion car. Linking LaSalle to Cadillac's reputation was an important factor to LaSalle's initial success. LaSalle was always linked to the parent company in one way or another. At first, advertisements listed the Cadillac Motor Car Company rather matter-of-factly. Later, LaSalle was linked more boldly to the luxury and features found in Cadillac: "Manufactured completely by the Cadillac Motor Car Company within its own plants"; "the Royal Family of Motordom, LaSalle, Cadillac and Fleetwood"; and "LaSalle is fashioned side by side with Cadillac."

Kinship was also evident in the use and ownership of manufacturing facilities. LaSalle automobiles were assembled in a separate plant from 1927 through part of the 1933 model year. The Cadillac-LaSalle Dealers Manual published in 1928 stated: "The LaSalle plant covering forty acres of ground is situated on McGraw Avenue, Detroit, and was purchased by the Cadillac Motor Car Company in 1927." "Floor space of this plant is 2,927,873 square feet." "While the parts are made in the Cadillac plant, the assembling of the LaSalle is carried out entirely at the LaSalle plant."

During those early years, bodies for the LaSalle were primarily by Fisher, but Fleetwood offerings were also popular. Bodies for V-windshield open and closed jobs and the seven-passenger touring models were typically done in Pennsylvania; the more conventional body types were executed during the early 1930s in the Fisher/Fleetwood plant on West Fort Street and West End Avenue in Detroit.

For LaSalle's 1934 model year only, all LaSalle bodies were fabricated by Fleetwood craftsmen in the Fisher/Fleetwood plant. Final assembly took place on Cadillac's Clark Avenue line. From then on, the process of producing Cadillacs and LaSalles on the same line at Clark Avenue would remain in place through 1940.

Cadillac has always tried to find ways of increasing its share of the luxury car market. Creating and introducing LaSalle as its companion car was a clever approach to entice those climbing the economic ladder into a Cadillac product. Once in a LaSalle, then the next step would be to upgrade that customer the next time into a Cadillac. True to that objective, LaSalle helped Cadillac increase or maintain its overall market share during very difficult economic times.

Year	LaSalle Production	Cadillac Production
1927	16,850	36,369
1928	9,954	40,000
1929	22,961	18,004
1930	14,986	19,980
1931	10,095	10,709
1932	3,386	4,698
1933	3,482	3,173
1934	7,232	5,819
1935	8,653	3,636
1936	13,004	12,880
1937	32,005	14,152
1938	15,501	9,268
1939	23,002	13,581
1940	24,130	13,046
TOTAL	205,241	205,315

During the "Great Depression," it was not in vogue for most Americans to be driving a new luxury car. It was a matter of image. LaSalle had the luxury car quality but without the luxury name. As Cadillac's production volume decreased, LaSalle was able to keep the overall volume up by selling Cadillac quality without an expensive sounding name. LaSalle was the ideal answer, and it served that purpose admirably. From 1927 to 1940, production of LaSalle branded automobiles equaled the total production figures for all Cadillacs. The existence of a separate LaSalle line also allowed Cadillac to concentrate on preserving the prestige associated with its own name. It could be said that LaSalle, under the companion car concept, saved Cadillac.

In 1940, LaSalle presented Cadillac with a ready-made customer base, allowing the parent company to drop the LaSalle name and market all of its automobiles under the Cadillac name. Cadillac history has been one of marketing innovation, styling leadership and customer loyalty. It is that rich history which can enable Cadillac to continue building its future.

Today, Cadillac is being served well by such names as DeVille, Eldorado and Seville, just as Cadillac was served well in the past by LaSalle, Cadillac's Companion Car.

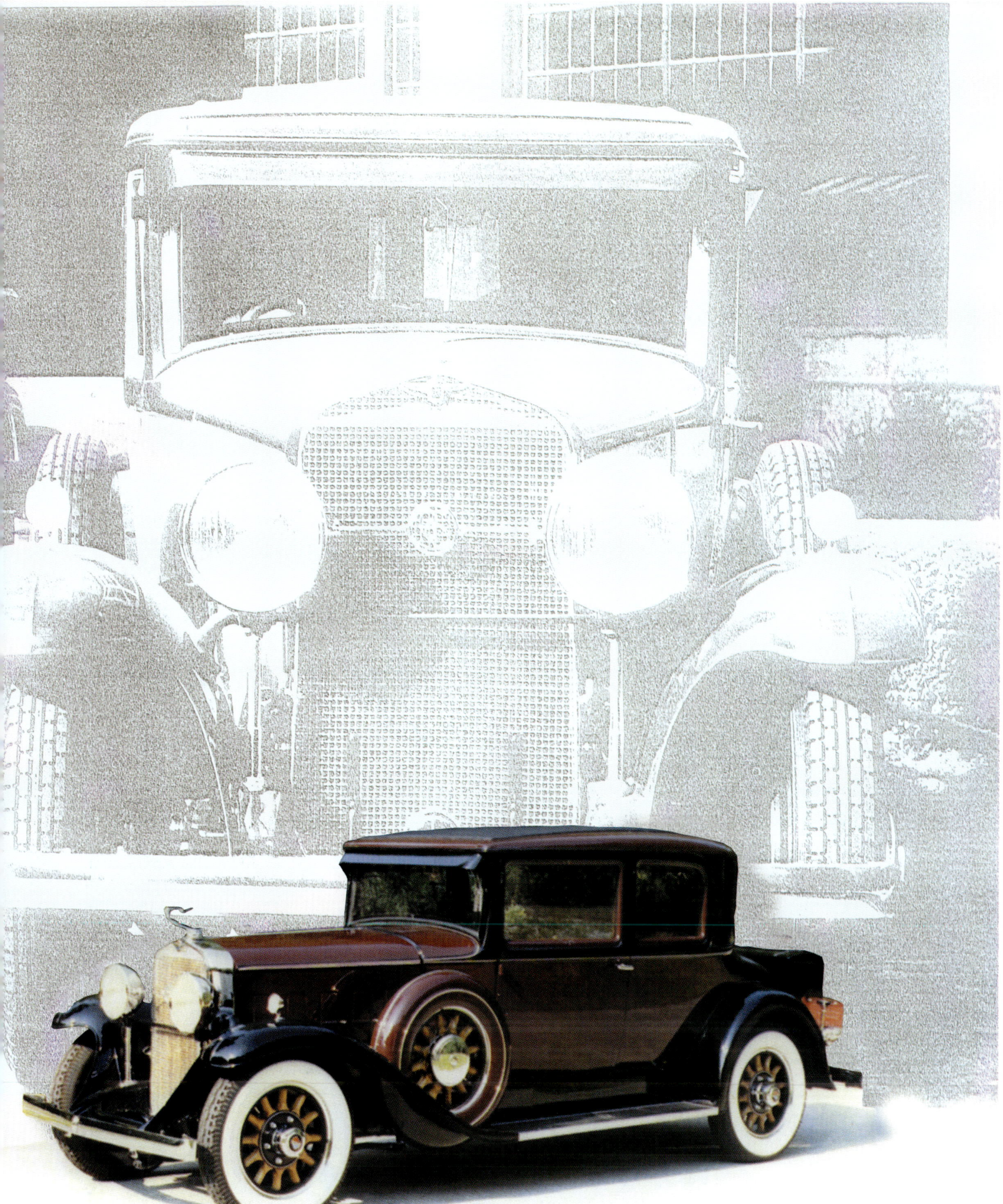

OVERVIEWS

Specifications Overview

Condensed specifications in greater detail are a part of most production year sections in this book from 1927 through 1940. A basic summary for easy reference has been compiled and placed in chart form on this page. This is the first time all statistics are based upon research from the actual factory records rather than from the promotional literature. Discrepancies may occur between this information and that collected by others. Included are all configurations and units such as CKD (Completely-Knocked-Down), partially built units and exported units are a part of all body numbers.

It is of note that, during the fourteen years of production, only one has two series of LaSalle during the same year, while others list only one series but made available Fleetwood custom or semi-custom bodies as well as Fisher models. For all practical purposes, these could have been called separate series during the same year.

Body or model configurations for each series are listed as actually found and delivered according to the records.

The series designation up through 1933 is commensurate to the cubic inch displacement of the engine. From 1934 through 1940 they are considered brake horsepower. The series designations beginning with 1934 are conceptual and have no relationship to engine size.

LaSalle used only three basic engine configurations, three V-8 and one Straight-8.

Throughout the fourteen years of production, 146 different body styles were built. LaSalle's smallest wheelbase was 119 inches in 1934 and the largest of 136 inches in 1932-1933.

Production runs are listed for each model year except 1927 that runs until December 31, 1927. The lowest production year was 1932 and the highest production year was 1937.

LaSalle Specifications Summary

Year	Series	Engine type	Engine bhp	Engine c.u.	Wheelbase small	Wheelbase large	Body[1] Fisher	Body[1] Fltwd.	Model Year Production[2]
1927	303	V8	75	303	125	134	14	4	16,850
1928	303	V8	75	303	125	134	17	4	9,954
1929	328	V8	90	328	125	134	14	4	22,961
1930	340	V8	90	340		134	7	8	14,986
1931	345	V8	95	353		134	7	6	10,095
1932	345B	V8	115	353	130	136	8		3,386
1933	345C	V8	115	353	130	136	10	1	3,482
1934	350	8	95	240	119			4	7,232
1935	50	8	105	248	120		5		8,653
1936	50	8	115	248	120		4		13,004
1937	50	V8	125	322	124		6		32,005
1938	50	V8	125	322	124		5		15,501
1939	50	V8	125	322	120		7		23,002
1940	50	V8	130	322	123		7		10,380
1940	52	V8	130	322	123		4		13,750

1) Body configurations are listed according to research of actual factory records and may differ with the numbers shown in sales brochures. Does not include CKD (Completely-Knocked-Down) units.
2) Production figures include CKD, chassis only and exported units.

Total Production   205,241

Price Ranges

LaSalle prices were positioned to fill a void between a low priced Cadillac and a high priced Buick. To fill that gap was a juggling act each and every year because of changing price structures for both Cadillac and Buick, due to changing economic conditions. In order to meet those changing market conditions, LaSalle often sold at a loss.

Quality and luxury at a slightly lower price than Cadillac helped the sales personnel in potential prospects on LaSalle. Internally, for the Cadillac Motor Car Division, LaSalle helped Cadillac maintain market share. Unfortunately, selling below or near cost had become a necessity and was often the means that justified the end in competing effectively with certain Auburns, Chryslers, Packards and Studebakers.

The F.O.B. Price Range information was taken from the factory production data at the end of each series chapter in the book. There, each model is listed with its price and a plethora of additional information. Over a span of fourteen production years for LaSalle, there were thirteen that had Fisher bodies; one where LaSalle had Fleetwood only bodies and no Fisher bodies; eight where no Fleetwood bodies were built for LaSalle at all; and six years where both Fisher- and Fleetwood-bodied LaSalles were built.

LaSalle Price Ranges—F.O.B. Detroit

Year	Series	Fisher Bodies low high	Fleetwood Bodies low high
1927	303	$2495-2995	$3600-5000
1928	303	$2350-2975	$4275-4800
1929	328	$2345-2875	$4800-5200
1930	340	$2490-2925	$2385-3995
1931	345	$2195-2595	$2245-3245
1932	345B	$2395-2795	none built
1933	345C	$2245-2645	price unknown
1934	350	none built	$1595-1695
1935	50	$1225-1370	none built
1936	50	$1175-1255	none built
1937	50	$ 995-1485	none built
1938	50	$1295-1825	none built
1939	50	$1240-1395	none built
1940	50	$1180-1730	none built
1940	52	$1320-1825	none built

These prices apply to factory assembled LaSalles only.
CKD or chassis units are not included in the ranges.

Power Plants

LaSalle used four basic engine configurations throughout its fourteen production years. At times, improvements to these basic configurations were made during a model year, based on new technology or field experience.

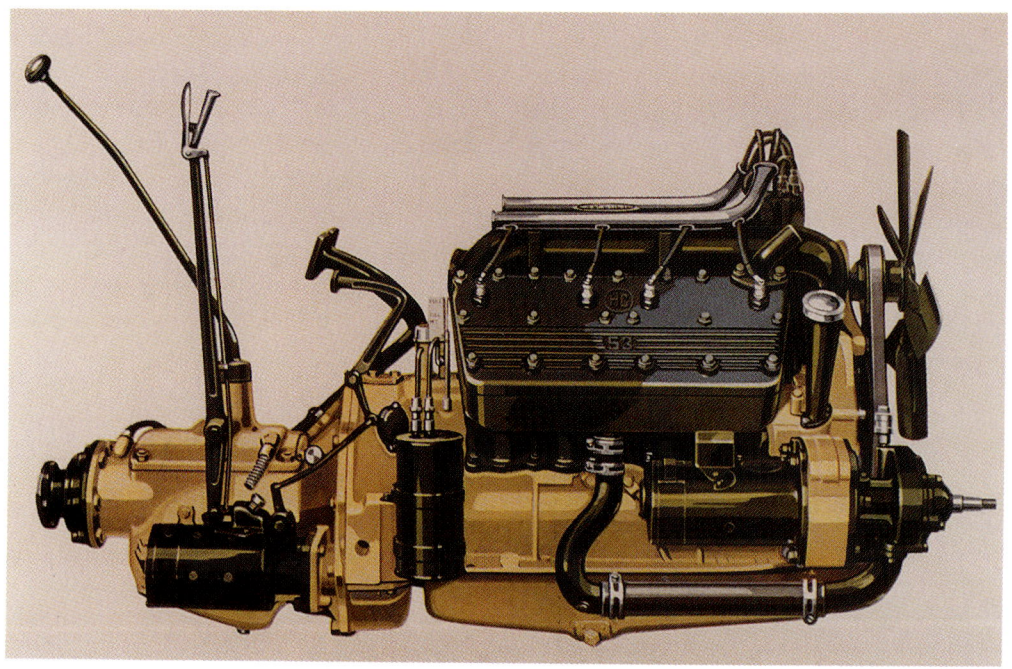

LaSalle used Cadillac's famous 90 degree V-type 8-cylinder engine with a slightly smaller bore for three years: 1927, 1928 and 1929.

The same powerful V-type 8-cylinder engine with refinements powered the 1930 through 1933 LaSalles, utilizing higher compression heads, improved carburization and air filters to silence the intake noise.

A Straight-8 with L-head design was used for the 1934, 1935 and 1936 model years, primarily to reduce costs and to fit the very narrow and long engine compartment. Built by Cadillac, they performed well because they had to meet very high standards of precision and accuracy.

Built from the same materials, to the same standards, by the same craftsmen as Cadillac, LaSalle used the V-type 8-cylinder monobloc engine for 1937, 1938, 1939 and 1940.

Nomenclature

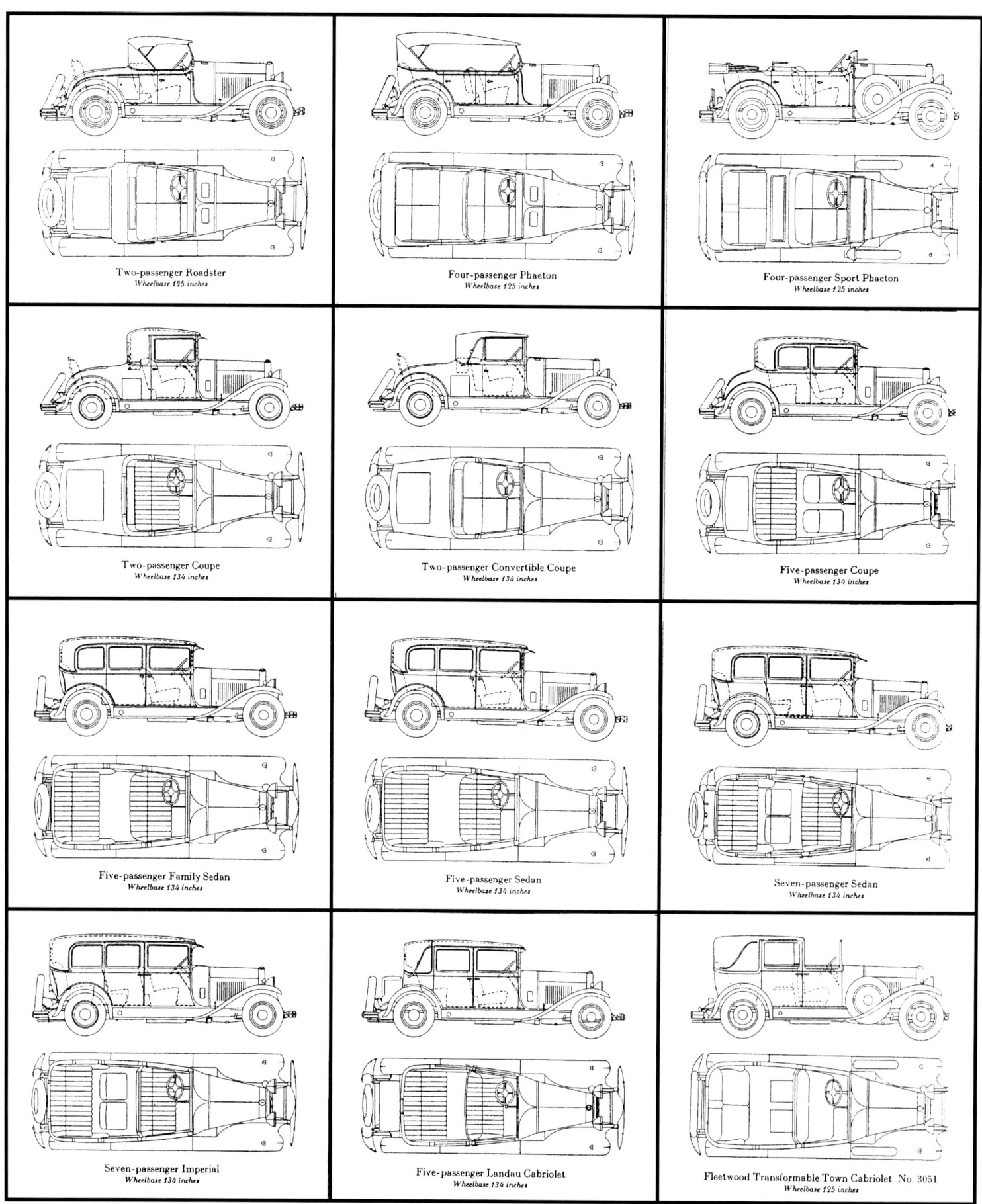

—*from the 1929 sales brochure*

Nomenclature of pre-1934 LaSalle models was reminiscent of the carriage trade. The multiplicity of body configurations and seating arrangements is very detailed. Post-1934 models assumed simpler nomenclature, such as a four- or five-passenger Sedan, two-passenger Coupe, Convertible Sedan, Convertible Coupe and a Formal or Imperial Limousine.

LaSALLE IDENTIFICATION GUIDE

Accurately identifying the year of a LaSalle series can be interesting. General differences are conspicuous, such as the earlier square front ensemble versus the later streamlined design, but that does not necessarily identify the model year. It becomes increasingly difficult when the basic body configurations are similar, requiring a detailed inspection of the design elements. To know and recognize the features of each LaSalle can lead to a greater appreciation of its qualities.

* body is boxy but with a lighter, more refined European look
* radiator has vertical louvers
* dish-type headlights
* LaS tiebar between headlights
* 12 wide vertical louvers on each side of hood panel
* parking lights on cowl
* glass sun visor on most models
* double flat bar bumpers

1927   Series 303

* same as 1927
* dish-type headlights
* LaS tiebar between headlights
* 28 narrow louvers on each side of hood panel
* parking lights on cowl
* glass sun visor on most models
* double flat bar bumpers

1928   Series 303

* same as 1927 and 1928
* dish-type headlights
* LaS tiebar between headlights
* 28 narrow louvers on each side of hood panel
* parking lights on front fenders
* glass sun visor on most models
* rounder double bar bumpers
* exterior brightwork is chrome plated

1929   Series 328

Front Ensembles

During the fourteen years of LaSalle production, there were seven basic designs. They were:

(1) 1927 and 1928 Series 303, 1929 Series 328
(2) 1930 Series 340 and 1931 Series 345
(3) 1932 Series 345-B and 1933 Series 345-C
(4) 1934 Series 350, 1935 and 1936 Series 50
(5) 1937 Series 50 and 1938 Series 50
(6) 1939 Series 50 and 1940 Series 50
(7) 1940 Series 52 Special.

Sooner or later in any discussion about automobiles, the name LaSalle will emerge. Even those who have only a remote interest in automobiles will have some personal recollection or will have heard someone else talk about LaSalle; everyone seems to remember the long nose or the very narrow grille. LaSalle styling was an anticipated event each year at new model introduction time. Seeing new ideas in fender design, radiator shape, window treatment, paint colors, interior trim and overall modernization was very exciting.

From the very first series introduced in 1927 until the last in 1940, LaSalle had very distinctive features that were readily identifiable. Each series was designed to attract the public with its own unique style. Ironically, that objective was successfully accomplished

* *body lines are somewhat softer than 1929, but still boxy*
* *radiator looks bigger and taller*
* *deeper than 1929 dish headlights*
* *LaS tiebar between headlights*
* *vertical louvers on each side of hood panel*
* *parking lights on front fenders*
* *shallow metal sun visor across windshield header*
* *double bar bumpers*

1930   **Series 340**

* *body lines are same as 1930*
* *radiator looks more refined and taller*
* *deep dish headlights*
* *LaS tiebar between headlights*
* *early models used vertical louvers, later models used vent doors on each side of hood panel*
* *parking lights on front fenders*
* *shallow metal sun visor across windshield header*
* *single bumper bar*

1931   **Series 345**

- *rounder body lines than 1931 and lower profile with 17-inch wheels*
- *waffle patterned radiator and chromed shell*
- *chromed headlight shell*
- *LaS tiebar between headlights*
- *vertical ventilation doors on hood panels*
- *parking lights on fenders*
- *horn trumpets*
- *single bar bumper*

1932   Series 345-B

- *body lines are same as 1932*
- *Vee'd radiator shroud, painted or chromed*
- *no tiebar between headlights; instead, branding iron LaS ornament on radiator*
- *horizontal louver doors on side of hood*
- *parking lights on top of fenders*
- *fenders are canted at the front and skirted*

1933   Series 345-C

---

by some very daring concepts, while maintaining some of the same refined and most recognizable elements associated with LaSalle.

Harley Earl, Director of Styling for General Motors and designer of the first LaSalle in 1927, concentrated on front ensembles as the feature that would set one model apart from another. LaSalle's design studio under his direction was constantly challenged to come up with a different look from the front, while the basic body shapes remained the same. Facelifting, as an expression, came from this concept which, by definition, required a certain familiar sameness of the grille and surrounding components while changing minute details to distinguish one model year from the next. A close look at the variations in detail within each group makes it obvious that the facelifting techniques used by the design studio was state of the art. The LaSalle owner could be readily identified with driving the very latest model.

Harley Earl made sure that LaSalle always had its own unique character. LaSalle was his favorite. It was often used as a styling development exercise and trial balloon.

Even though numerous designers worked daily in the LaSalle studio, it was Harley Earl who made the decision about LaSalle's looks and appearance. He had the uncanny ability to know what the public would like. Receiving public approval was no small accomplishment.

* new aerodynamic body lines covering all chassis components
* pontoon fenders with center crease
* very narrow, tall radiator grille with 6 horizontal dividers
* round branding iron LaS grille emblem
* headlights mounted to radiator shroud
* 5 chromed hashes at leading edge of catwalk
* recoiling biplane bumpers
* 5 round art deco ventilation pods on each hood side panel
* 3, unique to 1934, textured chevrons on leading edge of each front fender
* rear window has one center divider

1934   Series 350

* aerodynamic, rounded body lines similar (not identical) to 1934
* pontoon fenders with center crease
* very narrow, tall radiator grille with 6 horizontal dividers, same as 1934
* round branding iron LaS grille emblem
* headlights mounted to radiator shroud
* 4 chromed hashes at leading edge of catwalk
* 5 round ventilation pods on each hood side panel as in 1934
* single bumper bar
* 3 smooth chevrons on each fender
* all steel "turret-top"
* rear window has two Cadillac-like dividers

1935   Series 50

* same aerodynamic, rounded body as 1935
* pontoon fenders with center crease
* very narrow, tall one-piece diecast grille with 9 horizontal dividers
* round branding iron LaS grille emblem
* headlights mounted to radiator shroud
* new vent design with long horizontal eyebrow on each hood side panel
* single bumper bar
* 3 smooth chevrons on each fender
* 2 chromed hashes at catwalk
* all steel "turret-top"
* rear window has two Cadillac-like dividers

1936   Series 50

* *body is huskier than 1936 and slightly more angular*
* *very narrow radiator and radiator shroud*
* *new V-8 emblem mounted on grille*
* *simulated air intakes on each side of radiator shroud*
* *larger suitcase-like fenders*
* *larger windows*
* *headlights are mounted on radiator shroud*
* *last year for use of chevrons*
* *bumper emblem with LaS is flanked by vertical chromed ribs on the bumper bar*

1937   Series 50

* *same body as 1937*
* *wider grille than 1937*
* *exceptionally long nose (hood)*
* *4 decorative strips full length of hood panel adjacent to ventilation openings*
* *headlights mounted on 3 ribbed, chromed stanchions*
* *alligator hood opening*
* *no decorative chevrons on front fenders*
* *small, simple LaS bumper emblem*

1938   Series 50

* new slab-sided body design and larger windows
* very narrow one-piece diecast grille with off-white and gold LaSalle scripted emblem
* one-piece ventilation grille on each hood side panel
* large catwalk grille on each side of vertical grille
* headlights mounted back on radiator shroud
* chrome belt molding runs length of the car

1939   Series 50

* slab-sided body design same as 1939
* tall narrow grille with 44 thin horizontal bars and has LaSalle scripted emblem in off-white and gold
* three separate ventilator grilles on each side hood panel
* 6 vertical vent openings at the leading edge of the catwalk
* headlights integrated with front fenders, parking lights are mounted on top of the assembly
* chrome belt molding runs length of the car

1940   Series 50

* new rounded torpedo and wider body style
* radiator grille same in appearance as Series 50 but opens 4 horizontal bars down from the top
* no chromed belt moldings
* three separate ventilator grilles on each side hood panel
* 6 vertical vent openings at the leading edge of the catwalk
* headlights integrated with front fenders, parking lights are mounted on top of the assembly
* many models were fitted with optional grille guard units consisting of 1 vertical bar and 2 horizontal bars

1940   Series 52

LaSalle

Above: These two line drawings by Bob Eng depict the 1941 LaSalle proposals which, ultimately, were scrapped in favor of an all Cadillac line. Below: A family resemblance of the two 1941 proposals with the 1940 Series 50 production four-door Convertible Sedan.

Above: An interesting proposal by line artist Bob Eng for a current-day LaSalle with family resemblance to the 1930s. Below: A beautiful line drawing design perspective of a 1934 LaSalle Convertible Coupe.

A dramatic view of the radiator shield emblem on a 1930 LaSalle.

An artistic view of the new LaSalle emblem surrounded by the clean lines of the 1933 trunk.

There is nothing more graceful than the long, narrow nose of the 1937 LaSalle.

LaSalle heraldry in its emblems was consistently jewel-like throughout the production years.

The 1940 prow included all of the refinements to the hood ornament and LaSalle unmistakable identifiers.

The proud, the beautiful and the last.